Figure 2   Age Distribution of Central-City Population, 1970 and 1980

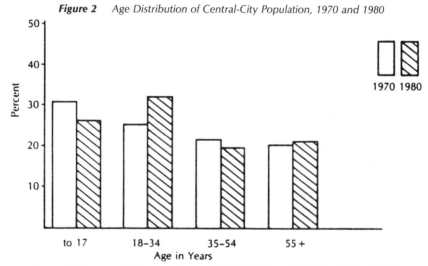

Source: U.S. Department of Commerce, Bureau of the Census. *Census of Population* (Washington, D.C.: Government Printing Office, 1970, 1980).

The postwar baby-boom generation, followed by the 1970s baby-bust generation, moves through the age distribution. In the 1960s and 1970s our cities were burdened with children in need of education. By 1980, the postwar babies had become young adults, the return-to-the-city generation. By 2000 they will be middle-aged parents—the prime age group for suburban living.

URBAN ECONOMICS

Fifth Edition

The HarperCollins Series in Economics

URBAN ECONOMICS

Fifth Edition

Edwin S. Mills
Northwestern University

Bruce W. Hamilton
Johns Hopkins University

HarperCollins*CollegePublishers*

Executive Editor: John Greenman
Project Coordination, Text and Cover Design: Proof Positive/Farrowlyne
    Associates, Inc.
Cover Photo: Andy Caulfield/The Image Bank
Photo Researcher: Nina Page
Production Manager: Kewal Sharma
Compositer: Black Dot Graphics, Inc.
Printer and Binder: R. R. Donnelley & Sons Company
Cover Printer: The Lehigh Press, Inc.

Urban Economics, Fifth Edition

Library of Congress Cataloging-in-Publication Data

Mills, Edwin S.
    Urban economics / Edwin S. Mills, Bruce W. Hamilton.—5th ed.
      p.   cm.
    Includes bibliographical references and index.
    ISBN 0-673-46867-4
    1. Urban economics.   I. Hamilton, Bruce W., 1946-   .   II. Title.
  HT321.M53   1993
  330.9173'2—dc20   93-11766
                                                                          CIP

93 94 95 96 9 8 7 6 5 4 3 2 1

Table of Contents

Preface

Urban Economics, Fifth Edition, is the third edition of this textbook to be published under joint authorship. It builds on the continuing success that grew from combining Edwin Mills's text, *Urban Economics,* and Bruce W. Hamilton's urban economics course, which has been offered at Johns Hopkins University for the past several years.

We have preserved almost intact the theoretical section from previous editions of this textbook. In the remainder of the book—chapters 1 through 4 and chapters 10 through 17—we have instituted several minor revisions and two major ones. In addition, the textbook has been updated to take account of the 1990 data from the Bureau of the Census and the most recent research results in urban economics. Moreover, there is a new chapter on housing finance—a topic that would have seemed uninteresting and out-of-place a few years ago, but which now is of great interest and importance.

As with previous editions, this book is intended for use as a core text in urban economics, and a reasonably solid foundation in microeconomic principles is a prerequisite. We have not used calculus notation in the book, and calculus is not a requirement. Nevertheless, students who are familiar with calculus will recognize these concepts as they appear. At several points we also describe regression analysis and results. The discussion is fairly basic, and we believe that it is accessible to students who are unfamiliar with techniques of regression analysis. We have, however, included an appendix on the rudiments of regression analysis to help students with these passages.

With the advent of personal computers and spreadsheet software, it is now quite easy for students to run their own statistical analyses. Urban economics is a particularly rich source of statistical relationships that can be explored by students. In several places in the book we point out possible student research projects that use basic regression analysis.

We hope that this text represents the state of the discipline as it really is, warts and all. We believe that economics contributes greatly to an understanding of how cities function, and we hope students will share our view after studying this book. At the same time, however, there are poorly understood phenomena and facts that are at odds with our theoretical predictions. We discuss many of these uncomfortable facts. This process ought not to leave students confused. Rather, we hope to convey the message that there are important questions that remain to be studied.

As is always the case with such a venture, we have received generous support from many quarters. By now, this support extends back over several editions. We extend our thanks to three generations of research assistants: Molly Macauley (third edition), Mohamed Elhage (fourth edition), and Mukti Upadhyay (fifth edition). Molly Macauley and Bob Schwab served as patient sounding boards, almost to the point of co-authorship, particularly on the third and fourth editions.

We extend thanks to several reviewers who provided many helpful suggestions:

Ralph Braid, *Columbia University*

Anne E. Bresnock, *California State Polytechnic University, Ponoma*

Gabriella Bucci, *DePaul University*

Louis Cain, *Loyola University of Chicago*

Mark Dynarski, *Mathematica Policy Research*

Gerald Goldstein, *Northwestern University*

Vernon Henderson, *Brown University*

Irving Hoch, *University of Texas*

Robert Inman, *University of Pennsylvania*

Theodore Keeler, *University of California at Berkeley*

Richard Muth, *Emory University*

Jolyne Sanjak, *State University of New York at Albany*

Steven Sheppard, *University of Virginia*

Robert Singleton, *Loyola Marymount University*

Kenneth Small, *University of California at Irvine*

William Vickrey, *Columbia University*

Ann Witte, *University of North Carolina*

Many people also provided us with unpublished information:

Ronnie Davis, *National Association of Realtors*

William Geppart, *Geppart Demolition Contractors of Philadelphia*

Nelson James, *Society of Industrial Realtors*

Macy Whitney, *Knott Remodelling, Washington, D.C.*

Richard P. Davis, *Baltimore City Department of Housing and Community Development*

Edwin S. Mills
Bruce W. Hamilton

Part One

Basic Ideas and Historical Background

1

The Nature of Urban Areas

☐ The city is one of humanity's earliest and most productive inventions. The first true cities arose along the Nile, the eastern Mediterranean, and the Fertile Crescent, approximately 5,500 years ago. By 2000 B.C., the city had spread throughout the Mediterranean basin and the Arabian Peninsula and on to the Indus River valley in India and the Yellow River valley in China.

Since that time, the advances and declines of civilization have been intimately connected with advances and declines of urbanization. The episode of urbanization that began along the Nile and the Fertile Crescent reached its apex with the Roman Empire. With the sacking of Rome in A.D. 476, both urbanization and the quality of life went into a steep decline throughout southern Europe. Recovery from this decline began in approximately the tenth century, with the emergence of the medieval city. With some setbacks, urbanization and economic progress proceeded slowly until the late 1700s and the beginning of the Industrial Revolution.

At this point, it is useful to ask two questions: First, what conditions are necessary for the formation of cities, and second, what is to be gained from urban life? These questions can be answered initially by noting what types of economic activities took place in cities, even in the earliest times.

From these early times onward, the city has been the home of specialists—in particular, specialists in nonagricultural activities. These specialists cannot survive without the produce of the land, so the first prerequisite for a city is the presence of an agricultural sector that produces a surplus—more than enough food to sustain itself. The second prerequisite is that the urban dwellers must induce the farmers to part with their surplus—either by exchange or by force.

Before and after the initial formation of cities, one of the crucial requirements for urbanization is the improvement of agriculture. Techniques of irrigation and the use of metal implements are among the first such innovations.

To thrive in an economy that is based on exchange rather than force, cities had to be productive—to provide something for the agricultural sector that the latter could not provide as well for itself. This ability of cities to provide something with which to trade for produce is dependent on scale economies. The city's unique attribute is *large scale.* In other words, the city is distinguished from the *hinterland* (the rural area served by the city) by the fact that the city concentrates large numbers of people, and large amounts of physical capital, in a confined area. As explained in this book, this concentration has proved to be a most productive way of providing many of the fruits of civilization. This concentration, however, has created problems that are virtually absent in rural areas and small villages.

This book is concerned with the economic opportunities that cities present to humanity. In addition, attention will be concentrated on the economic problems that arise with the existence of cities and with possible ways of handling these problems.

Most people make intuitive distinctions between urban and rural areas and between big cities and small towns. For many purposes, the intuitive distinctions are adequate. Nevertheless, it is worthwhile to start with some careful definitions and distinctions, because data sources depend on them.

☐ WHAT ARE URBAN AREAS?

Among the many examples of urban concepts are town, city, urban area, metropolitan area, and megalopolis. Some have legal definitions. *Towns, municipalities,* and *cities* are built-up areas designated as political subdivisions by states, provinces, or national governments. Practices in designating urban government jurisdictions vary greatly from country to country and, in the United States, from state to state. What one country or state designates a city, another may designate a town. More important, the part of an urban area included in a city or other political subdivision varies from place to place and from time to time. In 1980, the city of Boston contained only 20 percent of the 2.8 million people in its metropolitan area, whereas the city of Austin contained 64 percent of the 537,000 people in its metropolitan area. In metropolitan areas in the United States, the largest city contains, on the average, less than half of the residents of the metropolitan area. Other countries tend to expand city boundaries as the metropolitan area expands so that the city includes all or nearly all of the metropolitan area.

To the political scientist studying local government, the legal definitions of local government jurisdictions are of primary importance. They are also important to the economist studying economic aspects of local government. Much of Chapter 14 discusses the causes and effects of arrangements of local government jurisdictions. These jurisdictions, however, have been chosen largely for historical and political reasons, and they have little to do with the economist's notion of an urban area. They are, therefore, of secondary concern in urban economics.

Much more fundamental for urban economists than legal designations is variability in population and employment density from one place to another. A country's **average population density** is the ratio of its population to its land area. In 1990, the average population density in the United States was about 70 people per square mile. It is conceivable that every square mile in the country might have about the same number of residents.

The study of urban economics begins with the observation that population density varies enormously from place to place. In 1990, about 320 places in the United States had a population density that reached extremely high levels relative to the average level and relative to levels a few miles away. The most dramatic example occurred in New York City, where the population density was more than 23,700 people per square mile. Fifty miles away, in Sussex County, New Jersey, it was 250. A less dramatic, but instructive, example was found in Wichita, Kansas. In 1990, its population density was 2,639 people per square mile. The adjoining county of Kingman had a density of less than ten. Both New York City and Wichita are clearly urban areas. Such places contain more than half the country's population and constitute the popular image of a metropolitan area, but they do not exhaust the list of urban areas. Hundreds of small cities and towns, many of which have population densities that exceed those of surrounding rural areas by factors of 50 or 100, are also urban areas.

The fundamental and generic definition of *urban area,* or *metropolitan area,* is a place with a much higher population density than elsewhere. At least a few urban areas have existed since the beginning of recorded history and now these areas are found in every country in the world. For some purposes, this crude definition is adequate. For purposes of data collection and analysis, however, more careful definitions are needed.

The generic definition of an urban area is a relative concept. A place with a population density that is high relative to the average density in one region or country might not be high relative to the average density in another region or country. To cite an extreme example, the average population density in Japan was 860 people per square mile in 1990. This density is higher than the densities of many metropolitan areas in the United States. Thus, a minimum density that would define an urban area needs to be higher in Japan than in the United States. Similar situations arise within the United States. The average population density in the Phoenix metropolitan area is only about 61 percent that of the entire state of New York. Urban areas, therefore, cannot be defined exclusively by population density.

To be designated urban, a place must have not only a minimum population density but also a minimum total population. An isolated half-acre lot lived on by a trapper's family in Alaska may have as great a density as many urban areas, but no one would call it a one-family urban area. Many small places have densities that are high relative to surrounding areas. Official statistics necessarily employ an arbitrary population cutoff in defining urban areas: between 2,500 and 25,000 people in most countries.

A final problem arises in counting urban areas. As urban areas grow, they frequently encompass places that were formerly separate urban areas. Metropolitan areas encompass what were formerly separate small towns. On a larger scale, metropolitan areas gradually grow together. The New York-northeastern New Jersey-Connecticut area encompasses nine metropolitan areas, and the Chicago-Gary area encompasses six metropolitan areas. Such amalgamations create no problems in counting the urban population, but they do cause problems in counting the number of urban areas. When metropolitan areas grow together, the Census Bureau wisely presents data separately for each metropolitan area so that users can put the data together as they please. The Census Bureau also uses its criteria indicating which metropolitan areas are integrated sufficiently to be thought of as one large area, and it publishes the combined data. For example, several metropolitan areas across the Hudson River from New York City are closely related to the New York metropolitan area, although they are in some ways distinct.

☐ NOTE ON STATISTICAL DATA

Many data on the United States available to the urban economist, as well as most of those that are comparable among urban areas on a nationwide basis, come from the censuses of population and housing, manufacturers, business, and government. Every student of urban economics should learn about these data sources. Despite their many inadequacies, no better sources exist in the world.

Most federal government data pertaining to urban areas in the United States now are based on the same set of definitions regarding the area covered. The federal government, however, distinguishes among several urban concepts, depending on the way data became available and the purposes for which measures are intended.

An **urban place** is any concentration—usually in an incorporated town, borough, or city—of at least 2,500 people. Because an urban place is usually defined by political boundaries, it does not correspond to the economist's notation of an urban area. Data pertaining to urban places, therefore, are of relatively little value to the urban economist. In fact, an urban area usually contains many urban places. In the 1980 census of population, there were 8,765 urban places containing 154 million people, which was about 68 percent of the country's population of 226.5 million at that time.

The concept that corresponds to the economist's notion of an urban area is called an *urbanized area* by the federal government. An **urbanized area** consists of one central city (or sometimes two) of at least 50,000 residents and the surrounding closely settled area. Thus, an urbanized area is the physical city, defined without regard for political boundaries. In 1980, the census identified 366 urbanized areas in the United States. They contained 139 million people, or 61 percent of the country's population.

By far the most important urban concept for urban data users is the Metropolitan Statistical Area (MSA). An MSA normally contains a central city (sometimes two or three) with at least 50,000 people, as well as any contiguous counties that are metropolitan in character, as determined by the percentage of the labor force that is nonagricultural and by the amount of commuting between the counties and the central city. Thus, MSAs do not include parts of counties. There are about the same number of MSAs as there are urban areas, but MSAs include large rural parts of contiguous metropolitan counties. Thus, MSAs have somewhat more people and much more land than urbanized areas.

Some MSA counties, particularly in the West, contain large amounts of land, although their rural land contains few people. A dramatic example is the Riverside-San Bernadino MSA in California, which extends through the desert to the Nevada border.

Especially in high population areas of the country, MSAs have either grown together or, in some counties that were formerly parts of an MSA, have acquired enough metropolitan characteristics that the government has identified them as separate MSAs. In such cases, an individual MSA is referred to as a Primary Metropolitan Statistical Area (PMSA) and the set of contiguous PMSAs is referred to as a Consolidated Metropolitan Statistical Area (CMSA). A freestanding MSA is referred to simply as an MSA, but an MSA that is part of a CMSA is referred to as a PMSA. In 1990, the New York–Long Island–northeastern New Jersey–southwestern Connecticut CMSA consisted of nine PMSAs, which were more PMSAs than in any other CMSA. The Chicago-Gary-Lake County-southeastern Wisconsin CMSA consisted of six PMSAs. In 1990, the Government recognized 17 PMSAs.

The urbanized area corresponds much more closely to the generic concept of an urban or metropolitan area than does the MSA or CMSA. Why then should an economist be interested in MSA data? The answer is because much more data are available for MSAs than for urbanized areas. Some data become available by county and, therefore, can be put together for MSAs but not for urbanized areas.

The term *megalopolis* sometimes is applied to the part of the Eastern Seaboard from Boston to Washington or Richmond or to part of the West Coast from San Francisco to San Diego. The term also is applied to the

Pacific coast of Japan from Tokyo to Osaka and to the stretch of England from London to Manchester. The term is popular and somewhat descriptive but it is unofficial. It is also somewhat unreal. The four megalopolises do indeed contain many people. The Japanese megalopolis is the largest, with more than 40 million residents. Yet the term is unreal in that the metropolitan areas within a megalopolis are not united by the usual criterion of people commuting from one to another. The term is also unreal in that each of the megalopolises, especially the ones in the United States, contain large amounts of rural land.

Overall density data indicate that the urbanized area is a significant urban concept. In 1980, population density for the United States was 64 people per square mile. In urbanized areas it was 2,675. By contrast, in PMSAs the density was 299.

In this book, the term *urban area* refers generically to places of high population density. The term *city* refers to the legal city, while *urban place, urbanized area, MSA, CMSA,* and *PMSA* refer to the concepts used in federal government data sources.

☐ WHY URBAN AREAS?

If an urban area is defined by dramatically high population densities relative to those found elsewhere, why do we have urban areas? There is no single answer. Historians, geographers, sociologists, political scientists, and economists tend to emphasize different sets of causes in explaining why urban areas exist.

One proposition is that urban areas exist because people have found it advantageous to carry on various activities in a spatially concentrated fashion. Most of the differences of opinion result from the fact that these activities may be very different, such as military activities, religious practice or the administration of religion, governmental activities, and private production and the distribution of goods and services. At various times in history, many urban areas had defense as their major function. It was simply more economical and effective to defend a large group of people if they were spatially concentrated. (The word *was* is used intentionally, because weapons technology in the nuclear age may make it easier to defend a dispersed population than it is to defend a concentrated one.) In such urban areas, people commuted out of the city to carry on the predominant economic activity, farming. Colonial North America provides one interesting example of this phenomenon. During the first several decades after the original settlement of the British North American colonies, the fraction of the population that was urban actually declined, with the gradual reduction in fear of attacks by native people. Some urban areas began as cathedral towns or centers for the administration of religion. Finally, some cities grew because they were seats of civil government. Washington, D.C., is the most obvious example, in the United States of the latter.

However, most urban areas today do not owe their existence or size to military, religious, or governmental activities. In countries where economic decisions are predominantly made privately, *the sizes of most urban areas are mainly determined by market forces.* Households have found that income and employment opportunities, as well as prices and the availability of consumer goods, are more favorable in urban areas than in other areas. Business firms have found that returns are higher on investments made in urban areas than in rural areas.

In the United States, seats of government are almost the only substantial exceptions to the determination of urban sizes predominantly by market forces. Washington, D.C., is a clear exception. To some extent, most state capitals also are exceptions. Most of them were intentionally located in small towns away from major centers, and many have remained small towns. European national capitals, such as London, Paris, and Rome, are harder to classify. They certainly owe part of their size to their being seats of government. The opposite, however, is also true: They were made seats of government partly because they were major cities.

People unsympathetic to *economic location theory* sometimes claim that historical, rather than economic, forces have determined the locations of major urban areas. They claim, for example, that a certain urban area is where it is because that was where some settlers first happened to land. This idea, however, assumes that settlers or other founders were unresponsive to the advantages and disadvantages of alternative locations. Much more important, maps are dotted with places where people happened to settle. Some locations became major urban centers. Most remained just dots on the map despite elaborate local plans and efforts to make them metropolitan centers. Locations that developed into major centers did so in large part because their economic potential induced thousands of people and institutions to work, live, and produce there. Chapter 2 describes what forces other than the simple economic superiority of one site over another have at times played crucial roles in urban locations. The best assumption is that economic factors affect decisions about location to about the same extent that they affect other types of decisions, such as pricing by firms and demand for goods and services by consumers. Employers who choose locations in the wrong places find that they cannot compete for employees or customers. Workers who make poor locational choices find that their living standards suffer.

Scale Economies, Input Substitution, and Urban Areas

How do market forces generate urban areas? Most urban areas arise because of the economic advantages of large-scale activities. The economist's term for this phenomenon is *indivisibilities,* or, more generally, **scale economies.** General price theory states that a firm's production function displays scale economies if a proportionate change in all inputs leads to a greater proportionate change in output. With all input prices constant, scale economies exist at any level of output at which the long-run average total cost is falling. Thus, **diseconomies of scale** exist if the long-run average cost is rising.

What is the relationship between scale economies and spatial concentration? Economists usually assume that most scale economies are realized within a plant, which is often a contiguous set of production facilities. Even if they are contiguous, however, they may be more or less concentrated—that is, the ratios of capital or other inputs to land may be high or low. Which ratio entails lower costs?

In some cases, the mechanism by which proximity provides scale economies is clear. When a raw material is subject to several processing stages, greater spatial separation of the stages entails more movement of the material. This aspect is particularly significant when material must be at extreme temperatures during processing: To move molten steel over substantial distances would be highly impractical. Contiguity, however, does not always seem to be a requirement for scale economies. It is easy to imagine that a firm with two plants might find it economical to provide a service facility, such as maintenance, for its plants. In this way, it might have lower average costs than a firm with one plant that either bought maintenance services from another firm or produced them itself. Although examples are easy to come by, economists to date have paid relatively little attention to the spatial aspects of scale economies.

Closely related to scale economies is the concept of *scope economies,* which result if a single firm produces a variety of products or services instead of several firms producing just one product or service each. Just as it is more efficient to produce undergraduate education in a college with 2,000 students than in one with only 200 students, so it is more efficient to produce the education in a single college that has a range of departments than if each college had only one department. Scale and scope economies are pervasive and are difficult to separate in many cases. The term *scale economies* is used in this book with the understanding that it includes scope economies as well.

Scale economies are crucial for the existence of urban areas. In the absence of scale economies, goods and services could be produced on an arbitrarily small scale to satisfy the demands of small groups of consumers. That plan would permit consumers to scatter themselves across the land and yet to consume the desired bundle of goods and services, all produced closest to consumers' residences. Then, both transportation of goods and services and commuting could be kept to negligible amounts.

The movement of goods and people is expensive. More will be written about the issue in Chapter 13, although the concept is obvious. The combination of transportation costs and scale economies motivates producers and worker-consumers to locate close to production facilities that are large enough to produce on a scale that can satisfy the demands of many consumers in the surrounding area.

In fact, scale economies are pervasive. No commodity or service can be produced as efficiently on an arbitrarily small scale as on a somewhat larger scale. Of course, the extent of scale economies—the amount by which unit costs fall as production is increased and the range of production over which unit costs fall—varies greatly from one production activity to another.

The final consideration that motivates urban concentration is input substitution. According to the theory of the firm, production isoquants slope downward and are normally convex to the origin. Then, firms economize on relatively expensive inputs by using more of the less expensive inputs. Urban concentrations, resulting from scale economies and transportation costs, raise land values in the urban area relative to land values in surrounding rural areas. High land values induce producers to economize on the high-priced input—land—by using large amounts of capital, labor, and other inputs relative to land.

An activity in which input productivities vary little as input proportions change is the production of office space. In fact, for given rates of construction-worker wages, costs of construction machinery, and prices of construction materials, the production cost per square foot of office space is hardly greater in a 70-story building than in a 7-story building, even though both buildings sit on the same size lot. Those findings mean that there is a tenfold difference in the capital to land ratio and almost no difference in unit cost.

Much of the same is true of residences. Production costs per square foot of apartment space are hardly greater in a 50-story apartment than in a 5-story apartment. Such input substitutability also occurs in manufacturing, but most modern manufacturing plants are only 1 to 3 stories high. There may be other floors in the same building, but they are usually offices. Input substitutability also occurs in agriculture—as seen by contrasting farm production in Japan and Iowa—but substitutability is much more limited.

The ability to substitute other inputs for land permits the extremely great densities of production and residences that are observed in the world's great cities. Scale economies and transport costs motivate market participants to concentrate production and consumption on a large scale. Since workers and customers economize on transportation costs by proximity to employment and production facilities, they are willing to pay more for land that is close to production facilities than for land that is far from them. Competition for proximate land raises land values, inducing substitution of structural capital for land and resulting in high densities.

Not only do workers and customers benefit from proximity to production facilities, but also producers that buy from and sell to each other benefit. Thus, urban areas consist of concentrations of a variety of producers, workers, and consumers. Such concentrations bid up land values, inducing greater substitution of nonland for land inputs the larger the urban area. You can judge the amount of substitution by how much the heights of downtown office buildings vary with the size of the metropolitan area during flights into and out of many metropolitan airports.

The foregoing description is perhaps the simplest model of urban areas. The model is an elaboration of a group of models known as *central place theory,* which has had a long and distinguished history. (One of the curiosities of that history is that, until after World War II, most contributions were made by German-speaking writers, and central place theory was practically unknown to English-speaking economists. August Lösch, the father of modern location theory, was the most important contributor. The English translation of his *Economics of Location,* published in 1954, familiarized many English-speaking economists with central place theory.) This class of models can be developed now in a somewhat more formal way.

The relationship between pricing and transport cost in the presence of scale economies can be seen in Figure 1.1. The horizontal axis depicts distance from the plant. The vertical axis measures cost. The location of the plant is shown on the vertical axis labeled I.[1]

Suppose the unit cost of producing a commodity is A if we do not employ a scale economies technique and B if we produce a sufficient quantity to capture scale economies. Regardless of where consumers live, they can acquire the good at price A. If a firm sets up a large plant, it will be able to sell its output at price B and still cover costs. But not all consumers will find this price cheaper than A because of the transport cost involved.

Suppose that it costs $\$t$ per mile to transport the good from the factory to the home. This is depicted by the upward-sloping lines labeled BB' emanating from the plant, with a slope of t. The height of the line, at each distance, now represents the price of the good *inclusive of transport cost.* Transport cost obviously rises with distance from the factory until finally, at distance $\bar{u}$, transport cost has eaten up all the scale economies. Beyond this point, consumers are better off producing the good locally, at cost A. Thus, everyone who lives inside the circle whose center is the scale economies plant and whose radius is $\bar{u}$ will purchase from the plant rather than produce locally or do without. This circle is called the firm's *market area* (see Figure 1.2).

It is important at this point to note two features of the model. First, the scale-economies producer might charge a price above the average cost in an attempt to extract some monopoly profit. Second, consumers living close to the plant are better off than those living far from the plant, because they can get the commodity cheaper. Thus, it can be expected that consumers compete with one another for sites near the plant. From this competition, it can be expected that land values are higher for sites close to the plant than sites far from the plant. This basic relationship

---

1.   The vertical line labeled II is the site of a second, competing plant. Ignore it for now.

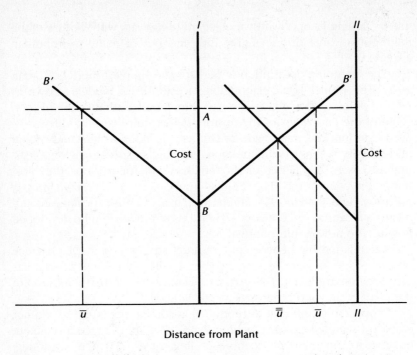

Figure 1.1   *Relationship Between Pricing and Transport Cost with Scale Economies*

between accessibility and rent pervades the study of urban economics. The price of land varies geographically to offset other advantages of location. It is also easy to understand that dwellings close to the plant will use more structural capital relative to land than those farther from the plant.

Spatial competition.   If a firm can charge a price above the average cost, it makes a profit. This example attracts imitators, and like the original, imitators carve out market areas limited by transport cost. Eventually, all the land from which circular market areas can be carved could be occupied, and the world, when viewed from above, might look like the diagram in Figure 1.2, with each circular market area tangent to the four adjacent market areas and with interstices between the circles that are too remote to be served. Each plant is indifferent to the existence of the others; in no sense does competition exist, even though there are large numbers of producers.[2]

It is possible (although not certain), however, that genuine competition could spring up. Consider point *a* in the middle of an unserved

2.   Actually, there is some dispute over the strength with which market forces would cause these circular market areas to be tightly packed. They might arise with bigger gaps between the circles.

region in Figure 1.2. Suppose an entrepreneur opens a plant there, at the same scale (and therefore at the same cost) as the existing plants in the centers of each circle. The entrepreneur attracts all customers who live closer to point *a* than to their former shopping centers, and carves out the market inside the dashed square.[3] The market area is smaller than the original circles, but it still may be large enough to earn the entrepreneur a positive profit. This entry shrinks both the market area and the profit of competitors. The most efficient outcome of this spatial competition is a world filled with hexagonal market areas, with the size of the hexagons just sufficient to permit each entrepreneur to cover costs,[4] as shown in Figure 1.3.

Returning to Figure 1.1, there is now a competing plant at *II,* and the edge of the market area is no longer the point at which home production is cheaper; instead, it is the point at which purchasing from a competing, large plant is cheaper ($\bar{\bar{u}}$ in Figure 1.1).[5]

3. All the points inside the square are closer to the plant at point *a* than to any other plant.

4. The hexagonal packing, in addition to being efficient, is an equilibrium in the sense that if the world should happen to find itself in such a configuration, no agents would have an incentive to change their location or other behavior. The world, however, might not find itself in such a configuration, as will be shown.

5. This spatial competition model is essentially that described by Lösch (1954), who has a relatively readable discussion in Friedmann and Alonso (1964). His model is much richer and more flexible than the one discussed. For example, this model assumes an L-shaped average cost curve—average cost is either *A* or *B* in Figure 1.1, depending upon whether or not the plant has scale economies. In Lösch's work, average cost curves are smoothly downward sloping. His model, in fact, is essentially the Chamberlain monopolistic competition model, with spatial separations providing the product differentiation.

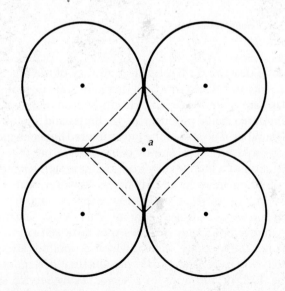

Figure 1.2   *Market Areas*

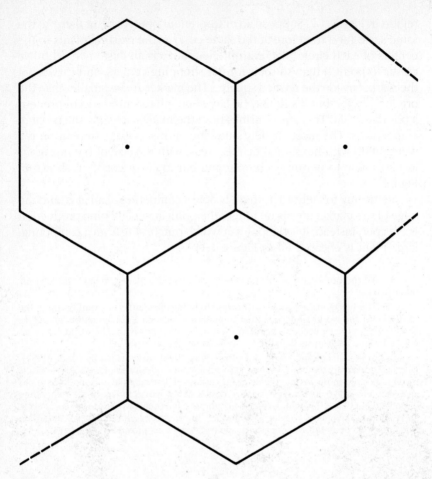

Figure 1.3   *Equilibrium Market Areas*

A complete description has been given now of the organization of economic activity in a world in which there are scale economies in one industry. Maps are dotted with autarkic cities, each trading its specialty good for the agricultural products in its hinterland but no one city trading with another. The size of the city is limited by the degree of scale economies, by transport cost, and by competition from other cities.

Specialization of a kind results from the next step toward reality in this model of urban areas. As already noted, however, scale economies are pervasive in all sectors, at least at low levels of output. In retailing, wholesaling, and services, scale economies also exist, but they may be exhausted when employment reaches only a dozen or a few dozen people. It is not the absolute scale at which economies are exhausted, but rather *the scale relative to market demand* that determines whether there can be 1, 2, or 100 firms in a sector. Many service sectors, for example, are highly specialized and have extremely low per capita demands. Scale economies may prevent such industries from locating in towns and small cities or may permit so few firms that those that exist have substantial monopoly power. Thus, large urban areas provide specialized cultural, legal, medical, financial, and other services that are not available in small urban areas.

The fact that scale economies exist in all sectors rather than in just one, and that scale economies may be exhausted at different levels of output or employment in different industries, greatly enriches our hypothetical landscape. All sectors tend to concentrate spatially to some extent, and transportation costs can be kept low if the sectors concentrate near one another. Thus, it is now possible to account for the variety in size among urban areas, as well as for a certain kind of trade between large and small urban areas. The small urban areas would contain only those sectors with scale economies that were exhausted by the demands of small populations. The large urban areas would contain, in addition to small-scale sectors, sectors with scale economies that were exhausted only by the demands of a large population. The large urban areas would supply such products not only to their own residents but also to residents of small urban areas. The largest urban areas would contain all types of sectors and would be the only urban areas to contain sectors with scale economies that required the demands of the largest population to exhaust them.

Thus, urban areas of a given size would export to urban areas of smaller sizes, but there would be no other kind of trade between urban areas. In particular, it is not yet possible to account for mutual trade, in which one urban area both exports to and imports from another.

In this model, big cities export to small cities but do not import anything in return. Thus, it appears that some balance-of-trade principles are violated. If small cities have nothing big cities want, how do they pay for their purchases? The answer is that exports from small cities to big cities are roundabout—via the rural sector. Small cities export their output to the agricultural sector, which exports to the big cities, which export to the small cities. This pattern completes the circular flow of trade. Superimposed on this flow, of course, are direct-trade circles involving only farms and small cities, as well as farms and large cities.

An interesting implication of this hierarchical view of cities is that there are many small cities and few large cities. In other words, the number of cities of a given size is inversely related to city size. The theory does not tell us how rapidly the number of cities declines as city size increases; that rate depends on empirical details of the degree of scale economies in various sectors, the density of demand, and transport costs. Chapter 4 will show that the empirical relationship between the number of cities and city size is remarkably stable.

Export base. According to this scale economies-based theory, cities arise because scale economies enable them to produce a good or goods that can be exported profitably to a hinterland. The demand for the export good and the ability of the city to supply it through scale-economies production are the reasons for the existence of the city. Initially, this prototype city can be thought of as populated only by people who work in the scale-economies plant. These people subsist on imports of agricultural goods from the hinterland.

Of course, it can be expected that these workers consume something in addition to food imports. For example, they also demand services and manufactured goods. The existence of a labor force with these demands, concentrated in a city, attracts suppliers of services and manufactures for home consumption. Thus, the city ultimately will be substantially larger than the export sector that gave rise to its existence in the first place.

Employment in the export sectors of a city's sectors with scale economies frequently is called *basic employment,* or *export base employment,* and the remainder of employment (that which satisfies local demand) is called *nonbasic employment.* As cities (or regions or nations) get bigger, the ratio of nonbasic to basic employment tends to rise. If some of the home-consumption goods are produced subject to scale economies (which is surely the case), then, as a city gets bigger, it finds itself able to substitute home production for imports of these goods. This feature, which is known as *import substitution,* will play an important role in the discussion of regional shifts in Chapter 2. The result of import substitution is that big cities are more self-reliant than small cities.

Space in microeconomic theory.   It is interesting at this point to note how standard microeconomic theory must be modified to accommodate the existence of space and transport cost. First, however, notice how completely spaceless most economic models are. Even the theory of international trade pays little attention to the friction of space and distance. In very advanced treatments of theory, in which consideration of time is basic, economists typically assume that space can be overcome costlessly or that all economic activity takes place at the same point. The introduction of space creates some nasty problems for economists, but it also solves a few. First, in a spatial world, plant size under constant returns is no longer indeterminate—it is zero, or instead, just big enough to satisfy one household's demand. Without increasing returns, there is no reason to incur transport cost. Casual observation reveals that this finding is correct: Activities that can be done as cheaply at home as in a factory, such as brushing teeth and washing dishes, are done at home to save the transport cost. Firms that produce for more than one household have scale economies, at least over some range.

Second, a spatial model solves the problem of pricing under increasing returns. In the absence of a spatial model, increasing returns and efficient pricing are incompatible, because marginal cost is less than average cost. Furthermore, the existence of competition is in doubt both as a descriptive model and a normative model, because bigger is always better, both socially and privately. But once we introduce space and location, firms with increasing returns take on a different look. Even if production cost falls with output, average transport cost generally rises with output, because the only way to increase output is to ship the increment a greater distance. Hence, the existence of transport cost is likely to give firms a "normal" U-shaped average cost curve, with the upward-sloping average transport cost curve eventually outweighing the downward-sloping average production cost, even if there are increasing returns in production.

The introduction of space and transport cost also causes problems for microeconomic theory. The most important is that the equilibriums that emerge might not be optimum or unique. The first case in which spatial competition does not lead to an optimum was analyzed by Hotelling (1929). Suppose there is a beach along which sunbathers are evenly distributed, and on this beach there are two ice-cream vendors, each of whom wants to locate to maximize sales. Every sunbather buys one ice-cream cone per day (that is, demand is perfectly inelastic), walking to the nearest vendor. The optimum location is obvious—the vendors should locate respectively one-fourth and three-fourths of the way from one end of the beach (at points *a* and *b* in Figure 1.4). Even if they start at these locations, however, each vendor has an incentive to move toward the other. To take an extreme case, the vendor at point *a* might move to point *a'* next to point *b*, thus capturing all the market to the left of point *b*, which is three-fourths of the beach. The vendor at point *b*, of course, would hop over the vendor at point *a'*. This leapfrogging would continue until the vendors were next to one another at the midpoint of the beach (points *a''* and *b''*). This result is the only stable equilibrium, yet the average trip length is twice as long as at the optimum location.

The Hotelling model has been applied to a wide range of problems, some of which have nothing to do with geographic space. It has been cited, for example, as the reason both major political parties tend to stake out platform positions near the political center.

There is some dispute over the practical importance of the Hotelling finding. The presumption of a nonoptimum equilibrium is greatly weakened when there are more vendors (in particular, when there are at least four). When there are many vendors on the beach, a move toward one competitor is a move away from another, so a vendor's optimum location is midway between the neighboring vendors. This is also the socially optimum location, since it minimizes average transport cost. The model is most appropriate when large numbers are precluded for

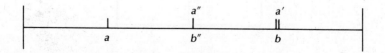

Figure 1.4   *Competition Along a Line*

some reason (as in the case of political parties). But even in this context, the model contains some assumptions that are odd from an economist's perspective. First, demand is perfectly inelastic with respect to price (the customers at the end of the beach do not curtail their demand when the vendors move toward the middle). Second, it apparently never occurs to the vendors that they can compete with one another on price as well as location. You may want to think about what happens to the model's results when one or both of these assumptions are relaxed.

Some technical considerations.* Even in the case of a large number of competitors, in the spirit of the central place theory model previously discussed, there is some dispute as to whether an economy will tend to arrive at the optimum hexagonal configuration seen in Figure 1.3. Consider the world of Figure 1.3, in which hexagonal market areas represent an optimum. Now suppose that the plants are oriented in such a way that the actual market areas are squares. It is easy to see that this configuration is not an optimum. If a market area of the same size were served by a hexagon, average transport cost would be lower. A hexagon more closely approximates a circle than does a square, so the average distance from a point in the polygon to the center is less for a hexagon than for a square. The corners are less remote.

However, the configuration of square market areas might be an equilibrium. To see this possibility, note that a new entrant would establish a plant at a point like *a* in Figure 1.5. In the original configuration, the side of a market square is 1, so the market areas also are 1. But the new entrant, at point *a,* carves out a market square with a side of 0.7 and, therefore, an area of 0.49. It is possible that this area will be too small to generate positive profit, even if the original (unit) market

---

* The material presented in this section, up to "Agglomeration Economies," is not central to material in the remainder of the book. Some readers may wish to skip this section.

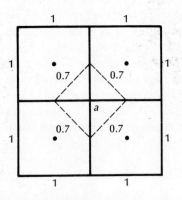

Figure 1.5   *Inefficient Equilibrium Market Areas*

area is profitable. If this supposition is true, there will be no new entrants (because they would experience a loss). The original participants in the market have no incentive to change their behavior, so the square configuration is an equilibrium. Profit has not been eliminated; market areas have not achieved their optimum (transport-minimizing) shape. Whether the world is carved up into optimum hexagons or nonoptimum squares, rectangles, or triangles appears to be a matter of historical accident rather than the efficient direction of an invisible hand.[6]

In the configuration of square market areas, no firm has an incentive to move or to enter or leave the industry. Thus, the outcome appears to be an equilibrium, even though it is not an optimum. The result is that freedom of entry and spatial competition do not necessarily yield an optimum location pattern.

Some economists dispute this result. The new entrant, at point *a* in Figure 1.5, carves out an unprofitable market area of 0.49 and, therefore, decides not to enter, recognizing that his or her entry might not drive an established producer out of business. It is plausible, however, that the potential new entrant, recognizing that this is a profitable industry, might enter at point *a,* set a price below cost, and thus carve out a market area bigger than 0.49. This bigger market area exists at the expense of the established merchants adjacent to the entrant. If the entrant's price were low enough, he or she might drive all neighboring merchants out of business and then be able to charge a price high enough to recoup early losses. Only when the world is carved into efficient hexagons is this predatory behavior definitely unprofitable.

This analysis can shed light on location patterns within urban areas. Customer densities vary greatly within an urban area, so market areas cannot be expected to be perfect hexagons or other polygons. However, some urban activities appear to have spatial patterns roughly in accord with this analysis. Supermarkets and shopping centers are good examples. What about drugstores, doctors, and lawyers? You can plot the locations of these activities on a street map using the yellow pages of the telephone book as a data source.

Other activities tend to concentrate near one another instead of spreading themselves out to be near customers. Most garment manufacturers and wholesalers in the New York City area are concentrated in a small area below midtown Manhattan. The reason is that they produce fashion goods, and customers—mostly retail buyers—like to do comparison shopping. In many cities, especially New York, stockbrokers also are concentrated in a small area. That they do business by phone and mail reduces the need to be near customers, but it does not explain why they are close to one another.

---

6. These arguments are fully developed in a discussion by Eaton and Lipsey (1976) that is very interesting and not as difficult as it may appear to be.

Agglomeration Economies

So far, the existence of urban areas has been explained entirely in terms of scale economies in production, a concept economists understand relatively well. Urban economists also often refer to the **agglomeration economies** of urban areas. In part, they interpret the term to mean the advantages of spatial concentration resulting from scale economies. Of course, it must be remembered that scale economies exist not only in private sectors, but also in mixed public-private or regulated sectors, such as transportation, communications, and public utilities. Also, scale economies may exist in such public sector activities as education, police protection, water supply, and waste disposal.

Urban economists also use the term *agglomeration economies* to refer to the advantages of spatial concentration that result from the scale of an entire urban area, but not from the scale of a particular firm. The first, and most important, of such agglomeration economies is statistical in nature and is an application of the law of large numbers. Sales of outputs and purchases of inputs fluctuate in many firms and industries for random, seasonal, cyclical, and secular reasons. To the extent that fluctuations are imperfectly correlated among employers, an urban area with many employers can provide more nearly full employment of its labor force than can an urban area with few employers. Likewise, a firm with many buyers whose demand fluctuations are uncorrelated will have proportionately less variability in its sales than a firm with few buyers. It can hold, therefore, smaller inventories and employ smoother production scheduling.

A second such agglomeration economy is complementarity in labor supply and in production. Different kinds of labor are to some extent supplied in fixed proportions. For example, industries with large demands for female workers are attracted to areas where women live. Complementarity in production works the same way. If two commodities can be produced more cheaply together than separately, users of both commodities will be attracted to areas where they are produced.

A third agglomeration economy has been emphasized by Jane Jacobs (1969). Although her argument is complex, it is based on the contention that spatial concentration of large groups of people permits a great deal of personal interaction, which in turn generates new ideas, products, and processes. She views urban areas generally as the progressive and innovative sectors of society. Hers is a fascinating theory that ties in with economists' interests in sources of technical progress, and it deserves careful attention.

Other types of agglomeration economies have been claimed, but on analysis, they usually turn out to be special cases of the mechanisms just described.

The final major economic rationale for the existence of cities and the comparative advantages or inherent differences in attributes of different regions is taken up in Chapter 2.

☐ LIMITS TO URBAN SIZE

To be viable, a city must be able to produce one or more products cheaper than its hinterland, after accounting for the cost of transporting the export good or goods to the hinterland and agricultural products to the city. Throughout history, city size has been constrained by transport cost. The size of cities that owe their existence to market forces also is constrained by the degree of scale economies relative to market demand. Another constraint on city sizes and configurations is the cost of carrying on activities within the city itself—special costs that arise as a result of urban life. Most important among these is commuting to work, which is much less important in agriculture. Other such costs, not uniquely urban but more problematic in cities, are the delivery of water and the disposal of waste and sewage. An important portion of the history of urban areas in the last two centuries is the progressive relaxation of these constraints on viable city sizes through a series of inventions and innovations. A brief summary of this history follows to emphasize the constraint relaxations that have permitted the dramatic changes in urban form.

Preindustrial Cities in the United States

Buildings in early nineteenth century cities were frame (though not of the modern style; see "Construction Innovations" ahead), brick, or stone, with residential structures generally limited to two or three stories. Overland transport, both in commuting and in trading with the outside world, was either by foot or by horse (either on horseback or by some form of conveyance). The cheapest form of bulk transport was by water (overland transport by horse and wagon was perhaps 100 times more costly than travel by ship or by barge). Water was provided to urban residents largely through private wells, and sewage was carried away on the (generally dirt) surfaces of streets or in the streams that ran through the cities. (Prior to the development of concrete and asphalt around 1900, the only way to hard-surface a street was with cobblestones. For most streets, the cost of laying a cobblestone surface was prohibitive.) Since almost all commuting was by foot, it was impractical for workers to live more than about three miles from their jobs (about a one-hour walk, at a moderate pace). Employment was almost necessarily centered along a navigable waterway to reap the cost advantage of water versus overland bulk transport. Thus, the city could extend no more than about three miles inland. Given the relatively low construction density that was feasible, it was, therefore, not possible to house a very large labor force within commuting distance of a central employment district.

The technology for the underground delivery of water and disposal of sewage was available, though expensive, at this time.[7] Typically, other constraints prevented cities from reaching sufficient size to require their use. In any case, a combined lack of pure water and efficient sewage disposal was a major contributor to health problems and above-average mortality in nineteenth-century cities. Well water was particularly contaminated in low-lying areas, where it was more seriously exposed to the runoff of sewage from higher elevations. It was well known at the time that mortality was high in these low-lying areas (although it was thought that the cause was the quality of the air rather than the water), with the result that almost all upper-class housing was built on high ground. The causes of such epidemic diseases as yellow fever, malaria, cholera, and tuberculosis were not widely understood until approximately 1900, but the effects were apparent during the early phases of urbanization. New York's death rate almost doubled from 1810 to 1859, surely due to increases in density with no proper means of providing water or removing waste.[8]

At the beginning of the nineteenth century, the real constraint on city size was not the limit on the infrastructure of the city. Rather, it was the cost of trade with the hinterland. Output was exported and food was imported over dirt roads by horse and wagon. Water transport, as noted, was much cheaper, but only a tiny hinterland was accessible to water. In fact, water transport was so cheap that most American manufactured goods came from Europe (especially Britain). Manufacturers in the United States frequently could not compete with British manufacturers, even after accounting for the cost of transatlantic shipping.

In fact, the major cities in the United States in 1800 were not manufacturing centers at all but commercial centers. They were largely collection points for agricultural products bound for export and distribution points for imported manufactures. For this reason, most cities of consequence were located on or below what is called the *fall line*— basically, the farthest upriver point that can be reached by oceangoing vessels. This distribution provided access to the maximum amount of land while still retaining access to the ocean.

Preindustrial Cities Elsewhere

It was not impossible to build large cities with preindustrial technology, although cities with a population of more than 100,000 were

---

7. Colonial New York City had a rudimentary water delivery system, with hollowed-out logs for pipes.

8. Glaab and Brown quote the editor of the *New World:* "The offal and filth, of which there are loads thrown from the houses in defiance of an ordinance which is never enforced, is scraped up with the usual deposits of mud and manure into big heaps and left for weeks together on the sides of the street."

rare before 1800. From the time of Christ to approximately A.D. 300, Rome's population ranged from 500,000 to one million. But this size was not achieved again in the West until London reached one million in 1800. It is clear that Rome achieved this size only at great cost to its population. Streets ranged in width from about 6 to 20 feet; they were apparently used all night by wagoneers and cattle drovers (who were excluded from the streets during the daytime). Dwelling units were about five stories high (apparently somewhat beyond safe limits, since there are many accounts of buildings collapsing). The standard method of disposing of human waste was to pitch it out the window (sometimes chamber pot and all). Juvenal wrote, "Anyone who goes out to dinner without making out a will is a fool. You can suffer as many deaths as there are open windows to pass under." Population density was approximately 185 people per acre (118,400 per square mile), although the figure would be much higher if we were able to deduct properly for the land, which was occupied by public buildings and temples. By comparison, Athens at its peak had a population of only about 40,000.

Rome was able to achieve this population because of a combination of technical advances (primarily in engineering) and willingness to suffer. Foremost among the technical advances were aqueducts and roads to the hinterland and the system of artificial harbors at Ostia. Astonishingly, classical Rome consumed twice as much water per capita as does modern Rome.

In Europe, both cities and civilization went into general decline after the fall of Rome, with the recovery of both beginning in approximately the tenth century. By the late Middle Ages, the biggest cities in Europe were Palermo (300,000) and Cordoba (500,000), which were still at that time under Moslem domination. Of cities that were later to attain prominence, Paris and Milan each had populations of about 200,000.

Infectious diseases played a role in keeping urban populations in check. In the light of this observation, it is interesting to examine the case of Rome, and of the subsequent decline and slow recovery of urban Europe. The average age at death among adults (i.e., for those who survived childhood) was apparently just under 30 years in Rome (McNeill, p. 286). This mortality record existed before the arrival of the major killer epidemic diseases in Europe. Smallpox and measles apparently arrived in the second or third century A.D. (about the time the decline of the Empire began), and bubonic plague first appeared in Europe in 1346. According to McNeill, the emergence of modern urban Europe had to await society's accommodation—part immunological and part alteration of behavior—to these epidemic diseases.

Industrialization

On the eve of the Industrial Revolution, the technology of city-building was not much advanced over what it had been in Roman times.

Industrialization fundamentally altered both the demands on cities and the means of building cities. With industrialization, the benefits of large cities grew enormously. At the same time, the technical progress that underlay an industrial revolution offered new solutions to the fundamental problem of how to crowd so much activity into so little space.

Industrialization in the United States

Manufacturing became big business in northern cities during the first half of the nineteenth century, after the initial establishment of cities as commercial centers and also after the first major innovation in this history—a swift and dramatic improvement in overland bulk transportation.

Canals and railroads, as well as the introduction of the steamboat on the Mississippi and Ohio rivers (and somewhat later on the less-navigable Missouri), reduced the cost of overland bulk transport by well over 90 percent, on the average, between 1800 and 1850 (Tolley and Krumm, 1983). These innovations transformed the United States from a coastal society to a nation with a genuine, integrated heartland. Eastern cities now could trade profitably with areas hundreds of times larger than those that had been accessible previously. With the geographic expansion of viable markets, it became possible for East Coast cities to profitably reap the advantages of scale economies in industrial manufacturing. The key to the Industrial Revolution was specialization and scale, and it could only be exploited by a city with a large market. Once a region began to industrialize, it would also gain population. With this larger population, the local economy could support larger-scale manufacturing, replacing former imports with domestic production. This process is called *import substitution,* and it is one of the recurring fundamental themes in the discussion of regional shifts within the United States (Chapter 2). Basically, import substitution occurs when the domestic market reaches sufficient size to support scale-economies manufacturing.

With the opening of the Erie Canal in 1825, New York City could trade by water with upper New York State, as well as with the northern part of Ohio bordering on Lake Erie. Philadelphia, via the Delaware River Canal, had access to the upper Delaware valley. In addition, Baltimore, with the B&O Railroad, was linked with the Ohio valley.[9]

The significance of these changes in overland transport is apparent from Table 4.1 in Chapter 4. In 1790, New York City had a population of just under 50,000, and Philadelphia, the second largest city in the United States, had a population just under 30,000. No other city at that time had as many as 20,000 people. By 1850, New York City housed over half a

---

9. Washington, D.C., also was linked with the Ohio valley via the C&O Canal, but the canal was costly to maintain and was subject to flooding and damage. It never competed successfully with the B&O Railroad.

million people, and six cities had populations over 100,000. The methods of building cities and of transporting goods and people within cities were not very different from what they had been in 1790. New York City, by this time, had water and sewer lines. Baltimore, however, was not to have generally available water until the 1880s, nor a sewer system until 1906 (Olson, 1980).

The growth of cities, fostered by improved access to the hinterland, placed great strain on the urban infrastructure and environment and led to improvements in the efficiency of conducting urban functions. Walking was no longer an adequate means of commuting. In a city of 200,000 people, with employment still concentrated along a small section of waterfront, a commute would have required something like a two-hour walk each way.

The 1830s saw the introduction of the omnibus, a horse-drawn vehicle carrying 12 passengers. It was not much of an improvement over walking, however. The fare was somewhere between one-eighth and one-half of the average daily wage, and an omnibus traveled only about 50 percent faster than a pedestrian. In short, the omnibus served only the rich. The same was true of commuter railroads (also introduced in the 1830s), which were expensive and also were banned in several major cities because of smoke and noise. The first breakthrough for the masses was the two-horse streetcar, which ran on rails in the streets and was introduced in the 1850s and 1860s. A streetcar could haul three times more passengers, at speeds one-third greater than the omnibus. (The streetcar was successful because friction is almost 75 percent less on rails than on a well-paved street. Rails, however, were too expensive until the development of cheap smelting of iron and steel around the middle of the century.) This breakthrough substantially increased the radius of feasible development. For a given time spent commuting (e.g., an hour), the radius of the city could be twice as great as under the walking mode; therefore, the area could be almost four times as great.[10] Except in New York City, Boston, Philadelphia, and Chicago (all of which built subways around 1900, or shortly thereafter), the streetcar (and walking) remained the dominant mode of commuting until the arrival of the automobile and the bus. The source of power changed from horse to electricity (see "Subway and Electric Trolleys" ahead), but the mode remained the same.[11] Interestingly, the horse-drawn streetcar was adopted much more quickly in the United States than in Europe, in part because American streets were more primitive and in part because American land was more plentiful and, therefore, cheaper. This difference meant that expansion of the urban radius was a more attractive option in the United States than in Europe.

10. The reason for the "almost" modifier is that it was not practical to serve every point with trolley lines.

11. The discussion and data from this paragraph draw heavily on LeRoy and Sonstelie (1983).

In addition to facilitating great expansion of our cities, streetcars had a profound effect on the shapes of cities. Because of the fixed-rail, mass-transit nature of streetcars, they are relatively good at only one thing—collecting people along "spokes" and dropping them off at work in the "hub." The system was well suited, in other words, to delivering a large labor force to a small area—a *central business district* (CBD). Any tendency firms already had to locate at the central node—access to the port, to interurban rail lines, or to other firms—was enhanced by the obvious tendency to locate at the one place in the city to which the transport system could deliver the labor force. The streetcar, in other words, was not suited to the crosstown or reverse-direction commuting that can be done by an automobile-based system.

Steel

After the introduction of the streetcar, many urban-form innovations relied heavily on steel, which is considerably stronger and lighter than iron. The first economical steel-making process was developed by Bessemer in England in 1856 and was quickly adopted by the Carnegie Company of Pittsburgh. Prior to the adoption of the Bessemer process, steel was so expensive that some firms attempted to produce and market iron railroad rails with a steel cap, thus providing a steel surface for contact with the wheels.

The advantages of steel can perhaps be seen most clearly in bridge-building. The maximum length of an iron span is approximately 500 feet; with steel, the span is 1,500 feet. Since cities tend to be built at a body of water, the ability to span these bodies with long bridges considerably improved the ability to build big cities. In addition, without bridges across the great rivers of the interior, the railroad network of the second half of the nineteenth century would have been much less efficient at tying the nation together.

Construction Innovations

The second half of the nineteenth century also saw crucial innovations in the construction of both commercial and residential buildings. The breakthrough for commercial buildings was the development of the high-rise building, and the key innovations underlying the high rise are structural steel (developed in the 1880s) and elevators (first installed in New York in 1857). The replacement of brick with a skeleton of steel made it possible to build higher buildings more quickly and cheaply than before and to reduce the lower-floor space devoted to thick supporting walls.[12] The high rise essentially substituted vertical for

12.   This method was first employed in Chicago, in 1884, in the aftermath of the 1881 fire. One of the motivations for using steel instead of brick was apparently a desire to break the bricklayers' union, which was on strike at the time. The advantage of steel over brick is that higher buildings can be constructed with less lower-floor space given over to thick supporting walls.

horizontal transportation and expanded the feasible populations of cities for a given transportation network. Even though high-rise construction was more costly (especially before the introduction of modern construction machinery, much of it since 1945), it became worthwhile in big cities because of the savings in commuting that could be realized. The emergence of viable high-rise construction was stimulated by the transport system, which specialized in delivering people to the CBD. This transit system raised the value of CBD sites and encouraged the substitution of capital for land (as will be detailed in Chapter 6). Chapter 16 will address how the development of the high rise contributed to another crucial change in urban form—the implications of which are still being worked out today. The high rise has made it possible for office activity to outbid manufacturing for valuable downtown land.

The big advance in residential construction took the form of balloon (today known as frame) construction. This is the now-familiar method whereby 2″ × 4″ (or larger) rafters, studs, and joists are nailed together to form the shell of a house. Prior to this, wood construction required a mortise-and-tenon system of carefully fitting beams into one another. This method was slow and intensive in both wood and skilled carpenters. The balloon technique made it possible to put up a large number of houses quickly.[13] It was on the strength of balloon construction that Chicago went from virtually nothing to a city of one million between 1830 and 1880. This episode is surely the most rapid of city-building anywhere in the world prior to the twentieth century.

Subways and Electric Trolleys

Probably the most important constraint on city size in the latter quarter of the nineteenth century, even with the existence of the streetcar, was urban transit. In the absence of rapid mechanical transit, it was difficult for cities to spread out, either to relieve crowding or to expand population. The importance of the transport constraint can be inferred by reading contemporary accounts of these cities. A reporter for the *New York Tribune* counted the number of horse-drawn conveyances going up and down Broadway over a 13-hour period in 1867. One such vehicle went by, in each direction, every 1.3 seconds.[14] In London in 1820, merchants complained that their produce rotted in the sun while they were trying to transport it across town.

Mechanical transit, to be viable, had to await the development of electric traction. Coal-fired locomotives were banned from most city streets and were even more impractical in subways. The London

13.   The crucial component of the balloon method, which was absent before about 1830, was the mass-produced steel nail.

14.   This rate was a dramatic increase over traffic volume 15 years earlier, when a vehicle passed the same intersection, in each direction, every 13 seconds. (These numbers are cited in Bobrick, 1981).

underground, which opened in 1863, was for a time powered by coal-fired locomotives. The air was so bad, however, that many deaths from asphyxiation were reported.[15] Underground, the problem of effluents is compounded by the fact that the coal fire depletes the oxygen.

Electric traction, a product of the last decade of the nineteenth century, permitted the running of clean subways and trolley cars. The electric trolley represented the first truly radical departure from the methods of city-building, which had existed for centuries. (The only competitor for this honor would be the high-rise building.)

America's first electric trolley line opened in Cleveland, in 1884. This development was followed by a period of rapid innovation and experimentation, as developers searched for the most efficient technology. The real problem was how to deliver the electricity to the trolley. Early experiments included batteries and at-grade cables. Batteries were too heavy and at-grade cables delivered nasty shocks to people and lethal shocks to horses (the difference in severity apparently due to horseshoes). The overhead power line, which became ubiquitous in American cities in the first half of the twentieth century, was developed by Frank Sprague, a former Edison employee. His first installation of this system was in 1887, in Richmond. The speed with which electrification was adopted was almost beyond belief. By 1890 20 percent (914 miles) of American trolley lines were electrified. Within another decade, total mileage had increased to 30,000, with 98 percent of the trolley lines electrified. The rapid adoption was due to the fact that service was approximately twice as fast, and half as costly, as horse-drawn trolley service. In addition, electric trolleys could negotiate grades between two and three times as steep as horses could manage.

The electric trolley was adopted with much less speed and enthusiasm in Europe than the United States, largely because of public concerns over the aesthetics of overhead wires. Europe lagged behind the United States by some 15 years, but the trolley wave ultimately swept Europe's cities as well.

If the trolley was the innovation that permitted small cities to become big, the subway was the revolution that permitted big cities to become giants. New York City opened its first subway line in 1904.[16] This mechanism of fixed-rail transit greatly expanded the reach of commuting

15.   Incredibly, the first New York City subway was constructed and operated for a time clandestinely. The infamous Boss Tweed would not permit a subway franchise to be issued on the pretext that it was infeasible. In fact, a substantial portion of his income was extorted from ferry and omnibus franchises. In 1870, therefore, Alfred Ely Beach built his subway at night. Only 312 feet long, it was of pneumatic power driven by a reversible fan at one end of the tunnel (thus, the tunnel was pollution free). He had hoped that popular demand would force the legislature to grant him a franchise for a line all the way to Central Park. A combination of political intrigue and the Panic of 1873, however, ultimately ended the project.

16.   The Boston subway opened earlier, on a smaller scale, in 1897. Also, New York City had elevated trains in the last two decades of the nineteenth century.

networks, but it was still best suited to delivering a large number of workers to a fixed point—the CBD.[17]

The primary economic distinction between the subway and the trolley is in the degree of scale economies. Subways require massive capital investments, with the result that they are viable only with very high volumes of traffic. (See Chapter 13 for more detailed discussion.)

With the mechanization of commuter traffic, the remaining major bottleneck in urban travel was the delivery of materials—goods (both finished and in process) and solid waste. As recently as 1910, almost all such materials were moved by horse and wagon. In addition to the cost consideration, this method was very space intensive. The transport revolution wrought by electric traction was almost exclusively to the benefit of personal transport. The next major transport innovation—the internal combustion engine—revolutionized urban freight transit as well.

Electric Power

Before discussing the internal combustion engine, note should be made of one other urban consequence of the development of electric power transmission—the first major wave of manufacturing decentralization.

The urban innovations of the nineteenth century greatly expanded the ability of the city to deliver a large labor force to the CBD and export goods to a far-flung hinterland. Manufacturing was still tied to CBD location, in part because of the presence of the port or railhead and in part because of the presence of the labor force. In large measure, much manufacturing was tied to the CBD because of its reliance on steam power—and, therefore, its reliance on coal. Access to the railhead was valuable in part because it meant access to coal. With the advent of electric power transmission toward the end of the nineteenth century, however, power could be delivered anywhere. In particular, power could be delivered to sites on the outskirts of the city where land was cheap and regulation of smoke and noise was nonexistent. Largely on the strength of electric power, the suburban rings outside central cities were the manufacturing growth centers beginning as early as 1900.[18]

Internal Combustion Engines

Compared with the steam engine, the internal combustion engine is small. It can be used to power much smaller vehicles, such as cars and

17. A more complete discussion of the history of the New York subway and Beach's clandestine pneumatic tube can be found in Bobrick (1981).

18. From 1899 to 1904, suburban manufacturing employment increased by 32.8 percent, as opposed to 14.9 percent for central cities. For the next five-year period, the numbers were respectively 48.8 percent and 22.5 percent (see Glaab and Brown, p. 277).

trucks. With this innovation, mechanized transport no longer had to be mass transport, which in particular meant that it was no longer necessary that everyone be going to or coming from the same place. Automobile transport is both faster (generally) and more flexible than the fixed-rail mass transit systems powered by steam or electricity.[19] Also important were complementary innovations that permitted low-cost construction of paved streets.

The automobile substantially expanded the feasible range of the city, both by increasing the range of commuting and by permitting residential location in places unserved by rail transit. Initially, of course, the automobile was available only to the rich, so the initial wave of automobile-spawned suburbanization was largely upper-class.

To some extent, the automobile eased constraints on firm location as well. With the automobile, cities have a transit system that can deliver labor to virtually any point. Thus, firms no longer are tied to central locations because that is where the labor force is brought every morning. For some types of firms, the development of the truck may have been equally important. With the advent of the truck, materials transport was no longer tied to railheads and ports. Material inputs and outputs now could be shipped from almost anywhere. Railheads and ports still may have a cost advantage for some firms, but it is generally not the overwhelming advantage it was 50 years ago. Many firms may find that cost advantages are outweighed by the high land rents of prime locations.

Thus, the invention of the automobile and the truck did two things. First, it increased the feasible size of cities by reducing transport cost and expanding the range of the transport network, both for commuters and materials. Second, by introducing flexibility in the pattern of origins and destinations, it reduced the center orientation of cities and gave an impetus to the decentralization that had begun well before these inventions.

□ Summary

An urban area is a place in which economic activity is highly concentrated. Both population and employment density are much higher than in surrounding areas. A major benefit of this concentration is the realization of scale economies, and a major cost is the necessity of transporting materials both to and from the urban area. With the technical progress of the past two centuries, the benefits of urbanization have increased, and the costs have been reduced.

19. See Chapter 13 for a discussion of the relative speeds and costs of the various modes of transport.

Questions and Problems

1. Suppose there are economies of large-scale production so that large urban areas export to small urban areas but not vice versa. How can small urban areas pay for their imports?

2. In the central place theory analysis embodied in Figures 1.1 and 1.3, how would you expect each of the following to influence the distance between production sites?

    a.   A rise in income (an outward shift in the demand curve for the output)

    b.   A decline in the cost of transporting the good

3. Commuting times and distances are greater in large urban areas than in small urban areas. Is this difference evidence of diminishing returns in large urban areas?

4. Suppose urban areas produce just one commodity, X. Each urban area produces $x = AN^a$ units, where N is the labor force in an urban area and A and $a > 1$ are constants. Thus, there are increasing returns in producing a large amount of Commodity X in each urban area. However, each urban area must supply Commodity X to the rural residents who live closer to it than to another urban area. Rural residents have a fixed density (D), and each consumes a fixed amount (x) of Commodity X. If urban areas are too small, the advantages of large-scale production are missed; if they are too large, scale economies will be more than offset by the costs of transporting Commodity X from urban areas to rural consumers. Find the optimum size of each urban area. (Assume each unit-mile of transportation of Commodity X requires y workers. The optimum-sized urban area minimizes the sum of workers needed to produce and ship units of Commodity X.)

References and Further Reading

Beckmann, Martin. *Location Theory* (New York: Random House, 1968). A short and elementary, but very abstract, statement of modern location theory.

Blinder, Alan. "The Economics of Brushing Your Teeth." *Journal of Political Economy* 82 (1974): 887–891. A clever spoof on the tendency of economists to describe everything in terms of economic models. Blinder forgot to discuss the location patterns of toothbrushing establishments.

Bobrick, Benson. *Labyrinths of Iron: A History of the World's Subways* (New York: Newsweek Books, 1981). A very good popular book on the history of subways, subway construction and engineering, and the character of cities during the period when subways were built.

Eaton, B. Curtis, and Richard G. Lipsey. "The Non-Uniqueness of Equilibrium in the Löschian Location Model." *American Economic Review* 66 (1976): 77–93. A discussion of the possibility that some configuration other than efficient hexagons might be a location equilibrium.

Friedmann, John, and William Alonso, eds. *Regional Development and Planning: A Reader* (Cambridge, Mass.: MIT Press, 1964). Contains a very readable chapter by Lösch (Chap. 5, pp. 107–115) on his spatial theory, entitled "The Nature of Economic Regions."

Glaab, Charles N., and A. Theodore Brown. *A History of Urban America* (New York: Macmillan, 1967). This is an excellent discussion of the history of the development of urban America. It is a superb companion to Chapters 1 and 2.

Hotelling, Harold. "Stability in Competition." *Economic Journal* 39 (1929): 41–57.

Jacobs, Jane. *The Economy of Cities* (New York: Random House, 1969). A wise and perceptive essay by a noneconomist on economic aspects of urban life.

LeRoy, Stephen, and Jon Sonstelie. "Paradise Lost and Regained: Transportation Innovation, Income, and Residential Location." *Journal of Urban Economics* 13 (1983): 67–89. A very good theoretical discussion of what happens if different income groups use different transport modes, backed by a nice historical discussion of technical changes in urban transport. The theoretical section should not be attempted before reading Chapter 7 of this book.

Lösch, August. *The Economics of Location* (New Haven: Yale University Press, 1954). Probably the most important contribution ever made to location theory. The book can be very difficult in some places.

McKay, John P. *Tramways and Trolleys* (Princeton: Princeton University Press, 1976).

McNeill, William H. *Plagues and Peoples* (Garden City, N.Y.: Doubleday, 1976). A fascinating account of the role of infectious disease in history.

Olson, Sherry. *Baltimore: The Building of an American City* (Baltimore: Johns Hopkins University Press, 1980). A history of the development of Baltimore from colonial to modern times.

Perloff, Harvey, E. S. Dunn, E. E. Lampard, and R. Muth. *Regions, Resources and Economic Growth* (Baltimore: Johns Hopkins University Press, 1960). An influential study of the causes and consequences of differences in economic growth rates among regions of the United States.

Tolley, George, and Ronald J. Krumm. "On the Regional Labor-Supply Relationship." In *The Urban Economy and Housing,* edited by Ronald Grieson, 203–237 (Lexington, Mass: D. C. Heath, 1983). A good, readable survey paper.

U.S. Department of Commerce, Bureau of the Census. *Census of Population* (Washington, D.C.: Government Printing Office). Published for every year ending in zero. It presents the most complete urban data available anywhere and provides careful definitions of concepts.

2

Comparative Advantage and Regions

☐ Chapter 1 describes a system of cities that would emerge as a result of scale and agglomeration economies. In this model, there are no interregional differences in resource endowments, and there is no trade among cities of equal size. The topography of the natural landscape plays no role in the placement of, or interaction among, the cities discussed in Chapter 1.

Once the fiction of the featureless plain is dropped, however, and the notion of interregional differences in endowments (comparative advantage) is introduced in its place, the world becomes more interesting and more realistic. In this chapter, the world has rivers, mountains, and mineral deposits. The locations of these features have a dramatic effect not only on the location of cities but also on the manner in which they interact.

The first part of this chapter lays out the principles governing location decisions of interregional firms. The second part presents a brief history of regional shifts in the United States.

☐ THEORETICAL PRINCIPLES OF INTERREGIONAL FIRM LOCATION DECISIONS

The principle of comparative advantage states that if two different regions (or workers, or nations, or machines) differ from each other in their *relative* abilities to produce two goods, the value of output is maximized if the region that is relatively good at (has a comparative advantage in) producing one good specializes in producing that good. Adherence to this rule is equivalent to being on, rather than inside, the nation's production possibility curve. As Chapter 8 will explain, competition and profit maximization induce factors to pursue their comparative advantages.

The principle of comparative advantage is illustrated in Figure 2.1. Panels (a) and (b) are, respectively, the production possibility curves for Regions 1 and 2 (note that Region 1 is better at producing *both* goods than is Region 2). The aggregate production possibility curve is in panel (c). As can be seen, efficient production requires that Region 1 specialize in x_1 and Region 2 specialize in x_2, to the extent the mix of demands permits this. Ignoring transport cost, aggregate social welfare is maximized if Region 1 imports its x_2 from Region 2, even though Region 1 is actually better at producing x_2 than is Region 2.

As can be seen from Figure 2.1, specialization improves aggregate production possibilities only when the shapes of the region-specific production possibility curves differ. These changes, in turn, happen only when regions have different mixes of inputs. Thus, trade among regions would be expected to occur when the regions have different mixes of inputs. Even when the input mixes differ, trade will only occur if the gains from trade are sufficient to overcome transport cost.

Comparative advantage and the specialization that follows from it give an economic rationale for trade between regions or between cities of different or of equal size. As in the case of scale economies, trade occurs only if comparative advantage is strong enough to justify the transport cost.

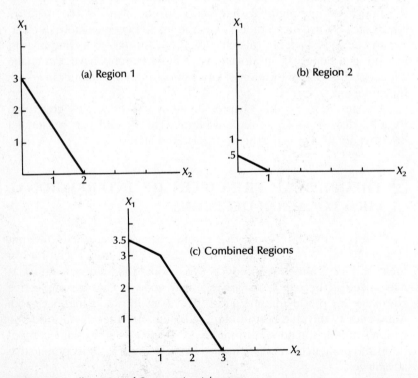

Figure 2.1   *Illustration of Comparative Advantage*

Economists frequently argue that comparative advantage is a rationale for the existence of cities. This is not true: It is a rationale only for trade among regions. If there were no scale economies in transportation, interregional trade could take place between the individual agents in the various regions without the intervention of cities.

There are, however, scale economies in transport—in vehicles, rights-of-way, and facilities for loading and unloading. These scale economies, along with regional comparative advantage, give rise to transport-node, or port, cities. The location of port cities is governed largely by the technology of freight transport. Two principles characterize this technology: First, water transport is much cheaper, but slower, than any other mode; and second, loading and unloading are substantial portions of total transport cost; hence, shipping cost per ton-mile declines with distance.

Determinants of Firm Location When Regions Differ

If regions differ from one another, in either natural or manufactured aspects of their economic environments, the differences affect locations of economic activities. This section lays out some principles governing these location decisions.

Cost considerations. A profit-maximizing firm is also a cost-minimizing firm, but in the spatial context, it must be remembered that cost includes both production cost and transport cost. Furthermore, transport cost includes the cost of transporting both inputs, if they are not locally available, and outputs. In general, there are geographic variations in both transport and production costs, so a profit-maximizing firm must look at both of these sources of interregional cost variation. What follows is a rough taxonomy of firms based on the types of cost considerations that most heavily influence their optimum locations.

The first step is to dichotomize firms into either *production-cost orientation* or *transport-cost orientation*. A production-cost-oriented firm bases its location decision on regional differences in production cost, largely ignoring transport cost. The reverse is true for a transport-cost-oriented firm. A firm is likely to be production-cost oriented if both of the following are true:

1. Transport cost is a small fraction of total cost—in general, because inputs and outputs are light in weight relative to their value or because inputs are available everywhere (ubiquitous) and outputs are light in weight.
2. The production process is intensive for some input in which there is substantial geographic variation in cost—such as labor or, more recently, energy.

The textile industry is production-cost oriented. Textiles are light in weight per dollar of value, so total cost is not very sensitive to the transport component. The industry is intensive in unskilled labor, so a low-wage region offers a large cost saving. Thus, the textile industry moved from New England to the South when the development of steam power (used in the operation of power looms) freed it from water power. (For the same economic reasons, the textile industry has more recently moved to developing countries and the Pacific rim.)

At the opposite end of the spectrum is transport orientation. For such firms, the following statements are true:

1. Transport is a large fraction of cost—in general, because either an input or an output is heavy and bulky relative to its value.
2. Interregional differences in input prices are relatively less important.

Examples are steel and beer. In the case of steel, the raw material inputs—iron ore, coal, and lime—are heavy relative to the value of the final product, and it is worthwhile to locate to economize on transportation of these inputs. This consideration means it is most economical to smelt steel at sites to which it is relatively cheap to transport the inputs. In the case of beer, the heaviest input is water—which also is costly to transport relative to its value. In the latter case, it is most economical to brew beer near the market to avoid trucking water all over the country.

In the first example given (steel), transport-cost considerations induced the firm to locate at an input source; in the second example (beer), the firm located at the market where the output was to be sold. These examples represent two subcategories of transport orientation, known respectively as *materials orientation* and *market orientation*. A firm is materials oriented if it is cheaper to ship the output than the input; hence, the output is produced at the input site. The catchword for "cheaper to ship the output than the input" is *weight losing,* although, as will be seen, not all materials-oriented firms are technically weight losing. If the production process begins with an input available only at certain sites (a localized input, such as coal or iron ore) and yields a relatively lightweight output (steel is light in weight compared with the amount of coal and ore required to produce it), transport cost is minimized by locating the plant at the site where the localized input is available.[1] Other products, such as beer, are *weight gaining.* In the most straightforward cases of "weight-gaining" production, a ubiquitous input (water, in the case of beer) is added to raw materials or to an intermediate product to yield the final product. Transport cost is minimized by shipping the localized inputs to the market and then adding the ubiquitous input.

As noted, *weight losing* does not necessarily mean "weight losing" in the literal sense, as the history of livestock slaughtering demonstrates. Prior to about 1960, the majority of hogs and cattle raised in Indiana,

---

1. In the case of more than one localized input, such as in the case of steel, the optimum site minimizes the total cost of shipping inputs. In general, this site will be where the localized input is the heaviest.

Illinois, and Iowa were shipped to the Chicago stockyards for slaughter. Chicago, in Carl Sandburg's famous phrase, was "hog-butcher to the world." But slaughtering was not weight gaining—only about 60 percent of live weight is prepared as meat for consumption.[2] In addition, cattle lost weight in transit; on both counts, it was better to slaughter cattle in the feedlot than in the stockyards of Chicago.

Why, then, did farmers ship live animals to Chicago rather than only the meat? Until the invention of the refrigerated truck, the meat would have spoiled in transit. With refrigerated trucking, however, the shipment of meat to market became cheaper than shipping livestock. Beginning in the 1960s, the Midwest was dotted with small slaughterhouses, and Chicago was no longer hog-butcher to the world. Indeed, it was no longer hog-butcher to Chicago; its last stockyard closed in 1971. Thus, with the change in technology, slaughtering shifted from market orientation to materials orientation.[3]

As a rough characterization, the historical trend in the United States has been away from materials orientation in particular (contrary to the pattern noted for beef slaughter) and from transport orientation in general. The reason for the shift from materials orientation is simply that, with the more complicated production processes that have come with technical progress, fewer processes are weight losing. In general, transport orientation has declined because of rapid declines, throughout the history of the United States, in the cost of transport.

An example: The steel industry. The history of the steel industry illustrates well the decline in the importance of materials and transport orientation. The transport orientation of the steel industry has been greatly reduced over the past century, first because of improvements in bulk transport, and second because of dramatic technical improvements in steel production. Between 1879 and 1919, the coal requirement per ton of steel fell 67 percent, from 3.93 to 1.31 tons. Over the same period, ore requirements decreased 45 percent, from 2.11 to 1.16 tons (Harper, 1976). By 1980, coal and ore requirements had fallen to 0.57 and 0.104 tons, respectively.[4] The reduction in coal use came from more efficient use of heat in mills; the reduction in ore use resulted partly from the

2. Furthermore, shipment of live cattle reduced their weight and meat yield. This effect was, of course, even more pronounced during the days of cattle drives in the 1870s and 1880s.

3. The same locational principles govern earlier stages in the production of beef. Cows give birth to calves on the high-plains grasslands just east of the Rocky Mountains. These calves are then fattened into beef cattle on a diet of corn—which must be grown farther east in Iowa, Illinois, and adjacent states. Fattening beef cattle is weight-losing (it takes about ten pounds of corn to produce one pound of beef), so after weaning, calves are shipped from the grasslands to the cornfields for fattening.

4. The 1980 data come from the 1981 *Annual Statistical Report* of the American Iron and Steel Institute. The ability to produce a ton of steel from one-tenth of a ton of ore results from the use of scrap and iron-bearing by-products of mining and smelting.

discovery of richer ores in Minnesota and partly from the increased use of scrap iron as an ore substitute.

To illustrate how the importance of transport cost has declined, consider that Japan, with neither coal nor ore deposits, has become a major steel exporter. Indeed, when the World Trade Center was built on the Baltimore waterfront in 1977, the structural steel was imported from Japan, despite the fact that Bethlehem Steel's Sparrows Point mill was fewer than five miles away by barge.

Technical progress in steel manufacture itself represented only part of the story. In 1879, railroad rails constituted 44.8 percent of steel mill output (in tons). By 1919, the rails' share had fallen to 9.5 percent and to 2.1 percent by 1980. Structural steel took up much of the slack, rising from 8.3 percent in 1879 to 22 percent in 1919 (and down to 15 percent in 1980). Rails were finished products, but the overwhelming bulk of steel output in 1980 was of intermediate products (14.5 percent of output went to the auto industry and 14.2 percent went to construction). In other words, in 1879, most of the value that was added to iron ore took place at the steel mill. Today, however, because more complicated things are being done with steel, the bulk of value added has taken place after the steel leaves the mill. The location of most production, even if it uses steel as a major input, has been independent of the fact that steel smelting is a weight-losing industry.

The production of steel is currently more footloose (a term that will be explained in the following section), both because technical progress has reduced its input requirements and because of improvements in bulk transport. Furthermore, the manufacture of steel *products* is more footloose than in the past because the steel itself has become a smaller part of the value of final products.

Footloose Industries and Amenity Orientation

If transport orientation has declined, is it necessarily true that production-cost orientation has increased? The secular decline in transport cost has left firms more able to seek locations where production cost is low. One side effect of firm movement to areas of low production cost, however, is the raising of production costs in the receiving area and the lowering of production costs in the sending area. If firms move from a high-wage to a low-wage area to take advantage of cheap labor, wages are driven up in the low-wage area and depressed in the high-wage area. This gradual reduction in interregional input-price differentials (which will be documented for labor in the next section) implies that production-cost orientation is declining. When interregional production cost differences are small, they should not have a big effect on firm location.

What does it mean to say that both transport-cost orientation and production-cost orientation have declined historically? Basically, it means that for a large range of firms, interregional cost differences are very small, and location decisions are less important than they were several decades ago. Increasingly, according to this view, firms are *footloose*—largely free from traditional location constraints. This state has led to *amenity orientation,* a firm-location criterion based on pleasant locational attributes—such as climate or culture—rather than on transport or production cost.

In fact, amenity orientation is production-cost orientation in another guise. As will be discussed more fully in Chapters 7 and 14, most interurban wage differences appear to be related directly to interurban amenity differences. Basically, labor can be attracted to a high-amenity environment more readily (and hence, for a lower wage) than to a low-amenity environment. Thus, even in a world of perfect mobility, wage differences persist as compensation for amenity differences. Firms now may be attracted to high-amenity sites because labor there is cheaper, which is to say because workers are attracted to high-amenity sites. This trend may continue until high-amenity regions begin to suffer amenity declines with rising population. Such declines may be the result of pollution and congestion or, in the case of the Southwest, water shortages.

☐ REGIONS AND REGIONAL SHIFTS IN THE UNITED STATES, 1790 TO 1990[5]

This section gives an overview of the economic forces governing the location of economic activity and urbanization in the United States since colonial times.

Colonial Times

When the United States was founded, most manufactured goods consumed in this country came from Europe. A few small iron foundries, which had been established during the Revolution, continued to operate, but they were the major exception. Cities formed along the North Atlantic seaboard to serve as collection points for grain exports and manufactured imports. The market initially was not sufficiently dense to support much local manufacture.

Manufactured goods tended to be imported from Europe rather than produced domestically because of scale economies (coupled with the fact that ocean transport was cheap). The American population was not large enough to support home production.

With the growth of cities and the decline in overland transport cost in the first half of the nineteenth century (see Chapter 1), the economic feasibility of domestic manufacturing emerged. Manufacturing devel-

5. This discussion relies heavily on Mieszkowski (1979), which provides for a fuller treatment of these topics.

oped initially in the North—but not in the South—because of higher concentrations of people, which, in turn, was in part due to the difference between the technologies for exporting grain and tobacco. Grain, which was produced in the North, was transported overland from farms to port cities, where it was loaded onto ships. (This costly overland transport was justified because of the high value of grain relative to its weight.) By contrast, tobacco produced in the South was loaded directly onto ships at the plantation's wharf. In part, this procedure was due to the high bulk-to-value ratio of tobacco and in part to the fact that southern rivers are generally navigable farther inland (the fall line is farther inland) than are northern rivers.

Geography played another important role in determining the differences between northern and southern development. Most of the Carolina coast is bounded by barrier islands, which prevent oceangoing ships from reaching the coast. Produce from the Carolina region was sent up the coastal waterway in special shallow-draft barges to Norfolk, Virginia, where it was loaded onto oceangoing vessels.[6] On the eve of the Revolution, Norfolk was one of the major colonial cities, but it was virtually destroyed during the war. For reasons to be given, Norfolk did not regain its former prominence during the nineteenth century. The early emergence of northern cities was also influenced by the wider availability of water power, which enabled it to take advantage of the manufacturing opportunity presented by its colonial growth.

Northern colonial cities flourished as a result of exploitation of some exportable resource. Boston exported fish from Cape Cod, New York exported furs from the Hudson River valley, and Philadelphia and Baltimore exported wheat from nearby land. Until approximately 1750, all were primarily import-export depots—commercial rather than manufacturing centers. Contact among colonial cities, particularly until about 1850, was probably less significant than contact with England. (Recall the model from Chapter 1, in which cities of equal size do not trade with one another.)

Early Development

By the beginning of the nineteenth century, many northern cities had become large enough to support home production of manufactured goods, thus replacing some imports. This process, known as *import substitution,* is one of the central themes of this chapter. The self-feeding process works as follows: Population increases sufficiently to permit home production of some goods, causing population to rise more (due to the home-production–induced demand for labor), causing more import substitution, and so on. This process was well underway in the cities of the eastern seaboard by 1810. By 1850, the Northeast not

---

6.   The inland Carolina waterway was also the home of the pirate Blackbeard, so for a considerable period transit of produce to Norfolk was quite hazardous.

only had replaced many European exports with its own production, it also had become a major exporter of manufactured goods to the South and the emerging Midwest. As will be seen, this process of import substitution was repeated in the Midwest, the Far West, and more recently, in the South.

Finally, it should be noted that the emergence of northern cities as manufacturing centers was stimulated in part by the cutoff of British goods during the Revolution and, again, during the War of 1812. Indeed, the War of 1812 seems in some ways to have been connected with New York's emergence as America's premier city (before the war, it was a toss-up between New York and Philadelphia). As the war ended, British manufacturers saw the threat from American manufacturing, and set out to flood the American market, through New York, to bankrupt American manufacturers. Many were bankrupted, but with the flood of goods, New York realized an era of prosperity in its old role as a commercial center. Part of the fruit of this prosperity was invested in the Erie Canal. At almost the same time (1817), a group of merchants offered the first *scheduled* transatlantic shipping service (the so-called packet service). These two innovations placed New York in the lead among eastern cities as a commercial center, from which base manufacturing soon re-emerged.

Import substitution could be seen clearly in the growth of Pittsburgh. Founded as Fort Duquesne by the French, it was renamed Fort Pitt after the French and Indian War. It became a commercial center after the Revolution by supplying the needs of migrants into the Northwest Territory. Pittsburgh purchased all manner of manufactured goods from Baltimore and Philadelphia and resold them to homesteaders. The road from Philadelphia to Pittsburgh saw a steady stream of Conestoga wagons hauling this material.[7]

As the trade down the upper Ohio River increased, it became economically feasible to replace the imported manufactured goods with home production. As early as 1820, Pittsburgh began to sprout foundries, glass factories, and machine shops.[8]

Chapter 1 described a series of innovations that reduced intracity transport costs by a factor of approximately ten. The initial innovations came in around 1850, but the most dramatic progress was made between about 1890 and 1940, with the adoption first of electric power and later of internal-combustion power. These innovations were preceded by approximately 50 years by a series of innovations that marked an absolute revolution in interregional transport. The development, and

---

7.   The Conestoga wagon was built with a watertight box so that it could stay afloat while fording a deep stream. When railroads replaced the wagon trains, these Conestogas became surplus, available to be recycled into their better-known trips across the Great Plains.

8.   For an excellent discussion of the early development of Pittsburgh, see Glaab and Brown (1967).

the changing location pattern, of cities was intimately connected to those innovations.

The first of those innovations was the Erie Canal and rail links between eastern cities and the Ohio valley. The Erie Canal vastly expanded New York's hinterland, and it pushed the effective fall line to Detroit and ultimately to Chicago. By bypassing Niagara Falls, all the Great Lakes except Superior became essentially coastal.[9] Like New York before it, Detroit began as a commercial and transshipment center. Once again, the process of import substitution allowed Detroit gradually to replace New York manufactures with home production and, ultimately, to become a manufacturing exporter itself.

The big boom town was Chicago. The Erie Canal gave it access to the Atlantic, and by 1847, Chicago had a canal connecting Lake Michigan with the Illinois (and, therefore, the Mississippi) River. Chicago quickly emerged as the preeminent city of the heartland.[10]

What the Erie Canal did for Detroit and Chicago, the steamboat did for New Orleans and St. Louis.

New Orleans was not established as a commercial or manufacturing city, but rather as part of a grand French design to dominate North America. The plan was to have an empire that ran up the St. Lawrence River, through the Great Lakes basin, and down the Mississippi, thus isolating the British colonies on the eastern seaboard. New Orleans was established for this military purpose in 1721.

Even before the advent of the steamboat in about 1820, New Orleans was a major commercial center. Goods were floated down the river on rafts, then loaded onto oceangoing vessels. Of course, trade was two way, and upriver travel was very costly. Consequently, the steamboat cut the cost of river travel by perhaps 90 percent, and its advent assured the emergence of New Orleans. Between 1810 (seven years before the first steamboat) and 1860, New Orleans grew in population from 17,000 to 168,000. In 1840, it was the third largest city in the nation.

St. Louis was founded in 1764, under orders from France, for the purpose of developing trade on the Missouri River. Located on the first high ground south of the confluence of the Missouri and Mississippi rivers, it served this precise role for the next century.[11]

The first steamboat arrived from New Orleans in 1817. From this time on, St. Louis had direct and inexpensive access to the great water routes of the world. For the first half of the nineteenth century, the major

9. With the opening of the Soo locks in 1855, Lake Superior also gained access to the coast. This availability gave the American steel industry access to the rich iron mines of Minnesota.

10. Glaab and Brown vividly describe land-value escalation in Chicago, including a 100-fold increase between 1834 and 1837. They state, "As the real estate boom neared its climax, early in 1837, daily advances in land values of twenty to twenty-five percent were not unusual."

11. The French founded St. Louis just at the time they were losing their North American empire, so the city was originally governed by Spain. It came into the possession of the United States, as did New Orleans, with the Louisiana Purchase.

product St. Louis offered to the world was furs.[12] The fur traders left St. Louis every spring with provisions and barter material for the trappers and Indians, returning in the fall with furs.[13] The Missouri was considerably more treacherous than the Mississippi, with the result that steamboat navigation was delayed until the late 1840s. Early travel up the Missouri was by keelboat, powered by poles and ropes. A round trip from St. Louis to the fur-yielding regions of the upper Missouri required a full season—departure from St. Louis in the early spring and return in the late fall. The steamboat not only reduced cost but also increased the probability of returning at all.

The importance of St. Louis was further enhanced by the opening of navigation between the Mississippi and Chicago, which enabled it to send and receive goods from that direction as well. In the absence of the steamboat, river travel would not have been sufficiently economical to permit St. Louis to become more than a minor regional center.[14]

A city's ability to flourish was critically determined by its ability to develop a trading hinterland and access to the outside world; until the Civil War, this success depended critically on water navigation routes.

The Railroad Era and Beyond

The railroad, which came into widespread use in the decades after the Civil War, significantly weakened the advantage of water as a medium for bulk transport. In prerailroad days, overland transport was perhaps a few hundred times more costly than water transport, but the railroad reduced this gap to something considerably less than a ratio of ten to one.

With the railroad, east-west transport across the country became feasible. In addition, within fairly broad limits, railroads could be built anywhere. The location of cities, at least in detail, became tied less to accidents of geography and more to the locations of railroad lines. Particularly in the West, many cities were placed where they are, in large measure, because of effective boosterism on the part of city founders.

A prime example of this boosterism placement was Kansas City, even though the confluence of the Missouri and Kansas rivers was hardly the stuff of which locational advantage is made. The city became a major meat-packing center shortly after several business leaders persuaded (bribed) the Hannibal and St. Joseph Railroad to build its connection with the Union Pacific through Kansas City rather than Leavenworth.

12.   Recall that fur-exporting is precisely the economic role played by New York a century earlier.

13.   As a lesson in economics, it is fascinating to read in *The American Fur Trader of the Far West* by Chittenden (1935) of the disdain the Indians and traders felt for one another, and each for the same reason. In the exchange of furs for beads, blankets, metalware, and other manufactured goods, each party to the trade thought the other side was giving up something of great value in exchange for something almost valueless.

14.   For an excellent and colorful discussion of this material on New Orleans and St. Louis, see Chittenden.

This connection was the first bridge across the Missouri, completed in the late 1860s. Similar stories, with approximately equal parts geographical imperative, chance, and hucksterism, surrounded the locations of many other Western cities, including Denver, Omaha (another bridge across the Missouri), and Los Angeles. In each instance, the existence of an exportable surplus ensured that a city would arise, but the location of the city, up to a radius of nearly 100 miles or more, was a matter of choice.

The element of choice added noticeable color to the development of the West. The location of future cities lay in considerable measure in the hands of the railroad barons. Given that the value of urban land was close to several hundred times greater than that of rural land, landowners from all over the West went to frantic lengths to secure the railroad links that held the hope, if not the promise, of great wealth.

The rise of the railroads reduced the significance of the Mississippi and its main tributaries as the only viable transport link to the Great Plains. Of the water-based cities of the first half of the nineteenth century, the ones that flourished in the second half were those that developed important rail links. Thus Chicago, not St. Louis, became the hub of the upper Midwest. New Orleans, which had been the fifth largest city in 1860, fell to fifteenth by 1910.

The railroads did much more than determine the location of western cities. The railroads also reduced overland transport cost sufficiently to make trade between these regions and the rest of the world viable.

Until about 1940, the South did not challenge the Northeast in manufacturing, nor did many low-paid, low-skill workers migrate to higher-paying jobs in the North. The failure of industry to move south, where incomes and wages were lower, may have resulted from scale economies and the larger initial population in the North, as well as from the more fully developed railroad network in the North. (See Figure 2.2, which shows the gradual convergence of real incomes among regions.) The failure of southern low-skill workers to migrate to the high-wage North surely resulted in part from racial barriers in the North. In addition, the jobs in the North that might have been claimed by migrating southerners were claimed, for several generations, by European immigrants.

Although the South did not compete with the Northeast, the Far West did. From the start, the Pacific (and later the Mountain) states were a high-wage area for both supply and demand reasons. Initially, the population was small, so manufactured goods had to be imported from Europe or the Northeast. Wages had to be high to compensate for the high cost of living. Employers, however, were willing to pay high wages, because labor was scarce relative to the abundant supply of resources (largely timber and minerals). Indeed, the wage premium offered by employers was apparently more than sufficient to compensate for higher prices. The high wages induced migration, and eventually, the popula-

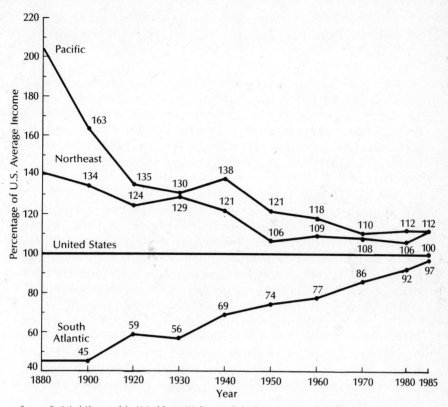

Source: *Statistical Abstract of the United States.* Washington, D.C.: Government Printing Office, 1981, 1987.

Figure 2.2   *Regional per Capita Income, 1880 to 1985 (Selected Regions, Percentage of Average in United States)*

tion of the Far West began to grow. By 1910, the population of the West was growing faster (in absolute numbers, not just in percentage) than in the Northeast. Figures 2.3, 2.4, and 2.5 document these population shifts for American-born whites and blacks and foreign-born whites. Note the following important features of these figures:

1. For whites, net migration to the Northeast has been negative since 1930; the outflow has grown in nearly each succeeding decade.
2. There was a modest net outflow of whites from the South from 1910 through 1950. Beginning in about 1960, the inflow of whites to the South has been very rapid.
3. There has been a positive net flow of whites to the West in every decade since 1880, although the pace has slowed considerably since the peak years immediately following World War II.
4. Blacks left the South in modest numbers up through 1910, and at an increasing pace in the next 20 years. There was an enormous

outflow of blacks from 1940 through 1970, but since the mid-1970s, there has been very little interregional movement of blacks.

With population growth came the ability to take advantage of scale economies locally and to substitute home production for imports from the Northeast. This process fed on itself in the West, as it had earlier in the Northeast—up to a point. The more home production, the larger the population that can find jobs. The larger the population, the more it is possible, because of scale economies, to substitute home production for imports.

The export base continues to be the rationale for the West's economy, as in the gold rush days. With today's larger population, however, the region is more nearly self-sufficient, and the ratio of nonbasic to basic (export) employment has risen. The result of these forces is that the West's wage premium over that of the Northeast gradually has been eroded, first because migration has reduced the labor shortage, and second because the gradual substitution of home production for imports has reduced the West's cost-of-living premium.

The increasing local production of the West gradually has robbed the Northeast of one of its export markets. A substantial portion of the Northeast's comparative advantage over the history of the United States has been derived from both its access to Europe and its size (population). The gradual erosion of both advantages began almost with the founding of the nation.

It is important to note that the flight from the Northeast to the West, which has received so much attention over the past few years, has been going on for two centuries. There are two major differences between the flights from 1970 to the present and in the previous 200 years. First, until about 1970, the emigrants from the Northeast always were replaced by immigrants—from Europe until about 1930 and then, beginning with the Great Depression and World War II, by southern blacks. Beginning in the early 1970s, however, the wave of black migration from the South to the Northeast stopped, and in fact, reversed. As can be seen in Figure 2.4, the out-migration of blacks from the Northeast began in the first half of the 1970s. About one-third of the migration of blacks to the Northeast in the 1960s was undone by migration from the Northeast (basically a return to the South and a move to the West) in the 1970s. At this time, the long-standing pattern of migration from the Northeast to the West began to result in population declines for the Northeast.

The second difference is that in the years after World War II, the West has achieved sufficient size (population) to be roughly comparable with the Northeast. In short, the Northeast no longer has its initial advantage—scale—compared with the rest of the country. Also, it no longer serves as a major processing region for immigrants.

While much of this shift between the Northeast and the West was in progress, the South was languishing in the aftermath of the Civil War and

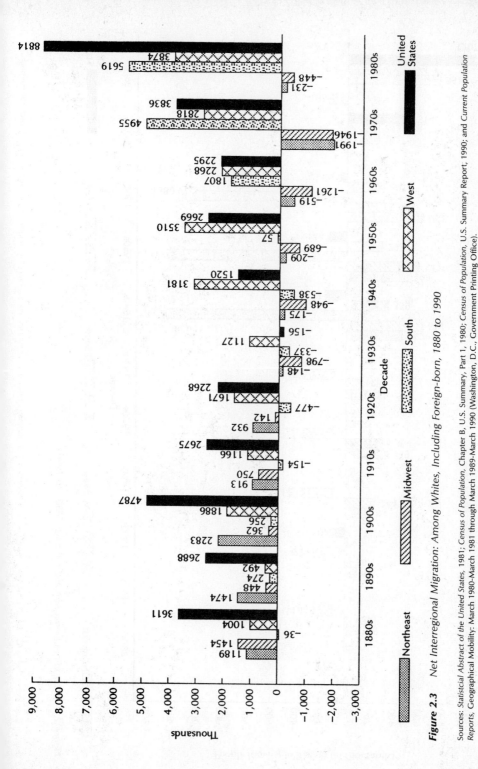

Figure 2.3   Net Interregional Migration: Among Whites, Including Foreign-born, 1880 to 1990

Sources: *Statistical Abstract of the United States*, 1981; *Census of Population*, Chapter B, U.S. Summary, Part 1, 1980; *Census of Population, U.S. Summary Report*, 1990; and *Current Population Reports, Geographical Mobility:* March 1980–March 1981 through March 1989–March 1990 (Washington, D.C., Government Printing Office).

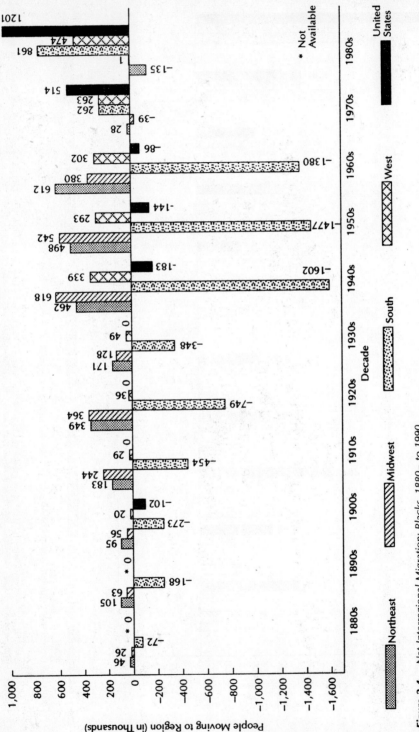

Figure 2.4   Net Interregional Migration: Blacks, 1880– to 1990

* Not available.

Sources: Statistical Abstract of the United States, 1981, 1987; Census of Population, U.S. Summary, 1990; and Current Population Reports, Geographical Mobility: March 1980–March 1981 through March 1989–March 1990 (Washington, D.C., Government Printing Office).

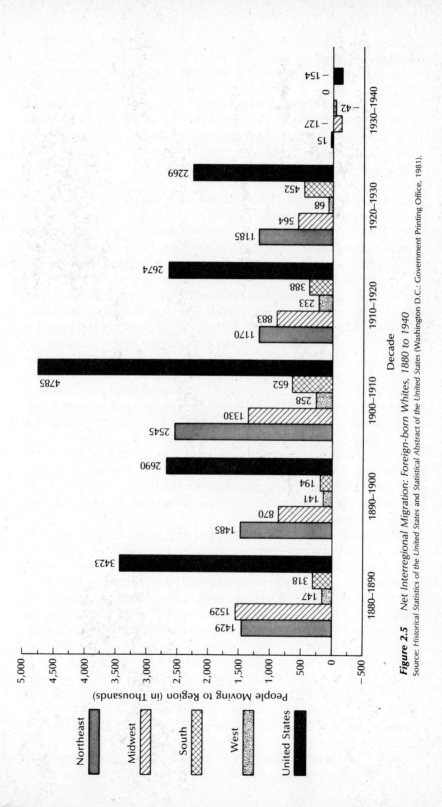

Figure 2.5   *Net Interregional Migration: Foreign-born Whites, 1880 to 1940*

Source: *Historical Statistics of the United States* and *Statistical Abstract of the United States* (Washington D.C.: Government Printing Office, 1981).

Reconstruction. As late as 1940, as much as 40 percent of the southern population worked in agriculture (compared with 23 percent nation-wide). The failure of the South to show much economic growth before World War II, even though its low wage structure should have attracted industry, resulted from a number of causes. First, the Northeast contin-ued to dominate the South in terms of size and transport network. Thus, the Northeast continued to be the location of choice for market-oriented firms with scale economies (it is cheaper to ship a small amount of output to the South than a large amount to the North). Second, although this is hard to document, regional prejudice may have played a role in industries locating in the North rather than in the South.

Until the development of modern sanitation and medicine, disease may have been a more serious impediment to southern urbanization than northern urbanization. The drier summers and colder winters of the North provided a check on the spread of infectious diseases, and mosquito-borne diseases (most notably yellow fever) took a heavy toll in the South in the nineteenth century. There is no reason to believe that yellow fever was much worse in urban than in rural areas, but the same would not be true for diseases carried by air- or water-borne germs.

The industrial awakening of the South began with a dramatic shift out of agriculture—partly in a shift to southern manufacturing but largely in a migration of southern blacks to the Northeast. By 1970, only 6 percent of the southern population was in agriculture (compared with 4.8 percent nationwide). Interestingly, the migration of southern blacks to northeastern cities began after the flow of European immigrants had almost halted. The massive migration of blacks (3.4 million between 1940 and 1970) was caused by a combination of push and pull. The mechanization of southern agriculture forced many low-skill workers off the farm, and, at the same time, wages were higher in the North (and for the first time since Emancipation, these jobs were not being taken by European immigrants).

Almost simultaneous with this out-migration of blacks from the South was a substantial net in-migration of whites, largely from the Northeast. Between 1950 and 1970, the net in-migration of whites to the South was 1.9 million, which was followed by another 2.3 million in the first half of the 1970s. These generally high-skilled whites apparently were attracted to the South by its manufacturing boom. The manufactur-ing boom may have resulted in part from the availability of a low-wage, nonunion work force (although the boom was not sufficient to absorb all the people released from agricultural work).

All the flows of labor described are expected—from low-wage regions to high-wage regions. The continual flow of people from the Northeast to the West follows this pattern, as does the earlier flow of blacks from the South to the Northeast. Figure 2.2 shows American per capita income, by region and decade, as a percentage of the national average. The figure reveals that the West always has been a high-wage region and the South has been a low-wage region relative to the

Northeast. The most striking feature of the figure is the convergence of incomes over the past century. This convergence, according to Mieszkowski, is even more nearly complete if regional difference in living costs is accounted for.

This characterization of the economic interactions among regions pleads to the following observations regarding cities and urban economics:

1. The flight from the Northeast to the Sun Belt is of long duration and has been driven, in part, by predictable interregional wage differences. These wage differences had been largely eliminated by 1990, which resulted in a significant slowdown in the pace of migration.
2. The major reason for the increased visibility of the flight to the Sun Belt is the lack of replacement migration to the Northeast. With the cessation of black migration from the South in about 1970, gross outflows have been net outflows.
3. The emergence of the modern southern urban sector has been in progress since at least 1950. The rapid out-migration of blacks in the 1950s and 1960s tended to conceal from view the almost equally rapid in-migration of highly skilled whites.
4. The rapid migration of blacks into northeastern cities, which began after World War I, reached its peak between 1940 and 1960 and completely stopped shortly after 1970. Few blacks (or whites, for that matter) live in rural areas of the South, so another such wave of migration cannot be expected. This finding should lead to the question of whether some of our urban racial problems are due in part not to race, per se, but to the disruptions and tensions associated with the one-shot, massive migration.[15]

☐ Summary

This chapter began by exploring the determinants of firm location in a world with geographic variety in endowments. Next, it used this theory to examine the economic history of the development of regions in the United States.

When regions differ from one another in their resource endowments, the world becomes more interesting than had been described in Chapter 1. First, the profitability of firms varies with location; hence, different types of firms will locate at different types of sites. Second, both profitability and efficiency dictate that regions trade with one another, because they tend to produce different types of goods.

15. Absorption of waves of migrants, and problems associated with this absorption, is hardly a new phenomenon for American cities. Through the second half of the nineteenth century, New York was dominated by immigrants. In 1890, for example, 80 percent of the residents of New York were either foreign born or the offspring of foreign born.

Questions and Problems

1. This chapter explained that transport-oriented firms tend to locate either at sources of raw materials or at markets. Would it ever pay a firm to locate midway between its materials sources and markets? Why?

2. Name cities that have locations that can be explained by the following:
   a. Materials-oriented firms
   b. Production cost-oriented firms
   c. Market-oriented firms

3. First in the Northeast, then in the West, and most recently in the South, industrialization and urbanization progressed quite slowly for a while and then accelerated. Can you think of a reason for this pattern?

4. From 1950 to 1970, most of the rapidly growing metropolitan areas in the United States were near the edges of the country, with easy access to ocean transportation (including the ports of the Great Lakes). How do you explain this finding in a country in which international trade is relatively unimportant?

References and Further Reading

American Iron and Steel Institute. *1981 Annual Statistical Report* (Washington, D.C., American Iron and Steel Institute, 1982).

Chittenden, Hiram M. *The American Fur Trade in the Far West* (Lincoln: University of Nebraska, 1935).

Courant, Paul N., and Alan V. Deardorff. "International Trade with Lumpy Countries." *Journal of Political Economy* 100 (1992): 198–210. This paper is quite advanced. For students who have had a rigorous course in international trade, it offers some interesting insights into the relationship between interregional and international trade.

Fogel, Robert, and Stanley Engerman, eds. *The Reinterpretation of American Economic History* (New York: Harper & Row, 1971). A collection of essays by several scholars on various aspects of economic history in the United States.

Glaab, Charles N., and A. Theodore Brown. *A History of Urban America* (New York: Macmillan, 1967). This is a superb discussion of the history of the development of urban America. It is an excellent companion to Chapters 1 and 2.

Harper, Ann. *The Location of the American Iron and Steel Industry: 1879–1919.* Ph.D. dissertation, Johns Hopkins University, 1976.

Isard, Walter. *Location and Space Economy* (New York: Wiley, 1956). A technical discussion of location theory.

Mieszkowski, Peter. "Recent Trends in Urban and Regional Development." In *Current Issues in Urban Economics,* edited by Peter Mieszkowski and Mahlon Straszhein (Baltimore: Johns Hopkins University Press, 1979). An excellent and highly readable discussion of regional shifts, as well as the basis for much of the discussion in this chapter. Other survey papers in this volume are also very good and frequently will be referred to at the appropriate places.

Temin, Peter. *Iron and Steel in 19th Century America* (Cambridge, Mass.: MIT Press, 1964).

Weber, Alfred. *Alfred Weber's Theory of Location of Industries,* translated by Carl Friedrich (Chicago: University of Chicago Press, 1929).

3

Urbanization and Economic Growth in the United States

☐ Very poor countries, without exception, are largely agricultural, because food is the prime requirement for life. Economic development consists, in part, of the transfer of labor and other inputs from predominantly rural agriculture to predominantly urban manufacturing and service sectors. Thus, economic growth everywhere is associated with urbanization.

During the nineteenth century, rapid economic growth in Europe and North America resulted in rapid urbanization. The United States, having industrialized somewhat later than western Europe, also lagged in urbanization. Much of Europe was highly urbanized by the early decades of the twentieth century. Since about 1925, even more rapid industrialization and urbanization have taken place in some countries in Asia and South America. (Urbanization in developing countries will be discussed in Chapter 17.)

One prerequisite for the urbanization of the past two centuries was technical progress in various aspects of urban life, which was discussed in Chapter 1. Equally important, however, was technical progress in agriculture, which enabled a small farm population to feed an urban population many times its size. (The effects of this change will be documented ahead in the section on long-term trends.)

☐ A DIGRESSION ON DISEASE

The nature of the agricultural revolution that facilitated modern urban growth need not be a concern to this discussion, although it is interesting to note that advances in agriculture have been behind previous waves of urbanization. Indeed, until modern times, the rural sector had to produce not only a surplus of food but also a surplus of people. Urban death rates were sufficiently high, until the advent of modern sanitation, that cities were demographically unable to sustain themselves. In some parts of the world, rural populations were sufficiently disease ridden that they could not produce this surplus of food or people. According to McNeill (1976), the unhealthy environment in tropical Africa was one of the major reasons that large urban areas did not emerge there, although they did emerge later in the 1970s and 1980s. Rather, urbanization had to await the migration of humans from their apparent birthplace in east Africa to less humid, more temperate regions. This migration gave people a respite from the killing and debilitating diseases of the tropics, which in turn allowed the rural sector sufficient health to produce a surplus of food and babies and enabled cities to grow with at least some hope that they would not be wiped out by epidemics.

To a degree, this respite was only temporary. The major debilitating parasitic diseases of the tropics have never effectively penetrated the temperate regions, because the parasites require warmth and humidity in order to travel from host to host. Infectious diseases, however, ultimately caught up with humanity's northward migration.

Europe appeared to have been free of such epidemic diseases as measles, smallpox, and bubonic plague throughout classical times.[1] The first epidemic disease to reach Europe was apparently smallpox, probably carried by Roman troops, in about A.D. 165. This outbreak of smallpox, and other epidemic diseases that were to follow, ushered in an era of European population decline and deurbanization that was to last 500 years (McNeill, p. 103). In the city of Rome, it was said that 5,000 people per day died at the height of the original epidemic. Even before the arrival of bubonic plague, there were many recorded instances of a single epidemic killing 90 percent of a city's population.

A new infectious disease damages a population more severely than an established one for a variety of reasons and after a few generations, populations tend to adapt. So it was with smallpox and measles. Then came bubonic plague in the fourteenth century; it is said to have reduced the population of Europe by 35 percent. These infectious diseases were apparently much more severe in urban areas than in rural areas, simply because of the density of people and the consequent ease of transmission.

During the period when these infectious diseases were establishing themselves in Europe and China, it became virtually impossible to build and sustain urban areas anywhere near the size of classical Rome or Hangzhou, China, which achieved a population of approximately one million in the twelfth century (before the fourteenth-century arrival of plague in China).

Thus, the modern era of urbanization has resulted, in part, from its ability to accommodate to, and limit, the killer diseases of the past. Part

---

1. Even without these killers, the average age at death in Rome, for those who survived childhood, seems to have been just under 30 years.

of this accommodation was immunological, and it was well underway before the beginning of the nineteenth century. The last major outbreak of plague in London was in 1665, one year before the great fire. (There is some speculation that the fire killed many of the rats harboring the disease, and that the methods used during rebuilding were less hospitable to rats than previous construction methods.) The real breakthrough, however, came with the understanding of the causes of these diseases, which began in the middle of the nineteenth century when the role of germs in infectious diseases was discovered. This understanding ultimately led to the construction of sewer systems, attention to clean water and chlorination, and the development of vaccinations and antibiotics. There was a worldwide epidemic of a killer influenza at the end of World War I, and AIDS has threatened similar devastation since the 1980s. All told, the taming of disease is one of the most important prerequisites to modern urban society.

☐ LONG-TERM TRENDS

Although the pattern of urbanization and economic growth has not differed greatly in the United States from that observed in Europe, its scale and speed have been as dramatic here as anywhere. During a period of less than two centuries, the United States was transformed from a rural and agricultural society into an urban and industrial society. Urbanization has been one of the most prominent, widely studied, and controversial trends throughout America's history. This chapter and the next discuss the broad trends of urban growth and the sizes and structures of urban areas. These chapters present a historical context, begun in Chapters 1 and 2, for the analytical chapters that follow in Part Two and for the policy chapters in Part Three.

The simplest statistical picture of the growth and urbanization of the population in the United States is presented in Table 3.1, which shows the growth of the urban and total populations from 1790, the time of the first national census, to 1990.[2] The urban population consists of people living in urban places. According to Chapter 1, most urban areas consist of many urban places, so the population of an urban place is not an indication of the size of an urban area. However, the population of all urban places is the proper measure of the urban population of the entire country. Remember that an urban place can contain as few as 2,500

---

2. Interestingly, the percentage of urban population apparently declined from early colonial times until about 1790. Glaab and Brown (1967) report that almost 10 percent of the population in 1690 had been urban. There were two reasons. The first was safety. Only after the native Americans were pushed beyond the Alleghenies could farmers live alone in relative safety. Second, the Crown apparently encouraged urban living, possibly thinking that urban colonists would be easier to control. The Crown was wrong; most revolutionary leaders were urban.

Table 3.1   *Urban Population of the Coterminous United States, 1790 to 1980 (Population in Millions)*

Year	Total Population	Urban Population	Urban Percentage
1790	3.9	0.2	5.1%
1800	5.3	0.3	5.7
1810	7.2	0.5	6.9
1820	9.6	0.7	7.3
1830	12.9	1.1	8.5
1840	17.1	1.8	10.5
1850	23.2	3.5	15.1
1860	31.4	6.2	19.7
1870	38.6	9.9	25.6
1880	50.2	14.1	28.1
1890	63.0	22.1	35.1
1900	76.2	30.2	39.6
1910	92.2	42.1	45.7
1920	106.0	54.3	51.2
1930	123.2	69.2	56.2
1940	132.2	74.7	56.5
1950	151.3	90.1	59.6
1960	179.3	113.1	63.1
1970*	203.2	149.3	73.5
1980*	226.5	167.1	73.8
1990*	248.7	187.1	75.2

*Based on the new urban-place definition; not comparable with earlier data. See the source for definitions.
Source: Data from U.S. Department of Commerce, Bureau of the Census. *Census of Population* (Washington, D.C.: Government Printing Office, 1972, 1982, 1992).

people, and urban places, therefore, include many villages and small towns.

The total population in the United States grew from 3.9 million in 1790 to 248.7 million in 1990. In 1790, only 5 percent of the country was urban, even under the inclusive measure reported in Table 3.1. In 1960, the urban population was 63 percent. Since 1950, the Census Bureau has used a new, and somewhat broader, definition of *urban places* that increases the urban percentages for 1950 and 1960 in Table 3.1 by about 7 percentage points. Only data based on the new definition are available in the 1970 and subsequent national censuses.

The percentage of the population in the United States that is urban has grown steadily from 1790 to 1990. The country's total population, however, has grown fast enough that the number of people in rural areas also has increased each decade, even though its percentage of the total population has declined. Indeed, the number of rural residents in 1960 exceeded the country's entire population in each census year up to 1900.

Table 3.1 also suggests the close historical relationship that has existed between urbanization and industrialization. Historians place the beginning of rapid industrialization in the United States at about 1840.

Table 3.1 shows that between 1790 and 1840, the urban percentage of the population increased by about 1.1 percentage points per decade. Between 1840 and 1930, the increase averaged about 5 percentage points per decade. Urbanization thus proceeded very rapidly during the second half of the nineteenth century and the early part of the twentieth century, when industrial employment and output also were increasing rapidly.

It is not widely appreciated that *urbanization has decelerated since about 1930*. Between 1930 and 1960, the percentage of the population that was urban increased by an average of only 2.3 percentage points per decade. Industrialization has become more widespread, and the growth rate of employment in manufacturing has slackened relative to that in other sectors. Also, despite the massive urbanization of society, rural areas are by no means drained of people. Even under the new urban-place definition, more than 60 million people still live in rural areas. Another popular misconception is that most rural people live on farms. In 1990, the farm population in the United States was about 5 million (2 percent of the national population). Because the rural population was 61.6 million, about 92 percent of the rural population was nonfarm.

In the early years of history in the United States, the cities and towns in which the urban population lived were very small indeed. In 1790, only 62,000 people lived in the only two cities (New York City and Philadelphia) with populations that exceeded 25,000. By 1840, three cities (New York City, Baltimore, and New Orleans) had populations in excess of 100,000, but the three cities together contained slightly more than 0.5 million people. In 1840, Chicago had fewer than 5,000 people. During the last half of the nineteenth century, statistics on the growth of cities became difficult to interpret because of the common tendency to annex suburban areas to the central city. For example, between 1890 and 1900, New York City's population had increased from 1.5 million to 3.4 million, mostly as a result of the consolidation of the five boroughs that now constitute the city. By 1900, however, six cities (New York City, Chicago, Philadelphia, Baltimore, St. Louis, and Boston) had at least 0.5 million people each. Los Angeles, now the nation's largest PMSA (second largest CMSA), had slightly more than 100,000 people.[3]

Employment data are fragmentary for the early years of the nation's history, but they make it possible to trace the rough outlines of the industrialization process. Table 3.2 shows the number of gainful workers in the total labor force and in agriculture and manufacturing for selected years from 1820 to 1989.

Table 3.2 shows vividly the transformation of the economy in the

---

3. All statistics in this paragraph are from the U.S. Department of Commerce, Bureau of the Census. *Census of Population* (Washington, D.C.: Government Printing Office, 1960). For a more complete list, see Table 4.1.

United States. Farm workers fell in number from 71.9 percent of all workers in 1820 to a mere 2.7 percent in 1989. Conversely, manufacturing workers increased in number from 12.2 percent to 27.1 percent in 1960. Even in 1820, many rural people did not live on farms. As seen in Table 3.1, in that year, 92.7 percent of the population was rural, but only 71.9 percent of the workers were on farms. Table 3.2 also shows that the period of rapid industrialization was between about 1840 and 1920. During that period, the percentage of all workers employed in manufacturing increased by an average of 1.4 percentage points per decade. Between 1920 and 1960, however, the percentage of all workers in manufacturing hardly changed. By 1970, it had fallen below its 1920 value. By 1989, manufacturing absorbed a smaller fraction of the labor force than it had in 1900. (The 1940 figure is strongly influenced by the large amount of unemployment that still existed that year.) The figures in Table 3.2 are workers, not labor force, and employment decreased much more in manufacturing than in agriculture during the Great Depression. Therefore, the 23.6 percent of the workers in manufacturing in 1940 would be closer to the 1920 and 1970 percentages had there been full employment in 1940.

Table 3.2 shows the magnitude of the agricultural revolution that has been in progress during the last century. As a result of mechanization and other changes, productivity per farm worker has risen at an unprecedented rate. Despite the fact that food consumption has increased substantially, agricultural workers have decreased, not only as a

Table 3.2 *Sectorial Distribution of Gainful Workers, 1820 to 1989 (Employment in Thousands)*

		Workers					
Year	Total (No.)	Agriculture (No.)	(Pct.)	Manufacturing (No.)	(Pct.)	Other and Not Allocated (No.)	(Pct.)
1820	2,880	2,070	71.9%	350*	12.2%	460	16.0%
1840	5,420	3,720	68.6	790*	14.6	910	16.8
1860	10,530	6,210	59.0	1,930*	18.3	2,390	22.7
1880	17,390	8,610	49.5	3,170	18.2	5,610	32.3
1900	29,070	10,710	36.8	6,340	21.8	12,020	41.3
1920	41,610	11,120	26.7	10,880	26.1	19,610	47.1
1940	45,070	8,449	18.7	10,650	23.6	25,971	57.6
1950	56,435	6,909	12.2	14,685	26.0	34,841	61.7
1960	64,639	4,257	6.6	17,513	27.1	42,869	66.3
1970	78,678	3,463	4.4	20,746	26.4	54,469	69.2
1980	99,303	3,364	3.4	21,942	22.1	73,997	74.5
1989	117,342	3,199	2.7	21,652	18.5	92,491	78.8

*Includes construction.

Sources: 1820 to 1920 data from *Historical Statistics of the United States,* 1976; 1940 to 1960 data from U.S. Department of Commerce, Bureau of the Census, *Census of Population,* 1972, 1982; 1970 to 1989 data from *Statistical Abstract of the United States,* 1991 (Washington, D.C.: Government Printing Office).

percentage of all workers, but also in numbers. Between 1950 and 1989, more than half of the jobs in agriculture disappeared. Because the rural population grew or, under the new definition, remained about constant during the period, nonfarm people have become an increasingly large percentage of the rural population.[4]

The provision of food has the highest priority in every society. A poor society must devote most of its labor force to the production of food or of exports to get the foreign exchange needed to import food. In wealthy societies, however, high productivity in agriculture and low price and income elasticities of demand for food free much of the labor force to produce other goods and services. In the latter societies, increases in agricultural productivity come from technical progress in both agriculture and industry. In the United States, large increases in agricultural productivity have resulted from technical progress in the design and production of farm machinery, which is part of the manufacturing sector. The process of freeing workers from food production has gone much farther in the United States than in other countries that produce enough food to nourish their population, and the United States is a large net exporter of agricultural products.

Nonagricultural workers can, and often do, however, find rural employment in manufacturing and other sectors. Rapid urbanization has occurred because manufacturing and other employers found it increasingly advantageous to locate in large population centers. Since about 1920, there has been a deceleration of growth in manufacturing employment. One consequence has been a deceleration in the growth of urban areas. Another consequence has been an acceleration of urban employment in other sectors.

☐ RECENT TRENDS

This section discusses recent trends in employment and population across both sectors and regions.

National Employment

As seen in Table 3.2, the fraction of the labor force in manufacturing grew steadily from 1820 to 1960 and then began a fairly steep decline. As Table 3.3 shows, this decline continued in the 1980s. In the period from 1980 to 1985, manufacturing employment fell in absolute numbers (by 4.3 percent), not just as a percent of the total. Manufacturing's share of total employment was down to 18.5 percent in 1989. Also according to Table 3.3, the major growth industry in the 1980s

---

4.   The agricultural revolution is far from complete. It appears that the number of farm workers may fall by half again by the turn of the century. Even if this does happen, the effect on the urban sector will be trivial, as the total number of people involved is very small.

Table 3.3 *Growth of Population and Selected Employment Categories,
United States and Regions (Percentage Change)*

| | Population 1980-90 | Nonagricultural Employment (1980-89) | | | | | |
| | | Total | | Manufacturing | | Services* | |
		1980–89	1985–89	1980–89	1985–89	1980–89	1985–89
United States	9.8%	19.9%	11.2%	−4.3%	0.9%	28.1%	14.4%
New England	7.0	20.2	8.6	−14.6	−10.6	32.1	14.5
Mid-Atlantic	2.2	13.8	7.5	−18.7	−6.5	23.3	10.5
E. North Central	0.8	11.2	10.4	−9.4	1.2	19.0	13.2
W. North Central	2.8	14.5	10.5	1.5	6.3	19.5	12.2
South Atlantic	17.9	32.3	15.8	4.6	3.2	41.5	19.5
E. South Central	3.5	18.6	13.2	5.2	8.1	26.3	15.9
W. South Central	12.4	11.4	1.5	−7.6	−1.4	22.9	6.3
Mountain	20.1	24.7	9.9	13.9	5.1	32.3	13.7
Pacific	23.0	26.2	14.8	8.4	6.5	30.5	16.1

*Includes transportation and public utilities; trade; finance, insurance and real estate; government; and all other services.

Source: Data from *1991 Statistical Abstract of the United States* (Washington, D.C.: Government Printing Office, 1992).

had been services. The service sector of every region of the country registered at least a 15 percent growth in employment. Manufacturing was stagnant virtually everywhere except for healthy growth in the Pacific states. Manufacturing declined most severely in the Middle Atlantic and the eastern North Central states. The shift from manufacturing to services and the regional bias associated with this shift were important forces shaping the destinies of individual urban areas. You will note these trends several times in later chapters, culminating with a discussion in Chapter 16.

MSA Population

Much more accurate and comprehensive data regarding urbanization are available for the period since 1940. Most important has been the publication by the Census Bureau of comprehensive demographic and economic data for MSAs (see Table 3.4). These data confirm the observation that the populations of urban places and MSAs are of similar magnitude. Some urban places are outside MSAs, and some parts of each MSA are rural. There is a large overlap, however, between MSA and urban-place populations, and the two nonoverlapping groups approximately cancel each other out.

The MSA data provide the best picture of the metropolitan character of the population in the United States. Table 3.4 shows that, in 1990, more than 77 percent of the American population lived in metropolitan areas, which places the United States among the world's most urbanized countries. Almost certainly, the percentage of the population living in MSAs will increase only slowly during the coming decades.

Table 3.4 *Population of the United States and MSAs, 1940 to 1990 (Population in Millions)*

Year	United States	MSAs	Percentage in MSAs
1940	132.2	72.8	55.1%
1950	151.3	89.3	59.0
1960*	179.3	112.9	63.0
1970	203.2	139.4	68.6
1980	226.5	169.4	74.8
1985	238.7	182.5	76.5
1990	248.7	192.7	77.5

*1960 and subsequent data include Alaska and Hawaii.
Sources: U.S. Department of Commerce, Bureau of the Census. *Census of Population,* 1982, 1992; and *Statistical Abstract of the United States,* 1987 (Washington, D.C. Government Printing Office).

MSA Employment

By and large, MSAs are labor market areas. Most people who work in an MSA also live there, and vice versa; however, there is some commuting between MSAs. Some people live in Gary and work in Chicago, and some people live in Newark and work in New York City. For this reason, the Census Bureau has created CMSAs. There is relatively little commuting, however, between MSAs and non-MSA areas. The number of workers employed in MSAs is, therefore, about the same as the number of workers living in MSAs. In other words, it is not necessary to distinguish workers by place of employment from workers by place of residence, although the distinction is crucial in discussing data on suburbanization (see Chapter 4).

Table 3.5 shows employment in 1950, 1970, 1980, and 1990 for 12 major industry groups in the United States and in MSAs. For 1950 and 1970, the MSA entry refers to employment in MSAs larger than 100,000. For 1980, the figure is more inclusive—all MSAs. In addition to those included for 1950 and 1970, the 1980 tabulation includes small MSAs that have populations ranging from 50,000 to 100,000 people. The expansion of the definition adds about 5 percent of the labor force to the urban total. Thus, the 1980 numbers show more urbanization of employment, in part, because of an expanded definition of the urban sector.

Aside from those that did not report the industry in which they were employed, the groups are exhaustive; that is, they include all workers. The names of the groups are self-explanatory.

For each year, Table 3.5 shows the percentage distribution of total employment by industry in the United States and in MSAs; it also shows the percentage of all workers found in MSAs in each industry. For any industry and year, the percentage figure in the last column of Table 3.5 exceeds the national total at the bottom of the table if, and only if, the percentage figure in the MSA column exceeds that in the United States column. In other words, if the percentage of the workers in a certain

Table 3.5 Industry Groups of Employed Persons: United States and MSAs (Employment in Thousands)

Industry	1950 United States No.	Pct.	1950 MSAs No.	Pct.	Pct. in MSAs	1970 United States No.	Pct.	1970 MSAs No.	Pct.	Pct. in MSAs	1980 United States No.	Pct.	1980 MSAs No.	Pct.	Pct. in MSAs
Agriculture, forestry, and fisheries	7,034	12.5%	826	2.5%	11.7%	2,840	3.7%	782	1.5%	27.5%	2,913	3.0%	1,194	1.5%	40.9%
Mining	931	1.6	251	0.8	26.9	631	0.8	240	0.5	38.0	1,028	1.1	460	0.6	44.7
Construction	3,458	6.1	2,004	6.1	57.9	4,572	6.0	2,978	5.6	65.1	5,740	5.9	4,193	5.5	73.0
Manufacturing	14,685	26.0	10,021	30.5	68.2	19,837	26.0	13,722	25.8	69.1	21,915	22.4	16,613	22.0	75.8
Transportation, communication, and utilities	4,450	7.9	2,911	8.9	65.4	5,186	6.8	3,832	7.2	73.8	7,087	7.3	5,653	7.5	79.7
Wholesale and retail	10,507	18.6	6,834	20.8	65.0	15,373	20.1	11,026	20.7	71.7	19,934	20.4	15,677	20.0	78.6
Finance, insurance, and real estate	1,920	3.4	1,508	4.6	78.5	3,838	5.0	3,129	5.9	81.5	5,898	6.0	5,057	6.7	85.7
Business and repair services	1,308	2.3	888	2.7	67.8	2,395	3.1	1,904	3.6	79.4	4,018	4.1	3,482	4.6	86.6
Personal services	3,465	6.1	2,154	6.6	62.1	3,537	4.6	2,356	4.4	66.6	3,076	3.6	2,327	3.0	75.6
Entertainment and recreation	493	0.9	382	1.2	77.4	631	0.8	492	0.9	77.9	1,007	1.0	855	1.1	84.9
Professional and related services	4,826	8.6	2,899	8.8	60.0	13,511	17.6	9,606	18.0	71.0	19,812	20.3	15,509	20.0	78.2
Public administration	2,514	4.5	1,727	5.3	68.6	4,202	5.5	3,175	6.0	75.5	5,147	5.3	4,103	5.4	79.7
Not reported*	843	1.5	435	1.3	51.6	—	—	—	—	—	—	—	—	—	—
Total	56,434	100.0%	32,840	100.1%	58.1%	76,553	100.0%	53,242	100.1%	69.5%	97,575	100.4%	75,123	97.9%	76.9%

*"Not reported" category not applicable to 1970 and later years.

Sources: Data from U.S. Department of Commerce, Bureau of the Census. *Census of Population* (Washington, D.C.: Government Printing Office, 1951, 1972, 1982).

sector who are in large MSAs exceeds that for all workers, then the workers in that sector must constitute a larger percentage of workers in the MSA than of workers in the United States.

This relationship is easiest to see by considering an example, such as manufacturing, in Table 3.5. In 1950, the United States had 14,685,000 manufacturing jobs, which constituted 26 percent of total employment. There were 10,021,000 MSA manufacturing jobs, making up 30.5 percent of the MSA jobs. The next column shows that 68.2 percent of manufacturing jobs were in MSAs. At the bottom of this column, it can be seen that 58.1 percent of all jobs were in MSAs. Thus, manufacturing was more urbanized than overall employment in 1950. (Note that by 1970 this was not true, nor was it true in 1980, even with the expanded definition of *urban*.)

It should be expected that some sectors are predominantly located in MSAs, whereas others are predominantly outside MSAs. In 1970, the percentage of workers living in large MSAs ranged from less than 28 percent in agriculture, forestry, and fisheries to more than 81 percent in finance, insurance, and real estate. By 1980, agriculture, forestry, and fisheries remained the least urbanized sector, but even this sector was 41 percent within MSAs. Mining was next with 44 percent. Finance, insurance, and real estate remained the most urbanized in 1980, at 85.8 percent.

Although manufacturing is the largest employer in both the United States and in large MSAs, it was not among the most highly urbanized industries by the measure in Table 3.5. In both 1970 and 1980, seven industries had larger percentages of their employment in large MSAs than did manufacturing. Manufacturing was slightly less urbanized than total employment.

If 1950 is compared with 1970, the percentage of total employment that was in large MSAs rose from 58.1 to 69.5. Manufacturing employment fell from 30.5 percent of MSA employment in 1950 to 25.8 percent in 1970 and to 22 percent in 1980. However, the percentage of manufacturing employees who were in MSAs rose slightly from 68.2 to 69.2. The increase in urbanization of manufacturing from 1970 to 1980 (75.8 percent urbanized in 1980) was almost entirely due to the expanded definition of the urban sector.

In percentage terms, the largest growth in employment both in the United States and in MSAs was in service sectors: finance, insurance, and real estate; business and repair services; personal and professional and related services; and public administration. Together, these sectors grew from 29.2 percent of the work force in 1950 to 40.8 percent in 1980. (As noted in Table 3.3, this trend accelerated between 1980 and 1985. By 1985, 45.8 percent of employment was in the service sector.) These industries not only grew rapidly, but they also became increasingly urbanized. The data presented in the foregoing section on "Long-Term Trends" suggests that, since 1950, the service sector has been the major growth industry in urban areas, and since 1980, manufacturing has actually declined.

The major lesson obtained from Table 3.5 is that manufacturing and other industrial jobs (construction, transportation, communication, and utilities) are no longer the major sources of MSA employment growth. A secondary lesson is that highly urbanized service sectors are not only major sources of increased MSA employment; they also are becoming more urbanized. The MSA shift of employment toward services parallels the national trend and results mainly from high-income elasticities of demand and the slow growth of productivity in service sectors, as well as rapid labor-saving technical progress in manufacturing. One reason for the increased urbanization of service sectors is that they find it increasingly advantageous to locate near hospitals, medical laboratories, law courts, financial markets, and other institutions found mainly in large population centers. Another reason is that improved transportation and communication have increased the ability of service sectors to provide services to customers whose residences are far away.

An anomaly in Table 3.5 is the percentage of agricultural, forestry, and fisheries employment in large MSAs, which rose from 11.7 percent in 1950 to 40.9 percent in 1980. Only a relatively small part of this increase is due to the expanded urban definition, as can be seen by noting the growth between 1950 and 1970. There was a smaller drop in MSA than in total employment in this sector in the United States, probably because of three factors. First, land prices in the rural parts of MSAs most likely have risen relative to prices of other factors of production in agriculture, so MSA agriculture has become increasingly labor intensive. Second, there appeared to be a tendency near population centers to substitute production of labor-intensive agricultural products. Third, nurseries are part of agriculture, and the rise in MSA employment in agriculture probably reflects the growth of nurseries in suburbs. Indeed, approximately 10 percent of agricultural employment takes place in central cities, and another 10 percent occurs in the urbanized portion of suburban rings. Surely, this figure is almost exclusively nursery and other specialty activities.

Note also that mining is 44.7 percent urban. Like agriculture, approximately 10 percent of mining employment takes place within central cities. This figure is apparently just an artifact of small numbers; only 1 percent of total employment in the United States and 0.6 percent of MSA employment are in mining.

MSA Manufacturing Employment

In 1950, manufacturing was by far the largest employer of MSA workers, employing 30.5 percent of the urban workforce. In second place was wholesaling and retailing, employing 20.8 percent. In a virtual tie for third place were transportation sectors (8.9 percent) and professional and related services (8.8 percent). By 1970, however, professional and related services had grown substantially to 18 percent, and manufacturing had shrunk to 25.8 percent. Manufacturing continued to be the leading urban employer, but its lead over both wholesaling and retailing and professional services was very modest. Nevertheless, the dominance of manufacturing indicated that it was worth special attention. In this section the manufacturing sector of Table 3.5 has been broken down into the various components reported by the Census Bureau.

Most industrial statistics from the federal government now are based on a consistent industrial classification scheme. The data in Table 3.5 are based on what is called the *one-digit standard industrial classification* (SIC) *code.* The next level of detail is the two-digit level. For example, all manufacturing industries are in one-digit Groups 2 and 3. Two-digit numbers are numbers from 20 to 39 that represent 20 more-detailed categories of manufacturing industries.[5] These two-digit groups are successively divided into three-, four-, five-, and seven-digit groups. For example, food processing is the two-digit manufacturing industry bearing the SIC Code 20. Within the food-processing category are several three-digit industries, one of which is meat products, which has the three-digit Code 201. Within the three-digit meat products category are several four-digit industries, including slaughterhouses, which is given the four-digit Code 2011. Altogether, there are 149 three-digit industries and 427 four-digit industries. There also are five- and seven-digit codes. Disclosure rules limit the detail governmental agencies can publish. In addition, most five- and seven-digit data are too detailed for economists' purposes. Only at the two-digit level are comprehensive data available for large MSAs, and even at this level of aggregation, the data are not broken down between urban and rural after 1972.

Table 3.6 provides complete two-digit data for manufacturing. The table shows employment data in the United States and in large MSAs for all two-digit manufacturing industries for 1947 and 1972, as well as the national totals for 1982 and 1987. The set of MSAs included consists of those with at least 40,000 manufacturing employees. The set contains only about one-third of the MSAs included in Table 3.5.

It should not be surprising to find that some two-digit manufacturing industries are much more urbanized than others. In 1972, large-MSA employment ranged from a low of 6.1 percent of total employment in tobacco products to a high of 70.7 percent in printing. In general, the figures in Table 3.6 confirm what would be predicted based on the location theory described in Chapter 2. Materials-oriented industries would be expected to be less urbanized than market-oriented industries, because markets almost invariably are concentrated in urban areas, but

---

5.   In 1963, a new two-digit industry (ordinance, with SIC Code 19) was added, but it is not included in the data discussed in this section.

Table 3.6 Manufacturing Employment by Industry Group (Employment in Thousands)

Industry	1947 United States	1947 MSAs	1947 Percentage in MSAs	1972 United States	1972 MSAs	1972 Percentage in MSAs	1982 United States	1987 United States	1972–82 Percentage Change	1982–87 Percentage Change	1947–87 Percentage Change
Food*	1,442	717	49.7%	1,569	764	48.7%	1,488	1,449	-5.2%	-2.6%	0.5%
Tobacco*	112	33	29.5	66	4	6.1	58	45	-12.1	-22.4	-59.8
Textiles*	1,233	384	31.1	953	327	34.3	717	672	-24.8	-6.3	-45.5
Apparel	1,082	759	70.1	1,386	721	52.0	1,189	1,081	-14.2	-9.1	-0.1
Lumber products*	636	87	13.7	691	143	20.7	576	698	-16.6	21.2	9.7
Furniture*	322	158	49.1	462	219	47.4	436	511	-5.6	17.2	58.7
Paper*	450	207	46.0	633	300	47.4	606	611	-4.3	0.8	35.8
Printing	715	511	71.5	1,056	747	70.7	1,291	1,494	22.3	15.7	109.0
Chemicals*	632	370	58.5	837	482	57.6	872	814	4.2	-6.7	28.8
Petroleum refining	212	133	62.7	140	68	48.6	151	116	7.9	-23.2	-45.3
Rubber products	259	176	68.0	618	342	55.3	682	831	10.4	21.8	220.8
Leather*	383	159	41.5	273	84	30.8	200	129	-26.7	-35.5	-66.3
Stone, clay, and glass products*	462	203	43.9	623	305	49.0	531	524	-14.8	-1.3	13.4
Primary metals	1,157	839	72.5	1,143	727	63.6	854	701	-25.3	-17.9	-39.4
Fabricated metals	971	698	71.9	1,493	1,001	67.0	1,460	1,458	-2.2	-0.1	50.2
Nonelectrical machinery	1,545	1,018	65.9	1,828	1,107	60.6	2,189	1,844	19.7	-15.8	19.4
Electrical machinery	801	614	76.7	1,662	974	58.6	1,915	1,565	15.2	-18.3	95.4
Transportation equipment	1,182	901	76.2	1,719	747	43.5	1,596	1,817	-7.2	13.8	53.7
Instruments	232	184	79.3	454	257	56.6	624	982	37.4	57.4	323.3
Miscellaneous	464	339	73.1	446	296	66.4	383	374	-14.1	-2.3	-19.4
Total	14,292	8,490	59.4%	18,052	9,615	53.3%	17,818	18,950*	-1.3%	6.4%	32.6%

*Less urbanized than overall manufacturing.

Source: U.S. Department of Commerce, Bureau of the Census. Census of Manufactures (Washington, D.C.: Goverment Printing Office, 1947, 1973, 1983, 1988).

localized materials frequently are available only in rural locations. Of course, to some extent urbanized areas would be expected to grow up around materials-oriented manufacturing plants, so a dramatic difference would not be expected in urbanization between materials- and market-oriented industries. The industries that are starred in Table 3.6 are less urbanized than the average of all industries; with the sole exception of transportation equipment, they are all either definitely or plausibly materials oriented. In general, the more urbanized industries are those that process intermediate goods rather than raw materials.

From 1972 to 1987, the degree of urbanization of the various manufacturing industries cannot be traced, but overall employment trends could be noted. Total manufacturing employment was about constant during this period, but variation across industries was striking.[6] Several sectors, such as tobacco, textiles, apparel, leather, and primary metals, suffered large declines. Seven industries recorded growth. In general, employment shifted to later stages of processing. In part, this shift was due to the tendency to do more complicated things with primary materials (noted in Chapter 2); in part, it was because earlier production stages have been carried out increasingly in other countries. The United States, with its literate and skilled labor force, has a comparative advantage in the later, more complicated stages of production.

Table 3.6 shows a drop of 6 points in the percentage of manufacturing employment in large MSAs from 1947 to 1972. This finding is in contrast with data in Table 3.5, which shows a slight increase in the percentage of manufacturing employment in large MSAs. Neither the years nor the MSAs are the same in the two tables. Table 3.5, which represents the larger set of MSAs, shows that the percentage of manufacturing employment that is in MSAs has been stagnant, whereas the percentage of the population in MSAs has grown. The contrast between Tables 3.5 and 3.6 shows a dramatic shift of manufacturing from large to smaller MSAs.

If changes in urbanization among particular two-digit industries were considered, an interesting pattern would emerge. The percentage of employment that was in large MSAs fell in most two-digit industries and in those employing most manufacturing workers. The percentage fell in 16 of the 20 two-digit industries. In 1947, the 16 industries employed 89.6 percent of manufacturing workers in large MSAs and 80.5 percent of manufacturing workers in the United States. Furthermore, the percentage decreases were much larger in the industries that became less urbanized than in the industries that became more urbanized.

How do most manufacturing industries become substantially less urbanized at a time when the total changes relatively little? This apparent

---

6. The 1982 figure is depressed somewhat by the severe 1981–1982 recession.

paradox occurs frequently in economics statistics, and it is worthwhile to explore. Although it has not happened, it is logically possible for urbanization to decrease in every manufacturing industry at a time when urbanization increases in total manufacturing employment. An example will make this phenomenon clear. Suppose a country has two industries, A and B (see Table 3.7 for MSA and total employment data for years 1 and 2). Between years 1 and 2, urbanization decreases from 80 percent to 71 percent in Industry A and from 20 percent to 7 percent in Industry B, although urbanization of total employment increases from 50 percent to 52 percent. This peculiar pattern is made possible by a shift in employment in the direction of the more highly urbanized industry. Thus, even though a smaller percentage of workers is in MSAs in Year 2 than in Year 1 in each industry, the percentage of all workers in MSAs has increased, because the more urbanized industry employs a larger percentage of all workers in Year 2 than in Year 1.

A less extreme form of the phenomenon is illustrated in Table 3.6. In 1947, there were 39.7 percent of manufacturing employees in two-digit industries with an urbanization below the national average of 59.4 percent. By 1972, these particular industries employed only 33.9 percent of manufacturing employees. Thus, as seen in Table 3.7, manufacturing employment has shifted in the direction of relatively urbanized two-digit industries.

So much for the apparent statistical paradox. Why does employment shift toward the more highly urbanized industries? Once again, it is what would be predicted based on the location theory presented in Chapter 2. Technical change is pervasive and rapid in manufacturing. An inevitable characteristic of technical progress is an increase in the number of processing stages through which raw materials go before they reach the final consumer. Indeed, the Industrial Revolution itself imposed the factory between the farmer as producer and the farmer as consumer. Current technical change continues to create additional stages of raw-material processing. The greater the number of processing stages, the greater the number of workers who will be found in those two-digit industries representing later processing stages. As has been seen, however, industries engaged in later stages of processing are precisely

Table 3.7 *Increasing and Decreasing Urbanization*

	Year 1			Year 2		
Industry	National Employ-ment	MSA Employ-ment	Percent-age in MSAs	National Employ-ment	MSA Employ-ment	Percent-age in MSAs
A	25	20	80%	35	25	71%
B	25	5	20	15	1	7
Total	50	25	50%	50	26	52%

those that are not tied to location near predominantly rural sources of raw materials.

Increased fabrication of raw materials explains the shift of employment toward urbanized two-digit industries, but it does not explain the decreased urbanization of these industries. All two-digit industries have substantial employment outside urban areas. There is no reason to expect that the percentage of employment in large MSAs will remain constant in any industry. Nevertheless, the particular pattern of decreased urbanization of the most highly urbanized industries calls for study and explanation.

There are, of course, special explanations for changes in particular industries. The decreased urbanization of the textile industry is part of the migration of that industry from New England to predominantly rural parts of the South. The movement has been extensively studied. Decreased urbanization in the apparel industry is explained partly by the movement of that industry out of New York City. There undoubtedly are reasons peculiar to other industries, but it would be interesting to know the importance of factors that are common to most industries.

The pattern observed in this section is one of rather modest increases since World War II in the percentages of population, total employment, and manufacturing employment found in MSAs. There is evidence in all three categories, however, of a slowing down in urbanization. At the same time, there has been a dramatic trend away from manufacturing, particularly at early stages of production, and toward service employment. No one knows what future censuses will show, but it seems likely that the trends since 1940 will persist during the remainder of the twentieth century.

☐ Summary

In less than 200 years, the United States has been transformed from a country in which 95 percent of the population was rural to one in which three-fourths is urban. In broad outlines, the transformation has been associated with dramatic decreases in agricultural employment and with industrialization of the economy. Since about 1920, urbanization has proceeded steadily, even though the percentage of the labor force in manufacturing has remained roughly constant.

There is great variation in the extent of urbanization among industries. Manufacturing is more urbanized than most industries but less urbanized than many service industries. Within manufacturing, industries that process raw materials are the least urbanized, whereas those that process materials previously processed are more urbanized. Since World War II, there has been a shift in manufacturing employment toward more highly urbanized industries but a decrease in urban location in most manufacturing industries.

Questions and Problems

1. Do you think that the manufacturing industry will be less urbanized in 2000 than it is now? Why?

2. What part of the population do you think will live in MSAs in 2000? Do you expect the service sector to become urbanized more rapidly than the total population during the remainder of the century?

3. In the late 1970s, about two-thirds of the population of industrialized countries was urban, whereas only about one-third of the population of less-developed countries was urban. How will these figures change by the end of the century?

4. In many industrialized countries, a larger fraction of the nonfarm population is urban than in the United States. How would you explain that fact?

References and Further Reading

Davis, Kingsley. "The Urbanization of Human Populations." *Scientific American* 213, No. 3 (1965): 41–53. A provocative survey of long-term trends in urbanization in industrialized and less-developed countries.

Handlin, Oscar, and John Burchard, eds. *The Historian and the City* (Cambridge, Mass.: MIT Press, 1963). Papers by historians and other scholars on urban history.

McNeill, William H. *Plagues and Peoples* (Garden City, N.Y.: Doubleday, 1976). This fascinating book discusses the role of disease (particularly communicable and epidemic disease) in shaping world history. The book makes the compelling argument that the process of urbanization was profoundly influenced by the relationship between people and disease-causing microorganisms.

Perloff, Harvey, et al. *Regions, Resources and Economic Growth* (Baltimore: Johns Hopkins University Press, 1960). An influential study of the causes and consequences of regional shifts in population and production.

Thernstrom, Stephan, and Richard Sennett, eds. *Nineteenth-Century Cities* (New Haven: Yale University Press, 1969). Fascinating historical essays on life in nineteenth-century cities.

4

Trends in Sizes and Structures of Urban Areas

☐ The first three chapters have presented the broad outlines of trends in the urbanization of people and jobs during more than 200 years of history in the United States. This chapter completes the historical survey with a discussion of two other important characteristics of urbanization: the sizes of urban areas and suburbanization.

Urban areas vary enormously in total population. Many millions of people live in the largest metropolitan areas; only a few hundred inhabit each of many small towns. Documenting and explaining the facts has been a favorite pastime of urban specialists for decades. With a significant qualification, the facts are easy to come by. Total populations of cities are published by more national censuses and for more years than are almost any other data except for national population totals. The important qualification is that the most common data are populations of legal cities, and as has been discussed, these often do not include the entire urban area. Persuasive explanations of the observed data are much more difficult to come by. This chapter concentrates mainly on the data; comments on explanations are reserved for Chapter 16.

Also important, but outside the scope of economics, is the effect of the size of the urban area on attitudes and life-styles. Life in New York City or Los Angeles differs in many ways from life in Broken Bow, Nebraska, or Monroeville, Alabama. Anyone raised in one place or the other is forever stamped by the experience. In terms of economists' measures, however, such differences are less important than they were previously. Incomes are lower in small towns than in metropolitan areas, but living standards vary less by size of urban area than they did in earlier times. The kinds and brands of products bought and the work done also differ much less from place to place than before.

Suburbanization refers generically to the dispersion of population from the centers to the peripheries of urban areas. People in the United States associate the phenomenon with the outward movement of people across central-city boundaries. This feature is indeed an important aspect of the phenomenon. It profoundly affects the ways local govern-ments function in urban areas. This public-finance aspect of the issue will be analyzed in Chapter 14. The generic notion of suburbanization, or dispersion of population, however, does not depend on the locations of central-city boundaries. Careful measurement of the phenomenon will be discussed in Chapter 16. This chapter relies on jurisdictional data.

However measured, suburbanization is one of the most pervasive and important urban phenomena of the twentieth century. It is pervasive in that it has been important in all industrialized countries and has proceeded since at least the beginning of the twentieth century—and well before that, at least in countries where the phenomenon has been documented. Thus, the first lesson about suburbanization in the United States is to stop thinking of it as exclusively a post–World War II phenomenon resulting from racial turmoil, high taxes, and poor public schools in central cities. The phenomenon also occurs when and where these causes are absent. They are undoubtedly important in the Ameri-can context, but are hardly fundamental causes. Nevertheless, suburban-ization has proceeded far in postwar U.S. urban areas. The final task of this chapter is to trace this process and to point out some of its implications.

☐ SIZES OF U.S. URBAN AREAS

The two most important measures of the size of an urban area are its total population and its total land area. The former is more important and better documented than the latter. In this section, the size of an urban area always refers to its total population.

The primary characteristic of the sizes of urban areas is diversity. In most countries large enough to have more than a few urban areas, the largest urban areas are 100 or 1,000 times (two or three orders of magnitude) as large as the smallest. In the United States, the largest urban area is the New York City CMSA, with about 18 million inhabitants. It is more than 300 times as big as the smallest MSA, Enid, Oklahoma, with 56,000 people. The world's largest urban area is the Tokyo metropolitan area, with about 25 million residents, almost 40 percent larger than the New York CMSA.

Table 4.1 provides data on sizes of selected U.S. cities at 20-year intervals from 1790 to 1990. The table contains data for the 15 cities that were largest in 1990. The first column at the left shows each city's rank in 1990. The data refer to legal cities, not urban areas, but the distinction is mostly unimportant before World War II. Even with the restricted number of cities included in the table, the wide range of sizes can be seen. The tenth-largest city in 1990, Baltimore, is just 10 percent as large as the largest city, New York City.

Although all the cities in the table grew a great deal during the

Table 4.1 Population of Selected Cities for Selected Years, 1790 to 1990 (Population in Thousands)

City	Rank 1990	Rank 1980	Rank 1970	1790	1810	1830	1850	1870	1890	1910	1930	1950	1970	1980	1990	Percentage Change 1970–80
New York City	1	1	1	49	120	242	696	1,478	2,507	4,767	6,930	7,892	7,896	7,072	7,323	−10.4%
Los Angeles	2	3	3	…	…	…	2	6	50	319	1,238	1,970	2,812	2,969	3,485	5.6
Chicago	3	2	2	…	…	…	30	299	1,100	2,185	3,376	3,621	3,369	3,005	2,784	−10.8
Houston	4	5	6	…	…	…	2	9	28	79	292	596	1,234	1,595	1,631	29.3
Philadelphia	5	4	4	29	54	80	121	647	1,047	1,549	1,951	2,072	1,949	1,688	1,586	−13.4
San Diego	6	8	14	…	…	…	…	…	…	…	…	…	697	876	1,111	25.7
Detroit	7	6	5	…	…	2	21	80	206	466	1,569	1,849	1,514	1,203	1,028	−20.5
Dallas	8	7	8	…	…	…	…	…	38	92	260	434	844	905	1,007	7.2
Phoenix	9	9	20	…	…	…	…	…	…	…	…	…	584	790	983	35.3
Baltimore	10	10	7	14	47	81	169	267	434	558	805	950	905	787	736	−13.0
Washington, D.C.	11	15	9	…	8	19	40	109	189	331	487	802	757	638	607	−15.7
Boston	12	20	16	18	34	61	137	251	448	671	781	801	641	563	574	−12.2
Cleveland	13	18	10	…	…	1	17	93	261	561	900	915	751	574	506	−23.6
Pittsburgh	14	30	24	…	5	13	47	86	239	534	670	677	520	424	370	−18.5
Miami	15	41	42	…	…	…	…	…	…	5	111	249	335	347	359	3.6

Sources: U.S. Department of Commerce, Bureau of the Census. *Census of Population*, 1972, 1982; *Statistical Abstract of the United States*, 1991 (Washington, D.C.: Government Printing Office).

country's history, there is great persistence among ranks. New York City was the nation's largest city in 1790 and has been ever since.

Chicago, the nation's second-largest city until 1984, occupied that rank for about 100 years. Ranks do change, but slowly. Philadelphia was the second-largest city in 1790, but it fell to third place about a century ago and to fourth place after World War II. In 1790, Baltimore was the fourth-largest city (it moved up briefly to second in 1840); it was seventh in 1970 and tenth in 1990. Los Angeles, Dallas, Houston, and Miami are relative newcomers to the ranks of large cities and have moved up in rank rapidly during the twentieth century. San Diego moved from fourteenth to sixth position between 1970 and 1990, and Phoenix went from twentieth to ninth.[1]

Cities not only change ranks slowly, but demonstrate even greater persistence in the relative size of cities in particular ranks. The largest city may continue to be twice as large as the second-largest city, even though different cities occupy those ranks. In fact, New York City was 2.3 times as large as the second-largest city in 1870 and 2.1 times as large as the second-largest city in 1990, although a different city had come to occupy second place. More about the relative sizes of cities of different ranks will come at the end of this section.

The final important observation about the data in Table 4.1 is that the majority of the cities declined in population between 1950 and 1990; the decade of the 1970s accounted for most of the decline. Most of the cities that suffered population decline in the 1970s continued to do so during the 1980s, although for almost all of these cities, the rate of decline was much smaller than during the 1970s. It is also worth noting that population decline during the 1970s was concentrated in the Northeast and Midwest regions. Although this pattern continued in the 1980s, New York and Boston bucked the trend. Chapter 16 discusses the economic causes and consequences of these facts.

Population decreases in central cities have been common during the postwar period, reflecting in part, massive suburbanization and interurban migration. Even metropolitan areas that have grown rapidly throughout the postwar period have had declining central cities. (Chicago is an example.) In fact, many central cities that have recorded postwar growth have done so by annexing land adjacent to the city as population grows. Annexation is especially common in southwestern states (for example, Texas). The tendency to annex land in certain regions of the country makes comparisons difficult. The subject of

1.   Chapter 1 emphasized that historical accident is an inadequate explanation for the location and growth of urban areas. Accident does play some role, however, as can be seen by looking at the population figures for Baltimore and Philadelphia in 1850 and 1870. In 1850, the Baltimore and Ohio Railroad had put Baltimore well ahead of Philadelphia in the race to be the leading Middle Atlantic port. During the Civil War, however, pro–South Baltimore was occupied by federal troops, and Philadelphia moved ahead and has remained ahead ever since.

Table 4.2 *Rank and Population of Ten Largest MSAs, 1950 to 1990 (Population in Thousands)*

Rank	1950 MSA	Pop	1970 PMSA	Pop	1980 PMSA	Pop	1990 PMSA	Pop	Percentage Growth* 1970-80	Percentage Growth* 1980-90	1990* CMSA Pop
1	New York City	9,556	New York City	9,077	New York City	8,275	Los Angeles	8,863	-8.8%	7.1%	14,532
2	Chicago	5,178	Los Angeles	7,042	Los Angeles	7,477	New York City	8,547	6.2	14.3	18,087
3	Los Angeles	4,152	Chicago	6,093	Chicago	6,060	Chicago	6,070	-0.5	0.2	8,066
4	Philadelphia	3,671	Philadelphia	4,824	Philadelphia	4,717	Philadelphia	4,857	-2.2	3.0	5,899
5	Detroit	3,016	Detroit	4,554	Detroit	4,488	Detroit	4,382	-1.4	-2.4	4,665
6	Boston	2,414	San Francisco	3,110	San Francisco	3,251	Washington, D.C.	3,924	13.6	20.7	...
7	Pittsburgh	2,213	Washington, D.C.	2,861	Washington, D.C.	3,251	Dallas	3,885	...	32.5	...
8	San Francisco	2,136	Boston	2,887	Dallas	2,931	San Francisco	3,687	4.5	13.4	6,253
9	St. Louis	1,755	Pittsburgh	2,348	Houston	2,735	Houston	3,302	...	20.7	3,711
10	Cleveland	1,533	St. Louis	2,429	Boston	2,806	Boston	2,871	-2.8	2.3	4,172

*The order of PMSAs is according to their rank in 1990.

Sources: U.S. Department of Commerce, Bureau of the Census. *Census of Population*, 1972, 1982; *Statistical Abstract of the United States*, 1991; *State and Metropolitan Area Data Book*, 1991. (Washington D.C.: Government Printing Office).

suburbanization and its measurement will be discussed at the end of the chapter. Central-city population loss will be examined in Chapter 16.

As has been pointed out, comprehensive MSA data are available only since 1940. Table 4.2 shows rank and population of each of the ten largest MSAs for 1950, 1970, 1980, and 1990. Ranks of MSAs are of greater interest than are ranks of central cities, since MSAs correspond more closely to the notion of the generic urban area. Table 4.2 also indicates considerable stability of ranks, at least during the relatively brief period covered. New York was the largest PMSA until 1990. Chicago and Los Angeles switched places between 1950 and 1970. Philadelphia and Detroit retained their ranks. Four of the five smallest PMSAs in 1950 lost rank by 1990. One—San Francisco—rose in rank. Cleveland, Pittsburgh, and St. Louis dropped out of the ten largest PMSAs by 1990, whereas Washington, D.C., entered the top ten in 1970. By 1980, Houston and Dallas were among the top ten. Between 1980 and 1990, only one of the large PMSAs lost population—Detroit.

What Table 4.1 shows for cities, Table 4.2 shows for PMSAs: There is greater persistence in the relative sizes of PMSAs of given ranks than in the identities of the PMSAs that occupy those ranks. The New York PMSA was 1.85 times as large as the second-largest MSA in 1950 and 1.29 times as large in 1970. By 1980, however, it was only 1.11 times as large as the second largest. The regional shifts underlying this convergence were discussed in Chapter 2. Likewise, the fifth-largest PMSA was 1.97 times as large as the tenth largest in 1950, and 1.53 times as large in 1990. In fact, these ratios suggest that the largest PMSAs have grown less rapidly than somewhat smaller PMSAs during the postwar period. In particular, the New York PMSA lost ground to its nearest competitors during the period. The PMSA data understate the size differences between the top three metropolitan areas (most particularly, New York and Los Angeles) on the one hand and the others in Table 4.2 on the other. Each of the top three MSAs is a part of a larger urban area, which is designated a *CMSA* (see Chapter 1).

☐ ESTIMATES OF MSA SIZE DISTRIBUTIONS

The best way to think systematically about sizes of urban areas is to think of them as a frequency distribution. Urban area sizes can be arrayed in various categories from the largest, just as a frequency distribution of incomes or of almost any economic variable can be displayed. Such frequency distributions are published in every population census. It has been shown that the size distribution of cities or PMSAs is characterized by a small number of very large ones and a much larger number of small ones. In other words, the frequency decreases continuously as the sizes of urban areas increase. Such distributions are said to be "skewed to the right." They contrast with the more familiar normal, or Gaussian, distribution, which is symmetrical around its highest point. Many economic variables—incomes, firm sizes, and urban-area sizes—follow distributions that are skewed to the right. Statisticians and economists have studied carefully the properties of several such distributions.

The distribution most commonly employed to study urban sizes is the **Pareto distribution.** It can be written as follows:

$$G(x) = Ax^{-a}, \tag{4.1}$$

where $G(x)$ is the number of urban areas with at least x people, and A and a are constants to be estimated from the data. Thus, $G(x)$ is the rank of an urban area with x people. For some reason, the Pareto distribution usually is written as in Equation (4.1), which is a cumulative distribution, cumulated from the top. That is, $G(x)$ is the number of observations *at least as large as x,* whereas the usual way to write a cumulative distribution is the number of observations at least *as small as x.*

Scholars in many disciplines have estimated Equation (4.1) from data on urban populations taken from U.S. and many other national censuses. Frequently, a is estimated to be about 1. Then, the Pareto distribution can be written as follows:

$$G(x) = Ax^{-1}, \tag{4.2}$$

which is known as the **rank-size rule.** Putting $G(x) = 1$, we see that $x = A$; that is, A is the population of the largest urban area. Multiplying both sides of Equation (4.2) by x,

$$xG(x) = A. \tag{4.3}$$

That is, the product of an urban area's rank and population is a constant equal to the population of the largest urban area. Thus, the rank-size rule implies that the second-largest urban area is half the size of the largest, that the third-largest urban area is one-third the size of the largest, and so on. There is no theoretical reason to expect the rank-size rule to hold with precision for urban sizes. It is such a simple distribution, however, that it is remarkable how close the fit is for urban area sizes in very different countries and at many different times in history.

An indication of the accuracy of the rank-size rule can be obtained from the data in Table 4.3. It shows the population, rank, and rank times population for every tenth entry in the census list by size of urbanized areas for 1990. Do those data confirm or refute the rank-size rule? Of course, no theory in economics is exactly confirmed by significant bodies of evidence. The most that can be hoped for is that deviations of actual values from theoretical values are small and random.

There is a tendency for the product of rank and size or of urbanized areas in the table to cluster, and the average of the entires in the last column is 18,411. There are, however, also substantial and apparently systematic departures. The smallest entries are at the top and bottom of the column. Entries rise smoothly from the top to the third entry, and they fall almost continously after the sixth entry. The best way to test the

Table 4.3   *Population and Rank of a Sample of U.S. Metropolitan Areas, 1990*

Metropolitan Area	Population Rank	Population (Thousands)	Rank × Population
New York-northern New Jersey-Long Island, New York-northern New Jersey-Connecticut	1	17,953	17,953
Miami-Fort Lauderdale, Florida	11	3,193	35,123
Tampa-St.Petersburg-Clearwater, Florida	21	2,068	43,428
Indianapolis, Indiana	31	1,250	38,750
Oklahoma City, Oklahoma	41	959	39,319
Honolulu, Hawaii	51	836	42,636
Fresno, California	61	667	40,687
Bakersfield, California	71	543	38,553
Columbia, South Carolina	81	453	36,693
Colorado Springs, Colorado	91	397	36,127
Fort Wayne, Indiana	101	364	36,764
Reading, Pennsylvania	111	337	37,407
Rockford, Illinois	121	284	34,364
Brownsville-Harlingen, Texas	131	260	34,060
Savannah, Georgia	141	243	34,263
Hickory, North Carolina	151	222	33,522
Bremerton, Washington	161	190	30,590
Asheville, North Carolina	171	175	29,925
Muskegon, Michigan	181	159	28,779
Jackson, Mississippi	191	395	75,445
Monroe, Louisiana	201	142	28,542
Greeley, Colorado	211	132	27,852
Bloomington-Normal, Illinois	221	129	28,509
Hagerstown, Maryland	231	121	27,951
Santa Fe, New Mexico	241	117	28,197
Lawton, Oklahoma	251	111	27,861
San Angelo, Texas	261	98	25,578
Bismarck, North Dakota	271	84	22,764
Enid, Oklahoma	281	57	16,017

Note: Areas with ranks 1 and 11 are CMSAs (consolidated metropolitan statistical areas); others are MSAs.
Source: U.S. Department of Commerce, Bureau of the Census. *State and Metropolitan Area Data Book*, Table 2, pp. xx–xxiii (Washington, D.C.: Government Printing Office, 1991).

rank-size rule is to return to the Pareto distribution, Equation (4.1). Take logs of both sides:

$$\log\ G(x) = \log A - a \log x. \tag{4.4}$$

The Pareto distribution can be estimated by computing the least-squares regression of Equation (4.4).[2] Equation (4.5) presents an estimate of

2.   Least-squares regression means using as estimates of log A and a values that minimize the sum of squared differences between values of log $G(x)$ calculated from Equation (4.4) and those in a sample of data. See the Appendix for a more detailed discussion of regression analysis.

Equation (4.4) calculated, not from the data in Table 4.3, but from the full census list of ranks and populations of the 366 urbanized areas:

$$\log G(x) = 6.833 - 0.905 \log x. \quad R^2 = 0.99.$$
$$\qquad\quad (0.025) \quad (0.005) \qquad\qquad\qquad (4.5)$$

The numbers in parentheses are estimated standard errors of the coefficients above them. In a sample as large as this one, the probability is less than 0.05 that the true and estimated coefficients differ by at least as much as twice the standard deviation. R^2 in Equation (4.5) is the squared correlation coefficient between $\log G(x)$ and $\log x$. The reported R^2 means that the regression equation explains 99 percent of the variance of $\log G(x)$.

Two important observations should be made about Equation (4.5). First, the Pareto distribution provides a very accurate description of the distribution of population sizes of urbanized areas. An R^2 of 0.99 means that the data all lie very close to the estimated Pareto distribution. It is remarkable that, in country after country and in decade after decade, the Pareto distribution fits urban-area-size distribution data so well. Second, the rank-size rule (the special case of the Pareto distribution where $a = 1$) can be rejected for the American 1990 data. The previous paragraph implies that the true value of a is unlikely to be above 0.915, or 0.905 + 2(.005). That amount is still well below the unit value of a implied by the rank-size rule.

The estimated value of a of 0.905 in Equation (4.5) means that populations of urbanized areas far down in the size distribution are smaller than is indicated by the rank-size rule. This feature reflects the fact that, in moving down most of the final column in Table 4.3, the product of rank and population falls. Unfortunately, few countries have measures of urban size as good as those provided in the urbanized area data for the United States. In a recent study employing data on legal cities, Rosen and Resnick (1980) have estimated Pareto distributions of city sizes for all countries in the world that had a substantial number of cities and published the needed data. Their estimated value of a for the United States is somewhat above the average estimated a in the worldwide sample, indicating that city sizes are somewhat more evenly distributed here than in most countries. The most important of Rosen's and Resnick's findings from the data, however, is that city sizes in the United States are distributed in a manner typical of many countries.

Chapter 1 discussed the gradual relaxation of technological and economic constraints on the sizes of urban areas. The skewed size distribution of urban areas revealed in Table 4.2 and Equation (4.5) indicated that only a small number of urban areas have fully exploited the possibilities for urban growth that were created by this technical progress. This finding was to be expected. One of the improvements that has permitted growth of cities has been in long-distance goods transport. As long-distance transport (both of city exports and of food from farms) became cheaper, it became feasible to concentrate some activities in only a small number of widely dispersed urban areas. Urban areas have varied in size because variations in scale economies, density of demand, and transport cost mean that the optimum market area is larger for some goods and services than others.

☐ SUBURBANIZATION

Despite its familiarity, suburbanization is not really a simple concept. As has been stated, people in the United States tend to think of it in terms of numbers or percentages of people living or working in central-city and suburban jurisdictions of urban areas. The concept, however, is more basic than locations of jurisdictional boundaries. A basic definition is that an urban area is more *suburbanized* the more dispersed are residences and jobs around the center of the urban area. This definition does not rely on jurisdictional boundaries but still admits to several possible quantitative measures of the concept.

Jurisdictional measurements of suburbanization are unavailable in most countries because central-city boundaries are moved out as population expands, thus keeping all, or nearly all, the urban area within the boundaries of the central city. During the period of rapid urban growth in the nineteenth century, it was common to expand central-city boundaries as population expanded, even in the United States. In the twentieth century, the process of boundary movement stopped in much of this country, thus permitting the measurement of suburbanization by concentration of people and jobs in central-city and suburban jurisdictions. By this measure, an urban area is said to have suburbanized between years 1 and 2 if a larger percentage of the urban area's residents lived or worked in suburban jurisdictions in Year 2 than in Year 1. That measure will be exploited in this section. Data are easily available and, for that reason, jurisdictional measures of suburbanization almost always are used in popular discussions of the subject in newspapers and magazines. More sophisticated measures will be introduced in Chapter 16 after their theoretical basis has been laid in intervening chapters.

It is important to keep in mind several limitations of jurisdictional measures as they are discussed in this section. First, jurisdictional measures do not permit careful cross-sectional comparisons. If one urban area has a larger percentage of its population living or working in the central city than in another, it may indicate only where central-city boundaries happen to have been drawn many decades ago. Second, even time-series comparisons are imprecise, because some central-city boundaries still are moved outward as population and employment expand, especially in the South and the Southwest. Each census presents population data within central-city boundaries as they existed at the time of the previous census, but making the comparison among several decades is laborious and approximate.

Table 4.4 contains some comprehensive data on postwar subur-

Table 4.4 Suburbanization of Population and Employment in Selected MSAs, 1950 to 1980

	1950		1960		1970		1980	
	Central City	Suburban Ring	Central City	Suburban Ring	Central City	Suburban Ring	Central City	Suburban Ring
Population	57.3%	42.7%	49.2%	50.8%	43.1%	56.9%	39.89%	60.11%
Employment[a]								
Manufacturing	63.3	36.7	56.5	43.5	51.0	49.0	46.15	53.85
Retailing	74.4	25.6	65.3	34.7	52.2	47.8	46.64	53.36
Service	80.8	19.2	75.2	24.8	64.2	35.8	58.25	41.75
Wholesaling	87.1	12.9	80.4	19.6	65.5	34.5	57.33	42.67
Total	70.1%	29.9%	63.1%	36.9%	54.6%	45.4%	49.54%	50.46%

[a]Employment data are from 1977 for a random sample of 18 MSAs. Employment data are averages of data for census years from the relevant employment census.
Sources: Data from the U.S. Department of Commerce, Bureau of the Census. Census of Population, 1950, 1960, 1972, 1982; Census of Manufactures, 1947, 1954, 1958, 1963, 1967, 1972, 1977; Census of Business, 1948, 1954, 1958, 1963, 1967; Census of Retail Trade, 1972, 1977; Census of Selected Service Industries, 1972, 1977; Census of Wholesale Trade, 1972, 1977 (Washington, D.C.: Government Printing Office).

banization, making use of jurisdictional data. Keep in mind that the data understate postwar suburbanization, since they take no account of boundary movements. The problem of differing central-city boundary locations was avoided by basing Table 4.4 on the same set of MSAs for each year included. The MSAs represent the 168 MSAs defined by the census in 1950 minus the MSAs in the three CMSAs that had been defined by 1970. The reason for eliminating the CMSAs is that one MSA may, in a sense, be a suburb of another within a CMSA. The exclusions leave 135 MSAs, which contained nearly two-thirds of the total MSA population in 1970. The 1980 numbers are based on a subsample of 18 of the MSAs that make up the sample for the previous years.

Despite the limitations of the data, Table 4.4 shows the massive suburbanization that has taken place in the United States since World War II. In 1950, of the residents of the metropolitan areas included in the table, 57.3 percent lived in central cities. The percentage had fallen to 49.2 in 1960, to 43.1 by 1970, and to 39.89 by 1980.

The employment data included in Table 4.4 are incomplete. Some private service jobs are excluded from the service category, but the most important exclusion is government service employment. Government employment is probably more concentrated in central cities than is total employment, so its exclusion may exaggerate the impression of employment suburbanization given in the table.

Employment is less suburbanized than population, as should be expected. Like population, employment has become much more suburbanized during the postwar period. In 1950, of the jobs in the metropolitan areas included in Table 4.4, 70.1 percent were in central cities. By 1980, the percentage had fallen to 49.5. By the census, employment was almost evenly divided between central cities and suburbs.

In the employment sectors, manufacturing and retailing are more suburbanized than services and wholesaling. None of the employment sectors, however, is as suburbanized as population. All four employment sectors have suburbanized a great deal since 1950. By one measure, the four employment sectors have come to be more nearly equally suburbanized since 1950. In 1950 almost 24 percentage points separated the percentage of jobs in central cities in the wholesaling and manufacturing sectors. By 1980, the range was just over 12 percentage points. This finding implies that postwar employment suburbanization has been most rapid in the employment sectors that were least suburbanized in 1950.

A final point is worth noting regarding the suburbanization of jobs and people. Between 1950 and 1980, the fraction of people living in suburbs increased by 17.4 percentage points. During the same period, the fraction of jobs in the suburbs increased by 20.5 points. The suburbanization of jobs has been modestly faster than that of people, suggesting a slight reduction in central-city jobs per capita over the postwar era.

Table 4.5 Central-City Employment in Three U.S. Cities, by Sector, for 1953, 1970, 1980, and 1989 (Figures in Thousands)

Central City and Sector	Number of Jobs				Percentage of Total			
	1953	1970	1980	1989	1953	1970	1980	1989
New York								
Total employment[a]	2,977	3,350	2,866	2,048	100%	100%	100%	100%
Agriculture and mining	5	5	5	3	*	*	*	*
Mfg. and construction	1,176	971	650	268	40	29	23	13
Retail and wholesale	805	779	596	355	27	23	21	17
Selected services								
Information processing[b]	646	1,172	1,302	1,284†	22	35	45	63
Other services	344	424	314	138†	12	13	11	7
Philadelphia								
Total employment[a]	788	772	628	614	100	100	100	100
Agriculture and mining	0.7	0.7	0.5	0.8	*	*	*	*
Mfg. and construction	398	291	171	111	51	38	27	18
Retail and wholesale	206	180	134	136	26	23	21	22
Selected services								
Information processing[b]	98	220	271	323†	12	28	43	53
Other services	85	81	52	42†	11	10	8	7
Boston (Suffolk County)								
Total employment[a]	402	465	437	520	100	100	100	100
Agriculture and mining	2	0.9	0.5	0.5	*	*	*	*
Mfg. and construction	130	105	77	53	32	23	18	10
Retail and wholesale	132	111	82	85	33	24	19	16
Selected services								
Information processing[b]	87	194	232	341†	22	42	53	66
Other services**	51	55	46	41†	13	12	11	8

[a]Total classified employment and industry subcategories, excluding government employees and sole proprietors.
[b]Service industries (excluding government, retail, and wholesale) in which more than one-half the employees hold executive, managerial, professional, or clerical positions.
*Less than 1.
†Finance, Insurance, and Real Estate; and "Services."
**Transportation and public utilities and unclassified establishments.
Sources: U.S. Department of Commerce, Bureau of the Census. County Business Patterns, selected years; Occupation by Industry statistics, 1970, 1980 (Washington, D.C.: Government Printing Office).
Figures are rounded.

Two crucial aspects of employment decentralization are not evident from Table 4.4. First, note that manufacturing in central cities fell from 63.3 percent in 1950 to only 46.15 percent in 1980. Since manufacturing is the largest urban sector, this figure represents a massive loss of central-city jobs. Second, concealed within the service sector is a sector that has enjoyed extremely rapid growth in central cities. Categorized as "information processing,"[3] this sector includes legal, financial, banking, and other professional services. As can be seen in Table 4.5, this sector has grown so fast that it is by far the leading employer in each of the sample cities (bear in mind that these cities are old-line *manufacturing* cities). For these central cities, manufacturing and construction together are only about half as big as information processing. During precisely the time when manufacturing has been fleeing to the suburbs, information processing has been racing to central cities (and to central business districts, in particular).

The reasons for these moves are not hard to find. Before the days of trucks and electricity, manufacturing was tied tightly to railheads in the core of the city. Neither coal nor the steam power produced from it could be transported readily from the railhead; in addition, the nineteenth-century transport network was designed to deliver the work force to the railhead. All of this changed with the advent of electric power, the automobile, the truck, and the declining energy intensity of manufacturing.[4] These changes weakened the advantages of central locations for manufacturing and allowed manufacturing to take advantage of some real benefits offered by suburban locations, the most important of which were cheap land and an escape from narrow streets that were laid out before the era of the car and truck. Cheap and plentiful land is important, because with modern manufacturing techniques, one-story plants offer tremendous advantages.

Suburbanization has been among the most dramatic and widely discussed phenomena of recent history. Analyzing its causes and consequences will occupy a large part of both the theoretical and applied chapters of this book. Although this section has presented only the most basic measures, they are adequate to show that suburbanization has occurred on a large scale.

☐ Summary

This chapter has reviewed trends in the sizes and structures of urban areas. There is great persistence in the ranks of metropolitan areas and

---

3. In the accompanying Table 4.5, information processing is defined as service industries excluding government, for which more than half of the employees hold executive, managerial, professional, or secretarial positions.

4. Energy intensity has declined due to technical progress and also because more complicated things are done with raw materials, which require more processing but less energy. See the discussion of steel production in Chapter 2.

even more persistence in the relative populations of metropolitan areas that occupy particular ranks in the metropolitan size distribution. The Pareto distribution closely approximates the metropolitan size distribution for many countries and for many times in history. Furthermore, the exponents of the Pareto distribution cluster around 1.

The decentralization of residences and employment around the centers of metropolitan areas is also characteristic of many countries and of many times in history. Metropolitan dispersion has proceeded especially far and fast in post–World War II metropolitan areas of the United States. By 1980, American metropolitan areas were probably as dispersed as metropolitan areas anywhere in the world.

Questions and Problems

1. Find out what government data are available on incomes, prices, and consumption patterns for particular metropolitan areas. What additional data do you think the government should collect and publish?

2. Would you expect greater persistence in relative sizes of central cities or of PMSAs of particular ranks?

3. Would you expect the exponent in the Pareto distribution of metropolitan populations to become larger or smaller as time passes? Why?

4. Do you think employment suburbanization has caused population suburbanization or vice versa? What do you think has caused whichever movement you believe was the catalyst?

5. Which regions of the country do you think have the most suburbanized metropolitan areas? Why? Check your prediction with census data.

6. What industries would you expect to be most concentrated in big urban areas? Why?

References and Further Reading

Beckmann, Martin, and John McPherson. "City Size Distributions in a Central Place Hierarchy: An Alternative Approach." *Journal of Regional Science* 10 (1970): 25–33. A theory of city-size distributions based on the work of Lösch. It provides an explanation of why the distribution is approximately Pareto.

Chinitz, Benjamin. *City and Suburb* (Englewood Cliffs, N.J.: Prentice-Hall, 1965). A collection of essays on the causes and consequences of suburbanization.

Kasarda, John. "Urban Change and Minority Opportunities." In *The New Urban Reality,* edited by Paul E. Peterson (Washington, D.C.: Brookings Institute, 1985). Kasarda discusses the effects of employment shifts on the availability of various types of jobs in the central city. Other essays in this book also are excellent.

Lösch, August. *The Economics of Location* (New Haven: Yale University Press, 1954). A classic on location theory; parts are highly technical.

Moses, Leon, and Harold Williamson. "The Location of Economic Activity in Cities." *American Economic Review* 57 (May, 1967): 211–222. A fine empirical study of employment suburbanization in Chicago.

Rosen, Kenneth, and Mitchel Resnick. "The Size Distribution of Cities: An Examination of the Pareto Law and Primacy." *Journal of Urban Economics* 8, No. 2 (1980): 165–186. An analysis of city-size distributions for many of the world's countries.

Part Two

Theoretical
Foundations

5

Introducing Land and Land Rents Into Price Theory

☐ Chapter 1 showed that urban areas are places where market activities result in much higher production and employment densities than are observed elsewhere. Tall, closely spaced buildings and crowded streets and sidewalks are visible manifestations of high densities. To the urban economist, however, urban land, buildings, and human labor are inputs in producing commodities and services. The observation that population and employment densities are high in urban areas translates into the economic statement that ratios of capital and labor to land inputs are high in those areas. Thus, the key observation in urban-economic model building is that input proportions in urban areas are systematically and dramatically different from those elsewhere.

Analysis of input proportions and input prices is part of the microeconomic theory of production and supply.[1] Textbooks on modern price theory, however, hardly mention land, land prices, or land rents except in the context of agricultural examples. Hence, the first task is to incorporate land into production theory. This chapter carries out that task. The second task is to use the theory of production, modified by the inclusion of land, to analyze the particular spatial relationships that characterize urban areas. Chapter 6 accomplishes that task. Together with the discussion of welfare economics in Chapter 8, these chapters provide a broad theoretical framework within which urban problems can be analyzed in Part Three.

Just as the wage is the price of labor services, so land rent is the price of land services. Also, just as a large part of labor-market theory is concerned with wage determination, so much of land-market theory is concerned with land-rent determination. Prices are, of course, instruments for rationing the uses of inputs and outputs in a market economy. This concept is no less true of land than of any other commodity or service. The special character of land rent as the price of a nonproduced

1. For review, Mansfield (1979) offers a good discussion of production theory.

input, however, has stimulated some of the most interesting scientific and political controversy in history. Some comments on this controversy are made later in this chapter.

☐ SOME TERMS

It is necessary at this point to define carefully several closely related terms. *Land value and land rent* are related in the way that the price of any asset is related to the price of the service it yields. Stocks of physical assets are valuable because they yield flows of services during many years. **Land rent** is the price of the services yielded by land during a specific time period. It depends on the time period covered as well as on the unit in which land is measured. *Land price* is the present value, or capitalized value, of the rent the asset will yield throughout the future. For example, if a tract of land will yield a rent of R dollars per year in perpetuity, and if the appropriate interest rate to use in discounting is $100i$ percent per year, the price (V) of the land is as follows[2]:

$$V = R/i. \tag{5.1}$$

The asset price (V) has the dimension only of the unit in which the asset is measured (for example, dollars per acre).

Assets, such as buildings and machinery, inevitably deteriorate with time and use, and they eventually cease to be valuable. Land used—or rather, abused—in agriculture also may deteriorate. Most urban land uses, however, do not cause physical deterioration, and the land, therefore, yields a perpetual stream of services, as Equation (5.1) assumes.

The second set of terms to define are *unimproved and improved land values*. Most urban land uses require that structures be built on the land. In other words, urban production of goods and services normally requires both land and produced capital, among other factors of production. **Unimproved land value** means the price of the land with no structure on it, whereas **improved land value** means the price of the land and the structures on it. Because structures are usually expensive to move or demolish, it is often difficult to estimate the unimproved value of land that has structures on it. Furthermore, in many urban areas very little unimproved land appears on the market, especially near city centers. There are, therefore, few transactions from which to estimate unimproved land values, which are among the scarcest and poorest of the data needed by urban economists.

There also are many ways to improve land in addition to building on it, if the term *improve* is taken literally. Land can be drained and graded,

---

2.   The present value at Time 0 of a stream of R dollars per year in perpetuity, discounted at interest rate i, is as follows:

$$V = \sum_{t=1}^{\infty} \frac{R}{(1+i)^t} = \frac{R}{i}$$

provided with pipes for water supply and waste disposal, and planted with or cleared of trees. These ways simply represent different kinds of capital investment in land, and like buildings, they can affect its market value. Some of the ambiguity of unimproved-land-value data results from the fact that various amounts of nonbuilding capital may have been invested in it.

Although nonstructural land improvements present real problems in applied research, as well as in real-estate tax assessment, they are not important in this book. The terms *land value and land rent* refer here to the prices and rents of unimproved land, that is, before any capital has been invested in it. *Improved land values* include the value of buildings and other capital invested in the land. Much of the analysis here is concerned with equilibrium situations, in which land values and land rents are proportionate to each other, as in Equation (5.1).

☐ THEORY OF LAND RENT AND LAND USE

In this section, and throughout much of the book, *it is assumed that input and product markets are perfectly competitive*—that is, that each market participant can buy and sell unlimited quantities without affecting the price set by the market. There are two compelling reasons for this assumption. First, most urban phenomena and problems can be best understood and analyzed within the competitive framework. Although monopoly and oligopoly may worsen some urban problems, they are not important *explanations* of most urban phenomena. Racial discrimination, poverty, poor housing, congestion, and pollution would hardly be less serious problems in competitive than in non-competitive markets. (The analysis to support this claim is presented in Part Three.) Second, spatial models, such as those used to analyze urban markets, are usually much simpler to formulate and analyze if perfect competition is assumed than if other market structures are considered. There are basic difficulties (discussed later on) that economists have not yet solved in formulating spatial relationships in noncompetitive markets.

It is also assumed, as it is in other branches of economic theory, that people own productive land and capital assets because of the return they yield. Owners, therefore, seek the use of the asset that yields the greatest return available.

These assumptions are powerful, and they yield many insights. Among them is the inference that, in equilibrium, *all equally productive units of land command the same price*—which does not imply that all urban land has the same price or rent. Productivity may vary greatly from one unit of land to another within an urban area.

Suppose a firm in a competitive industry produces a single commodity with the aid of several inputs—for example, land, labor, and capital. The firm can vary its production continuously by appropriate variations in its inputs. The firm's production function represents input combinations that can be used to produce each output volume. Input and output prices are given to the firm, so it need only find the input and resulting output volumes that maximize its profit level at those prices. Intermediate price theory textbooks show that profit maximization requires that the firm use input quantities that equate the *value of the marginal product (VMP)* of each input to its price or, in the case of an asset, to its rental rate. This important result can be established in the following explanation.

The *marginal product (MP)* of an input is the change in output that results from a small change in the input quantity employed. The VMP is the product price multiplied by the MP of the input. It shows the change in the firm's revenue resulting from a small change in the employment of an input, holding constant the amounts of other inputs. The input price shows the change in the firm's cost resulting from a one-unit change in the employment of the input. If the *VMP* exceeded the input price, it would mean that the employment of additional units of the input would add more to revenue than to cost. Profit, therefore, would increase. If the *VMP* were less than the input price, a decrease in employment of the input would reduce cost by more than revenue. Profit, therefore, would increase. It follows that profit is largest when an amount of the input is used that equates the *VMP* and the input price.

The result is illustrated in Figure 5.1. The term n stands for the amount of the input—such as labor—employed. S_n is the perfectly elastic supply curve of labor, and w is the competitive wage rate. VMP_n decreases as n increases, because the labor MP falls as more labor is employed with fixed amounts of other inputs. The term $\bar{n}$ shows the profit-maximizing employment of labor for the firm, in that it equates VMP_n to w.

The result in Figure 5.1 also can be stated algebraically. Suppose three inputs—land, labor, and capital—are used to produce a product.

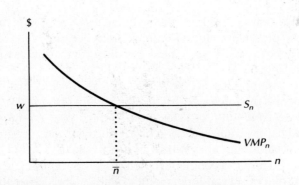

Figure 5.1   *Determination of Equilibrium Wage and Employment*

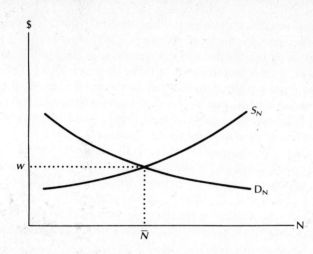

Figure 5.2   *Equilibrium with Rising Supply Curve*

Then, the conditions for profit maximization can be written as follows:

$$p \cdot MP_1 = R, \quad p \cdot MP_k = r, \quad p \cdot MP_n = w,$$

or

$$MP_1 = R/p, \quad MP_k = r/p, \quad MP_n = w/p, \qquad (5.2)$$

where p is the price of the product, R is the rental rate of land, r is the rental rate of capital, w is the wage rate (the rental rate of labor), and the MPs are the marginal products of the inputs indicated by the subscripts. By the assumption of perfect competition, the product price and each input price are given to the firm. Each MP depends not only on the quantity of the input designated, but also on the quantities of the other two inputs. Thus, each of the equations involves all three input quantities, and these equations must be solved simultaneously to ascertain the profit-maximizing input levels, as shown in Figure 5.1.[3]

Until now, the discussion has been concerned entirely with the firm. In a competitive input market, input price is given to the firm and is determined by industry supply and demand. To understand land-rent determination, we, therefore, must discuss the industry as a whole. Industry-input demand is computed by adding the demands of all firms for the input at the fixed input price. The industry input-demand schedule is obtained by repeating the procedure at each input price. Like the firm's *VMP* curve, it is downward sloping. Although the input-supply curve is horizontal for the firm, it is normally upward sloping for the industry. The input price is determined by the equality of demand and supply for the input in the industry as a whole.

---

3.   As Figure 5.1 indicates, the *VMP* is the firm's demand curve for the indicated input, if quantities of other inputs are constant. Otherwise, it must be adjusted as quantities of other inputs change.

Input-price determination is illustrated in Figure 5.2. N refers to labor employment in the entire industry. S_N and D_N are the labor supply and demand curves for the entire industry, w is the equilibrium wage rate, and $\overline{N}$ is total employment of labor in the industry. The term w equals the common value of VMP_n in all the firms in the industry.

The only peculiarity of land is that, being a nonproduced input, its total supply is fixed. Therefore, its supply curve to the industry is vertical, or perfectly inelastic. However, the competitive supply to the individual firm is nevertheless horizontal, or perfectly elastic. Thus, the foregoing analysis applies in full and is shown in Figure 5.3. L is land used by the entire industry, D_L is industry demand for land, and S_L is the vertical industry supply curve. R and $\overline{L}$ are the equilibrium land rent and land employed in the industry, respectively. As with labor or any other input, land rent equals the common value of its VMP in all land-using firms.

☐ WELFARE AND ETHICAL ASPECTS OF LAND RENT

During the nineteenth century, some economists and social philosophers held passionate views about land rent. Many people still feel that land is basically different from other inputs and should be treated differently by governments. Two basic considerations account for these views. First, David Ricardo (1821), Henry George (1879), and others thought land rents would absorb all the fruits of economic progress. Second is the view that land, not having been produced by people's efforts, should yield no return to its owners. Each view should be analyzed with care.

Ricardo's view rested on Thomas Malthus's population theory and on an inadequate appreciation of the importance of technical change. Ricardo believed that high birthrates would increase the labor supply and keep wage rates at the subsistence level in the long run. Land rent,

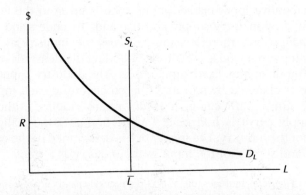

Figure 5.3   Supply and Demand for Land

being a residual, would absorb all revenues left over after paying workers—and perhaps capital owners—the input prices necessary to induce their supply. Thus, Ricardo believed, land rents would become an increasing share of total revenue as technical progress occurred. However important Malthusian theory may be for some parts of the world, it is not a threat for the foreseeable future in western Europe, North America, and some other parts of the world. Birthrates there have fallen for many decades, and many countries now have virtually stationary populations. Thus, *wage rates have risen rapidly in real terms as capital accumulation and technical change have occurred.*

On the conceptual level, the relationship between land rents as a residual and land rents as a return to the owner of a productive input proceeds as follows. Suppose the production function has constant returns to scale and that input and output markets are competitive. Then Euler's theorem[4] shows that all combinations of inputs and outputs satisfy the following identity:

$$x \equiv MP_1 \cdot 1 + MP_k \cdot k + MP_n \cdot n. \tag{5.3}$$

Here, x is the output level, and l, k, and n are amounts of land, capital, and labor, respectively, employed by the firm. Eliminating the MP terms from Equation (5.3) by substituting from Equations (5.2) and multiplying both sides by p yields this result:

$$px = R \cdot 1 + r \cdot k + w \cdot n. \tag{5.4}$$

Equation (5.4) shows that the sum of competitive payments to the three inputs is equal to total receipts from the sale of the product in a competitive market. Thus, *the land rent that pays landowners the value of land's marginal product is precisely the amount left over after paying owners of other inputs the values of their marginal products.* This remarkable result shows that there is no conflict between the notion of land rent as a residual and as a payment based on input productivity in the conditions stated. The result does not depend on the number of inputs.

The result also does not depend on the restrictive assumption of constant returns to scale in the firm's production function. Suppose that input and output markets are competitive and that fixed competitive input prices yield a conventional U-shaped long-run average cost (LAC) curve, as Figure 5.4 shows. The term LMC represents the firm's long-run marginal cost curve, p is the industry's long-run equilibrium price, and $\bar{x}$ is the firm's long-run equilibrium output. Thus, price equals both average and marginal cost, and competitively priced payments to inputs,

---

4. Euler's theorem is proved in many calculus and mathematical economics textbooks.

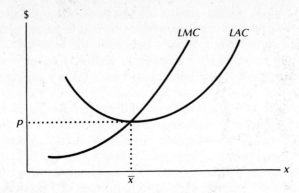

Figure 5.4   *Cost Curves and Competitive Pricing*

therefore, exhaust revenues. Once again, land rent, or any other input payment, can be viewed as a productivity-based payment or as a residual.

Equation (5.4) makes no distinction between land and the other inputs; each is paid the value of its *MP,* and each could be regarded as receiving the residual after other inputs are paid the value of their *MP*s. Total land rent is the box inscribed by the lines originating at R and $\overline{L}$ in Figure 5.3. Similar equilibrium supply-and-demand diagrams for the other inputs determine equilibrium prices and total payments to these inputs. For the United States, the supply curve of labor is probably nearly vertical. As in the case of land, an outward shift in the demand curve raises wages but brings forth, at most, a modest increase in labor supply. The fact that land rent can be thought of as either the value of the *MP* or the residual after other inputs have been paid will be of some importance in this book. Sometimes rent will be calculated one way, and sometimes it will be calculated the other way.

Constant returns to scale and U-shaped average-cost curves by no means exhaust the market situations that interest economists. They exhaust, however, those that are consistent with perfect competition. In recent decades, economists have considerably sharpened their tools for analyzing land rents in noncompetitive markets, but they appear to have lost interest in the subject. In fact, the best evidence is that the share of land rents in American national income has been between 6 and 8 percent since the middle of the nineteenth century (Keiper, 1961). The share probably fell slightly from 1850 to 1950. Thus, even if the Ricardo-George theory of a rising share of land rents were conceptually sound, it would be refuted by the facts.

Turn now to the second concern about land: Why should there be a return to landownership? Unlike labor and capital, land supply does not result from forgone leisure or consumption. No resources are used to produce land. Thus, many writers have felt that landowners should not receive a return on this asset. Many people still believe that owners should not be allowed to receive a return on a nonproduced asset.

George (1879) proposed a "single tax" on land. Since land supply is perfectly inelastic, he argued correctly that a tax equal to its entire rent would have no effect on its supply or use. He called it a *single* tax because he thought its yield would be sufficient to finance all government activity, making other taxes unnecessary. He was probably right in 1879, at the time he wrote, but the government now spends and taxes a much larger part of national income than the 6 percent or so that goes to land rent. Nevertheless, many economists believe that a very high tax on land rent would be a good idea and that it should replace other taxes to the extent that its yield would permit.

An analogy between land rent and wages may help to clarify the issues. Labor supply is more complex than land supply; it depends on choices between work and other activities and, in the long run, on birthrates and death rates. Labor, like land, however, is supplied quite inelastically, even over long time periods. Thus, taxes probably have little distorting effect on supplies of either input. Should income from land be taxed differently from income from labor? Not necessarily.

First is the equity issue. Income from land and other assets is more unequally distributed than income from labor. Thus a 100-percent tax on land rent would fall more heavily on high-income people than would an 8.5-percent tax on wages, which would yield government about the same revenue. The object of a progressive tax, however, should be to tax people with high incomes at higher rates than those with low incomes. The best way to levy a progressive tax is to tax high incomes at higher rates than low incomes. Income from land is by no means perfectly correlated with total income, so a high tax on land rent is a poor substitute for a progressive income tax.

Second, a large part of what is called *wage income* is really a return on investment in human capital, such as education and training. Taxes on wages reduce the return on investment in human capital and, hence, discourage it. It is also difficult, however, to separate the return on land from the return on capital investment, or improvements, on it. Thus, in principle, land and labor are similar. Both are typically "improved" by investments, which should not be discouraged. It is much easier to separate the return on improved and unimproved land than on improved and unimproved labor. The same kinds of problems, however, are present in both cases.

Third, a major justification for competitive pricing of any input is to provide its owner with an incentive to use it efficiently. A central result of modern welfare economics (demonstrated in Chapter 8) is that if all inputs are priced competitively, and if their owners use them where the return is greatest, goods and services will be produced efficiently. Thus, if wages are taxed heavily, owners of labor (that is, workers) lack incentive to find the occupation with the highest return. Again, the situation is nearly symmetrical with respect to land and labor. If central planners knew the best use for each plot of land and for each unit of labor, they could allocate both without the help of market transactions.

Central planners do not, however, know the best use of each unit of each input. Market prices, therefore, are used as rewards to encourage input owners to find the best uses. An important difference between land and labor is that people are much more bothered by bureaucratic controls over the use of labor than over the use of land. The former violates a human right, whereas the latter violates a property right.

The problem with the single tax remains, however. To levy the right tax, the assessor must know the best use and the resulting rent for each plot of land. If the assessor levies an excessively high tax, resource misallocation will result. Thus, *the single tax would assign to the tax assessor the task now assigned to real estate markets.* This is a serious matter, because urban land is a valuable resource, and it is important that it be used efficiently. Whatever the deficiencies in the ways competitive markets allocate land (discussed in Chapter 12), it is clear that the job should not be given to the tax assessor. Tax assessors are skilled at tax assessment, not at urban land allocation.

A final point is that a 100-percent tax on land rent is, economically speaking, the same as land confiscation. In the United States, it is neither desirable nor constitutional governmental policy to institute such a tax without the compensation of landowners at fair market values. If government and landowners held the same expectations of future land rents, however, compensation would equal the land's market price, i.e., capitalized future land rents, and the government would be in no better financial position with the single tax than without it.[5]

The theoretical merits of the single tax seem slight. Most concern with land rents probably is based on concern with the distribution of asset or wealth ownership. If that is the case, asset redistribution is more appropriate, and less drastic, reform than the adoption of the single tax.

Although the single tax may not be desirable, higher tax rates on land than on improvements may be justifiable. In the United States, real estate taxation is almost the preserve of local governments. They now tax both land and improvements at high rates, especially in urban areas. It can be argued that less distortion of resource allocation would result if land were taxed at higher rates and improvements were taxed at lower rates than they are at present. This practical policy issue is discussed in Chapter 10.

☐ Summary

Chapter 6 will use the basic theory of land rent and land allocation to develop the theory of urban spatial structure. It is worth emphasizing here that the theories of land rent and allocation and urban structure are

---

5. This statement assumes that the government's discount rate equals the land-owners' discount rate less the marginal income tax rate. It may not be quite true, because governmental and private risk premiums may differ.

tools to help people understand other urban phenomena and are not themselves of primary concern. Reasons for direct concern with land rents have been discussed in this chapter. Land otherwise is merely one of several inputs used in urban production, and its remuneration certainly accounts for less than 10 percent of total incomes.

The theory and social implications of land rent were among the most hotly debated subjects in economics during the nineteenth century. David Ricardo, the father of land rent theory, believed that land rent equals residual revenues remaining after other inputs are compensated at competitive prices. Modern economic theory shows that land rents, like other input prices, are set by marginal productivity. Marginal productivity and the residual theory are equivalent in competitive equilibrium.

Questions and Problems

1. Would you expect land rents to be a larger share of national income in the United States or in Japan? Why?

2. What would be the effect of a single tax in Iowa on Iowa land values and corn prices?

3. Property income is more unequally distributed than earned income. Do you think that landownership is more unequally distributed than ownership of other property?

4. Can you generalize Equation (5.4) to the case of a monopoly output market?

References and Further Reading

George, Henry. *Progress and Poverty* (1896; republished, New York: Robert Schalkenbach Foundation, 1954). George's basic exposition of his theory of land rents and his defense of a single tax.

Keiper, Joseph, et al. *Theory and Measurement of Land Rent* (Philadelphia: Chilton & Co., 1961). A fine survey of land rent theories and estimates of land rents in U.S. economic history.

Ricardo, David. *Principles of Political Economy and Taxation.* 3rd ed. (1821; republished, London: John Murray, 1886). A definitive statement of the views of the famous nineteenth-century economist.

Mansfield, Edwin. *Microeconomics* (New York: Norton, 1979). A good undergraduate microeconomics textbook that explains input-price determination in detail.

6

Theoretical Analysis of Urban Structure

☐ The goal in theorizing about urban structure is to understand how and why the urban economy ticks. Why are certain goods and services produced in urban areas? Why are some produced downtown and some in suburbs? Why do suburbs grow more rapidly than central cities? Why are certain urban areas developed much more intensively than others? Most important, what are the causes and cures of problems that afflict urban areas?

As Chapter 1 showed, urban areas are places where large amounts of labor and capital are combined with small amounts of land in producing goods and services. Intensive development of central cities is another way of saying that the ratio of nonland to land inputs is greater there than in suburbs. A major determinant of production location within an urban area is the extent to which large amounts of capital and labor can be combined economically with small amounts of land. If all else is equal, goods and services are produced downtown if their production functions permit the substitution of capital and labor for land. If not, goods and services are produced in suburbs or, as in the case of agriculture, outside urban areas altogether. Furthermore, goods and services that are produced both downtown and in suburbs are produced with higher ratios of nonland to land inputs downtown than in the suburbs. Therefore, understanding how the urban economy ticks is, in part, a matter of understanding how markets combine land with other inputs in varying proportions at different places to produce goods and services.

This chapter presents the basic ingredients of models of urban structure and puts them together in models of increasing complexity and realism. The models analyzed in this chapter provide insight into reasons for the gross spatial patterns of urban areas. How well the facts fit the models will be discussed in the next chapter. Many urban problems, however, relate only loosely, or perhaps not at all, to the spatial patterns of urban areas. These problems will be discussed in Part Three. In those chapters, the theoretical models will need to be augmented with considerable factual detail to gain insights into the problems.

☐ URBAN AREA WITH A SINGLE INDUSTRY

Suppose there is a region with a comparative advantage in the production of a certain commodity. The commodity is exported from the region at a certain point, which may be a port or a railhead. Wherever the commodity is produced in the region, it must be shipped to the point of export. Production of the commodity as close as possible to the point of export is, therefore, an advantage. Not only does production close to the point of export economize on transportation of the exports, but also needed material inputs probably can be brought to the production site by the same mode that carries exports to the other places.

A circle of radius u has a circumference of $2\pi u$ and an area of πu^2. Therefore, within u miles of the point of export, there are πu^2 square miles of space. Some of the space may be covered by water or have other topographical features that make it unusable for production. Some space may be needed for intraurban or interurban area transportation. Obviously, however, the greater the distance from the point of export, the more space is available for production. Quite generally, the supply of such space can be represented by a function showing the square miles of land within u miles of the export point. For simplicity, suppose that ϕ radians of the circle are available for production at every distance from the point of export. The supply of land for production within u miles of the point of export, then, is $(\phi/2)u^2$ square miles. Of course, ϕ cannot exceed 2π. For an urban area, such as Chicago, which fronts on an approximately straight-line waterfront, ϕ is about equal to π.

Production Conditions

Labor inputs and the production of housing services play no role in this model; they will be introduced in the next section. Here it is assumed that only one commodity is produced in the urban area. It also is assumed that all commodities have the same production functions. The commodity can be sold locally as well as exported, but it is assumed that all units of the commodity must be shipped to the point of export for distribution in all cases. Thus, the export point may also be a local distribution center. The demand for the commodity is a function of its price at the point of export.

The commodity is produced with land and capital. The production function has constant returns to scale and permits substitution between capital and land. For example, suppose a building has a certain number of floors and a certain number of rooms. The inputs and the output of usable floor space then can be doubled by constructing an identical building adjacent to it.[1] This is the meaning of *constant returns to scale.* Now suppose that the building is extended up rather than out to economize on land. Suppose, for example, that an identical second floor is added to a one-story building. The land input is unchanged, but the amount of capital has more than doubled; although the second story requires the same amount of materials as the one-story building, the walls of the first story and the foundation must be stronger to hold the second story as well as the first. In addition, the output of usable floor space is less than double, because part of each story must be used for stairs to provide vertical transportation between the floors. Similar considerations apply to additional floors in the building. Thus, *capital can be substituted for land, but with diminishing returns to the use of additional capital with a fixed amount of land.* For buildings more than five to ten stories, however, structural steel construction and elevators are justified. These techniques keep diminishing returns to increases in the structure to land ratio remarkably small until very tall building heights are reached.

It is assumed that input and output markets are perfectly competitive. A *competitive-output market* is one in which all units of the commodity must be sold at the same price at the point of export, wherever they are produced. *Competitive-input markets* are those in which producers take rental rates on land and capital as given at each location. It is assumed that the supply of capital (structure capital, not land) is perfectly elastic to the urban area as a whole. It also is assumed that the rental rate on capital is the same throughout the urban area. Land rent, in contrast, is determined by the model and will depend on distance from the point of export.

Finally, it is assumed that shipment costs of the commodity to the point of export depend only on the straight-line distance between the location of production and the point of export. This distance is an approximation, because shipments must follow the road network. Studies have shown, however, that actual transportation time and distance are strongly correlated with straight-line distance in urban areas. Thus, transportation cost per commodity-unit-per-mile is assumed to be constant—independent of the distance shipped and of the point of origin.

The dependent variables in the model are the amounts of capital employed on different plots of land, the rental rates on the various plots, and the total output and price of the commodity. Because transportation cost to the point of export depends only on distance and not on

---

1.   Some increasing returns are made possible by the sharing of common walls. For example, the construction cost per apartment is lower in an apartment building with several apartments than in a single-family house with the same floor space. The scale economy, however, becomes unimportant in a building that contains at least a modest number of rooms.

direction, it follows that all the land available at a distance u from the export point has the same rent; that is, land rent also depends only on distance and not on direction.

As Chapter 5 showed, in any place that production of the commodity occurs, producers use amounts of capital and land inputs that equate the *VMPs* of the inputs to their rental rates. We can write these equations as follows:

$$\textbf{\textit{MP}}_{\textbf{K(u)}}(\textbf{\textit{p}} - \textbf{\textit{tu}}) = \textbf{\textit{r}}. \tag{6.1}$$

$$\textbf{\textit{MP}}_{\textbf{L(u)}}(\textbf{\textit{p}} - \textbf{\textit{tu}}) = \textbf{\textit{R(u)}}. \tag{6.2}$$

$MP_{K(u)}$ and $MP_{L(u)}$ are the marginal products of the amounts of capital and land used at a distance u miles from the point of export. Each MP depends on the amounts of both inputs used. The term p is the price of the commodity at the point of export, and t is the unit-mile shipment cost to the point of export. The term $p - tu$ is, therefore, the price at the point of production for units of the commodity produced u miles from the point of export—that is, the price net of shipment cost to the point of export. The terms r and $R(u)$ are the rental rates per unit of capital and land.

The analysis leading to Equation (5.4) showed that a rent function, $R(u)$, that satisfies Equations (6.1) and (6.2) also makes profit exactly zero at each u. In fact, for given values of p, t, u, and r, a unique R makes average total cost (including transportation cost) equal to p. Thus, the competitive equilibrium rent function $R(u)$ makes profit just zero at each u if producers employ capital and land inputs that minimize average total cost. It is worthwhile to investigate carefully the shape of the resulting rent function. If no input substitution were possible, the inputs of land and capital per unit of output would be constants— independent of input prices and of u. Equations (6.1) and (6.2) would not need to be solved simultaneously. The land rent that equated profit to zero at each u would increase linearly as u decreased—just enough to offset the lower transportation cost as u decreased. In the model here, however, input substitution is possible. It is easy then to show that $R(u)$ must rise faster than linearly as u decreases; that is, $R(u)$ must have the general shape shown in Figure 6.1. The curve in Figure 6.1 is referred to

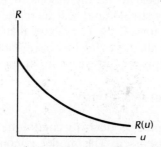

Figure 6.1   The Relationship Between Rent and Location

as the *land-rent function*. We will discuss the related housing-price and residential-density functions later.

To establish the result on the curvature of the land-rent function, suppose the contrary. Specifically, suppose $R(u)$ is at a level that makes profit just zero at some large value of u and that, as u decreases, $R(u)$ increases by just enough to keep profit zero at the input ratio that was most profitable at the initial value of u. The previous paragraph showed that the resulting $R(u)$ would rise along a straight line as u became smaller. The input proportion that was optimum at the large value of u, however, would not be optimum at smaller values of u. At small values of u, land is more expensive relative to capital than at large values of u, as $R(u)$ is rising linearly. This result means that at small values of u, production cost is lower if a larger capital to land ratio is used than the ratio appropriate at a large u. Therefore, if $R(u)$ increases linearly as u decreases, profit will be positive at small values of u. Thus, $R(u)$ must increase faster than linearly as u becomes small, if profit is to be just zero at each u. Of course, the more rapidly $R(u)$ rises at small values of u, the more capital is substituted for land. The urban area is in equilibrium when the capital to land ratio at each u is appropriate for $R(u)$, and $R(u)$ makes profit just zero at each u. To be a solution of Equations (6.1) and (6.2), $R(u)$ must satisfy both properties. Thus, $R(u)$ must increase faster than linearly as u becomes small.

Of course, the ratio of capital to land inputs is an increasing function of the ratio of land rent to capital rent. Therefore, *as land rent rises rapidly and* u *decreases close to the urban center, the capital to land ratio also rises rapidly*. The expression *rising capital to land ratio* is graphic, because it characterizes the rapid rise in the heights of buildings approaching the center of a large city.

The result is important, because if it were not possible to substitute capital for land, urban land-rent functions would be linear, and land used for each purpose would be used with the same intensity in all parts of the urban area. *Land rent, population density, and capital to land ratios, however, fall very rapidly as distance increases close to city centers and flatten out in the suburbs*. The pattern is a consequence of input substitution, and the precise form of the rent function depends on the ease with which capital can be substituted for land. Nonlinear rent functions sometimes appear to be mysterious in models with linear transportation costs. Why should land rent increase more with a move from three to two miles toward the city center than with a move from nine to eight miles? After all, the saving in transportation cost is the same in the two moves. The apparent answer is input substitution.

Market Equilibrium Conditions

So far, only the marginal-productivity conditions of Equations (6.1) and (6.2) have been discussed. The model is completed by several additional equations.

First, all the land available within the urban area must be used to produce the commodity. It would never pay to use land at a certain distance from the point of export if closer land were unused. Thus, for each u within the urban area, we must have $L(u) = \phi u$.

Second, the production function indicates how much of the commodity is produced by the land and capital employed at each u.

Third, overall demand and supply for the commodity must be equal for the urban area as a whole. Overall supply is the sum, or integral, of the amounts produced at each u within the urban area. The overall demand equation shows the amount that can be sold, both locally and for export, at each p. Although each competitive producer in the urban area takes p as given, p depends on the total amount produced by the entire area. A decrease in p increases exports in two ways. The commodity is then cheaper in the region in which it was previously sold, and customers there buy more. In addition, a decrease in p increases the size of the region in which the urban area's exports are competitive.

Finally, urban areas compete for land with nonurban users, such as agriculture. Suppose, for simplicity, that the nonurban land surrounding the urban area commands a rent of $\bar{R}$. The urban area then includes only the land that can be bid away from nonurban users. The edge of the urban area occurs at a distance $\bar{u}$ miles from the export point, where urban land rent falls to the level $\bar{R}$. The urban area has a radius of $\bar{u}$ miles where $R(\bar{u}) = \bar{R}$.

These equations complete the model. The two marginal productivity conditions, the equation relating land use to land available, and the production function give us four equations to determine land and capital inputs, output, and land rent at each u in the urban area. Then, the equation of overall demand and supply and $R(\bar{u}) = \bar{R}$ determine the price of the commodity at the export point and the radius of the urban area.

The model here cannot in any sense be considered a realistic model of urban structure. Its purpose is to introduce the use of land rent and allocation theory into models of urban structure. It is possible, however, to deduce from the model the most pervasive characteristics of urban structure—namely, high land rents and intensive land use near the urban center. Both fall rapidly near the urban center and much less rapidly in distant suburbs. Although the model contains many unrealistic simplifications, the most significant is that the described urban area has no people in it. Labor does not appear as an input, and households do not appear as consumers of housing and other outputs.

☐ HOUSEHOLDS IN AN URBAN SPATIAL CONTEXT

There are important similarities between the foregoing model of business location and the theory of household location. It is assumed that firms maximize profits by choosing a location for production and shipping the commodity they produce to the urban center. Likewise, it is assumed that households maximize their utility or satisfaction in choosing a residential location (among other goods and services). The employed members of households "get shipped," or commute, to workplaces at or near the urban center. Hereafter, this urban center, or transport node, will be referred to as CBD (see Chapter 1). Thus, the production of housing services is analogous to the production of goods and services by businesses, and commuting is analogous to the shipment of commodities. (Of course, not all workers actually work in the CBD, any more than all goods are really shipped to the CBD. More realistic assumptions along this line will be introduced later. It is assumed here that all commuting is to the CBD to maintain parallelism of the model with the model of business location.)

Housing services, like other goods and services, are produced with land, labor, and capital inputs. The provision of housing services bears the same relationship to the housing construction industry that the downtown provision of legal services bears to the office construction industry. In both cases, the construction industry produces a capital good that is used as an input in the production of a service to users of the space. The cost of housing services includes labor cost for maintenance and repairs, plus the rent on the land and capital used. Provided that competitive markets supply the inputs on the same terms to everyone, the cost of a given amount of housing services at a given location is the same to all, and the distinction between ownership and rental of housing is immaterial. Markets for real estate mortgages are highly competitive, and mortgages are highly secure loans, in that land and houses are durable, easily insured, and unlike cars, virtually impossible to remove surreptitiously. This chapter focuses on the price per unit of housing services, which is a rental rate analogous to that of land.

In the United States, there are only two important reasons for the cost of a particular house in a particular location to vary from person to person. First, and most important, is racial discrimination. In many parts of most urban areas, whites still sell or rent real estate to blacks only on premium terms, despite the fact that racial discrimination in housing is illegal. Second, for federal tax reasons to be discussed in Chapter 10, housing services are provided on more favorable terms to owners than to renters. (This factor is most important to people in a high-marginal-income tax bracket.) More is said about racial discrimination and tax considerations in housing markets in Chapters 10 and 11. Here, it is assumed that the cost per unit of housing services is the same for everyone at a given location.

Capital and land can be, and are, substituted for each other in the production of housing services in the same way as in commodity production. A downtown high-rise apartment has a high capital to land ratio, and a suburban ranch-style house has a low capital to land ratio. There is, however, an additional consideration that is more important in the production of housing services than it is in commodity production:

the value of housing services is affected by the amount of uncovered land surrounding the house. Presumably, householders are as well-off with a big house surrounded by a small amount of uncovered land as with a somewhat smaller house surrounded by a larger amount of uncovered land. That is, exterior and interior space can be substituted for each other. Although suburban industrial buildings sometimes have considerable amounts of uncovered land around them, it is usually held for parking, future expansion, or speculation.

Assumptions of the Model

A theory of household-location choice can be formulated as an extension of consumer-behavior theory. Suppose a household has a utility function or set of indifference curves that represent its tastes or preferences for housing services and for nonhousing goods and services. As is true of nonspatial consumer-behavior theory, the theory presented here depends in only minor ways on the number of goods and services available. To facilitate diagrammatic exposition, however, it is assumed that only one nonhousing commodity, called *goods* for short, is available.

The most general way to introduce location choice into the model would be to include u in the utility function. It then could represent all the subjective costs of commuting, such as time foregone from other activities, fatigue, strain, and boredom. Although little is known about some of these factors, it is reasonable to assume that the marginal disutility of additional time spent in commuting increases with the time spent commuting, at least beyond some number of minutes. (Some interesting research has been done on commuters' valuation of travel time; it is discussed in Chapter 12.) Almost no results can be demonstrated unless restrictions are placed on the way commuting affects utility. In this section, a very special assumption is used; it is assumed that commuting costs enter linearly into the budget constraint but do not otherwise affect utility. The important restriction implied by this assumption is that the marginal disutility of additional time spent commuting is a constant. Nevertheless, the disutility of a given amount of commuting may increase with income.

Households maximize their satisfaction with respect to the consumption of housing, goods, and commuting, subject to a budget constraint. The budget constraint says that expenditures on housing, goods, and commuting must not exceed income. It is assumed that the household can buy as much of the goods and housing services as it wants without affecting their prices. The price of goods is assumed not to vary with residential location, but the price per unit of housing services depends on u, since the price depends on land rents, which in turn vary with u. In addition to subjective costs, commuting entails monetary costs in the form of fares or vehicle-operating costs. The money cost per mile of commuting is assumed to be a constant, and commuting cost, similar to the cost of commodity shipment, is assumed to depend on the

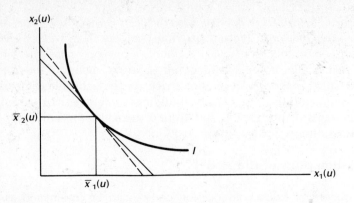

Figure 6.2   *Household's Equilibrium Consumption*

straight-line distance from the residence to the urban center. The coefficient of distance in the budget equation (t in Equation [6.4] in the next section) includes both the money and the money value of the subjective or time costs of commuting.

Wherever the household decides to live, it consumes the amounts of housing services and goods that yield the greatest satisfaction at that location. Figure 6.2 illustrates the equilibrium choice for a household located u miles from the center. The point $x_1(u)$ is the consumption of goods, and $x_2(u)$ is the consumption of housing services. The solid straight line is the budget line for a household living u miles from the center. The curve I, which is the highest indifference curve that can be reached, is attained by consuming $\bar{x}_1(u)$ units of goods and $\bar{x}_2(u)$ units of housing services. The equilibrium condition is the familiar equation between the marginal rate of substitution, or the slope of the indifference curve, and the ratio of the prices of the two consumer goods. If Δx_1 and Δx_2 are written for small changes in the consumption of x_1 and x_2 that keep the household on the indifference curve, the slope of the indifference curve is $\Delta x_2/\Delta x_1$, and the familiar tangency condition between the budget line and an indifference curve for consumer equilibrium requires the consumption of amounts of x_1 and x_2 such that

$$\frac{\Delta x_2}{\Delta x_1} = -\frac{p_1}{p_2(u)}. \qquad (6.3)$$

The household also must decide how far from the CBD to live. If its residence is close to the center, housing services are expensive,[2] but

---

2. It may seem counterfactual to talk about housing being more expensive close to the CBD than in more remote locations, since the tendency is for the more expensive houses to be in the suburbs and the more modest ones to be in the central city. As Chapter 10 will discuss more fully, the price of housing refers to the price of a given "amount" of housing. Suburban homes can be more expensive because they generally have bigger yards and more floor space. Any specified type of house, however, is generally cheaper in the suburbs than close to the CBD.

commuting is cheap. If its residence is far from the CBD, housing services are cheap, but commuting is expensive.

Now suppose that the workplaces in the urban center occupy a space that is small compared with the rest of the urban area, which is occupied by residences. Approximate the area occupied by workplaces with a point at the urban center. Suppose also that $(\phi/2)u^2$ square miles of land are available for housing within u miles of the urban center. Finally, suppose that all households have the same tastes or indifference curves and the same money income. Then, an equilibrium-location pattern requires that households achieve the same satisfaction level wherever they live. If they did not, some households could achieve greater satisfaction by moving. Locations and house rents would be out of equilibrium until enough households had moved so that nobody could increase their satisfaction by a move.

Suppose, for example, that households living five miles from the urban center could achieve a higher indifference level than those living ten miles from the center. By moving in closer, those living ten miles away could achieve the same satisfaction as those five miles away, since they have the same tastes and income and face the same market prices as people already at that location. Thus, some households would move in. These moves would increase land and housing prices at the closer location and reduce them at the more distant location. Thus, satisfaction levels would fall at the closer location and would rise at the more distant location. Movement ceases only when equal satisfaction levels are achieved at all distances from the center.

Implications of the Model

What shape of land-rent function is implied by this model? It is an interesting and important fact that *the model has a land-rent function that is steeper close to the city center than in the suburbs,* as did the model in the previous section. This shape can be seen as follows: The household budget constraint can be written as

$$p_1x_1(u) + p_2(u)x_2(u) + tu = w. \qquad (6.4)$$

Here, p_1 is the price of goods, which does not depend on u, and $p_2(u)$ is the price of housing services, which does depend on u. The term t is the cost per two miles of commuting. A worker who lives u miles from work must commute $2u$ miles per day. The term w is income. Now consider the effect on p_2, x_1, and x_2 of a small change (Δu) in u. Because the budget constraint must be satisfied at both values, Equation (6.4) implies that

$$p_1\Delta x_1(u) + \Delta p_2(u)x_2(u) + p_2(u)\Delta x_2(u) + t\Delta u = 0. \qquad (6.5)$$

Here, Δx_1, Δx_2, and Δp_2 are the small changes in x_1, x_2, and p_2 that result from the small change in u. If the Δ terms are sufficiently small, the cross product $(\Delta p_2 \Delta x_2)$ is nearly zero, so it has been ignored in Equation (6.5).

Equation (6.3) can be written

$$p_1 \Delta x_1(u) + p_2(u)\Delta x_2(u) = 0.$$

Subtracting it from both sides of Equation (6.5) yields

$$\Delta p_2(u)x_2(u) + t\Delta u = 0.$$

Rearranging terms, this equation can be written as

$$\frac{\Delta p_2(u)}{\Delta u} = -\frac{t}{x_2(u)}. \qquad (6.6)$$

Equation (6.6) is known as the **location-equilibrium condition.** It is important to understand it and to understand why it is intuitively appealing. We will use this equation several times in this and the next chapter to derive important results on the structure of cities. To see the intuition behind the equation, rearrange it once again as follows:

$$\frac{x_2(u)\Delta p_2(u)}{\Delta(u)} = -t.$$

Let Δu equal one mile. Now the left side represents the benefit of moving one mile farther from the CBD; it is the change in housing expenditure associated with the housing price decline, or

$$\frac{x_2(u)\Delta p_2(u)}{1}.$$

The cost of moving one mile from the CBD is the increase by t in commuting cost. Clearly, if the benefits of moving toward the suburbs exceed the costs, the household will move. If the opposite is true, the household will move toward the CBD. Only when the costs and benefits of a move are equal will the household be in location equilibrium. Satisfying the location-equilibrium condition, as shown in Equation (6.6), simply means that the costs and benefits are equal.

With the aid of Equation (6.6), how substitution leads to curvature of the housing-price function can be seen more clearly. The slope of the housing-price function is equal to $-t/x_2(u)$. Assume t is constant; if $x_2(u)$ also is constant, the slope of the price function will be constant as well. However, moving up the function (that is, toward the CBD), housing becomes more expensive. As this happens, people reduce their consumption of x_2; that is, they substitute away from x_2. With a smaller x_2, however, the function must be steeper to preserve location equilibrium. The more readily households can substitute away from x_2, the more quickly $t/x_2(u)$ grows. Thus, more substitution leads to more curvature of the function.

The left side of Equation (6.6) is the slope of the housing-price function. The minus on the right side shows that the slope is negative;

that is, housing is more expensive close to the urban center than in the suburbs.

Equation (6.6) implies that the housing-price function is steep wherever x_2 is small. Therefore, the housing-price function is steeper closer to the urban center than in the suburbs if suburban residents consume more housing than those living closer in. Suburban residents, however, must consume more housing, or they could not achieve the same utility level as those living closer in. Therefore, the budget line of a suburban resident must be less steep than that of a close-in resident in Figure 6.2, since the housing price is lower for the suburban resident. The suburban resident, however, also spends more on commuting. Since equilibrium requires that the suburban and close-in residents achieve the same indifference curve, the combined effect of increased commuting cost and lower housing prices must make the suburban resident's budget line tangent to the same indifference as that of the close-in resident. Thus, the broken line in Figure 6.2 is the budget line of a suburban resident, and the solid line is that of a close-in resident. It is clear from Figure 6.2 that *the suburban resident consumes more housing than the close-in resident.*

The foregoing result can be stated in terms of income and substitution effects. As people move farther from the urban center, the price of housing falls. The increased commuting cost, however, exactly offsets the income effect of the decline in housing price. Thus, the new budget line is tangent to the indifference curve achieved closer in. It follows that the only effect of the move on housing consumption is the substitution effect of the decrease in housing price. It is a basic theorem of consumer-behavior analysis that the substitution effect on the consumption of a product which has fallen in price is to increase the consumption of the product.

It is easy to see that the assumption that u does not appear directly in the utility function is crucial in the foregoing demonstration. If u did appear in the utility function, a move away from the urban center would shift the indifference curve in Figure 6.2, and it would not be possible to predict the effect on housing demand.

It has now been shown that suburbanites consume more housing than close-in residents in equilibrium. It follows from Equation (6.6) that the housing-price function must be steeper close to the urban center than in the suburbs. If nonland input prices do not vary with distance, housing price can be steep only where the land-rent function is steep. Thus, the land-rent function becomes steep close to the urban center in the consumer model, just as in the producer model.

The consumer model has two very realistic implications. First, suburbanites consume more housing than residents close to the urban center. Second, because land is cheaper relative to other housing inputs in the suburbs than it is close to the urban center, suburban housing uses lower capital to land ratios than does housing close to the center. These two implications entail lower suburban population densities than those near the urban center. (None of these implications suggest that suburbanites are better off than those living close to the urban center. In this model, all households have the same income, and all achieve the same satisfaction level. This assumption is dropped in the next section.)

☐ SEVERAL URBAN SECTORS

Two one-sector models in which the urban area contains only producers or only households have now been considered, thus developing the basic urban location theory of firms and households. In this section, the theory is extended to explain the location pattern of several sectors in one urban area. A *sector* is defined as a set of institutions that have the same rent functions. Rent functions of firms are affected by their production functions, prices of nonland inputs, and product-demand functions. Rent functions of households are affected by their incomes, their tastes for housing, commuting, and other goods and services, as well as by the prices of consumer goods other than housing. Thus, there are many distinguishable sectors in even a small urban area. For theoretical purposes, the number of sectors makes little difference; for applied research and for ease of exposition, however, it is important to keep sectors to a manageable number. This procedure necessitates the grouping of similar, but not identical, institutions as an approximation of a sector. In applied research, the way data are collected and published usually dictates the definition of sectors.

The key to understanding the location pattern of several sectors in an urban area is the notion introduced in Chapter 5. It states that land owners want the largest return possible from their asset and, hence, allocate their land to the sector that offers the highest rent.

Two Production Sectors

Suppose that two production sectors bid for land in an urban area. The rent that firms in each sector can offer for land at each distance from the center is found by using the method discussed at the beginning of the chapter. From here on, the rent that each sector can pay at each u will be referred to as the sector's **rent-offer curve.**

Designate the sectors as 1 and 2, and suppose that their rent-offer curves are as shown in Figure 6.3. At values of u less than u_0, Sector 1 can offer higher rent than Sector 2, and at values of u greater than u_0, the opposite is true. Land close to the urban center is used by Sector 1, and land beyond u_0 is used by Sector 2. At each u, the rent actually paid is that indicated by the higher of the two rent-offer functions. That is, the rent function is the "envelope" of the rent-offer curves.[3]

3. **Envelope** refers here to the curve that is tangent to the highest of the sectors' rent-offer curves.

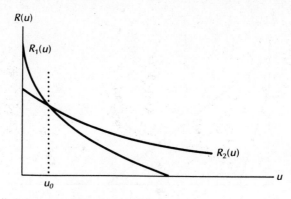

Figure 6.3   *Rent Functions for Different Sectors*

Why should firms in Sector 1 pay much more for land than $R_2(u)$ at small values of u? After all, Sector 1 firms can rent the land if they offer just a little more than Sector 2 firms. The answer is that Sector 1 firms compete not only with Sector 2 firms, but also with one another. Remember that the entire analysis here rests on the assumption that firms enter each sector until profit is just zero. Thus, the complete set of equilibrium conditions for our two-sector urban area is as follows:

1. Wherever firms in each sector locate, they must make zero profit.
2. Each plot of land goes to the highest bidder.
3. Supply and demand for land must be equal.
4. Supply and demand for the product of each sector must be equal.

A very simple rule applies for the urban-location pattern of sectors with linear rent-offer curves. Imagine an arbitrarily large set of sectors, each of which is able to bid successfully for land somewhere in the urban area, and each of which has a linear rent-offer curve. The sectors locate according to the steepness of their rent-offer curves. The sector with the steepest rent-offer curve is closest to the urban center, followed

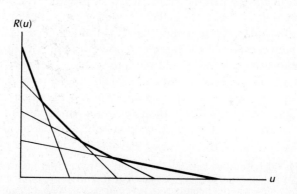

Figure 6.4   *Rent Function as Envelope of Sector Curves*

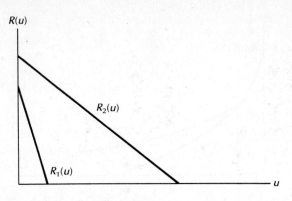

Figure 6.5   *Rent Functions for Different Sectors*

by the sector with the next steepest curve, and so on. This pattern is illustrated in Figure 6.4. The heavy line is the rent function, constructed as the envelope of the sectors' rent-offer curves. It is easy to see that in an urban area with a large number of sectors, the rent function would be nearly smooth and would become flatter the greater the distance from the center, even if each sector had a linear rent-offer curve.

Although Figure 6.4 shows the shape of the rent function, it does not indicate which sectors will locate in the urban area. It is not necessarily true that any one sector will locate in the urban area at all. This possibility is illustrated in Figure 6.5. Here, $R_1(u)$ is steeper than $R_2(u)$, but $R_1(u)$ is nowhere above $R_2(u)$, so Sector 1, therefore, does not locate in the urban area.

As we have seen, input and product substitution mean that business and household rent-offer curves are typically not straight lines. In that case, no simple rule indicates the locational pattern to be expected in the urban area. The locational pattern, however, must satisfy the four equilibrium conditions listed previously.

Figure 6.6 illustrates a realistic possibility. Here, the Sector 1 rent-offer function is steep near the urban center, and it flattens as distance from the center increases, whereas the Sector 2 function is more nearly linear. The result is that Sector 1 locates at values of u less than u_0 and at values of u greater than u_1, whereas Sector 2 locates at distances between u_0 and u_1. There are, however, some reasonable sets of assumptions that preclude multiple intersections. Suppose that each sector has a Cobb-Douglas production function.[4] Suppose further that the two sectors differ only in that their production functions have different land intensities. Then, their rent-offer functions cannot intersect twice. Alternatively, if the sectors differ only in the demand elasticity

---

4.   The Cobb-Douglas constant-returns-to-scale production function in which inputs L and K produce output x can be written $x = AL^{\sigma}K^{1-\sigma}$, where A is a scale factor and σ and $1-\sigma$ represent the intensities of land and capital. We must have $A > 0$ and $0 \leq \sigma \leq 1$.

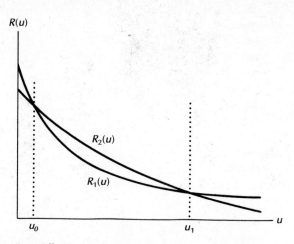

Figure 6.6   *Rent-Offer Curves that Cross Twice*

for their products, their rent-offer functions cannot intersect twice. There are situations, however, in which multiple intersections can occur.

Households and Production Sectors

A sector's rent-offer function is unique because zero profit is a well-defined notion. In considering the rent-offer functions of households, however, zero utility is not a sensible notion. In fact, in modern ordinal utility theory, any "bundle" of goods and services whatsoever can be assigned zero utility. All that matters is whether one bundle yields more or less utility than another. For a group of households with given tastes, income, and prices for nonhousing goods and services, a rent-offer curve exists for each utility level. The lower the rent-offer curve, the higher the utility level, since paying less land rent leaves more money to spend on housing and on other goods and services. This theory is illustrated in Figure 6.7, where $R_1(u)$ is the rent-offer curve

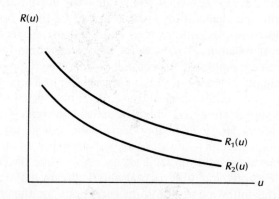

Figure 6.7   *Rent-Offer Curves for Different Utility Levels*

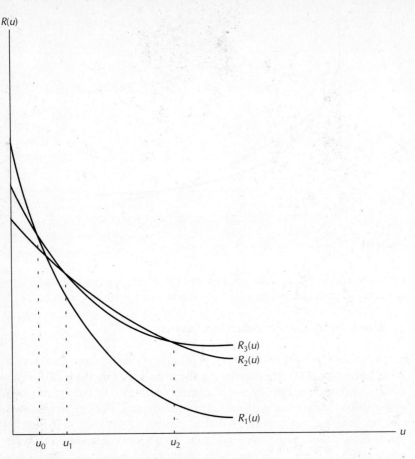

Figure 6.8   *Rent-Offer Curves for Interacting Sectors*

corresponding to a low utility level for the set of households represented, and $R_2(u)$ corresponds to a high utility level.

Which rent-offer curve is relevant? The relevant curve is the one that
equates supply and demand for labor provided by these households.
Figure 6.8 illustrates this notion. Here, $R_1(u)$ is the rent-offer curve of a
sector that employs labor. $R_2(u)$ is a rent offer curve for households that
supply labor to the employment sector; it represents a high utility level
and a small supply of labor. $R_3(u)$ is another household rent-offer curve
representing a low utility level and a large supply of labor. If labor
demand and supply are equal when the household rent-offer curve is
$R_2(u)$, it is relevant. However, if labor demand exceeds supply, and if the
wage rate is high enough to attract more workers to the urban area from
elsewhere, the household rent-offer curve rises to one like $R_3(u)$, the
labor supply expands, and utility of households already in the urban area
falls. Thus, the following equilibrium conditions for the location of
households are similar to those for business location:

1. Wherever households with given tastes and income reside, they must achieve the same utility levels.
2. Each plot of land goes to the highest bidder.
3. Supply and demand for land must be equal.
4. Supply and demand for labor provided by the households must be equal.

Condition 4 implies that household utility levels in this urban area must be equal to those that can be achieved elsewhere. For some kinds of labor, the lowest rent-offer curve that commands land anywhere in the urban area may be so high that the households to which the labor belongs achieve a lower utility level than the utility levels that the households can achieve elsewhere. Households of this type simply do not locate in this urban area. Farmers rarely reside in large urban areas, and highly specialized labor, such as eye surgeons, is rarely found in small towns. This topic will be discussed ahead in the section on the open city model.

As Figure 6.6 showed, not all the firms in a sector necessarily locate in a contiguous area. The same is true of households. In Figure 6.8, $R_1(u)$ is the rent-offer curve of a production and employment sector, and $R_2(u)$ and $R_3(u)$ are rent-offer curves of residential sectors. In this example, the production sector locates at values of u between o and u_o. Residents of Sector 2 locate at values of u between u_1 and u_2, but residents of Sector 3 locate both in close-in neighborhoods between u_o and u_1 and in suburban neighborhoods beyond u_2.

☐ FIRM AND HOUSEHOLD LOCATION WITH DECENTRALIZED EMPLOYMENT

The models of this chapter are built around the notions that access to the CBD is valuable and that the market for land arbitrates the competing desires for this access. In the case of households, access reduces commuting.[5] What about firms? We began our discussion of household location by assuming all firms were located at the CBD, because it is an export node. If all firms are not arbitrarily assigned to the CBD, what can be said about the determinants of their location decisions?

The first thing that can be said is that access to the CBD is valuable, even to a non-CBD firm. If this access were not valuable, firms would be unwilling to endure the cost of locating anywhere on the urban rent curve. Willingness to pay urban land rent means that, either directly or indirectly, access to the CBD must be valuable. Even a firm located in a distant suburb could find much cheaper land outside the urban area

5. This observation needs some elaboration now that the discussion concerns the fact that some employment is located away from the CBD. It will be seen, however, that the basic properties of consumer equilibrium are unchanged by this fact.

altogether. For non-CBD firms, just as for CBD firms, there are two basic reasons that such access is valuable. The first is agglomeration economies, and the second (already discussed at the outset of the chapter) is access to the CBD export facility. (More realistic models would include the value of access by CBD firms to other CBD firms.)

Suppose a manufacturing firm realizes agglomeration economies because of financial, legal, and other business service sectors in the CBD. These services are more costly to obtain the farther away the firm is located. There is no reason to believe that agglomeration economies are lost entirely if firm locations are not contiguous. The more rapidly agglomeration economies decline with distance, however, the steeper the firm's rent-offer curve and the more central its location.

Now suppose the same firm exports its output through the CBD. It can locate at the CBD, incurring high land rent. In exchange, its output is already at the CBD and does not have to be transported downtown for export. By moving to the suburbs, the firm saves on land rent but suffers an increase in output (and perhaps input) shipping costs.

The firm saves, however, on more than land rent by locating away from the CBD. The wage rate it must offer its workers is lower at a suburban location than in the CBD. Workers do not have to commute as far to get to a suburban as to a CBD job site; thus, they accept a lower wage. To see this, consider a firm located five miles from the CBD, at point F in Figure 6.9. Any household living on the way between F and G (the suburban side of a line going through both F and the CBD) would save a five-mile commute by working at F instead of at the CBD. As long as there are more workers living on or near this line segment than the firm at F wants to employ, it can attract workers by offering a wage as much as $5t$ less than the CBD wage (recall that t is the cost of one mile of *round-trip* commuting). That is, with this wage discount, workers living on the line segment FG are indifferent to working at F and at the CBD. Thus, in addition to the rent function, the urban area displays a *wage function,* the slope of which equals $-t$.

Also, notice that jobs at F are most attractive to households living on

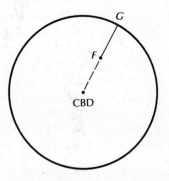

Figure 6.9   *Commute to a Non-CBD Job*

the segment *FG*. For anyone else, the commute saving is less than $5t$. For some people, *F* is farther from home than is the CBD.

The introduction of a wage function, leaving appropriately located households indifferent between CBD and non-CBD jobs, preserves the applicability of the monocentric model in the face of decentralized employment. Many people feel that the monocentric model of household location is inappropriate, given that only a small fraction of the typical urban area's employment is located in the CBD.[6] The description of household equilibrium, however, is unaltered by decentralized employment. Workers still commute up the rent gradient every morning, some all the way to the CBD and some only as far as their suburban jobs. The location-equilibrium condition in Equation (6.6) still holds and still determines the shape of the rent function. The fact that the same location-equilibrium condition holds in a world with decentralized employment leads to a somewhat counterintuitive result: *the shape of the rent function is not affected by the fact of employment decentralization.* Because workers must be indifferent between CBD and suburban jobs, rent functions of households are not different if there are suburban jobs than if all jobs are in the CBD. Remember that only job location and not residential location affects wages.

The historical process of increasingly suburbanized jobs and residences results from changes in transportation costs and other parameters of the spatial model. These parameter changes have caused changes in the spatial equilibriums of urban areas. The result has certainly been the flattening of urban rent, population, and employment-density functions. The point of the previous paragraph is that, for given parameter values, the household equilibrium-location conditions are not different whether there are or are not jobs located away from the CBD. The causes of suburbanization will be discussed further in the last section of this chapter and in Chapter 16.

Returning to the firm's location problem, we see that the firm is attracted to the suburbs because of cheap labor and land, and it is attracted to the CBD because of agglomeration economies and access to the CBD export node. Here is another way of expressing the decision facing the firm: It can locate in the suburbs (where the workers live and hence where labor is cheap) or in the CBD (where the export terminal is and hence where output shipment is cheap).

This concept can be expressed formally with an equation similar to the location equilibrium for the household.[7] The firm's location equilibrium is

$$\frac{L(u)}{X(u)}\frac{\Delta R(u)}{\Delta u} + \frac{N(u)}{X(u)}\frac{\Delta w(u)}{\Delta u} = -t. \qquad (6.7)$$

---

6. As Chapter 4 showed, in 1990, less than half of urban employment was located in central cities, and only a fraction of even this figure was in the CBD.

7. The following material is somewhat difficult. Some readers may want to skip to the next section.

Here $X(u)$ is output produced at u, $L(u)$ and $N(u)$ are land and labor inputs, $R(u)$ is land rent, and w is the wage rate. The term t is the extra cost of producing and shipping a unit of output associated with a one-mile increase in distance of the firm from the CBD; it includes both the extra cost of output shipment and the reduction of agglomeration economies resulting from a move one mile farther from the CBD. The derivation of Equation (6.7) is similar to that of Equation (6.6) and will not be discussed here. It is apparent, however, that it is indeed the firm's location-equilibrium condition. $L(u)/X(u)$ and $N(u)/X(u)$ are usages of land and labor per unit of output. Thus, the two terms on the left side of Equation (6.7) are the reductions in land and labor costs per unit of output from moving one mile farther from the CBD; the right side is the cost per unit of output of moving the extra mile. The firm locates when the benefit equals the cost of a short move.

Equation (6.7) can be rearranged and written as

$$\frac{\Delta R(u)}{\Delta u} = -\frac{t}{L(u)/X(u)} - \frac{N(u)}{L(u)} \cdot \frac{\Delta w(u)}{\Delta u}. \qquad (6.8)$$

The left side is the slope of the firm's rent-offer curve. It is negative because $R(u)$ is smaller at larger values of u, as has been shown in the simpler models. $R(u)$ is the steeper function—that is, the larger the left side in absolute value, the more strongly the firm is attracted to the CBD. A rise in t steepens the rent-offer curve, since an increase in t means an increase in the cost of getting the firm's product to the CBD from any given distance. An increase in $N(u)/L(u)$, the labor input per acre of land, flattens the rent-offer curve, since $N(u)/L(u)$ is multiplied by the negative term $\Delta w(u)/\Delta u$. ($\Delta w(u)/\Delta u$ is simply minus commuting cost per mile, so it is negative.) The rise in $N(u)/L(u)$ reduces the attractiveness of proximity to the CBD and pulls the firm toward cheap labor, which is in distant suburbs. It follows that an increase in commuting cost pulls the firm away from the CBD and closer to workers at distant residences.

The outcome of this process can be characterized as follows: If it is cheaper to ship the workers than their output to the CBD, the firm locates in the CBD; in the reverse case, the firm locates in the suburbs. The cost of shipping freight has declined much more dramatically than has the cost of commuting (faster commuting has been largely offset by increases in the value of time as wages have risen), so this shift in relative prices has led to an increase in the tendency for firms to decentralize during the past several decades. This pattern, of course, is just what has been observed, although it is impossible to say how much firm decentralization has resulted from rapid improvement in freight transport.[8]

---

8. Mills (1972, Chap. 5) has developed a model of firm location that basically works along the lines of these paragraphs.

If there are several production sectors and several types of households, the variety of possible location patterns becomes bewildering. No matter how many business and household types there may be, however, the following must be true. One of the production sectors that exports from the urban area through the CBD will occupy the land surrounding the export node. Suppose the contrary, that a household group occupied the land surrounding the export node and that the group's workers commuted outward to firms that produced things that had to be shipped to the export node. Then, it is clear that the firms and households can trade places, reducing the firms' shipment costs and not increasing the households' commuting costs. Thus, the firms can outbid the households for land nearest the export node. Centrality is worth more to businesses than to households, and CBDs are invariably predominantly occupied by firms.

☐ EQUILIBRIUM WITH OTHER CITIES: THE OPEN-CITY MODEL

So far, the discussion has been restricted to one city, but the possibility of migration among cities has been in the background. Because interurban migration equalizes supply and demand for labor within an urban area, this section examines the effects of interurban migration.

After taking into account any wage, rent, and commuting cost differences, anyone in Urban Area B who concludes that Urban Area A is preferable to Urban Area B can be expected to move to A. Thus, in considering the interaction of one urban area with the rest of the country, the following equilibrium condition is needed: no household can achieve a higher utility by moving to a different urban area.[9] This concept is known as the **open-city model** because it assumes that the urban area is open to migration to or from the rest of the country. Of course, interurban migration occurs gradually, but over time, Americans respond to important differences among urban areas.

An important prediction emerges from the open-city model: Wages vary among urban areas as compensation for differences among urban areas in land rent, commuting cost, and other amenities. Chapter 14 will discuss the other amenities; here, attention is limited to rents and commuting costs.

The first observation is that rent is higher in large urban areas than in

9.   As will be shown, this notion is the same as Assumption 4 in the "Households and Production Sectors" section, which states that the supply and demand for labor must be equal.

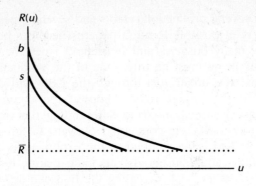

Figure 6.10   *Rent Functions for Large and Small Cities*

small ones.[10] The steepness of the function should not be affected by the size of the urban area, since there is nothing in Equation (6.6) that varies with urban area size.[11] Because the rent functions of both large and small urban areas must start at the agricultural rent at the rural-urban boundary, and since they both have the same shape, the rent function for the large urban area lies everywhere above that for the small urban area, as depicted in Figure 6.10.

Now consider workers deciding whether to live adjacent to the CBD of the large Urban Area B, or adjacent to the CBD of the small Urban Area S. In B they must pay rent b, and in S they must pay rent s. To induce them to choose B, employers in B must offer them a wage premium sufficient to compensate them for the difference between rents b and s. The same wage premium must be paid to all workers in Area B, since the land market there ensures that all households in Area B obtain the same utility level as the workers living adjacent to the CBD.

Note an implication of this result for firm location. If firms find locations in Area B advantageous, perhaps because of agglomeration economies, they must endure both the high land rents and the high wages in Area B. These features are the signals that production is costly in large urban areas and should be undertaken sparingly. At sufficiently large size, an urban area's rents and wages signal markets that the urban area should not grow.

Chapter 7 will explore the statistical evidence on the relationship between wages and urban size, and Chapter 14 will look at the relationship between wages and amenity levels.

---

10.   Although this result does not rest on the open-city assumption, it is the starting point for the discussion on compensating wage differences.

11.   This is not entirely right; the commuting cost per mile may rise with the size of the urban area, as congestion would be expected to be greater in large than in small urban areas.

☐ COMPARATIVE STATICS: THE EQUILIBRIUM EFFECTS OF CHANGES IN INCOME AND TRANSPORT COST

Changes in income (w) and commuting cost (t) bring about changes in the equilibrium shape of the urban area. First, a change in w or t brings about a change in the shape of the housing-price function, and a shift in the function induces entrepreneurs to alter their land-use decisions. Thus, this section begins by examining the effect of changes in w or t on the housing-price function. For both effects, the starting point is, again, the household's location-equilibrium condition, Equation (6.6).

Rise in Income

To determine the effect of a rise in income, begin by dividing both sides of Equation (6.6) by $p_2(u)$:

$$\frac{1}{p_2(u)} \frac{\Delta p_2(u)}{\Delta u} = - \frac{t}{p_2(u)x_2(u)}. \tag{6.9}$$

The left side expresses the *percentage rate* of housing price decline per mile that preserves the location equilibriums of households at every location. In other words, this value is the percentage rate of decline in the household's rent-offer curve. If the urban area contains only one type of household, Equation (6.9) also gives the percentage rate of decline in the equilibrium-rent function.[12] The question to be answered now is, Does the percentage rate of decline in the price of housing increase or decrease as income rises; that is, does the price function get steeper or flatter?

A change in income affects the right side of Equation (6.9), because consumption of housing (x_2) rises with income. If this were the only effect, the right side of Equation (6.9) would get smaller with a rise in w, and the left side of the equation, to preserve location equilibrium, would have to do the same. In other words, the price function would get flatter. For reasons that will be given, the land-rent function also gets flatter, as does the density function, because the substitution to high density is induced by high rent.

Income, however, affects t as well as x_2; a rise in the wage rate causes a rise in the opportunity cost of time spent commuting. This raises the time cost of commuting, which raises the overall cost of commuting. The increase in t tends to offset the increase in x_2 in Equation (6.9). Thus, whether the right side gets bigger or smaller is unknown. Consequently,

---

12.   It has been noted that the rate of decline, $\Delta p(u)/\Delta u$, should get smaller in absolute value as distance increases due to substitution. Reasonable assumptions about the production and demand functions for housing, however, lead to the conclusion that the percentage decline in population density per mile of distance from the CBD will be constant. Chapter 7 will examine evidence on this and related considerations.

whether the rent function gets steeper or flatter and whether the city becomes more or less dense are unknown as well.

The answers hinge on whether the cost of transport or the demand for housing rises more rapidly with income. In particular, if the elasticity of transport cost with respect to income is greater than the income elasticity of demand for housing, then a rise in income makes the price function steeper (the reverse occurs in the opposite case). The best available evidence suggests that the income elasticity of commuting cost is only modestly smaller than the income elasticity of demand for housing. If time cost is roughly half of the commuting cost, a 10 percent rise in income brings about a 5 percent rise in commuting cost (out-of-pocket costs are unaffected). Thus, the income elasticity of commuting cost is 0.5. Direct estimates of the demand for housing give income elasticities of around 0.7 (see Chapter 10). These two figures together suggest that the rent-offer curve gets slightly flatter as income rises. The margin of error in these estimates, however, is sufficiently large that great weight should not be placed on this prediction.

Wheaton (1977) has estimated rent-offer curves directly for various income groups and has found no evidence that rent-offer curves get flatter as income rises. In summary, a rise in income may be associated with a flattening of the housing price gradient, but the evidence is mixed and the effect, if any, is small.

This observation is important for another subject: income segregation. It was previously noted that the land market tends to segregate economic activities, with sectors with steep rent-offer curves locating closer to the CBD than sectors with flat rent-offer curves. The past few paragraphs have addressed the question, Does the rent-offer curve get steeper or flatter as income rises? If high incomes are associated with flat rent-offer curves, this factor would at least partially explain the tendency for high-wage earners to live farther from the CBD than low-wage earners. In fact, no definitive prediction can be made as to whether the rich or the poor have steeper rent-offer curves. Thus, the explanation for income segregation probably lies elsewhere (a topic to which the next chapter will return).

Transport Cost

A decline in transport cost (t) has an unambiguous impact on the rent function; it makes it flatter. Again, this feature is clear from Equation (6.9). If the numerator of the right side of the equation gets smaller, the whole term gets smaller, and so must the rent function in order to sustain location equilibrium. Indeed, this result is apparent even without recourse to Equation (6.9). The cost of urban transport gives rise to urban land values in excess of rural land values in the first place, and a reduction in commuting cost reduces the premium a household is willing to pay for a central location. In fact, if urban transport became free, urban and rural land values would be uniform.

If the rural-urban boundary does not move in response to the decline in t, the rent function shifts from Curve 1 to Curve 2 in Figure 6.11. The rural-urban boundary, however, is expected to shift outward, thus giving a rent function like Curve 3. To see why this is so, consider the open-city effects previously discussed. Consider workers who live adjacent to the CBD (who incur no commuting cost but pay high land rent). Figure 6.11 shows that before the decline in t, their rent was a. When the rent gradient shifts to Curve 2 (before the boundary shift), their rent has fallen to b. That the workers were indifferent to living in this and in another urban area before the rent gradient declined can be known, because location equilibrium among urban areas had been achieved. However, with the decline in Urban Area A's CBD rent, this equilibrium is disturbed. Now, more people prefer to live in Area A; at every location, the sum of transport cost and land rent is lower than before. Thus, outsiders bid up the price of land in Area A, and developers rebuild the city at higher density.

The rent function, however, is not likely to shift all the way back up to rent a at the CBD. As the work force in Area A expands, the money wage offered by employers declines (employers have a downward-sloping demand curve for labor in the urban area). This decline chokes off expansion in Area A before the intercept of the rent function is driven up to rent a, leaving an equilibrium function like Curve 3.

Thus, the effect of a transport cost decline is the generation of a new rent function in which central-city rents are lower and suburban rents are higher than before. The economic reason for this is straightforward. The value of suburban sites rises because they have obtained an increase in valuable accessibility to the CBD. Central-city sites have declined in value because the total supply of land accessible to the CBD has increased, so the value of access from any given distance from the CBD has been eroded. This feature is an important part of the explanation of

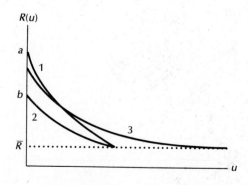

Figure 6.11   *Response of Rent Function to a Transport Cost Decline*

the large decline in central-city real estate prices relative to suburban prices after World War II.

It is important to note that the change in land value is *not* an indication of the social value of the reduction in transport cost. Whether total land value has increased or decreased cannot even be determined, because in general, it increases in the suburbs and decreases in more central locations. The reason changes in land value cannot be used as measures of the value of transport improvements lies in the offsetting effects on land values previously discussed. First, transport improvements improve accessibility of individual sites, increasing their value. If this were the end of the story, changes in land value would be a good measure of the value of transport improvements. Because transport improvements, however, also increase the total supply of accessible sites, the value of access is diminished. It is this diminution of the value of access that breaks the link between changes in aggregate land values and the value of transport improvements. The most extreme case has already been noted: by some act of magic, urban transport becomes costless. Clearly (assuming the magician does not have to be paid), this aspect would be beneficial. Equally clearly, urban-land values would drop, since access would be free.

There is one case in which changes in land value reflect the value of transport improvements. The case is one in which the transport improvement does not extend to the edge of the urban area and, hence, does not increase the supply of accessible sites. Figure 6.12 depicts such a case. The new rent function, Curve 2, is an equilibrium after a transport improvement that is available only to the people who live less than five miles from the CBD.

Finally, note that there may be differences among households in transport cost. Most obviously, two-worker households incur a higher commuting cost per house than do one-worker households; with other things being equal, two-worker households should be expected to have

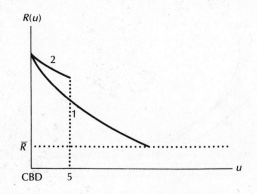

Figure 6.12   *Effect of Transport Improvement for Distances Less than Five Miles from the CBD*

bid rent curves that are steeper than those of one-worker households. Many two-worker households are also childless. Because children increase the demand for space (and for access to suburban schools), the difference in gradients between one- and two-worker households may be greater still.

☐ REALISTIC URBAN-LOCATION PATTERNS AND URBAN-SIMULATION MODELS

The model of urban land use developed in previous sections is important. (Basically, the model is referred to as *the monocentric model,* even though it easily admits dispersed employment.) The model and its various generalizations have been developed by many scholars during the past 25 years or so. The model provides valuable insights. It shows how and why land is used, and why virtually all land very close to urban centers is used for employment instead of for housing. The model shows how and why population density falls as people move away from urban centers. It provides a possible reason why high-income people live farther from urban centers than low-income people. Finally, it provides a basic explanation for the urban decentralization that was shown in Chapter 4 to have been occurring for several decades. The next chapter will show that the model also yields remarkably accurate quantitative predictions on the behavior of density, land rent, and housing prices.

The monocentric model, however, has severe limitations as a description of reality. Some of the limitations can and will be removed by further research, but some are inherent in the model. One limitation is the fact that all employment is assumed to be concentrated in the urban center. As was shown, the model can be extended to the case in which there is a concentration of employment at the CBD and a diffusion of other employment scattered throughout the urban area. There does not appear, however, to be any way to extend the model to cover the realistic case of large concentrations (subcenters) of employment some miles removed from the CBD. The problem arises because the model contains only a one-dimensional description of location; that is, it contains distance but not direction from the urban center. It might be possible to introduce a two-dimensional description of location into the model, but that would make the model extremely complex.

Such complex models yield few analytical results. In general, it is necessary to estimate or assume numerical values for the elasticities and other parameters of the model and to solve them on a computer. The idea of using powerful modern computers to solve or simulate urban models has opened up a large area of research since the early 1960s.[13] Computers have an enormous capacity to solve large systems of equa-

---

13. *Simulation* means the repeated solution of a model with different parameter values to test the effects of parameter changes on the model's solution.

tions and inequalities. Since the late 1960s, several urban models have been published that make use of this capacity and are closely related to the urban models discussed in this chapter.[14]

All computer-simulation models start with a discrete description of locations in the urban area. A set of locations is defined (each might be a census tract), and the computer keeps track of where each location is in relation to all the others. Typically, the computer records a great deal of information about housing and employment at each location. Important characteristics of the existing housing stock might include the numbers, sizes, kinds, and ages of dwellings at each location. Employment information might include numbers, sectors, and occupational descriptions of jobs. Housing-demand equations might relate residents to desired housing, making use of such information as family size, income, race, and education. The model takes into account considerations that induce people to move: their present dwelling is unsatisfactory, employment changes, or the family status changes. New construction is brought into the picture via a supply curve of new housing. Then, the movers are matched up with the available housing supply according to a market-clearing equation.

The great advantage of computer-simulation models is the detail that they can employ regarding housing demand and supply in relation to locations of housing and workplaces. A major purpose of such models is to analyze the effects of alternative national housing policies. Suppose, for example, that a national program is proposed to subsidize housing of low-income people in a specific way. What would be the effect of the program on the amounts, qualities, and locations of housing they inhabit? What would be the effect on housing inhabited by those with incomes too high to be eligible for the program? Existing simulation models are designed to answer such hypothetical questions.

The most important limitation of existing simulation models is their limited success in making amounts and locations of employment endogenous to the model. Usually, the models' solutions are conditional, depending on forecasts of exogenous amounts and locations of employment.[15] Simulation models thus have not yet succeeded in incorporating one of the important determinants of the speed and direction of urban growth or decline.

Urban-simulation models are expensive. A small team of experts and at least two years of work are required to formulate the model, collect the data, estimate the parameters in the model, program a computer to solve it, and simulate alternative governmental programs. Gradually, however, available models have become more sophisticated and com-

14.   For information on these urban models, see Kain (1987), deLeeuw and Struyk (1975), and Kain and Apgar (1985). For a different approach, see Mills (1972).

15.   The works of Birch, et al. (1974) and Mills (1972) are partial exceptions to this conclusion. An endogenous variable is determined within a theoretical model, whereas an exogenous variable is determined outside the model.

puters have become much more powerful and much easier to use than before. The models can analyze not only housing programs but also transportation investments; local governmental taxation, spending, and regulatory programs; national environmental protection programs; and more.

☐ Summary

This chapter has shown how to extend theories of consumer and producer behavior to an urban spatial context. The result is an urban land-use model that provides important insights into urban spatial characteristics.

Most analytical models assume that everything produced in an urban area must be shipped to the urban center for sale inside or outside the urban area. Spatial production theory then shows how production is distributed around the urban center. Spatial consumer theory shows how employees and their families distribute their residences around the employment locations. Such models can provide results that show how land values, land uses, input ratios, and population density vary with distance from the urban center.

Such analytical models are simplified and long-run in character. Computer-simulation models have been formulated to analyze in detail the way households distribute themselves among the available housing stock in an urban area. Simulation models can incorporate much locational detail, many demand determinants, and many characteristics of the housing stock.

Questions and Problems

1. How would you introduce real estate taxes into an urban land-use model?

2. Is it possible in equilibrium for land rent to increase with distance from the urban center?

3. Evaluate the argument that employment has moved to suburbs because CBD land values have become so high that employers can no longer afford to locate there.

4. Some urban areas (for example, Indianapolis) have essentially a full circle of land surrounding the CBD available for urban development. Others (for example, Chicago) have only a half-circle available because the CBD is on the lakefront. How would you expect these topographical differences to affect rent and density gradients? (Some students might want to look at the estimated density gradients in Mills [1972] or Muth [1969] to see whether their predictions are confirmed.)

5. Suppose lakefront land adjacent to the Chicago Loop is worth $1 million per acre. The city proposes to dump nontoxic garbage into the lake to create more land to sell. The cost of dumping and grading is only $200,000 per acre for the newly created land, leaving the city with a net profit of $800,000. Would you recommend that the city do this? Why or why not?

References and Further Reading

Birch, David, et al. *Patterns of Urban Change* (Lexington, Mass.: Lexington Books, 1974). A complex urban simulation model that determines not only housing location and consumption, but also employment location.

deLeeuw, Frank, and Raymond Struyk. *The Web of Urban Housing* (Washington, D.C.: Urban Institute, 1975). A computer-simulation model designed to investigate alternative national policies to subsidize housing for the poor.

Kain, John, and William Apgar. *Housing and Neighborhood Dynamics* (Cambridge, Mass.: Harvard University Press, 1985). A large computer-simulation model to investigate a variety of government housing programs.

Mills, Edwin S. *Studies in the Structure of the Urban Economy* (Baltimore: Johns Hopkins University Press, 1972). A research monograph in which congestion is introduced into an urban land-use model.

Mills, Edwin S. "Planning and Market Processes in Urban Models." In *Public and Urban Economics,* edited by Ronald Grieson (Lexington, Mass.: Lexington Books, 1976). An urban-simulation model based on linear and nonlinear programming.

Muth, Richard. *Cities and Housing* (Chicago: University of Chicago Press, 1969). A modern classic in urban economics.

Wheaton, William C. "Income and Urban Residence: An Analysis of Consumer Demand for Location." *American Economic Review* 67 (September, 1977): 620–631.

7

A Critical Examination of the Monocentric Model

☐ Urban areas are obviously much more complicated than the monocentric models described in Chapter 6. In fact, urban areas are too complicated to describe fully, which is the reason for developing an abstract model. As with all models, the hope is that the abstraction captures important features of reality. The purpose of this chapter is to see how well this hope has been realized. The first part will examine the monocentric model's predictions of the characteristics of urban areas and compare the predictions with evidence. The second part will examine some of the model's specific assumptions and ask whether more realistic assumptions might lead to different results.

☐ STATISTICAL EVIDENCE

The monocentric models developed in the previous chapter yield a number of predictions about urban form. Checking how well the predictions agree with the facts is a way to get a better feeling about whether the model is a good mimic of reality. This section discusses evidence on geographic variation in population density, the price of housing, and land rent to see whether the density and rent gradients of the last chapter really exist. It also calculates the predicted magnitude of the wage gradient and compares the prediction with estimates. Then, it explores the question of interurban wage variation. Finally, it examines the model's predictions of commuting behavior and compares them with actual commuting patterns.

Fortunately, many specific predictions can be extracted and understood from the monocentric models presented in Chapter 6, even without solving the entire model of urban structure. The crucial feature of the model is the location-equilibrium equation (6.6). (Be sure to re-read "Implications of the Model" in Chapter 6 before proceeding with the material in this section.)

Housing-price gradient.   Begin by rewriting Equation (6.6) with the percentage rate of decline in the price of housing on the left side:

$$\frac{\Delta p_2(u)/p_2(u)}{\Delta u} = -\frac{t}{p_2(u)x_2(u)}. \tag{7.1}$$

The right side of this expression now consists solely of numbers with values that can be learned (at least in principle). By filling in reasonable numbers on the right side of Equation (7.1), a predicted value can be calculated for the percentage rate of decline in the price of housing. Consider a household earning $10 per hour, giving an annual income of about $20,000 (close to the national average for 1990). If it spends 20 percent of its income on housing, then there is $4,000 for $p_2(u)x_2(u)$.[1] Now assume transport cost is $0.75 per round-trip mile (including the value of time used for commuting).[2] Now it is necessary to calculate the *annual* cost of a round-trip mile, as the housing expenditure term is in annual units. Assuming there are 220 workdays per year, t is 220 × $0.75, or $165. Now, the calculation is

$$\frac{\Delta p_2(u)/p_2(u)}{\Delta u} = -\frac{\$165}{\$4,000} \left(= -\frac{t}{p_2(u)x_2(u)}\right) \cong -0.04.$$

Thus, if the model of the last chapter is basically right and if the numbers used in this calculation are correct, it should be expected that *the price of housing declines roughly 4 percent per mile of distance from the CBD.* This percentage rate of decline is referred to as the *gradient.*

Land-rent gradient.   Housing is constructed from land and capital with the use of labor. The price of capital (bricks and boards, for example) does not vary much by location in an urban area. Furthermore, although it has been argued that the price of labor varies, its variation is not nearly sufficient to bring about the variation in the price of housing just predicted. If the price of housing is to vary over space, then, the reason must be that the price of the land input varies. According to most estimates, the value of land is between 10 and 20 percent of the value of housing (for example, an $80,000 structure on about a $20,000 lot yields a property worth $100,000). This estimate means that 80 to 90 percent of the cost of housing does not vary with location, and the entire geographic variation in the price of housing is due to variation in the

---

1.   If the price elasticity of demand for housing is −1, the fraction of income spent on housing does not vary with $p_2(u)$; hence, it does not vary with u. Thus, we do not need to worry about the effect of a change in $p_2(u)$ upon the calculations.

2.   See Chapter 12 for a discussion of the cost of commuting.

Table 7.1   *Calculated CBD Land Value as a Function of Urban Area Radius*

$\bar{u}$	$R(0)$[a]	Area
10	15,000	314
15	40,000	706
20	109,000	1,256
25	297,000	1,962
30	807,000	2,826
35	2,193,000	3,846

[a]CBD land value per acre.

price of land. If 20 percent of house value is due to land value, a 4-percent-per-mile decline in the price of housing must be generated by a *20-percent-per-mile decline in the price of land*.[3] In contrast, if the land's share were 10 percent, a land-rent gradient of 40 percent per mile would be predicted.

Even a 20-percent-per-mile change in the price of land is extremely rapid, as Table 7.1 shows. This table shows CBD land value for various urban area sizes, assuming that land value at the periphery of the urban area is $2,000 per acre and that land value rises 20 percent per mile until the CBD is reached. Columns 1 and 2 show, respectively, the radius of the urban area, or $\bar{u}$, and the predicted CBD land value per acre, or $R(0)$. Column 3 shows the amount of land contained within the urban area, assuming it is a full circle. To give perspective, an urban area with a 15-mile radius generally has a population that is slightly in excess of 2 million people. An urban area with a 30-mile radius has four times as much land as an urban area with a 15-mile radius and might house as many as 15 million people due to its higher density.

Density gradient.   As Chapter 6 explained, a city would display a downward-sloping rent function even if it were impossible to substitute away from the use of expensive land. If this substitution were impossible, however, density would be uniform. Density rises as the CBD is approached only because rising land values induce developers to substitute away from land in the production of housing and because households substitute away from housing in their consumption bundles. Thus, the steepness of the density function depends on the steepness of the rent function and on the ability of producers and consumers to substitute. The willingness of consumers to substitute away from housing as it gets more expensive is measured by the price elasticity of housing demand. The ability of housing producers to substitute away

---

3. Consider the $80,000 structure on the $20,000 lot. The price of the house (including the lot) declines from $100,000 to $96,000 if it is moved one mile farther from the CBD. The cost of the structure does not change, so the price of the lot must decline from $20,000 to $16,000.

from land is measured by another elasticity, called the *elasticity of substitution*.[4]

Under reasonable assumptions regarding these elasticities, the density function has the same gradient as the land-rent function.[5] It has already been argued that the rent function should fall about 20 percent per mile, or possibly more, so the simple model predicts that the *density function also falls about 20 percent per mile*.[6]

Wage gradient.   Suburban employers can offer lower wages than CBD employers because the suburban job location reduces the required commute. For any given occupation, the wage rate is expected to fall at the rate t per mile, where t is the commuting cost per mile. With the numbers stated at the beginning of this chapter, t is $165 per year; at an average annual wage income of $16,000, a *wage decline of about 1 percent per mile* is expected.[7]

Summary.   The proper way to read the predictions made so far is as follows: The price of housing should decline a few percentage points per mile; a function flatter than about 1 to 2 percent per mile or greater than 6 to 7 percent per mile is inconsistent with the model. The land-rent function should be between five and ten times steeper than the housing-price function, since land value is between 10 and 20 percent of house value. The density gradient should be in the same range as the land-rent gradient, although uncertainty regarding substitution possibilities means that considerable uncertainty surrounds this prediction. The wage gradient should be quite small—no more than about 25 percent of the housing-price gradient, or about 1 percent per mile.

Evidence

To compare reality with prediction, a rent, price, density, or wage gradient must be estimated; in general, this estimate is done via regression analysis. Under reasonable assumptions, both rent and den-

---

4. The elasticity of substitution is a measure of the curvature of the producer's isoquant (see Layard and Walters, 1978).

5.   In particular, this is the case if the price elasticity of demand for housing is −1.

6.   Actually, a somewhat steeper density gradient than this should be expected. Rich people tend to live farther from the CBD than do poor people, and the rich also consume more housing. Thus, in addition to the forces already discussed, density declines with distance because income rises with distance. This probably adds about five percentage points to the gradient, leaving a prediction that density declines at about 30 percent per mile.

7.   The prediction of a wage gradient of approximately 1 percent per mile is not tied closely to the example of a worker earning $16,000 per year. For a worker earning more income, we would expect transport cost to also be higher (since an important component of transport cost is the value of time).

sity decline by roughly a constant percentage per mile. Such a pattern can be expressed by either of these two (equivalent) equations:

$$X(u) = X_o e^{-\gamma u}, \text{ or equivalently}$$

$$1nX(u) - 1nX_o - \gamma u. \tag{7.2}$$

$X(u)$ is the density, price, rent, or wage rate (as the case may be) at distance u, and γ is the percentage rate of decline per mile. These observations, which could be plotted in a scatter diagram like Figure 7.1, form the basis for a regression equation like Equation (7.2).

Considering the case of density, suppose there are many observations on density at different distances from the CBD, as plotted in Figure 7.1. There are two things to know about this scatter diagram: What is the average rate of decline in density and, on the average, how well does Equation (7.2) predict the actual variation in density? Regression analysis answers both of these questions. First it finds the curve that best fits the scatter, subject to the restriction that the equation for the curve satisfies Equation (7.2). Technically, the regression finds the parameter values X_0 and γ that minimize the sum of the squares of the distances of points from the curve (see the Appendix for a more nearly complete discussion). Second the R^2 statistic indicates the percentage of the variation in density that is "due to" the variation in distance. By way of illustration, the scatter diagram in Figure 7.1 yields an R^2 of 0.501.

Thus, the first step in estimating the gradients previously described is to gather observations on density, land rent, the price of housing, or wages, as the case may be.

Density gradient.   The first thorough study of residential density was carried out by Muth (1969) using 1950 Census Bureau data. For a

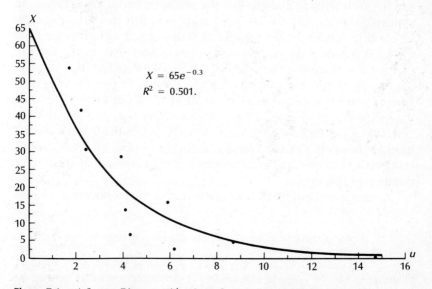

Figure 7.1   *A Scatter Diagram with a Least-Squares Log-Linear Regression Curve*

sample of U.S. metropolitan central cities, he used a regression equation like Equation (7.2) and found that density declined by an average of 41 percent per mile.

Using the same regression technique, Mills and Ohta (1976) found that density gradients had become much flatter by 1970, averaging 20 percent per mile. Evidence from more recent years is discussed in Chapter 16. For a sample of Japanese cities, where transport cost is much higher (largely due to congestion), the average population-density gradient was 64 percent—3.2 times as steep as for the sample of U.S. cities.

The evidence indicates that density declines with distance at essentially the rate that would be predicted (about 20 percent per mile) when reasonable numbers are put into the monocentric model of the last chapter. The steeper density gradients for Japanese cities are what would be predicted based on the higher commuting cost in Japan.

The preceding pattern appears to hold equally well in developing countries. Dowall (1989) estimates a population-density gradient for Bangkok, an extremely rapidly growing third-world city. For 1977, he has calculated a gradient of 19.2 percent per mile; for 1986, his estimated gradient is 16.9 percent per mile. On the other hand, Kahimbaara (1986) estimates an extremely steep gradient—100 percent per mile for Nairobi, Kenya (remember compounding; the city extends for more than one mile). Kenya is one of the poorest countries in the world, with a per capita income of $360 in 1989, and, from 1980 to 1989, the fastest population growth rate of any country in the world—3.9 percent. (By comparison, Thailand had a per capita income of $1,220 and a population growth rate of 1.9 percent.)

In all of these studies, the R^2 (see Appendix) has been between 0.4 and 0.6, indicating that about half the variation among observations in density is due to distance.[8] It is not surprising that there is substantial variation in residential density that is unassociated with distance from the CBD. Cities, after all, are more complicated than the models of Chapter 6 indicate. For the observations used in these studies, residential density is measured by dividing the number of people living in a **census tract** (a small segment of an MSA with about 4,000 people) by the land area of the tract. One reason tracts vary in density—not corrected for in these studies—is that tracts vary in the fraction of land used for housing. On the average, about 59 percent of urban land is residential,[9] but even casual observation reveals substantial geographic variation in this fraction.

At least qualitatively, another prediction of the monocentric models

8.   By way of visual reference, the exponential curve through the scatter diagram in Figure 7.1 gives an R^2 of 0.5.

9.   The remainder of urban land is divided as follows: open space, 7.5 percent; public-semipublic, 13.5 percent; industrial, 10.2 percent; commercial, 5.1 percent; and transportation and utilities, 4.6 percent.

Table 7.2 *Average Gradients for Population-Density Functions of Four Metropolitan Areas*

Year	Average Gradient
1880	1.22
1890	1.06
1900	0.96
1910	0.80
1920	0.69
1930	0.63
1940	0.59
1948	0.50
1954	0.40
1958	0.35
1963	0.31

is borne out by looking at residential density patterns. As Chapter 1 discussed, commuting cost has fallen substantially throughout the history of the United States. Looking at Equation (7.1), this leads to the prediction that density gradients also would get flatter with the passage of time. Mills (1972) has estimated density gradients for four cities as far back as 1880[10]; the average gradient for selected years is shown in Table 7.2. Density gradients have been getting flatter for at least a century in these cities. The well-known suburbanization of U.S. cities after World War II is merely a continuation of the little-known suburbanization of at least the previous 70 years.

Housing-price gradient.   The price of housing can be expected to vary according to many variables other than distance from the CBD. Property taxes, school quality, air quality, and neighborhood racial mix, to mention a few, have been found to influence the price of housing. As Chapter 10 will show, it is inherently difficult to measure the price of housing.[11] The result of these problems is that it is difficult to get a scatter diagram like the one in Figure 7.1, which would be the basis for estimating a housing-price gradient.[12]

Many researchers have tried to overcome these difficulties, with mixed results. Most have found the predicted downward-sloping gradient, but some have found upward-sloping gradients, and others have

10. The cities are Baltimore, Philadelphia, Milwaukee, and Rochester, NY.

11.   The readily observable value of a house is in units of total expenditure, or price times quantity. The tendency for house values to be higher in the suburbs than in the central city arises from the idea that the nicer houses are in the suburbs, not because the price of a house of constant quality is higher in the suburbs.

12.   When the dependent variable (the price of housing, in this case) is influenced by more than one variable, the appropriate statistical technique for estimation is not simple-regression analysis (as depicted in Figure 7.1), but rather a slightly more complicated analogue, multiple-regression analysis (discussed in the Appendix). The analogue between the scatter diagram and the regression line is also somewhat different, although the intuition is the same.

found no variation with distance. It is likely, although far from certain, that these mixed results are due to the inability of the researchers to hold constant other determinants of the price of housing. In fact, a study by Jackson (1979) that took extreme care to hold other price determinants constant found a downward-sloping gradient of about 2 percent per mile.[13]

The model also predicts that downtown housing prices will be higher in large urban areas than in small ones. The model predicts that housing prices rise at a certain rate—call it γ percent—per mile from the edge of the urban area. It is a straightforward matter to calculate the value of housing adjacent to the CBD as a function of the radius of the city and then to determine how much centrally located housing prices are predicted to rise with city size. If the housing price gradient is assumed to be 4 percent per mile, the prediction is that a 10 percent rise in the land area of the city leads to a 2.4 percent rise in downtown housing cost. (If the assumption is that γ equals 6 percent, then the same 10 percent rise in the land area would lead to a 3.6 percent increase in the price of downtown housing.) The relationship between land area and downtown housing cost is not the same as the relationship between population and downtown housing cost, because population is not proportional to land area (since population density rises with city size). Nevertheless, the calculations reported here give a good idea of the relationship we should expect between population and central housing prices.

Asabere and McGowan (1987) have questioned the accuracy of this prediction. They obtained data on the rents charged for downtown apartments in 49 cities around the world and discovered via regression analysis that a 10 percent increase in population is associated with a 4.6 percent increase in rents for centrally located apartments. Once again, the facts are remarkably close to those predicted by the model.

Wage gradient.   Wage gradients are difficult to measure, because the predicted variation in wages is small and because it is difficult to obtain data on wages by the location of the *employer.* In other words, few samples are available from which to plot the scatter diagram of Figure 7.1.

Eberts (1981) solved the latter problem by using data on public-sector wages paid by various jurisdictions in the Chicago metropolitan area. Essentially, he obtained a scatter diagram like that in Figure 7.1 by observing the wage and location (distance from the Chicago Loop) for each of five different occupations (for example, police and fire fighters) for each of the jurisdictions in his sample. For each of these occupations,

---

13.   The gradient Jackson found is considerably more complicated than the simple negative exponential. The peak is slightly off-center from the CBD, and the equal-rent contours bend away from the peak along freeway routes. This finding seems to indicate that the housing market incorporates information on differences in commuting costs along different corridors.

he was able to estimate a wage function. He found a wage decline of between 0.95 and 1.6 percent per mile for four of the five occupations studied (Eberts 1981, pp. 57–58).[14] This finding compares very well with our predicted rate of decline of about 1 percent per mile.

Land-rent gradient.   It is difficult to get data on land rent (or land value) in urban areas, because there are very few transactions in undeveloped land. There are very few studies in which a researcher has gathered the data for a scatter diagram of land value versus distance from the CBD like that in Figure 7.1, because adequate samples are so rare. The reason for their scarcity is simply that the vast majority of urban land is already built on, so there are very few sales of uncovered land. Nevertheless, a few of the bigger metropolitan areas in the United States have yielded samples large enough to warrant careful statistical work. The earliest careful work, on Chicago, was done by Hoyt (1933). Hoyt found Loop land values of about $1 million per acre in 1892 and about $1.9 million by 1928. More recent statistical analyses of his data by Mills (1969) and Kau and Sirmans (1979) yield estimated rent gradients of about 40 percent per mile in 1836 and just over 20 percent per mile in 1928. By the 1960s, according to an estimate by Mills, the land-rent gradient had flattened sufficiently that the rate of decline was only 11.5 percent per mile.

Chicoine (1981) has examined sale prices of farmland at the periphery of the Chicago metropolitan area using multiple-regression analysis to explore simultaneously a large number of determinants of land value. Of most importance for the purposes of the present discussion, sale price per acre was found to fall 41.3 percent per mile of distance from the Chicago Loop. Because the observations are all of farmland, they are far from the CBD; this study does not indicate whether this steep gradient persists as the CBD is approached. This 41.3 percent gradient is at the upper end of the range predicted at the outset of this chapter.

The paucity of transactions in undeveloped urban land makes it very difficult to estimate land-rent gradients, as noted. The model of Chapter 6, however, predicts enormous variation in land value as a function of distance from the CBD. It also predicts that, for any given distance from the CBD, land will be much more valuable in big metropolitan areas than in small ones. Since the predicted effects are so large (see Table 7.1), it is possible to look for these land price effects with less sophisticated statistical techniques than those previously described. If it is predicted that CBD land in a city with a 35-mile radius is worth $2.2 million an acre, whereas CBD land in a city with a 10-mile radius is only $15,000, the effect should be pretty easy to discern.

The anecdotal evidence in favor of this prediction has been

---

14.   The fifth occupation, fire fighters, also displayed a downward-sloping gradient, but it was smaller and statistically insignificant.

overwhelming; everyone knows that land values are very high in New York and Tokyo. In 1970, the most expensive land in the United States—prime sites in Manhattan—was worth over $50 million per acre. The most expensive land in Tokyo has been worth around $100 million per acre. The world's highest land prices apparently occur in Hong Kong, with some sites commanding over $200 million per acre. It is almost impossible, however, to make firm quantitative statements because of the difficulty of getting comparable data on land values for different cities.

In a very interesting study, Rose and La Croix (1980) obtained data on home sites in the top 40 (by population) metropolitan areas in the United States for 1980. They were particularly interested in evaluating Honolulu, where the 1980 average sale price was $373,600 per acre (for only the lot and not the house). The average for the top 40 urban areas was $75,360. Taking data from all of these cities, they used regression analysis to estimate the following relationships:

1. A 1 percent increase in population results in a 0.3 percent increase in the value of a home site.
2. A 1 percent increase in the population *growth rate* results in a 0.28 percent increase in the price of a home site.
3. A 1 percent increase in average income results in a 0.2 percent increase in the price of a home site.
4. A 1 percent increase in the fraction of the area surrounding the CBD that is available for building results in a 0.69 percent decrease in the price of a home site.
5. A 1 percent increase in the degree to which zoning power is concentrated in a small number of authorities results in a 0.14 percent increase in the value of a home site (a finding that will be revisited in Chapter 14).

The authors concluded that Honolulu is expensive because of its high income, its rapidly growing population, the fact that there is so little land around the CBD available for building, and the fact that the entire island of Oahu is controlled by one zoning authority.

Table 7.3 provides sale prices (per acre) for prime industrial sites in 1982. Industrial sites generally are located some distance from the CBD, so these figures do not very accurately indicate CBD land values (that is, values of prime commercial sites). Nevertheless, the figures confirm that high-proximity urban land values are hundreds of times higher than nearby rural land values. There also is a tendency (with some marked exceptions) for big-city sites to have higher site values than sites in smaller cities.[15]

15. You should not make too much of the comparison among cities; there is no presumption that the sites in the various cities are equally distant from the CBD. For example, Chicago industrial sites are surely farther from the CBD than are Portland sites due to the massive commercial district in the Chicago CBD and the large concentration of industrial plants around O'Hare International Airport.

Table 7.3 Sale Price per Acre of Central City Prime Industrial Sites, 1991 (Improved Land, Less than Two-Acre Sites, in Dollars)

Rank	City	Sale Price	Rank	City	Sale Price
1	New York City (Brooklyn/Queens)	$1,089,000	21	El Paso	$130,680
2	Seattle	653,400	22	Kansas City (Missouri/Kansas)	125,235
3	Los Angeles, East	522,720	23	Atlanta (Suburban)	108,900
4	Portland (Oregon)	326,700	24	Denver (Suburban)	108,900
5	Northern New Jersey	304,920	25	Miami	108,900
6	Nashville	261,360	26	Baltimore	104,544
7	Los Angeles (San Bernardino)	228,690	27	Cleveland	98,010
8	Birmingham (Alabama)	217,800	28	St. Louis	91,476
9	Indianapolis	217,800	29	Charlotte	87,120
10	Pittsburgh	185,130	30	Fort Worth (Suburban)	87,120
11	Minneapolis	174,240	31	Wichita	87,120
12	Chicago	163,350	32	Omaha	78,408
13	Houston	163,350	33	Des Moines	65,340
14	Albuquerque	152,460	34	Columbus (Suburban, Ohio)	64,251
15	Charleston	152,460	35	Syracuse	60,984
16	Detroit	141,570	36	Memphis	49,005
17	New Orleans	141,570	37	Little Rock (Suburban)	43,560
18	Orlando	141,570	38	Milwaukee	40,075
19	Cincinnati	130,680	39	Philadelphia	39,857
20	Dallas (Suburban)	130,680	40	Akron	39,204

Source: Data from *Industrial Real Estate Market Survey* (Washington, D.C.: Society of Industrial Realtors, Spring, 1988).

Interurban wage differences. Chapter 6 noted that wages are predicted to be higher in big metropolitan areas than in small ones. The argument already given is that a worker who lives adjacent to the CBD has to pay higher rent in the big urban area and must be compensated. The workers who live at the edges of the big and small urban areas also might be compared. Viewed this way, the big-city workers must be compensated for the fact that their commutes to the CBD are longer than if they lived in a small metropolitan area. It is difficult to establish a firm prediction of the magnitude of the relationship between the wage rate and urban area size, so for this section the procedure previously followed will be reversed; we will describe the statistical findings and ask whether the magnitude is reasonable.

In a study that will be described more fully in Chapter 15, Rosen (1979) estimated the relationship between (among other things) wages and urban area population, as well as between wages and population density. He found that a 10 percent increase in population leads to an average $48 increase in annual wages and that a 10 percent increase in population density (holding population constant) leads to a $120 reduction in wages (Rosen 1979, Tables 3.4 and 3.5). Although this discussion concentrates on Rosen's findings, other researchers have found the same pattern.

Is it plausible that these wage differences are due to the intercity equilibrium conditions discussed in Chapter 6? Consider a metropolitan area with a population of 2 million people and a radius of 15 miles (roughly the correct numbers for Baltimore). Now suppose the population increased by 20 percent to 2.4 million. According to Rosen's estimates, this would lead to a wage increase of just under $100. We have estimated the annual round-trip cost of a 1-mile increase in the commute at $165, so the observed $100 wage increase would be reasonable if the population increase from 2 million to 2.4 million were associated with about a 1-mile increase in the radius of the metropolitan area.

In fact, the area of a circle (or partial circle—it makes no difference) with a radius of 16 miles is 13.8 percent greater than that of a circle with a 15-mile radius. If the metropolitan area grew to the 16-mile size, its average density also would increase somewhat, so it seems quite reasonable that a 13.8 percent increase in land area, achieved by a 1-mile expansion of the radius, would be associated with a 20 percent increase in population. Also, this 1-mile expansion in radius should lead to an annual wage increase of about $165—close to the observed $100.

An increase in population density is associated with a wage reduction, according to Rosen's findings. Qualitatively, this relationship also makes sense. The higher the density for a given population, the smaller is the radius of the city and the shorter is the commute of the worker who lives at the edge.[16] To see if this can explain Rosen's findings, return to the previous example. Shrinking the radius of a city from 16 to 15 miles reduces land area (and, therefore, increases density) by 12.1 percent. The reduced radius should reduce wage demands by about $165 (the annual cost of a 1-mile round trip); from Rosen's estimates, it can be calculated that it actually reduces the average wage by $145 ($120 times 1.21). Thus, the observed pattern of interurban wage variation agrees remarkably well with predictions based on the theory of Chapter 6. Overall, the density, land rent, housing price, and wage patterns conform very nicely to the predictions coming from the monocentric model of Chapter 6.

No model perfectly characterizes reality, however, and it should not be surprising to learn that some aspects of reality are very much at odds with the predictions of the model. One troubling set of findings follows.

Commuting patterns.   The monocentric model predicts that all workers commute straight toward the CBD, even if they work at a suburban job. The reason is simple: workers are willing to commute because housing is cheaper at the home end of the commute. In fact, it is the inexpensive housing that compensates the workers for their commutes. (This situation is depicted in Figure 6.9.)

With a modest amount of statistical information, it is possible to calculate how far workers would commute, on the average, in any metropolitan area, assuming that everyone commutes straight toward the CBD. Begin by calculating the mean commute if everyone works at the CBD. The mean commute is the mean distance of residences from the CBD, which can be calculated from the residential-density gradient.[17] Hamilton (1982) has estimated this number for a sample of medium-sized and large urban areas; the average over the sample is 8.70 miles. In other words, for these urban areas, if all jobs were in the CBD, the mean one-way commute would be 8.70 miles.

Not all jobs, however, are at the CBD, as Chapter 4 explained. Using the same technique used for home sites, Hamilton has estimated the mean distance of jobs from the CBD. For the same sample of urban areas, the average distance is 7.58 miles. On the average, jobs, are therefore almost as decentralized as the population and are not far from the

---

16.   Higher average density does not necessarily mean smaller average lot size. It also can result from more "orderly" development, with little leapfrogging, and preserving rural land uses within the area of urban development.

17.   Basically, the calculation can be shown in the following equation:

Mean distance $= \dfrac{[N(1) \times 1] + [N(2) \times 2] + \ldots + [N(\bar{u}) \times u]}{N}$, where $N(1)$ is the number of people living one mile from the CBD, $N(2)$ is the population two miles from the CBD, and so on. N is the sum of the $N(u)$ variables in the numerator and is the total population. The integration (basically, the sum depicted in the equation) of the density gradient multiplied by u yields this mean distance from the CBD.

workers' homes. Because jobs are an average of 7.58 miles from the CBD, the average length of commute should be reduced by this amount, as compared with the mean commute of 8.70 miles if all jobs were in the CBD. This finding means that, for this sample of urban areas, it would be possible for all workers to commute to their jobs—given the current locations of homes and jobs—with a mean commute of only 1.12 miles (8.70 minus 7.58). It is possible to convert all the movement of jobs to the suburbs into commuter savings. Furthermore, if everyone commuted straight toward the CBD, as the monocentric model predicts, all of these potential savings would be realized. In other words, the monocentric model predicts an average one-way commute of 1.12 miles for this sample of urban areas.

In fact, the average commute for these metropolitan areas is 8.70 miles, the same as it would be if all jobs were in the CBD. None of the potential commuter savings resulting from job decentralization has occurred. By this calculation, about 85 percent of commuting in the sample metropolitan areas is wasteful.

The simple logical extension of the monocentric model, which implies that all workers can commute directly toward the CBD, is unrealistic. Non-CBD jobs, like CBD jobs, tend to be concentrated in specific places. In addition, the urban transportation network is not ubiquitous. Recently, White (1988) has reestimated the amount of wasteful commuting for Hamilton's sample of metropolitan areas and has concluded that only about 11 percent of commuting is wasteful. Small and Song (1992), however, have reexamined both Hamilton's and White's analyses and have concluded that the volume of wasteful commuting is very substantial.

These studies show that the simple model is inadequate to describe commuting patterns, which is the key issue here. Underlying that issue are the following questions: What model would adequately explain metropolitan commuting patterns, and would it imply waste? The answers are still needed on that deeper issue.

Conclusion

This section began by noting that no model fits reality perfectly; the monocentric model is no exception. The gradients, with respect to density, housing price, land rent, and wages, conform remarkably well to predictions generated by the model and reasonable, assumed numbers. In particular, no other model has predictions for these patterns that come so close to reality. Actual patterns of commuting, however, appear to be at odds with the predictions of the model. This finding suggests the need for more sophisticated models in which the cost of commuting toward the CBD is not responsible for the entire shape of the urban landscape. The findings on commuting tell us that residential and job locations are more complicated than those described in the models of Chapter 6. Despite the obvious need for further research on the determinants of home and job locations, however, the monocentric model of Chapter 6 correctly predicts many important features of urban form.

☐ CRITICISMS AND EXTENSIONS

The models of the previous chapter are static; by assumption, the urban area has no history. Today's circumstances determine the shape of the present urban area. To describe it somewhat differently, the models deal only with urban areas in which everything has achieved equilibrium. This statement, however, is obviously false: Urban areas have durable inventories of housing, office and manufacturing structures, and transport networks. The rapid declines in transport cost over the past several decades have led to declines in the steepness of *equilibrium*-density gradients for U.S. cities. The best available evidence indicates that actual gradients have become flatter, as was already shown. However, the process of converting to lower central-city density is far from instantaneous; it can take decades.

The conversion process frequently necessitates the demolition of buildings. The full cost of this demolition is greater than the fee that must be paid to the wrecking company; it also includes any income the building would have generated if it had been allowed to stand. It is worthwhile to incur this cost only if the value of the vacant land exceeds the demolition cost plus the present value of forgone profit on the demolished building. Thus, even if the equilibrium density has declined, a market economy may achieve this density reduction only very slowly. Also, it is economically more difficult to convert from high density to low density than the other way around for two reasons. First demolition of low-density structures is cheaper than demolition of high-density structures. Second the reason people would want to convert from high density to low density initially is that raw land value has fallen. If, however, the cleared land is not worth very much, the payoff to demolition is low. Thus, conversion from high density to low density has high costs and a low payoff. This finding means that high-density urban areas are likely to persist long after they are economically and technologically obsolete.

Table 7.4 *Demolition Cost per Acre as a Function of Building Height*

Building Height (Stories)	Demolition Cost per Acre[a]	Critical Distance (Miles)[a]
2	$91,476	19
3	137,214	21
4	365,904	26
5	457,380	27

[a]See text for assumptions.

Demolition cost can be a serious impediment to redevelopment, as the figures in Table 7.4 indicate. Demolition costs about $0.15 per cubic foot for brick buildings one- to three-stories tall and about $0.30 per cubic foot for taller buildings.[18] Table 7.4 shows demolition cost per acre of cleared land for various building heights, assuming that 70 percent of the land is covered by the structures. If raw land is worth less than this amount, demolition is not worth the cost, even if the buildings currently occupying the land are worthless.

To add perspective, Table 7.4 defines *critical distance* in the following way: Assume, as before, that rural land is worth $2,000 per acre and that urban land value rises 20 percent per mile from the edge of the metropolitan area. The critical distance entry in Table 7.4 gives the distance from the edge of the urban area at which land value is sufficient to justify the demolition of unwanted buildings. Take the case of two-story buildings. Urban land value achieves a level of $91,476 per acre 19 miles from the edge, meaning that the land to be cleared must be at least this far from the edge if proceeds from the sale of vacant land are to cover the demolition cost. Five-story buildings must be at least 27 miles from the edge. For an urban area with a radius smaller than this critical distance, demolition is not justified, even at the CBD. In such circumstances, it is cheaper to abandon structures than to demolish them and sell the vacant land. The numbers in Table 7.4 reveal that abandonment is economically preferable to demolition in many actual conditions.

As noted, the demolition contractor's fee is typically only part of the cost of demolishing a building. Demolition also involves forgoing the income the building could have earned; even for buildings that have fallen on hard times, this impediment can be more serious than the demolition charge. Consider a standard 18- by 50-foot row house occupying 1,286 square feet of land (assuming 70 percent coverage). Suppose the building yields income after operating and maintenance (but excluding interest) of $25 per month, or $300 per year. At a 10-percent discount rate, the discounted value of this stream of income is nearly $3,000, if maintenance and repair expenditures give the house a long useful life, so the market price of the row house is $3,000. Thus, the current use of the land has a present value of $2.33 per square foot ($3,000/1,286), or $101,600 per acre. In other words, an acre of row houses that are worth $3,000 each has an aggregate market value of $101,600. When this amount is added to a demolition cost of another $100,000 or more, the decision to demolish is not to be taken lightly. Even when the current buildings are worth little or nothing, the cost of adjusting to the new equilibrium land use can be prohibitive. It is

18. These figures were supplied by William Geppert of Geppert Demolition Contractors of Philadelphia. The figures assume an entire block is demolished. The cost is much higher if a single building is to be demolished while surrounding buildings are protected. The cost rises for buildings four or more stories high, because these buildings typically have steel reinforcing rods and thicker walls.

readily apparent that in most of the cities listed in Table 7.3 it would not be profitable to tear down an acre of row houses and sell the land on the prime industrial-site market, even if the acre were a prime site.

It would be wrong to infer that this analysis provides justification for governmental programs to demolish slum housing. Demolition cost and forgone rents are net costs, and markets value them correctly in the analysis here. There may be other costs of slums not yet included in the analysis that would justify governmental intervention. This issue will be pursued in Chapter 11.

A second observation that emerges from considering an urban area's past concerns residential-location patterns. It has already been noted that income tends to rise with distance from the CBD. As noted in Chapter 6, the static monocentric model can explain this observation provided the income elasticity of demand for housing is greater than the income elasticity of transport cost. Modern evidence, however, suggests that these two elasticities are quite close to one another, casting doubt on the static model explanation of income segregation.

Once it is realized that urban areas have histories and that, to a good approximation, they are built from the middle out, there is at least a partial explanation of segregation patterns that is straightforward. Low-income housing tends to be old housing (because it was built at a time when incomes, in general, were lower than they are today and because quality and rents fall as time passes), and old housing tends to be located in the central parts of U.S. cities. According to one study (Cooke and Hamilton 1984), these forces are more than sufficient to explain the existing pattern of income segregation.[19]

Rural-Urban Boundary

According to the models presented in Chapter 6, urban development extends out to the point at which urban land users no longer can outbid rural land users. The typical interpretation of this observation is that urban expansion should take place along a thin line, like an advancing glacier. In fact, however, the edges of most urban areas are characterized by a band up to several miles wide in which rural and urban uses commingle. Judging by census data on the locations of houses of various ages, this configuration appears to have been the pattern at least as far back as the 1930s.

There are three important reasons for this thick, fuzzy boundary between rural and urban uses (sometimes referred to as *urban sprawl*). The first two are discussed here and the third is covered in the next section. The first reason comes from a careful, rather than a casual, interpretation of the monocentric model. Agricultural land is not homogeneous; its productivity varies dramatically from one plot to the next, depending on aspects of the soil—conditions, topography, drain-

19. Chapter 11 will address this topic in more detail.

age, and the like. Peterson (1988) has found that parcels with low farm productivity tend to be converted to urban use first, which means that some farmland is skipped over—at least temporarily—because of its high farm productivity.

The second reason for the fuzzy boundary is that farmland tends to come on the market at specific times in the lifetime of the farmer (particularly if the farm is occupied by the owner). A farmer is much more interested in selling at his or her retirement than ten years before, for example. Also, there are tax advantages to selling land to a developer when the owner dies. Finally, of course, farmers simply vary in their desire to remain in business. Thus, not all parcels in the path of urban development are for sale at the same time and price, which means that, at any given time, developers have a limited number of sites to choose from. The result is that urban land uses extend far into the countryside, or agricultural uses extend far into the urban area, depending on the perspective.

Speculation

Many parcels of land for development are held back from urban use because a speculator is holding the land in anticipation of future capital gains. Many downtown parking lots, suburban farms, and vacant lots are examples. This speculative withholding of land from the market means that today's development must take place at a more remote location than would otherwise be the case. This practice, in turn, increases many of the costs associated with urban life. The provision of water, sewer, road, and other services is more costly when development is scattered than when it is concentrated. Personal travel (commuting, shopping, and the like) probably increases as well. These social costs of scattered development and the speculation that helps bring it about are well known.

What is less well known is that there are often important benefits associated with speculation. It was shown that the full costs of demolition (the demolition contractor's fee plus the forgone income from the old structure) can be prohibitive when compared with the value of the cleared land. The decision to develop a parcel of land is frequently irreversible. An efficient development criterion will recognize this fact; if optimum current and future uses of a parcel of land are different, it is necessary to consider the trade-off between present and future development.

The following example illustrates this point. The present density function for some urban areas is depicted by the solid curve in Figure 7.2(a). The optimum density function 20 years hence also includes the segment AC. Segment BC of the dashed function represents wealthy people who demand large lots and are willing to live at remote locations. The adjacent section (AB) represents middle-income people who demand smaller lots and more access. Suppose that the middle-income people (the AB segment) are predicted to arrive in the urban area in ten

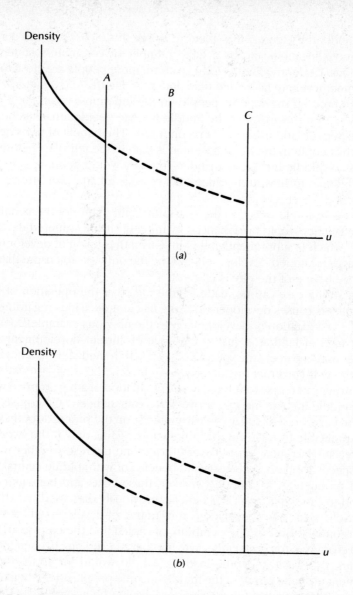

Figure 7.2   *Density Functions with Growth: (a) with Speculation; (b) without Speculation*

years but that the wealthy people (segment *BC*) are already there demanding housing. Developers could build housing for the wealthy people on the innermost vacant land, beginning at *A,* which would mean that when the middle-income people arrived ten years hence, their housing would be relegated to the *BC* segment. The density gradient would look something like Figure 7.2(b), with the higher-density housing more remote than the lower-density housing.

Chapter 6 showed that this pattern is not optimum. Among other things, total commuting is greater under the Figure 7.2(b) configuration than under the Figure 7.2(a) pattern. To see this, note that high density at remote locations means a large number of commuters at remote locations. Under the Figure 7.2(a) pattern, more people are close to the CBD and fewer are far from it than under the Figure 7.2(b) pattern. The cost of housing the wealthy people on the innermost vacant land is as follows: After the arrival of the middle-income people ten years hence, the pattern of land use will not be optimum. The benefit of housing the wealthy people in the innermost land is that, in the ten years before the arrival of middle-income demanders, the city would be more compact. This plan, in turn, would reduce such costs as urban travel, streets, and water and sewer mains.

This example indicates the possibility (although not the certainty) that efficiency would be enhanced by initially having scattered development, which is subsequently filled in. Given the timing of development demands, scattered development may be the only way to ensure that the ultimate shape of the city is efficient.

A strong case can be made for the idea that the operation of land speculators causes developers to make efficient decisions regarding the timing and location of development. In the previous example, consider the parcel of land at A, just at the edge of current development. The owner of this parcel (the speculator) can sell immediately to a developer, who will construct low-density, high-income housing. Alternatively, the owner can refuse to sell today, in anticipation of a higher price when the middle-income people arrive ten years hence.[20] Of course, the speculator who sells today can earn interest on the proceeds of the sale. It is profitable to hold out for future capital gains only if the expected appreciation is sufficient to cover this forgone interest. In other words, the speculator faces both costs and benefits of withholding central land from production; in a perfect market, these costs and benefits correspond to the social costs and benefits previously discussed.

Note that the speculation and timing-of-development problem arises only because of the durability of capital and the costs associated with changing from one land use to another. If everyone lived in mobile homes, the wealthy people in the example would locate on the AB segment until the arrival of the middle-income people; then, they would move without cost to the BC segment, having been outbid for the AB land.

The point of the previous paragraphs has been that the optimum timing of real estate development is a complex and interactive process; an optimum temporal sequence of development does not necessarily occur at sequential distances from the center of an MSA. The final point to be made is that real estate-development decisions are among the most complex economic decisions that people make. Real estate is the

---

20.   The land will appreciate, because it no longer will be at the urban periphery; it will, therefore, command a location premium over land at the edge.

longest-lived among major kinds of capital investments. Industrial capital may last 10 to 25 years; much real estate capital lasts at least 50 years. Modern high-rise office buildings of structural steel may still be around after 100 years, implying that real estate-development decisions must be based on the longest forecasts of technical and market developments that humans now make. Inevitably, judgments differ as to optimum timing and nature of development. One reason that there are parking lots on land surrounded by properties worth one million dollars an acre is that owners of adjacent properties simply make different judgments about optimum timing of development.

Topography

Another assumption underlying the monocentric models of Chapter 6 is that as long as there is land it is possible to build cities on it. The effect on cities of variations in the character of the land itself is virtually never given serious consideration by urban economists. Two examples will help to illustrate the importance of considering the underlying terrain when attempting to describe the shapes of cities.

New York.   According to the models of Chapter 6, a city should have a single high-density CBD, with density falling off gradually in all directions. But anybody who has viewed the skyline of Manhattan knows that Manhattan has two CBDs—one around 34th Street (the Empire State Building) and the other around Wall Street (the World Trade Center). Between the two, looking like a mountain pass, is Greenwich Village. At least in a casual way, many urban economists have tried to discover the explanation for "what went wrong" with the models of Chapter 6. It turns out that the answer lies not in economics but geology.

The bedrock underlying Manhattan lies close to the surface from about 30th Street north. But south of 30th Street, it sinks to several hundred feet (deep enough that the builders of the Brooklyn Bridge eventually gave up looking for bedrock and rested the pilings on sand). At the south end, the bedrock again rises to only about 100 feet below the surface. The entire surface is composed of former New Jersey land that was deposited during the last Ice Age. This material is not a suitable substrate for high-rise buildings; hence, Greenwich Village. (See Mc-Phee [1982] for a detailed discussion.)

New Orleans.   Until recently, New Orleans has had considerably less in the way of high-rise buildings than one would predict for a city of its size. The reason, again, has to do with the substrate. For all practical purposes, there is no bedrock under New Orleans; rather, the city is built over a layer of Mississippi River silt about 20,000-feet thick. The instability of this material precluded high-rise construction until the last couple of decades.

☐ Summary

The monocentric model of Chapter 6 does an excellent job of predicting geographic patterns of land value, housing prices, residential density, and wages. However, for poorly understood reasons, it and its natural extension do a poor job of predicting commuting patterns.

Many assumptions underlying the basic model of Chapter 6 are unrealistic. Most notable among them is the assumption of continuous (static) equilibrium with no adjustment costs. The recognition of adjustment costs alters and enriches the perception of urban form, but the original model remains the frame of reference.

Questions and Problems

1. How would you expect fees at parking lots to vary with distance from the CBD? Would the rate of variation depend on whether the facilities were street-level lots or multistory parking structures? See whether you can test your prediction by gathering data on parking fees.

2. The 1970s witnessed a rise in the proportion of two-worker, childless households. How do you think this finding would affect an urban area's housing-price and density gradients?

3. In many developing countries the rich live close to the CBD and the poor live at the periphery. What do you think explains this pattern?

4. Many states have "use-value" property taxation for agricultural land. Taxes are based not on the market value of the property, but rather on the estimated value of the property in its *current use*. The taxes are designed to make it easier for farmers to remain in business, even if their farms are in the path of urban development and, hence, would command high sale prices to developers. Discuss the distributional and efficiency aspects of use-value taxation. Would you expect urban areas in states with use-value taxation to look different from those in other states? How would you test your hypothesis?

5. It was noted in the text that a 1 percent rise in population is associated with a 0.3 percent increase in the value of a home site. Quantitatively, is this finding consistent with the model of Chapter 6? From the real estate sections of newspapers, obtain data on apartment rents in the downtown districts of several major cities (most university and public libraries have newspapers from other cities). Then, for the same cities, gather data on average income, population, air pollution, and any other variables you think might be relevant. Predict the effect of these variables on rents, and run a regression analysis to check your predictions. (It is very easy to run multiple regressions on most spreadsheet computer-software packages, such as Lotus.)

References and Further Reading

Asabere, Paul K., and Carl McGowan. "Some Factors Explaining Variations in Rents of Downtown Apartments for 49 Cities Around the World." *Urban Studies* 24 (1987): 279–284.

Chicoine, David L. "Farmland Values at the Urban Fringe: An Analysis of Sale Prices." *Land Economics* 57 (1981): 353–362.

Cooke, Timothy, and Bruce W. Hamilton. "Evolution of Urban Housing Stocks: A Model Applied to Baltimore and Houston." *Journal of Urban Economics* 12 (November, 1984): 304–323. A model of urban form that takes account of the fact that housing is highly durable and thus cannot be readily changed in character when economic conditions change.

Dowall, David. "Bangkok: A Profile of an Efficiently Performing Housing Market." *Urban Studies* 26 (1989): 327–339.

Eberts, Randall W. "An Empirical Investigation of Intraurban Wage Gradients." *Journal of Urban Economics* 10 (1981): 50–60.

Hamilton, Bruce W. "Wasteful Commuting." *Journal of Political Economy* 90 (1982): 1035–1058. A comparison of "optimal" and actual commuting behavior in a sample of U.S. and Japanese cities.

Hoyt, Homer. *One Hundred Years of Land Values in Chicago* (Chicago: University of Chicago Press, 1933). A classic study of land values.

Jackson, Jerry R. "Intraurban Variation in the Price of Housing." *Journal of Urban Economics* 6 (1979): 465–479.

Kahimbaara, J. A. "The Population Density Gradient and the Spatial Structure of a Third World City: Nairobi, A Case Study." *Urban Studies* 23 (1986): 307–322.

Kau, J., and C. Sirmans. "Urban Land Value Functions and the Price Elasticity of Demand for Housing." *Journal of Urban Economics* 6 (1979): 112–121.

Layard, P. R. G., and A. A. Walters. *Microeconomic Theory* (New York: McGraw-Hill, 1978). A good microeconomics textbook, cited here for its discussion of the elasticity of substitution. It would also be excellent background for Chapter 8.

McPhee, John. *In Suspect Terrain* (New York: Farrar, Straus, and Giroux, 1982). Describes the formation of Manhattan and the geological problems associated with building there.

Mills, Edwin S. "The Value of Urban Land." In *The Quality of the Urban Environment,* edited by H. Perloff. (Washington, D.C.: Resources for the Future, 1969). One article of an important collection of theoretical and empirical studies.

Mills, Edwin S. *Studies in the Structure of the Urban Economy* (Baltimore: Johns Hopkins University Press, 1972). A theoretical section develops several models of urban form, and an empirical section estimates population and employment density gradients for a sample of U.S. cities, some as far back as the late nineteenth century.

Mills, Edwin S., and Katsutoshi, Ohta. "Urbanization and Urban Problems," Chap. 10. In *Asia's New Giant,* edited by Hugh, Patrick, and Henry Rosovsky (Washington, D.C.: Brookings Institute, 1976). 673–752. A discussion of urbanization and urban form in Japan, with interesting comparisons to the United States.

Muth, Richard. *Cities and Housing* (Chicago: University of Chicago Press, 1969). An exhaustive study of the ability of models like those of Chapter 6 to explain actual patterns of urban land use.

Peterson, George E. *Federal Tax Policy and Urban Development* (Washington, D.C.: The Urban Institute, 1988). An investigation of several features of federal tax policy on urban form.

Rose, Louis, and Sumner J. La Croix. "Urban Land Price: The Extraordinary Case of Honolulu, HI" *Urban Studies* 26 (1989): 301–314.

Rosen, Sherwin. "Wage-Based Indexes of Urban Quality of Life." In *Current Issues in Urban Economics,* edited by Mieszkowski, Peter, and Mahlon Straszheim (Baltimore: Johns Hopkins University Press, 1979). A theoretical and empirical discussion of the relationship between a city's wage rates and the various costs and amenities associated with life in the city.

Small, Kenneth A., and Shunfeng Song. " 'Wasteful' Commuting: A Resolution," *Journal of Political Economy* 100 (1992): 888–898.

Wheaton, William. "Urban Residential Growth Under Perfect Foresight." *Journal of Urban Economics* 12 (July 1982): 1–21. An estimation of the shapes of rent-offer curves for various income groups.

White, Michelle J. "Urban Commuting Journeys are not Wasteful." *Journal of Political Economy* 96 (1988): 1097–1110.

8

Welfare Economics and Urban Problems

☐ The preceding chapters have built a theoretical and empirical framework within which to analyze urban processes and trends. Part Three focuses its attention on the analysis of urban problems and the alternatives open to society to solve them. Welfare economics is the link between the positive analyses and the normative, or policy, analyses. A brief discussion of this field is included to emphasize certain topics that are important in urban policy analysis. Fuller treatment can be found in a good intermediate-price theory textbook.

☐ WHAT IS WELFARE ECONOMICS?

Welfare economics is a branch of economic theory concerned with evaluating the performance of the economic system. To decide whether the system is performing well and whether a change in governmental policy would improve its performance, a yardstick is needed by which to measure performance. Such a yardstick is called a *value judgment*. Some people believe that economics becomes unscientific, or at least less scientific, when value judgments are introduced into analysis, but the feeling is misplaced. Economic theory is the deduction of implications from assumptions or axioms. There is no reason for economists to exclude value judgments among their assumptions and, hence, judgments about the performance of the economy among their conclusions. It is important that economists make their value judgments as clear and explicit as possible so that others can decide whether to accept these value judgments and, hence, the concluding evaluation of performance. A major element of progress in welfare economics during recent decades has been to make value judgments explicit rather than implicit in the analysis. This practice has been part of an important trend in economics to make all assumptions as explicit as possible.

Conversely, it is not possible to judge the performance of the economy without value judgments. Whenever someone judges that an economy is performing well or badly, that person is explicitly or implicitly using a value judgment as to what constitutes good or bad performance. The implication is that if economics did not involve value judgments, it would be an entirely academic discipline incapable of advising society on solutions to economic problems.

What value judgments should economists use in evaluating the economy's performance? In a free society, people can make whatever value judgments they wish. Economists have spent enormous amounts of time and effort discussing and clarifying value judgments that would be interesting and acceptable to many people, or at least to many thoughtful people. The value judgments underlying modern welfare economics are the result of decades of thought and analysis. Nevertheless, they are value judgments, and the conclusions of analysis can be no more persuasive than the value judgments and other assumptions from which they follow.

Welfare economics begins with the idea that the purpose of economic activity is to produce goods and services for people to use. It leads to the broad judgment that *the economic system should be evaluated by the efficiency with which it produces goods and services as well as by the efficiency and equity with which it distributes them for people's use.* For many purposes, *goods and services* can be defined narrowly as inputs and outputs traded on markets. For other purposes, however, it is desirable to broaden the definition. To take the most important example, suppose that the production and consumption of traded goods and services affect the environment in undesirable ways. Then, the definition of *goods and services* can be broadened to include the quality of the environment, and this can be included in the analysis. Of course, the broader definition may require a somewhat different and more complex analysis than the narrow definition.

The foregoing value judgment is not sufficiently precise for purposes of analysis. A crucial step toward precision is the assumption that each individual has a set of preferences for goods and services that leads to indifference curves that have the properties postulated in consumer-behavior theory, as well as the assumption that a person's welfare is measured by the indifference or utility level attained. This value judgment usually is expressed by the assumption that each individual is the best judge of his or her own welfare. No one accepts that value judgment without qualification. Everyone makes mistakes, and a few people are persistently incapable of judging their self-interest. For many people, however, the attractiveness of this value judgment as a broad guide to governmental policy is clinched by the following consideration. People make mistakes in choosing cars to buy, plays to see, and people to marry. Who, however, is qualified to make such decisions for others? *The value judgment that each person is the best judge of his or her own welfare underlies all the subsequent analysis in this book.*

☐ CRITERIA OF ECONOMIC PERFORMANCE

The foregoing consideration leads economists to two specific criteria for evaluating the performance of an economy. The economy is said to perform well if, given the productive resources and technology available to it, (1) no reallocation of inputs and outputs can improve the welfare of some without worsening the welfare of others, and (2) income and wealth are equitably distributed. Criterion 1 is known as the **efficiency criterion,** or the **Pareto efficiency criterion,** after the economist who first proposed it. Criterion 2 is known as the **equity criterion.**

Most people find these criteria easy to accept. Objections come from the fact that Criterion 2 does not specify what distribution of income and wealth is equitable. Utilitarian economists of the nineteenth century believed that a society's welfare was the sum of the utilities of its members. Add to that belief the assumptions that all people have the same utility functions and that marginal utility decreases with income, and it is easy to derive the utilitarian conclusion that social welfare is maximized if income is equally distributed. Modern theory of consumer behavior, however, does not attach any meaning to the sum of people's utilities. Specifically, if a utility function can be found that represents a person's preferences, any utility function that is an increasing function of the first one will represent that person's preferences equally well. In particular, the sum of all people's utilities can be made any number by choosing appropriate individual utility functions.

Despite this theory, everyone has strong feelings about the distribution of income. At present, however, economics is able to provide very little help in forming or evaluating such feelings. About all that can be said is that each person's evaluation of governmental policy proposals should depend on the effect of the proposals on income distribution. Of course, a citizen can unhesitatingly support a policy proposal that improves the economy's efficiency without worsening its income distribution, given the citizen's feelings about income distribution. Likewise, a citizen can support a proposal that improves the income distribution without worsening efficiency. The difficult choices involve proposals that would improve efficiency at the expense of equity or vice versa.

Disagreement about equity issues, however, should not be exaggerated. Nearly all U.S. citizens agree that government should raise the living standards of society's neediest people by taxing those with substantial incomes for the purpose. Nearly all people in the United States also agree that high-income people should pay a larger percentage of their incomes in taxes to support government than should middle-income people. There is a great deal of disagreement on the specifics of these matters, but it occurs mainly within a broad consensus on basic issues. How societies do or should make equity evaluations is the subject of advanced expositions of welfare economies.

The assumption that each person is the best judge of his or her own welfare has an important and controversial implication: *Governmental programs to improve equity by raising living standards of the poor should provide them with money and not commodities or services.* People cannot be made worse off by providing them with the money value of commodities or services instead of the actual commodities or services. Most people probably accept this general principle. The political process continues, however, to provide or subsidize food, health care, housing, and other things for the poor instead of providing them with money. Direct provision of commodities and services for the poor is justified only if there is market failure in private provision of the commodities or services. An important task of this and subsequent chapters will be to analyze arguments for the direct provision of commodities and services to the poor. The first task is to lay out criteria for market efficiency.

☐ CONDITIONS FOR ECONOMIC EFFICIENCY

The efficiency criterion has implications for the allocation of both outputs and inputs. The basic ideas are most easily understood by considering the simplest situation in which a problem of resource allocation can be posed—a model of pure consumption.

Pure Consumption Model

Suppose a society must allocate fixed amounts of two consumption goods per unit of time between two of its members. Shortly, it will be assumed that the commodities are produced with scarce inputs, but for now it is assumed that they simply appear in fixed amounts. X units of one good and Y units of the other are available. Designate the two people A and B and the amounts of the two goods allocated to each by X_A, X_B, Y_A, and Y_B. The allocation of the goods must satisfy the following conditions:

$$X_A + X_B = X, \text{ and } Y_A + Y_B = Y, \qquad (8.1)$$

and all the allocations must be nonnegative.

Individuals A and B have indifference maps representing their tastes for the two goods, as shown in Figure 8.1. Society's allocation problem is usually represented as shown in Figure 8.2. The horizontal and vertical axes of the indifference diagrams in Figure 8.1 have been extended to lengths X and Y, and the indifference diagram for B has been rotated so that its origin is in the upper right corner of the rectangle. Each point in Figure 8.2 corresponds exactly to one of the possible allocations of X and Y between A and B. Society's problem is, therefore, to choose a point in the rectangle that satisfies the efficiency criterion.

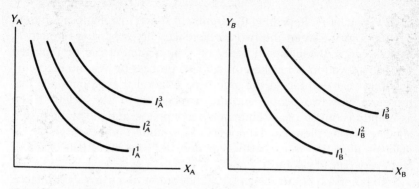

Figure 8.1   *Indifference Maps for Two Consumers*

Unless the tastes of A and B differ greatly, there will be some allocations at which the indifference curves for A and B have the same slope. Assume that such allocations exist and can be represented by a continuous curve, designated cc in Figure 8.2. The cc curve represents all the allocations such that

$$MRS_A(X_A,\ Y_A) = MRS_B(X_B, Y_B),\qquad (8.2)$$

where *MRS* stands for one person's marginal rate of substitution between the two goods. The **basic welfare theorem** in the pure consumption model is that the set of allocations that satisfies the efficiency criterion is precisely the set that satisfies Equation (8.2).

To prove the theorem, consider an allocation P_1 (not on cc in Figure 8.2). There must be exactly one of the indifference curves for A and one for B passing through P_1, but they cannot be tangent. Then, any reallocation from P_1 to a point like P_2, which lies between the indifference curves passing through P_1, must place all individuals on higher indifference curves than they were on at P_1. Thus, each person is better

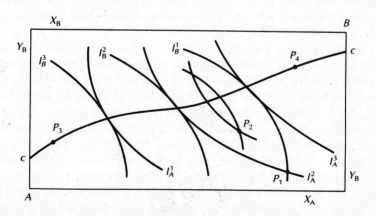

Figure 8.2   *Edgeworth Box with Two Consumers' Indifference Maps*

off at P_2 than at P_1. Repeating the argument shows that reallocation from P_2 to a point between the two indifference curves passing through P_2 makes both individuals still better off. The argument can be repeated until an allocation is reached on cc. This process proves the theorem.

Note that nothing in the argument rests on the assumptions that there are only two people and only two goods in the society. If the assumption consists of any finite number of people and the problem is to allocate among them fixed amounts of any finite number of goods, an efficient allocation must satisfy Equation (8.1) for every pair of goods and every pair of people.

All points on cc are efficient, but they are by no means all equitable. At allocation P_4, A has practically all of both goods and B has almost nothing, whereas at P_3 the opposite is true. Thus, a person who thought that A was relatively deserving would prefer P_4 to P_3, whereas a person who felt that B was relatively deserving would prefer P_3 to P_4. The efficiency criterion narrows society's choice from the set of points in the rectangle in Figure 8.2 to the set of points on cc. The equity criterion narrows the choice from the set of points on cc to one or a few of those points.

What kinds of institutions might society develop to solve its allocation problem? If someone knew each person's indifference map, that person could compute the set of efficient allocations. Of course, no one has the required information. Recall from price theory that if goods are allocated on markets and if the price each person pays for each good is independent of the amount bought, all individuals maximize their welfare by buying amounts of goods that equate their marginal rates of substitution to the price ratios of pairs of goods. Thus, all buyers who face the same prices choose amounts of goods that equate to each other every person's *MRS* for a particular pair of goods. Competitive markets, in particular, will allocate goods to satisfy Equation (8.2) and, hence, allocate efficiently. In the pure consumption model, monopoly is also efficient, but it will be shown that only competitive markets, among all market allocations, satisfy the efficiency conditions when input allocations are included in the model.

Are competitive markets equitable as well as efficient? Not necessarily, as competitive markets ensure only that the allocation will be on cc, not that it will be at any particular point on cc. Equity depends on how much purchasing power or income A and B bring to the market. Suppose, for example, that A and B each inherits amounts of the two commodities. Their inheritances put them at a point like P_1, and they then trade the commodities on competitive markets and end up on cc between I^2_A and I^1_B. The point P_1 is entirely determined by the legacies, and the amounts A and B inherit determine where on cc they end up after trading. Thus, competitive markets can guarantee only to get the society to cc, not to an equitable point on cc. In this simple example, society could ensure equity as well as efficiency by enacting inheritance laws that reallocated purchasing power in an equitable way and then letting individuals trade on competitive markets.

Production-Consumption Model

The model now can be enriched by recognizing that X and Y are produced with scarce inputs. Suppose there are two inputs, labor and land, with fixed amounts of each available to society. There are N units of labor and L units of land. Both inputs can be used to produce each output. The amounts of the goods produced are related to the amounts of the inputs used by the following two production functions:

$$X = F(N_X, L_X), \text{ and } Y = G(N_Y, L_Y), \qquad (8.3)$$

where F and G are different functions. Subscripts indicate the amounts of the inputs used to produce the commodity indicated, so the use of inputs is limited by the following:

$$L_X + L_Y = L, \text{ and } N_X + N_Y = N. \qquad (8.4)$$

Society now has two problems. First it must allocate the inputs to production of the two commodities. Second it must allocate the commodities to the two individuals. The production function can be represented by their *isoquants,* as shown in Figure 8.3. An isoquant shows all of the combinations of two inputs (here, land and labor) that produce the same amount of output. A representation of the input allocation problem can be formed from Figure 8.3 in precisely the same way that Figure 8.2 was formed from Figure 8.1. The result is Figure 8.4, where the horizontal sides of the rectangle have length L and the vertical sides have length N. The origin for the production of Y is at the upper right corner of the rectangle.

Given an understanding of the proof of the theorem in the pure consumption model, it is easy to see how inputs must be allocated in the production-consumption model to satisfy the efficiency criterion. Any allocation of the two inputs between X and Y corresponds to a point in

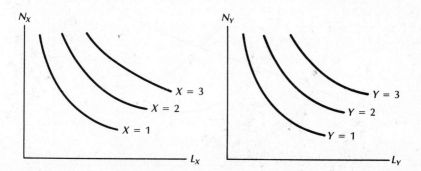

Figure 8.3   *Isoquant Maps for the Production of Goods X and Y*

Figure 8.4. The curve *dd* connects all the points of tangency between pairs of isoquants. Price-theory texts show that the slope of an isoquant is the ratio of the marginal products of the two inputs. Thus, *dd* is the set of input allocations such that the ratio of the marginal products of the two inputs is the same for the production of both commodities at a given point—that is, *dd* is the set of input allocations such that

$$\frac{MP_{LX}}{MP_{NX}} = \frac{MP_{LY}}{MP_{NY}}. \tag{8.5}$$

The basic efficiency theorem in the production-consumption model is that the set of input and output allocations that satisfies the efficiency criterion is precisely that which satisfies Equations (8.2) and (8.5). The theorem and its proof are analogous to those in the pure consumption model. Suppose that the input allocation is at a point like P_1 in Figure 8.4, not on *dd*. Then the same amounts of the two inputs can be reallocated so as to produce more of both X and Y by moving from P_1 to a point like P_2, which is between the isoquants passing through P_1, because P_2 is on higher isoquants for both X and Y than is P_1. Clearly, P_2 represents more output of both X and Y than does P_1. Thus, it is possible to improve the welfare of both individuals (A and B) by moving from P_1 to P_2, since each can receive more of both goods. Repeating the argument shows that reallocations of inputs can improve the welfare of both individuals as long as the input allocation is not on *dd*.

The set of efficient input allocations is the set on *dd*. Given the total outputs of X and Y, however, efficiency also requires that the outputs be allocated efficiently between A and B. Thus, Equation (8.2) is also a condition for efficiency, just as in the pure consumption model. Therefore, input and output allocations are efficient only if Equations (8.2) and (8.5) are both satisfied. Once again, it is easy to see that the argument applies if there are more than two inputs or outputs. If more than two inputs are used to produce X and Y, Equation (8.5) must hold

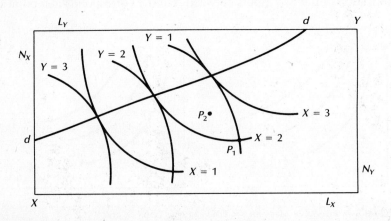

Figure 8.4   Edgeworth Box with X and Y Isoquant Maps

for each pair of inputs taken separately. Then, there would be many equations like Equation (8.5). If there are more than two outputs, input allocations must satisfy Equation (8.5) for those outputs as well as for X and Y.

The conditions for efficient allocation of inputs and outputs have been derived without reference to social institutions that might undertake production and distribution. It now can be shown that allocations of inputs and outputs by competitive markets do satisfy the efficiency conditions. It is shown in price-theory textbooks and in Chapter 6 that the necessary conditions for profit maximization for producers who deal in competitive input and output markets are the following:

$$MP_{LX} \cdot p_X = R \text{ and } MP_{NX} \cdot p_X = w \qquad (8.6)$$

for an X producer, and

$$MP_{LY} \cdot p_Y = R \text{ and } MP_{NY} \cdot p_Y = w \qquad (8.7)$$

for a Y producer. MP is the marginal product of each of the two inputs in producing the two outputs; p_X and p_Y are the prices of X and Y; R is the rental rate of land; and w is the wage rate.

It only remains now to show that Equations (8.6) and (8.7) imply Equation (8.5). If the first equation is divided by the second in Equations (8.6) and (8.7), the result is

$$\frac{MP_{LX}}{MP_{NX}} = \frac{R}{w} \text{ and } \frac{MP_{LY}}{MP_{NY}} = \frac{R}{w}. \qquad (8.8)$$

Thus, the two ratios of marginal products are equal to the same input price ratio, and hence to one another. This equation shows that competitive profit-maximizing firms employ inputs in amounts that satisfy the efficiency criterion of Equation (8.5). The pure consumption model showed that competitive output markets satisfy Equation (8.2). Thus, competitive input and output markets satisfy both sets of efficiency conditions.

A corollary to the foregoing discussion is that efficiency requires outputs of both X and Y to be such that their marginal costs are equal to their respective prices. This condition, of course, is satisfied by competitive (but not by monopoly) markets.

The efficiency criterion tells society that, among all the points in Figures 8.2 and 8.4, it should choose input and output allocations on cc and dd. As in the pure consumption model, there are many efficient input and output allocations, but not all of them are equitable. Suppose (within the two-input model) that every worker is equally productive, and thus in competitive markets, receives the same earned income. Suppose further that ownership of land is determined by inheritance. Then, each unit of land receives the same rental rate, but the overall distribution of income or purchasing power is affected by the distribution of land ownership. In this model, society can obtain efficient and equitable input and output allocations by using an inheritance tax to produce an equitable distribution of land ownership and by permitting competitive markets to allocate inputs and outputs. The inheritance tax might, for example, tax those whose incomes exceed the average and distribute the proceeds to others.

Variable Input/Output Model

The pure consumption model assumed that the amounts of the two consumer goods available to society were fixed. The assumption was relaxed in the production-consumption model and replaced by the assumption that the amounts of inputs were fixed. In the model here, the assumption of fixed input quantities is relaxed. It is replaced by the assumption that workers can vary their supplies of labor freely, within limits.

This assumption is, of course, an approximation, since many jobs require more or less rigid hours of work. Hours of work, however, are more flexible than is sometimes realized. Over a period of a decade or two, hours of work change substantially, falling as incomes rise. Even within short periods of time, however, there are many ways to vary hours of work. Moonlighting, overtime, and part-time jobs are available. Many professional and self-employed workers have flexible hours of work, as do, to some extent, many commission and piece-rate workers.

Leisure, a catchall for whatever is done during nonwork hours, is valuable, just as consumer goods are valuable. Assume that each individual has a set of indifference curves between leisure and each commodity, as illustrated in Figure 8.5. $\overline{N}_A$ represents hours of leisure for A per unit of time, just as X_A represents the amount of X consumed by A per unit of time. If N_A is hours of work for A, then $N_T = N_A + \overline{N}_A$ is the total hours available to A for work and leisure. The indifference curves in Figure 8.5 depend only on the tastes of individual A. Now introduce the

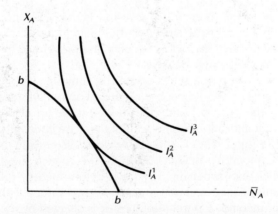

Figure 8.5   Household's Production-Possibilities Curve and Indifference Map

production side by supposing that A produces X at work. The output of X depends on A's hours of work, and, therefore, it varies inversely with the amount of leisure he or she takes. The relationship is shown by bb in Figure 8.5. Since bb shows how the production of X by A varies with his or her hours of leisure, its slope is minus the marginal product of an extra hour of work by A in producing X. If bb is concave, as in Figure 8.5, it means that the marginal product of A falls as he or she works more hours producing X.

The final criterion for efficient resource allocation now can be derived. It says that the hours of work by A should equate his or her marginal rate of substitution between X and leisure to his or her marginal product in producing X—that is,

$$MRS_A \, (X_A, \bar{N}_A) = MP_{AX}. \tag{8.9}$$

The curve bb is like a budget constraint for A, showing the combinations of leisure and X available to him or her. Individual A achieves the highest possible indifference curve by choosing a combination of X and leisure that places him or her at the point of tangency between bb and an indifference curve. A's wage, w, may be higher in one sector than in another. If so, A should work in the sector in which his or her wage is greatest and work a number of hours in that sector such that his or her production-possibility curve is tangent to an indifference curve. Since the movement of A to the point of tangency from another point on bb does not affect the welfare of other members of society, the move satisfies the efficiency criterion—that is, it makes A better off without making anyone else worse off. Going up bb means working more hours, and concavity implies that each additional hour results in a smaller increase in production of X.

It only remains to show that competitive markets satisfy this efficiency criterion, as well as those already discussed. If A sells his or her labor and buys X and Y on markets, the budget constraint is

$$p_X X_A + p_Y Y_A = w(N_T - \bar{N}_A), \tag{8.10}$$

where $N_T - \bar{N}_A$ is the number of hours A chooses to work, and w is the hourly wage rate. If the labor market is competitive,

$$w = MP_{AX} \cdot p_X.$$

Substituting for w in Equation (8.10) and rearranging terms, the budget constraint can be written as follows:

$$X_A = (MP_{AX} N_T - \frac{p_Y}{p_X} Y_A) - MP_{AX} \bar{N}_A. \tag{8.11}$$

Thus, in a competitive labor market, the slope of the budget constraint of A is MP_{AX}, the same as that of bb. It follows that the market choice by A will lead him or her to the tangency point in Figure 8.5 that has been shown to satisfy the efficiency criterion.

The production-consumption model showed that society could obtain an efficient and equitable resource allocation by choosing an appropriate initial distribution of input ownership and permitting exchange of inputs and outputs on competitive markets. In the model, input supplies were fixed, and therefore, redistribution of their ownership did not affect resource-allocation decisions. However, matters are more complicated in the model with variable inputs. In this model, only a wage rate equal to the value of the worker's marginal product results in an efficient allocation of labor resources. If many workers have a variety of skills and abilities, the wage of each must be equal to the value of the worker's marginal product. Thus, in the variable-input model, the efficiency conditions imply a distribution of earned income, which will be referred to as an *efficient distribution of income.*

Some characteristics that affect worker productivity are innate, but some result from education and training, now referred to as accumulation of human capital. To a considerable extent, workers acquire human capital on the basis of employment and earnings considerations. Thus, a long-run characteristic of competitive markets is that they provide strong incentives for human capital accumulation. Returns to human capital are designated as earned income, even though they are really property income. Physical assets also provide returns to their owners in the form of profit, interest, dividends, and rents. Such returns are referred to as property, or unearned, income. Nevertheless, physical assets are accumulated as a result of people's economic decisions, and competitive markets also provide incentives for optimum physical capital ownership.

Thus, the most general concept of an efficient distribution of income depends on the pattern of competitive input and output prices. It also depends on the pattern of inheritance of physical capital and on the extent to which parents finance human capital accumulation of their children. In the United States, labor income is about 80 percent of total income. Most of the labor income is a return to human capital, which careful research concludes, exceeds the stock of physical capital.

Is the overall efficient distribution of income also equitable? It can hardly be. Some adults have no salable skills at all because of physical or psychological disabilities. Even among adult males without severe disabilities, earnings vary by more than a factor of 1000, say from $5,000 to $5 million per year. Adding in property income, the range is much greater. Almost no one doubts that governments should attempt to narrow this range, at least somewhat. Most people believe that high-income people should be taxed at higher percentages of their incomes than are low-income people and that some of governments' revenues should be used to provide transfers and human capital accumulation (especially education) to low-income people.

☐ SOME CAUSES OF RESOURCE MISALLOCATION

The discussion of the social efficiency of competitive markets is now complete. There are several reasons to believe that markets are less efficient than the preceding discussion has indicated. This chapter concludes with a general classification and analysis of reasons for resource misallocation. Succeeding chapters will analyze specific problems of efficiency and equity in the urban economy. Each problem requires facts and analysis specific to that problem, and they are presented in the appropriate chapters.

Monopoly and Monopsony

It is easy to show that *monopolists and monopsonists misallocate resources.* A monopolist maximizes profits by employing input quantities that satisfy equations similar to Equations (8.3) and (8.4), but with product prices replaced by marginal revenues. Because a monopolist's marginal revenue is less than price, profit maximization requires that marginal products be greater for the monopolist than for the competitive firm for given input prices. The monopolist, therefore, employs smaller input quantities and produces less output than is efficient from society's point of view. Similar reasoning shows that Equation (8.7) also is violated if the employer is a monopoly, and therefore inefficient amounts of labor are supplied. (As an exercise, it should be possible to show that monopsony power also leads to inefficient resource allocations.)

The quantitative importance of resource misallocation from monopoly and monopsony is a subject of debate among specialists in industrial organization economics. If misallocation is substantial, it must be substantial in urban areas, since most economic activity occurs there. It is claimed in following chapters, however, that monopoly is unimportant in understanding most serious urban problems; poverty, poor housing, congestion, pollution, and inadequate public services result only to a minor extent from monopoly power. They would be serious problems even if all markets were perfectly competitive. Many people resist this conclusion, in part because they use the term *monopoly* more broadly than economists do, and in part because of the human tendency to search for villains to blame for problems.

External Economies and Diseconomies

For decades, economists have analyzed **externalities,** a closely related set of considerations that entail resource misallocation, even in competitive markets. Despite important recent progress in clarifying the concept, there is still considerable disagreement among economists about the causes and effects of externalities. The result is that the term tends to be used somewhat loosely in applied studies. Especially in urban economics, the term is badly overused and abused.

The basic idea behind the notion of an **external effect** is that *the actions of one person or institution may affect the welfare of another in ways that cannot be regulated by private agreements among the affected parties.* As has been discussed, if a firm buys and sells on competitive markets in certain assumed circumstances, market prices and profit maximization induce the firm to behave efficiently from society's point of view. It employs just the inputs and produces just the outputs that are in society's interest. Now suppose that one of the firm's activities affects people's welfare in a way not based on agreement or market transaction. The classic example, used by generations of writers, is smoke emission. Suppose a certain fuel is among the firm's inputs and that burning the fuel creates smoke that spreads over the neighborhood and reduces residents' welfare. If the fuel is an important input and its smoke is not too harmful, some smoke may be worth its cost to the firm and to the public. There is no market, however, on which to register the advantages of smoke production to the firm and its disadvantages to the neighbors. If the smoke maximizes profits, it fails to take into account the cost that its smoke imposes on others. Even though some smoke may be worth the cost, too much is produced. The smoke is then said to be an **external diseconomy.** The resulting resource misallocation—too much smoke—is no less serious just because the firm buys inputs and sells outputs in competitive markets.

In fact, smoke is a less serious problem than it used to be, but nearly all economists agree that air pollution is a serious public problem because of its external effects. In a general way, almost everyone would agree on the underlying explanation that private agreements cannot allocate resources to abate air pollution efficiently. Disagreement comes when people try to establish exactly why private agreements do not work.

The basic reason that private agreements do not work is that *private transaction costs sometimes exceed the potential gain from the agreement.* The reason is not hard to understand in the example of smoke emission. Many people suffer more or less harm from the smoke, and many sources may be more or less responsible for the smoke damage to each person and to each person's property. Thus, a private agreement to abate smoke discharges would require negotiations among large numbers of people and factories, and the public would have complex and poorly understood interests in abatement by particular sources. Obviously, a private agreement on such an issue would be extremely difficult and costly to specify and negotiate. That is the meaning of the statement that the transaction costs of such an agreement are high.

Exactly what circumstances entail transaction costs so high as to prevent otherwise desirable agreements? There is no satisfactory answer at present, and the result is that many studies of externalities are merely anecdotal. About all that can be said is that transaction costs may be high regarding agreement about an activity, if the activity affects large numbers of people in complex ways. Any study of an apparent externality, however, should include a careful investigation of the kinds and amounts of transaction costs that prevent agreement.

Once an important externality has been identified, the next question is what to do about it. The usual answer is that the government should tax or subsidize so as to create an appropriate market, or it should regulate so that private activity approximates the missing market. In the example of smoke emission, the government can tax emissions, subsidize abatement, or regulate emissions. The first question that needs to be asked, however, is whether transaction costs will be lower if the government intervenes than if private parties try to reach agreement. If not, the transaction costs are unavoidable, and the agreement is not worth having. In the example of smoke emission, the disadvantage of the smoke may be smaller than the cost of doing something about it. In many cases, however, the government can adopt policies that at least approximate the results of private agreements, and with relatively small transaction costs. In each case, however, the facts must decide the issue. Sometimes governmental programs become cumbersome because the government must bear exactly the transaction costs that prevented the private sector from undertaking the transactions in the first place.

If transaction costs are low enough that governmental intervention is justified, the appropriate policy is easy to specify in principle. In the example of smoke emission, the efficient amount of smoke is the amount such that the cost to the neighbors of a little more smoke equals the cost to the factory of a little more abatement. In other words, the amount of smoke should be such that marginal costs and marginal benefits of abatement are equal. The goal might be achieved by an appropriate tax on smoke or by regulation of smoke discharges. Which policy should be chosen depends on the transaction costs of the policies and on the extent to which they approximate efficient resource allocation. Of course, in practice, the benefits of abatement may be difficult to estimate.

Externalities in an Urban Context

What are the important externalities in urban areas? There is no agreement on this matter in the relevant economics literature. Environmental pollution commands the greatest agreement. Almost all economists agree that polluting discharges to air and water result in resource misallocation and that government should tax or regulate such discharges. Consensus probably also could be reached on housing. Most people's welfare is affected by the quality of housing in the neighborhood where they live. Also, most economists probably would agree that governmental interference in housing markets is justified. However, there is little agreement as to the best kind of governmental interference. In fact, we have a panoply of taxes, subsidies, codes, and controls on housing markets.

What about urban transportation? Most economists would agree that a street or subway system must be planned as an integrated whole in an entire urban area. This plan justifies governmental ownership or regulation of the basic infrastructure. But how should the use of the streets or tracks by vehicles be controlled? Chapter 13 will show that congestion is an external diseconomy that might justify government intervention in the use of rights-of-way by vehicles.

These and other resource allocation problems raise complex issues about whether and how government should intervene. Many of the issues will be discussed in subsequent chapters. The logical sequence of the argument is the same with every issue: What is the justification for governmental intervention, and what is the best kind of intervention? Both questions are important.

Taxes

Governments must raise large amounts of money by taxing citizens to finance the public services and transfers demanded of them. In fact, total tax payments to all levels of government in the United States are almost one-third of the Gross National Product (GNP). An important goal of tax policy should be to employ taxes that cause as little resource misallocation as possible.

Price-theory texts show that a change in the price of a consumer good has an income effect and a substitution effect. Almost all taxes are directly or indirectly taxes on particular kinds of goods and services. They alter, therefore, the prices of the taxed items relative to the untaxed items. The income effect is the desired effect of the tax, and it represents no misallocation of resources. The purpose of a tax is to transfer resources from the private to the public sector, and the income effect measures the value of the resources transferred. If the resources are less valuable in the public sector than in the private sector, there should be no tax and no transfer. If the resources are more valuable in the public sector, however, the transfer should be made, and the income effect of the tax is the desired reduction of private purchasing power. The income effect may reduce demands for private goods and services by varying amounts, but it represents the least costly way of transferring the purchasing power represented by the tax.

The substitution effect of a tax on the demand for the taxed goods and services represents a loss of welfare to consumers beyond that which is necessary to transfer purchasing power. The substitution effect leads to what is called the *excess burden* of the tax—that is, the excess welfare loss over that necessary to transfer the purchasing power to the public sector. *Among all the taxes that have a given income effect in transfer-*

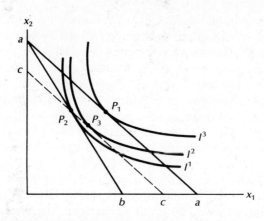

Figure 8.6   *Consumer Response to a Price Change*

ring given resources to the public sector, the best is the one with the smallest excess burden, or substitution effect.[1]

These ideas can be illustrated with the property tax (discussed in detail in Chapters 10 and 14). Here, it is necessary to note only that the property tax is a high sales tax on housing services. Figure 8.6 shows a household's set of indifference curves between housing services (x_1) and another commodity (x_2) for a given amount of a public service provided by the government. Suppose that x_1 and x_2 are produced by competitive firms and that *aa* would be the household's budget line in the absence of any tax. Then P_1 would be the household's equilibrium, and it would be efficient. However, P_1 is not available, because it does not provide resources to the government necessary to produce the public service. Suppose then that the government finances the public service with a property tax and that the entire tax is paid by the consumer of housing services. The household's budget line is shifted to *ab*. Its new equilibrium is P_2. Budget line *cc* is drawn parallel to *aa* and passes through P_2. P_3 is the household's equilibrium position for budget line *cc*. The movement from P_1 to P_3 is the income effect of the tax—that is, it represents the household's loss of welfare if the government had taken the resources it needed without affecting the relative prices of x_1 and x_2. The movement from P_3 to P_2 represents the substitution effect of the tax. The fact that the property tax has a substitution effect causes an excess burden of the tax on the household that reduces its welfare from I^2 to I^1.

What kinds of taxes would have no excess burdens? In principle, the answer is only taxes that do not affect relative prices. *A "head" tax, which simply charges the same amount of tax to each person, is probably the only tax that has no excess burden.* The property tax is presumed to have

---

1.   See Scitovsky (1971) for a complete discussion of the issue in this and the preceding paragraph.

a large excess burden, since it is a high tax on a narrow range of activities, namely, housing consumption. A broadly based sales tax is probably somewhat better. A sales tax that taxed all consumer goods and services at the same rate would be a flat-rate consumption tax. It would leave unaffected the relative prices of goods and services. Most sales taxes, however, fall far short of this ideal. Most sales taxes are levied on a narrow set of consumer goods, excluding almost all services and some commodities. Some also are levied on a few intermediate goods, which entails double taxation of the final goods they are used to produce.

Some economists take a more generous view of the property tax to the extent that it is levied uniformly on business real estate as well as on housing. In that case, it is a tax on all, or nearly all, kinds of capital. Then, distortion arises only to the extent that the property tax increases current consumption at the expense of capital accumulation, that is, savings. Many economists believe that savings are insensitive to modest taxes on capital or on capital income. However, existing real estate taxes are poor approximations to uniform taxes on property. They vary greatly by local government jurisdiction and from one kind of real estate to another. Finally, the Tiebout hypothesis, to be discussed in Chapter 14, is germane to the controversy about distorting effects of real estate taxes.

An income tax, like a broadly based sales tax, leaves relative prices of goods and services unchanged, which accounts in part for the strong preference of most economists for income taxes over other taxes. An income tax and a broadly based sales tax, however, do have an excess burden. An income tax is a tax on the result of hours spent working but not on hours of leisure. In Figure 8.5, an income tax changes the relative prices of goods and leisure, and, therefore, the slope of the budget line *bb*. The substitution effect of an income tax is an inefficiently large amount of leisure. The total effect that an income tax has on hours of work and leisure depends on the relative sizes of the income and substitution effects.

Is the excess burden of an income tax large? The best study on the subject, by Harberger (1964), concludes that the burden is substantial, but probably small relative to the excess burdens of existing sales and property taxes. Sales and property taxes, like income taxes, affect the relative prices of goods and leisure. Unlike income taxes, however, they also affect the relative prices of goods and services.

It should be emphasized that this entire discussion has been about the efficiency aspects of taxes. Taxes, like other public policies, also have important equity effects. A major goal of governmental tax policy is to redistribute income, specifically to reduce income inequality. That goal requires progressive taxes of transfer payments, and the income tax is almost the only tax that can be made to be progressive. Thus, *if equity considerations require progressive taxes, they are an important reason for the use of income rather than other taxes.* It is also possible that equity considerations indicate the desirability of one kind of tax, whereas efficiency considerations indicate the desirability of another. In such cases, a compromise between equity and efficiency is necessary.

☐ Summary

Welfare economics is a branch of economic theory concerned with evaluating the performance of the economic system. Economists evaluate the system's performance by its efficiency and equity in meeting people's economic wants.

An elaborate system of conditions for economic efficiency has been worked out by economists during recent decades. A major result obtained in welfare economics is that competitive markets allocate resources so as to satisfy the efficiency conditions, if strong assumptions are made. Competitive markets, however, may not produce distributions of income and wealth that meet people's senses of equity.

Monopolies and monopsonies misallocate resources, although neither is likely to be an important source of urban problems. External economies and diseconomies imply that even competitive markets misallocate resources. Pollution and congestion are examples of external diseconomies in urban areas.

Governments raise large sums of money by taxes to finance public services and to transfer payments. Taxes should be equitable and should cause as little resource misallocation as possible. Most economists believe that sales and property taxes are both less efficient and less equitable than are income taxes. There may well be conflict, however, between efficiency and equity in the tax policy.

Questions and Problems

1. Show that price discrimination violates the requirements for efficient resource allocation.

2. Economists tend to argue that activities causing external diseconomies should be taxed, whereas governmental officials tend to regulate such activities. Which strategy is better on equity and efficiency grounds?

3. The do-it-yourself movement, in which homeowners repair and maintain their houses instead of hiring craftspeople, has blossomed since World War II. Do-it-yourself labor is not subject to income tax, whereas a craftsperson's wages are. Do you think the do-it-yourself

movement is a distortion in resource allocation resulting from high income tax rates?

4. Governments tend to provide or subsidize goods and services to the poor, despite economists' advice that money transfers are preferable. One possibility is that taxpayers prefer to provide goods and services instead of money. Another possibility is that interest groups determine the form of transfers. For example, farmers like food stamps and builders like housing subsidies. What do you think the real reason is for providing or subsidizing goods and services?

References and Further Reading

Harberger, Arnold. "Taxation, Resource Allocation, and Welfare." In *The Role of Direct and Indirect Taxes in the Federal System,* edited by John Due (Princeton: Princeton University Press, 1964): 25–70. A thorough study of distorting effects of taxes.

Just, Richard E., Darrell Hueth, and Andrew Schmitz. *Applied Welfare Economics* (Englewood Cliffs, N.J.: Prentice-Hall, 1982). A fine modern text covering every aspect of the subject.

Mishan, E. J. *Cost-Benefit Analysis.* 2nd ed. (New York: Praeger, 1981). A classic study of the use of welfare economics to analyze the benefits and costs of proposed government projects.

Scitovsky, Tibor. *Welfare and Competition* (Homewood, Ill.: Richard D. Irwin, 1971). A microeconomics text with a strong welfare economics orientation.

Part Three

Urban Problems and the Public Sector

9

The Problem of Poverty

☐ Poverty is among the most urgent and widely discussed domestic problems of our time. The 1960s witnessed a vast outpouring of literature on the subject, much of it written as though poverty had just been invented or discovered. Although the subject has not been, and should not be, the exclusive preserve of economists, they have contributed their share to the analysis of causes and cures of poverty. Many of the great nineteenth-century economists were deeply concerned with the most fundamental issues related to poverty. Beginning about 1900, some of the best applied economic research was on consumer-demand and family-budget studies, which were motivated by a concern with poverty and related nutritional problems. During the 1930s, much of the profession's effort was devoted to public and private measures to alleviate poverty, especially that caused by the massive unemployment that dominated the decade.

Nevertheless, there was a rapid growth of concern with poverty during the 1960s among economists, public officials, and the general public. Both a cause and an effect of this concern was a rapid improvement in the data available about poverty. As the 1970s progressed, the subject of poverty became gradually less fashionable. Serious research on poverty has continued, however, and it is now possible to present the dimensions of the subject in a way that was impossible even in 1970. Poverty has not disappeared as a subject of public debate. Successive presidents have proposed reforms in national programs to aid the poor, and successive Congresses have increased federal appropriations to raise living standards of the poor. Although the subject now appears less frequently in newspaper headlines than it did a decade ago, there is more to be said about poverty than ever.

One thing to remember when considering poverty or any other urban problem is that the appropriate solution varies enormously according to the nature of the problem. For example, slum housing may be caused by poverty or it may be caused by market failure. The urban economist, therefore, must use analytical tools, such as those developed in Part Two, to identify urban problems and determine the true cause-and-effect relationships before proposing solutions.

☐ MEASURES OF POVERTY

What is poverty? The easy answer is that it is a lack of money income. Like most easy answers, it is in the right direction but inadequate. Many undergraduate and graduate students have relatively low money incomes, but, for the most part, they are not poor in the sense that many blacks and Puerto Ricans who live in places like the South Bronx in New York City are poor. Most college students know that they are preparing themselves for a status that will give them the option of making a good income (whether they choose the option or not). Also, in an emergency, many may be able to obtain money from parents, a spouse, or an employer. *To be poor requires not only that people have little money income, but also that they have no prospect of substantially greater income,* at least in the near future. Unfortunately, official data sources are not able to ascertain the extent of voluntarism among the country's low-income population, although it is an important issue and will be discussed ahead.

Furthermore, *money income is only one means to a high living standard,* although it is the most important means. Many poor people in the United States receive *in-kind income,* which is income in the form of commodities or services that are provided directly—especially by governments—instead of money that recipients can spend as they choose. Most of the commodities and services provided—food, housing, and health care—are valuable, and recipients would have purchased some amounts of them if they had been given money. The commodities and services, however, may not be worth as much to recipients as their money cost to taxpayers. Again, this issue will be discussed later.

Finally, *assets must be taken into account.* A family with a temporarily low income can maintain a high living standard by drawing down assets. More important, many elderly people with low incomes own a house, furniture, and a car. Such assets provide services and contribute to living standards, although the services are not included in income, as ordinarily measured. The notion of welfare recipients driving Cadillacs is largely fanciful. Some people with low money incomes, however, are able to maintain higher living standards than their incomes would indicate because of assets that yield direct services. Again, governmental data generally do not include such services.

However it is measured, poverty is a matter of degree. A family with an income of $3,000 per year would be better off if it had $4,000, and better off yet if it had $6,000. *There is no natural dividing line such that people below it can be said to be poor and people above it can be said not to be poor.* Regarding the substance of the problem, no poverty line is needed. Data should be available on the entire size distribution of incomes, and society should decide through the democratic process what groups it wants to tax and to whom it wants to give the proceeds.

In fact, great controversy surrounds the notion of an official poverty line and where it should be drawn. The main reason government is urged to draw a poverty line is political: Raising everyone's income to the government's poverty level inevitably becomes a social goal. Thus, those who favor a great deal of redistribution of incomes from rich to poor want a poverty line to be established at a high income level. Those who favor little income redistribution want it established at a low income level.

In the early 1960s, the federal government adopted an official poverty line, and raising low incomes to at least that level has been a quasi-official goal of government ever since. The official poverty income level is computed in a relatively simple way. The Department of Agriculture computes the annual cost of a nutritious diet for low-income families. Various studies have shown that poor families spend about one-third of their incomes on food. Thus, the poverty line is defined as three times the calculated low-income food budget. As food prices change, the poverty income is adjusted accordingly. In 1960, the poverty income for a family of four was $3,022 per year; in 1970, it was $3,968; and in 1990, it was $13,359.

A more sophisticated measure of poverty is the poverty gap, which is simply the total amount of additional income that the poor would need to escape poverty. It can be written as

$$G = \sum_{i=1}^{p} (y_p - y_i). \tag{9.1}$$

In Equation (9.1), y_p is the poverty income. People are ranked inversely by income level, starting with Person 1 at the lowest income. Thus, the sum in Equation (9.1) is more than the incomes of all poor people. In 1990, the average poverty income per poor person was $1,401.

The poverty population and the poverty gap measure different concepts and need not move together. The poverty gap may increase when the poverty population decreases, if the number of poor people were fewer but they were poorer than before. Poverty gaps have been calculated for data in the United States and for many other countries.

The poverty income in the United States is about 20 percent of the country's median income. By a worldwide standard it is high—ten times the average income in some of Asia's and Africa's poorest countries. Surely, however, that should be little comfort for people in the United States. Presumably, the living standard to which we should aspire to bring the poorest members of our society should be defined by average American living standards, not those in societies much poorer than ours. A more relevant comparison is with countries in northern Europe, where average living standards are roughly the same as in the United States. Although exact comparisons are difficult, it is likely that the poorest people in the United States have lower living standards than the poorest people in several northern European countries. That fact alone does not imply that we should have more income redistribution, but it does make the subject worth discussing.

☐ DEMOGRAPHY OF POVERTY

How many people in the United States are poor? The numbers of people living below the official poverty line have been computed only back to 1959, and these figures are shown for selected years in Table 9.1. It is possible, however, to calculate approximate poverty measures for much earlier years. Allowing for changes in the price level, 1929 income per capita was about the same as the present official poverty level. Thus, roughly half the country was poor in 1929, by the current official poverty standard. By a somewhat better measure, about one-third of the country was poor in 1947. Table 9.1 indicates that the number of poor decreased from 22.4 percent of the population in 1959 to 11.6 percent in 1979, with no decline since.

Not only the percentage but also the number of poor decreased during the half-century since 1929. Half of the 1929 population was about 60 million people, and one-third of the 1947 population was 48 million people. Table 9.1 shows that the number of poor decreased from about 40 million in 1959 to about 34 million in 1990.

The data show remarkable progress in reducing poverty during the period from 1929 to 1969. From 1959 to 1969, the percentage of the population living below the poverty line fell about 1 point per year. From 1969 to 1979, however, there was a slight increase in the number of people and only a slight decrease in the percentage of the population

Table 9.1 *Poverty in the United States, 1959 to 1989*

Year	Poor Population Number in Millions	Percentage	Poverty Cutoff Family of Four (Dollars per Year)	Median Income Per Family (Dollars per Year)
1959	39.5	22.4%	$ 2,973	$ 5,417
1969	24.1	12.1	3,743	9,433
1974	24.3	11.6	5,038	12,836
1977	24.7	11.6	6,191	16,009
1979	25.3	11.6	7,412	19,715
1985	33.1	14.0	10,989	27,735
1989	31.5	12.8	12,675	28,906
1990	33.6	13.6	13,359	29,943

Source: Data from U.S. Department of Commerce, Bureau of the Census. *Statistical Abstract of the United States* (Washington, D.C.: Government Printing Office, 1978, 1981, 1987, 1991).

living below the poverty line. Both the number and the percentage of people living below the poverty line were greater in 1990 than they were in 1979, despite a brief improvement in 1984 and 1985.

What happened? Part of the answer is cyclical. Poverty inevitably worsens during recessions, and the number of poor rose during the recession of 1980 and during the much more severe recession of 1982. A more fundamental answer is that the entire economy has grown more slowly since the mid-1970s than it had previously. The shares of various income groups in total income change only slowly from one decade to the next. Thus, when the overall growth rate slows, income growth slows at least as much for poor and near-poor people as for higher income people. But even that accounting does not explain why the percentage of the population in poverty in 1990 was as great as it has been in nearly 25 years. Sentiment in the national government for antipoverty programs became less favorable during the 1980s, but actual expenditures on programs that favor the poor did not decline enough to account for the retreat in the war against poverty.

The 1980s witnessed a steady increase in earnings inequality. It had virtually nothing to do with the two major national tax changes in the 1980s. The growth of earnings inequality was pretax and was true regardless of gender, race, or age. It represented a large increase in the returns to investment in human capital or education and experience. The earnings of well-educated workers increased rapidly during the 1980s, while the earnings of poorly educated workers fell in real terms.

What caused the increase in the returns to education? Nobody knows; however, it seems nearly certain that it was intimately related to the increasingly widespread use of computers: the electronic storage, manipulation, and transmission of data and documents. Clearly, every facet of computer technology—manufacture, programming, servicing, data entry, data analysis, and the interpretation and use of computer output—favors educated workers.

In addition, in recent years international trade barriers have eroded greatly. On a worldwide basis, poorly educated workers are extremely abundant and highly educated workers are extremely scarce. Thus, the relaxation of trade barriers served to benefit highly educated workers in the United States and to harm those who are poorly educated.

Who are the poor? Table 9.2 presents basic demographic data concerning poverty. The column headed "Incidence of Poverty" shows the percentage of people in the groups in each row that are poor. The incidence should be distinguished from the percentage of the poor in each group. For example, the first numerical column shows that about 66 percent (22.3 million of 33.6 million) of the poor were white, but the second numerical column shows that the incidence of poverty among whites was nearly one-third its incidence among nonwhites (10.7 percent compared with 31.8 percent).

Table 9.2 shows the uneven incidence of poverty among various demographic groups. The data under "Family status" show that 20

Table 9.2 *Number of Poor and Incidence of Poverty in the United States, 1979 and 1990*

Characteristics	1979		1990	
	Number of Poor (Million)	Incidence of Poverty (Percentage)	Number of Poor (Million)	Incidence of Poverty (Percentage)
Total*	26.1	11.7%	33.6	13.5%
Family status				
Family head	5.5	9.2	7.1	10.7
Family members under age 18	10.0	16.0	12.7	20.0
Other family members	4.5	6.1	5.4	6.7
Unrelated individuals	5.7	21.9	7.4	20.5
Race				
White	17.2	8.9	22.3	10.7
Black	8.1	36.8	9.8	31.8
Residence				
MSA central city	9.5	15.7	3.0	16.0
MSA suburb	6.2	7.2	2.1	6.5
Non-MSA	9.6	13.7	2.0	13.0
Persons age 65 and older	3.7	15.2	3.7	12.2

*Includes races and members of unrelated subfamilies not shown separately.
Source: Data from U.S. Department of Commerce, Bureau of the Census. *Statistical Abstract of the United States* (Washington, D.C.: Government Printing Office, 1981, 1991).

percent of children were in poor families in 1990. Why is the incidence of poverty among children greater than among the entire population? In part, it is because low-income parents tend to have more children than do high-income parents. Also, it is because women with many children cannot undertake paid work; hence, income is low in families with many children. Moreover, it is simply that, for a given family money income, having many children makes the family poor, since poverty depends both on the amount of income and on the number of people the income must support. Table 9.2 shows that the incidence of poverty among the elderly is less than that among the population as a whole. In fact, the most remarkable trend in poverty statistics during the last two decades is a dramatic decrease in the incidence of poverty among the elderly in contrast with a dramatic increase in the incidence of poverty among children. Private pensions and savings available to the elderly have improved as an increasing fraction of the elderly have spent most of their working lives during the prosperous postwar years. In addition, social security and Medicare benefits have improved greatly. By contrast, children have suffered from rising birthrates to unwed mothers and from rising divorce rates. Yet, it remains surprising that support for the elderly has improved even though they have been an increasing share of the population, whereas support for children has deteriorated even though they have become a decreasing share of the population.

The data under "Race" show the crushing burden of poverty borne by nonwhites in the United States. Although there are more than twice as many poor whites as blacks, the incidence of poverty is four times as high among blacks as among whites. Blacks suffer disproportionately when the economy performs weakly, as well.

The data on residence in the table show that poverty is by no means entirely a phenomenon of large cities. Taking metropolitan areas as a whole, income levels are higher and the incidence of poverty is lower than elsewhere in the country. Within metropolitan areas, however, the poor are strongly segregated. The incidence of poverty is nearly three times as great in metropolitan central cities as in suburbs (16 percent compared with 6.5 percent).

Many of our commonly identified urban problems are directly linked with poverty. The main explanation for the existence of slum housing is the poverty of its inhabitants. Violent crime is closely linked with poverty. Children of poor families are at a disadvantage in school and in labor markets. Poverty, however, was not invented in urban slums, and it is a mistake to focus public policy entirely on the urban poor.

As Chapter 2 discussed, during the late 1940s, 1950s, and 1960s, there was a rapid migration of poor people and blacks from the rural South to cities in all parts of the country. Migrants left desperately poor and, for blacks, oppressive rural areas to seek better lives for themselves and their children in the cities. Agricultural employment was declining, and urban employment was expanding. This massive movement of people succeeded in increasing living standards for many poor people, and it was a crucial step in the struggle of blacks in the United States to attain political rights and recognition. It also moved some of the nation's poverty, however, from rural areas to metropolitan central cities. The result was that, during the 1970s, the incidence of poverty in central cities for the first time exceeded that in rural areas.

Many people are concerned about the concentration of the poor in metropolitan central cities. Concentrations of the poor certainly cause problems, which will be discussed in subsequent chapters. The poor are highly visible in city slums, and many people are appalled at the sight. It must be remembered, however, that the poor have come to the cities for good reasons. Poverty is worse, although less visible to others, in the rural South. Urban migration has increased job opportunities for the poor and their children. It has enabled them to organize and demand political rights. In addition it has enabled society to increase living standards of the poor by governmental transfer payments in ways that are not possible if the poor are scattered in rural areas.

The incidence of poverty is much lower in MSAs than elsewhere. It is only in central cities that the incidence is high. It is much more constructive to show concern about the discrimination and exclusion that keep the poor concentrated in central cities than about the movement of the poor from rural to urban areas.

☐ RACE AND POVERTY

In his 1944 classic, Myrdal described race relations in the United States as "an American dilemma." It is no exaggeration to say that race relations became "the American trauma" during succeeding decades. The elemental and brutal fact is that blacks in the United States have been forced into demeaning and subservient status by legal and extralegal means since they arrived in the holds of slave ships. As with the broader issue of poverty discussed in the last section, however, the rapid postwar urban migration of blacks has made their status better, not worse. Black urbanization has made racial disparities much more visible to both blacks and whites and has increased the tension and conflict between them. It has, however, indisputably raised the economic and political status of blacks.

Table 9.3 shows the magnitude of postwar black metropolitanization. By 1950, the percentage of blacks living in metropolitan areas was 59, as compared with 63 percent of whites. By 1990, the black percentage had grown to 81 (up from 75 as recently as 1977), whereas the white percentage had grown only to 73. Thus, by 1990, blacks were much more concentrated in metropolitan areas than were whites. Blacks were, and are, much more concentrated in central cities than whites. The percentage of blacks in the United States who lived in central cities increased from 44 in 1950 to 58 in 1990. The percentage of blacks living in metropolitan suburbs also increased, from 15 to 28. The increase was concentrated in the 1970s, indicating that blacks were beginning to acquire suburban housing in some places. Although suburban blacks are strongly concentrated in a few segregated suburbs, most suburbs now contain at least a sprinkling of blacks in many metropolitan areas.

Living standards of both blacks and whites are higher in metropolitan areas than elsewhere. Table 9.4 shows the incidence of poverty by race in metropolitan and nonmetropolitan areas. Blacks have a much higher incidence of poverty than whites in all areas. For both blacks and whites, however, the incidence of poverty is between one-third and one-half greater outside than inside metropolitan areas. Within metro-

Table 9.3   *Racial Composition of Metropolitan and Nonmetropolitan Areas, 1950 and 1990 (Percentage)*

	1950		1990	
	Black	White	Black	White
Metropolitan areas	59%	63%	81%	73%
Central cities	44	35	58	25
Suburbs	15	28	23	48
Nonmetropolitan areas	41	37	19	27
Total	100%	100%	100%	100%

Source: Data from U.S. Department of Commerce, Bureau of the Census. *Statistical Abstract of the United States* (Washington, D.C.: Government Printing Office, 1981, 1991).

Table 9.4 *Incidence of Poverty by Race: Metropolitan and Nonmetro-politan Areas, 1979 and 1990 (Percentage)*

	1979		1990	
	Whites	Blacks	Whites	Blacks
Metropolitan areas	7.8%	28.3%	9.9%	30.1%
Central cities	10.7	31.1	14.3	33.8
Suburbs	6.2	21.1	7.6	22.2
Nonmetropolitan areas	11.2	39.5	13.5	40.8

Source: Data from U.S. Department of Commerce, Bureau of the Census. *Statistical Abstract of the United States* (Washington, D.C.: Government Printing Office, 1981, 1991).

politan areas, the incidence of poverty is higher for both blacks and whites in central cities than in suburbs. Even in central cities, the incidence of poverty among blacks is less than outside metropolitan areas.

Thus, poverty is much more common among blacks than among whites everywhere, but urban migration from the rural South has helped blacks reduce their incidence of poverty. Table 9.5 shows that racial disparities in income pervade the income distribution. The table shows family incomes of whites and blacks in 1990 dollars for 1975 and 1985. In both years, incomes of blacks were much more concentrated toward the low end of the distribution than were those of whites. Whereas real family income increased somewhat among whites, family incomes of blacks were about the same in 1985 as in 1975. Although earnings per worker rose somewhat for blacks relative to those of white workers during the period, the number of employed blacks rose more slowly than the number of employed whites. Most social and economic statistics tell about the same story: Blacks started the postwar period with large disadvantages compared with whites; during the postwar period, they made substantial absolute and moderate relative gains, at least up to about 1970. In 1950, life expectancy was 69.1 years for whites and 60.8 years for blacks, a difference of 8.3 years. In 1990, the figures were 76.0 and 70.3 years, respectively, a difference of 5.7 years. In 1950, the median educational attainment was 9.6 years for whites and 6.8 years for blacks, a difference of 2.8 years. In 1991, the figures were 12.8 and 12.4 years, a difference of only 0.4 years. During the postwar period, black unemployment rates have consistently averaged about twice those of whites, and the disparity increased during the 1980s.

Careful studies have documented a gradual narrowing of wage differences between blacks and whites. For men, the black to white wage ratio increased from about 45 percent in 1940 to about 60 percent in 1980. For women, the gap is even narrower. The gap is also lower for young people with comparable amounts of schooling. These figures are consistent with the low ratios of overall median income previously quoted, because relatively few blacks are in the highly educated groups.

Table 9.5 *Percentage Distribution of Family Income, 1975 and 1985 (1985 Dollars)*

	Under $5,000	$5,000–$9,999	$10,000–$14,999	$15,000–$19,999	$20,000–$24,999	$25,000–$34,999	$35,000+	Median
1975								
White	6.0	12.2	11.3	11.1	10.1	19.0	29.8	$24,665
Black	15.0	22.0	14.0	12.3	10.6	13.5	13.0	$14,807
Hispanic	9.3	16.6	16.8	13.9	11.4	17.5	14.4	$17,719
1985								
White	6.4	11.7	11.2	10.8	10.1	17.5	32.3	$24,908
Black	17.6	18.8	14.0	12.4	8.5	12.9	15.7	$14,819
Hispanic	10.8	17.9	14.7	12.2	10.8	15.2	18.3	$17,465

Source: Data from U.S. Department of Commerce, Bureau of the Census. *Statistical Abstract of the United States* (Washington, D.C.: Government Printing Office, 1987).

As will be noted in Chapter 14, there has been dramatic improvement in high-school completion among blacks since World War II.

We can be either encouraged or discouraged by the statistics presented in this section. That there has been progress toward racial equality cannot be denied. It also cannot be denied, however, that there are many blacks—concentrated among older and poorly educated groups—who have hardly been touched by the progress. The explanation for the progress is extremely controversial. Part of the explanation is certainly a reduction in discriminatory attitudes by the white majority. Another part is the efforts by blacks to break down barriers to education, employment, and political representation. A third part is the federal civil rights acts and expenditure programs that have helped blacks. A final part is court decisions that have extended constitutional protections to blacks. Sorting out the importance of these explanations will be a complex and controversial activity.

☐ PUBLIC PROGRAMS FOR REDUCING POVERTY

Macroeconomic Policies

By far the most important factor in the gradual reduction of poverty in the United States has been the overall growth of the economy. It has already been stated and will be shown in more detail in the next section that the percentage distribution of income has changed little during the postwar period. Poverty has been reduced rapidly when the economy has prospered and slowly when economic growth has faltered, especially from the early 1970s to 1990.

The most obvious beneficiaries of economic growth are the employed and their families. However, economic growth also reduces poverty among retired people and others not in the labor force, because it is easiest to save for retirement and contingencies during working years if income is high and rising and unemployment rates are low. Finally, economic growth increases revenues received by governments at fixed tax rates. Governments thus have more money to finance public services such as education and transfers such as unemployment compensation, welfare, and social security, all of which help reduce poverty.

Thus, our most important weapon in reducing poverty is monetary —fiscal and other policies that promote full employment and economic growth. Such policies are beyond the scope of this book but are discussed in macroeconomics textbooks.

Income-Maintenance Policies: Theory

The best way to organize thinking regarding income redistribution programs is to consider the often-proposed *negative income tax* (NIT). The NIT works just like the ordinary income tax except that, below some cutoff level of income, a household receives a payment from the government. The size of the payment depends on pretax income (just like the size of a household's income tax liability depends on pretax income) and is depicted in Figure 9.1. Aftertax income is plotted on the vertical axis against pretax income on the horizontal axis. In the absence of any income taxation, pretax and aftertax income would be the same, as depicted by the 45-degree line. The ordinary income tax alters the relationship to make aftertax income less than pretax income above some point determined by the tax schedule, exemptions, and deductions. The NIT makes aftertax income greater than pretax income below that point. Of course, the relationship need not be linear, but these kinds of cases are easier to analyze, so mainly linear tax laws will be discussed.

The equation for Line A is

$$Y_{at} = a + (1 - t)\ Y_{pt}, \tag{9.2}$$

where Y_{at} is aftertax income, Y_{pt} is pretax income, a is the lump sum given to a household with no pretax income, and t is the tax rate. The equation simply says that aftertax income is a plus the fraction $(1 - t)$ of pretax income that is left after paying income taxes.

According to the standard proposal, the tax-and-grant law embodied in Figure 9.1 and Equation (9.2) would replace all existing income redistribution programs and the federal income tax. In other words, tax revenue (tY) would have to be sufficient, along with other revenue sources, to finance the grants and other activities of the federal government.

A critical observation regarding the NIT (or, as will be seen, any redistribution program) can be made by plugging numbers into Equation (9.2). Suppose a equals $4,000, indicating that a family with no pretax income has an aftertax income of $4,000. Now suppose the tax rate is 25 percent. Under such a program, aftertax income would be

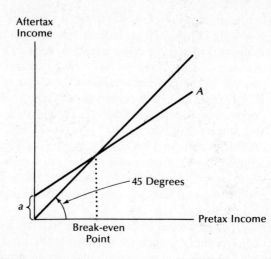

Figure 9.1 *Negative Income Tax*

higher than pretax income for everyone with less than $16,000 of pretax income. This point (the intersection of the 45-degree line with Line A, where pretax income equals aftertax income) is called the *break-even point*.[1] Notice that under the program just outlined, which sounds reasonable, the break-even point is very high—in fact, it is nearly half the mean per-household income in the United States.

Aside from the fact that taxpayers may not want to subsidize households with incomes as high as $16,000, this high break-even point indicates that the NIT might be a very expensive program. In fact, for the linear tax structure considered here, the following result can be established: If the break-even point is equal to mean household income, the entire proceeds from the federal personal income tax are required to finance the program of grants, at least with linear tax schedules. Clearly, if the NIT is to be financially viable, either the tax rate must be larger or the maximum grant must be smaller. Neither is an attractive option; the maximum grant in the example is already quite low for a household with no income, and a tax rate too much above 25 percent could have serious effects on incentives. At all levels of income, a high income tax rate reduces incentives to work and to purchase productivity-enhancing training and education. The inescapable fact is that an NIT program must have either a tax rate sufficiently high to distort incentives seriously or a maximum grant level sufficiently low to redistribute income only modestly.

Some recent experiments provide evidence on the cost-and-incentive effects of the NIT. The NIT was most recently tested in Seattle and Denver. To mitigate the disadvantages previously discussed, participants

---

1. The break-even point is that income level at which $Y_{at} = Y_{pt}$ and can be solved for by setting $Y_{at} = Y_{pt}$ in Equation (9.2). This result yields $Y_{at} = a + (1+t)Y_{at}$ (since $Y_{at} = Y_{pt}$). Solving for this equation, $Y_{at} (= Y_{pt}) = a/t$.

received guaranteed payments based on family income before the experiment; they were reimbursed for federal, state, and local taxes; and they were not allowed to receive other transfers, such as food stamps. The results indicated that a nationwide NIT with a guaranteed payment equal to 50 percent of the poverty level and a tax rate of 70 percent would cost $5.3 billion (in 1978 dollars) less than current welfare programs (an expenditure savings of about 41 percent).[2] In contrast, an NIT with a guaranteed payment of 100 percent of poverty income ($9,287 for a family of four in 1981) and a tax rate of 50 percent was projected to increase welfare expenditures by $40.5 billion (about a threefold increase over current expenditure). All of these comparisons would be very different if an NIT also substituted for the largest transfer program of all, social security.

Interestingly, congressional debate over the NIT has focused on its surprisingly negative effect on marital stability. Unlike Aid to Families with Dependent Children, for example, which accrues only to households without a father present and, hence, has been criticized as encouraging family breakups, the NIT applies to households regardless of family status.[3] Marital dissolution, however, was about 60 percent higher (and significantly so) among NIT participants than among the control groups in the Seattle and Denver experiments. Researchers hypothesize that the NIT causes marriage partners to feel less bound by nonpecuniary family ties, because the administration of the NIT is more impersonal and its nonwage income is less stigmatized than other, often locally administered, welfare sources. Ironically then, the NIT's administrative efficiency reduces not only explicit transaction costs of welfare, but implicit costs of family separation, too, with net effects that Congress, at least, considers undesirable.

Redistribution Programs in the United States

Detailed discussion of the NIT may seem like a waste of time; the United States does not have such a program, and there seems little prospect that one will be enacted. The theory of the NIT, however, is an ideal vehicle for discussing real-world redistribution programs for the following reason: Every income-redistribution program specifies a (legal) relationship between preprogram and afterprogram income, and thus the redistributive aspect of the program can be plotted in a graph like the one in Figure 9.1.[4] This finding means that a tax rate, a maximum grant level, and a break-even point are inherent in any redistribution

2. Current welfare programs accounted for here are Aid to Families with Dependent Children and food stamps.

3. A newer program bases eligibility on the father's employment.

4. Many income redistribution programs do other things as well, such as specifically encourage the consumption of food, housing, or medical care.

program or, indeed, in the whole constellation of redistribution programs.

If all income-redistribution programs, however, have the basic properties of the NIT (the maximum grant level, the tax rate, and the break-even point), all are subject to the same trade-off between generosity to the very poor on the one hand and tax rate-induced distortion or expense on the other. The dilemma of the NIT is that (1) it may be extremely expensive or (2) the tax rates on income may be so high that they do grave damage to incentives. Note that this is not the dilemma of the NIT, per se, but rather of any package of income-redistribution programs in general.

Income-Maintenance Policies: Facts and Institutions

Governmental expenditures are either purchases of goods and services or transfer payments. Many goods and services, such as national defense and highway construction, are for the general public, and it is almost meaningless to estimate the extent to which they benefit the poor. However, transfer payments such as unemployment compensation and social security, as well as goods and services such as public housing and Medicare, are provided by governments for identifiable groups of people. In principle, it is possible to estimate the income classes of the beneficiaries of such programs.

In practice, the number and complexity of such programs make accurate imputation to particular income groups difficult. Some programs, such as the welfare and food stamp programs, were designed to aid particular groups of needy people. Others, however, such as social security and veterans' benefits, were designed to aid groups thought to be worthy, regardless of need. It is possible, however, to identify programs that are *means tested.* To be eligible for a means-tested program, people must meet a test of need—usually some measure of income. The particular test varies from program to program, but tests invariably require that recipients be quite poor, although not always poor enough to meet the official poverty criterion.

Table 9.6 shows transfer program expenditures, classified by whether they are means-tested and by whether they provide cash or services, for 1960, 1977, and 1986. Most program names are self-explanatory. Aid to Families with Dependent Children and supplementary security income are important welfare programs. "Old Age, Survivors, and Disability Insurance" in the table is the social security program. The public service employment program provides government jobs for the unemployed. Medicaid and Medicare are governmental health-care programs for the poor and elderly. The child nutrition program provides food for the children of poor people. Many programs are cooperative federal-state undertakings. The table shows only federal expenditures, but they are much larger than state expenditures.

Table 9.6   *Federal Expenditures for Income-Security Transfer Programs (Billions of Dollars)*

Program	1960	1977	1986
Cash programs	$22.0	$140.9	$249.5
Means tested	2.1	12.3	20.2
Aid to Families with Dependent Children	0.7	6.3	9.9
Supplemental security income	1.4	6.0	10.3
Not means tested	19.9	128.6	229.3
Old Age, Survivors, and Disability Insurance	12.9	87.2	179.6
Federal Civil Service retirement	0.9	10.1	11.6
Veterans compensation pensions	3.4	8.4	14.4
Unemployment compensation	2.7	18.4	17.8
Coal miners' "black lung" benefits	. . .	1.2	1.0
Public service employment	. . .	3.3	4.9
In-kind programs	0.6	42.1	123.3
Means tested	0.6	21.6	53.1
Food stamps	0.1	6.0	11.6
Medicaid	0.2	9.4	25.0
Child nutrition	0.2	3.1	3.8
Housing assistance	0.1	3.1	12.7
Not means tested	. . .	20.5	70.2
Medicare	. . .	20.5	70.2
Total	$22.6	$183.0	$372.8

Source: 1960 and 1977 data from *Setting National Priorities: The Next Ten Years,* edited by Henry Owen and Charles Schultze (Washington, D.C.: Brookings Institution, 1976). Reprinted by permission. 1986 data from *The Budget of the United States* (Washington, D.C.: Government Printing Office, 1987).

Three things are remarkable about the data in Table 9.6. The first is the rapid growth in total expenditures. During the 26-year period, expenditures on income-security transfer programs grew from 4.5 to 14.3 percent of the GNP. The 1977 expenditures were 8 times those in 1960, and the 1986 expenditures were 3.3 times those in 1977. The second is that means-tested programs have grown faster than other programs. In 1986, expenditure on means-tested programs was 27.1 times the 1960 expenditure, whereas expenditure on programs not means tested was only 15.1 times its earlier level. Thus, transfer expenditures are becoming better focused on the needy. Third, in-kind program expenditures have grown much faster than cash-transfer programs. The 1986 expenditures on cash programs were 11.3 times their 1960 level, whereas those on in-kind programs were 205.0 times their 1960 level. Thus, we have moved away from the notion of helping the needy by giving them money and toward the notion of providing them with particular goods and services.

Including state contributions, total governmental expenditures on income-security transfers cannot be less than 15 percent of the GNP. People certainly differ as to whether the total is too much or too little. No one should believe, however, that the American effort is negligible. Governmental efforts to help people are substantial and have increased rapidly since the early 1960s. Those who believe that further efforts should be made to help the needy have two options. The easy option is to continue to expand transfer programs. That is the option that has been followed for two decades, and it encounters increasing taxpayer resistance. The hard option is to focus transfer programs more accurately on the needy. In 1977, less than 20 percent of the transfers in Table 9.6 were means tested. Of course, much of the remainder nevertheless goes to the needy. Much does not, though. The large programs that are not means tested are social security, Medicare, and unemployment compensation. Introducing means-tested programs would be controversial in all three. If transfers to the needy are to be increased, however, either middle-class and upper-middle-class workers must bear a large tax burden or these programs must be reformed. Notice that increasing the focus of these programs on the poor involves a reduction of benefits as income rises—either a gradual reduction of benefits or a termination of eligibility above some cutoff point. This tying of benefit levels to income is precisely the income tax rate that was discussed in relation to the NIT. The more rapidly benefits are reduced as income rises, the more heavily program benefits are concentrated on the poor. The same rapid benefit reduction, however, represents a very high income-taxation rate (in fact, approaching 100 percent over some income ranges). Without question, tax rates of the magnitude that currently exist seriously diminish the incentive to work and engage in training and education.

There can be no doubt that federal governmental expenditures tend to reduce income inequality in the United States. There is much more doubt about the effects of state and local governmental expenditures, which have increased relative to federal governmental expenditures during the postwar period. Furthermore, not only governmental expenditures, but also governmental taxes, affect the distribution of income. The government has a greater effect in mitigating poverty the more progressive are taxes. Thus, the basic question is, What is the net effect of governmental taxes and expenditures on the distribution of income?

The issue is complex. Governmental taxes and expenditures affect the income distribution in many complex and poorly understood ways. Some very high quality research, however, has been done on the subject in recent years. Table 9.7 summarizes the results of a study by Reynolds and Smolensky (1977). It shows the percentage of total income received by the lowest and highest income quintiles of the population, as well as by the 60 percent between the extreme groups. If each quintile had 20 percent of total income, everyone would have the same income. In fact, as the table shows, the richest quintile has much higher income than the poorest quintile. As Table 9.1 showed, the bottom 20 percent was about the same as the poverty group in 1959, but the poverty group was much less than 20 percent in 1969. The first numerical columns of Table 9.7 provide income percentages before taxes and governmental expenditures are taken into account (the factor income). The last two columns show income percentages after effects of taxes and governmental expenditures have been allowed for—the *postfisc income* (income after accounting for taxes and transfers).

Table 9.7   *Income Shares of Quintiles, 1950 and 1970*

Percentile Share	Factor Income		Postfisc Income	
	1950	1970	1950	1970
Share of lowest 20 percent	3.6	2.9	6.4	6.7
Share of middle 60 percent	48.5	46.5	53.7	54.2
Share of highest 20 percent	48.0	50.6	39.9	39.1

Source: Data from Reynolds, Morgan, and Eugene Smolensky. *Public Expenditures, Taxes, and the Distribution of Income* (New York: Academic Press, 1977).

Two facts stand out from the data given in Table 9.7. First, *the distribution of income before taxes and governmental expenditures are taken into account became somewhat less equal between 1950 and 1970.* The income of the lowest quintile dropped from 3.6 to 2.9 percent of the total. Table 9.5 shows much the same trend for a longer period, but it is restricted to families. The most important reason for this was an increase in the percentage of people in traditionally low-income groups (female-headed households, for example). However, such demographic changes account for only part of the observed shift. Both Tables 9.5 and 9.7 suggest that the rapid growth of transfers shown in Table 9.6 may have reduced the incentive of the poor to earn income. Second, *governmental taxes and expenditures greatly reduced the inequality in the income distribution.* For example, governmental taxes and expenditures more than doubled the income share of the lowest quintile in 1970, increasing it from 2.9 to 6.7 percent. Contrary to some popular belief, the postfisc-income share of the middle 60 percent increased between 1950 and 1970. Thus, income redistribution has been at the expense of the highest income quintile, not the middle class.

Unfortunately the careful analysis that produced the data in Table 9.7 has not been updated. The more recent data in Table 9.5, however, strongly indicates that the factor-income distribution has become more unequal since 1970. Since that time, taxes have not become more progressive. Although transfers have increased relative to GNP, most of the increase has gone to the non-means-tested social security and Medicare programs. Thus, it seems very likely that the postfisc-income distribution has become more unequal since 1970.

The income share of the poorest group depends very much on how government transfers to them are valued. The official poverty statistics in Table 9.1 include only some transfers in the measure of income of the poor. The data in Table 9.7 include estimates of all transfers received by people in each quintile. Paglin (1979) claims that careful valuation of transfers implies that only 3.8 percent of the population was living below the poverty line in 1974 instead of the 11.6 percent reported in Table 9.1.

☐ FURTHER POSSIBLE STEPS FOR REDUCING POVERTY

Where does the United States stand in the national effort to eliminate poverty? What additional steps should be taken by government? These are complex questions with answers that depend on detailed notions of equity as well as on economic analysis. The variety and complexity of governmental tax and expenditure programs is enormous. Some programs are federal, but increasing numbers are federal-state or state programs. The intended beneficiaries, the rules of eligibility, and the amount and kind of help provided vary greatly from program to program. Each program, as well as the total effort, is controversial. Specific program evaluations cannot be attempted here, but several general comments can be made.

First although people can differ in their evaluations of attempts in the United States to redistribute income, no one should sneer at the effort. Redistributive expenditures are now large in the United States, and they have grown rapidly since the beginning of the national effort in the early 1960s. The result has been a clear and substantial increase in living standards of the poor, although exact measures are not available.

Second programs vary greatly in the extent to which they help the poor. Means-tested programs, such as welfare and food stamps, are targeted accurately on the neediest people. Other programs, such as unemployment compensation and social security benefits, benefit unemployed and elderly people with little regard to need. Beyond a doubt, the elderly have been the biggest group of beneficiaries of the dramatic increases in transfers since the 1960s. Indeed, living standards of the elderly are now somewhat higher than those of the nonelderly.

Third many programs have become extremely complex. Successive congresses modify programs to take into account new circumstances or to increase assistance to particular groups. In some cases, programs have become so complex that legal assistance is required to establish eligibility. An excessive burden is placed on prospective beneficiaries, especially those who are poorly educated. Administrative costs of some programs are far too high, and the door is opened to manipulation of programs by experts both within the administrative agency and within recipient groups. Social Security, housing programs, and welfare programs are examples of programs that have become extremely complex.

Self-help has been at the center of traditional ways to reduce poverty in the United States, yet the white majority has used discriminatory obstacles to block efforts of the black minority to lift themselves from poverty. Gradually and painfully, a national consensus has emerged that discrimination is unconscionable. The consensus was embodied in the civil rights bills of the 1960s. Evidence has been presented that discrimination indeed has been reduced, yet it still exists in public service provision, housing, employment, and union membership. It is still true that one of the most important antipoverty measures is reduction of racial discrimination, yet the most important obstacle to self-help by the poor during the 1970s and early 1980s has been the instability and slow growth of the macroeconomy. It will take much longer to eliminate poverty, as well as be much more painful, if the economy continues to grow slowly.

Another approach to the reduction of poverty that has received increasing recent attention is programs to increase the income-earning capacity of the poor. Better health services may help, but the key is improved quality of education, especially in inner-city schools. Educational problems will be discussed in Chapter 14.

The current political mood suggests that the percentage of the GNP devoted to income-security transfers during the 1990s will not be much larger than it was in the 1980s. If so, the most important antipoverty program—next to increasing the growth rate of the entire economy—will be to simplify and focus transfer programs. *Poverty, as officially measured, could be eliminated by a moderate improvement in the focus of transfer programs on the poor.* Unemployment compensation, Medicare, and social security payments are the important candidates for such reform.

☐ Summary

Poverty is a matter of degree. Although the United States has virtually no poverty of the kind widespread in developing countries, many people here are poor by reasonable standards in an affluent society. The incidence of poverty is especially great among blacks. Poverty decreased rapidly during the 1960s and more slowly during the 1970s. Since the early 1960s, the U.S. government has mounted an elaborate, complex, and expensive set of programs to redistribute income. The effect has been to increase the income share of the lowest quintile and to reduce the income share of the highest quintile, but the magnitudes of the redistribution are subject to debate.

During the late 1970s, interest focused on the reform of transfer programs. Many economists favor substituting an NIT for many present income-security transfer programs.

Questions and Problems

1. To what extent do you think the poor would benefit from a wage-price freeze that curtailed inflation without raising the unemployment rate?

2. Calculate the cost of an NIT proposal of your choice and compare it with the cost of recent transfer expenditures. Make explicit your

assumptions about incentive effects of the NIT and the present transfer programs you propose to abolish.

3. Do you think local real estate taxes are progressive or regressive?

4. What contribution would the elimination of racial discrimination in housing make to eliminating poverty among blacks?

References and Further Reading

Freeman, Richard. "Black Economic Progress After 1964; Who Has Gained and Why." In *Studies in Labor Markets,* edited by Sherwin Rosen (Chicago: University of Chicago Press, 1981). A survey and analysis of trends in incomes of blacks and whites since the passage of the civil rights laws in the 1960s.

Kain, John, ed. *Race and Poverty* (Englewood Cliffs, N.J.: Prentice-Hall, 1969). A collection of essays on the relationship between race and poverty in the 1950s and 1960s.

Myrdal, Gunnar. *An American Dilemma* (New York: Harper & Row, 1944). A classic study of American racial problems by the Swedish economist.

Owen, Henry, and Schultze, Charles, eds. *Setting National Priorities* (Washington, D.C.: Brookings Institution, 1976). An annual volume by the Brookings Institute staff analyzing the president's budget proposals to Congress.

Paglin, Morton. "Poverty in the United States: A Reevaluation." *Policy Review* (Spring, 1979): 7–24. An attempt to include in-kind transfers in measuring income of the poor.

Reynolds, Morgan, and Smolensky, Eugene. *Public Expenditures, Taxes, and the Distribution of Income* (New York: Academic Press, 1977). A careful statistical study of the effects of governmental taxes and expenditures on the distribution of income.

Robbins, Philip K., Spiegelman, Robert G., and Weiner, Samuel, eds. *A Guaranteed Annual Income: Evidence from a Social Experiment, 1980* (Washington, D.C.: Urban Institute, 1980).

U.S. Department of Commerce, Bureau of the Census. *Statistical Abstract of the United States* (Washington, D.C.: Government Printing Office, 1987). A useful compendium of governmental statistics.

10

The Market for Housing

☐ Housing is important, especially in cold climates where dwellings are crucial for survival. Everywhere, dwellings are essential components of living standards, comfort, security, and social status. People devote not only large shares of their incomes to housing, but also extensive amounts of their time and energy to acquiring, financing, maintaining, repairing, improving, and operating their homes. Americans devote about 15.5 percent of personal income to housing and another 12.5 percent to household operation (e.g., utilities, insurance, maintenance, and repair).

Needless to say, housing also is a valuable asset. In fact, housing is the largest category of privately owned assets. The market value of dwellings is more than 40 percent of the market value of all privately owned fixed capital. (In addition to housing, fixed capital includes consumers' durables, business equipment, and nonresidential real estate.) The market value of housing is about 1.8 times annual disposable income. Although Americans complain endlessly about the cost of housing, most are better housed, and at lower costs relative to incomes, than are people in almost any other country.

Not only is housing this country's largest asset category, but also it is among the most durable. The average American dwelling lasts about 40 to 50 years. Many houses last 100 years, and some last longer than 200 years. Much depends on the material from which the house is constructed—brick and stone houses last longer than wooden ones. Much also depends on the care, maintenance, and repair history of the house, and on economic considerations. Some houses are converted to nonresidential uses—stores and offices—because the most valuable use of the structure shifts. In addition, many houses are demolished intentionally, either because the most valuable use of the land has shifted or because the value of the land has risen enough to justify much more intensive use of the land, for high-rise apartments, for example.

Consumer and producer equipment tends to last only 5 to 20 years, in comparison. Modern structural-steel office buildings are constructed to last longer than houses. Few structural-steel office buildings were built before the 1920s, but some of these 70-year-old buildings are still functional. Structural-steel office buildings, however, represent the only class of assets that is built to last longer than houses. Durability is advantageous in keeping housing costs low relative to construction costs, but it also causes social problems, which will be discussed subsequently.

This chapter provides an introduction to the analysis of markets for housing. The next chapter analyzes housing finance and personal decision-making regarding homeownership. Chapter 12 analyzes housing problems in the United States and housing issues that relate to the low-income segment of the population.

☐ QUANTITY AND PRICE MEASURES FOR HOUSING

Earlier chapters have referred to the price and quantity of housing, and the usual assumption was made that the quantity demanded and supplied depended on price. That assumption is appropriate whether the reference is to housing or eggs, but the concept of quantity is much more complex with housing than with almost any other commodity. Before a discussion on housing issues can continue, the meanings of price and quantity must be sorted out. For example, the statement that poor people consume less housing than wealthy people is meaningful only if price and quantity can be distinguished.

What is the difference between a $100,000 house and a $200,000 house? Is the price per unit of housing in the second house twice as high as the price of the first, does the second house represent twice as much house as the first, or is the difference a combination of price and quantity? Perhaps, the first house is twice as expensive as the second because it is closer to the CBD, it may be a difference in price, or it might simply be twice as much housing at the same price per unit. Only housing asset values can be observed directly, not price or quantity.

The measurement problem is further complicated by the extreme durability of housing and by the existence of both rental and homeowner markets. Who is paying a higher price for housing, an owner who occupies a $100,000 house or a renter who pays $700 per month for an identical house?

Quantity

Consumers value many characteristics of residences, such as floor space, number of rooms, internal layout, structural quality, decoration, appliances, and yard space. Assume that only two characteristics matter,

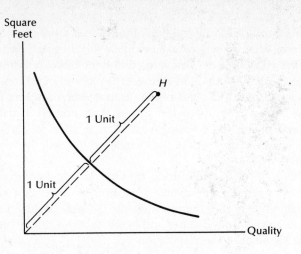

Figure 10.1   *Measuring "Units" of Housing*

floor space and an undefined quality concept. Making the usual assumption that consumers have coherent and consistent tastes, they have indifference curves between floor space and quality, one of which is shown in Figure 10.1. All combinations of floor space and quality on the indifference curve are equally desirable to the consumer. Hence, an indifference curve can be selected and the dwellings represented by the points on that indifference curve can be defined as containing one unit of housing.

We can call the indifference curve by which we have defined one unit of housing the *reference curve*. This reference curve is arbitrary. The theory of consumer behavior assumes that exactly one indifference curve passes through each square feet-quality combination. Because indifference curves can be arbitrarily numbered or renumbered, the indifference curve through any square feet-quality combination can be selected and the dwellings on that indifference curve can be defined as one unit of housing. Now, consider the house labeled *H* in Figure 10.1 as containing amounts of floor space and quality that are indicated by its coordinates on the graph. Draw a line from *H* through the origin and assume that *H* consists of twice as much floor space and quality as the house situated where the line through the origin crosses the reference curve. Then, if *H* is a two-unit house, it represents twice as much housing as a house on the reference curve. Note that, although the choice of a one-unit dwelling is arbitrary, once a one-unit house has been designated, a two-unit house is well defined. A *two-unit house* is any house on the indifference curve that passes through *H* and is twice as much house as a one-unit house. Thus, a two-unit house is a quantitative concept—twice as much house as a one-unit house—even though both one- and two-unit houses include a variety of square feet-quality combinations.

How could this representation be generalized to account for the many dimensions of housing quantity in addition to floor space and the many components of quality that matter to consumers? Economists have developed a technique called *hedonic price-index analysis* to estimate quantity and quality in realistically complex cases, and many studies have applied hedonic analysis to housing.[1] For example, a recent study concludes that central air conditioning adds about 5.4 percent to a dwelling's value and that a detached home is worth about 6.7 percent more than an attached home, assuming all other characteristics are fixed. The implication is that a non-air-conditioned detached home and an air-conditioned attached home are on indifference curves that represent nearly the same quantity of housing.

Price

Having measured quantity (relative to an arbitrary unit *quantity*), price now can be measured by dividing house value by quantity. This number is a price measure in that it captures the variation in house value that remains after correcting for differences in quantity. Returning to the example of the $200,000 and the $100,000 houses, if the quantity measures showed that the first had twice as many units as the second, we would find that $200,000 divided by 2 equals $100,000 divided by 1; that is, the price per unit of the two houses is the same. More specifically, this measure is defined as the *asset price,* as it is calculated by dividing the value of the house by quantity.

By similar means, *rental price* can be calculated by dividing monthly (or annual) rent by quantity. The rental price tells how much it would cost to rent a dwelling relative to one with characteristics that place it on the reference indifference curve.

Both value prices and rental prices, of course, may vary from time to time and from place to place. Chapter 6 introduced the possibility of spatial variation in housing prices, and this chapter looks at variations over time. The reason for going through the previous analysis is to be sure that *price* is observed in the same sense that economists and others generally use the term.

Relationship Between Value Price and Rental Price

The market relationship between value price and rental price is probably the most important concept in the analysis of housing markets.

---

1. Basically, hedonic analysis regresses (see the Appendix) dwelling price on a function of many dwelling (and neighborhood) characteristics. The estimated equation can be used to calculate combinations of characteristics that result in the same sales price. The technique is made feasible by the availability of large data sets of many dwelling characteristics and prices at which the dwellings were sold. Hedonic analysis was introduced by Griliches (1971) to disentangle price and quantity-quality changes in automobiles. The definitive, but difficult, theoretical report is by Rosen (1974). A pragmatic application is written King and Mieszkowski (1973). Many hedonic analyses of housing prices appear in the *Journal of Urban Economics.* The example in the following text sentence is from Mills and Simenauer (1992).

Table 10.1 *Movements in Value Prices, Rental Price, Real Interest Rates, and Nominal Interest Rates, 1965 to 1990*

Year	(1) Value Price	(2) Average Mortgage Rate	(3) Rental Price	(4) Real Interest Rate	(5) Real After-tax Mortgage Rate
1965	100.0	5.83	100.0	5.09	3.63
1966	101.4	6.40	98.5	5.24	3.64
1967	101.4	6.53	97.5	5.19	3.56
1968	102.3	7.12	95.8	5.03	3.25
1969	104.6	7.99	93.9	5.88	3.88
1970	101.6	8.52	92.3	5.88	3.75
1971	102.7	7.75	92.6	4.64	2.70
1972	105.9	7.64	92.8	4.40	2.49
1973	108.6	8.30	91.1	5.05	2.98
1974	107.0	9.22	86.2	4.85	2.55
1975	107.8	9.10	83.0	5.17	2.90
1976	110.5	8.99	82.8	4.08	1.83
1977	116.1	8.95	82.4	3.68	1.44
1978	123.1	9.68	81.8	4.58	2.16
1979	127.2	11.15	79.0	5.27	2.48
1980	123.7	12.25	75.7	5.43	2.37
1981	121.2	16.52	74.5	9.78	5.65
1982	117.0	15.79	75.8	9.90	5.95
1983	116.0	13.43	76.8	8.15	4.79
1984	116.0	13.80	78.0	8.80	5.35
1985	114.3	12.28	79.4	8.80	5.73
1986	117.6	10.07	82.3	8.97	6.45
1987	120.2	10.17	82.7	5.74	3.20
1988	119.6	10.30	82.8	5.88	3.30
1989	118.3	10.21	82.9	5.56	3.00
1990	114.0	10.08	82.3	3.97	1.45

Notes: Column 1 shows the real value price of housing: the price index of new one-family homes divided by the Consumer Price Index (CPI) and set equal to 100 in 1965.
Column 2 shows the average conventional new-home mortgage rate.
Column 3 shows the CPI rent component divided by the CPI, set equal to 100 in 1965.
Column 4 shows the estimate of the real mortgage rate.
Column 5 shows the estimate of the real after-tax mortgage rate.
Sources: Data from U.S. Department of Commerce, Bureau of the Census; Bureau of Labor Statistics; *Federal Reserve Bulletin* (Washington, D.C.: Government Printing Office); and Hulten, Charles, and Robert Schwab. "Income Originating in the State and Local Sector." Working paper (College Park: University of Maryland, 1987).

Confusion over these concepts has resulted in errors in analysis and governmental policy. Table 10.1 shows some general information that is relevant to the subject.

In principle, the relationship is straightforward: *asset price* is the present value of rent minus the present value of costs of operation.[2] In fact, the relationship is rather complicated because of considerations of

2. The remainder of this discussion will use the terms *value* and *rent* rather than the more cumbersome *asset price* and *rental price*. This substitution will cause no problems if the reader remembers that *asset value* and *rental* each refer to dwellings with the same characteristics.

taxation, capital gains, inflation, maintenance, and depreciation, as well as interest.

We begin with the simple case in which rent and value are linked only by the interest rate. In this simple model, assume that housing lasts forever, with no depreciation, maintenance, capital gains, or taxes. In this unrealistic case, if rent is to cover the landlord's costs,

$$R = iV, \tag{10.1}$$

where R is rent, i is the interest rate, and V is value. Given the simplifications assumed, the landlord's only cost is the annual interest on the investment.[3] If the rental market is competitive (and therefore the landlord makes no abnormal profit), annual rent (R) just covers annual cost (iV).

Note that the relationship between R and V has been described in two equivalent ways: R is the annual cost of holding a house of value V, embodied in Equation (10.1), or V is the present value of future R (assumed to be a constant stream forever). This version of the relationship can be found by rearranging Equation (10.1):[4]

$$= \frac{R}{i} = \sum_{t=1}^{\infty} \frac{R}{(1 + i)^t}. \tag{10.2}$$

The rent is the amount that a competitive landlord charges a tenant for the right to occupy the dwelling for one year. The rent, then, is the relevant price term when a renter's demand function for housing is considered. It is important to note that *the rent is also the price a homeowner faces for the right to occupy housing.* This amount can be seen in two ways. First note that the homeowner's annual cost is iV. Second the opportunity cost of occupying a house is obviously the annual rent the homeowner could charge if the owner moved out and rented the house to a tenant.

Thus, just like the renter's, the homeowner's cost of housing is the rent, and it is the rent—not the value—that enters the homeowner's demand function and governs the amount of housing he or she consumes. The value makes no difference either to the homeowner or to the renter except through its influence on the rent (via Equation [10.1] or

3.   It does not matter how much of the house is financed by a mortgage. That which is not financed by the mortgage is the owner's equity. By having some of his or her wealth tied up in the house, the homeowner is foregoing interest that could be earned by selling the house and investing the equity at the market rate of interest. "Interest" includes interest paid on the outstanding mortgage plus foregone interest on the homeowner's equity. Of course, borrowing rates are actually somewhat greater than lending rates for most homeowners, but that difference is ignored here.

4. t indicates the year number. The right side of Equation (10.2) is a shorthand expression for the discounted sum of future rents:

$$\sum_{t=1}^{\infty} \frac{R}{(1 + i)^t} = \frac{R}{(1 + i)} + \frac{R}{(1 + i)^2} + \frac{R}{(1 + i)^3} = + \ldots + \frac{R}{(1 + i)^\infty}.$$

[10.2]). By way of example, if the value rises 10 percent and the interest rate falls 10 percent, the rent does not change, and neither the owner-occupant nor the renter is induced to change behavior. If the house is occupied by the owner, the expression "implicit rent" is sometimes used.

☐ COST OF CAPITAL: COMPLICATIONS

The coefficient linking R and V is known as the *cost of capital,* because it measures the cost of holding a unit of capital for a year. In the previous case, the only cost is interest; if the interest rate is 10 percent, the cost of holding $1.00 of capital for a year is $0.10. This section's task is to modify the cost-of-capital term to account for costs other than interest that are associated with holding housing capital.

If the house is subject to a property tax, at the tax rate T, operating costs (maintenance, repair, insurance, utilities), at the rate c, and expected capital gains net of depreciation, at the rate g, the rent becomes

$$R = iV + TV + cV - gV$$

$$= (i + T + c - g)V. \qquad (10.3)$$

Each of the terms multiplied by V is an item in the landlord's cost and is assumed to be proportional to value. For a house of value V and unit costs given by i, T, c, and g, R is the rent that must be charged to cover costs. R is the total cost incurred by holding the house for a year, whether the owner occupies the house or rents it to a tenant. If the owner rents it to a tenant, the owner must recover these costs in rent; if the owner occupies it, he or she incurs these costs for housing. Most of the costs included in Equation (10.3) are cash outlays. The part of iV that represents interest payments to the mortgage lender is a cash outlay. (Why are mortgage-principal payments not included in Equation [10.3]?) The part of iV that is not mortgage-interest payments is an opportunity cost, but not a cash outlay. gV is an unrealized capital gain or loss (until the house is sold), so it is a "paper" or opportunity cost, which is negative if g is greater than zero.

Inflation

The incorporation of inflation into Equation (10.3) is critical to understanding housing markets as inflation rises and falls. Incorporating inflation requires an understanding of the relationship between interest rates and inflation.

Ignoring federal income taxes, the true cost of borrowing is the interest payment less the inflation that occurs between the time of borrowing and repayment. The reason is that inflation renders the repaid dollars less valuable than the borrowed dollars. Thus, the repayment of principal does not return to lenders all of the purchasing power they lent out sometime earlier. To maintain the real value of the borrowed principal outstanding, or to keep the principal whole, competitive markets tack on an *inflation premium* to interest rates.

Expressing this observation in terms of rates of inflation and interest,

$$i = i^r + \pi, \tag{10.4}$$

where i is the interest rate, π is the inflation rate, and i^r is the true cost of borrowing in terms of purchasing power, called the *real interest rate*.[5] For example, suppose there is 4 percent inflation, and a lender demands a 3 percent real return on investment. The "nominal" interest rate (i) must be 7 percent (3 percent plus 4 percent) to keep the capital whole and yield 3 percent.

Suppose now that the nominal interest rate rises one percentage point for each percentage point of inflation and that the rate of capital gains does likewise. That is, suppose the real interest rate and the real rate of capital gains are independent of the rate of inflation. This concept can be represented by replacing i by ($i^r + \pi$) and g by ($g^r + \pi$) in Equation (10.3) (g^r stands for real capital gains). How does this influence the cost-of-capital expression? It gives the following:

$$R = [(i^r + \pi) + T + c - (g^r + \pi)]V$$
$$= [i^r + T + c - g^r]V. \tag{10.5}$$

Since there is the same inflation premium on interest and capital gains, inflation is canceled and the cost-of-capital is unaffected by inflation. Thus, "pure" inflation is neutral with respect to the rental price of housing, just as pure inflation is neutral with respect to all relative prices.

This result is important. It says that a rise in the interest rate brought about by a rise in inflation expectations does not depress the demand for housing. In other words, an 8 percent mortgage when inflation is 6 percent is no more costly than a 2 percent mortgage when inflation is zero. In the former case, the homeowner anticipates a 6 percent capital gain (due to the 6 percent inflation), which can be used to pay all but two percentage points on the mortgage. Of course, if the mortgage rate is 8 percent and inflation is zero, the true cost of borrowing is the full 8 percent. Many people expressed surprise over the fact that the high interest rates of the 1970s and early 1980s failed to choke off housing demand. An important part of the reason is that interest rates were not high after accounting for inflation.

---

5. Equation (10.4) is not quite right, as it does not allow for continuous compounding. The correct expression is $1 + i = (1+i^r)(1+\pi)$. Multiplying out the right side $i = i^r + \pi + i^r\pi$. The product ($i^r\pi$), however, can be ignored unless either i^r or π is very large.

Federal Income Taxation*

The reason that many people think that inflation is good for homeowners is that they concentrate on the capital gains and not on their interest payments (and, of course, not on foregone interest on their equity). These days, interest rates quite fully reflect the market's anticipated inflation rates. Homeowners benefit from inflation if they obtained a fixed-interest rate mortgage and if inflation that the lender did not anticipate when the mortgage was originated occurs during the life of the loan. That requires the owner-borrower to be lucky or to outguess a market in which thousands of smart people pay careful attention to all publicly available information that is relevant to trends in interest rates and inflation. Don't depend on outguessing the market! More on this subject will be discussed in the next chapter.

The next step is to introduce federal income taxation. Federal tax law treats owner-occupied and rental housing differently. This section provides a brief introduction to taxation of owner-occupied housing. A full discussion of taxation of owner-occupied and rental housing will be presented in the next chapter.

As was pointed out, what has been referred to as interest payments consists of two parts: mortgage-interest payments and the foregone interest on the homeowner's equity in the house.[3] As a good approximation, the assumption will continue to be that the interest rates on the two parts are the same. Mortgage-interest payments are deductible on the federal income tax form, provided that the taxpayer itemizes. Interest on an investment, such as a federal government or corporate bond, that the homeowner could have made instead of investing his or her equity in the home is fully taxable. (Interest on state and local government bonds is not taxable by the federal government, but interest rates are lower on such investments by about the top marginal income tax rate.) Thus, whether the homeowner has a large mortgage or a large equity in the home, it is aftertax interest that represents his or her cost. If the interest is paid on a mortgage, the federal government pays a fraction t of the interest, where t is the homeowner's top marginal tax rate. Thus, the homeowner's after-deductibility interest rate is $i(1-t)$. If the interest is foregone interest on the homeowner's equity, it would be taxable, so the owner's opportunity cost is $i(1-t)$. Thus, the new rent to value equation becomes

$$R = [i(1-t) + T(1-t) + c - g]V, \tag{10.6}$$

where t is the homeowner's marginal income tax rate. This expression recognizes that interest (but not principal) payments and property taxes are tax deductible. Thus, the homeowner's cost is interest payments or foregone interest plus property tax minus the income tax reduction that

---

* This section is somewhat difficult and can be skipped without loss of continuity.

results from the deductions, plus the other terms in Equation (10.6) that are the same as in Equation (10.5). Equation (10.6) specifies that the aftertax rent is what the homeowner cares about.

A simple example will suggest magnitudes. Suppose you own a $200,000 house, for which the mortgage and foregone interest rates are 8 percent, so i is .08. Annual property taxes are 1.0 percent of the property's value, and the items included in c are 2 percent of the house's value. You anticipate a 4 percent appreciation of the house per year. (Realistically, you might anticipate 3 percent inflation, so the real interest rate $[i^r]$ is 5 percent and the real capital gain $[g^r]$ is 1 percent.) Then, using either form of Equation (10.5), your rent to value ratio (R/V) is .07. It costs you .07(200,000) or $14,000 per year to rent your house from yourself. Using the same numbers for Equation (10.6) and assuming your income puts you in the 31-percent tax bracket, your rent to value ratio becomes .0621. Taking account of federal (and local) taxes, the cost of renting the house to yourself comes down to $12,420 per year. Readers should do similar calculations for other data to gain a sense of the importance of the tax status of owner-occupied houses.

The fact that the homeowner's imputed rent is not taxed (yet mortgage-interest and property-tax payments are deductible) and that capital gains are nearly tax free are two important ways in which owner-occupants are favored over landlords and renters in the federal tax law. Although few countries tax the homeowner's imputed rent or capital gains, most countries do not permit deductions of mortgage-interest and real-estate tax payments on national income tax forms.

Inflation and Income Taxation Combined*

The neutrality of inflation disappears when the interaction of inflation and taxes is included. Federal tax law treats the two inflation entries differently, creating a situation in which inflation does not cancel out in the rent to value equation. To see this, remember that interest and capital gains both have an inflation component and a real component.

As has been stated, both the real and inflation components of capital gains on owner-occupied houses are virtually untaxed. For mortgage-interest payments, both the real and inflation components are deductible. Again, separating interest and capital gains into real and inflation components, the rent to value equation now becomes

$$R = [(i^r + \pi)(1-t) + T(1-t) + c + (g^r + \pi)]V$$
$$= [(i^r + T)(1-t) - \pi t - g^r + c]V. \tag{10.7}$$

Now it can be seen that the deductibility provisions do indeed make inflation the homeowner's friend. Equation (10.7) is the same as

---

* This section is somewhat difficult and can be skipped without loss of continuity.

Equation (10.6), except that in Equation (10.6) the real and inflationary components of interest and capital gains are separated. Thus, with the parameters in the previous example, it can still be concluded that the rent to value ratio is .0421 when the inflation rate is .03. Now, suppose that the inflationary component of interest and capital gains rises to .05, with the real components of interest and capital gains remaining at .05 and .01. In this more inflationary environment, the rent to value ratio falls to .0359. Inflation has substantially reduced the rent to value ratio. The reader can verify that an inflation rate of .1658 would reduce the rent to value ratio to zero. The reason that inflation is the homeowner's friend is that the inflationary component of interest is deductible, whereas the inflationary component of capital gains is not taxed.

☐ THE MARKET FOR HOUSING

The cost-of-capital expression, despite its complexity, is the crucial link between the supply and demand sides of the market for housing, and it is apparent that the market for housing cannot be analyzed without an understanding of the cost of capital. The following section will designate the cost of capital as ρ, recognizing that it incorporates all the terms in the square brackets in Equation (10.7).

Demand for Housing

So far, the discussion has been on rent for owner-occupied housing. Rent for renters is similar and somewhat simpler, as none of the foregoing deductibility analysis applies to rental markets. Specific differences in rent for renters will be covered in the next chapter. Meanwhile, rent will be referred to as ρV, where ρ is the cost of capital—the annual cost of occupying an owner-occupied house per dollar of its asset price.

Economists always say that demand for a commodity or service depends on its price and on income. That is as true for housing as for anything else. However, as seen in the previous sections, the notion of a price per unit of housing is complex. If there were no inflation (or if there were no taxes!) and if house value were proportionate to the number of housing units (as defined at the beginning of the chapter) in the dwelling, then ρ would be the price per unit of housing. Indeed, in those ideal circumstances, the rent per unit of housing would be the same for owner-occupiers and for renters.

In the real world, the rent per unit of housing is different for owners than for renters, different for people in high tax brackets than for people in low tax brackets, different in periods of high and low inflationary rates, and different depending on where one lives. (The value of a given house is lower in small than in large metropolitan areas and may be lower in suburbs than in central cities.)

In any case, the basic equation is that the rent of a dwelling is the cost of capital multiplied by the value of the dwelling, $R = \rho V$. In principle, the rent per unit of housing is R divided by the number of units of housing in the dwelling, as defined at the beginning of the chapter. Thus, we can write

$$\bar{R} = \frac{R}{H} = \frac{\rho V}{H}. \tag{10.8}$$

In Equation (10.8), H is the number of housing units in the dwelling and $\bar{R}$ is the rent per unit of housing. $\bar{R}$ is the price on which the consumption demand for housing depends.

The decision to occupy a house is a consumption decision; it gives the occupant the right to consume the housing services provided by the housing asset for a period of time, such as a month or a year. The decision to buy a house is an investment or portfolio decision. One asset (the house) is exchanged for others (the mortgage and the down payment). The demand for housing also is a consumption decision. The investment decision will be discussed in the next chapter.

Empirical Estimates of Demand for Housing

Despite the complexity of the preceding discussion, $\bar{R}$, the rent per unit of housing, is the price concept that is relevant to the demand for housing consumption. Then, the demand curve for housing, making the usual assumption that it is downward sloping, is as shown in Figure 10.2. In addition to rent per unit, a household's housing demand depends on its income and on its demographic characteristics, such as how many children, how many workers, and life-style. Finally, there are costs of changing housing consumption; substantial changes typically require a move. Moving entails transaction costs, which are costs that are incurred by virtue of moving but do not depend on the amount of housing

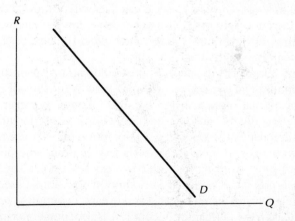

Figure 10.2   *Demand Curve for Housing Services*

consumed. Examples are search costs, costs of moving possessions, and costs of negotiating a sale, purchase, or lease. These costs will be discussed in detail in the next chapter. Here, it is important to recognize that the transaction costs imply that households may be considerably out of equilibrium much of the time, consuming more or less housing than is indicated by their demand equation.

The foregoing suggests that estimating housing-demand equations may be complex and frustrating. Indeed, some of the most ingenious and persistent applied research in economics during the last century has been carried out in this area. Such hard work has been motivated not just by scholarly curiosity but also by the social importance of the subject, especially the housing plight of low-income people.

Progress in estimating housing-demand equations has been especially rapid since the late 1950s, the result of better theoretical understanding, more and better data, better estimating techniques, and vastly more powerful computers.

To estimate the effect of price on demand, it is necessary to have data in which the price varies. Chapter 6 showed that urban-location theory provides an intriguing possibility. Thus, as was shown, in ideal circumstances, rent per unit of housing would vary by distance from the CBD, so as to keep households with the same money income on a given indifference curve. Those circumstances should enable economists to estimate the income-compensated demand equation for housing, the gold ring of demand estimation. Chapter 12 will show that the world is more complex than the ideal circumstances, but that careful work can nevertheless provide estimates of demand equations.

Another intriguing possibility relates to interest rates. An example earlier in this chapter showed that the interest rate is the biggest component of the cost of capital. Since governments have at least some control over interest rates, it would be very desirable to know how much housing demand would be stimulated by a reduction in interest rates. However, at any given time, interest rates hardly vary within or among metropolitan areas. Thus, cross-sectional data will not reveal the world's secrets to the curious housing economist. Many interest rates vary greatly through time; however, real interest rates affect the cost of capital, and real rates vary much less through time.

Income varies greatly among households at any given time. Even taking community averages, income may vary by a factor of 5 within a given metropolitan area at a given time. Income, however, must be measured carefully. Because of the transaction costs of moving, households do not change their housing consumption in response to small or temporary changes in income. Nevertheless, high-income people consume much more housing than do low-income people. The answer is that households make housing consumption decisions based on forecasts of their average income over several years. Economists refer to this income measure as permanent income. It is, of course, not permanent but is more nearly permanent than current income. Although what households forecast as their income for the next several years is not normally known, it has been found that approximations of permanent income (for example, average income during the last three years), provide much better explanations of housing demand than does current income. Not surprisingly, permanent-income measures suggest higher income elasticities of housing demand than does current income. Households with very high or low current income probably have current incomes above or below their permanent income. Because housing demand depends on permanent income, housing consumption adjusts little to fluctuations that are thought to be temporary.

Coping with these and other problems, a gradual consensus has emerged about the important parameters of housing-demand equations. Price elasticity appears to be in the vicinity of −0.65 and income elasticity appears to be in the vicinity of +0.75. No theorem says that all households or all communities must have the same price elasticities, or the same income elasticities, so these figures must be taken as approximations. Nevertheless, nearly all housing specialists now agree that housing demand is inelastic with respect to price, and most agree that the income elasticity is somewhat less than one.

Such estimates have important consequences. In one example, it has been observed that the poor spend larger percentages of their permanent incomes on housing than do the rich. That observation is a consequence of an income elasticity less than one, which implies that the share of income spent on housing increases as income decreases. If, in addition, the poor are concentrated closer than the rich to the city centers, where land and housing prices are high, it is easy to explain much larger income shares spent on housing by the poor.

Housing Supply

In the short run, housing supply is dominated by the nearly fixed standing stock. The supply of dwellings can be increased in less than a year, mainly by splitting one large dwelling into two or more small ones and by converting stores, offices, warehouses, or churches into dwellings. Although it may take only three to six months to build a dwelling, it takes much longer to plan, obtain required permissions, and arrange financing for new construction. Thus, the short-run supply curve is quite, but not completely, inelastic. This is depicted in Figure 10.3.

Table 10.2 reports annual housing starts from 1959 through 1990. Note that housing starts fluctuate by as much as 50 percent over very few years.

In the short run, housing prices and rents are determined primarily by demand. Demand depends on rents. Rents translate into house values via Equation (10.7), which is simply another way of saying what is true for any asset with a supply that is fixed in the short run: Its price is that at which the public is willing to hold the stock. With housing, the public is willing to hold the stock at a price at which rents compensate owners for

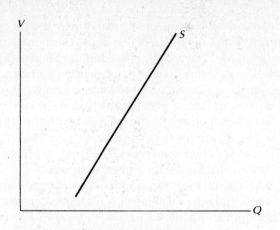

Figure 10.3 *Supply Curve for Housing Services*

the cost of capital. Remember, assumptions have been made that imply that the cost of capital is the same, whether the owner is the occupant or a profit-seeking landlord. We also noted that the cost of capital depends on prospects for capital gains, which depend on supply and demand prospects. Capital gains will be discussed more extensively in the next chapter.

In the long run, housing prices are set by construction and land costs or development costs. If the short-run price at which the public is willing to hold the existing stock exceeds development costs, then developers build houses and make a profit equal to the difference

Table 10.2 *Housing Starts by Year (Millions of Dwelling Units)*

Year	Millions of Dwelling Units	Year	Millions of Dwelling Units
1959	1.55	1975	1.17
1960	1.30	1976	1.55
1961	1.37	1977	2.00
1962	1.49	1978	2.04
1963	1.63	1979	1.76
1964	1.56	1980	1.31
1965	1.51	1981	1.10
1966	1.20	1982	1.07
1967	1.32	1983	1.71
1968	1.55	1984	1.76
1969	1.50	1985	1.75
1970	1.47	1986	1.81
1971	2.08	1987	1.62
1972	2.38	1988	1.49
1973	2.06	1989	1.38
1974	1.35	1990	1.19

Source: Data from U.S. Department of Commerce, Bureau of the Census. *Construction Reports;* and *Statistical Abstract of the United States* (Washington, D.C.: Government Printing Office, 1991).

between sale prices and development costs. If the short-run price is less than development costs, developers cannot make money by building new houses and development slows down.

The foregoing needs some elaboration. Developers, of course, try to anticipate demand a year or more in advance, so they can have enough houses available to match the demand. To the extent that anticipations are accurate, supply can increase to match an increase in demand with almost no increase in prices above the long-run equilibrium level. The process also works in reverse. Housing starts dropped almost 50 percent from their peak in 1986 to the worst months in the 1991 recession. During that period, median prices for new homes rose about as fast as the overall price level, and the vacancy rate showed no upward trend. Developers apparently anticipated quite accurately the dramatic and painful decrease in demand that occurred during that period. Changes in housing demand that are not anticipated by developers can, however, result in much larger price charges.

A second elaboration relates to land values. At given input prices, the long-run supply of housing is perfectly elastic. The important input prices in housing construction are construction labor, building materials, and land. As was shown in Chapter 6, land prices at the periphery of a metropolitan area equal the value of the land in nonurban use, typically agriculture. As a metropolitan area grows, most new housing is added at the periphery. The periphery gradually moves out, but land values at the periphery do not change unless agricultural or some other opportunity cost of land in the surrounding area changes. Thus, new home prices do not rise as the metropolitan area grows. As was illustrated in Figure 6.10, however, land and, therefore, house prices in the interior of the metropolitan area increase as the metropolitan area grows. Thus, average house prices in a metropolitan area increase with the size of the metropolitan area even though development costs, land values, and house prices at the periphery are unaffected by the size of the metropolitan area.

Market Equilibrium

At this point, the supply and demand analysis can be put together to describe housing-market equilibrium. The key to understanding the complexity of this issue is to note that housing supply depends on the asset price of housing (developers build more housing the greater the asset price relative to development costs), whereas demand depends on rent. Equation (10.7) links rent and value via the cost of capital.

Figure 10.4 demonstrates the linkage. The top graph shows supply and demand in value terms, and the bottom graph shows supply and demand in rent terms. The supply curve in the top graph shows supply (S) as an increasing function of value per unit of housing, for values in

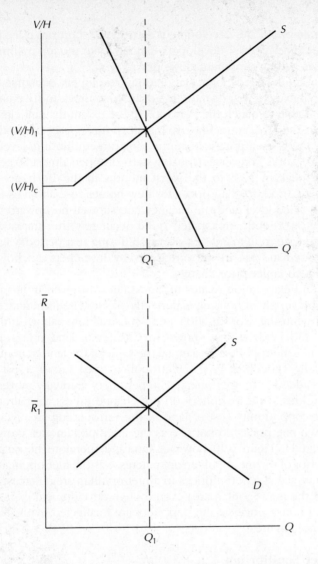

Figure 10.4   *Housing Market Equilibrium*

excess of construction costs ($[V/H]_c$). The bottom graph shows housing demand (D) as a function of rent ($\bar{R}$). For fixed ρ, Equation (10.7) permits supply to be expressed as a function of rent in the bottom graph and demand as a function of value in the top graph. Both rental and asset markets must be in equilibrium for the housing market to be in equilibrium.

As an exercise, the reader should trace the shifts in the curves and in market equilibrium that result from a change in the cost of capital, perhaps because of a change in the interest rate.

It was argued that housing supply is almost completely inelastic in the short run. The reader can draw the curves implied by this assumption. It was also argued previously that housing supply is perfectly elastic at development cost $(V/H)c$ in the long run. In that case, the supply curves in Figure 10.4 are horizontal, the equilibrium value equals development cost, and the equilibrium rent is the rent that Equation (10.7) gives when V/H is $(V/H)c$. It must be remembered, however, that, if the market is a metropolitan area, the supply of new housing at the periphery of the metropolitan area is likely to be perfectly elastic, but the value of the average house in the metropolitan area increases as the metropolitan area enlarges. This force is important because it limits the sizes of metropolitan areas. For example, in the late 1980s, growth of the Los Angeles and New York metropolitan areas was limited by the very high housing prices in those metropolitan areas.

Development Sector

So far, housing supply has been discussed without indicating who does it: Who actually builds houses? The answer is developers.

A *residential developer* is a firm that develops residential real estate. The residential developer is the entrepreneur who takes the responsibility and risks of building residences. Developers acquire building sites, decide what kinds and mixes of dwellings to put on the site, obtain legal permission to develop the sites, design the dwellings to be built, arrange financing, deal with interior and external environmental issues, build the dwellings, market the dwellings, and ascertain customer satisfaction so as to do a better job next time. In many suburban communities, developers also take pains to confer with business, residential, and governmental groups already in the community in which they wish to build to facilitate obtaining zoning and other provisions, to avoid public opposition to the proposed development, and to learn about local market potential.

Developers are extremely diverse in size and function. The smallest are "pickup truck" developers who acquire a few sites when they see a good buy and build just a few dwellings a year. Typically, they subcontract much of the plumbing, electrical, and other specialized construction work; use architectural plans "off-the-shelf"; employ local attorneys, as they need them; obtain construction financing from a friendly local bank; and employ local realtors to sell the completed houses. Although each of these developers builds only a few dwellings, there are many of them, and a large part of housing development is their work. The largest developers, in contrast, perform most of the above functions with their own personnel, and each may build many thousands of houses per year. Small developers tend to work in a small number of suburban communities of a single metropolitan area; the largest developers operate nationally, but even some quite large developers are regional firms. The need for detailed knowledge of local laws, regulations, and markets restricts the geographical diversification of all but the largest developers.

Developers relate to their customers in a variety of ways. Most residences are built "on spec," which means that the developer may have sites for several dozen houses, but builds them a few at a time and builds subsequent dwellings at a speed that depends on how quickly and at what prices the first ones sell. Often, the construction of subsequent houses is financed, at least in part, by sales of the houses that have been completed. A "contract" builder does not start building until a contract has been made for the house with a buyer. Typically, the contract requires the buyer to make "progress payments" as construction proceeds.

Developers, large or small, are notoriously short of money and engage in a range of strategies to finance development. Often, the buyers (of previously built houses in the case of a spec developer and of the house being built in the case of a contract builder) provide partial financing. A purchaser of a contract builder's dwelling must carefully monitor the developer's progress to avoid paying for work not completed. Even if the work has been completed, the developer's reliability must be carefully judged. It is very expensive to hire a builder to finish the construction on a project on which the developer has declared bankruptcy before finishing the job. When a developer is in financial trouble, his or her focus may be more on lenders and lawyers than on the speed and quality of work on the building sites.

In any case, developers typically obtain at least some financing through "construction loans," usually from a bank. Construction loans are typically for no more than five years, and they carry considerably higher interest rates than "permanent" mortgage financing on the completed and sold home. Construction lenders also are wary of having to foreclose on a loan on a partially built home, if the developer declares bankruptcy.

It may seem odd that banks are willing to finance the riskiest part of the residential real-estate market. The reason is that the bank's commitment is short term, in contrast to a usual mortgage on a finished home. Sometimes, a construction loan is accompanied by a promise of permanent financing on the finished home, provided, of course, that the buyer meets the bank's underwriting standards. Developers then use the availability of financing as a strategy for marketing the homes.

Homebuilding is among the most unstable businesses in the country, as will be documented in the next chapter. One reason is a simple accelerator effect. The durability of dwellings means that construction to replace houses that leave the stock because of demolition, disaster, or conversion is small relative to the stock. There are about 105 million dwelling units in the country (housing a population of about 250 million people); the average dwelling has a life of 40 to 50 years; and the average age of the stock is less than 17 years (reflecting large construction rates during the 1970s and early 1980s). Only about 1 percent of the stock needs to be replaced per year, so replacement demand is little more than one million dwellings per year.

In the 1990s, the population of the household formulation age group (20 to 29 years old) will shrink. Thus, the growth demand for housing will be small and will come mostly from increased longevity of the population.

The implication of the foregoing data is that the relatively steady replacement demand for housing is about one million units per year. Growth demand is much more volatile. Young people stay with parents and double up in hard times. (Baby boomers who return to their parents' homes after college, divorce, or job loss are sometimes referred to as "baby boomerangers.") In the worst periods of the 1990 to 1991 recession, home building was about 900,000 per year, which is a little less than replacement demand, having fallen from 1.8 million in 1986, or 50 percent in about 5 years. No sector outside construction is the victim of such instability!

Not surprisingly, instability has affected the organization of the housing-development sector. Instability places a premium on small organizations that can contract out many functions and on organizations that rent construction machinery instead of buying it. These characteristics would not be efficient in a more stable world, but are adaptations to the world that has existed and will probably continue to exist. Housing development is not a business for people with weak hearts!

Stock of Housing

The stock of housing is the legacy of past construction, alteration, depreciation, and retirements. The stock depreciates quite slowly, probably little more than 1 percent per year. Furthermore, alterations are a relatively minor source of changes in the housing stock. Home improvement expenditure runs about 1 percent of the value of stock, but this figure overstates the volume of upgrading; much of this expenditure should properly be called *maintenance*. Thus, the most important means of altering the housing stock are construction and retirement, and even these processes operate on the massive housing stock rather slowly.

For an idea of the quantitative impact of construction and demolition on the housing stock, consider the data in Tables 10.3 and 10.4. These remarkable data provide a complete picture of changes in the housing stock in the ten-year period between 1973 and 1983. Much more detailed data are available in the source. The first column in each table shows the total number of dwellings that existed in the year and places indicated. The second column shows the parts of the stock that existed in both years. The third column is the difference between the first two in each table, except that the data are all estimates from samples, so the arithmetic is inexact. For example, the first row of Table

Table 10.3 *Sources of 1983 Housing Stock by Region (Thousands of Dwelling Units)*

	1983 Stock	Same in 1973	Total Addition	New Construction
United States	94,421	70,739	21,972	16,171
MSA	62,603	48,472	12,970	10,157
Central city	27,240	22,556	3,962	2,990
Outside	35,363	25,916	9,008	7,167
Northeast	20,256	16,942	2,726	1,743
MSA	15,205	12,964	1,786	1,172
Central city	6,623	5,766	603	257
Outside	8,582	7,198	1,183	915
Midwest	24,067	19,205	4,474	3,291
MSA	15,102	12,411	2,446	1,993
Central city	6,539	5,688	672	496
Outside	8,563	6,724	1,773	1,497
South	31,782	21,773	9,484	7,257
MSA	18,099	12,731	5,051	4,076
Central city	8,287	6,481	1,586	1,371
Outside	13,683	6,251	3,465	2,705
West	18,316	12,819	5,288	3,879
MSA	14,197	10,365	3,687	2,916
Central city	5,791	4,621	1,100	865
Outside	8,406	5,744	2,587	2,051

Source: Data from U.S. Department of Commerce, Bureau of the Census. "Components of Inventory Change." *Census of Housing* (Washington, D.C.: Government Printing Office, 1983).

10.3 shows that there were about 94.4 million dwellings in 1983, of which approximately 70.7 had existed in 1973. These two numbers imply that 23.7 million units were added to the stock between the two years, whereas the third column records additions of nearly 22 million. Thus, there is a discrepancy of about 1.7 million units.

Of the nearly 22 million additions reported, almost 16.2 million were constructed during the seven-year period. The remainder were conversions from nonhousing uses (hospital to apartments, warehouses to residential lofts in Greenwich Village in New York City) and from the separation of one dwelling unit into two or more (a three-story town house, for example, is converted to three apartments). Table 10.3 shows that new construction provided approximately 16 million of the nearly 22 million dwellings added to the stock during the ten years. Thus, although construction accounted for about 74 percent of the additions to the stock, nearly 6 million dwellings were added by conversion and separation. Such nonconstruction additions are sometimes an important source of growth in the supply of low-income housing and are entirely separate from the filter-down source to be discussed in the next chapter.

Table 10.4 shows that almost 6.1 million dwellings disappeared from the 1973 stock by 1983, but that only about 2.4 million had been demolished (including disasters, such as fire and flood, which often

Table 10.4   *Disposition of 1973 Housing Stock by Region (Thousands of Dwelling Units)*

	1973 Stock	Same in 1983	Total Losses	Demolition and Disaster
United States	78,484	70,739	6,097	2,444
MSA	52,885	48,472	3,243	1,510
Central city	25,087	22,556	1,731	1,009
Outside	27,797	25,916	1,512	500
Northeast	18,501	16,942	979	442
MSA	14,123	12,964	695	341
Central city	6,545	5,766	477	252
Outside	7,579	7,198	217	89
Midwest	21,126	19,205	1,502	671
MSA	13,507	12,411	603	461
Central city	6,425	5,688	513	351
Outside	7,082	6,724	290	110
South	24,758	21,773	2,552	983
MSA	14,080	12,731	1,080	449
Central city	7,163	6,481	485	270
Outside	6,917	6,251	595	180
West	14,099	12,819	1,064	348
MSA	11,175	10,365	665	258
Central city	4,955	4,621	256	137
Outside	6,220	5,744	409	122

Source: Data obtained from the U.S. Department of Commerce, Bureau of the Census. "Components of Inventory Change." *Census of Housing* (Washington, D.C.: Government Printing Office, 1983).

precede demolitions). The remaining 3.7 million units of the 1973 stock that had disappeared by 1983 were converted to nondwelling uses (such as stores and offices) or were merged (gentrification, for example, may result in the merger of three apartments in a town house into one dwelling). Thus, for the country as a whole, additions to and subtractions from the housing stock by conversion and merger and separation just about balanced at around 6 million units during the ten years. In net terms, construction accounted for virtually the entire growth of the stock, about 16 million units.

☐ Summary

The unifying theme of this chapter is the relationship between the value and rental prices of housing. The rental price is the price of occupying a standard-size house for one year; the value price is the price of the right to permanent ownership. Consumers basically care only about the rental price, while suppliers are concerned only about the value price, making analysis of the market somewhat complicated. This chapter also traces recent movements in value and rental prices of housing, and examines the reasons for these movements.

Questions and Problems

1. Is it possible that dwellings last too long, in that tastes and technology change so that nobody wants to live in the oldest dwellings?

2. Does the discussion at the beginning of the chapter imply that the data in Tables 10.3 and 10.4 understate the increase in the stock of housing from 1973 to 1983?

3. Although housing construction fell dramatically during the late 1980s and early 1990s, the housing vacancy rate hardly increased. That finding is in contrast with earlier housing recessions, when the vacancy rate rose considerably. Why was the recent recession different?

4. Does the cost of capital concept also apply to businesses? If so, do you think that the cost of capital for businesses is greater or less than that for housing? Why?

5. In housing, demand instability shows up mostly in instability in the production of new units, whereas in agriculture it shows up mostly in price instability. Why?

References and Further Reading

Aaron, Henry. *Shelter and Subsidies* (Washington, D.C.: Brookings Institution, 1972). A very good review of housing policies (including the tax law) and the relative costs for homeowners and renters.

Becker, Gary. *The Economics of Discrimination* (Chicago: University of Chicago Press, 1971). A classic analysis of discrimination.

Berry, Brian. "Ghetto Expansion and Racial Residential Segregation in an Urban Model." *Journal of Urban Economics* 3 (1976): 397–423. A statistical study of blacks' and whites' housing costs in Chicago.

Carron, Andrew. *The Plight of the Thrift Institutions* (Washington, D.C.: Brookings Institution, 1982).

Chinloy, Peter. "The Effect of Maintenance Expenditures on the Measurement of Depreciation in Housing." *Journal of Urban Economics* 8 (1980): 86–107.

Chinloy, Peter. "Estimation of Net Depreciation Rates on Housing." *Journal of Urban Economics* 6 (1979): 432–43.

deLeeuw, Frank. "Demand for Housing." *Review of Economics and Statistics* 53 (1971): 1–10. A careful survey of housing demand studies.

Dougherty, Ann, and Robert Van Order. "Inflation, Housing Costs, and the Consumer Price Index." *American Economic Review* 72 (1982): 154–64.

Dynarski, Mark. "The Economics of Community: Theory and Measurement." Ph.D. dissertation, Johns Hopkins University, 1981.

Ellwood, David, and A. Mitchell Polinsky. "An Empirical Reconciliation of Micro and Grouped Estimates of the Demand for Housing." *Review of Economics and Statistics* 61 (1979): 199–205. The best and latest evidence on the parameters of the demand function for housing.

Friedman, Milton. *A Theory of the Consumption Function* (Princeton, N.J.:

Princeton University Press, 1957). Contains the original discussion of permanent income.

Griliches, Zvi. *Price Indexes and Quality Change* (Cambridge, Mass.: Harvard University Press, 1971). A detailed discussion of hedonic price indexes.

Hulten, Charles, and Robert Schwab. "Income Originating in the State and Local Sector." Working paper (College Park: University of Maryland), 1987.

Kain, John, and John Quigley. *Housing Markets and Racial Discrimination* (New York: Columbia University Press, 1975). A thorough analysis of effects of racial discrimination on blacks' housing.

Kaiser Committee. *A Decent Home* (Washington, D.C.: Government Printing Office, 1969). A good summary appears in Kaiser Committee. "The Nation's Housing Needs." *Readings in Urban Economics,* edited by M. Edel and J. Rothenberg (New York: Macmillan, 1972). Has fair amounts of detail on the housing inventory and the character of construction and operating cost.

King, A. Thomas, and Peter Mieszkowski. "Racial Discrimination, Segregation, and the Price of Housing." *Journal of Political Economy* 8 (1973): 590–601. A very careful study of race differences in housing costs. Chapter 12 will refer to this work; it is cited here as a readable example of the use of hedonic price analysis.

Muth, Richard. "The Demand for Nonfarm Housing." *The Demand for Durable Goods,* edited by A. Harberger (Chicago: University of Chicago Press, 1960). One of the first studies of housing demand to use the permanent income concept. It makes excellent reading, as it is easy to see the mechanics of the research strategy.

Pechman, Joseph. *Federal Tax Policy* (Washington, D.C.: Brookings Institution, 1982). An annual publication giving a careful description of the federal tax law.

Peterson, George. "Federal Tax Policy and the Shaping of Urban Development." *The Prospective City,* edited by A. P. Solomon (Cambridge, Mass.: MIT Press, 1980).

Polinsky, Mitchell. "The Demand for Housing: A Study in Specification and Grouping." *Econometrica* 45 (1977): 447–462. An abstract conceptual analysis of housing demand that requires considerable knowledge of econometrics.

Rosen, Kenneth. "The Affordability of Housing in 1980 and Beyond." Working paper (Berkeley: University of California at Berkeley, 1979).

Rosen, Sherwin. "Hedonic Prices and Implicit Markets." *Journal of Political Economy* 82 (1974): 34–55. A fundamental theoretical contribution to hedonic price analysis that requires advanced economics knowledge.

Sternlieb, George. *The Tenement Landlord* (New Brunswick, N.J.: Rutgers University Press, 1969). A study of slum landlords in Newark, New Jersey.

Tanzi, Vito. "Inflationary Expectations, Economic Activity, Taxes, and Interest Rates." *American Economic Review* 70 (1980): 12–21.

U.S. Department of Commerce, Bureau of the Census. "Components of Inventory Change." *Census of Housing.* Table HC (4) (Washington, D.C.: Government Printing Office, 1970).

11

Housing Finance and Investment

☐ The last chapter painted the broad picture of the housing sector in the United States. In this chapter, the focus is narrowed to discuss housing finance and investment. The United States has one of the world's most complex and sophisticated systems of housing finance. The financial system services an enormous and diverse clientele of dwelling owners. Home ownership is the most dispersed form of asset ownership in the nation, far more dispersed than ownership of corporate stocks or of bonds. Nearly two-thirds of dwellings are owner-occupied, and rental dwellings are mostly owned by small proprietorships and partnerships that own only a few dwellings each. This chapter explores how markets and tax considerations motivate and facilitate such diverse ownership.

There is a mystique to home ownership in the United States and in most other countries. Governments and private groups emphasize that home ownership is "the American dream." It is widely believed that home ownership is a superb investment, that it provides an important element of control over owners' lives, and that it is the source of important pride of ownership. House occupancy is a consumption decision, as has been emphasized in the previous chapter. Home ownership is an investment or portfolio decision. An important task of this chapter will be to dissect the dream into its components.

An important consideration regarding home finance is that dwellings are superb collateral. A home owner can help finance the investment with a mortgage that has an interest rate which is about the same as that on a high-grade corporate bond. Furthermore, an enormous variety of mortgages is available to home owners. These facts will be important in helping to answer a key question in the chapter: Is home ownership a good investment?

☐ DEFINING SOME TERMS

People tend to think that everyone knows what is meant when they refer to commonly used terms. Because it is important to avoid confusion, some of the terms used in this discussion are defined as follows:

1. *Dwelling* is a place where an individual or people in a household live. In the United States, it normally consists of a kitchen, one or more bathrooms, and living areas for the exclusive use of the members of the household.
2. *Single-family structure* describes a building that contains just one dwelling.
3. *Single-family detached structure* is a single-family building that is not attached to another structure.
4. *Apartment* is a dwelling in a building that contains at least two dwellings.
5. *Condominium* (condo) is a dwelling that is either an apartment or an attached structure (row house, town house, semidetached house, and the like) that is separately owned and is in a group of such dwellings in which the owners elect a management board that administers common areas (e.g., entry ways, outer walls, roofs, grounds) and levies maintenance fees on condo owners to finance upkeep, repairs, and insurance of common areas.
6. *Cooperative* (coop) describes a dwelling that is either an apartment or an attached dwelling in which coop owners own shares in the entire coop complex, usually proportionate to the square feet of the owner's dwelling.
7. *Owner-occupied dwelling* is a dwelling that is owned by its occupant(s).

It is important to note that a condo or coop may or may not be owner-occupied; its owner may live in it or rent it to a tenant. Likewise, a single-family detached dwelling may be owner-occupied or rented to tenants. In fact, ownership forms are not perfectly related to any structure type. Most commonly, single-family detached dwellings are owner-occupied and apartments are rented. Property rights in apartments and town houses, however, are now well enough defined that they may be owned separately or jointly. Unfortunately, property rights in apartments are still not well enough defined and there are proportionately more disputes and litigation among condo and coop owners than among owners of detached dwellings.

☐ HOUSING OWNERSHIP FORMS AND FINANCE

Ownership Forms

Most private fixed capital in manufacturing, mining, and utilities is owned by corporations.[1] The stock of private housing, which is half of the fixed capital in the country, is almost entirely owned by proprietorships and partnerships. A proprietorship is a single-owner business and a partnership is a business owned by two or more partners. The key legal characteristic of a corporation is that its owners have limited liability; their responsibility for the corporation's debts extends only to the value of their shares. In contrast, proprietors and partners have unlimited liability; all their personal assets can be seized to pay debts of the business. Limited partnerships are common ownership forms for commercial real estate (offices, shopping centers, rental apartment houses); it is a special kind of partnership in which most owners are limited partners—that is, their liability is limited to the value of their ownership certificates. It should be noted that a marriage is a special kind of partnership, governed by many special state laws and court decisions.

Housing Finance

Nearly all fixed capital in business is financed by a combination of debt and equity. Corporate debt consists of a variety of instruments such as bonds and commercial paper. Corporate equity is ownership shares. Real-estate proprietorships' and partnerships' debts are invariably mortgages. A *mortgage* is a loan secured by real estate. Limited partnerships' equities are often ownership certificates, very similar to corporate shares, and many limited partnership shares are traded on stock exchanges. There are normally no equity certificates for proprietorships or for small unlimited partnerships.

A mortgage is similar to a corporate bond. In both cases, the borrower agrees to pay back the loan to the lender on a stipulated schedule. The monthly payment on a mortgage is normally part interest and part principle, which are set so that the debt is retired during the life of the mortgage. Bond borrowers usually make two interest payments per year and pay the principle to the holder at maturity. Thus, most bonds are like interest-only mortgages. Bonds are typically offered for sale to the public, whereas mortgages are typically negotiated between a borrower and a small number of lenders. A bond may contain a call option, giving the borrower the right to pay the entire outstanding value of the bond at any given time, perhaps including penalty payments for early prepayment. A mortgage also contains a call option; the borrower can prepay at his or her discretion. Mortgages on commercial real estate

---

1. Fixed means normally not moved. The important kinds of nonfixed capital are transportation equipment and inventories.

typically require penalty payments for early prepayment. States regulate the ability of lenders to collect prepayment penalties on mortgages on owner-occupied houses, and they are now rare. Prepayment penalties are not permitted on mortgages insured or guaranteed by the Federal Housing Administration or by the Veterans Administration.

The ratio of debt to debt plus equity, or total-asset value, is referred to as leverage. For example, a dwelling worth $100,000 with a $50,000 mortgage has a leverage of 0.5. If leverage is 0.0, the asset is entirely financed by equity. If leverage is 1.0, it is entirely financed by debt. When originated, mortgages are often 70 to 90 percent of the dwelling's value, so leverage is 0.7 to 0.9.

Fixed rate mortgages.

Until about 1970, almost the only kind of mortgage available to dwelling owners was a fixed-interest rate, fixed payment, fully amortized mortgage (FRM, for short). Under an FRM, a fixed periodic, invariably monthly, payment is made such that, after a stipulated number of payments, the principal and the periodic interest on the principal are paid off. For example, a $100,000 mortgage at 9 percent interest will be paid off in 30 years, 360 months, with a monthly payment of $804.60. The monthly payment for a FRM depends on the amount borrowed, the term, and the interest rate. Any hand-held calculator with a financial program will calculate the fourth number if any three of these numbers are punched in. In a FRM with a long term, the first few payments are mostly interest. Principal payments dominate toward the end of the term.

Adjustable rate mortgages.

An adjustable rate mortgage (ARM) is more complex. It also has a fixed term and an initial interest rate that is set by the mortgage contract for a stated period, such as six months or one year. The contract states that, after the initial period, the interest rate will be adjusted periodically in relation to some publicly available interest rate. For example, the initial interest rate might be 7 percent for the first six months, and after that the interest rate might be adjusted every six months to 2 percentage points (200 basis points) above the index of interest rates on Treasury securities with one year to maturity. A variety of such indexes is published in financial newspapers and magazines. Finally, an ARM contract usually stipulates annual and lifetime caps, maximum amounts that the interest rate can move in a year or during the lifetime of the mortgage regardless of the movement of the index. Caps might be 2 percent in a given year and 5 percent over the lifetime of the loan.

An ARM contract is defined by more parameters than an FRM: amount borrowed, term, initial interest rate, interval between changes, index to which the interest rate is tied after the initial period, margin between the index and the ARM interest rate, and annual and lifetime caps.

FRM and ARM contracts account for nearly all home mortgages. Other types are available, however, and should be mentioned briefly.

Shared appreciation mortgages. A shared appreciation mortgage (SAM) is a fixed-rate, fixed-term mortgage, in which the borrower and lender receive contractual shares of the dwelling's appreciation when the dwelling is sold, the mortgage is paid off, or at some other stipulated time. The borrower obtains a lower fixed-interest rate in exchange for the agreement to share capital gains with the lender. SAMs are unpopular, in part because owners often make substantial investments in the home during the life of the loan (adding a bedroom or finishing an attic, for example), and it is difficult to estimate how much appreciation is capital gains and how much results from the new investment.

Reverse annuity mortgages. A reverse annuity mortgage (RAM) is sometimes obtained by retirees who own their home free of any mortgage. With a RAM, the lender sends the borrower a monthly check for a stipulated period, at the end of which the borrower must pay the lender an agreed amount or the lender takes title to the dwelling. In one RAM specification, the owners receive checks and retain occupancy until both die or they sell the dwelling. The terms of a RAM depend on the implicit interest rate, on the anticipated appreciation of the dwelling, and with lifetime tenure, on the life expectancies of the owners. RAMS may involve what economists call adverse selection, in that borrowers who know something about their health that the lender does not know may use the information to obtain a RAM on terms that are actuarially disadvantageous to the lender. In addition, RAM borrowers may be loathe to enter a nursing home when they should because they may lose rights to subsequent checks.

Price-level-adjusted mortgages. A price-level-adjusted mortgage (PLAM) is a fixed-rate, fixed-term mortgage in which the outstanding balance on the mortgage is adjusted periodically to reflect the rate of inflation. If you have a PLAM with a balance of $50,000 on December 31 and the CPI has risen 3 percent during the year, then your balance would rise to $51,500 on January 1. The implication is that the lender can lend at the real rate of interest and need not add on the inflation factor discussed in the previous chapter.

Comparisons. Nearly all home mortgages are FRMs or ARMs. An important reason is that only those mortgages can be sold on the secondary mortgage market, to be discussed. A crucial distinction between FRMs and ARMs is who bears prepayment risk. Most home mortgages have terms of 30 years, but the average life of a mortgage is between 10 and 15 years. Frequently, borrowers prepay because a job change, divorce, death, family growth or shrinkage such as the birth or departure of children, or a large change in permanent income makes the family want a different home. Prepayments for these reasons occur when the call option on an FRM is "in the money" (current interest rates are below the FRM contract rate) or when the call option is "out of the money" (current interest rates are above the FRM contract rate). For example, a couple prepaid a 6.25 percent FRM mortgage and took out an 8.75 percent mortgage when they moved from Princeton to Chicago, an exchange that was painfully out of the money! (Virtually all mortgages have a due-on-sale provision.) Such prepayments occur almost at random relative to the level of current interest rates, which are relative to FRM contract rates. Thus, borrowers tend to prepay FRM mortgages when the prepayment option is in the money.

The FRM borrowers, however, increasingly prepay mortgages when interest rates are below their FRM contract rates. Very roughly, if current FRM interest rates are at least 2 percentage points below the fixed rate on an FRM contract, and there is still at least five years to pay on a mortgage, it is likely to benefit the borrower to refinance. (If there were no transaction costs of refinancing—application fees, closing costs, points —it would pay to refinance, if current rates were only slightly below your contract rate. Sometimes, lenders have "sales" on mortgages, in which they forgive some of the transaction costs.) If there are significant prepayment penalties, current interest rates must be farther below the contract rate.

With the stated caveats, lenders bear prepayment risks with an FRM. If interest rates rise above contract rates, investors take a capital loss, but cannot force prepayment, and borrowers celebrate at an expensive restaurant! If interest rates fall much below contract rates, borrowers prepay. Why do lenders care? One reason is that lenders may bear transaction costs that borrowers do not reimburse if a new mortgage must be originated. However, that would be the lenders' fault: Lenders are free to charge all of their transaction costs to borrowers. (Borrowers are also free to take their business elsewhere.) Much more important is that, to the extent that mortgages are prepaid because interest rates have fallen, lenders get money back exactly when it is not wanted. Lenders must lend the money again at current low rates. Statistically, borrowers tend to prepay FRMs when the call option is in the money, but not when the call option is out of the money. The borrowers' gain is the lenders' loss.

With an ARM, the interest rate goes up and down with market rates, subject to the contractual interval between interest rate changes and to caps. With those provisos, ARMs shift the interest-rate risks to borrowers. Interest-rate risks are large, since interest rates can move several percentage points during a year or so. Inevitably, people must be paid to assume risk. Thus, we should expect interest rates over mortgage lifetimes to be lower on ARMs than on FRMs. With FRMs, lenders bear the risks and must be compensated with higher interest rates. With

ARMs, borrowers bear the risk and must be compensated with lower interest rates.

Comparing interest rates on ARMs with those on FRMs is tricky because those on ARMs move through the life of the mortgage. In addition, the initial interest rate on an ARM is frequently set below what it would be if it were above the initial value of the index by the contractual margin. Such low-interest rates are referred to as "teasers," suggesting that low initial rates may tease borrowers into contracts without borrowers being aware that the interest rates are almost certain to increase in a few months. Nevertheless, typical FRM interest rates are above ARM rates calculated by adding the margin to the index. Borrowers are compensated for bearing the interest-rate risk, but probably not by much. The comparison is difficult, in that ARM contracts can be complex. Some ARMs have initial interest rates that may be fixed for a year or two and may contain an option on the part of borrowers to convert to an FRM.

One might guess that prepayments would be less common with ARMs than with FRMs, since ARM interest rates go down with market interest rates without prepayment. The opposite, however, is the case; prepayments are more common with ARMs than with FRMs. The reason seems to be the teaser rate. Consider a young university graduate who becomes a first-time home buyer in a new job. Having just paid off college loans, there is little money for a down payment, and the initial salary is low. The job's prospects, however, are good, and the graduate expects to stay in the dwelling only two or three years. The graduate takes an ARM with the initial interest rate locked in for two years, and is relatively unconcerned about the rate after the lock-in period. By that time, the buyer expects to be about ready to "buy up." The ARM may be a good choice.

Choosing among mortgages. How should a potential buyer choose among the large menu of mortgages currently available? The answer is shop around and calculate. In many cities, the real estate section of the Sunday newspaper presents data on a variety of mortgages currently offered by local lenders. Lay out a plan that states the likely price of the dwelling you may buy, the likely closing costs, your anticipated length of stay, and the combinations of down payments and monthly mortgage payments you feel comfortable with. (You should be willing to make larger monthly payments and smaller down payments, or smaller monthly payments and larger down payments. Remember, interest rates may be higher for a highly leveraged investment.) Then, use a computer to calculate the present value of a variety of payment options that the newspaper menu provides. You may need to phone a few lenders to obtain details not provided in the newspaper. For example, lenders have underwriting standards to qualify lenders: monthly mortgage payments relative to take-home pay, leverage limits, and so on. The object is to find the mortgage among those available that has minimal present value of payments and satisfies the plan you have laid out. Once you have found a solution, shop around. Use the telephone to find out if some lenders may be willing to do better than the conditions in the newspaper. They may be intending to have a "sale," or they may be willing to provide more attractive terms to an especially high-quality borrower.

Secondary Mortgage Markets

Three distinct functions must be performed in connection with mortgages: origination, investing, and servicing.

Origination is a marketing activity. The availability of mortgages must be advertised, applications must be accepted and evaluated, loans must be approved, contracts must be drawn up, and loans must be issued and financed.

Investing refers to the fact that someone must hold the mortgage during its life. Investors hold a mortgage for the same reason that investors hold bonds: because of the interest income that it yields.

Servicing refers to collecting monthly payments, keeping accounts, and answering borrowers' inquiries. Among the important tasks of the servicing organization is the administration of escrow accounts. An *escrow account* is an account held by the servicer and into which the borrower pays funds that the servicer uses to pay real estate taxes and hazard insurance premiums when they are owed. Most mortgage contracts specify that an escrow account is to be maintained. Borrowers make monthly escrow account payments (along with their debt-service payments) equal to one-twelfth of the taxes and insurance premiums that the servicing organization estimates will be owed during the next 12 months. At closing, borrowers make an initial payment to the escrow account, such that with monthly payments, the account balance will be adequate to pay the bills when they come due, plus a reserve of one or two months' escrow payments. The mortgage servicers must manage the escrow account and answer borrowers' inquiries about the account. Escrow accounts provide a service to borrowers and protection for investors.

Until about 1970, all three functions were typically performed by the same institution, most often a local savings and loan association to which buyers applied for a mortgage. During the last quarter century, the development of a secondary mortgage market, plus gradual deregulation of financial markets, have revolutionized the housing finance sector. The key development is that originators no longer need to be substantial investors. That need restricted mortgage origination to institutions with large amounts of assets to invest in the mortgages they originated, almost exclusively depository institutions. Now originators can sell the mortgage to an institution that packages similar mortgages and issues bonds that are backed by the mortgages. The most important of such institutions are two governmental or quasi-governmental institutions, the Federal National Mortgage Association and the Federal Home Loan Mortgage Corporation. The bonds are sold on bond markets, just like other governmental and corporate bonds.

The secondary mortgage market is now extremely large, with trillions of dollars worth of bonds outstanding. The growth of the market has been highly advantageous to home buyers. Most important is that it has gotten mortgages into the national and international bond markets, helping to integrate financial markets and helping to mitigate regional and cyclical variations in mortgage interest rates. Also important is the entry of nondepository institutions into the mortgage-origination sector, making it more competitive. Lending institutions can sell their mortgages soon after origination, so they can turn their money over quickly (on very tight margins) and thus originate mortgages even if they have only modest assets. Finally, the characteristics that make mortgages saleable in the secondary market—15- or 30-year terms, FRMs and ARMs, common underwriting criteria—have enabled borrowers to shop for mortgages on the basis of important characteristics and to compare alternatives precisely.

The mortgage-origination sector is highly dispersed. Depository institutions are still the largest originating groups. However, many mortgage-banking firms and other financial firms now originate mortgages. Mortgage investing is also dispersed, as much as the bond-holding sector. Insurance companies, pension funds, and large industrial corporations invest in mortgage-backed bonds. Depository institutions still invest in mortgages, especially in mortgages that they originate but cannot be sold on the secondary market. Depository institutions are large investors in mortgage-backed bonds; they are preferable to mortgages because they can be bought and sold at any time with minimal transaction costs. Mortgage servicing is dispersed, but computerization gives an advantage to large servicers who handle thousands of mortgages. An efficient servicer should be able to bring the details of a mortgage and escrow account onto a computer screen, answer queries, and settle problems in one phone call with the client. The largest servicer services only about 2 percent of mortgages that are outstanding. The secondary mortgage market handles almost exclusively home mortgages; a secondary market is developing slowly for mortgages on commercial real estate. Mortgage-backed bonds can, however, be issued, backed by mortgages on apartment houses.

☐ TAXATION OF HOUSING

Rental housing is taxed differently from owner-occupied housing. Some housing is both: A landlord may live in one of the apartments in the building. In that case, part of the building is taxed as owner-occupied and part is taxed as rental housing. Usually, the division is in terms of square feet of floor space. Taxation of housing is complex in detail, but simple in basic outline. Almost all privately owned housing is subject to real estate taxes. Local governments assess the dwelling, usually at a fraction of its estimated market value. In some places, the law states that assessments should be at full-market value; in other places, the law may state a target fraction of market value as an assessment goal. Nevertheless, assessment is rarely at full-market value. Assessment is an administrative matter; the local legislature sets a tax rate per dollar of assessed value. In many jurisdictions, rental housing is assessed at a larger fraction of market value than owner-occupied housing. In metropolitan communities, annual real estate taxes tend to be 1 to 2 percent of the dwellings' market values.

The remainder of this section is about federal income taxation. Most states also have income taxes, and state taxes invariably include income on rental dwellings. Provisions vary, but state income taxes on income from rental dwellings are deductible on the federal tax form. State income taxes are mostly 5 to 20 percent of the taxpayer's federal income tax liability.

Rental Housing

Virtually all privately owned rental housing is owned by proprietorships or partnerships. These are *pass through* organizations, meaning that all their income is passed through to the organizations' owners, and the owners are taxed at personal income-tax rates. Proprietorships and partnerships, unlike corporations, do not pay taxes, but all their income is subject to tax by their owners, whether the income is distributed to owners or retained by the business.

Taxable income from operating rental housing is based on rents received minus all normal and necessary costs of doing business. Costs include mortgage interest, insurance, maintenance, repair, depreciation, utilities (if paid for by the owner) and costs of marketing the apartments. Annual depreciation for tax proposes is straight line over 27.5 years. That means that $100 \ (1/27.5) \cong 3.6$ percent of the basis can be subtracted from rents each year for 27.5 years in computing the owner's yearly taxable income. The basis on which depreciation is calculated is purchase price plus transaction costs at time of purchase. The annual tax liability is taxable income multiplied by the owner's tax rate, which was 0, 15 percent, or 31 percent in 1992, depending on the owner's taxable income.

On sale, the owner pays capital gains tax. The capital gains tax base is ([sale price − transaction costs of sale] − [purchase price + transaction cost of purchase − accumulated depreciation since purchase]). Capital gains tax liability is the capital gains tax base multiplied by the taxpayer's income-tax bracket.

If either taxable income from operating the property or the capital-gains tax base is negative, the loss can be carried forward under complicated rules.

Owner-Occupied Housing

Because there is no market rent, the federal government does not levy income taxes on owner-occupied housing. For the same reason, owner-occupied houses cannot be depreciated for tax purposes. Real estate tax payments and mortgage interest, however, can be deducted on the federal personal income-tax form, provided the owner itemizes. It is worthwhile for most owner-occupiers to itemize.

Owner-occupied housing receives favorable treatment regarding capital gains taxation. If an owner-occupier sells the home and purchases another home to occupy within two years, and pays at least as much for the new home as was received for the old home, then capital gains taxation is deferred.[2] An owner-occupier can continue to defer capital gains taxes on principal residences by such sales and purchases, provided the requirements are satisfied. In addition, once at least one owner-occupier spouse reaches 55 years of age, a once-in-a-lifetime capital forgiveness of up to $125,000 on owner-occupied property may be taken. If capital gains tax is paid on an owner-occupied dwelling, the tax equals the capital gains times the tax-payer's tax rate.

Finally, unrealized capital gains on owner-occupied housing or on any other asset are forgiven at death. For tax purposes, heirs value the property at its market value at the time of the owner's death, but neither the deceased owner's estate nor the heirs pay capital gains tax on the asset.

Comparison

Federal taxation of real estate is absurdly complex. Congress tries to make so many distinctions in the tax status of various groups that the laws, regulations, and important court decisions would fill a good-size room.

---

2.   The correct terms are the bases, not the purchase prices, of the old and new properties. The bases take account of transactions costs of purchase or sale, and of some other items. In addition, the home must be the principal residence and must have been occupied by the owner for a stipulated period prior to sale. There is a somewhat similar provision for capital gains tax forgiveness on rental dwellings (and other commercial real estate) called a Section 1031 like-kind exchange, but the eligibility conditions are much more restrictive than those for capital gains tax deferment on owner-occupied homes.

There are three important differences between taxation of owner-occupied and rental dwellings. First, net rental income is taxed for rental dwellings but its counterpart, net imputed rental income, is not taxed for owner-occupied dwellings.[3] As with landlords, owner-occupiers are permitted to deduct real estate taxes and mortgage interest despite the fact that net imputed rent is not taxed. Second, landlords can deduct depreciation, whereas owner-occupiers cannot, and the permitted depreciation is considerably greater than actual depreciation.[4] This tax shelter is also available to owners of depreciable commercial real estate. Third, capital gains are virtually untaxed on owner-occupied dwellings, whereas they are taxed on realization at income-tax rates for rental dwellings.

Do these tax differences affect the rent landlords must charge compared with the inputed rent that homeowners charge themselves? The answer is yes. Return to the example of the owner-occupier's inputed rent just following Equation (10.6) in Chapter 10. In that example, the rent to value ratio (R/V) was .07. To compare that with the competitive rent on the same dwelling if it was rental instead of owner-occupied, take out the capital gains in both cases. If one assumes that the ownership by the landlord or owner-occupant is long term, capital gains and capital gains taxes will not be cash flows for many years, so the present values of those flows will be small. Thus, the rent to value ratio for the owner-occupier becomes .082, and the inputed rent becomes $16,400 per year, or $1,370 per month.

For the rental option, the calculation is a little more complex. Assume that the landlord's after-tax cash flow must yield a return of 8 percent, or an after-tax return of $.08\,(1.00 - .31) = .055$ on the landlord's equity. Then, competitive rent must be

$$R = \text{costs} + .055\,(V - M), \tag{11.1}$$

where M is the landlord's mortgage balance. Then, the calculation

---

3. If Congress wanted to tax inputed rental income on owner-occupied dwellings, the cost of capital formula in the previous chapter would be the place to start. Capital gains would need to be removed from the formula, since it is taxed separately. The Swedish government has made a half-hearted attempt to tax inputed rental income of owner-occupied housing, but it appears to be the only country that has made the attempt.

4. If a dwelling lasts 50 years, real depreciation averages 2 percent per year. With an inflation rate of 2 to 4 percent per year, most dwelling prices increase in an average year. It has been pointed out that the accumulated depreciation since purchase is added in computing the landlord's capital gains tax base on sale of the property. Thus, if all else is equal, each dollar of depreciation during the ownership period increases the taxable capital gains at the time of sale by one dollar. Depreciation is thus best viewed as a loan by the government to the landlord that must be repaid at the time of the sale. Thus, the benefit of depreciation to the landlord is the after-tax interest that can be saved because of the depreciation loan.

indicates that the rent to value ratio (R/V) is .097, the annual rent is $19,390, and the monthly rent is $1,620.[5]

The conclusion from this realistic example is that the inputed rent for a $200,000 owner-occupied dwelling is about 15 percent lower than the competitive rent for the same dwelling, because of the differences in tax status. Different parameters would yield different conclusions, but the 15 percent difference is typical for American dwelling values and the other parameter values in the early 1990s. The reader can redo the calculation for other parameter values. Owner-occupancy is indeed a tax-favored ownership status.

☐ IS OWNER-OCCUPANCY A GOOD INVESTMENT?

Dwelling occupancy is a consumption decision; home ownership is an investment or portfolio decision. The demand for housing has been discussed extensively; this section analyzes the portfolio decision. In earlier decades, apartments were almost impossible to own separately and were almost always rented. Now, property rights have become well-enough defined so that any physical type of dwelling can be owner-occupied or rental. The division between the two forms of occupancy is demand driven.

The most common answer to the portfolio question is the rhetorical question: Why pay it to a landlord when you can pay it to yourself? The fallacy in this question is that housing entails large and real costs, such as taxes, interest, and insurance. Indeed, as has been shown, the same kinds of costs are incurred by owner-occupiers as by landlords. Neither owner-occupiers nor landlords have any monopoly power, so neither group can expect to receive more than competitive returns on the investment. The only component of housing cost that an owner-

---

5. Equation (11.1) can be written

$$R = iM + (T+c)V + \text{income tax} + .055\ (V-M).$$

The landlord's income tax liability is

$$\text{income tax} = t[R - iM - (T+C)V - dfV],$$

where d is the depreciation rate for tax purposes and f is the fraction of the property value that is structure (the land cannot be depreciated).

Using the parameter values used in Chapter 10, the parameter definitions and values are as follows:

$$V = \text{market value of dwelling} = \$200,000$$
$$i = \text{mortgage-interest rate} = .08$$
$$T = \text{real estate tax rate} = .01$$
$$c = \text{all other recurrent costs} = .02$$
$$t = \text{income-tax rate} = .31$$
$$M = \text{mortgage balance} = 150$$
$$d = \text{depreciation rate} = 1/27.5 = .036$$
$$f = \text{fraction of property value that is structure} = .8$$

occupant pays to himself or herself is the return on equity in the dwelling. As we have also seen, landlords also must receive a competitive return on their equity; otherwise, they would not hold the asset.

Homeowner advocates sometimes take a different stance. Someone may say, "The next President of the United States is likely to follow policies that will raise the rate of inflation and interest rates, so this is a good time to buy a house and get a mortgage, while house prices and interest rates are low." The fallacy in this stance is that it assumes that the speaker can outguess the market. To the extent that homeowners and mortgage lenders anticipate inflation, prices and mortgage-interest rates take the anticipated inflation into account. If you can outguess the market, if you can forecast inflation better than others, then you can make money in the housing market, or in many other markets. But remember, thousands of market participants are trying to do the same thing!

In fact, about 65 percent of Americans are owner-occupiers, and 35 percent are renters. Is one group rational and the other irrational? That seems unlikely. If not, what circumstances make it rational for one group to be owners and the other to be renters?

In the long run, MSA housing prices tend to increase about one percentage point faster than the rate of inflation. The important reason is that the metropolitan population grows faster than the overall population and, therefore, MSA land values rise a bit faster than the rate of inflation. That finding suggests a real rate of return on housing investment of about 1 percent, whether you are an owner-occupier or a landlord. That return is not very high on an illiquid and risky investment. Stocks listed on the New York Stock Exchange provide an average real return of 8 or 9 percent.[6] Now suppose that the dwelling purchase is financed by a 75 percent mortgage and that the mortgage-interest rate is about the return that the dwelling investor could earn on an alternative and similarly risky investment. Then the landlord or owner-occupier receives the entire 1 percent real return on his or her 25 percent equity, or a total real return of 4 percent. That is not as good as the stock market, but better than an unleveraged investment in corporate or government bonds.

The preceding example is meant to identify the ball park for housing returns, but does not distinguish between owner-occupancy and rental status. In fact, there are two important differences between the two forms of occupancy: tax status, which has been discussed, and transactions costs. Transactions costs refer to the costs of buying, selling, or renting a dwelling. They are incurred by the occupant, at the time of moving in or out. They are one-time costs, not recurrent, so they are not part of the cost of capital, and have not been included in the cost of capital equations in the previous chapter.

---

6. See Brealey and Myers (1991), p. 131.

Transactions costs of both renters and buyers include the financial and time costs of searching for a dwelling and the cost of moving possessions and people from one dwelling to another. Movers incur much greater costs searching for a dwelling to buy than for a dwelling to rent, since the investment is much greater. In addition, for a renter, transactions costs include the interest cost of a security deposit. For a buyer, transactions costs also include fees and points on a mortgage, and any other fees and taxes that must be paid when buying a dwelling. When the dwelling is sold, a buyer must be found, and a realtor is normally retained for the purpose. Legal advice may be needed for the purchase or sale, or both. Transactions costs vary from person to person and from move to move, but on the average, the transactions costs of buying a home are probably about 5 percent of the value of the dwelling, and perhaps 2 percent of the value of the dwelling for a renter. Transactions costs for selling the owner-occupied dwelling are probably about 10 percent of the dwelling's value, the big difference being that the realtor's fee is paid by the seller. For a renter, the transactions of moving out are probably about the same as those of moving in, about 2 percent of the dwelling's value.

We have seen that the cost of capital is lower for owner-occupiers because of differences in tax status, and we have now seen that transactions costs are higher for owner-occupiers than for renters. An easy implication of these facts is that people who expect to stay in the dwelling for many years are much stronger candidates for owner-occupancy than are those who anticipate short stays. Longer stays mean that the lower capital costs can dominate the one-time transactions costs.

To make the comparison precise, we employ Equation (11.2) for the buyer's total costs,

$$PV_{H0} = \sum_{t=1}^{T} \frac{R_{Ht}}{(1 + r)^t} + (C_{H0} + V_0 - M_0) - \frac{V_{HT} - M_T - C_{HT}}{(1 + r)^T};$$

(11.2)

and Equation (11.3) for the renter's total costs;

$$PV_{L0} = \sum_{t=1}^{T} \frac{R_{Lt}}{(1 + r)^t} + C_{L0} + \frac{C_{LT}}{(1 + r)^T}.$$

(11.3)

In these equations, the move-in date is designated 0 and the move-out date is designated T. The two equations are the discounted costs of occupancy for the buyer and renter for the T periods of occupancy. H refers to the homeowner and L to the renter (R has been used, so L, for landlord, is used, although the costs are those of the tenant.) C stands for transactions costs and the subscripts indicate whose transactions costs are represented and when they are incurred.

R_H refers to the owner's periodic cost of capital,

$$R_{Ht} = r_m M_t (1 - T_y) + T_{Rt} V_t (1 - T_y) + e V_t - DM_t. \qquad (11.4)$$

Equation (11.4) is similar to Equation (10.6). *VM* is the mortgage-interest rate and *Mt* is the mortgage balance. Because mortgage interest is deductible, the after-tax mortgage interest cost is $1 - Ty$ times the interest payment, where *Ty* is the owner's marginal income tax rate. *TR* is the real estate tax rate, relative to the property's value *V*. It is also deductible. *e* is nondeductible maintenance, insurance, and repair costs per dollar of the dwelling value. *DM* is the mortgage principal payment.

At time of purchase, the home buyer must lay out the transactions costs C_{H0} plus the downpayment $V_0 - M_0$. At the time of sale, the seller receives the sale price less the terminal mortgage balance and the transactions costs C_{HT}. The discount rate is *r*, and it should equal the owner's foregone (that is, the return the owner foregoes by investing in the home) after tax return on the equity in the home.

Equation (11.3) is much simpler, since none of the renter's costs are deductible. *Rt* is simply the rent the tenant pays the landlord, and the two transactions costs are incurred at the beginning and at the end of occupancy.

For any given anticipated occupancy length, the tenure status should be chosen that has the smaller PV_0. Because the subject here is the portfolio choice, not the consumption decision, it is assumed that the two dwellings are similar and have the same value *V*. As has been shown, the division between owner-occupancy and rental status is demand-driven, and any dwelling will be sold to a landlord or to an owner-occupant according to who offers the largest amount for the dwelling, which depends only on the *PV* comparison.

If the purchase decision is made, the dwelling must be financed. It is assumed that the buyer obtains a conventional fixed-interest fixed-term mortgage. The periodic payment for principal and interest is

$$P = r_m M_{t-1} - DM_t. \qquad (11.5)$$

The first term on the right side is the interest payment and the second is the principal payment (*DM* is the principal payment, so it is negative, and $-DM$ is the principal reduction. Any calculator with a financial mode can calculate *P* if *rM*, M_0, and the term of the mortgage are entered.)

Unlike Equation (10.6), Equation (11.2) does not include the capital gains term. The reason is that Equation (11.2) contains explicit time trends, and capital gains are recorded when they are received. The capital gain (or loss) on the dwelling is $V_{HT} - V_{H0}$, and the discounted value, if there is any increase in price, is included in Equation (11.2).

A numerical example will illustrate how the equations can be used to make the decision to rent or buy. The parameter values used are shown in Table 11.1. The parameters chosen are realistic, but they vary from one situation to another. Dwellings with a purchase price of

Table 11.1 *Base Case Parameter Values (Flow Parameters at Annual Values; Dollar Figures in Thousands)*

V_0	Purchase price	$200.0
M_0	Initial mortgage	$150.0
r_M	Mortgage interest rate	0.1
t_y	Marginal income tax rate	0.28
t_r	Real estate tax rate	0.02
r_E	After-tax discount rate	0.072
n	Nondeductible ownership costs	0.02
V_{Ht}	Property value in year t	$V_0(1.05)^t$
R_L	Rent to value ratio	0.07
C_{H0}	Transaction cost at purchase	$0.05V_0$
C_{L0}	Transaction cost at time of renting	$0.02V_0$
C_{HT}	Transaction cost at sale	$0.1V_T$
C_{LT}	Transaction cost at end of rental	$0.02V_T$

$200,000 are considered. That price is about twice the national average, but the conclusion is unchanged in this analysis if V_0 and M_0 are both raised or lowered in the same proportion. It is assumed that a mortgage for $150,000 is obtained if the purchase option is chosen. The mortgage is for 30 years, at a 10 percent interest rate, which is a little high at the time of this writing. A lower mortgage-interest rate, however, would lower not only the homeowner's costs but also the landlord's costs, and competition would force the landlord to pass the savings on to tenants.

How long an occupancy should a family expect to make a purchase a better form of tenure than a rental? The answer is the smallest value of T for which Equation (11.2) is less than Equation (11.3). For the parameter values in Table 11.1, the answer is 7.5 years. For any shorter occupancy, the higher transactions costs of owner-occupancy outweigh the fact that P_{Ht} is less than P_{Lt}. Of course, other parameter values give different results. Perhaps most surprising, if the tax rate is 15 percent and all other parameters retain their values in Table 11.1, it does not pay to buy, regardless of the length of occupancy.[7] The deductibility provisions are simply not worth enough in tax savings to justify the higher transactions costs of purchasing than renting. Of course, other parameter values might justify ownership for a sufficiently long residency. However, a lower priced dwelling with a proportionately smaller mortgage would not change the result, as has been pointed out.

Finally, it must be pointed out that people do not become owner-occupiers simply as a financial investment. Other reasons can be summarized by the term "pride of ownership." That term covers several feelings. One is simply the ability to tell friends that you are a more substantial community member than others are. Probably more important is the greater control over one's life that owner-occupancy provides. It enables one to move at one's wish instead of at the landlord's wish, it

---

7. The discount rate r is the after-tax rate, so it must be raised if the tax rate is reduced.

avoids small squabbles with landlords, and it avoids periodic disputes over lease terms. Of course, owner-occupancy has its problems, specifically being responsible for repairs, maintenance, and hazard insurance. Each person must weigh these issues on an individual basis. The numerical analysis, however, indicates that if you have a modest income, owner-occupancy is probably justified only in unusual circumstances.

☐ Summary

Housing finance is extremely sophisticated in the United States. Many kinds of mortgages are available. Which is the most desirable depends on personal and market circumstances. Homeownership is a large investment. It is risky both because real estate asset prices fluctuate and because ownership is usually highly leveraged. Careful calculations are needed to determine whether ownership is justified and what is the best kind of mortgage to obtain.

Under the twin pressures of high inflation and financial market deregulation in the 1970s, an explosion of new and sophisticated mortgage instruments occurred. These new instruments have greatly increased the efficiency of the mortgage market by offering consumers a wider array of options and by enabling lending institutions to diversify their portfolios by selling their mortgages on the securities market.

Questions and Problems

1. Some people have proposed that the federal government institute a tax credit for first-time homebuyers. The buyer would be allowed to deduct a percentage of the home's value before computing tax liability. What would be the effect of such a credit on the decision to rent or buy? What would be its effect on housing demand?

2. How would you compute the optimum leverage for an owner-occupied home?

3. In inflationary times, ARMs become more common relative to FRMs. Is that because of the borrowers' or the lenders' preferences? Why?

4. Suppose the federal government wanted to revise the personal income tax system to make tax liability neutral with respect to owning and renting. What would you suggest?

5. Canada does not provide the tax preferences for owner-occupancy that the United States provides, yet ownership in both countries is about the same. Why?

References and Further Reading

Brealey, Richard, and Stuart Myers. *Principles of Corporate Finance,* 4th ed. (New York: McGraw-Hill, 1991). A fine text on corporate finance.

Joint Center for Housing Studies of Harvard University. *The State of the Nation's Housing* (Cambridge, Mass.: Harvard Joint Center for Housing Studies, annual).

Mills, Edwin, and Ronald Simenauer. "Homeownership as an Investment." *The Biskind Report* (Evanston, Ill.: Northwestern University, 1991). An analysis from the Center for Real Estate Research at the Kellogg Graduate School of Management of recent trends and prospects for economic returns to owner-occupancy.

Mortgage Bankers Association of America. *Mortgage Banking Basics* (Washington, D.C.: Mortgage Bankers Association of America, undated). An excellent introduction to modern mortgage markets.

12

Housing Problems and Policies

☐ Major housing problems—slums, low quality and high prices for poor people, abandonment, and race segregation—are apparent to everyone. Before looking at these and other problems, however, it is important to put the matter into perspective.

Americans are housed better than at any time in our history, and surely better than the citizens of almost any other country. The available statistics, summarized in the following tables and figures, indicate truly remarkable improvements in the quality of housing since 1940. Note, for example, in Table 12.1 that 55.4 percent of dwelling units in 1940 lacked at least one component of basic plumbing (usually a toilet or hot water, and sometimes both). By 1980, the incidence of incomplete plumbing had fallen to 2.7 percent.[1] In 1940, a total of 9 percent of the units had more than 1.5 persons per room; by 1980, this figure had fallen to 1 percent, and even the number of units with more than one person per room was 4.1 percent. In fact, by 1980, as many as 60 percent of the units had fewer than 0.5 person per room (up from 50 percent in 1970).

Blacks lag behind whites in obtaining quality housing, but they also have made rapid improvements. The fraction of units with more than 1.5 persons per room fell between 1970 and 1980 from 6.9 to 2.2 percent (roughly the same improvement achieved by the population at large between 1950 and 1970).

As can be seen in the table, the obvious and easily quantifiable indices of housing deficiency—crowding and inadequate plumbing—had been virtually eliminated by 1980. This means, among other things, that measurement of subsequent changes in housing quality will be

---

1. It sometimes is argued that these figures overstate the improvement in the quality of plumbing because of frequent breakdowns. For 1978, however, only 2.8 percent of all households reported at least one breakdown of water supply, 0.8 percent reported sewer breakdowns, and 7.5 percent reported heating system breakdowns. Although earlier data are unavailable, it is unlikely that they would show recent deterioration.

Table 12.1   *Housing Characteristics, 1940 to 1980*

Characteristic	1940	1950	1960	1970	1980
Percentage of stock lacking					
complete plumbing	55.4	34.0	14.7	5.5	2.7
Percentage of stock with					
more than 1.5 persons per room	9.0	6.2	3.8	2.0	1.0
Blacks only	n.a.	n.a.	14.1	6.9	2.2
1 to 1.5 persons per room	n.a.	9.4	7.9	6.0	3.1
Blacks only	n.a.	n.a.	14.3	12.5	6.9
0.5 to 1 person per room	79.8[a]	82.9[a]	46.6	42.0	35.0
Blacks only	n.a.	n.a.	40.9	40.5	41.8

[a]Percentage for fewer than one person per room.
Source: Data from U.S. Department of Commerce, Bureau of the Census. *Census of Housing* (Washington, D.C.: Government Printing Office, 1983).

more difficult. We are now at the state of eliminating structural and other defects that are less easily measured. But even taking account of these problems, the best available evidence shows that the quality of housing has continued to improve during the 1980s. In particular, it appears that the quality of low-income housing has continued to improve. Figure 12.1 shows the fraction of the housing stock (respectively, all occupied

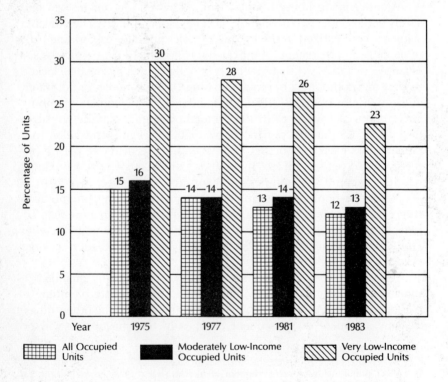

Source: Data from "Low and Moderate Income Housing: Progress, Problems and Prospects" (Washington, D.C.: National Association of Home Builders, 1986).

Figure 12.1   *Percentage of Units that Are Inadequate, by Year and Income Level*

units, moderately low-income units, and very low-income units) judged to be adequate. For both moderately low and very low-income households, the incidence of inadequate housing fell by about 25 percent during the period covered in the figure. As shown, this trend continued in the early 1980s (See Clemmer and Simonson [1983] for detailed discussion of the variables and trends).

Table 12.2 shows that renters, including low-income renters, have been beneficiaries of the improvement in housing quality over the past decade. A somewhat longer, if less quantitative, perspective can be obtained from the *First Report* of the Tenement Housing Commission of New York (1903). The commission estimates that New York City's 82,000 tenements housed some three million people—about 88 percent of the city's population. Although the report lacks statistical summaries, it has vivid descriptions: ". . . conditions . . . so bad as to be indescribable in print, . . . sewer gas throughout houses . . . rooms so dark one cannot see the people in them. . . ." (In a later section, the commission reports filthy conditions the tenants were unaware of because of complete lack of light.) They continue: ". . . [dirt floor] cellars occupied as sleeping quarters, . . . [sinks and cellars] with garbage and decomposing fecal matter. . . ."

Whatever else can be said of housing in the United States, conditions have improved dramatically within the last several decades. If the 1903 Tenement Housing Commissioners could see the housing stock today, they surely would be happy beyond their wildest dreams.

The picture that emerges from these facts is one of dramatic improvement in housing quality over at least the past 80 years, with strong evidence that the quality improvement has continued through the early 1980s. This finding raises the obvious question—What caused this almost continuous rapid improvement?

During most of the twentieth century, real income per capita rose about 2 percent per year, and much of the improvement in housing quality is certainly the result of growth in housing demand caused by rising real incomes. Starting about 1973, however, real earnings growth ceased in the United States. By 1986, real earnings per worker were well below levels in the early 1970s. Why would housing continue to improve if income growth has ceased?

The basic answer is straightforward, although not widely understood. Although real earnings per worker have not grown since the early 1970s, real income per capita has continued to grow. The explanation of the paradoxical pattern has been a rapid increase in the fraction of the adult population that is working. Millions of young women whose mothers stayed home at similar ages are out working. That fact, combined with steady decreases in fertility, means that income per capita has continued to rise almost as fast as earlier, even though earnings per worker have been flat. That process, however, was nearing completion in the early 1990s. By that time, labor force participation rates were very high among young women. Further increases in female

Table 12.2   Characteristics of Rental Units by Household Income, 1974 and 1983

Income in 1983 Dollars	Median Number of Rooms		Percentage of Units with							
			Complete Kitchen		Complete Plumbing		More than One Bath		Air-conditioning	
	1974	1983	1974	1983	1974	1983	1974	1983	1974	1983
$ 3,000– 6,999	3.6	3.7	91.9%	96.7%	88.8%	94.4%	4.3%	8.0%	28.5%	37.3%
7,000– 9,999	3.8	3.9	94.4	98.0	92.5	96.1	5.7	11.5	32.8	45.9
10,000–14,999	3.9	4.0	95.8	98.7	95.4	98.3	8.7	15.2	41.2	51.5
15,000–24,999	4.1	4.1	97.7	99.1	97.6	98.7	13.2	20.3	48.8	58.7

1974 incomes were adjusted to the 1983 basis using the GNP deflator for personal consumption expenditures. Linear interpolation was used to assign households to 1983 brackets.
Source: Data from Annual Housing Survey, Part C, Financial Characteristics of the Housing Inventory (Washington, D.C.: National Association of Home Builders, 1974, 1983).

labor force participation will be limited to the replacement of aging women by younger women who have higher participation rates. Per capita income will soon grow only slowly unless earnings per worker increase.

What about the relative price of housing? The net capital cost of housing rose during the 1980s, because of the rise in real mortgage rates. The result has been, as would be predicted from the price inelasticity of housing demand, an increase in rents paid, but little effect on housing consumption. Remember that rent is the product of price and quantity, so it increases as the price increases, if demand is inelastic. Rents paid by renters rose from 20 percent of income in 1970 to 26 percent in 1991. This dramatic increase results in part from rising real rents per unit of housing. The percentage of households who are owner-occupiers rose somewhat during the 1970s but has fallen slightly during the 1980s. Since owner-occupiers tend to be high-income groups, an increase in owner-occupancy means that renters are increasingly concentrated at the low end of the income distribution. That increase alone cannot be the explanation, however, for the increase in rents relative to incomes in the 1980s and early 1990s. During that period, the correct explanation is that the real incomes of the bottom 20 to 40 percent of the income distribution have declined since the early 1980s. Together with the price inelasticity of demand, that finding explains rising ratios of rent to income since about 1980 (Figure 12.2).

Housing costs per unit of quality-quantity-adjusted housing appear not to have risen during the 1980s and 1990s. There appears to be no comprehensive index of rents per unit of housing. The Harvard housing survey for 1992, however, presents a constant quality housing-cost index for first-time buyers, whose housing demands are similar to those of higher income residents. The Harvard index shows about a 20 percent decline in after-tax ownership cost from 1982 to 1991. It also presents, however, an estimate of the owner's expected appreciation, which has also declined, so ownership costs, including the non-cash flow item of anticipated appreciation, has fallen only about 13 percent. It is likely that quality-quantity-adjusted rents have fallen about as much.

☐ HOUSING PROBLEMS

None of these statistics or descriptions is intended to convey the impression that the United States has no housing problems. Indeed, it takes only a drive through any large city slum to see that the worst-housed 5 or 10 percent of Americans, nearly all of them minorities, are housed abominably. Indeed, one cannot find such bad slums in Northern Europe. We should, however, remember—even as we hope for improvement in the future—that we are in a much better position than we were a generation or two ago.

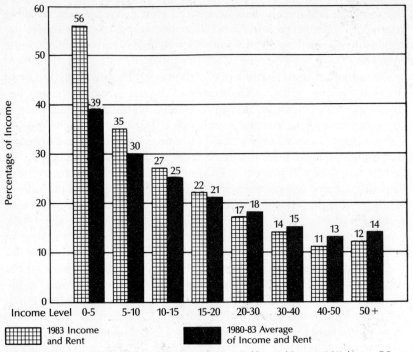

Source: Data from "Low and Moderate Income Housing: Progress, Problems and Prospects" (Washington, DC: National Association of Home Builders, 1986).

Figure 12.2   *Rent-Income Ratios by Income Level, 1983 and 1980-83*

Many of the important social problems surrounding housing—abandonment, slums, displacement, homelessness, and segregation—are linked to two peculiarities of housing. The first is that housing is the most durable capital asset. On the average, housing appears to depreciate about 1 percent per year, and under the right circumstances, a well-constructed house can last indefinitely (many houses in this country are well over one century old, and show no signs of imminent retirement).[2] The second peculiarity is that a dwelling unit, once constructed, is quite inflexible. It is very expensive physically to move a house, and it is also very costly to alter the quality of an existing house—in particular, it is difficult to upgrade a house very much.

Individual dwelling units may be inflexible, but demands are not. As society becomes richer, the demand for housing services increases, which means that there is constant pressure to improve the quality of the housing stock.

Although some upgrading of individual units occurs, the cheaper way to improve the quality of the stock is generally to retire the old

2. Margolis (1982) estimates that housing depreciates at 0.39 percent per annum.

low-quality housing and build new. To see why this is so, recall that the shell of a dwelling unit represents only about one-sixth of the cost. Upgrading frequently means putting a new interior into an old shell. This change involves replacing plumbing and wiring, removing walls to make bigger rooms, modernizing the kitchen and bathrooms, upgrading the heating plant, and installing air-conditioning and thermal insulation. Often, the cost of working around the existing structure—for example, stringing wiring, pipes, and air-conditioning ducts through interwall spaces—makes this finishing work far more costly in an existing house than in a new one.

If a building needs a complete rehabilitation job, known as a "gut-rehab," the cost per square foot is at least 80 percent as high as the cost of new construction. If the foundation or exterior walls need work, gut-rehab may be no cheaper than starting from scratch (assuming that starting from scratch takes place on vacant land and entails no demolition cost).[3]

The last chapter concluded by discussing the notion that construction and retirement form the major mechanism whereby the housing stock is upgraded. In the United States and in other developed countries, the demand for this upgrading comes largely from income growth and from the fact that the demand for housing rises with income.

Durable, hard-to-alter houses and growing incomes, however, result in an excess supply of low-quality housing and an excess demand for high-quality housing. Figure 12.3 illustrates this result. The solid line depicts the size distribution of income at an initial time (a small number of very poor people, a large number of middle-income people, and a small number of very rich people). If the housing stock is tailored to satisfy the demands of these people, there are a small number of very low-quality houses, a large number of middle-quality houses, and a small number of very high-quality houses. At a later time, the size distribution of income has shifted to the right (the dashed curve in Figure 12.3), reflecting secular income growth. Now there is an excess supply of low-quality houses and an excess demand for high-quality houses. Note that this pattern of excess supply and demand is chronic in a society with rising incomes. Put slightly differently, the quality of the housing stock inherited from the 1930s, 1940s, and 1950s inadequately satisfies today's demands, because we are a richer society today, and our housing demands have grown accordingly. To bring the housing stock inherited from past decades up to current standards (governed by current demand, which, in turn, is governed by current and recent incomes), we must either upgrade existing dwelling units or retire them and replace them with better ones.

---

3.   The gut-rehab numbers were provided by Macy Whitney of Knott Remodeling, Washington, D.C.

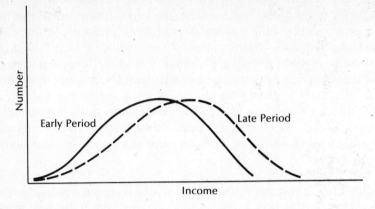

Figure 12.3   *Size Distribution of Income and Housing Demand*

At the end of Chapter 10 it was noted that about two-thirds of housing construction accommodates population growth, with the other one-third serving as replacements for units retired from the stock. It is now easy to see why there is a steady stream of retirements from the housing stock at the same time as new housing is constructed. Indeed, the more rapid the pace of construction, the more rapid is the pace of retirement (holding the number of households constant). It is entirely plausible that much of the retired housing is perfectly sound and inhabitable. Many people express surprise and dismay over the fact that houses are retired from use before they wear out. At least part of this phenomenon, however, is a natural consequence of the durability and inflexibility of the housing stock, along with rising incomes.

☐ ABANDONMENT

In every major U.S. city there are some abandoned dwelling units for which no one claims title. As cited elsewhere in this book, Baltimore has about 7,000 abandoned units; Philadelphia has about 30,000 units; and New York City has about 100,000 units. Each case represents about 3 to 5 percent of the stock. Why this abandonment occurs and what might be done to prevent it are important policy and research questions.

The previous section discussed housing retirement, not abandonment. Abandonment, of course, is one of the ways to retire a dwelling unit—the other way is to reuse the site, either through conversion of the house to a nonresidential use or demolition of the house and sale of the vacant land to another user. Unlike these other methods of retirement, abandonment essentially means throwing away the title—simply relinquishing all rights and responsibilities to the property. This action involves concealing ownership to keep the tax collector and code enforcer away; but in our society, that is not difficult to do.

An Economic Decision

Why would property owners abandon title? Stated in its starkest form, they are likely to do so whenever (1) current and prospective income from the property cannot cover costs and (2) the value of the cleared land is less than the demolition cost. The negative effect of abandonment on neighbors and the possibility that abandonment begets more abandonment will be discussed ahead. For now, however, it is important to recognize that even in the absence of slum externalities, it may be possible that demolition and clearing costs are sufficiently high and urban land values are sufficiently low for abandonment to become the most economical way for a landlord to retire property. The discussion at the end of Chapter 7, culminating in Table 7.3, demonstrates that demolition is frequently not economically justified—even for worthless buildings.

One thing that adds to the relative attractiveness of abandonment is the administration of the property tax in many cities. The typical annual central-city property tax liability is about 2 percent of true market value. However, low-quality housing tends to be overassessed, and high-quality housing tends to be underassessed. Although this regressive assessment policy may be deliberate policy on the part of local governments, at least part of the cause is that reassessments occur, on the average, only every three to five years. Infrequent reassessment while low-value houses are declining in value (the effects of excess supply depicted in Figure 12.3) and high-value houses are appreciating or holding their own means that low-quality houses tend to be overassessed.

In many cities, it is possible to escape property taxation for a few years in anticipation of abandonment. A property tax of about 3 percent for low-income housing represents a substantial fraction of the operating cost of a dwelling unit—about one-third of the total, if the cost of capital is 9 percent. Landlords make a decision several years before they anticipate retiring buildings as to whether the better means of retirement is demolition and sale of the cleared land or abandonment. If they plan to sell sites, they must keep paying their property taxes to retain clear title. If they intend to abandon sites, they stop paying property taxes, immediately reducing their operating expenses by roughly one-third. Closer to the expected abandonment date, they completely stop maintenance, reducing costs by about another third. Finally, they stop paying bills altogether and stop attempting to collect rent. Over a period of five years, it is possible for a landlord to save approximately 25 percent of the initial value of the property in operating expenses, as compared with the demolition and resale strategy.

Another contributor to the attractiveness of the abandonment option, particularly in old Eastern cities, is the gradual decline in central-city land values.[4] In Eastern cities, housing that is ripe for retirement is at least several decades old and built on land near the CBD. At the time the housing was built, the land was quite valuable, so the development was at relatively high density. High density means high-demolition cost per acre (and, of course, it is the per-acre cost that matters, since the end product to be reused is vacant land). In the meantime, however, the land has lost some of its accessibility value, reducing the benefit of demolition and increasing the attractiveness of abandonment. A major component of urban renewal in the 1960s was slum clearance. The strategy was to acquire large tracts through eminent domain, clear the land, and sell it to a private developer.[5] To the surprise of the agencies involved, these programs invariably lost money.[6] But in the light of this discussion, it should be expected that slum clearance is a money-losing proposition, independent of whether it is a good idea.

Finally, consider the effect of the federal tax code, which taxes owner-occupied housing more favorably than rental housing. It is also advantageous to new rental housing, relative to used, to permit more rapid tax depreciation (relative to the actual useful lives) of new structures. The 1986 tax act improved the situation, but depreciable lives are still shorter relative to economic lives for new than for old rental dwellings. This provision increases the attractiveness of new housing relative to old, which in turn encourages replacement construction—construction beyond that which is required by increases in the number of households. For every unit of replacement construction, a unit must be retired. Favorable tax treatment of new housing, by simple logic, brings about retirements from the stock.[7] In an economic environment in which abandonment is a viable retirement strategy, the favorable tax treatment of new dwellings leads to the abandonment of old housing.

Using regression analysis, Peterson (1979) has concluded that for every 100 replacement units constructed in the suburbs, about 10 units are abandoned in the central city. Thus, if the number of households increases by 1,000 and there are 1,500 housing starts in the suburban ring (1,000 housing starts for net growth and 500 for replacement), 500 units will be retired. According to Peterson's estimates, of the 500 retirements, 50 will be central-city abandonments. Peterson counted a unit as abandoned if the Census Bureau classified it either as "standing, uninhabitable" or "vacant, dilapidated." This description, of course,

4. Recall from Chapter 6 that transport improvements can be expected to erode the land-value premium of central locations. This erosion occurs because improvements in transport make city and suburb more alike in terms of accessibility.

5. See Chapter 14 for a discussion of eminent domain.

6. For more complete discussion of urban renewal, see Rothenberg (1972).

7. There is one missing link in this logic. Favorable tax treatment of new dwellings could encourage household formation. In this case, there would be less than one retirement for each induced-tax housing start. This housing price-induced household formation, however, must be small and temporary.

means that 450 units were retired by demolition, merger, or conversion to another use.[8]

In a recent study of New York City, White (1986) has provided important evidence on two other policy questions surrounding abandonment. White begins by noting that properties ripe for abandonment are generally declining in value and, therefore, are typically, overassessed, as assessments are done only every few years. As a consequence, property taxes represent a large portion of the operating cost of low-income housing.[9] If taxes fail to decline with property values, the tax burden enhances the incentive to abandon. Exploring the empirical relationship between the likelihood of abandonment and property tax assessments, White concluded that the relation between the assessed and market property values is an extremely strong determinant of the rate of abandonment. She finds that a policy of speedy reassessment in blighted neighborhoods, coupled with quick foreclosure on property in arrears on taxes, would lead to very large reductions in abandonment. In her analysis of the Brownsville section of Brooklyn, she finds that a 6 percent reduction in assessed value would reduce abandonments by 13 percent. Approximately 80 percent of the property tax revenue lost by the rollback of assessments would be made up by increased collections from the properties that are saved from abandonment. The other 20 percent of lost revenue is more than made up by reduced administrative cost of handling abandoned buildings.

This information suggests a policy whereby cities can reduce abandonments and make money too. White's policy advice is surely sound, and it is encouraging to see that the statistical relationship is so strong. It is not clear, however, that the results would be as striking as they appear on first examination. It may be that White's proposed tax cut would actually reduce abandonment, but another possibility is that it would simply *relocate* abandonment. An examination of abandonment across neighborhoods within a city cannot shed any light on the determinants of abandonment for the city as a whole. To see the entire picture, suppose that local actions (tax assessments and speedy foreclosure) have no effect on the total number of abandonments in the city, but determine only where the abandonments take place. A study such as White's would still show a strong relationship between abandonment and tax assessments, since the observations are of individual neighborhoods. The way to learn whether tax assessment can reduce the overall rate of abandonment in a city would be to carry out an analysis like White's using a cross-section of cities (or MSAs), to see whether cities

8.   Always bear in mind that regression analysis demonstrates correlation, not causation. It is possible that at least some of the causation works in the other direction: the abandonment of dwelling units itself leads to further abandonments because of the unattractiveness of neighborhoods with abandoned housing. This aspect, in turn, leads to an increase in replacement construction in the suburbs.

9.   For low-income housing in Newark, New Jersey, in 1971, Sternlieb and Burchell (1973) estimated that property taxes accounted for 33 percent of rent.

with low-tax rates on low-income housing fare better than cities with higher tax rates (and less aggressive foreclosure policies).

To an important degree, the replacement of old housing with new is stimulated by income growth. Abandonment occurs because replacement construction stimulates housing retirement and because, under some conditions, abandonment is the most profitable retirement strategy. In many cases the administration of the local property tax adds to the profitability of abandonment relative to demolition or conversion. And the federal tax code, with its relatively favorable treatment of new housing, gives an additional impetus to the replacement cycle and, indirectly, to abandonment. This finding suggests two urgent policy questions. The first question, after considering all the costs and consequences, is, do we want to tax new housing more favorably than old—that is, do we want artificially to speed up the replacement cycle? Perhaps instead we should slow down the replacement cycle. In principle, the correct policies are taxation of implicit rents on owner-occupied dwellings and the requirement that depreciable lives equal economic lives for all dwellings, plus a capital gains tax on real capital gains. A less drastic policy change would be to give tax incentives for rehabilitation. The second question, given that some significant rate of replacement is an almost inevitable (and desirable) consequence of rising incomes, is, what is the most efficient encouragement for retirement of old housing and reuse of the land?

Some Effects of Abandonment

So far this discussion of abandonment has focused on a narrow issue: The abandonment method of retirement is a profitability decision, and retirement itself is the natural consequence of rising incomes. Abandonment, however, has serious adverse external effects on the neighborhood containing the abandoned property. For example, Sternlieb (1973) notes that abandoned residential buildings accounted for 21.2 percent of all severe fires in Newark, New Jersey, in 1970 and 1971. Although it is difficult to quantify, it is easy to see how the problem feeds on itself. Abandoned houses reduce the safety and attractiveness of a neighborhood (most likely, a neighborhood that contains a good deal of housing ripe for retirement), which in turn, depresses property values. This deterioration in property value increases the relative profitability of abandonment for the houses that are the next candidates for retirement by reducing the value of cleared land relative to the cost of demolition. In addition, residents are encouraged to move out of the neighborhood, implying that the retirements (which would have occurred somewhere) are likely to be concentrated in the neighborhoods where abandonment first took root. In a few cases, such as the worst slums of New York City and Chicago, the externalities are so damaging that even completely cleared land has no market value, even though land a few miles away is worth several hundred thousand dollars per acre.

Causation, however, need not go simply from old houses to abandonment to more abandonment. Suppose that the underlying problem is high violent-crime rates in a neighborhood of old dwellings; that type of problem would make the neighborhood an undesirable place to live and do business, causing a pervasive fall in land and property values. Then, the entire neighborhood would be ripe for abandonment, and each dwelling might be abandoned as its rents fall below the level of operating costs.

Indeed, there exists the logical possibility that the cycle will become even more vicious. Abandonment, through its effect on the neighborhood amenity level, reduces the quality of neighboring dwellings. This quality reduction stimulates the demand for new housing in suburbs and further increases the rate of retirement. Some of this abandonment-induced retirement would be in the form of abandonment.

The odds are that a variety of factors interacts and exacerbates the abandonment problem in marginal inner-city neighborhoods. The preceding paragraphs are more a statement of concern and research agenda than a description of economists' knowledge about the links among abandonment, neighborhoods, and cities. In fact, very little quantitative knowledge is available about the interaction between abandonment and neighborhoods.

☐ FILTERING

The notion of *filtering* in the housing market is basically the observation that most people—and particularly most poor people—live in hand-me-down housing. As every younger sibling knows, hand-me-down consumption is a mixed blessing. So it is with housing.

Figure 12.3 shows how filtering works. As a dwelling ages, the rent it can command falls. One reason is that old houses produce fewer housing services than new houses, simply because of the ravages of time. More important, as the discussion of abandonment emphasized, income growth means that people demand better and larger housing as time passes. Thus, rents of old houses must fall to levels that induce people to occupy them. The lowest quality houses, as has been seen, cannot be rented at rents that cover costs, and they are retired. Filtering is a natural consequence of deterioration and income growth. Filtering helps explain several important phenomena.

First it makes clear why almost all unsubsidized construction is of high-income housing. Rents and values are, of course, related by Equation (10.6) for both new and old housing. As we have seen in Chapter 10, dwelling value must equal the present value of its rents during its remaining economic life, plus the present value of the site less demolition costs at the end of its life. Values of old dwellings decline for two reasons. First, as has been stated in the previous paragraph, rents decline. Also, the remaining economic life is shorter for old than for new housing. For these reasons, values of filtered dwellings are far below construction costs. Thus, new housing cannot compete with filtered housing of acceptable quality in supplying the low-income market.

Second the housing-cost savings resulting from the filtering mechanism mean that low-income people, to avail themselves of this saving, must live where the used housing is. Old low-quality (and thus filtered-down) housing is mostly located in the central parts of metropolitan areas, for the simple reason that metropolitan areas were built sequentially from the center out. The housing that was built earliest is generally of the lowest quality (here *quality* means the number and sizes of rooms, in addition to other amenities). According to one recent estimate (Cooke and Hamilton, 1984), the tendency of old, low-income housing to be located in central cities can fully account for the observed tendency for the poor to live closer to the CBD than the rich. In other words, filtering and the location patterns it implies are a sufficiently powerful means of income segregation to explain the entire city-suburban income discrepancy for Baltimore and Houston, the two metropolitan areas Cooke and Hamilton examined. Nevertheless, some segregation results from the fact that blacks are frequently offered suburban housing, only on worse terms than are whites. Because blacks have lower incomes than whites, racial segregation is related to income segregation. This issue will be discussed more fully later in the chapter.

☐ NEIGHBORHOOD EFFECTS

Slums and Neighborhood Effects

So far, housing has been discussed as if the quality of housing services was definable solely by the characteristics of the dwelling unit and its proximity to the city center. In fact, however, the quality of life offered by a dwelling unit depends to an important degree on the character of the neighborhood in which it is located. The economic theory brought to bear on this problem is that of externalities, discussed conceptually in Chapter 8. Qualitatively, the proposition is straightforward: The utility that housing occupants derive from their homes depends in part on the actions of their neighbors—whether they maintain their properties and whether they generate noise, crime, or fire hazards. Particularly in high-density (generally low-income) neighborhoods, residents are keenly aware of the actions of their neighbors. In such a world, suboptimum maintenance of structures is predicted, as some of the benefits of maintenance accrue to neighbors.

If these neighborhood effects are quantitatively important (a topic that will be discussed later), they are likely to have the most serious consequences in the lowest income neighborhoods. First if anything generates adverse neighborhood effects, abandonment does. We have seen that abandonment is concentrated in the lowest income neighborhoods, and it probably spawns more abandonment. Indeed, abandonment may be the catalyst that transforms a stable low-income neighborhood into a slum in which the social fabric comes unwoven. Abandoned housing attracts the most alienated of any city's population, and it is easy to imagine how the social contract governing rights of property and people break down under such circumstances.

The second reason for the importance of neighborhood effects in slums is that much of the low-income housing stock is destined for retirement in the near future. Even if the landlord does not intend to abandon it, the imminence of retirement means that maintenance is reduced, ultimately to the vanishing point. This process makes good sense from the perspective of the entrepreneur: If the roof leaks and the building is to be demolished in five years anyway, buckets are cheaper to buy than shingles, and buying clear plastic is cheaper than reglazing broken windows. The problem is that these visible signs of poor maintenance indicate that a structure is on the way down. This deterioration, in turn, depresses maintenance on neighboring houses, and tenants who can afford to move out do so. In this view, slums, like abandonment, are the messy end product of filtering.

Among the general public, the importance of these neighborhood effects is almost beyond dispute. All of us have seen neighborhoods in which we would not wish to live, even in a mansion. Attempts by economists to document the quantitative significance of neighborhood effects, however, have been largely unsuccessful.

The first attempt to quantify these neighborhood effects statistically was by Crecine, Davis, and Jackson (1967). They reasoned that if certain activities are harmful to neighbors, the existence of these activities in a neighborhood should have an adverse effect on property values. To test for this, they regressed sale prices of single-family homes in Pittsburgh on several variables that describe the character of the neighborhood (the *neighborhood* was defined as the block on which the sold house is located).

By including appropriate variables and grouping observations, they corrected for other determinants of house value, such as accessibility and the characteristics of the house itself. Their findings were surprising. The presence of "undesirable" neighboring land uses, such as row and multiple-family housing, parking lots, light industry, wholesaling, and railroad lines had no systematic effect on the sale prices of single-family homes. Both the magnitude and direction of the effect shifted from one part of the sample to another, and in general, the magnitude of the effect was small.

This finding has proved to be remarkably robust. Other researchers, using more detailed samples and more powerful statistical techniques, have almost uniformly failed to find significant and consistent effects of neighboring activities on property values.

Another branch of neighborhood research provides at least a partial answer to the puzzle of no empirically observable neighborhood effects. The answer, it seems, is that most neighborhood effects are extremely localized geographically. Tideman (1969) estimated the probability of affected parties attending a local rezoning hearing. He found that the probability of attending declines by 50 percent with each additional 80 feet of distance from the site of the proposed rezoning. This finding suggests that even if houses next door to one another are strongly affected by the externality, households a couple of doors away will be almost indifferent. If neighborhood effects are so localized, it is not surprising that statistical studies have failed to uncover systematic effects on property values.

Another reason for the failure to find quantitative evidence of neighborhood effects may be that none of the studies uses slums as its primary data base. As we have seen, these effects are likely to be most important in slums. Neighborhood effects might be unimportant in stable and moderate-to-low-density neighborhoods because of the low density itself, as well as the absence of the worst kinds of neighboring disamenities, such as abandoned and badly deteriorated housing. In the same context, property value might be the wrong dependent variable in these regressions. Neighborhood effects may work as follows: An abandoned building reduces the value of a neighboring building, which in turn is allowed to deteriorate. In this case, the adverse neighborhood effect has revealed itself not in reduced house value (holding quality constant), but rather in reduced quality (and attendant reduced value). If house value is regressed on quality and neighboring land use, quality explains everything and neighboring land use explains nothing. Researchers interested in neighborhood effects and slums must take these interactions into account, although they have not yet done so.

Neighborhood Effects in Stable Neighborhoods

Even in stable, middle-class neighborhoods, there is reason to believe that neighborhood effects are more important than property-value studies indicate. Recently, researchers have begun to explore the possibility that nonconforming uses have little effect on property values for the simple reason that not everyone has the same attitude toward a specific set of neighboring uses. What matters for property-value determination is not whether most people find a neighboring activity distasteful, but whether the marginal bidder finds it distasteful. To take a concrete example, consider a neighborhood through which a railroad runs. Even if 90 percent of the population detests railroads, there is no effect on property values as long as it is possible to sell all the affected houses to the remaining 10 percent who like or is indifferent to railroads. If tastes are sufficiently diverse, this phenomenon can explain the lack of association between property values and neighborhood characteristics of their neighborhoods.

Thornton (1978) obtained interesting evidence supporting this view. He examined several neighborhoods in which high-rise apartment buildings were constructed; in some cases, the construction caught the neighbors by surprise, whereas in other neighborhoods the construction was probably anticipated (as the land had been zoned for apartments for a long time). In the cases in which the apartment buildings were not anticipated, Thornton found that homeowners who lived within 250 feet of the apartment building were about 40 percent more likely to move within the next eight years than were homeowners who lived beyond 250 feet from the new building. Interestingly, the difference in the probability of moving did not emerge until about five years after the apartments were constructed. This finding suggests that, whereas the construction of the apartments encouraged people to move, they tended to wait until the move made sense for other reasons, such as a change in household structure (children moving away, for example) or job location. The evidence, however, also indicates that the nonconforming use (a relatively innocuous one in this case) was distasteful to a significant portion of the population. Presumably, the people who were induced to sell found buyers who were less concerned by the existence of the apartment building.

Given this view, as it stands now, there is little reason for economists or policy makers to be concerned about neighborhood effects, except in slums. People who do not like apartment buildings do not live near them. If one were to be built in a neighborhood, such people sell and move out; they suffer no capital loss, because there are enough people who do not dislike apartments. The market mechanism, according to this story, leads to an efficient sorting-out of people according to tastes.

This conclusion, however, could be too strong. Middle-class communities not only are less vulnerable to neighborhood effects than slums, but they also are better protected. Most middle-class communities have land-use controls, one of whose purposes is to exclude land uses that would have negative externalities. If local government keeps out the most harmful land uses, it is no wonder that scholars cannot find deleterious effects of land uses that are permitted.

Neighborhood Attachment

Many of the economic problems that arise as a result of neighborhood effects occur when there is change in the character of a neighborhood. If a new land use comes in and some residents find it distasteful, they must either suffer the consequences or move. Even if it is possible to move without taking a capital loss on the house, as suggested by the evidence referred to, moves impose high costs on households. People form emotional attachments to their neighborhoods, and moving away to avoid a new neighboring land use necessitates the breaking of these attachments. Obviously, the buyer of the house must compensate the seller for the market value of the property, but not for the psychic losses involved in moving away from friends and familiar surroundings.

Accumulating evidence indicates that many people place a high value on the familiarity and attachments of their neighborhoods and are willing to endure substantial capital or income losses to avoid moving to a strange new neighborhood. The Roskill Commission (1970), studying the possibility of a third London airport, conducted a survey in which they asked people how large a premium over the fair market value of their homes they would insist on before moving voluntarily. The mean value was just under 40 percent—that is, they would not willingly leave their neighborhoods unless they were paid 140 percent of the market value of their houses. A similar result was found by Dunn (1979), who found that residents of a small town in the rural south, on the average, were willing to accept a 14 percent wage reduction (after the local mill went bankrupt) to avoid moving to another town where they could avoid the wage reduction.

Using a more complicated statistical technique, Dynarski (1981) also estimated the amount of money people were willing to forgo to remain in their neighborhoods. Unlike the other authors, he was able to examine the variation in this community attachment among types of people. He found that this "value of community," or value of familiar surroundings, is relatively high for older people (over age 56), blacks, low-income people, and people with friends and relatives in the neighborhood.

This set of findings is important because it tells us that change in the location of various activities imposes serious adjustment costs on people and that these adjustment costs are not recovered in the sale prices of houses.

None of this information constitutes an apology for the status quo. Change, including change in the character of neighborhoods, is the major vehicle on which progress arrives. In any event, it is inevitable. The external costs associated with change, however, are important.

☐ RACIAL SEGREGATION AND DISCRIMINATION

Racial segregation and discrimination are quite different from one another. *Segregation* refers to the physical separation of the races—the tendency of both blacks and whites to live in racially homogeneous neighborhoods. *Discrimination* refers to the situation in which housing is offered on different terms to blacks and whites—or not at all to blacks. Segregation, of course, might be a consequence of discrimination, but it also might be a consequence of benign forces, such as the preferences of both races to live among like people. An important observation in this context is that even people's mild preferences for living with their own race can lead to extreme segregation. Suppose, for example, that everyone were racially tolerant but did not want to live in a neighborhood in which he or she was in the minority. The only outcome that would satisfy this rather weak version of racial preference is complete racial segregation.

Segregation

It is obvious that urban housing markets are highly segregated by race; typically, blacks occupy enclaves in central cities, and whites are distributed between all-white areas of central cities and suburbs. Some of this segregation is due to the facts that blacks tend to be poorer than whites and that there is income segregation for the reasons discussed in Chapters 6 and 7. In fact, however, racial segregation is far greater than could be explained by income differences alone, as Taeuber and Taeuber (1965) have shown. They constructed an index of racial segregation (to be discussed ahead) and a similar index of the segregation that would emerge just because of income segregation and interracial income differences. By comparing the two indexes, they concluded that only about one-third of actual race segregation in 1960 was due to income differences.

This segregation, even if it is voluntary and a reflection of blacks' preference for living among other blacks, imposes significant costs on the black populations of our cities. Black neighborhoods are almost exclusively located in central cities rather than suburbs, and they are frequently located near downtown. Manufacturing jobs have suburbanized rapidly during the postwar era, as has already been shown. A central-city residential location, however, diminishes blacks' access to suburban jobs and, of course, precludes access to suburban schools. We will explore this problem in some detail at the conclusion of Chapter 16.

Measuring Segregation.   For a variety of reasons, it is important to be able to measure the extent of segregation. In part, this process is necessary if we are to do quantitative research on the subject, and in part, it is useful to have an objective measure of whether patterns of segregation are changing over time. The measurement of segregation, however, is more difficult than it might seem, as will be seen.

The most frequently employed measure is the so-called segregation, or dissimilarity, index:

$$D = \frac{\sum_i N_i |(b_i - b)|}{2Nb(1 - b)} \cdot 100, \tag{12.1}$$

where D is the value of the dissimilarity index, N is the urban area population, and b is the fraction of the population that is black. The urban area is divided into areas (census tracts, blocks, or whatever), and the population of each area and the fraction of the population that is black are measured. These are, respectively, N_i and b_i. For each tract i we construct the variable $N_i(b_i - b)$. If $b_i = b$, the fraction of the tract that is black is identical to the fraction for the entire urban area. For that tract, $N_i(b_i - b) = 0$. If this variable equals zero for each tract, then the whole index equals zero, meaning that there is no racial dissimilarity among tracts. This value is, of course, the lowest value the index can take. A value of zero for the index means no segregation (i.e., blacks have the same representation in each tract).

As an alternative, suppose each tract is either all black or all white. For each tract, the numerator takes the value either of $N_i b$ or $N_i(1 - b)$. This situation gives the largest possible value for the index, namely $D = 100$.

This index is the most widely used one in measuring discrimination. Although there are a variety of problems with it, it is useful to point out two in particular. The first problem concerns the selection of the entire reference area, and the second concerns the selection of the subareas.

As regards the selection of the entire reference area, typical practice is to construct an index either for a legal city or for an entire MSA. For either definition, one purpose of constructing the index is to determine whether segregation has increased or decreased through time. If the index is defined for a legal central city, measures of changes in segregation can be badly distorted by migration between the city and suburbs. To take an extreme case, suppose that in 1970 the city has two tracts—one all black and one all white. The value of D is 100— complete segregation. By 1980, all the whites have moved out of the central city to the suburbs. Both city tracts are now all black—the same as the city-wide total. D has fallen to 0—no segregation within the central city at all. The result, which emerged from this example, does not require the extreme assumptions made here. It is quite easy for a city's segregation index to decline simply as a result of the movement of whites out of the city. In general, comparisons of segregation indexes over time are valid only if the race mix of the entire area remains roughly the same. This finding, of course, means that MSA segregation indexes are much more informative than central-city indexes.

The value of the index also depends crucially on how the city is divided into subareas. Consider the following example. Every city block is all black or all white, and the blocks are arranged checkerboard fashion. If the blocks are used as the units of observation in constructing the segregation index, $D = 100$ (complete segregation). Instead, if the units of observation are two-block areas, $D = 0$, since each subarea contains the same racial mix as the entire city. In general, the smaller the subarea chosen, the higher is the value of D.

It must be kept in mind that there is no "right" way to divide a city into subareas for purposes of constructing a segregation index. As a practical matter, most segregation indexes are constructed on the basis of census tracts (typical population, about 3,000 people) or blocks.

We have already noted one of the prime findings to emerge from the study of segregation indexes. The distribution of blacks in metropolitan areas is far from random. Furthermore, by comparing actual values of D

with those that would emerge if low-income people were randomly assigned to low-income housing (and vice versa), how much of black segregation is due to the fact that low-income housing is segregated can be determined. The answer, as noted, is that only about 30 percent of racial segregation can be explained by geographical segregation of housing by quality.

In 1980, Chicago's segregation index was 91.9 (based on blocks) and 86.3 (based on census tracts), giving it a position it had long held—the most segregated city in the nation, although Cleveland was almost identical. Even this extremely high value showed a slight decline from 1970 (93.0), although it may have been solely due to white suburbanization, as discussed. (By contrast, San Francisco's block index was 68.2.) All of these numbers are reported by Kain (1984).

The general pattern is that dissimilarity indices have shown at least modest declines in American cities and MSAs during the past 40 years. Scholars, however, have not yet calculated dissimilarity indexes based on the census of 1990, so little concrete information is available on recent trends. (Calculation of these indexes is straightforward; students who wish to do research projects might find this a fruitful area for study.)

Discrimination

A naive interpretation of the standard microeconomic model would lead to the prediction that race discrimination cannot exist in a competitive economy. The reason is simple: Discrimination is costly. In the labor market, an entrepreneur who refuses to hire blacks would be driven out of business. In the case of housing markets, a person who refuses to sell or rent to blacks would suffer an economic loss. The naive model, however, is clearly inadequate: Blacks and other minorities obviously face discrimination in housing, job, and other markets.

Before exploring problems with the microeconomic model, it is worth noting that there is an important element of truth to the observation that competitive forces place restraints on the practice of discrimination. If black-white housing price differentials become large enough, there is profit to be made in arbitrage (blockbusting), and this practice reduces the price difference. If wage differences are sufficiently large, nonbigoted entrepreneurs (or at least entrepreneurs whose greed exceeds their bigotry) can hire black labor at a lower wage than can their bigoted competitors, thus achieving a competitive advantage.[10] A side effect will be the reduction of the wage spread. Nevertheless, there are

---

10. There is direct evidence of this practice in major league baseball. When the color barrier was broken in 1947, most teams began recruiting black players, but a few remained all-white for several years.

important reasons to believe that competitive forces will not completely eliminate discrimination.

One of the problems with the microeconomic model in this context is its assumption of perfect information. Information is not perfect, however, and its acquisition is expensive. In the housing market, this can make a major difference. A potential homeowner must be found creditworthy, and a landlord must judge whether a potential tenant can pay the rent and keep down wear and tear on the property. For whatever reason, blacks *on the average* have more unstable income prospects, as well as larger families with more children and fewer adults than do white families. They are worse risks as both tenants and homeowners. Judgments about creditworthiness and likely treatment of the property must be made by landlords and lending institutions if they are to remain in business, yet the information required to make these judgments is difficult and expensive to obtain. A proxy for the information—race—is, however, readily observable. Profit-maximizing entrepreneurs would be throwing away free information if they were blind to the race of prospective borrowers or tenants, and if the entrepreneurs' competitors are not blind to race, the entrepreneurs will be driven out of business. Competitive forces, that is, may place a lower limit, as well as an upper limit, on the price discrimination faced by blacks.

Racial discrimination in job and housing markets has been illegal since the mid-1960s. Since then, earnings of blacks have risen relative to those of similarly qualified whites, but there is spirited debate as to the extent to which the narrowing of the earnings gap has resulted from the legal prohibition of labor-market discrimination. Blacks have also increasingly bought and rented housing in formerly all-white neighborhoods. Discrimination, however, continues to exist in housing and housing-finance markets. Several experiments, summarized by Yinger (1992), have sent matched pairs of black and white applicants to housing sale and rental offices. All such studies conclude that blacks are discriminated against. Likewise, in the late 1980s and early 1990s, many studies analyzed data collected pursuant to the Home Mortgage Disclosure Act of 1975. Nearly all concluded that blacks are discriminated against in home-mortgage applications. The evidence on segregation indicates that blacks and whites can be thought of as facing two separate housing markets. To a good approximation, both restrict their search for housing to neighborhoods of their own race. Predictions can be made about black-white housing price differences based on hypotheses about the interactions between the segregated neighborhoods.

The easiest case to deal with is the one in which there are no interactions: Blacks live on one island and whites live on another. In this case, the price depends on the interaction of supply and demand on each island, and there is no reason to expect a price premium for one race or another. In a more realistic model, however, there is no moat separating the neighborhoods. Rather, there is a thin boundary—a street or a block—and depending on the institutions and the forces, the boundary can move.

The first formal model of housing markets with a boundary is that reported by Bailey (1959), who postulated that blacks are willing to pay a premium to live near whites, but that whites are willing to live near blacks only if they get their housing at a discount. Despite the chauvinistic assumptions concerning preferences, the model is important and revealing. Figure 12.4 shows the price of housing in two neighborhoods and at the boundary under the Bailey assumptions. It depicts the assumption that blacks pay a premium and whites pay a discount to live at the boundary. As illustrated, the prices in the interiors of the two neighborhoods are the same.[11]

The price, however, is higher on the black side than on the white side of the boundary, and this difference generates an incentive to convert housing at the boundary from white to black occupancy—that is, to shift the boundary to the right. Ignoring conversion costs of any sort, this incentive to shift is eliminated only when prices are the same on both sides of the boundary, as depicted in Figure 12.5. Now, of course, blacks in their interior receive their housing at a discount, as compared with whites in their interior.

Putting aside the assumption that everyone wants to live near the whites, this model properly focuses our attention on the boundary and what happens at the boundary. If prices are higher on the black side, will conversion occur until the differential is eliminated? If so, how quickly? A number of general observations can be made.

1. The stronger white neighborhood attachments are, the greater is the sustainable cross-border price difference. In fact, ethnic neighborhoods have been found to be much more resistant to conversion than nonethnic ones.
2. The greater the difficulty of physically altering housing to satisfy black demand (probably to lower quality, given the tendency for blacks to have lower income), the greater is the sustainable price difference.
3. The greater the rate of population growth in the ghetto the greater is that boundary price pressure. Even if boundary shifts completely eliminate any price difference in the long run, the adjustment process might be slow enough that it fails to keep up with population growth. Conversely, the faster the rate of white departure, the more readily are prices equalized.

The standard method of testing empirically for the existence of housing price discrimination is to use hedonic regression analysis, as discussed in Chapter 10. Monthly rent, or house value, is regressed on a

---

11. Remember that this amount is price per standardized unit—roughly per square foot—rather than house value.

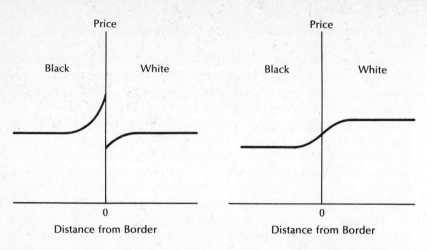

Figure 12.4   *Housing Price in Black and*   **Figure 12.5**   *Housing Price in Black and*
                 White Neighborhoods: *White Neighborhoods:*
                 Disequilibrium   *Equilibrium*

variety of characteristics of the house, of the neighborhood, and of the household itself. The main purpose of the multiple regression is to "hold constant" other determinants of rent (or value) so as to isolate the effect of race. The major difficulty is in gathering a sample with reliable data and making sure that all important determinants of rent variation have been accounted for. There are a number of such studies, and the pattern that emerges from them is interesting.

Studies from the late 1960s and early 1970s tend to find blacks paying rent premiums of 10 to 15 percent.[12] More recent studies, however, drawing their samples from the middle to late 1970s, have failed to find consistent evidence of a housing price markup for blacks.[13] Perhaps the cessation and partial reversal of black migration to Northern cities from the South, beginning about 1970, has reduced ghetto growth rates sufficiently that boundary adjustments have had a chance to reduce or, in some cases, eliminate the substantial price premiums that blacks surely were paying in the late 1960s.

None of these findings indicate that race-related housing problems are behind us, or even that price discrimination has disappeared. First the finding of a declining or disappearing racial housing price premium continues to be the subject of research and dispute. Second other aspects of housing discrimination are important and appear to be in place. Third it is important to realize that this discussion does not touch on the important questions of job-market discrimination and race differences in access to quality schooling.

12.   In one such study, King and Mieszkowski (1973) also found that both blacks and whites prefer to live in homogeneous rather than in border or mixed neighborhoods.

13.   For a good review of this literature, see Yinger (1979).

Homelessness

Homelessness became a public issue in the early 1980s. Residents of large cities became more and more aware of increasing numbers of poorly clothed people begging or wandering the streets aimlessly. Although data do not permit the identification of trends, the numbers of homeless people appear to have grown rapidly in the early 1980s and to have stabilized by the late years of the decade.

What does it mean to be homeless? The number of people who have no shelter to sleep in on a given night is a narrow definition and is relatively small, especially on a January night in a northern city. If one adds the people who spend the night in shelters—mostly run by cities and churches—the number becomes larger. If one adds the women and children in homes for battered women and the residents of single-room-occupancy dwellings—mostly walled part way to the ceiling, with a bed and a common bathroom, renting for a few dollars a night—the number becomes larger. If one adds the people who sleep in abandoned dwellings, cars, and detoxification centers, the number becomes still larger. Finally, if one adds the people who are not discharged from hospitals and other institutions because they have no place to go, we get the largest number.

How many homeless people are there in the United States? Estimates range from fewer than 200,000 to more than one million. The most careful estimate, by Burt and Cohen for 1989, is about two-thirds of one million. Some estimates are ideologically biased, upward and downward, but the number of homeless people is difficult to count. Some are uncommunicative, and the population turns over and moves from day to day.

Who are the homeless? A few are teenage runaways who are likely to return to their families or move in with friends after a night or two in the cold. Some are battered women who have escaped with their children from violent men. A few are intact families. The largest group are adult males who are more or less physically fit. Some, but not most, of these men are schizophrenic or alcoholic.[14] Many are simply poorly educated and so unstable, either as cause or consequence of homelessness, that they cannot hold jobs.

Why are there so many homeless? All the problems that homeless people have now were around long before 1980, and do not appear to have become worse since 1980. An exception may be drug abuse, which accounts for an unknown amount of the increased incidence of homelessness during the 1980s. It is unlikely, however, that many homeless people are taking hard drugs; they are too expensive. A well-documented trend in the 1980s was the increasing inequality

---

14. For a variety of reasons, it became increasingly difficult to compel people to stay in mental institutions against their will in the 1950s and 1960s. That process, however, was complete long before the early 1980s.

of earnings. It has been pointed out that real earnings per worker hardly grew after the early 1970s. Real earnings of the bottom 10 or 20 percent of the earnings distribution, however, fell during the 1980s. Some physically able men may simply have fallen below the earnings level at which they could afford much housing. They may simply have become too discouraged in their efforts to maintain a household.

Contrary to much popular writing, homelessness does not seem to be mostly a housing problem. Inner cities have housing surpluses, as has been pointed out. The Harvard study estimates that average real rent of renters rose about 14 percent from 1980 to 1988. Some of that represents increased housing consumption, not just increased rent per unit of housing. Although it is impossible to be certain, it appears that even in the late 1980s considerable amounts of low quality but cheap rental housing were available in most inner cities. Perhaps the blame should be split about evenly between low earnings and high-rental housing costs.

What should be done about homelessness? The short run, or Band-Aid, solution seems obvious. In a compassionate society, people should not be forced to sleep in doorways, regardless of the nature of their problems. Adequate shelters, that are clean and safe should be provided for the homeless, along with a meal. There is probably no feasible way to collect rent from tenants in such facilities, but shelters are not very costly. Many exist now, and the needed expansion is probably not great.

The long-run solution is much less easy. A stronger labor market than the one that existed in the early 1990s would certainly help, at least to curtail increases in the number of homeless people. Job training, health care, and various kinds of counseling are the common suggestions. These issues are beyond the scope of this book, but no one should underestimate the difficulty of dealing with at least many of the homeless people in the suggested ways.

☐ HOUSING POLICIES

Owner-Occupied Housing

Quantitatively, the most important housing program is the favorable tax treatment of owner-occupied dwellings discussed in the previous chapter. There it was estimated that the favorable tax status of owner-occupied housing reduces its rent by some percent relative to rental housing, and Peterson (1979) believes that the tax subsidy is directly responsible for raising the owner-occupancy rate by about 15 percentage points.[15] White and White (1977) estimate that the tax subsidy to owner-occupied housing cost the U.S. Treasury about $10 billion in 1970. A major consequence of this program has been to divert investment from other activities into housing, and indeed this objective was seen as a major one during the 1950s. Savings and loans were created and given special privileges precisely to help channel money into owner-occupied housing.[16] In the 1980s, however, many observers felt that this had gone too far—noting that the diversion of investment to housing has been a diversion of investment from manufacturing and other sectors. The 1970s was a decade of very low productivity growth in the United States (and in the rest of the industrialized world, which might lead us to doubt that housing is the only culprit), and many have argued that some of the investment that went into housing could more usefully have gone into plant and equipment. Also, recall Peterson's argument that the encouragement of housing investment decreases our incentive to preserve the standing stock. A recent paper (Mills, 1988), however, has estimated that the gap between social returns to other investments and to housing, although still substantial, is becoming smaller.

Other important housing programs exist, and many have been designed explicitly to address the problems discussed in the first part of this chapter. The following sections will look at some of these programs and at empirical estimates of their effectiveness in light of the discussion of the problems in the first part of this chapter. Federal housing programs over the postwar era have been directed largely at three goals: (1) the improvement of the quality of housing for low-income people, (2) the removal or improvement of blighted or slum neighborhoods, and (3) the elimination of racial discrimination in the housing market.

Housing the Poor

Programs designed to improve the housing of the poor have been of two types. The first type approaches the problem by increasing the supply of low-income housing and the second by increasing the ability and willingness of poor people to demand higher-quality housing.

15.   In 1940, just over 45 percent of housing was owner-occupied; by 1970, the figure had risen to 65 percent. Some of this increase is due to rising incomes, but most of it appears to be due to tax advantages of owner-occupancy, which became important only after personal income tax rates were raised substantially during World War II. Canada, however, has about the same percent owner-occupancy, and it does not provide the deductibility advantages present in the American tax code.

16.   Another stimulus to owner-occupancy, instituted in the mid-1930s, was federal mortgage insurance. This stimulus led to the standardization of mortgages described in Chapter 11.

Supply subsidies.   The oldest and best known of the programs to supply low-income housing is public housing, which was first instituted in 1937. The federal government provides construction subsidies to state and local housing authorities, who own and operate the units, renting them out (below cost, because of the federal subsidy) to low-income people. Eligibility requirements, which change from time to time, are established by Congress.

Public housing is not an entitlement program, which means there is no requirement that a unit be provided to every eligible applicant. This flexibility, of course, means that the housing authorities have discretion over which applicants they accept as tenants. The authorities, however, frequently have been taken to court over their use of this discretion; their response typically has been to reduce the top income limits for eligibility (thus reducing the pool of applicants). The result, contrary to congressional intent, has been that public housing has been occupied by only the poorest households.

Much of the political support for public housing has come from the construction industry. In fact, the whole program has been terminated more than once, only to be revived during the next downturn in construction activity. For example, the Nixon administration canceled the public housing program in 1973 (a boom year in housing and a year of highly publicized public housing failures), and it was reactivated in 1976 (by which time the bottom had fallen out of construction). In 1982, there were 1.2 million public housing units, just over 1 percent of the stock. The average annual federal subsidy in 1979 was about $2,000 per unit. The Reagan-Bush administrations proposed no more public housing construction, and in fact they recommended the sale or demolition of some of the highest-cost units ("HUD Subsidized Housing Overview," 1982).

By contrast, Section 236 of the 1968 Housing and Urban Development Act made interest subsidies available to private developers of low-income rental housing. This provision was replaced by Section 8 of the 1974 Housing and Community Development Act. Again, rent limits and quality standards are imposed by the federal government. The subsidy for this program has run about $4,000 per unit.

Supply-side programs, almost of necessity, are not entitlements. It is hard to imagine that public housing will be built for every eligible person who might apply. The only way the programs can benefit the poor in general (as opposed to those who just happen to get into the subsidized units) is through the effects of increased supply on the price of available units. These benefits, however, would be expected to be quite modest; the price of low-income housing is already well below replacement cost as a result of filtering. It is possible that public housing does not reduce the price of existing units to any substantial degree, but only increases the rate of retirement from the stock. Some of this retirement surely takes the form of abandonment, if Peterson's estimates are roughly correct. And in a few famous cases, the public housing units themselves were retired within a few years. In the early 1990s, Congress began to fund large-scale rehabilitation of public housing, some of which was more than 25 years old and in abominable condition.

Demand subsidies.   A combination of high-cost, highly publicized failures and doubts about the effectiveness of solutions led people to look for alternatives to the supply-side approaches to low-income housing problems. This reexamination culminated in the Housing and Community Development Act of 1974. It has already been noted that Section 8 of this law provided subsidies to private developers of low-income rental housing. The big departure, also funded through Section 8, was the initiation of rent subsidies to low-income households. The first step in the calculation of the subsidy is the determination of market rent for a "standard" (as opposed to substandard) dwelling in the urban area. If this figure is more than 30 percent of the income of an eligible household, the government makes up the difference with a payment directly to the household.[17] The subsidy is tied to the household—not to the unit—and is designed to stimulate consumption rather than production of new units.

For a household that would have lived in a standard unit anyway, the subsidy program is a pure income transfer. For others, however, the income transfer is conditional upon the applicant's moving into a standard-quality unit. One benefit of this program is that it encourages participants to seek out the cheapest available housing. The tenants are the ones who save if they are able to find a housing bargain.

In 1983, the Reagan administration proposed cancellation of the Section 8 New Housing Program. Almost all subsidized-housing money was proposed to go into a modified Section 8 demand-side program, known as the Housing Certificate Program. The administration anticipated supporting almost one million housing certificates at a cost of $2,000 each by 1988.[18] Congress, however, had not enacted a new housing program by the 1992 election.

Housing allowances.   Housing allowances do not exist in this country except for limited experiments in a few localities. As most frequently proposed, there are two differences between housing allowances and the Section 8 rent subsidy. The first is that the housing-allowance program would be an entitlement. It thus could improve the

17.   Actually, the subsidy is paid by the federal government to the local housing authority, which in turn pays it to the landlord. The subsidy goes with the tenant, however, not with the unit, in the event the tenant moves.

18.   For a more complete discussion, including the rationale for various policy changes, see "HUD Subsidized Housing Overview" (1982). For an excellent survey, along with a good background discussion, see "Low and Moderate Income Housing: Progress, Problems, and Prospects" (Washington, D.C.: National Association of Home Builders, 1986).

housing standards of all eligible households, not just those whose applications were accepted. The second difference is that the subsidy formula might be somewhat different. Under some proposals, the housing-allowance program would pay a certain fraction of rent to an eligible household rather than the difference between "fair market rent," as determined by the authority, and 30 percent of income. This difference is important. Under Section 8, the subsidy does not vary with housing consumption, except that eligibility is contingent on the household's ability to satisfy minimum quality standards. Thus, only its income effect increases housing consumption once the minimum standard has been met.[19] The "fraction of rent" housing-allowance subsidy, however, is a pure price reduction and thus encourages housing consumption by both an income and a substitution effect, even after the standard has been met. A national housing-allowance program could employ either formula.

Housing allowances, or an entitlement version of the Section 8 rent-subsidy program, would be an important step in providing consumer sovereignty to recipients of federal housing subsidies. For that reason, they are opposed by spokespeople for builders, banks, and local governments, all of whom now share in government programs to subsidize low-income housing.[20] Housing allowances would circumvent such groups, placing money in the hands of the poor, subject only to the restriction that they inhabit housing deemed adequate. Because only the poor would benefit, the proposal is opposed by groups that are traditional lobbyists for government housing programs!

Effectiveness of the programs. In some ways, any program targeted at a specific good is less efficient than a cash-grant program costing the same amount of money. To see this view, suppose that the government decides to give a $1,000 housing subsidy to a poor person in the form of a rent rebate conditional on the person occupying some minimum quality of housing. If the person were simply given the $1,000 in cash, he or she could buy that minimum house quality, or if preferred, something else. Thus, one of the costs of a housing-subsidy program is that it causes people to spend their money differently from the way they prefer.

Perhaps this consumption distortion should not be counted as a cost, since the objective of the program is to induce more housing

---

19. In the absence of a requirement that the recipient live in adequate housing, the Section 8 rent subsidy does not differ in concept from an NIT. The cost of adequate housing is analogous to the intercept in the NIT formula—the subsidy payment, if the family has no income. The percentage of income deemed reasonable to spend on housing is analogous to the marginal tax rate in the NIT; each dollar of additional income reduces the subsidy by that amount.

20. The opposition of builders has a somewhat different basis. Public housing and the supply-side Section 8 programs do stimulate housing production, to the obvious benefit of the building industry.

consumption. But two other types of cost are unambiguous. The first is administrative and needs no further explanation. The second, particularly for supply-side programs, is production cost. This amount is the difference between the cost the government incurs by producing new or rehabilitated subsidized housing and the cost of acquiring the same quality of housing on the open market.

Mayo and associates (1980) have discovered that supply-oriented programs are almost twice as expensive as demand-oriented programs. With new construction and public housing, it costs about $2 to provide a unit with a market value of $1, whereas the same $1 worth of services can be provided through a housing allowance or Section 8 rent subsidies for approximately $1.15. Therefore, if the objective is to provide housing services to poor people, a given budget will go much farther (almost twice as far) if it is devoted to demand-oriented programs.

This finding should come as no surprise, given what we already know about the housing market. In most cities there is a surplus, not a shortage, of low-income housing. The available housing stock, as a result of this surplus, already sells for low prices. Not surprising, a major effect of new construction of low-income housing is that this glut becomes more serious, and the new units provide housing services worth only a fraction of their production cost. As was noted, the construction probably also aggravates the abandonment program and certainly hastens housing retirement in other neighborhoods.

By contrast, the various rent subsidies address the true problem— poverty. Improving the ability of people to buy housing increases housing consumption, and it does so in a reasonably efficient manner.[21]

Rent control.   Another program, or rather a series of local programs, designed to help low-income renters is *rent control.* Rent control generally takes the form of a statutory ceiling on annual rent increases, sometimes with allowances for extraordinary cost increases such as fuel, major repairs, and taxes. New York City has had rent control, with various exemptions, throughout the postwar era. Many other cities adopted rent control measures during the mid-1970s.

The benefit of rent control seems obvious: Some citizens get housing more cheaply than they otherwise would. It is not totally as straightforward as that. The cost of rent control is the adverse effect on the supply of rental housing.[22] If government simply controls rents by edict, it ultimately reduces the supply of rental housing. If the supply of rental housing is elastic in the long run, even a modest price reduction

---

21.   It was claimed in the previous chapter that the long-run supply of housing is almost perfectly elastic because it is competitive and is produced under roughly constant returns. The elasticity of supply of rental housing should be higher yet, because it is easy to shift resources between rental and owner-occupied housing.

22.   See the discussion of the rental price of housing in Chapter 10.

leads to a substantial decline in quantity. If the supply elasticity is equal to 2 (a conservative estimate), a 10 percent price reduction ultimately will lead to a 20 percent decline in available supply! This problem is recognized by both proponents and opponents, and it must be addressed if rent control is to be effective. The possibilities for maintaining supply are fiat or subsidy, and localities have relied almost exclusively on fiat. It is extremely difficult, however, to enforce such a fiat. It is difficult to prevent landlords from inadequately maintaining buildings, and laws that prohibit conversion to condominiums and other uses are difficult to enforce and of questionable constitutionality.

Much of the support for rent control apparently comes from the belief that landlords make large profits and that the major effect will be to remove these profits (with little effect on supply). There is little evidence for this view, and little reason to believe it to be true. In every U.S. city, being a landlord is a highly competitive business, and it is hard to imagine how entrepreneurs would be able to keep prices above costs.

Another element of support for rent control results from some highly publicized episodes of "regentrification" of inner-city neighborhoods. One of the results of this process has been a rapid increase in both property values and rents in the redeveloped neighborhoods. Rent control is seized on as a tool to prevent this displacement, but it probably will not prevent the displacement in any case. Conversion to owner-occupancy, abandonment, or in some cases, demolition and sale of the vacant land becomes a viable option if rents are kept below market levels.

It is curious that rent control became popular during the 1970s, a decade when rents fell relative to the cost of living. Perhaps people have "money illusion"; rapid nominal rent increases, even though they failed to keep up with inflation and income growth, aroused the ire of the public.

If rent control is effective, rents are driven below market-clearing levels (i.e., below the levels the units could command in the absence of rent control). This practice brings up a difficult policy question: Are landlords permitted to raise rents to the market-clearing level when tenants move out? As will be seen, each answer leads to unsatisfactory consequences.

If rent adjustment is permitted when new tenants move in, landlords have an incentive to force current tenants out as soon as the controlled rents fall below market rents. If that does not work, tenants can agree to move out on the condition landlords pay them off. Of course, it is possible (but unlikely) that adequate law enforcement will prevent either tenants or landlords from holding the other hostage. If so, one of the main consequences of rent control is that current tenants have a strong incentive not to move (since tenants will be unable to replicate controlled rents after moving). In this event, (1) the benefits of rent control accrue only to those who occupy units at the time the law is passed, and (2) rent control diminishes mobility because tenants cannot take the benefits with them. In New York, an underground market has developed in subleasing rent-controlled apartments. The subleasees do not benefit from the controls, and the underground market is inefficient.

If landlords are not permitted to raise rents for the next tenants, then tenants can frequently collect a finder's fee, called *key money,* from the next tenants. As an example, suppose the market rent is $800 per month and the controlled rent is $500 per month. By gaining access to a rent-controlled apartment, the prospective tenant expects to save the present value of $300 per month forever.[23] This present value is the maximum amount he or she is willing to pay for access to a rent-controlled apartment, and any renter moving out of a controlled apartment will be sure to charge this amount.

In light of the discussion of key money, rent control has a surprising consequence. The only beneficiaries of rent control are those who have leases at the time the law is adopted. To the extent that key money represents the present value of savings, all subsequent tenants pay not the controlled rent but rather the market rents. (Also, market rents are higher than they would be in the absence of rent control, because rent control depresses the supply.) Seen in this light, rent control is a law that transfers part of the ownership rights of a rental property from landlords to the original tenants. Among other things, this ought to make it clear that any income redistribution emanating from rent control bears little resemblance to the income redistribution that would emerge from a conscious policy to help the poor. Even if all renters are poor, rent control helps the first generation of renters at the expense not only of landlords but also of subsequent generations of renters.

Of course, the institutions and facts are not as simple as the foregoing conceptual discussion. The distortions from rent control, however, are not small. In New York City, rent control has caused a massive transfer of assets from owners to early tenants. Many of these tenants pay rents that are a fraction of market rents and retain legal tenant status long after they vacate the dwelling, subleasing it at about market rates.

Why Subsidize Housing?

All the programs discussed so far—the tax subsidy for owner-occupied housing, public housing and construction-subsidy programs, rent-supplement programs and rent control—take as a given the notion that consumption of housing should be subsidized. Indeed, to many this idea seems self-evident. Housing satisfies a basic need, like food and clothing, and it is one of the most visible indicators of standard of living.

---

23.   It may seem that prospective tenants would pay key money only equal to the present value of rent savings during their own expected period of occupancy, but this is not the case. One of the benefits new tenants acquire on getting their rent-controlled apartments is the ability to charge key money when they move out. This key money, in turn, represents the present value of rent savings after the new tenants move out.

Also, without question, too many people live in housing that is deplorable by modern standards.

The economic question, however, is not whether we would like to see poor people live in better housing. The question is whether housing warrants favorable treatment *relative* to other goods. Subsidization of housing encourages housing consumption *at the expense* of something else. For low-income housing programs, the best way to pose the question is, Why do we subsidize housing rather than just redistribute income directly and let the people choose how they want to spend their money? The answers that suggest themselves follow:

1. The donors prefer giving their money for housing to giving it for income transfers.
2. Poor people somewhat undervalue housing when making their consumption decisions.
3. The market does not work smoothly, probably because of capital-market imperfections. Subsidies are required to restore the efficiency conditions that would exist in a perfect market.
4. There are externalities associated with housing consumption (neighborhood effects, essentially) that imply that individual households spend too little on their housing.
5. Particularly in the case of the supply-side programs, donors are simply unaware of the high cost of these programs.
6. Again, in the case of supply-side programs, as has already been noted, the housing industry is an important beneficiary and lobbyist on behalf of programs.

Economists can say little about donor preferences for housing, except to note that if that is what donors want to do, that is what they will do. Still, it is a little implausible to believe that donors have specific preferences for supporting housing unless it is because they believe that the second through fourth reasons are important. Economists also have little to say about the second possibility—that poor people "should" want more housing relative to other goods. This concept seems impossible to measure and impossible to know. The only thing to point out is the obvious, but frequently forgotten, fact that more housing means less of something else.

Market imperfections abound in housing in the form of imperfect access to borrowing and rental markets and extremely imperfect information regarding housing prices in various parts of a city.[24] The subsidization of housing, however, does nothing to eliminate these imperfections. Open-housing laws have helped promote equal access to capital and real estate markets and could help more if governments

24. Among other researchers, deLeeuw and Struyk (1975) have found that substantial housing price differences among neighborhoods can exist and be maintained for long periods of time. Perhaps these differences reflect genuine differences in the attractiveness of the neighborhoods, or perhaps a lack of information inhibits migration among neighborhoods so as to eliminate the price difference.

enforced them, but there is no reason to believe that subsidization of housing can redress these inequities.

Neighborhood effects certainly exist, although, as previously noted, they are extremely difficult to measure. Here again, housing subsidies do not seem to be the answer. Indeed, it can be argued that subsidies only make the problem worse. As has been seen, one of the major effects of public housing or construction subsidies is to create vacancies and retirements, as well as to put downward pressure on the asset price of low-income housing. Also, it is plausible that the retirement process—the awkward end-product of filtering—is responsible for the most deleterious neighborhood effects. There is no reason to doubt that every unit of public housing or subsidized private construction generates at least as much abandonment as does any other type of housing.

The point applies not only to construction-side subsidies. Demand subsidies also speed up the filtering process and increase the pace of retirements. Unlike the supply-side subsidies, however, demand-side subsidies do not necessarily create new low-income dwellings. They may simply help finance existing housing that can be maintained at a sufficiently high quality to avoid adverse neighborhood effects and abandonment. Even if housing subsidies improve housing for the recipient and improve the neighborhood for the neighbors, the same subsidies surely leave a wake of abandonment and decay elsewhere in the city.

If the problems of neighborhood effects are to be addressed in the areas where the problems are most serious, a more efficient mechanism for retirement or reuse of housing is needed than a consumption or production-subsidy program.

☐ Summary

This chapter has shown that an important contributor to many of our housing problems is the extreme durability of the housing stock, and that both demolition and modification are quite expensive. This finding makes it hard to adjust the stock to new conditions.

Questions and Problems

1. Suppose a house costs $100,000. Inflation is 5 percent, the mortgage rate is 7 percent, and property taxes are 2 percent. Depreciation and maintenance are 1 percent each. There are no expected capital gains.

   a. What rent must the owner of this house charge to cover expenses?

   b. If inflation remains at 5 percent and the mortgage rate rises to 9 percent, what changes would you expect in rent or house value?

2. What do you think is the reason for the enormous variation in housing cost in the following table? Can you think of a way of testing whether your ideas are right?

Metropolitan Area Housing Costs (Detached Single-Family Home)

Metropolitan	Cost per Square Foot
Area	$105
San Francisco	89
Los Angeles	82
Miami	58
Seattle	56
Chicago	55
Dallas	51
Boston	50
Baltimore	47
Cleveland	45
Pittsburgh	44
Nashville	42
Atlanta	42
Tampa/St. Petersburg	41
All surveyed metropolitan areas	55

Source: Reprinted with permission from National Association of Realtors. *Real Estate Status Report* (March, 1982):4.

3. This chapter discussed some peculiarities of the housing market when income is growing and population is fairly stable (as in the United States during the latter half of the twentieth century). How would the housing market be different if populations were growing quickly and incomes were stationary (as in the case in many developing countries)?

4. What do you think is the explanation for the patterns in the following table?

Median Home Size by Type (Square Feet)

Type	New	Existing	All
Detached single family	2,000	1,640	1,700
Apartment condominium	1,100	1,020	1,020
Townhouse	1,620	1,430	1,500

Source: Reprinted with permission from National Association of Realtors. *1980 National Homebuyers Survey.* (Washington, D.C.: National Association of Realtors, 1981):13.

5. The following graph shows almost a 60 percent decline in existing home sales between September 1980 and February 1982. Why do you think this happened? Now note that private housing starts displayed roughly the same pattern. Would you generally expect these two series to move together or is this a coincidence that would not be repeated in other periods?

Existing Home Sales and Housing Starts

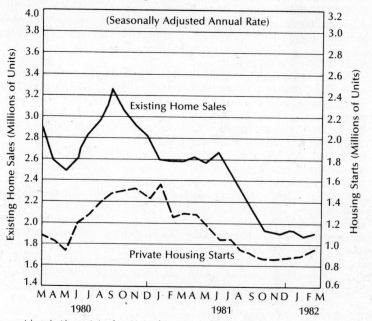

Source: Adapted with permission from National Association of Realtors. *Real Estate Status Report* (March, 1982).

References and Further Reading

Aaron, Henry. *Shelter and Subsidies* (Washington, D.C.: Brookings Institution, 1972).

Bailey, Martin J. "A Note on the Economics of Residential Zoning and Urban Renewal." *Land Economics* 35 (1959): 288–292. The original presentation of the housing-price boundary effects discussed in this chapter.

Burt, Martha, and Barbara Cohen. *America's Homeless* (Washington, D.C.: Urban Institute Report, 1989): 89–93.

Clemmer, Richard B., and John C. Simonson. "Trends in Substandard Housing." *AREUEA Journal* 10 (Winter, 1983): 442–464.

Cooke, Timothy, and Bruce W. Hamilton. "Evolution of Urban Housing Stocks: A Model Applied to Baltimore and Houston." *Journal of Urban Economics* 17 (1984): 317–337.

Courant, Paul. "Racial Prejudice in a Search Model of the Urban Housing Market." *Journal of Urban Economics* 5 (1978): 329–345. An interesting discussion of the manner in which reasonable house-search strategies might lead to extreme segregation.

Crecine, John, Otto Davis, and John Jackson. "Urban Property Markets: Some Empirical Results and Their Implications for Municipal Zoning." *Journal of Law and Economics* 10 (1967): 79–100. The original study of the relationship between neighboring land uses and land values. This paper spawned a great deal of subsequent research because of its surprising findings that deleterious neighboring land uses do not depress property values.

deLeeuw, Frank, and Raymond Struyk. *The Web of Urban Housing* (Washington, D.C.: Urban Institute, 1975). A simulation model of the urban housing market that takes account of the durability of housing.

Dunn, L. F. "Measuring the Value of Community." *Journal of Urban Economics* 6 (1979): 371–382.

Dynarski, Mark. *The Economics of Community: Theory and Measurement.* Ph.D. dissertation, Johns Hopkins University, 1981. Discusses and measures the economics of attachment, current residence, and the inertia caused by limited willingness to move.

"HUD Subsidized Housing Overview." In *Major Themes and Additional Budget Details: 1983 Budget of the United States Government* (Washington, D.C.: Government Printing Office, 1982). A detailed discussion of current programs, proposed changes, and rationales.

Joint Center for Housing Studies. *The State of the Nation's Housing 1992* (Cambridge: Harvard University Press, 1992).

Kain, John. "Housing Segregation, Negro Employment, and Metropolitan Decentralization." *Quarterly Journal of Economics* 82 (1968): 175–197.

Kain, John F. "Black Suburbanization in the Eighties: A New Beginning or a False Hope?" Paper presented at conference. The Agenda for Metropolitan American, 1984. Center for Real Estate and Urban Economics, University of California at Berkeley.

King, A. Thomas, and Peter Mieszkowski. "Racial Discrimination, Segregation, and the Price of Housing." *Journal of Political Economy* 8 (1973): 590–601.

Margolis, Stephen. "Depreciation of Housing: An Empirical Examination of the Filtering Hypothesis." *Review of Economics and Statistics* 64 (1982): 90–96.

Mayo, Stephen K., Shirley Mansfield, W. David Warner, and Richard Zwetchkenbaum. *Housing Allowances and Other Rental Assistance Programs: A Comparison Based on the Housing Allowance Demand Experiment,* revised (Cambridge, Mass.: Abt. Associates, Inc., 1980). A very thorough study comparing the various housing programs that have been either employed or seriously considered in the United States during the 1980s.

Mills, Edwin. "Are Real Estate Markets Becoming More Efficient?" *Journal of Real Estate Finance and Economics* 1 (1988): 75–83. Estimates that the divergence between the social and private return to housing narrowed in the 1980s.

Peterson, George. "The Effect of Federal Taxes on Urban Form." In *The Prospective City,* edited by A. Solomon (Cambridge, Mass.: MIT Press, 1979). Discusses several ways in which peculiarities of the federal tax code influence the housing market. Its topics include abandonment and suburban sprawl.

Peterson, George, and George Reigeluth. "Conservation of the Central City." Working paper (Washington, D.C.: Urban Institute, 1977).

Roskill Commission. *Report on the Third London Airport* (London: Government of Great Britain, 1970). A royal commission report on the feasibility, and possible location, of a new London airport.

Rothenberg, Jerome. "The Nature of Redevelopment Benefits." In *Readings in Urban Economics,* edited by M. Edel and J. Rothenberg (New York: Macmillan, 1972).

Sternlieb, George. *The Tenement Landlord* (Newark, N.J.: Rutgers University Press, 1966). An analysis of the economics of tenement ownership.

Sternlieb, George, and Robert W. Burchell. *The Tenement Landlord Revisited* (New Brunswick, N.J.: Rutgers University Press, 1973).

Taeuber, K. E., and A. F. Taeuber. *Negroes in Cities* (Chicago: Aldine Publishing, 1965). One of the first careful and detailed studies of residential segregation patterns. It continues to be a valuable source despite the fact that the data are somewhat old.

Tenement Housing Commission of New York. *First Report* (New York: Tenement Housing Commission, 1903). Little statistical analysis, but vivid descriptions and photographs of housing conditions in New York City's tenements at the turn of the century.

Thornton, Craig. *Zoning, Apartments, and Land Use Interactions.* Ph.D. dissertation. Johns Hopkins University, 1978.

Tideman, T. N. *Three Approaches to Improving Urban Land Use.* Ph.D. dissertation. University of Chicago, 1969. Three very readable and provocative essays on the land market and land-use interactions.

Weicher, John. *Housing: Federal Policies and Programs* (Washington, D.C.: American Enterprise Institute, 1980). An excellent historical summary of federal housing programs.

Wheaton, William C. "Housing Policies and Urban 'Markets' in Developing Countries: The Egyptian Experience." *Journal of Urban Economics* 9 (1981): 242–256. A fascinating discussion of the effects of rent control upon the housing market in Cairo.

White, L. J., and M. J. White. "The Tax Subsidy to Owner-Occupied Housing: Who Benefits?" *Journal of Public Economics* 7 (1977): 111–126.

White, M. J. "Property Taxes and Urban Housing Abandonment." *Journal of Urban Economics* 20 (1986): 312–330. A study of housing abandonment in New York City.

Wienk, Ronald, Clifford Reid, John Simonson, and Frederick Eggers. *Measuring Racial Discrimination in American Housing Markets: The Housing Market Practices Survey* (Washington, D.C.: Government Printing Office, 1980). A compendium of the results of the Department of Housing and Urban Development 1980 survey described in the text.

Yinger, John. "Prejudice and Discrimination in the Urban Housing Market." In *Current Issues in Urban Economics,* edited by P. Mieszkowski and M. Straszheim (Baltimore: Johns Hopkins University Press, 1979). A survey article describing current research in the field.

Yinger, John. *The Choice to Discriminate: Evidence from the 1989 Housing Discrimination Study* (New York: Syracuse University, 1992). An excellent report on discrimination against blacks in notched pair experiments in housing markets from the Metropolitan Studies Program.

13

Urban Transportation

☐ The theoretical analysis in Part Two showed that the function of an urban area is to facilitate the exchange of goods and services by proximate locations of diverse economic activities. Firms with products that are exported from the urban area have an incentive to locate near ports, railheads, highway interchanges, or other places from which intercity trade can be conducted economically. Households that provide the work force in export industries or that consume goods imported into the urban area have a similar incentive, as do firms that produce inputs for the export industries or consumer goods for local residents. Thus an urban area consists of large numbers of specialized economic institutions that produce goods and services, with large ratios of other inputs to land, and that locate close to each other to facilitate exchange.

The exchange of goods and services entails the movement of goods and people. Thus, the size, structure, and efficiency of an urban area are influenced by the transportation system on which goods and people are moved. *Commuting*—that is, the transportation of people for the exchange of labor services—is the most studied kind of urban transportation. Households also use the urban transportation system for noncommuting trips for shopping, recreation, and social activities. The movement of goods, or freight, within urban areas has been studied much less than has the movement of people. Many writers assume explicitly or implicitly that an urban transportation system that is adequate for commuting is also adequate for all other demands made on it. Although this assumption may be justified for the analysis of an overall urban transportation system, it is not necessarily valid with respect to all the details of the system.

There is a substantial body of engineering research on urban freight transport, but economists have given the topic little attention. The bulk of this chapter, therefore, concerns personal transport (with emphasis on commuting). Following this discussion is a brief section on freight transport.

☐ PERSONAL TRANSPORT

Commuting constitutes about 25 percent of personal urban travel (in miles), with shopping, recreation, and personal trips (largely visiting friends) making up the bulk of the remainder. Commuting is important, however, because it is concentrated during the morning and evening rush hours. It is commuting that strains the capacity of the transport network, and in part, it is commuting needs that dictate the extent of road and public-transit capacity.

Urban transportation is one of the most interesting examples of a mixed public-private sector in the economy in the United States. The supply side is clearly a public sector responsibility. Streets and highways are constructed, maintained, and owned by governments. Public-transit facilities such as buses, subways, and commuter trains are either owned or regulated by governments.

The demand side is more complex. Trucks and cars are privately owned, and they pay to use the public streets with user fees, such as taxes on motor-vehicle fuel and tires, and vehicle-registration fees. Public-transit riders pay fares. To the extent that both are available, urban residents choose without coercion between private cars and public transit, depending on the combination of fares or fees and services they prefer. In contrast, public education (for example) is supplied with an important element of coercion. Children are forced to go to school, and public schools are financed by tax revenues. Thus, parents cannot avoid paying for the public service, even if they refuse to consume it and instead send their children to private schools.

The difference is important. However bad public education is, large numbers of people consume it just because they cannot afford to pay for both the public and the private service. The use of private cars (either traveler owned or taxicabs), however, is generally a viable alternative to the use of public-transit systems. As will be detailed in Chapter 15, poor people in the central city represent an important exception to this statement regarding the availability of automobiles. If the combination of fares and service is sufficiently bad in public-transit systems, many people simply refrain from buying the service and use cars instead. Of course, governments can greatly influence the attractiveness of alternative modes of urban travel by the policies they follow. For example, public transit in the form of a subway system is relatively attractive if it provides frequent, economical, and safe service. Likewise, automobile travel is attractive if a system of urban expressways and adequate parking are available.

Thus, the basic decisions about the supply of urban transportation modes are the responsibility of the public sector. Consumers choose, however, among available modes according to the terms on which the modes are made available and according to their needs and tastes. The public sector's task is to provide the urban-transportation system that best serves the community. An important constraint on the public sector is that transportation services are bought by the public, and they can register dissatisfaction with one mode by purchasing the services of another.

A great debate has been under way regarding urban transportation since the 1960s. The issue is whether governmental policy should encourage the use of automobiles or public transit for urban commuting. One school of thought is that only large public investments in mass-transit facilities can save central cities from strangulation by congestion and pollution. Rapid inflation of fuel prices in the 1970s provided ammunition for transit advocates. Another school of thought believes that the advantages of the automobile to relatively high-income commuters are so great that no viable alternative exists to investment in urban expressways. A third school of thought advocates a balanced urban-transportation system, normally interpreted to mean substantial investment in both public transit and urban expressways. Almost inherent in this position is the advocacy of carefully planned and sophisticated pricing schemes to guide choices among modes.

The issues are complex. In part, complexity results from the availability of several related alternatives. Streets and highways must be available in urban areas, because movement by motor vehicles of practically all intraurban freight is by far the cheapest mode. The same is true for at least some intraurban passengers. To some extent, automobile commuters can share these facilities, as can at least one major form of public transit: buses. The other important kinds of public transit—subways and commuter railroads—require their own right-of-way, which is impractical for intraurban freight movement, given the great cost advantage of the truck. General railroad rights-of-way, however, can be shared among commuters, interurban freight, and interurban passengers. This debate will be discussed further in the "Cost and Supply of Urban Transit" section.

The details of urban-transportation investments must be tailored to the size, structure, and existing transportation facilities of each urban area. For example, transportation investments that are optimum for the metropolitan area of Philadelphia may not be appropriate for that of Los Angeles or Albuquerque. This chapter, therefore, explores the implications for government transportation policy of pervasive characteristics of urban areas in the United States and surveys systematic procedures for evaluating the benefits and costs of alternative transportation systems.

☐ TRENDS IN URBAN TRANSPORTATION

Overall travel in urban areas in the United States has increased rapidly since World War II. Rapid increases in urban population, incomes, automobile ownership, and suburbanization inevitably have led to a rapid growth of both passenger and freight transportation in

Table 13.1   *Urban Travel, 1940 to 1990*

	Public Transit Passengers (in Millions)					Automobile[b] (in Billions of Vehicle Miles)
	Railway	Subway[a]	Trolley	Bus	Total	
1940	5,943	2,382	534	4,239	13,098	129.1
1945	9,426	2,698	1,244	9,886	23,254	109.5
1950	3,904	2,264	1,658	9,420	17,246	182.5
1955	1,207	1,870	1,202	7,240	11,529	224.5
1960	463	1,850	657	6,425	9,395	284.8
1965	276	1,858	305	5,814	8,253	378.2
1970	235	1,881	182	5,034	7,332	920.0
1975	124	1,673	78	5,084	6,972	1040.0
1980	133	2,108	142	5,837	8,567	1122.0
1985	132	2,290	142	5,675	8,636	1270.0
1990	176	2,346	126	5,754	8,873	1439.0[c]

Notes: 1990 data are preliminary.
[a]Includes elevated railways; data for 1975 and later refer to reclassification as "heavy rail."
[b]Includes taxicabs and motorcycles
[c]Data for 1988
Sources: Data from American Public Transit Association. *Transit Fact Book;* and *Statistical Abstract of the United States* (Washington, D.C.: Government Printing Office, 1991).

urban areas. By far the most dramatic change in urban travel, however, has been the changing mix of modes.

Table 13.1 summarizes data of urban travel modes from 1940 to 1990. Public transit and passenger car figures, however, cannot be added. The transit data refer to total passengers, whereas the automobile data refer to vehicle miles. The ideal figures to have would be passenger miles, but they are not available, for either public transit or automobiles. Trip length per transit passenger and passengers per car probably have changed relatively little, so passenger miles today are about proportionate to the figures shown. The factors of proportionality, however, differ among modes. Another problem is that the 1945 figures are badly distorted by the effects of World War II. The suspension of automobile production and gasoline rationing caused many travelers to use public transit during the war. The 1940 figures, therefore, are a better base for postwar comparisons.

The stark message of Table 13.1 is that urban automobile travel in 1990 was more than 11 times its 1940 level.[1] Thus, the postwar growth of urban travel has been accompanied by a massive shift from public transit to private cars. Data from metropolitan transportation studies suggest that there are about 1.5 passengers per car on an average urban passenger car trip, and the average transit trip is about five miles. If those averages are applied to the 1990 data in Table 13.1, they indicate that more than 95 percent of commuter miles traveled were by car. Thus, popular writers do not exaggerate when they emphasize the dominance of the automobile in urban travel in the United States.

1. Note the steady rise in public transit ridership between 1975 and 1990.

The postwar decline of public-transit travel has been accompanied by shifts in the vehicle mix. Railroads and trolleys have nearly disappeared as modes of urban travel in all but a few cities in the United States. Subway travel declined only moderately from 1940 to 1975, and has increased somewhat since then, primarily because of the opening of subway systems in Atlanta, Baltimore, San Francisco, and Washington, D. C. Bus travel has been greater since World War II than it was in 1940. Although still far below its early postwar level, bus travel has increased about 14 percent since bottoming out in 1970.

Much of the urban transportation problem is a peak-load problem resulting from concentration of travel at morning and evening rush hours. (See Figure 13.6 and the accompanying discussion in a later section.) Most rush-hour travelers are on their way to or from work, and much concern with urban transportation, therefore, is focused on work trips. Chapter 4 showed that rapid suburbanization of both employment and residences has occurred in the postwar period. Considerable diversity, therefore, should be expected in origins and destinations of work trips. Table 13.2 presents comprehensive data for the ten largest MSAs as of 1980, with respect to destination by place of residence.

Approximately 21 percent of workers who reside in suburbs commute to the central city (including 6.1 percent who commute to the CBD), which is comparable to the nearly 29 percent of city dwellers who commute to the suburbs. Many people who live and work in suburbs, and some who live and work in central cities, commute crosstown (for example, around a circumferential highway) instead of toward or away from a CBD. The "Commuting Patterns" section in Chapter 7 showed that about 85 percent of commuting (for a different sample of cities) is either in the reverse direction or circumferential, rather than toward the CBD. Beyond a doubt, the growth of automobile ownership and improved urban expressways have contributed greatly to the diversity of origins and destinations since World War II. Not only are suburbs in the United States low in density compared with metropolitan areas in other countries, but workplace destinations are also more diverse here than elsewhere. All discussions of public transit must take account of the fact

Table 13.2 *Commuting Patterns in Ten Largest MSAs*

	Percent of all People who . . .		Percent of all Blacks who . . .[a]	
	Live in Central City	Live in Suburbs	Live in Central City	Live in Suburbs
Destination				
CBD	15.4	6.1	n.a.	n.a.
Central City	55.7	20.8	99.0	49.7
Suburbs	28.8	73.0	1.0	18.6

[a]Data not available

Source: Data calculated from U.S. Department of Commerce, Bureau of the Census. *1980 Census of Population and Housing; Census Tracts.* Tables P–9, P–14 (Washington, D.C.: Government Printing Office).

Table 13.3   *Commuting Mode in Ten Largest MSAs*

| Mode | Percent of all People who . . . | | | Percent of all Blacks who . . .[a] | |
	Live in Central City	Live in Suburbs		Live in Central City	Live in Suburbs
Drive alone	44.6	70.2	Drive alone	42.5	63.4
Carpool	15.3	19.1	Carpool	16.1	22.0
Public transit	. . .	. . .		41.4	14.6
Bus	15.0	3.7		. . .	. . .
Subway	16.7	3.0		. . .	. . .
Walk	8.4	3.9		n.a.	n.a.

[a]Data not available

Source: Data calculated from U.S. Department of Commerce, Bureau of the Census. *1980 Census of Population and Housing Census Tracts.* Tables P–9, P–14 (Washington, D.C.: Government Printing Office).

that public transit is relatively inconvenient for reverse-direction and circumferential commutes.

Note that black workers who reside in both cities and suburbs are much more likely to work in the central city than is the population as a whole. Almost half of the black suburbanites commute to the central city.

Modal choices (that is, decisions about which modes to use) for work trips are somewhat different from modal choices for other kinds of urban travel. Table 13.3 presents some data from 1980. As can be seen from data in Table 13.1 and facts presented in the text 95 percent of urban travel is by automobile, but Table 13.3 shows that slightly less than 60 percent of work trips originating in central cities were by automobile in 1980, and approximately 90 percent of suburb-originating trips were by car.[2] Public transit is much more heavily used by blacks than by the population as a whole, although the difference is much less striking for suburbanites than for central-city dwellers. Thus, automobile travel dominates metropolitan commuting, but less than it dominates other urban travel. Within metropolitan areas, the vast majority of those who commute by public transit either live or work, or both live and work, in central cities.

The data presented in Table 13.3 suggest that the major use of public transit is for commuting to (or, at least, toward) the CBD. For other commutes and for nonwork travel, the automobile is the overwhelming mode of choice. The reasons for this will be examined when cost and supply are discussed.

In most metropolitan areas, the worst crowding on roads is still in central cities, although suburban roads appear to have become much more crowded during the 1980s. As can be calculated from Table 4.4,

2.   If the sample underlying Tables 13.2 and 13.3 were expanded to include some smaller cities, the relative importance of public transit would decline somewhat, even for the central cities.

central city employment has increased only slightly in the postwar period. Crowding, however, has apparently become worse. It seems paradoxical that central-city crowding should worsen during a period when its employment has hardly changed.

Part of the resolution of the paradox is found in the data in Table 13.1. To the extent that crowding has worsened, the cause has been the massive switch from public transit to automobile travel in urban areas. Trains and subways do not use streets and highways, and trolleys and buses use them with much more passenger-intensity than do cars. Thus, the switch from public transit to cars increases travel on urban roads, and it changes use to a mode that generates more crowding. Urban-road capacity has increased since the early 1950s, mainly as a result of the construction of urban parts of the interstate highway system. The increased capacity, however, has not kept pace with the rapid increase in urban-automobile travel.

The same data in Table 13.1 suggest that, even in the absence of shifts in governmental policy, urban road congestion may have passed its peak. With 95 percent of urban passenger travel already by car, it is virtually impossible for the percentage to increase much in coming years. If, in addition, central-city employment continues to grow only slightly, it seems likely that demands placed on central-city streets and highways will grow little. If public transit use increases even moderately, crowding may decrease. In addition, as will be seen ahead, there is substantial room for improvement in the efficiency with which we use our existing facilities. If some of these potential gains are realized through changes in pricing and other policies, congestion also may be expected to fall. In fact, the suburbanization of jobs and people during recent decades suggests that the worst crowding on roads is moving to the suburbs.

☐ DEMAND FOR URBAN TRANSPORTATION

Concern about energy and environmental problems increased the intensity of the debate about urban transportation during the 1970s. Many people believe that high prices and unreliable supplies of gasoline, as well as pollution problems resulting from urban automobile driving, imply that more use should be made of public transit and less of automobiles in urban transportation. This matter is complex and cannot be settled in this chapter. It is possible, however, to indicate what is known and what needs to be studied to obtain answers.

As with the market for any commodity or service, there is a demand side and a supply, or production, side to the market for urban transportation services. Basic transportation facilities typically are constructed and owned by governments, and cost data are made available by engineering studies undertaken to plan new facilities. The demand side, however, is subtle, because of the complex interaction between government and private decision making. Only in the 1970s have economists undertaken high-quality demand studies.[3] The analysis will be couched in terms of *work trips,* since that is the subject of most available studies. However, the analysis that follows also applies to nonwork trips.

It is useful to divide work trips into three parts, referred to as residential collection, line haul, and workplace distribution. **Residential collection** refers to the trip from the residence to the vehicle on which the longest part of the trip is made, regardless of where the worker lives. If the trip is by car, residential collection entails no more than a walk to the garage or street. If the trip is by bus, residential collection refers to the walk to the bus stop. If the trip is by rail, residential collection may consist of a walk or a car or bus ride to the station where the worker boards the train or subway. **Line haul** refers to the trip by car, bus, subway, or train from the residential collection point to the distribution point. **Workplace distribution** refers to the part of the trip after the line-haul vehicle has been left. It is most commonly done on foot, but it may entail a bus or taxicab ride for some workers.[4]

Modal choice refers to choice of line-haul vehicle. In contemporary urban areas in the United States, the realistic choices are among car, bus, and subway. The mode chosen by a worker, however, depends on characteristics of all three parts of the trip. Ignoring this fact is the cause of much confusion in thinking about urban transportation. People sometimes conclude that subways are better modal choices than cars because subways are both faster and cheaper than cars. Whether they are faster and cheaper will be analyzed later. The point to be made here is that subway commuting entails collection and distribution trips that may be much longer or more irksome than those entailed by automobile commuting. If so, it will affect the modal choice of a rational commuter.

Trip characteristics that appear to have the greatest influence on modal choice are the time and money costs and comfort of each part of the trip. Certain modal characteristics, such as privacy and comfort, also may affect modal choice. In many studies, such data are either unavailable or indicate little effect on modal choice. They will be ignored here, but they easily can be included in Equation (13.1) in the next paragraph. In addition, certain characteristics of the worker, such as age, sex, and income, may affect modal choice. Once again, other variables can be included; however, income has been shown to be important, and only it will be included here.

What variable should be used to represent modal choice? There are advantages to the use of q_{ij}, the probability that a person of

---

3. Good references are Domencich and McFadden (1975) and Small (1992), on whose work much of this section is based.

4. A few commuting trips do not fit easily into this classification. Some workers walk or ride bicycles from their residences to their workplaces. Readers can make the necessary changes in the text to cover these possibilities.

characteristics i chooses commuting mode j. Then, the modal choice equation can be written as follows:

$$q_{ij} = f(pR_{ij},\ pH_{ij}, pD_{ij}, tS_{ij}, tH_{ij}, tD_{ij}, y_i). \qquad (13.1)$$

Here R refers to the residential collection part of the trip; H refers to the line haul; and D refers to the downtown distribution. The symbol p refers to the money cost of the part of the trip indicated by the subscript, and t refers to the time cost. The symbol pR might be bus fare for getting to the suburban rail or subway stop. The symbol pH is the fare on a line haul public-transit vehicle or the cost of operating a car. Transit fares are set by transit companies. Full costs of cars are the sum of depreciation, fuel, and other costs, and they might be $0.23 per mile in the early 1990s. The symbol y refers to income.

Care must be taken here. If the household would own the car anyway, interest and most depreciation should not be assigned as components of commuting cost. For such households, $0.23 per mile overstates the true operating cost. Depreciation per mile is $0.15 for a car that costs $16,000, lasts 11 years, and is driven 10,000 miles per year. If the car is needed mainly because of commuting, the properly calculated operating cost is in the neighborhood of $0.23. Parking costs have not been included, because most workers do not pay to park at work. A $5.00-per-day parking charge and a 20-mile round-trip drive, however, would add $0.25 per mile to the cost of a trip.

Of course, a unique suburban collection or downtown distribution mode does not correspond to a line-haul mode. For example, it might be possible to drive a car to a suburban railway station and leave it there or to take a bus there. For simplicity, Equation (13.1) ignores such choices.

Each p and t depends on both i and j. They depend on the person (i), because commuters have different origins and destinations, so the money and time costs of the trip vary from person to person, as well as by mode. Income (y) depends only on the person.

Domencich and McFadden (1975) have shown how Equation (13.1) can be used to analyze modal choices. In a large sample, q_{ij} can be replaced by N_{ij}/N_i, where N_i is the number of people in group i (they live and work in similar areas and have similar incomes), and N_{ij} is the number of them who choose mode j. Thus N_{ij}/N_i is the fraction of the people in group i who choose mode j.

Estimates of equations similar to Equation (13.1) have taught economists important lessons about modal choice. Most important is that people make substitutions between fares and travel time. Suppose, for example, that commuters who earn $15.00 per hour are observed to switch from bus to car if the time being saved is 10 minutes, even though the car trip costs $1.00 more than the bus trip. Then, the commuters are observed to value travel time at about $0.10 per minute, or at $6.00 per hour. In fact, this result is typical. Commuters typically value travel time in line-haul vehicles at between one-third and one-half their wage rates, although the proportion varies among studies.[5, 6] Several studies, however, have shown that time spent walking to or waiting at transit stops is valued at two to four times the value placed on line-haul travel time. Exposure to weather, noise, and fatigue probably account for the high value placed on such residential collection times. Presumably, the same is true of workplace distribution times, although evidence is lacking.

☐ CONGESTION AND PRICING

Controversy surrounds the pricing of both automobile and transit use in urban areas. Most controversy pertains to whether one mode or another is or should be subsidized. To understand these issues, it is necessary to investigate the effect of congestion on optimum pricing policy.

First it is important to distinguish between congestion and crowding. Congestion means excessive crowding. Crowding is appropriate on roadways built on expensive land for the same reason that high-residential densities are appropriate on expensive land. As was shown in Chapter 6, high-residential densities on expensive land economize on the relatively expensive input. So it is with roadways. Where land is expensive, crowding economizes on the transportation input that is expensive relative to vehicles and travelers' time. In the short run, road capacity is fixed, so the only issue is to optimize road use. In the long run, roadways and other transportation infrastructure are variable, so infrastructure is an issue. This section begins with an analysis of the short-run problem of optimal road use.

Short-Run Issues

It has already been noted that congestion slows travel. The theoretical analysis is the same for all modes. There are many cities in the world in which buses congest streets, but in the United States, emphasis is properly placed on congestion from cars.[7]

The basic theoretical issue can be posed in a simple example. Consider a divided, multilane stretch of road with no access or exits between points A and B. Suppose cars enter the road at A at a uniform rate per hour. Even if the rate is small, a maximum travel speed is imposed by legal speed limits and safety considerations. Associated with the maximum speed is a cost-per-vehicle mile of travel. It includes both time and operating cost, and it depends on the maximum travel speed

5. See Small (1992) for a discussion of estimation techniques and evidence.
6. Data in this section are from Small (1992).
7. It will be shown that trucks also add a substantial amount to urban congestion.

and on the characteristics of the vehicle. Now suppose there is an increase in the rate at which vehicles enter at A. When the number of vehicles entering per hour becomes great enough, congestion occurs and travel speed falls.

The critical rate of entry at which congestion begins depends on characteristics of the road such as its width, grade, curves, and surface. On any stretch of road, however, congestion occurs if the number of vehicles is great enough, because there are too many cars to permit the headway necessary for safety at high speeds, and cars must slow to a speed consistent with the available headway. Automobile-operating costs are relatively insensitive to speed, but time costs are inversely proportional to speed. Thus, slow travel caused by large numbers of cars entering at A increases the cost-per-vehicle mile of travel from A to B.

The foregoing ideas are illustrated in Figure 13.1, where T is the number of vehicles entering per hour at point A, and $AC(T)$ is the average cost-per-vehicle mile of travel between points A and B. $AC(T)$ is constant for values of T up to T_o, which can be called the *design capacity* of the road. Beyond T_o, $AC(T)$ rises rapidly with T. Economists have estimated several specific forms of $AC(T)$. $AC(T)$ is the cost per traveler that is borne by the traveler. It thus includes vehicle-operating costs and the traveler's time. Costs of providing the land and roadway are included only insofar as the traveler bears them. In the United States, the traveler

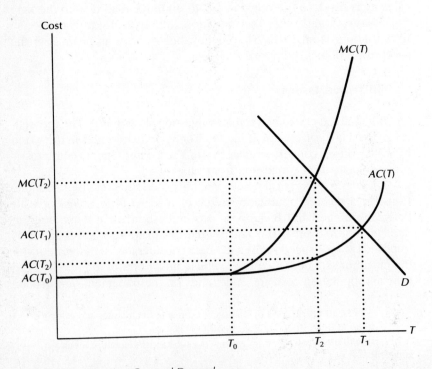

Figure 13.1   *Transport Cost and Demand*

does bear a substantial part of roadway provision costs, mostly through fuel taxes. The fuel taxes, however, are reflected in $AC(T)$, regardless of their relationship to roadway costs.

Now suppose, in the spirit of Equation (13.1), that the number of users of the road from point A to point B depends on the cost of travel. If travel on the road is too costly, people use a different route or mode, alter travel time, or change their places of work or residence to avoid the trip. The number of people who make the trip as a function of the travel cost is the demand curve for travel on the road from A to B, designated D in Figure 13.1. The equilibrium travel on the road is then T_1 vehicles per hour—the number of travelers willing to pay the cost of the trip. The equilibrium cost per vehicle is $AC(T_1)$. $AC(T_0)$ is the cost per vehicle in the absence of congestion, and $AC(T_1) - AC(T_0)$ is the congestion cost per vehicle. Crowding or congestion becomes costly at traffic volumes beyond T.

With a constant rate of entry at point A, all vehicles travel at the same speed and incur the same cost, or $AC(T_1)$. Thus, $AC(T_1)$ is the total cost of travel for those making the trip divided by the number of travelers, or the average cost per traveler. Elementary price-theory textbooks show that if an average cost curve is rising, the corresponding marginal cost curve must be above it. In the present context, *marginal cost* means the increase in travel cost to all travelers resulting from an increase in the number of vehicles using the road. In Figure 13.1, *marginal cost* is the curve designated $MC(T)$. It is important to understand exactly why $MC(T)$ is above $AC(T)$. If T exceeds T_0, speed decreases with increases in T, and $AC(T)$, therefore, exceeds $AC(T-1)$. Because everyone travels at the same speed, however, everyone goes slower if T cars enter per hour than if $(T-1)$ enter. Thus, the addition of a Tth user imposes costs on all T users because of the reduced speed. $MC(T)$ exceeds $AC(T)$ by the amount of the increased costs imposed on other travelers by the Tth entrant.

Expressing this in an equation,

$$MC(T) = AC(T) + [AC(T) - AC(T - 1)] \cdot (T - 1). \qquad (13.2)$$

Recall that the marginal cost is the increase in the total cost resulting from one additional road user. The right side of Equation (13.2) gives the components of this increase in total cost. First the marginal user incurs the cost of the trip, or $AC(T)$. In addition, the marginal user raises the trip cost of other users by slowing traffic. The total additional cost is the amount by which each other traveler's cost is increased, or $AC(T) - AC(T-1)$, times the number of affected travelers, or $(T-1)$. Clearly, the gap between average and marginal costs widens as the number of travelers (victims of congestion) increases. Thus, Figure 13.1 is realistic; as T increases, so does the spread between average and marginal costs.

The excess of $MC(T)$ over $AC(T)$ is an external diseconomy of the type defined in Chapter 8. Each traveler perceives and bears the average cost, or $AC(T)$. Travelers have no reason to consider the cost their travel imposes on others. Therefore, the equilibrium number of travelers (T_1) equates average cost to the price of the trip. As Chapter 8 showed, the situation represents an inefficient allocation of resources in that too many people use the road and there is too much congestion. T_2 entrants per hour, which equates marginal cost to price, represents efficient road use. Of course, if D intersects $AC(T)$ to the left of T_0 in Figure 13.1, there is no congestion and no misallocation of resources.

This analysis implies that a special method of rationing the use of the road is needed. How can it be done? Ignoring collection costs, efficient road use would be restored by charging a road-use toll equal to $MC(T_2) - AC(T_2)$ per vehicle mile in Figure 13.1. The appropriate toll equals the excess of social marginal cost over the cost perceived by the traveler, at the optimum use (T_2). If the government uses toll revenues to lower other taxes paid by users of the road, then everybody is made better off by the toll. If the government uses the toll revenue to lower taxes generally, or to provide service that residents want more than tax reduction, then the benefits exceed the costs of the toll policy, but toll payers and those deterred by the toll from using the road are made worse off and other residents are made better off. Only if the government uses the toll revenues wastefully does the toll program have a benefit-cost ratio less than one.

The actual collection of an efficient congestion toll is extremely difficult politically, and it poses some technical difficulties as well, for reasons that will be discussed. The nature of the argument on efficient tolls, however, is important, so for the moment the discussion ignores the problems associated with toll collection.

The congestion toll is efficient, because it discourages the use of a scarce resource; it encourages either doing without altogether or substituting other means of achieving the same end (other routes or modes, or other times, in the case of urban travel).[8] This result means that it is important for a congestion toll to vary with time of day (since congestion varies with time of day), as well as with location (since congestion is worse in some places than others). To state it differently, one of the important roles of an efficient congestion toll is to discourage people from taking shopping trips during rush hour. Only if tolls decline (or are removed) during off-peak hours do they properly encourage substitution between peak and off-peak travel times.

Long-Run Issues*

We have argued that the role of efficient pricing of road capacity is to internalize the congestion externality. Among noneconomists, however,

---

8. In the long run, efficient transport pricing also shifts the location of some economic activities away from the most congested areas.

*. This section is somewhat difficult, and some readers may want to skip it. The theory in this section is based on work done by Herbert Mohring (1976).

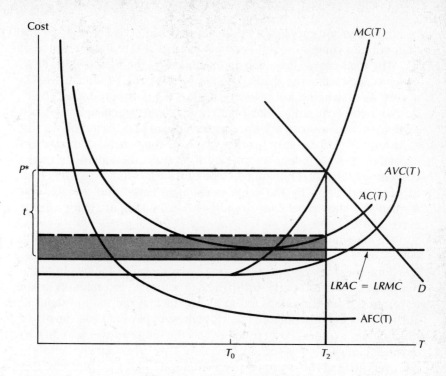

Figure 13.2   *Road Cost and Demand, Showing Capital Cost*

there is a widespread view that the use of tolls (or any prices, for that matter) is justified only to pay for the facility. Tolls, according to this view, should only cover interest, depreciation, and maintenance on the road itself.

In an important set of cases, there is a neat reconciliation between these two views, and the reconciliation is contained in the following statement: Under constant returns to scale in transport, if the economically efficient level of road capacity has been built, the optimum congestion toll is just sufficient to cover the cost of the facility (interest, maintenance, and depreciation).

To appreciate this concept, look at Figure 13.2, which is a reproduction of Figure 13.1, with some extra cost curves included. In comparing Figure 13.1 with Figure 13.2, the first thing to note is that the average cost curve of Figure 13.1, *AC(T)*, is labeled in Figure 13.2 as the average *variable* cost curve, *AVC(T)*. It is so labeled in recognition of the fact that the cost it depicts does not include the cost of the road capacity but only the (variable) costs incurred by the users themselves. The cost of the road capacity is depicted as a standard average fixed-cost curve, or *AFC(T)*. The curve shows how the average fixed cost varies with the number of users; it declines as a rectangular hyperbola, because, with a rise in *T*, fixed cost per user declines. The vertical sum of *AVC(T)* and *AFC(T)* gives the U-shaped average cost curve *AC(T)*. This curve is the standard U-shaped *short-run* average cost curve of producer theory.

If the demand curve is *D*, we already have seen (via Figure 13.1) that the optimum congestion toll is *t*. This variable will bring in revenue of $t \cdot T_2$. The total cost of financing and maintaining the road is $AFC(T) \cdot T_2$, which is depicted as the shaded box between the $AVC(T)$ and the $AC(T)$ curves. As drawn, the toll revenue exceeds the cost of the road.

With the realization that road capacity can be changed through investment, we now can ask whether society would be better off with an expansion of road capacity; in other words, do the benefits of investment exceed the costs? Under constant returns to scale, the long-run average-cost curve $LRAC(T)$ is horizontal, depicting the fact that expanding road capacity and users by the same percentage leaves the average cost unchanged. Thus, the $LRAC(T)$ curve is also the long-run marginal cost curve $LRMC(T)$.[9]

The height of the $LRAC(T)$ curve—which is equal to the $LRMC(T)$ curve—measures the cost of an increment of urban travel, assuming that it is done using the optimum amount of road capacity; the height of the demand curve measures the willingness to pay for an increment of urban travel. In the situation depicted in Figure 13.2, at the level of demand chosen with an optimum toll, the willingness to pay (P^*) is greater than the long-run marginal cost (which equals the long-run average cost), so expansion of capacity is socially desirable. This excess of willingness to pay over the long-run marginal cost will prevail until a position like that depicted in Figure 13.3, which looks like the (efficient) zero-profit, long-run equilibrium of a standard competitive firm, has been obtained.

Here, capacity expansion has allowed movement along the demand curve to the point where willingness to pay no longer exceeds long-run marginal cost. Thus, further investment would not be socially justified. As can be seen, this point is precisely where the optimum toll just equals the average fixed cost—that is, toll revenue covers the cost of the facility and no more. This same result can be stated somewhat differently: Under constant returns to scale, when capacity investment has been carried out to the optimum level, the optimum toll is also a fair market rent for the use of the facility.[10]

---

9. In terms of the curves of Figures 13.1 and 13.2, the upward-sloping portions of the $AC(T)$ and $MC(T)$ curves are shifted to the right, and the $AFC(T)$ curve is shifted away from the origin, yielding a new $AC(T)$ curve that is shifted to the right. Under constant returns, the minimum point on the new $AC(T)$ curve has the same height as the minimum point of the old one. As the $LRAC(T)$ curve is the envelope of these $AC(T)$ curves, it will be horizontal under constant returns. The horizontal $LRAC(T)$ curve coincides with the $LRMC(T)$ curve, since the marginal cost is always pulling the average toward it.

10. Of course, things do not work out so neatly if the $LRAC(T)$ curve is not horizontal (that is, if there are not constant returns to scale). Scholars disagree on this point. Keeler et al. (1975) found constant returns for highways; Vickrey (1963) and Walters (1961) found decreasing returns; and Meyer, Kain, and Wohl (1965) found increasing returns. Advanced students might want to explore the relationship between capital cost and long-run optimum tolls under these alternative assumptions regarding returns to scale.

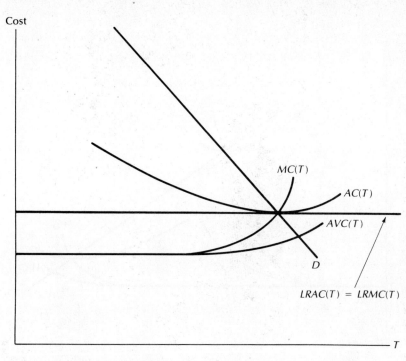

Figure 13.3   *Optimum Road Capacity*

Spatial Variation in Optimum Congestion

The distinction between crowding and congestion can now be used. The optimum long-run toll covers capacity costs, including land cost. Thus, the optimum toll is greater when land is more expensive. At that (optimum) toll, the road may be crowded, but it is not congested; there is no excess crowding.

Roadway crowding has been worse in central cities than in suburbs. In many metropolitan areas, there probably was no suburban congestion until recently. More roads were built there and delays were infrequent. Roadbuilding slowed in the 1980s, and suburbanization of people and jobs continued. Thus, there is now substantial crowding, and certainly some congestion, in many suburbs.

The relationship between crowding and distance from the CBD can be seen by studying the result previously derived: The optimum long-run toll is a fair market rent for the facility. Because land is an important component in a road network, the cost of the road rises with proximity to the CBD. In addition, roadbuilding requires more underpasses and overpasses, generally more careful design, and may require more demolition of valuable buildings in central cities than in suburbs. Hence, a toll sufficient to cover road costs also must be higher close to the CBD. Figure 13.4 depicts the optimum toll-and-investment outcome (for a given demand curve) where land is cheap (AC_2, MC_2, and AVC_2)

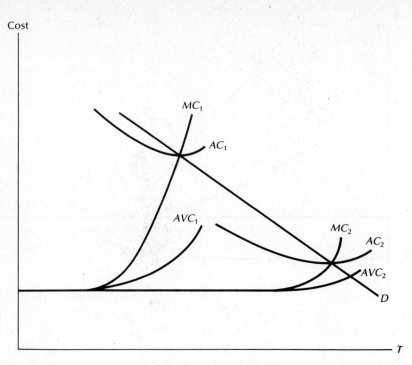

Cost

Figure 13.4   *Variation of Optimum Congestion with Land Cost*

and where land is expensive (AC_1, MC_1, and AVC_1). Clearly, where land is expensive the optimum decision is to have more crowded roads and less capacity.

Keeler et al. (1975) used this theory to estimate the optimum rush-hour toll for suburban roads ($0.11 to $0.30 per vehicle mile, depending on details of assumptions) and for central-city freeways ($0.38 to $1.09) for San Francisco.[11] (These figures have been converted into 1991 dollars by the authors.)

Realistic Pricing Possibilities

Subject to the uncertainties inherent in the estimates, the findings from Keeler et al. tell us that suburban road users impose congestion costs on others of about $0.11 to $0.30 per mile, on the average, and up to $1.09 per mile at the most highly congested central city times and places. It would be worthwhile to charge tolls to force consumers to recognize these costs, as long as the act of collecting the tolls is not more expensive than the original damage.

11.   San Francisco is more congested than many cities of comparable size and has higher land value, presumably because of its topography. Thus, optimum tolls in other large cities probably would be somewhat lower.

Tolls. As was noted, the ideal congestion toll should vary with time of day to encourage people to travel during off-peak times. It also should vary by location to encourage people to use less-congested routes. The standard mechanism for collecting tolls is the familiar tollbooth, but this is impractical for most urban-congestion pricing. Tollbooths use a large amount of land and disrupt traffic (and may well be more disruptive than the inefficient congestion they are trying to alleviate). In addition, they should be fairly closely spaced to allow for geographic variation in tolls. The ideal condition for using tollbooths to collect congestion tolls that vary by time of day is a fairly heavily traveled limited-access highway or a bridge. Here tolls can be collected cheaply and, using modern technology, with a minimum of traffic disruption. For many routes, however, the benefits do not justify the costs of administration and traffic disruption.

The major proposed alternative to tollbooths is automatic vehicle identification (AVI)—an electronic device on each vehicle that registers travel past certain points on a road network equipped with sensing devices. At the end of the month, all vehicle owners are sent statements of urban travels by location and time of day, and they are billed accordingly. Of course, there are many problems with such a proposal, but resource cost is not among the major problems.[12] One study estimates the total cost per one-way trip at $0.007.[13]

It would be quite feasible in many cities to establish time-of-day pricing for congested roads.[14] For whatever reason, however, time-of-day pricing for urban travel seems to have little political support. This factor has led to a discussion of other pricing policies that would approximate the efficient pricing previously discussed.

Gasoline taxes. In general, urban roads are more congested than rural roads, so some people propose higher gasoline taxes in urban areas. The optimum gasoline tax would be very large by current standards. At an average cost of about $0.20 per mile under optimum conditions and an average gas mileage of about 20 miles per gallon, the optimum tax would be $4.00 per gallon, or about $45 per tank, which

12. How to deal with occasional visitors (and, for that matter, how to apprehend operators without metering devices) and whether the system would be mandatory (some people object, on privacy grounds, to the creation of a record of travel patterns) are a couple of problems that have been discussed.

13. For a detailed discussion of congestion-pricing possibilities and problems, see Small (1992).

14. In the United States, there is no use of AVI and essentially no use of pricing of any sort to discourage road use during congested times and places. Such pricing is used, however, in other countries. Beginning in 1975, Singapore doubled its daytime parking fees and required a special license to enter the downtown area during the peak period. The plan is discussed briefly by Holland and Watson (1978). In addition, time-of-day pricing exists in the United States for many goods other than urban transport, such as restaurants; theaters; telephone service; and, in some cases, electricity.

would make gasoline in the United States the most expensive in the world.[15]

The problem with this approach is that it would discourage all urban automobile travel, not just the roughly 25 percent that takes place under congested conditions.[16] This aspect could be quite important. The demand for nonwork trips is much more price-elastic than that for work trips. Therefore, a gasoline tax might result in a drastic reduction in nonwork trips (when roads are uncongested anyway) and leave work trips relatively unchanged. Also, remember that an efficient price structure would (among other things) encourage people to shift travel to less congested times of day. A gasoline tax obviously cannot do this.

CBD parking taxes. It is possible to impose a tax on CBD parking that would vary with time of day in such a way that all-day parking would be much more expensive than evening or midday parking. Clearly, this plan discourages driving to the CBD for work and encourages the use of car pools and public transit.[17] With a 16-mile round-trip commute and an optimum toll of $0.20 per mile, the optimum parking tax would be about $3.20. The advantage of this system over the gasoline tax is that it can be restricted to the highly congested CBD and to people who travel during rush hour. Thus, unlike the gasoline tax, this system would encourage at least some types of efficient time and route substitution. A disadvantage is that it does not vary with length of commute. This disadvantage is not particularly serious. The greatest unpriced congestion is generally on routes near the CBD. Many long-distance commuters accumulate most of their long distance on relatively uncongested suburban roads; hence, failure to charge for this travel is not of great consequence. Another disadvantage is that the parking tax has no effect on drivers who simply pass through the CBD during rush hour. (During the morning rush hour, about one-third of vehicles traveling on Baltimore CBD streets are simply passing through, according to the Baltimore City Planning Department Traffic Study of 1983.)

Public-transit subsidization. For public transit, it is fairly easy to charge tolls that vary with time and place, because the collection of the tolls is an integral part of providing the service anyway. Here, however,

15. If the difference in gas prices is too great, city residents might find it worthwhile to drive to the country to buy gas. At $30 per tank, this is a real possibility for some drivers.

16. Overpayment for uncongested nonmetropolitan driving could be avoided by refunding part of the toll to nonmetropolitan residents who also worked outside the metropolitan area. Pump prices, however, would include the toll so that metropolitan residents would not make wasteful trips outside the metropolitan area to buy fuel.

17. It also might encourage firms to relocate to the suburbs.

another problem arises. In the absence of efficient road pricing for automobile users, congestion tolls for public transit might cause the wrong kind of substitution—namely, toward automobiles rather than toward different routes or times of day. In other words, a move toward marginal cost pricing for one mode might not lead to an efficiency gain. It is not certain that marginal-cost pricing improves efficiency except when all modes of travel at all times of day are subject to marginal-cost pricing. Therefore, many observers believe that rush-hour public-transit fares should be below marginal cost, as long as rush-hour highway pricing is below marginal cost to avoid distorting the modal-choice decision.

Although this idea may well be better than marginal-cost pricing of public transit and a subsidy to automobile travel (through the lack of a congestion toll), further welfare gains could be realized if it were feasible to have marginal-cost pricing for all modes. With no congestion toll for automobiles and with subsidized prices for transit, all (rush-hour) travel is priced below cost. The first result of this finding is that people travel too much. The second result, as Chapter 15 will discuss, is that urban areas are more decentralized than they otherwise would be. (This effect, as we will see, is rather modest.)

☐ COST AND SUPPLY OF URBAN TRANSIT

It appears that additional transportation infrastructure is justified if short-run marginal cost exceeds long-run average total cost. The optimum investment, however, may not be in roadways.

Nearly all people in the United States get to work by automobile, bus, or subway. An important question for planners is this: Which systems, if properly designed, could do the job most cheaply? In addressing this question, it is important to consider all costs, including out-of-pocket, time, and pollution costs. There are obvious trade-offs among these elements of cost; out-of-pocket and pollution costs would be very low if everyone walked to work, but the average commute would take about two hours. Thus, the now-standard procedure for comparing costs among modes begins with an assignment of dollar values to time and pollution costs, based on available statistical evidence. Then all costs are calculated in dollars, and we can look for the cheapest mode more straightforwardly.

Urban-travel analysis examines the cost of travel along a *corridor*—basically, an artery from a suburban residential area to the CBD. The cost comparison then looks at the full costs of travel along the corridor via each mode, assuming the optimum use of available technology for that mode.

Automobile

The cost of an automobile trip is made up of the following components: operating, time, roadway, pollution, and parking costs.[18] For a given number of users per hour, the only important trade-off is between time and roadway costs (with more roadway, people can drive faster). For a given amount of traffic, engineering studies tell how much extra speed can be obtained with any extra investment in road capacity. This process gives sufficient information to calculate the cost-minimizing way of carrying out automobile-based commuting. Empirically, the most important feature of an automobile-based system is that *scale economies are unimportant* beyond modest densities of travel.

Bus and Subway

The analyses for bus and subway systems are similar to each other, although obviously, the numbers are different.[19] As in the case of automobiles, the cost components are operating, time, roadway, and pollution costs (but no parking costs). The relationship among operating, time, and roadway costs, however, is much more subtle. Consider what is involved in a bus trip when there is a given volume of demand for travel along the corridor. Residential collection requires that people first get to the bus stop and then wait for the bus; the cost of this phase depends on the distance to the bus stop and the headway, or time, between buses. More closely spaced stops reduce distance to the bus stop, but they increase the number of times the bus stops, and therefore, increase the time cost once riders board the bus. Running buses more frequently reduces headway but increases the number of stops a bus makes before it gets full (or increases the fare it must charge to compensate for running half-full).[20]

After the line haul part of the bus trip, which occurs as the full bus travels along a freeway to a concentrated workplace, passenger distribution takes place. Costs of workplace distribution are much like residential collection costs; there is a trade-off among the number of stops, travel speed, and the required walk.

The residential collection and workplace distribution portions of bus and subway trips are subject to an important element of *scale*

18.   Recall that with an efficient system, the proper charge for the roadway is also a proper congestion toll, and congestion need not be listed as a separate cost.

19.   One difference between bus and subway systems is that a bus system can use a road network that also can be used by others (cars and trucks). This feature does not mean, however, that there are no road-capacity costs associated with a bus system.

20.   Walters (1982) states that this problem can be overcome in large measure by using smaller buses.

economies.[21] As demand increases, buses can be filled by making fewer residential stops or running with closer headways. Either of these reduces the time cost of this portion of the trip (and, as will be seen, the time cost of this portion is a major component of the total cost of a bus or subway trip).

Buses and subways are inherently inferior to the automobile in the residential collection and downtown distribution portions of the trip because of the necessity of making several stops and the imposition of waiting costs on riders. The automobile, however, is inferior as a line-haul vehicle, because subways (sometimes) travel faster, and buses have lower operating and roadway costs per passenger. Public transit's scale economies in residential collection and downtown distribution suggest the possibility that beyond some scale, these modes can offer cheaper overall transport than the automobile.

With available technological information, it is possible to calculate the minimum possible total per-passenger cost of a bus or subway trip for any given density of travel demand. Unlike the case of automobile travel, the cost for buses and subways depends on the number of people per hour demanding travel in the corridor because of scale economies in residential collection and workplace distribution.

Comparative Costs

Among the most careful cost comparisons is that provided by Keeler et al. (1975); Figure 13.5 depicts a representative set of their conclusions. For a six-mile line-haul trip (the average one-way commute in major cities in the United States is just over eight miles), the automobile is the cheapest mode at demand densities of less than 2,000 passengers per hour, but at any greater density a bus network is cheaper. A subway (San Francisco's Bay Area Rapid Transit [BART], in this case) is competitive with automobile travel when demand along the corridor reaches a bit over 20,000 passengers per hour. Even at 30,000 passengers per hour, however, the subway mode is about three times as expensive as a bus system.[22]

In the early 1960s, only New York City had an average corridor density of greater than 40,000 passengers per hour, and only Chicago had a density between 30,000 and 40,000. Five cities had densities between 13,000 and 30,000 (Philadelphia, Boston, Washington, Los Angeles, and San Francisco). Thirteen more cities had corridor densities

---

21.   Obviously, a bus has scale economies in that the demand must be sufficient to fill the bus (a subway also has these economies, although on a bigger scale). As will be seen, however, the scale economies associated with the mode extend far beyond this very modest size.

22.   Different assumptions regarding the interest rate, the opportunity cost of time, and the dollar cost of air pollution have only modest effects on the curves; the overall conclusions do not change.

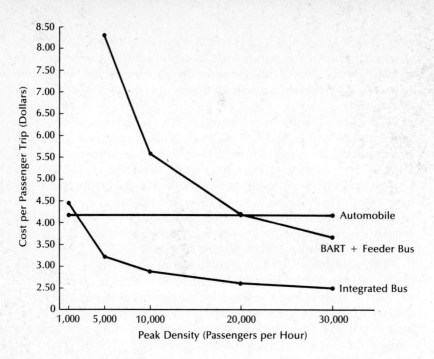

Source: Data adapted with permission from Keeler; Theodore, Kenneth Small, George Cluff, Jeffery Finke, Leonard Merewitz, and Randall Pozdena. *The Full Costs of Urban Transport*. Monograph No. 21, Part 3 (Berkeley, University of California at Berkeley, 1975): 128.

Figure 13.5   *Comparative Costs of a Six-Mile Line-Haul Trip Plus Collection and Distribution (Interest − 12 percent; Time Value − $3 in Vehicle, $9 in Walking and Waiting)*

in excess of 6,000 passengers per hour (Meyer, Kain, and Wohl 1965, Table 25). Since that time, corridor-travel densities have fallen significantly because of employment decentralization. For these 20 cities and possibly a few more, a cost-minimizing bus system is cheaper than an optimum automobile system *for persons who work in the CBD.* For all but New York City and Chicago, travel densities are generally not great enough to make bus service competitive for non-CBD workers.

The conclusion is that for roughly the top 20 urban areas (basically those with populations larger than one million), an optimum bus system is the cheapest way to deliver workers to the CBD. Except under special conditions, the automobile is a cheaper mode for smaller cities, for non-work travel, and for non-CBD work travel.

These calculations are slightly biased in favor of mass transit. They assume that the systems studied will be used only for work trips and will remain idle for the remainder of the day.[23] As Figure 13.6 demonstrates, this assumption is more valid for public transit than for automobiles.

23. Actually, Keeler et al. (1975) do assign a bit of the capital cost of the road-based and subway systems to nonpeak users.

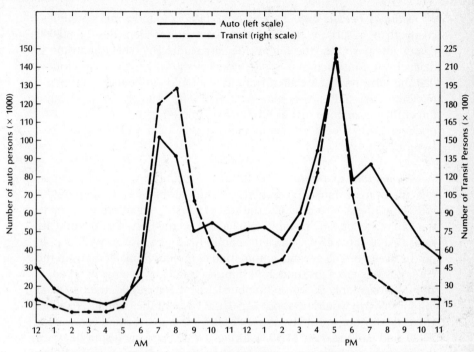

Source: Data derived from Figures A6, A7, A8, and A9 in Tittemore, L. H., M. R. Birsdall, D. M. Hill, and R. H. Hammond. *An Analysis of Urban Area Travel by Time of Day* (Boston: Peat, Marwick, Mitchell and Co., 1972).

Figure 13.6   *Number of Auto and Transit Persons in Motion, St. Louis, 1970*

Almost all nonwork trips are made by automobile for a variety of reasons. First origins and destinations are much more diverse than for work trips, so public transit routes rarely are convenient. Second as the density of demand drops during nonpeak hours, the optimum service frequency declines, which increases waiting time for public transit. Third the automobile is used to transport purchases of shopping trips. Fourth many nonwork trips are made by families. The cost of operating an automobile does not rise with the number of passengers, but bus fares are charged per passenger.

The problem of peak times revealed in Figure 13.6 is the source of one of the major financial difficulties facing public transit. Most transit systems are required to operate nearly 24 hours a day, even though they run relatively empty during nonrush hours. It is possible to cut service frequency during off-peak times, but this further discourages demand by increasing waiting time. For a transit system to operate without a subsidy, it must cover its capital costs (and even much of those operating costs that arise from off-peak operation) from its rush-hour traffic.

Subway versus bus.   Keeler et al. (1975) found a bus system less costly than a subway system, even for corridor densities of 30,000 passengers per mile (the highest density studied).[24] The conclusion is that subway construction is not economically justified; it does not follow that the subways that are already in place should not be used (although, in some cases, this also may be true). The studies do say—quite forcefully—that none of the subways constructed in the 1960s and 1970s operates with a cost even approaching that of a well-designed bus system.[25]

Numerical example.   The following example shows why it is so difficult for mass transit to compete with automobile travel except under ideal conditions. First calculate the cost of a rush-hour automobile trip to the CBD (the left side of Table 13.4) and then the cost of a bus trip (the right side of Table 13.4). The automobile is assumed to carry 1.5 people on the average. The average automobile commute in major cities in the United States takes just under 20 minutes and, as was already noted, is about 8 miles long. Based on numbers already referred to, the optimum toll for this trip would be about $1.50; the value of the commuter's time, at $6.00 per hour, would be about $2.00.[26] Vehicle operation costs about $1.20, and parking costs $1.50 (parking at $3.00 per day is split between the morning and afternoon trips). Multiply toll, operating, and parking costs by two-thirds to convert them from per-vehicle to per-capita costs to obtain a trip cost per passenger of $3.80.

Table 13.4   *Full Cost of an Eight-Mile Urban Rush Hour Trip*

Cost	Automobile		Bus	
	Per Vehicle	Per Passenger		
Toll	$1.50	$1.00	Walk and wait	$2.00
Time (at $6.00 per hour):				
20 minutes	3.00	2.00	On-bus time	3.00
Operation ($0.15 per mile)	1.20	0.80	Fare and toll	1.00
Parking	1.50	1.00	Walk to work	1.00
Total		$4.80		$7.00

24. As can be seen, the dominance of bus over subway continues well above 30,000 passengers per mile unless subway costs begin to decline very rapidly at higher densities.

25. The work by Keeler et al. (1975) and by other economists asks how to use existing technology most efficiently. The studies, by necessity, ignore the possibility that current subway systems (basically, BART and the Washington, D.C. Metro) have not been engineered efficiently. Vickrey believes that subways could be constructed much more cheaply than they are, and that taking this into account would tip the balance in favor of subways in a substantial number of cases.

26. Evidence cited by Keeler et al. (1975) indicates that commuters value time spent in an automobile at about one-third of their hourly wage, and they value time spent waiting for the bus at well over two-thirds the wage.

The bus trip begins with a walk to the bus stop and a wait, totaling 10 minutes ($2.00 at $12.00 per hour for walking and waiting time). On-bus time is assumed to be 30 minutes at $6.00 per hour—10 minutes longer than in-car time to account for the fact that the bus must make other stops and take a somewhat circuitous route to pick up and discharge other passengers. The value of this time is $3.00. Assume a fare of $1.00 and a 5-minute walk downtown for another $1.00, giving a total cost of the bus trip of $7.00. In this example, the automobile trip is a bit cheaper than the bus trip, although that conclusion could be reversed by a plausible change in the underlying assumptions. If a trip, however, has a destination other than the CBD, it is virtually impossible for a bus trip to be competitive with an automobile trip. Such a non-CBD trip generally would require a transfer, adding perhaps 10 minutes to waiting time at $2.00 and 5 to 20 minutes to on-board time. It is apparent that mass transit has trouble competing with the automobile on routes that involve transfers.

The obvious way to make buses more competitive with automobiles is to reduce the time cost of bus travel, because it is in the dimension of time cost that the automobile soundly beats the bus. For a given volume of demand, however, time cost can be reduced only by increasing money cost—basically by running buses more frequently and making fewer stops. This is why scale is so important. High-density demand permits reduced headway and fewer stops to fill a bus.

Example: The Washington, D.C., subway.   The first segment of the Washington, D.C., Metro opened in 1976; by 1981, it had six major lines running from the suburbs into the CBD. According to estimates by Keeler et al. (1975), such a system would be economically viable *compared with automobiles* at a peak corridor volume of at least 20,000 passengers per hour, for a total of 120,000 passengers per hour for the six lines. It is easy to see that such volumes are not feasible for Washington. The District of Columbia has about 670,000 jobs (about 15,600 of them in the Federal Triangle, a restrictive definition of the CBD). If all central-city workers rode the subway to work, there would be about 110,000 riders per corridor, or about 55,000 per hour over a two-hour rush hour. However, many central-city jobs and many homes (both city and suburban) do not have easy access to subway lines; only about 7 percent of the residential land area is within one mile of a subway stop. Also, a subway is superior to an automobile only on the line-haul portion of the trip. Clearly, for many people who both live and work in the central city, the line haul will be relatively short. The prime population for subway commuting is people who live in the suburbs and work in the city. In Washington, 21.2 percent of suburban residents work in the city. The conclusion is that Washington cannot have built a subway that is as efficient as automobile travel.

Washington did not, in fact, build an economically viable subway system. In 1981, the average weekday ridership was 290,000 (145,000 each way). Capital cost through 1981 was $4,828 billion; at a 10 percent cost of capital (interest and depreciation), the annual capital cost is $483 million. Dividing the capital cost by 250 (workdays per year) gives the daily capital cost at $1,932,000. Dividing by 145,000 riders gives an interest and depreciation cost of $13.32 per round trip.

Operating expenses were $94,200,000 for fiscal year 1981, which comes to $2.60 per round trip. Capital plus operating cost was $15.92 per round trip. To break even, the one-way fare would have had to be over $8.00. The total cost of the trip is, of course, much higher; we have ignored time costs and the commuters' out-of-pocket costs associated with residential collection and downtown distribution. These costs might add about $2.50 to the one-way total.

Could a rebuilt Washington, D.C., support a subway?   As has been seen, Washington's Metro is not economically viable; that is, there are much cheaper ways of providing the same bundle of services. Some observers conclude from this type of evidence that subway transit should not be used except in the very largest cities in this country. Others argue, however, that the evidence is flawed. Washington, D.C., was built as an automobile-based city; in addition, the city of Washington has a building height restriction of ten stories. If Washington had always had an efficient subway system (and no height restriction), the pattern of development and commuting would have been much different than it is now, and corridor densities might have been sufficiently high to tip the economic balance in favor of subways. This section asks, What would Washington, D.C., look like if it were built to make subway travel viable?

To be competitive with automobiles, a subway system must carry about 20,000 passengers per rush hour per corridor, or about 240,000 people each morning on a six-corridor route (assuming a two-hour peak). To be competitive with an efficient bus system, a subway system must carry at least twice this volume, or 480,000 passengers per peak period. This latter figure is about 70 percent of the central-city work force. Currently, only about 2 percent of the central-city labor force works in the Federal Triangle; a broader definition of the CBD would perhaps include 15 percent of the central-city work force, or about 6 percent of the metropolitan work force. The first step toward making Washington viable for subways would be to relocate almost all the jobs in the city in Washington into the CBD, increasing employment density there by some sevenfold.

In addition, residential patterns would have to be changed. The subway would be viable, hauling 480,000 workers per day. These workers would come from households with a total population of 1.2 million (assuming 40 percent of the population were in the labor force). When the system is completed, there will be 62 subway stops in basically residential areas and 194.7 square miles of land within walking distance of a residential subway stop, assuming people are willing to walk up to one mile to a stop.[27] To house 1.2 million people, the population density within the mile-radius circles surrounding the stops would have to average 7,200 persons per square mile, or about five households per residential acre.[28, 29]

If the city were to be rebuilt according to these specifications, subway travel (to the CBD) would be somewhat cheaper than automobile travel and about competitive with bus travel. The benefit would be a very modest saving in total travel cost, as compared with the present system, and the cost would be a substantial reduction in average lot size and a great increase in the density of CBD development, in addition to the enormous political and economic costs of rebuilding the city.

☐ EFFECTS OF TRANSPORTATION ON URBAN STRUCTURE

Most of the foregoing analysis has taken the origins and destinations of work trips as givens. In other words, it has assumed that the locations of residences and workplaces are unaffected by the urban transportation system. The assumption cannot literally be true. Indeed, the analysis in Chapter 6 showed that the residential-density pattern is affected by the relationship between housing prices and transportation costs. Thus, it is inevitable that a major transportation investment, such as the construction of a transit system, would have at least some effect on the locations of residences and workplaces. Some writers believe that the effect of transit systems on urban structure is profound. It is frequently maintained that a modern-transit system would stop or reverse the alleged decay of downtown business areas, eliminate urban sprawl, and solve the unemployment problem in urban ghettos.

The effects of transit systems on urban structure depend on the system and the metropolitan area in question. It is easy to see, however, that the strongest claims are exaggerated. Even the best-designed and best-operated public-transit system could have only a moderate effect in reducing the total time and money costs of commuting. Although there has been underinvestment in public transit in urban areas in the United States, the existing—mainly automobile-based—transportation system is simply not much more costly than one with a better mix of public transit and automobiles.

27.   This assumption is generous; a one-mile walk takes about 15 minutes. Added to even a modest wait, the residential-collection portion of the trip becomes almost 20 minutes.

28.   At present, the average population density for the Washington, D.C., urban area is roughly 1,900 persons per square mile.

29.   If instead the maximum walk to a subway stop is assumed to be 0.75 mile, the average population density rises within the circles to about 9 households per residential acre. If the maximum walk is a more realistic 0.5 mile, the density must be about 20 households per acre.

The purpose of a radial transit system is to make radial travel economical. With public transit improvement, people already employed in the CBD would find it advantageous to live farther out, on the average, to take advantage of low land (and therefore, low housing) prices. Chapter 6 showed that a decrease in transportation cost would flatten the population-density function of CBD workers.

The transit system would make the CBD more attractive for firms, because it would be more accessible to their employees. Thus, CBD employment would increase at the expense of suburban employment, making the employment-density function steeper. The transit system might also attract CBD employment that would not have located in the MSA at all in the absence of the transit system. Construction of the subway system in San Francisco was accompanied by a surge of downtown skyscraper construction, which has since been curtailed by government. San Francisco, however, was growing rapidly even before construction of the subway system. It is unlikely that large transit investments would have a large effect on total employment and population in the MSA.

Furthermore, it is unlikely that transit improvements would have a large effect in creating CBD jobs for the central-city unemployed. The main effect of the transit system is to increase accessibility to the CBD from suburbs. Thus, more jobs created probably would be for predominantly well-educated and well-paid suburbanites. The central-city unemployed already have access to the CBD, and a transit system would hardly increase the attractiveness of the CBD as a place of employment for them.

Based on the analysis of Chapter 6, it would be expected that this transit improvement would increase suburban residential property values and depress central-city residential property values. Given this expectation, it is interesting and disturbing that the nonfederal share of Washington, D.C., subway deficits is distributed as shown in Table 13.5.

In conclusion, major transit improvements would slow, but probably not reverse, employment decentralization, but the effect on total MSA employment would not be large. Transit investments would hasten the flattening of population-density functions.

Table 13.5   *Distribution of Nonfederal Share of Washington Subway Deficits*

Jurisdiction	Percent of Subsidy
District of Columbia	44
Montgomery County	13
Prince George's County	14
Arlington County	10
Fairfax County	13
Alexandria	5

☐ TRANSPORTATION AND URBAN POVERTY

Urban poverty enters into the consideration of urban transportation in two ways. First low-income housing sometimes is displaced by the construction of urban transportation facilities, especially expressways. In some ways, the problem is similar to the displacement of low-income housing by slum-clearance projects. Unlike slum clearance, however, urban expressways are not restricted to poor parts of central cities. In fact, much of the postwar construction of urban highways has been of circumferential roads (which pass only through suburbs) and radial expressways (which pass through both low- and high-income areas).

The problem is similar to that of slum clearance in that low-income people are affected differently by conventional compensation procedures than are high-income people. High-income residents tend to be owner-occupiers, and compensation of the property owner is therefore compensation of the resident. Low-income residents, however, tend to be renters, and therefore, they do not benefit when property owners are compensated under condemnation proceedings. Moreover, renters may suffer—whether they are displaced by slum clearance or by highway construction—if their homes and neighborhoods are destroyed. It seems indisputable that renters should be compensated for such losses, whether they are financial or psychic. The determination of psychic losses is not easy, but it is done in other equity proceedings. The cost of such compensation is a cost of the facility constructed, and it should be borne by those who benefit from the facility. Some federal programs now assist renters in finding places to live.

The second way in which urban poverty enters into consideration of urban transportation is more complex: An automobile-based urban transportation system has an *income bias,* in that the poorest people cannot afford cars. The problem is especially acute among blacks confined to central-city ghettos because of racial discrimination in housing markets. Some people advocate the construction of public transit systems to improve the access of ghetto residents to suburban-employment centers.

It can hardly be doubted that the problem is real. Many labor specialists believe that ghetto unemployment rates are high, partly because blacks who live there lack access to suburban jobs. Even if there were no effect of housing segregation on ghetto unemployment, segregation would nevertheless impose costs on blacks in the form of excessive commuting to suburban jobs, as Chapter 11 discussed.

First the problem is not basically one of transportation. If ghetto residents are deprived of access to suburban jobs because of housing segregation, the obvious answer is to open up suburban housing to blacks on the terms under which it is available to others. Special provisions for the transportation of ghetto residents to suburban jobs might be viewed as a way of maintaining all-white suburbs.

Second little is known about what transportation system would be best for ghetto residents. The mass transit systems now being planned clearly are designed to bring suburban residents to central cities rather than to bring central-city residents to the suburbs. This finding is at least suggested by the proposed locations of radial rights-of-way and of suburban line-haul stations. It is also clear that suburban bus systems are planned to bring suburban residents to line-haul stations, and not to bring central-city residents from suburban line-haul stations to suburban employment centers.

It is possible that the diversity of origins and destinations of ghetto residents who would commute to suburban jobs is such that an automobile-based system would be better for them than a transit system. If so, that the poor cannot afford automobiles implies that they are even less able to afford transit transportation. The foregoing comments are meant to raise questions rather than provide answers. The special transportation needs of the urban poor are simply not known.

☐ URBAN FREIGHT TRANSPORT

Almost all intracity freight is carried by truck.[30] Much interurban freight, of course, is carried by other modes—train, pipeline, water transport, and a small amount by air—but much of this freight is delivered to its ultimate urban destination by truck.[31] Hence, the analysis of urban-freight transport has concentrated on the truck.

A few basic facts underlie the discussion of the economics of urban truck travel. First truck miles make up about 20 percent of total urban-vehicle miles (Tittemore et al. 1972). Second terminal costs typically constitute over two-thirds of urban truck travel cost.[32] Third transport represents only about 10 percent of the total cost of producing and distributing goods in the United States.

The economic analysis of urban truck transport has concentrated on two questions. The first question is, Does industry minimize private truck costs, and if not, what could be done about it? The second question asks, Are there important externalities that warrant government intervention?

Private Costs

Casual examination strongly suggests the existence of important inefficiencies in the trucking sector, although a closer look leaves more

30. This freight excludes, of course, drinking water and sewage, as well as items purchased on personal shopping trips.

31. Examples are gasoline, home heating oil, new cars, and some department store merchandise.

32. See Hicks (1976). Much of the material on freight transport comes from his discussion, and all numbers, unless otherwise noted, are from his work.

doubt. Trucks in the United States average less than 3 hours on the road out of every 24, and in New York City about one-third of all trucks do not move at all on a given weekday. In addition to a large amount of idle time for a rig, trucks generally haul much less than a full load when on the move. In fact, survey numbers from Chicago and Columbus, Ohio, indicate that average urban truck cargoes are less than 20 percent of capacity. Obviously, if more intensive use were to be made of the truck fleet, the same freight could be delivered with many fewer trucks and probably with fewer miles driven.

There are important reasons to doubt, however, that this more intensive use of the truck fleet would make economic sense. Running trucks fuller and for more hours per day involves extra costs of handling, coordinating, and warehousing. In addition, it would surely increase time in transit. Imagine, for example, a retailer receiving shipments from three different wholesalers. It may be more efficient to dispatch three different trucks to the three different warehouses rather than hire one to make a circuit of all three. (In the latter case, for example, all three deliveries must be made on the same day, which may cause logistic problems.) In addition, given the high cost of terminal handling, it sometimes may be cheaper to use a truck trailer as a storage facility for a few days if the alternative is to unload the cargo into a warehouse and then reload it for shipment to its final destination.

The important point is that the line haul represents a minority of urban freight-shipping costs; although the cited numbers indicate substantial room for line-haul cost savings, such savings surely would be at the expense of further increases in terminal costs. In short, although doubts persist, there is no strong reason to believe that the freight transport sector fails to minimize private cost.

External Costs

As was seen in the "Personal Transport" section, the most important external cost of urban transport is congestion. Although trucks constitute about 20 percent of urban travel, they may contribute more than this share to total congestion. Trucks are larger and more unwieldy than cars, and they are more likely to obstruct traffic when loading and unloading.

Truck drivers, like car passengers, have no incentive to modify their behavior to reduce the congestion costs they impose on others. As noted, a truck imposes much higher congestion costs than a car; thus, its optimum congestion toll is higher as well. There are apparently no estimates of the optimum congestion toll for trucks, but it seems apparent that it would be several times that for cars, probably in the range of $1 to $5 per mile of downtown streets during rush hour. If trucks faced this rush hour road-use price, they would have an added (efficient) incentive to avoid the use of downtown streets during rush hour. We would expect some shifting to other times or fuller loads.

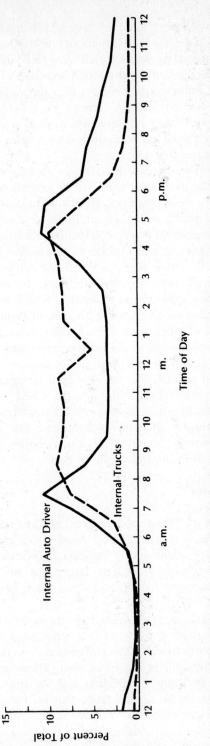

Source: Data reprinted from Tittemore L.H., M.R. Birdsall, D.M. Hill, and R.H. Hammond. *An Analysis of Urban Area Travel by Time of Day* (Boston: Peat, Marwick, Mitchell and Co., 1972).
Note: *Internal* means either origin or distribution in metro area.

Figure 13.7 *Hourly Distribution of Auto and Truck Volume, St. Louis, 1970*

Although time-of-day pricing would set up the incentives described, there is neither evidence on how much adjustment in fact would occur nor evidence on how much congestion would be reduced as a result of any adjustment. As Figure 13.7 shows, truck travel even now is not particularly concentrated during rush hour (although the figure does show that there is a substantial amount of truck travel during rush hours).[33] There is reason to believe, however, that there would be substantial response to an efficient toll. A toll of $3 per mile (taking the middle of the wide range of plausibility) at ten miles per hour is a toll of $30 per hour, or roughly a doubling of operation costs of a delivery van. At this cost, many operators might find it worthwhile to incur the inconvenience (and possible overtime pay) associated with making midday or nighttime deliveries. More information on this point would be extremely valuable.

Much (although no one knows how much) of the congestion caused by trucks is created when they stop for unloading. Here at least part of the problem may be one of changes in law and stricter enforcement of existing laws. A study of Toronto's city center noted that 19 percent of all recorded freight-vehicle stops were at office buildings with "good off-street facilities with good loading/unloading facilities" (Hicks 1976), yet 90 percent of these stops made no use of the facilities. Almost certainly these instances of street unloading represent a mild increase in convenience for operators at the expense of a substantial increase in congestion faced by others.

The efficient pricing of trucking road use—both for driving and unloading—possibly could lead to quite substantial improvements in the efficiency with which the urban transportation network is used. Hard evidence, however, is simply not available.

☐ Summary

The purpose of an urban transportation system is to facilitate the exchange of goods and services in the urban area. The optimum transportation system for an urban area depends on the area's size and structure, as well as on the historical development in the area.

Since 1940, the volume of urban transportation has grown rapidly, and there has been a massive shift from public transit to private automobile transportation. Total commuting in an urban area depends on locations of employment and residences. A person's choice of mode depends on time and money costs of alternative modes. Among realistic alternatives in urban areas in the United States, time is likely to be the dominant consideration. Any mode becomes congested if used by

---

33. In St. Louis (the city underlying the data in Figure 13.7), trucks account for 15 percent of vehicle miles during the morning rush hour, 18 percent during the evening rush hour, and 21 percent throughout the whole day.

enough passengers. Congestion costs are an important element in planning and pricing urban transportation systems. Both public transit and private automobile transportation are typically underpriced in metropolitan areas in the United States, at least during rush hour.

The major policy debate in urban transportation concerns the benefits and costs of public transit versus automobile travel in medium-sized metropolitan areas. The decision depends mainly on whether a combination of fares and conditions of service can be offered by public transit that will be attractive to enough commuters to make public transit economical. Subway systems surely cannot be economical for any but the largest metropolitan areas.

There is considerable doubt about the effects of urban transportation systems on the structure of urban areas. Public transit systems would probably increase CBD employment, but it is unlikely that the effect would be large. Very little is known about the urban transportation needs of the poor, but it is unlikely that the public transit systems being designed for many metropolitan areas will be valuable for low-income residents.

Questions and Problems

1. It is frequently proposed that New York City's subways and buses be free to all passengers. Evaluate the proposal on the grounds of efficiency and equity.

2. Suppose technological improvements made it possible for helicopter buses to carry 50 commuters each at 60 miles per hour and a fare of $0.20 per mile. What would be the effect on location of employment and housing in metropolitan areas during the remainder of the century?

3. Do you think it might be desirable to have one or more circumferential subway lines in large metropolitan areas at a future date?

4. Do you think low-income workers spend more or less time commuting than do high-income workers in metropolitan areas? Which group do you think commutes longer distances? Can you reconcile your answers with the theoretical analysis in Chapter 6?

5. Give the economic analysis underlying the following quotation, attributed to Yogi Berra: "Nobody goes to that restaurant anymore; it's too crowded."

6. Tittemore et al. (1972) studied traffic patterns on radial expressways for four cities (Boston, St. Louis, Seattle, and Louisville), and discovered the following: Between 6:00 and 9:00 A.M. about 70 percent of the traffic was going toward the CBD, whereas between

4:00 and 6:00 P.M. less than 40 percent of the traffic was flowing toward the CBD.

a. Does this traffic pattern suggest anything to you about efficient design and use of a roadway?

b. Do you see any problems with the road-use plans you discussed in part *a*?

c. The data from Tittemore et al. are from 1970. How do you think the numbers have changed since then, and what are the implications for efficient road use?

7. Suppose all transportation in the urban area were priced at peak-period pricing. If landlords could rent by the minute, what would happen to the rent gradient? What would happen if landlords could not rent by the minute?

8. Evaluate the effect of the following policies on equilibrium traffic flow:

a. "High-density vehicle" lanes, for example, traffic lanes open only to buses and cars carrying four or more passengers. (For an analysis of priority bus lanes, see Mohring [1979].)

b. Traffic information, for example, radio broadcasts from helicopters.

9. In March, 1986, a Staten Island congressman succeeded in obtaining Congressional legislation that eliminated the toll for vehicles crossing the Verrazano-Narrows Bridge in the eastbound direction, from Staten Island into Brooklyn. Instead, a double toll was imposed in the reverse direction. (After the change, tolls were $3.50 for cars and from $8.00 to $24.00 for trucks, depending on size.) The aim was to cut travel time for peak morning commuters travelling into Brooklyn and Manhattan, and to reduce the buildup of carbon monoxide on Staten Island from emissions generated by vehicles waiting in line to pay tolls.

a. One year after the legislation, annual toll revenue on the Verrazano-Narrows Bridge had declined by $7 million. Would you have predicted this decline in toll revenue? Why or why not?

b. Annual westbound traffic declined by about 1.2 million cars and 200,000 trucks. Where do you think all this traffic went?

c. Evening travel times increased an average of three to six minutes along the New Jersey-bound lanes of the Holland Tunnel. What does this reveal about commuters' value of time?

d. By March 1987, there was a proposal to rescind the original change in the toll collection. How would you vote if you lived on Staten Island? How about if you lived in Brooklyn, Manhattan, or New Jersey?

References and Further Reading

American Public Transit Association. *Transit Fact Book of 1981* (Washington, D.C.: 1982). A good annual publication giving data on public transit.

Baltimore City Department of Planning. *Traffic Study* (1983).

Domencich, Thomas, and Daniel McFadden. *Urban Travel Demand* (Amsterdam: North Holland, 1975). A definitive technical study using the probabilistic approach to travel demand.

Downs, Anthony. *Stuck in Traffic* (Washington, D. C.: Brookings Institution, 1992). A fine discussion of congestion problems.

Hensher, David. "Valuation of Journey Attributes: Existing Empirical Evidence." In *Identification and Valuation of Travel Choice Determinants,* edited by D. A. Hensher and M. Q. Dalvi (New York: McGraw-Hill, 1977). A very good source on consumer valuation of the time devoted to various aspects of travel, including a discussion of how economists estimate such things.

Hicks, Stuart. "Urban Freight." In *Urban Transport Economics,* edited by David Hensher (New York: Cambridge University Press, 1976): 100–130. The basis for most of our discussion on freight transport, this work includes substantially more detail than is in the text.

Holland, E. P., and P. L. Watson, "The Design of Traffic Pricing Schemes." In *Transportation Engineering* 23 (February, 1978): 32–38. A good review of pricing possibilities, including a discussion of experiences outside the United States.

Keeler, Theodore, et al. *The Full Costs of Urban Transport.* Monograph No. 21. (Berkeley: Institute of Urban and Regional Development, 1975).

Meyer, John, John Kain, and Martin Wohl. *The Urban Transportation Problem* (Cambridge, Mass.: Harvard University Press, 1965). A thorough analysis of the benefits and costs of alternative transportation modes.

Meyer, John, and John Kain, "Transportation and Poverty." In *Urban Economics: Readings and Analysis,* edited by Ronald Grieson (Boston: Little, Brown, 1973).

Mohring, Herbert. *Transportation Economics* (Cambridge, Mass.: Ballinger, 1976). A survey of transportation economics.

Quandt, Richard, ed. *The Demand for Travel: Theory and Measurement* (Lexington, Mass.: D. C. Heath, 1970). Technical papers on travel demand.

Small, Kenneth. *Urban Transportation Economics* (Philadelphia: Hammond Academic Publishers, 1992). An excellent summary of this subject.

Tittemore, L. H., M. R. Birdsall, D. M. Hill, and R. H. Hammond. *An Analysis of Urban Area Travel by Time of Day* (Boston: Peat, Marwick, Mitchell and Co., 1972). An excellent source of information on temporal variation in travel patterns.

Vickrey, William. "Pricing in Urban and Suburban Transport." *American Economic Review* 53 (1963): 452–465. One of the original discussions of innovative road-pricing mechanisms: very enjoyable reading.

Walters, Alan. "Theory and Measurement of Private and Social Cost of Highway Congestion." *Econometrica* 29 (1961): 676–699. A very good discussion on how to estimate real values for optimum tolls.

Walters, Alan. "Externalities in Urban Buses." *Journal of Urban Economics* 11 (1982): 60–72. Explores the possibility that smaller buses would be more efficient than larger ones, and has important implications for cost comparisons between cars and buses.

14

Local Government

☐ In the United States, state and local governments provide most of the governmental services that have a direct and immediate impact on people's lives and welfare. A large part of the federal government's budget is devoted to national security and other activities that affect the country's relationships with the rest of the world. Another part of the federal budget finances programs that affect the public only indirectly, such as research and space exploration. A third use of federal funds is to help finance programs that are the direct responsibility of state and local governments. State and local governments, however, administer almost all governmental services provided directly to the people. Important examples are public education, public health and welfare programs, police and fire protection, public transportation, and water supply and sanitation.

☐ SYSTEM OF STATE AND LOCAL GOVERNMENTS

Under the Constitution of the United States, sovereignty is shared between federal and state governments. Local governments are the creations of state governments. A characteristic of our federal system is that state governments have created a bewildering variety of local governments. Although this subject is mainly the concern of political science rather than of economics, some understanding of the systems of local governments is a prerequisite to understanding problems of local governments.

In 1988, there were nearly 83,000 local governments in the United States, almost all having limited power to levy taxes and spend the revenues collected. The best known of these governments are the 3,000 counties that nearly blanket the country and the 19,000 municipal governments. In addition, there are about 16,500 townships, 15,000 school districts, and 30,000 special districts. School districts are ordinarily empowered to levy property taxes to support public education. Special districts are established for specific purposes—most commonly water supply and waste disposal—and they levy taxes to finance their activities.

The functions assigned to particular governments vary greatly from state to state. Some state governments perform functions that county or municipal governments perform in other states. In some states, municipal governments provide public education, whereas school districts provide it in other states. Furthermore, there is little coincidence among boundaries of jurisdictions. School and special-district jurisdictions may overlap municipal and county boundaries. Thus, it is very difficult to obtain comparable data on state and local public finances. The fact, for example, that one state government has a much smaller budget than another may simply mean that municipalities in the first state finance services that are financed by the state government in the other.

As a result, many citizens are within the jurisdiction and taxing power of several local governments. Furthermore, an integrated economic area, such as an MSA, may contain an extraordinarily large number of local governments. The Chicago MSA has more than 1,100 local governments, and the New York City, Philadelphia, and Pittsburgh MSAs have more than 500 local governments each.

Political scientists tend to be critical of our complex system of local governments from the point of view of governmental operations. Although the issues go beyond the scope of economics, it is difficult not to conclude that the system is cumbersome and unwieldy. Some implications for governmental resource allocation are explored later in the chapter.

There has been a tendency to reduce the number of local governments during recent decades, although the reduction results entirely from school district consolidation. In 1952, there were almost 117,000 local governments in the United States, including 67,000 school districts. The number of special districts has more than doubled since the early 1950s, while the number of school districts has fallen by approximately 75 percent.

☐ FINANCE

In this section, we examine the broad outlines of federal, state, and local policies with respect to taxation and expenditure.

Trends in State and Local Finance

Table 14.1 summarizes twentieth century trends in governmental expenditure. Overall, government has been a major growth industry both in dollar expenditure and as a fraction of the GNP. In 1929, governmental expenditure at all levels accounted for 9.9 percent of the

GNP. Almost 60 percent of governmental expenditure was incurred by local governments; the federal government accounted for less than one-quarter of the total. Thus, state and local governments together spent 7.5 percent of the GNP.

The Great Depression and World War II reversed this pattern. By 1949, government spent 23 percent of the GNP, and federal expenditure was almost twice as large as state and local spending combined. From this point, total governmental expenditure grew fairly steadily, temporarily peaking at 34.5 percent of the GNP in 1975, declining mildly for the next five years, rising to 35.5 percent by 1982, and remaining fairly flat thereafter. In 1990, governmental expenditure was 34.9 percent of GNP. During this period, growth of state and local expenditures modestly outstripped that of federal; by 1975, state and local expenditures were about 70 percent as large as was the federal.[1] During this period, state and local expenditures rose from 7.8 percent of the GNP to 15 percent, thus representing one of the major growth sectors of the postwar economy. As with total governmental expenditure, state and local expenditures have been flat during the 1980s (14 percent of GNP in 1990 versus 13.5 percent in 1980).

The figures in columns 1, 2, and 3 of Table 14.1 appear to point to a resurgence of state and local governments in the postwar era, following dominance by the federal government from 1929 through 1945. To a degree this is true, but the role of the federal government at the state and local levels has grown dramatically during this period, as is apparent from Column 4, showing federal aid to lower levels of government as a percentage of the GNP. Federal aid rose from 0.9 percent of the GNP in 1949 to a high of 3.6 percent in 1976 and 1978. Thus, over one-third of the postwar rise in state and local expenditures (columns 2 and 3) was financed by grants from the federal government. Although it is difficult to sort out state and local finances, it appears that substantially more than half of the postwar growth in local expenditure has been financed by growth in federal aid.

The middle 1970s witnessed the end of the postwar growth of government, particularly at the local level. As a fraction of GNP, local governmental expenditure peaked in 1976, declined more or less steadily until the early 1980s, and has been flat since then. State expenditure followed the same pattern, except that it peaked a year earlier, in 1975. Federal aid continued to grow modestly for a few more years, peaking in 1978 and registering a fairly steep decline thereafter. By 1985, federal grants to state and local governments were only 78 percent as high as in the peak year of 1976, and remained at this level for the remainder of the decade. Since the 1950s at least, the pattern of growth and decline of local expenditures has closely tracked the

---

1.   In all of these discussions and in the figures in columns 1, 2, and 3 in Table 14.1, federal aid to state and local governments is excluded from federal expenditure but included in state and local expenditures.

Table 14.1   *Twentieth-Century Trends in Governmental Expenditure*

Year	(1) Total Governmental Expenditure		(2) State Governmental Expenditure	
	As a Fraction of GNP	Per Capita in Constant (1990) Dollars	As a Fraction of GNP	Per Capita In Constant (1990) Dollars
1929	9.9	$ 805	1.6	$ 131
1939	19.2	1473	3.3	253
1949	23.0	2362	3.0	306
1954	26.4	3117	2.9	343
1959	26.8	3401	3.4	431
1964	27.6	3937	3.8	537
1969	30.4	5086	4.5	758
1974	32.1	5841	5.3	961
1975	34.5	6321	5.8	1067
1976	33.5	6228	5.4	1005
1977	32.5	6427	5.6	1114
1978	31.6	6346	5.1	1030
1979	31.2	6337	5.4	1089
1980	33.1	6674	5.2	1048
1981	32.2	5981	8.0	1481
1982	34.4	6155	8.1	1447
1983	34.3	6293	7.9	1451
1984	33.3	6481	7.9	1541
1985	35.4	6951	8.1	1616
1986	34.9	7133	8.3	1683
1987	35.3	7226	8.3	1727
1988	34.9	7280	8.3	1786
1989	34.1	7418	13.5	2944
1990	34.9	7595	14.0	3043

	(3) Local Governmental Expenditure		(4) Grants from Federal to State and Local Governments	
As a Fraction of GNP	Per Capita In Constant (1990) Dollars		As a Fraction of GNP	Per Capita In Constant (1990) Dollars
5.9	$ 477		0.1	$ 9
7.3	555		1.1	81
4.8	499		0.9	90
5.3	624		0.8	94
6.2	786		1.4	178
7.0	995		1.6	231
8.0	1348		2.2	359
9.0	1635		3.1	555
9.2	1679		3.5	646
9.2	1716		3.6	658
8.5	1669		3.5	696
8.6	1741		3.6	721
8.1	1644		3.3	677
8.3	1685		3.4	680
7.8	1444		3.2	534
7.9	1418		2.8	474
7.8	1433		2.8	465
7.5	1464		2.6	480
7.7	1530		2.7	494
8.0	1619		2.7	511
8.1	1671		2.5	471
8.0	1722		2.4	490
n.a.	n.a.*		2.4	495
n.a.	n.a.*		2.5	523

*Data appearing in Column 2 (State) refer to the aggregate of state and local expenditures, which were not disaggregated for the indicated years.
Source: Data from the Advisory Commission on Intergovernmental Relations. *Significant Features of Fiscal Federalism,* various issues; U.S. Department of Commerce, *Survey of Current Business,* various issues (Washington, D.C.: Government Printing Office).

progress of the baby-boom generation through the educational system. We will return to this topic ahead.

Revenue.   Table 14.2 presents a detailed picture of the sources of state and local governmental revenue. The percentages refer to amounts the governments raise from their own sources. Intergovernmental transfers appear at the bottoms of the columns. Transfers to state governments are from the federal government. Transfers to local governments may come directly through state governments, or from funds raised by the state governments.

State governments raise almost 30 percent of their revenues from sales taxes. Personal income taxes represent the second-largest source of revenue for state governments, yielding about 60 percent as much revenue as the sales tax. The next-largest source, 16.9 percent, comes from charges such as tuition at state universities and license fees. (This percent is up dramatically from 1976 to 1977, when this source yielded only 12.5 percent of revenue.) The "other taxes" category, which accounts for 6.2 percent of state governmental revenues, includes motor vehicle taxes, death and gift taxes, severance taxes, and several other taxes.

Local governments receive about 37 percent of their revenue from property taxes (down from 50 percent in 1976 to 1977). Many also are permitted to levy sales taxes, and a few have income or payroll taxes. The

Table 14.2   *State and Local Government Sources, 1986 to 1987 (in Millions of Dollars)*

Source	State		Local		State and Local	
Property tax	$4,609	1.1%	$116,503	37.0%	$121,112	16.6%
Sales and gross receipts tax	119,838	28.9	24,725	7.9	144,563	19.8
Individual income tax	75,965	18.3	7,718	2.5	83,683	11.5
Corporate income tax	20,724	5.0	1,947	0.6	22,672	3.1
Other taxes, including licenses	25,797	6.2	7,400	2.4	33,197	4.6
Charges and miscellaneous	70,173	16.9	97,027	30.8	167,200	22.9
Utility and liquor store revenues	5,797	1.4	44,371	14.1	50,168	6.9
Insurance trust revenue	91,933	22.2	14,917	4.7	106,850	14.6
Total	$414,836	100.0%	$314,608	100.0%	$729,445	100.0%
Intergovernmental transfers	$102,381		$156,263		$114,857	

Source: Data from U.S. Department of Commerce, Bureau of the Census. *1987 Census of Governments.* Vol. 6, No. 1 (Washington D.C.: Government Printing Office, 1987): 12–15.

dependence of local governments on property taxes, however, is great and of long duration. No other tax yields nearly as much revenue. Local governments also raise substantial amounts of revenue from such charges as water bills, tuition at community colleges, parking fees, transit fares, and license fees. Table 14.2 shows that over half of all taxes and charges collected by state and local governments are collected by local governments.

Expenditure.   What do state and local governments do with the money they collect? Some comprehensive data appear in Table 14.3. Expenditures in the table refer to direct expenditures for the purposes indicated. State governments, for example, finance substantial parts of local governmental expenditures on public welfare. Such expenditures show up as a direct expenditure of local governments in the table and as an intergovernmental grant of state governments at the bottom of the table. It is important to recognize that these are expenditures made by the indicated level of government, with no presumption about the source of the funds. In the case of welfare, local expenditure frequently constitutes little more than local administration of a program financed at the state and federal levels.

Education constitutes 32.8 percent of state governmental expenditure—mostly higher education in state colleges and universities, which has grown rapidly in recent years. Many state governments also finance substantial parts of the cost of local elementary and secondary education, but expenditure is included in intergovernmental transfers in the state governmental budgets. State transportation expenditure is mainly construction and maintenance of state highway systems. Public welfare and health expenditures, which together account for roughly 24 percent of state budgets, grew very rapidly during the 1960s and 1970s, although the share declined modestly during the 1980s.[2]

Local governments spend 36.1 percent of their budgets on education. In addition to utilities and liquor stores, and administration and interest, the second-largest item is public safety, consuming 8.4 percent of local expenditure. Note that welfare makes up 4.5 percent of expenditure, but there are two things to remember in interpreting this number. First it fluctuates substantially over the business cycle, and second at least half of this figure is financed by the state government in most states. Of the other expenditure items, only transportation and health and hospitals exceed 5 percent (6.1 percent and 6.5 percent, respectively). It is important to note how heavily education dominates local budgets.

The dominance of education has diminished in recent years with the decline in the school-age population. From 1971 to 1972, education took 41.2 percent of local and 34.5 percent of state and local expendi-

---

2.   Much of this is federally mandated state expenditure on Aid to Families with Dependent Children.

Table 14.3 State and Local Governmental Expenditures, 1986 to 1987 (in Millions of Dollars)

Function	State		Local		State and Local	
Education	$150,486	32.8%	$168,216	36.1%	$318,702	34.5%
Transportation	41,712	9.1	28,519	6.1	70,231	7.6
Welfare	78,454	17.1	20,924	4.5	99,378	10.8
Health and hospitals	32,131	7.0	30,359	6.5	62,490	6.8
Public safety	18,677	4.1	39,034	8.4	57,711	6.2
Parks and natural resources	2,135	0.5	9,146	2.0	11,281	1.2
Sanitation	970	0.2	21,291	4.6	22,261	2.4
Housing and community development	2,129	0.5	10,492	2.3	12,621	1.4
Administration and interest	69,365	15.1	66,672	14.3	136,037	14.7
Utilities and liquor stores	8,442	1.8	60,666	13.0	69,108	7.5
Insurance trust	43,316	9.4	7,488	1.6	50,804	5.5
Other	10,686	2.3	2,610	0.6	13,296	1.4
Total	$458,503	100.0%	$465,417	100.0%	$923,920	100.0%
Intergovernmental transfers	$141,279		$5,251		$2,456	

Source: Data from U.S. Department of Commerce, Bureau of the Census. 1987 Census of Governments. Vol. 6, No. 1 (Washington D.C.: Government Printing Office, 1991): 12–15.

tures. This decline is entirely due to the decrease in the school-age population. The last 15 years have witnessed substantial increases in expenditure per pupil.

Table 14.2 shows that state governments collect about 32 percent more revenue than do local governments. Local governments, however, spend slightly more than state governments. The disparity between local government expenditures and tax collections is mainly financed by grants from federal and state governments.

Although total expenditures by state and local governments have grown rapidly since World War II, the proportions spent on important categories have changed relatively little. Contrary to much popular opinion, the proportion of state and local governmental expenditures used for health and welfare has changed little since 1945. As Chapter 9 showed, almost all income redistribution is carried out by the federal government. Among major expenditure categories, only education has increased substantially as a fraction of total state and local governmental expenditures in the past 50 years. As noted, this trend has been reversed as a result of the maturing of the postwar babies.

Systematic data do not exist for local governmental expenditure before 1929, but it is clear that the century from 1820 to 1920 constituted a period of rapid growth in the scope and cost of the responsibilities of local government. In 1820, New York City's budget was approximately one dollar per capita (and this figure was probably the highest in the country). At that time, government did not provide sewer, water, police, fire, or education. The increasing complexity of cities, which began in earnest in about 1820, placed new demands on the public sector in all of these areas.

To take one example, the increasing density of cities increased the risk of catastrophic fire, and indeed most major cities had several major fires during the nineteenth and early twentieth centuries. Many cities found volunteer brigades inadequate beginning in the 1840s, and took on fire prevention as a governmental task.

Public provision of water and sewer services also became fairly widespread before the Civil War, and the discovery that proper attention to clean water and proper sewage disposal reduced epidemic diseases added impetus to the movement.

The increasing scope of activity is reflected in the cost of government. New York's per capita expenditure, for example, was up to $6.53 in 1850 and to $27.31 in 1900.

Overview of Big-City Finances

Table 14.4 presents data on per capita revenues and expenditures for central cities and the entire MSA in six MSAs for which comprehensive data are available. The MSAs were chosen partly because they are representative of conditions in older, predominantly eastern, MSAs, but primarily because their local governmental structures are sufficiently simple to permit tabulation of data.

The top lines of the table show that central cities raise more revenue both from local taxes and charges and from intergovernmental transfers (provided by federal and state governments) than do suburbs in five of the six metropolitan areas. The exception is Roanoke, where the central city receives slightly less per capita intergovernmental aid than do suburban governments. On the average, the six central cities raise about 15 percent more from local sources and 25 percent more from all sources, on a per capita basis, than do all local governments in the MSAs.

It is well known that income is greater in suburbs than in central cities. In fact, per capita income is about 16 percent greater in suburbs than in central cities, a smaller spread than many people think. As Chapter 16 will show, however, other measures reveal a much greater city-suburb spread in economic well-being (see Table 16.4). Per-household income is about 39 percent higher in suburbs than central cities, and for northeastern cities, the spread is even larger—63 percent. (In the Northeast, that is, suburban per-household income is 1.63 times that of central cities.) Furthermore, the incidence of poverty is much higher in central cities. High central-city poverty, relative to suburbs, explains why central cities receive more intergovernmental aid than do suburbs, but it does not explain why they raise more revenue from their own sources. A poorer jurisdiction would be expected to spend less on both public services and private goods. As Table 16.4 reveals, ratios of city to suburban income deteriorated badly during the 1970s. During the 1980s, this deterioration continued in the Midwest and the West, although the ratio improved somewhat in the Northeast and the South.

There appear to be three reasons why central cities tax themselves more heavily than do suburbs. First central cities are relatively well endowed with nonresidential property. If half of the tax base is nonresidential, every dollar of property tax paid by a household is matched by one dollar paid by nonresidents. This process effectively cuts the price of public expenditure by 50 percent, which in turn, stimulates demand. Of course, the fiscal benefit of nonresidential tax revenue is reduced if the government makes expenditures explicitly for the benefit of nonresidential taxpayers. Most observers, however, believe nonresidential taxpayers pay much more in taxes than the cost of the services they receive from local governments.

Second many of the grants to local government have *matching provisions* (although this practice is less prevalent today than in the early 1970s). Under these matching conditions, receipt of grant money is conditional on some expenditure ("matching") of local funds. These matching provisions have the same stimulative effect as does nonresidential taxable property.

Table 14.4   *Local Government Finance in Six MSAs, 1986 to 1987 (Dollars per Capita)*

	New York		Philadelphia		Baltimore	
Revenues	City	Suburb	City	Suburb	City	Suburb
Intergovernmental	$1,356	$543	$ 904	$ 485	$1,285	$ 358
Own source	3,212	1,814	2,057	1,064	1,368	1,068
Total	4,568	2,357	2,961	1,549	2,653	1,426
Expenditures						
Capital outlay (18)	$343	$ 183	$130	$142	$348	$190
Educational services (19+20)	991	1,035	709	736	541	718
Public welfare (21)	478	116	84	70	1	2
Health and hospital (22+23)	345	159	107	37	56	19
Transportation (24+25)	215	84	79	78	202	66
Public safety (26+29)	385	206	295	105	304	135
Natural resources and parks (30+31)	50	47	43	14	69	25
Housing and community development (32)	206	23	102	24	203	16
Sanitation (33+34)	163	148	139	125	171	114
Administration and interest (35..37)	229	185	329	181	254	146
Utilities(39)	445	33	720	45	70	30
Liquor and insurance (40)	322	0	117	5	76	22
Other*	101	88	52	−44	−239	−75
Total (14)	$4,273	$2,307	$2,906	$1,518	$2,534	$1,558
Population (in thousands)	7,262.7	2,047.6	1,642.9	3,182.9	752.8	1,497.5

Note: Based on figures for the following cities and counties:
New York:
    Central city—New York City (Bronx, King's, New York, Queens, and Richmond counties)
    Suburban—Putnam, Rockland, Westchester counties in New York, and Bergen County in New Jersey
Philadelphia:
    Central city—Philadelphia county
    Suburban—Bucks, Chester, Delaware, and Montgomery counties in Pennsylvania and Burlington, Camden, and Gloucester counties in New Jersey.
Baltimore:
    Central city—Baltimore city
    Suburban—Anne Arundel, Baltimore, Carroll, Harford, and Howard counties

Table 14.4 (continued)   *Local Government Finance in Six MSAs, 1986 to 1987 (Dollars per Capita)*

	New Orleans		Richmond		Roanoke	
Revenues	City	Suburb	City	Suburb	City	Suburb
Intergovernmental	$501	$329	$726	$542	$540	$448
Own source	1,219	1,037	1,791	988	697	871
Total	1,720	1,366	2,517	1,530	1,237	1,319
Expenditures						
Capital outlay (18)	$216	$257	$262	$274	$186	$155
Educational services (19+20)	465	429	694	739	540	708
Public welfare (21)	27	13	216	39	79	33
Health and hospital (22+23)	13	257	69	34	0	0
Transportation (24+25)	132	85	119	54	108	33
Public safety (26+29)	184	138	285	161	226	114
Natural resources and parks (30+31)	43	60	73	23	39	16
Housing and community development (32)	94	7	211	9	98	0
Sanitation (33+34)	137	183	129	163	118	81
Administration and interest (35..37)	269	191	317	175	108	122
Utilities(39)	238	42	505	95	79	187
Liquor and insurance (40)	47	1	41	0	39	0
Other*	−157	−226	−248	0	−98	−57
Total (14)	$1,708	$1,437	$2,673	$1,766	$1,522	$1,392
Population (in thousands)	554.5	695.2	217.7	441.1	101.9	122.9

New Orleans:
   Central city—Orleans parish
   Suburban—Jefferson, St. Bernard, and St. Tammany parishes
Richmond:
   Central city—Richmond city
   Suburban—Charles city and Chesterfield, Goochland, Hanover, Henrico, New Kent, and Powhatan counties
Roanoke:
   Central city—Roanoke city
   Suburban—Botetourt and Roanoke counties and Salem city
* This category is the difference between total expenditure and the expenditure on the above categories.
Source: Data from U.S. Department of Commerce, Bureau of the Census. *1987 Census of Governments: Compendium of Government Finances.* Table 50 (Washington, D.C.: Government Printing Office, 1988).

Third many services are more costly to provide for poor central-city residents than for wealthy suburban residents. The prime example is education, which will be discussed in detail later. The basic point is that a given level of service quality (educational attainment, fire protection, and safety) requires more expenditure if the population is poor and the housing is high density.[3]

As Table 14.4 shows, central cities tend to outspend suburbs in almost all categories of expenditure. The only important exception is education, for which the central cities in the sample spend about 90 percent as much as the whole MSA. Even this figure is deceptive, however, because the data in the table are per capita. A smaller fraction of central-city populations is made up of school-age children, and a larger fraction of central-city children go to private schools. For these MSAs, the central cities have about 8 percent fewer school-age children than their suburbs. In addition, about 20 percent of central-city children use private schools, as compared with 10 percent in the suburbs. Making these adjustments, we see that per-pupil expenditure is approximately the same in these central cities as in their suburban rings.

Reasons for Central-City Fiscal Problems

The fiscal problems of central cities—rising taxes, taxpayer revolts, bankruptcies, and general perceptions of declines in service quality—received a great deal of attention during the 1970s and 1980s, and in particular, during the recession that began in 1990. A substantial portion of these problems can be traced to five causes. The first, which we have already discussed (and to which we will return in Chapter 16), is that central cities have increasingly become the home of low-income households for whom the provision of services is inherently expensive. The other four major causes are discussed here.

Declining economic importance of central cities. The improvement in intraurban transportation—both of people and goods—has led to a decline in the location advantage of central cities, as compared with their suburbs. The result of this decline has been a drop in central-city land rents relative to suburban rents, as Figure 14.1 depicts. (See chapters 6 and 7 for a full development of this point.)

The flattening land-rent gradient (see Chapter 6) depicted in Figure 14.1, indicates that firms' preferences for central locations are less strong than in the past. This lack of strong preference for central location means that firms cannot be taxed too heavily or they may leave the city. Back in the days when the CBD was the only feasible location for many activities, this concern was not serious. Recently, however, nonresidential activity has decentralized more rapidly than has residential activity. As a result, the nonresidential fraction of a city's tax base has declined over the past

---

3. Oates (1971) presents a very good discussion of the evidence on this point.

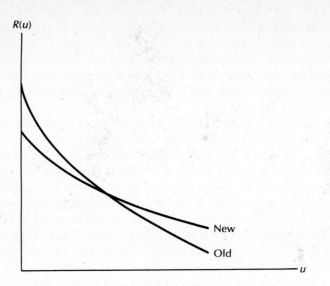

Figure 14.1   *Change in Land-Rent Function Over Time*

few decades. As previously noted, the higher the nonresidential fraction of the tax base, the lower is the effective price of public services. Thus, the decline in nonresidential property has increased the price of public services to residents.

Historically, central cities have had higher property values and a higher ratio of nonresidential to residential tax bases than have their suburbs. This pattern continues today, although in a much diminished form relative to 20 or 30 years ago. This city-suburban difference gives rise to the pattern of budget constraints depicted in Figure 14.2. The steeper budget constraint (line *A*) is faced by a central-city voter and reflects the fact that public services are relatively cheap and housing is relatively expensive. The flatter, suburban constraint (line *B*) shows that public services are relatively expensive and private goods are relatively cheap. As it is drawn, both constraints are tangent to the same indifference curve (*I*), which is to say that the price structure is such that it is possible to achieve the same utility in either place. Indeed, if all households were identical, that is the result that would be expected. The argument is identical to that used to derive the land-rent gradient in Chapter 6. If, at the given price structure, everyone prefers the suburbs, the price of central-city housing falls. This decline continues until households are again indifferent between living in the city and living in the suburbs. This concept is simply a generalization of the observation that a land-rent gradient soaks up any geographic utility differences that otherwise would exist. Thus, the difference between city and suburb is depicted in Figure 14.2 as a combination of a high central-city price for housing and a low central-city price for public services.

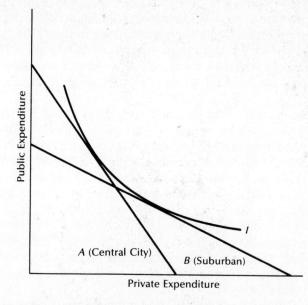

Figure 14.2   *City-Suburb Difference in Public Versus Private Expenditure*

Clearly, public expenditure would be higher in the central city (in Latin, *ceteris paribus*) than in the suburbs. As Table 14.4 shows, this prediction is borne out empirically. Per capita expenditure is about 15 percent higher in central cities than in their suburbs.[4]

The gradual erosion of the central cities' comparative advantages, particularly in the Northeast, has caused central-city budget constraints to become more like the suburban constraint depicted in Figure 14.2. With the shift to the constraint shown by line *B,* a given tax effort by a voter-taxpayer brings forth a smaller level of service than before. This result, not surprisingly, leads to voter pressure to cut taxes, as well as to complaints about service declines. The problem is that central cities put many plans into effect a few decades ago, when public expenditure was cheap (for voters). The dismantling or scaling-down of these programs, now that tax dollars are more expensive, is a painful and difficult process.

Central-city population decline. Chapter 16 will discuss the reasons for central-city population decline and will document its occurrence. At this point, the only concern is with the effect of population decline on central-city government. For this purpose, note

---

4.   The price differential that this section has discussed is by no means the only reason for this expenditure gap. For reasons that will be explained later, production costs are higher in central cities than in suburbs, so a given level of service costs more dollars. If demand is inelastic, this gives rise to higher expenditures. Also, as will be shown, federal aid has been targeted disproportionately to central cities, which has had a highly stimulative effect.

just that, for whatever reasons, central-city population decline went from being rare in the 1950s to being commonplace in the 1970s. A typical population loss for a northeastern central city during the 1970s was about 10 percent. For those cities that lost substantial population in the 1970s, population again fell in the 1980s, by about 5 percent on the average.

One would think that declining population would not impose a financial burden on a municipality—if population declines, there are fewer people demanding service, and it should be possible to cut costs. This reasoning is particularly sensible in light of the strong empirical evidence that most local public services are produced under constant returns to scale (see ahead, "Goods Provided by Local Governments"). The problem, however, is that returns are not constant in the *short run*. If the sewer and water systems were built for a city of one million, and population falls to 800,000, it is not possible to reduce immediately the stock of water mains, hookups, and treatment plants by 20 percent. The same point applies to streets and, to a lesser degree, to police and fire protection and to schools.

Notice that the problems caused by population decline are quite different from those caused by economic decline (discussed in the previous section). The erosion of the central-city comparative advantage causes a permanent shift in the ability to finance local public services. Population decline, in contrast, generates a temporary effect—the spreading of temporarily fixed costs over fewer people. In the long run, these costs become variable, and the problem can be expected to go away. One of the cost items that must be cut, of course, is labor—either through layoffs or (real) salary reductions. The real question that arises here is, How quickly and to what degree can the local government transform its fixed costs to variable (capable of being cut) costs and therefore return to production at minimum average cost?

Peterson (1976) has gathered a substantial amount of evidence on all of these problems. He has obtained spending figures for all central cities (except Washington, D.C.) that had populations that exceeded 500,000 either in 1960 or 1970. As compared with growing cities, the cities that were losing population from 1960 to 1973 spent almost 75 percent more per capita.[5] Cities that were growing between 1960 and 1970, but were declining after 1970, spent 28 percent more than growing cities. These figures are particularly striking because growing cities must, by virtue of their growth, make capital expenditures that frequently are not fully amortized. Clearly, something associated with decline greatly increases per capita expenditure. Most of this difference in

---

5. It is clear that only a part of this difference in expenditure is due to the phenomenon of fixed costs and declining population discussed here. If the population had declined even 30 percent recently and the expenditure remained unchanged, it would raise the per capita expenditure by 43 percent—just over one-half the observed difference between growing and declining cities.

expenditure, according to Peterson, is due to differences in the per capita number of public employees.

Thus, it appears that declining cities have had more trouble cutting back on employment than on capital expenditures. This finding is not surprising; most capital expenditure of a declining city is for maintenance and repair, and in bad times, the easiest thing to do simply may be to let the capital deteriorate. The public sector labor force, however, is not as easy to cut. Public employee unions are frequently strong in big cities, and public employees frequently represent a large fraction of voter turnout in local elections.

In the latter half of the 1970s, and more dramatically in the 1980s, the employment differences between growing and declining cities narrowed (see Table 14.5). Although data are incomplete, this narrowing was apparently accelerated during the 1980s. In part, this may be the kind of adjustment that would be expected after some lag. Part of it also is surely due to the shift in the focus of federal aid to cities. As the next section will show, prior to revenue sharing (which began in 1973), this aid was heavily targeted to declining cities. Relative to prior programs, however, the revenue-sharing program is more generous to growing cities. This finding also may explain the narrowing of the expenditure gap.

In addition to its effect on short-run average cost, population decline has a temporary adverse effect on revenue. If a city suffers a substantial population decline, almost of necessity it will be left with surplus housing. The existence of this surplus puts downward pressure on housing values. The depression of housing values will continue until the excess stock has been removed—a process that could take many years. According to one estimate (Hamilton and Schwab 1985), a decline of one percentage point in population growth leads to a 0.65 percent decline in the rate of increase of housing values. The effect on the property tax is obvious.

Thus, the process of population decline has serious adverse *short-run* consequences for local governments. Note that *being small* is not disadvantageous fiscally; rather, it is the process of converting from being a big city to a smaller one that is painful. Once the adjustment has been made, there is every reason to expect currently declining cities to be as viable as they ever were. The short run, however—the period of adjustment between a city's being big and small—may be quite long. In large measure, the adjustment process is one of retiring and refitting a capital stock—and a very durable capital stock, at that.

The role of the federal government should be one of easing the adjustment from big to small. As will be shown, however, federal aid over the past 25 years has had quite the opposite effect: It has made the adjustment much more painful, by encouraging the growth of local-government expenditure at precisely the time that local governments (particularly big cities) should have been accommodating to lower public-expenditure levels.

Table 14.5   *Central-City Patterns of Public Employment*

Type of City	Employees per 1,000 Population			Percentage Change in Total Employees	
	1964	1973	1980	1973 to 1975	1975 to 1980
Growing	22.2	24.0	23.4	+11	−13.5
Growing to 1970; declining thereafter	22.5	30.6	26.5	+ 4	−17.4
Declining	25.4	35.8	31.9	− 9	− 1.9
New York City	35.3	51.6	45.1	−13	+ 0.4

Note: The sample cities are those used by Peterson (1976). Three of the cities in his "growing to 1970; declining thereafter" category ultimately recorded positive population growth in the decade from 1970 to 1980. The inclusion of these cities in the "growing" category changes the numbers only modestly.
Sources: Data from Peterson, George E., "Finance." Table 6 In *The Urban Predicament*, edited by W. Gorham and N. Glazer (Washington, D.C.: Urban Institute, 1976); and U.S. Department of Commerce, Bureau of the Census. *Local Government Employment in Selected Metropolitan Areas and Large Counties* (Washington, D.C.: Government Printing Office, 1980).

Intergovernmental aid. The period from 1960 to 1976 witnessed rapid increases in federal aid to cities, sometimes administered directly and sometimes through state governments. Until 1973, much of this money was awarded in response to competitive applications and had rather specific strings attached. Some aid required either local matching or a specific level of tax effort on the part of the locality. On both counts, large declining central cities had an advantage relative to suburbs and small cities. For reasons already stated, large cities were already taxing themselves rather heavily. Furthermore, large-city bureaucracies, by virtue of their size, had an advantage over smaller governments in applying for federal grants. The result was that a large share of grant money went to big cities, and thus the period from the early 1960s to the mid-1970s was one of extremely rapid growth in big-city expenditures. Peterson (1976) reported that between 1962 and 1972, big-city expenditure rose 198 percent, whereas spending by all local government rose by only 142 percent. He further reported that almost two-thirds of this increase was financed directly by federal aid.

Beginning in 1973, the diverse set of federal transfers to states and cities was phased out, to be replaced by federal revenue sharing. This shift diminished cities' competitive advantage in attracting funds. Revenue-sharing money is dispersed according to a completely mechanical formula, with few strings attached and with only small weight given to tax effort. There is no longer any great advantage to skill at manipulating the federal bureaucracy. Revenue-sharing money sometimes is targeted to poor jurisdictions, but this is blunted by an upper limit on the per capita revenue-sharing grant.

The move to revenue sharing itself signaled a shift of grants away from big declining cities. In fact, however, the change was bigger than just this program shift would indicate. Shortly after the introduction of revenue sharing, the growth of total federal aid to cities and states came to a halt (adjusting for inflation). In more recent years, it actually has declined. Column 4 of Table 14.1 shows that real per capita aid to state and local governments peaked in 1978 at $231, declined by 25 percent by 1983, and remained flat during the 1980s.[6] This decline represents about 6 percent of state and local expenditures.

The effect of the growth and subsequent decline in federal aid on state and local expenditures is enormous. In 1954, state and local expenditures were 8.2 percent of the GNP; by 1974, the amount had risen to 14.2 percent. For local governments alone, some 35 percent of 1972 expenditure came from intergovernmental grants (not all was from the federal government, but many of the state grants were "pass-throughs" from the federal government). About 25 percent of state governmental expenditure came from the federal government. Thus, roughly 30 percent of 1972 state and local expenditures came from the federal government. Eliminating this source of funding and assuming that state and local tax efforts would not be any different, state and local expenditures in 1972 would have been 10 percent of the GNP—a modest increase over the actual figure for 1954 of 8.2 percent. It is fair to say that the explosion in state and local expenditures—and particularly big-city expenditure—was mostly due to the growth in intergovernmental aid.[7]

Whatever the growth of federal aid during the 1960s and early 1970s may have done, it certainly did not ease the transition of declining cities. During precisely the period when population declines were becoming commonplace and the need to adjust to smaller size was becoming apparent, federal-aid programs were put in place that encouraged local governments (particularly large central cities) to expand programs and offer expensive wage-and-benefit packages to their employees. When the decline in aid to big cities began in about 1975, the required adjustments were more painful than they otherwise would have been because of the extra expenditure programs cities had undertaken during the previous decade.

Sensitivity to economic cycles. The fourth financial problem local governments face is that their fiscal health is extremely sensitive to the business cycle. Almost unique among economic agents, state and local governments are constitutionally forbidden to run a current-account deficit during a recession.[8] The federal government, private businesses, and individual households can borrow (or increase borrowing)—with varying degrees of difficulty—to tide them over hard times. This option is not available for state and local governments. They are

---

6.   The $179 is in 1967 dollars, or about $810 in 1992 dollars.

7.   Intergovernmental aid, because of its matching provisions, may have stimulated local tax effort as well, but the evidence on this is less complete.

8.   The other major institution that is forbidden to run a deficit during a recession is the social security system. As with state and local governments, every recession brings cries of imminent bankruptcy for social security.

required to run a balanced current-account budget every year. Although they can engage in financial balancing acts to some extent, the constraint is quite rigid.

The restraint is a burden, because a recession has a strong tendency to increase local governmental expenditures and to reduce their revenues. On the revenue side, only property taxes are relatively unaffected by business cycles (although delinquency tends to rise in a recession). Income and sales taxes, fees, and user charges all decline. On the expenditure side, welfare, health, police, and housing expenditures all rise as unemployment rises. Thus, a locality that was running a healthy surplus in one year can find itself in a badly strained position a year or two later. During a recession, it is necessary either to cut expenditures or to raise taxes. Whatever effect these acts may have on the quality of public services, they do balance the books during a recession. They also set the stage for a very healthy fiscal recovery during the next boom. With high taxes and lean expenditures, the government will run a large surplus during the next expansion.

The recession of 1990 to 1992 clearly illustrates governmental sensitivity to the business cycle. Many localities curtailed pay raises for teachers and left positions open, and many of these same localities had appeared to be in a strong fiscal position in the late 1980s. It is a good prediction that they will look strong again by the middle of the 1990s.

Summary.   Given this list of central-city financial problems, it is not surprising that recent years witnessed some highly publicized state and local fiscal upheavals. The decline of central-city population, which began in earnest in the 1960s, continued (and, in some cases, accelerated) in the 1970s and 1980s. The economic importance of central cities relative to their suburbs declined, which reduced the tax bases of central cities. The growth of federal aid, which began in the early 1960s, came to a halt in the mid-1970s and then actually declined through 1983. The economy was unusually prone to recession. Finally, the reversal of the decade-old pattern of growing federal aid to big central cities coincided with the recession of 1975, making that episode especially painful for city governments.

☐ GOODS AND SERVICES

The "Finance" section of this chapter was concerned largely with the effects of various external forces on the ability of state and local governments to obtain revenues. This section examines the services local governments perform for their citizens. It is concerned largely with the nature of the goods provided—who receives them and who pays for them. Among other things, it discusses economic efficiency and income redistribution.

Goods Provided by Local Governments

One starting point is an examination of the goods local governments provide, beginning with reference to Table 14.3. A total of 36.1 percent of local expenditure is for education (almost entirely primary and secondary). Most of the remainder of the budget is split among transportation, police, fire, water, sewers, parks, hospitals, and welfare services. None of these items amounts to as much as 10 percent of the typical local budget.[9] Putting aside welfare for later discussion, we examine first the goods local governments provide to their citizens.

For a variety of reasons, the technology for producing many of these goods has not improved very much over the past few decades.[10] Unlike manufactured goods, the production of many local public services is not amenable to mass production, and therefore, it is not particularly amenable to technological improvement. Typically—although not universally—we expect more rapid technological progress in goods than in service production. The failure of technological progress in the local public sector to keep up with that in manufacturing means that the relative price of local public services has been rising and will probably continue to rise.

In general, during times of technical progress, the relative prices of some goods tend to rise. The benefit of technical progress is passed on to consumers in the form of lower prices. For some goods, technical progress is inherently infeasible, such as symphony orchestras and baseball games. (Innovation may make it possible to produce cars with fewer workers, but it is hard to imagine an innovation that will make it possible to play baseball without a shortstop.) Thus, it is natural to expect the relative cost of some goods, such as education and possibly police protection, to rise over time.

The second and most important observation about local public services is that they are not pure public goods in the sense, for example, of national defense. In other words, it is not true that a police force, water or sewer system, or school system of a given size can deliver the same quality of service to a city of 200,000 as it can to a city of 100,000. Unlike the case of pure public goods, additional residents do add to the cost of a given level of service. In fact, empirical evidence suggests that beyond a modest city size (around 10,000 people), local public services are produced under roughly constant returns to

9.   Aside from education, the largest items are administration and interest, utilities, and the like. Administration and interest is not payment for a direct service, and utilities are enterprises that sell products. Utilities are generally not financed by tax revenue.

10.   There have been important technological improvements in some services such as fire protection (see Getz [1979]) and police, but many services are provided with roughly the same technology as they were 20 years ago.

scale.[11] In other words, a population increase of 10 percent requires an expenditure increase of 10 percent, if services are to be maintained at a constant quality.[12]

If these goods are produced under constant returns to scale, why are they provided through the public sector rather than through private production and marketing as are food, housing, medical care, and a long list of other essential and nonessential goods? The answers vary from case to case.

In the case of most road networks, any method of collecting tolls to finance a for-profit firm would be so unwieldy that it would defeat the purpose of having an efficient network of streets.[13] In the terminology of public goods, even though roads are rival (one person's consumption reduces the amount available for others' consumption), they are nonexcludable, or at least exclusion is very costly. This finding means that the very act of collecting a price from users would be extremely costly. Such "nonexcludable" goods are different from the goods that usually appear in economics models as a result of this cost-of-pricing feature. Typically, such goods are provided by government and are financed not through the collection of an unwieldy fee but rather through taxation. For this reason, most roads are provided through the public sector, and they are financed through taxes rather than tolls. As was shown in Chapter 13, collection of tolls on some busy roads would yield benefits in terms of reducing congestion.

In the case of police protection, the problem is somewhat different. Police protection involves coercion (apprehension of criminal suspects, and the like). If the coercive power is not to be enforced by terror, it surely must be granted by the public sector.

Water, sewer, and fire protection, however, are like neither coercive police protection nor nonexcludable roads. It is easy to exclude someone from water service by shutting off the valve. The appropriate model here is *natural-spatial monopoly,* and it is best illustrated by way of example. Clearly, it is more efficient for the residents of one street to be served by one water main than by two. Thus, it is hard to imagine a

---

11. Inman (1979, pp. 296–298) notes that the evidence supporting the constant-returns claim is not fully convincing. Nevertheless, there is no evidence to contradict constant returns nor any inherent reason to believe that there would be important scale economies or diseconomies for most public services. (Mass transit is an important exception; see Chapter 13.)

12. Some people have argued that local public goods are unique because they can be congested, yet they have some of the characteristics of public goods. Up to some class size in a school, additional students do not diminish the quality of instruction; beyond some point, however, congestion sets in. This observation, although basically correct, in no way distinguishes local public goods from private goods. In the short run, output can be increased up to some point with no strain on fixed capacity. Eventually, the law of diminishing returns (that is, congestion) takes over and costs begin to rise. In fact, however, the same argument applies to any plant operating with short-run fixed capacity. When the capacity constraint becomes binding, the prescription is the same in both private and public sectors: build a bigger plant.

13. See Vickrey (1963) for a contrary view.

competitive water-supply industry. Even if it were imaginable, it would be inefficient, since it would involve duplication of water mains. Note that the existence of this natural-spatial monopoly is consistent with constant returns to scale; the extension of water service to 10 percent more people might increase the total cost by 10 percent, whereas serving one street with two water mains is twice as expensive as serving it with one. The natural-spatial monopoly does not arise from increasing returns, but rather from the avoidability—through monopoly—of duplication of capital. There are, of course, other natural-spatial monopolies, such as telephone service and electric power supply. The public has responded to these latter cases by regulating private industries, but in the other cases the most frequent (although by no means the only) response has been direct governmental takeover of the functions. Although this approach has disadvantages that will be discussed, it has the advantage of eliminating concern that the public will have to pay monopoly prices for services.[14]

Education is the most important and difficult case. Education is not a natural monopoly, nor does it involve the police power of coercion.[15] It is both rival (capable of becoming congested) and excludable (unlike roads). There is no reason to doubt that education could be provided efficiently through the private sector; indeed, in most cities private education exists and is a thriving and competitive industry.

The rationale for the public provision of education seems to be more philosophical and constitutional than economic. It derives from notions of equality, as expressed in the Declaration of Independence and the Constitution of the United States. More explicitly, most state constitutions require their subdivisions to operate "thoroughgoing and equal" primary and secondary educational systems. The purpose of the "thoroughgoing and equal" provision is that, whatever else *equality* might mean in the constitutional sense, it surely means at least some approximation of equal access to the basic skills needed for functioning in the adult world. If education were left to an unregulated private sector, the quality of education surely would vary significantly according to both the income and tastes of parents. Unequal access to education—particularly inequality based on parents' income—would serve as a significant barrier to upward mobility.

If the rationale for providing education, however, is to achieve some measure of equality in access, we must ask how well this objective is met through our current educational system. The best way to address this question is to look for a realistic theoretical model of the local public sector. The best-known and most complete model is known as the

---

14.   Governmental operation is by no means the only approach that offers at least some hope of competitive (average cost) pricing. For an excellent discussion of options, see Ely (1888).

15.   It is true that education is compulsory; unlike police protection, however, this feature does not prevent it from being provided in the private sector.

Tiebout hypothesis. A discussion of this model and an examination of its implications and realism ensue. Some special problems of providing education will be discussed later in the chapter.

Tiebout Hypothesis

In 1956, Charles Tiebout put forward a provocative hypothesis about the interaction of government and private decision-making in the context of the local governmental system of the United States. Since then, dozens of books and papers have elaborated, criticized, and tested the theory. No one can understand local government in the United States without understanding the Tiebout hypothesis.

In essence, the Tiebout hypothesis argues that "shopping" for a jurisdiction and its attendant offerings of education and other services is much like shopping for other goods. According to this model, competition fosters efficiency in the local public sector much as it does in the private sector. A crucial feature of this shopping model is the availability of a wide variety of jurisdictions offering different mixes of public services. In general, the better the services, the higher will be the costs in terms of taxes and housing (as will be seen). Thus, choice of jurisdiction represents choice of public service offering, along with an obligation to pay the cost. The details of this model will be worked out and its realism and implications will be examined.

Chapter 4 showed that metropolitan areas in the United States have been decentralizing for decades. In the nineteenth century, decentralization typically was accompanied by the outward movement of central-city boundaries. Since World War II, decentralization has occurred on a massive scale, but movement of central-city boundaries has become the exception instead of the rule.

Chapter 7 discussed the tendency for high-income residents to live farther from metropolitan centers than low-income residents, even in the absence of local governments. Consider a typical postwar metropolitan area that is growing and decentralizing rapidly. People with average or above-average incomes are moving into areas outside the central city in large numbers. At this point, one of three things must happen: These residents must petition to be annexed to the central city, new local governmental jurisdictions must be formed, or rural governments must be made into suburban governments. The central city is being populated with low-income people, crime and tax rates are rising, and public schools are deteriorating. The new suburban residents perceive that they would be better off having their own local government instead of being annexed to the central city. It is most advantageous if a group of perhaps 10,000 to 100,000 people with similar incomes and demands for local public services form a new jurisdiction. There, they can vote the bundle of local governmental services and the real estate taxes to pay for them that best suit their needs and tastes. In this way, several suburban governments are formed, within each of which live a few tens of thousands of people who are similar in income and family composition. Family composition is an important determinant of the demand for the most expensive local government service—public schools. The advantage to groups of people with similar demands for local governmental services in locating in the same jurisdictions is the essence of the Tiebout hypothesis.

The tradition in the United States of financing local governments by locally levied real estate taxes complicates the analysis in the last paragraph. As Chapter 10 showed, the income elasticity of housing demand is not far from 1. Thus, the relatively high-income residents of a particular suburb own relatively expensive homes. The real estate tax rate is set so that tax payments on the homes yield the revenues needed to finance the chosen bundle of local governmental services. A low-income family with a correspondingly modest housing demand, however, would be tempted to move to the community. Every resident pays the same tax rate, so the total taxes on a modest home would be small. Thus, the low-income family could obtain the local governmental services at a relatively small cost. Such a family is referred to as a "free rider," in that its share of local taxes is smaller than the share of local governmental services it consumes.

Communities have perceived that they can exclude free riders by land-use controls. The ostensible justification for land-use controls is to protect residents from nuisances such as noise, pollution, and congestion. State governments and courts, however, have given local governments wide latitude in choosing land-use controls. In the 1950s, 1960s, and 1970s, a common justification for land-use controls became "to protect the character of the community," which often means "to prevent free riders." Local land-use controls frequently specify minimum lot sizes and square feet of floor space, prohibit multifamily housing, and so on. A long list of such requirements effectively excludes from a community those whose homes would not pay the residents' shares of the cost of local-government services. Tiebout did not emphasize land-use controls to exclude free riders, but subsequent writers have.[16]

A large metropolitan area might have many suburban jurisdictions. Some might be inhabited by very high-income residents and have stringent land-use controls and very high-quality governmental services. Others might be inhabited by people with more modest incomes and have correspondingly modest governmental services and land-use controls. As an illustration, suppose there is a rich jurisdiction and a poor one—Jurisdiction A and Jurisdiction B, respectively. All houses in Jurisdiction A are worth $100,000, and the jurisdiction provides $2,000 per year in public services. The property tax rate is 2 percent. In Jurisdiction B, every house is worth $50,000, and the community

---

16. Tiebout's original model was not concerned with the manner in which local public goods were financed, hence, his lack of concern with zoning, property taxes, and so on. These details were left to be addressed by later researchers.

provides $1,000 in public services. Thus, Jurisdiction B's tax rate also is 2 percent. Obviously, all residents get what they pay for. The "price" of public services is equal to average cost, which in turn, is equal to marginal cost if there are constant returns. Equally obvious is the fact that there is no income redistribution.

For households that demand a $50,000 house and $1,000 in public services or a $100,000 house and $2,000 in public services, the consumption bundle in this primitive public economy is exactly what it would be if there were no taxes and people bought public services at a store. If a sufficiently rich variety of communities exists, every household receives the bundle it would demand in a private market, and the competitive (efficient) outcome is mimicked perfectly. Notice that a low-income person would rather live in Jurisdiction A than in Jurisdiction B; property taxes are the same in both jurisdictions, and public services are twice as high in Jurisdiction A. Of course, if all low-income people moved to Jurisdiction A, its tax base would be diluted, and taxes would have to be raised or services would have to be reduced. This process is why voters in Jurisdiction A would be expected to erect zoning barriers that prevent the construction of $50,000 houses (or, for that matter, houses worth anything less than $100,000).

Capitalization. This model is unrealistic; jurisdictions are far from homogeneous with regard to housing value, and therefore with respect to tax payment. The result that there is no income redistribution also seems to be an overstatement. It is true that there is no redistribution between the rich suburbs and the poorer central city. Surely, however, the poor who are in the suburbs are beneficiaries of public-sector redistribution, and surely there is redistribution between central-city wealthy and poor.

In the case of a representative suburb, the poor pay less in taxes than do the wealthy, and they probably have almost equal access to the public services. Precisely because of this apparent redistribution, however, the few low-income houses in the otherwise wealthy jurisdiction are unusually valuable. Suppose the suburb is Jurisdiction A of our previous example, and Jurisdiction B is the central city. Jurisdiction A is now dotted with a few low-income houses, although not enough to have any noticeable effect on the tax base. One of the low-income houses, which is physically identical to the $50,000 houses in Jurisdiction B, comes on the market. If poor people attach any value to the extra $1,000 of services offered in Jurisdiction A as compared with Jurisdiction B, the house sells at a premium above $50,000. If they value the service at the full $1,000, the premium is equal to the present value of this extra $1,000 of services ($10,000, if the interest rate is 10 percent).[17] Thus, in this case the house sells not for $50,000, but rather for $60,000. This housing value

---

17.   This calculation is not quite right; with the housing-value increase, the taxes will go up, and this will slightly depress the premium.

Table 14.6   *Toronto Zoning and Land Values*

Zoning Category	Units per Acre Permitted	Tax Revenue per Unit	Public Sector Cost per Unit	Land Price per Acre
R-2	2	$1,210	$800	$90,000
RM-2	12	361	800	150,000

Sources: Data from Hamilton, B. W., "Local Government, the Property Tax and the Quality of Life: Some Findings on Progressivity." In *Public Economics and the Quality of Life*, edited by L. Wingo and A. Evans (Washington, D.C.: Resources for the Future, 1977); after Peter Mieszkowski.

premium—the present, or capitalized, value of the extra services (or, in some cases, the tax savings)—is called *capitalization*. Once the housing market is in equilibrium, capitalization effects eliminate any utility differences that otherwise would exist between city and suburb. It is one more application of the land-rent gradient principle: If geographic differences in attainable utility exist, the tendency of people to migrate to the high-utility region will bring about housing price differences sufficient to soak up the utility differences.

The striking and important conclusion from this analysis is the following: If a poor household wants to become a beneficiary of income redistribution by moving into a wealthy suburb, it must purchase this right at a fair market price. What the tax-expenditure bundle gives, the housing market takes away.[18] Table 14.6 clearly illustrates the point (Hamilton 1977). The numbers are for fairly centrally located plots of vacant land in Toronto. Substantial effort was made to obtain data from parcels that are identical except for their zoning restrictions. The R-2 zoning category permits two dwelling units per acre, and RM-2 permits 12 units per acre. Clearly, R-2 houses will be nicer and more expensive than RM-2 houses, which is why the city anticipates $1,210 in tax revenue from an R-2 house and only $361 from an RM-2 house. At an annual per-house public sector cost of $800, it appears that wealthy people are subsidizing the poor. At a 10 percent interest rate, the present value of the extra taxes paid by an R-2, as compared with an RM-2, house

---

18. There is a potentially important qualification to this finding, namely, that supply adjustments may bring about some redistribution after all. This issue is treated only briefly here, because it is somewhat technical and because empirical evidence suggests that the account in the text is basically correct. The supply adjustment works as follows: In Jurisdiction A, a house otherwise worth $50,000 sells for $60,000 because of the fiscal advantage in Jurisdiction A. Because it only costs $50,000 to build, there is extra profit to be made in building low-income housing in Jurisdiction A. This extra incentive remains until the house in Jurisdiction A will cost only $50,000. This price is enough to drive the price in Jurisdiction B down to $40,000. The capitalization effect described above may or may not release a sufficient supply response to bring about this price reduction. If supply response is sufficiently large, low-income people get their housing plus public services at below cost throughout the urban area. This practice is financed by the fact that high-income people pay more than cost for their services, and the end result is that there is a measure of true income redistribution. In fact, as will be shown, this supply adjustment does not appear to take place to any important degree. The reason is that every jurisdiction—in an effort to protect or enhance its tax base—passes zoning ordinances that restrict the supply of low-income housing high enough to undo the redistribution through local taxation and expenditure.

is $8,490. This conclusion, however, is contradicted by the last column, which reveals that wealthy people pay a much lower price for the land on which their housing sits than do poor people. An R-2 lot (one-half acre) sells for $45,000, whereas the same quantity of land zoned RM-2 costs $75,000—a premium of $30,000. This makes the RM-2 tax break of $8,490 (present value) look like it is not such a good deal after all.

In the Toronto example, the zoning law restricts the supply of low-income housing. Many people are surprised to learn that land zoned for low-income housing sells at a premium, as compared with land zoned for high-income housing. The pattern has been observed in many cities, however, and in many cases the price differences are greater than those reported for Toronto. On reflection, the pattern of land-price differentials is what would be expected. In residential zoning, low-income (high-density) housing is always the excluded activity. If land were more valuable when devoted to high-income housing than low-income housing anyway, zoning would be superfluous.

If the poor are to be kept out, zoning is needed precisely because, in many circumstances, the poor would be able to outbid the wealthy for land in an unrestricted market. In the Toronto case, 12 poor households obviously can outbid 2 wealthy households for land. Zoning keeps the price of high-income housing low (and the price of low-income housing high) by setting aside a large amount of land for high-income development and preventing poor people from bidding on the land. It is somewhat like passing a law that sets aside a certain fraction of total food output for wealthy people.

The net effect of property taxation (which tends to redistribute from the wealthy to the poor) and zoning (which redistributes from the poor to the wealthy) is that there is little or no income redistribution at the level of local government. People receive public services from local government and pay for them with a combination of taxes and house-value premiums. Therefore, to a fairly good approximation, people get what they pay for in the way of public services.

Not only do people get what they pay for, there is considerable evidence that they get roughly what they demand. Statistical studies have shown that expenditure on both education and other public services rises with average income and the fraction of the tax base that is nonresidential, and that it falls with the relative cost of providing the service. This pattern is just what would be expected in analyzing the market demand for an ordinary good. Based on these estimates, demand for public services (most importantly education) appears to be mildly inelastic with respect to both price and income.[19]

Realism of the Tiebout hypothesis.   Is the Tiebout hypothesis realistic? Its preconditions are a substantial number of suburban governments in a metropolitan area, each with considerable local control over

---

19.   Inman (1979) provides a good summary of this evidence.

taxes, service provision, and land-use controls. Its implications are that such communities vary, but that within a community there are people with similar incomes, houses, and demands for local governmental services.

No one can drive through typical metropolitan suburbs and believe there is no truth to the Tiebout hypothesis. Many observers have commented—sometimes sarcastically—about the homogeneity of suburban communities. In addition, statistical studies have shown that there is more homogeneity by income and house value within suburban than within central-city neighborhoods, and more than would be expected in the absence of the motivations in the Tiebout hypothesis (Hamilton, Mills, and Puryear 1975).

Another set of statistical studies, pioneered by Oates (1969), shows that property values are higher in jurisdictions with high public expenditure than in low-expenditure jurisdictions, if all other things are equal. Similarly, low-tax jurisdictions have high property values. Interestingly, Oates found that property values are about $12 higher for each extra dollar of annual public expenditure. This amount would appear to be about the present, or capitalized, value of the extra expenditure. This finding is strong evidence that the *foot-voting* (deciding where to live based on public service offerings and taxes) that is the heart of the Tiebout model really does occur, since it is hard to imagine how property values would be affected by public-expenditure levels except through people's tendency to migrate from low- to high-expenditure jurisdictions. To state it a bit differently, high-expenditure jurisdictions are more valuable than low-expenditure jurisdictions because the high expenditure makes them more desirable. The previously postulated capitalization really does occur, and it is reasonable to believe it is part of the mechanism that ultimately stems the flow of migration to high-expenditure jurisdictions.

Of course, there is variety within suburban communities. People's choices of residential location depend on many things other than local taxes and government services provided. Suburbs are by no means as homogeneous as they would be if the Tiebout mechanism were the only force at work. However, recall what has been shown: Communities need not be perfectly homogeneous for the Tiebout hypothesis to work. Certainly, the Tiebout hypothesis contains important variables without which the residential pattern of suburbs in the United States cannot be understood.

Welfare economics and the Tiebout hypothesis. What about the normative characteristics of the Tiebout hypothesis? Do suburbs organized along Tiebout lines promote efficiency and equity in resource allocation? The question is important. Local governmental expenditures account for more than 10 percent of personal income in the United States. It is important to know whether they satisfy the conditions for efficient and equitable resource allocation discussed in Chapter 8. It is also important to know to what degree access to quality education is determined by income.

Many people are surprised to learn that a world like that in the Tiebout model might allocate resources efficiently to local governments. If there are enough local governmental jurisdictions, people can live in communities that provide the optimum bundle of local governmental services and corresponding taxes. By choosing the right communities and voting for officials who favor the appropriate services and taxes, all people can consume the quantity and quality of local governmental services they would consume if the services were sold on competitive markets. The requirement is that there be enough communities to provide each desired bundle of local governmental services, houses of a particular value, and location relative to workplaces. Of course, no metropolitan area has enough jurisdictions to satisfy this requirement. The Tiebout hypothesis, however, provides an approximation of both reality and efficient resource allocation.

An important corollary to the efficiency characteristic of the Tiebout hypothesis is that there is no resource misallocation from local real estate taxes. Shopping among different communities for the right bundle of local governmental services is just like shopping among car dealers for a car that combines the optimum combination of quantity, quality, and price for the customer. In both cases, the market satisfies the conditions for efficient resource allocation presented in Chapter 8.

This efficiency result must be qualified. First the limited number of metropolitan jurisdictions available means that the efficiency result is at best an approximation. That is, there simply is not enough variety so that all consumers are precisely on their demand curves. (Of course, there is also a limit to the number of available automobile types, as a result of scale economies. So many consumers are not able to find precisely the car they would like to buy either.) Second local governments must be free to choose their bundle of services and tax rates. In Europe, local governments are financed or tightly controlled by national governments. The Tiebout hypothesis cannot work there. It has been seen that in the United States, local governments are increasingly financed by grants from state and federal governments. This process prevents the Tiebout-like world from working efficiently. Third some government services cannot be provided by fragmented local governments, for example, metropolitan area-wide public transit and water supply systems. Such services must be provided by state governments or by agreements among local governments.

Fourth it is unlikely that competition among jurisdictions offers the same technological discipline as does competition in the private sector. In the perfect-competition model of the private sector, each firm earns zero profit; failure to operate with the best available technology results in bankruptcy. Thus, any technological improvement penetrates the industry relatively quickly. Since the method of shopping for local public services is so indirect, however, it is unlikely that any discipline imposed on inefficient producers would be either as swift or as certain in the public sector as in the private sector.

As will be discussed, technological progress tends to be relatively slow in the public sector (basically, because it is not amenable to mass production techniques to which technological improvements can be readily applied). The lack of market discipline noted above, however, may bring about a worse record on efficiency gains than is required by the nature of the product. Hulten (1982) has estimated that there actually has been negative technological progress in the provision of state and local services over the past 20 years—that we use more physical inputs now than 20 years ago to produce the same output.

Finally, the Tiebout hypothesis cannot ensure efficient resource allocation to local governments in metropolitan central cities. One reason is that most central cities were built before land-use controls became important, so land-use controls cannot perform their function of excluding free riders in central cities. Another reason is that central cities are too big and diverse for the Tiebout mechanism to work. In most metropolitan areas, it is not possible to find enough people with similar demands for local governmental services and location to populate a central city. This finding implies that real estate taxes have a much greater effect in distorting resource allocation in central cities than in suburbs.

To be specific, consider the following example. Suppose a worker is promoted, raising his or her take-home pay 25 percent. As a result, the worker's family wants a better house and better public education. If the family lives in a suburb, it can move to another suburb better suited to its higher economic status. If it moves from one house to another in the central city, it may obtain a better house, but the quality of public education is unlikely to be much better at one school than another within the central city (with the exception of so-called *magnet schools,* which cover large districts). Thus, higher taxes paid on the better house represent no higher-quality local governmental services. Such taxes distort resource allocation.

If the family does not like the central-city schools and taxes, why does it not move to a suburb? One reason may be that the central city is a much better location for it, given the breadwinner's workplace. Another reason may be that its income is not yet high enough to get the family over the barrier raised by exclusionary land-use controls in suburbs. A third reason may be that the family is black and is excluded from or made unwelcome in suburban communities by racial prejudice.

It is unfortunate that the efficiency characteristics of the Tiebout hypothesis are unavailable precisely where residents can least afford the loss of welfare caused by distorting real estate taxes—the central city. That, however, is not the end of the story. From an equity viewpoint, the basic purpose of people "voting with their feet" is to avoid paying more in real estate taxes than the local government services are worth to them. In other words, in a Tiebout world, local governments cannot redistribute income. If a suburban jurisdiction is homogeneous, there is no one within the jurisdiction to whom income must be redistributed. If the local government did levy significantly higher taxes on more valuable homes, either the residents would move to a jurisdiction in which local taxes reflected their demand for local governmental services or their houses would become cheaper. Given the approximate nature of the Tiebout hypothesis, local governments can engage in a small measure of income redistribution; given the mobility of upper-income households, however, this redistribution cannot be substantial.

The final aspect of the equity issue is that, in the postwar United States, land-use controls that exclude low-income central-city residents from suburban residences by and large exclude blacks and other minorities. The police power of suburban governments thus is added to other forms of discrimination against minorities in the United States (see "Inefficiencies in private land markets" for a discussion of police power).

One possible reaction to these equity issues is to decide that income redistribution should continue to be left to the federal government, as it mostly has been. Once that view is taken and it is believed that the enforcement of open-housing laws makes the racial exclusion unimportant, we can approve of our Tiebout-like suburbs. This case is one in which, for many people, there is strong conflict between efficiency and equity considerations.

Federal and state legislatures have shown little hostility to exclusionary suburbs. Strong attacks in the courts, however, have been partially successful. Some have contended that exclusionary zoning deprives central-city residents of access to governmental services—especially education—that are guaranteed by state or federal constitutions. Other attacks have been more broadly based, claiming that all residents have a right to live wherever they can bid successfully, as well as that land-use controls artifically raise housing costs beyond the reach of many (Mills [1979]; Rubinfeld [1979]).

Many attacks have not survived appeal. Some have, however, and courts are increasingly sympathetic to plaintiffs as their understanding of the implications of the Tiebout hypothesis improves. What influence the courts have is another matter. Courts do not build houses. They can say that a certain pattern of controls is unconstitutional and must be redone within certain guidelines. Local planners then redo the controls, and a new set of legal procedures is required to test their constitutionality. The point is that the courts have permitted local governments to have a wide range of land-use controls. To distinguish between constitutional and unconstitutional uses of those controls is a difficult task.

Summary of the Tiebout hypothesis.

The basic conclusions that emerge from the Tiebout model are (1) that it describes a mechanism for promoting economic efficiency (although surely quite an imperfect one) and (2) that it severely limits the ability of local government to redistribute income. Although the Tiebout model was introduced to examine education, the results apply across the whole range of local governmental activities, including welfare. If a jurisdiction has a particularly generous welfare program, the value of low-income housing can be expected to be relatively high and the value of high-income housing to be relatively low. The poor must pay (in higher housing costs) for the welfare they receive, and the wealthy are compensated (with below-market housing) for contributing to the welfare programs. It is easy to see why this result is so general: If there is perfect mobility between jurisdictions, it is impossible for the poor in one jurisdiction to be better off than those in another.

Some Special Problems of Education

As already noted, it is quite feasible to provide education in a purely private market, and there is every reason to believe that such a market outcome would be competitive rather than monopolistic. The public provision of education seems to rest on the view that people would not like the private market outcome for philosophical reasons.[20]

An examination of the actual outcome of the public education delivery system, however, shows that it is very much like a market outcome. Parents with a strong demand for education purchase high quality education for their children, and parents with lower demands actually purchase lower quality education for their children. Both types of parents pay about what it costs to educate their children. In other words, the Tiebout mechanism has given us an elaborate and cumbersome mimic of the outcome that would have emerged if education had been left in the private sector. If we retain the view that the market outcome in education is undesirable, we should be just as unhappy with the Tiebout outcome.

Displeasure with the Tiebout outcome has led to a number of proposals to reform education. The primary proposals are education vouchers and increased centralization (involvement of state and federal government) in the provision of education. Before examining these proposals, we need to note one special feature of the technology for providing education—namely, the role of students, parents, and peers in the production of education.

Up to this point, education has been discussed as if it were produced according to a technology just like any other good. Inputs (teachers, books, and buildings) are purchased, and they produce an output, education (which might be imperfectly measured as improvements in the test scores of students). A large body of evidence, however, indicates the production of education is much more complicated than

---

20.   Some have argued that education is provided publicly because of the external benefit of having an educated populace. This factor, however, does not require public provision; it merely dictates a subsidy.

that (Summers and Wolfe 1977). The discussion turns now to movements over time in the measured quality of education, and follows up
with a discussion of *how* education is produced.

The quality of education.   There is widespread concern that the
quality of education in the United States is bad and getting worse. The
most frequently cited evidence is a steady decline in test scores, as well
as a decline in the relative pay of teachers.

All of the popularly employed standardized tests began to show
declines beginning sometime between the late 1960s and 1970. What is
less well known is that after reaching a trough in the mid-1970s, all of the
test scores have shown a recovery that is approximately as rapid as the
original decline. When one plots the data by birth date, an interesting
pattern emerges. At all grade levels, pupils who were born between
about 1962 and 1964 perform worse than those who were born either
before or after this period. The data for fifth graders born in 1974 show
scores higher than at any previous time. Thus, the decline in test scores
seems to have been fairly short-lived, and largely concentrated on
children born in the early 1960s. This characterization of the facts is
pervasive—it applies to blacks, whites, segregated and integrated school
districts, and to all regions of the country.[21]

Beginning in 1985, there has been another significant decline in
verbal (but not math) standardized achievement test scores. But this
decline appears to be almost completely due to a rise in the fraction of
high school graduates taking the graduate record examination. (In 1980,
32 percent of graduating seniors took the test; by 1991, the fraction was
up to 41 percent.)

There are two significant but quantitatively small qualifications to
this pattern. One is that black students showed smaller declines than
whites; their scores stopped declining earlier; and the upturn in black
scores was sharper than that of whites. Thus, during the period from
1975 to 1984, the gap between black and white performance narrowed
by about 20 percent. (The same is true for performance by Hispanics.)
The second qualification is that this narrowing of the gap in test
performance took place both for blacks in integrated and heavily
segregated schools.[22] These trends raise fascinating and troublesome
questions: What went wrong with the birth cohorts of 1962 to 1964, and
what can we do to prevent a recurrence? To date, there is no research
even directed toward these questions, let alone answers to these
questions. Taken altogether, there seems little reason to conclude from
the history of test scores that the quality of education is declining.

---

21.   The decline in test scores during the 1970s was much more pronounced for
the verbal section than for mathematics and the recovery of verbal scores was much less
complete than for math scores.

22.   These facts on educational achievement come from *The Condition of Education 1992* (U.S. Department of Education, 1992).

Table 14.7   *Current National Educational Expenditure*

Year	Total Enrollment (in Thousands)	Expenditure 1989–90 (Dollars)*	
		Total (Dollars in Millions)	Per Pupil (Dollars)
1970	59,853	230,115	3,845
1975	58,626	266,404	4,544
1980	58,346	270,896	4,643
1985	57,226	297,316	5,195
1986	57,710	314,453	5,449
1987	58,121	333,123	5,732
1988	58,477	343,739	5,878

*Expenditure at all levels of government and by private sector. Source: Data from *Statistical Abstract of the United States* (Washington, D.C.: Government Printing Office, 1991).

Another concern regarding educational quality concerns expenditure levels in general and teachers' salaries in particular. In fact, real expenditure per pupil has risen steadily since 1970; it was about 50 percent higher in 1988 than in 1970. (See Table 14.7). This increase can roughly be decomposed into two components: changes in teacher salaries and changes in the pupil to teacher ratio. In the 1970s, teachers' salaries were lower, relative to all full-time workers in the economy, than they had been in the 1960s, as shown in Table 14.8. During the 1980s, the relative pay of teachers improved significantly. From 1972 to 1980, teachers' salaries declined from $31,700 (in 1991 dollars) to $26,400. By 1991, teachers' salaries had risen dramatically to $33,000.

Table 14.8   *Teachers' Salaries as Compared with Average Employee Earnings in All Industries*

Year	Elementary and Secondary Teachers' Salaries	Average Earnings of Full-Time Employees in All Industries	Percent Above Average Received by Teachers
1929–30	$1,420	$1,386	2.5%
1939–40	1,441	1,282	12.4
1949–50	3,010	2,930	2.7
1959–60	5,174	4,632	11.7
1969–70	9,047	7,334	23.4
1979–80	16,715	15,095	10.7
1984–85	24,666	20,626	19.6
1985–86	26,362	21,518	22.5
1986–87	27,707	22,432	23.5
1987–88	29,235	23,498	24.4
1988–89	30,969	24,483	26.5
1989–90	32,723	n.a.	n.a.
1990–91	34,456	n.a.	n.a.

Source: National Center for Education Statistics. *Digest of Education Statistics* (Washington, D.C.: Government Printing Office, 1991).

Average class size also declined significantly during the 1980s, although there was a mild upturn in 1990 and 1991 as localities responded to the recession by cutting teaching staffs. The numbers of teachers per 100 pupils rose from 3.6 in 1950 to 5.3 in 1980 to 5.8 in 1990. Interestingly, during the same period, the growth of non-teaching school employment has been even more dramatic. In 1950, 70 percent of school full-time-equivalent personnel were teachers. By 1990, this fraction had fallen to 53.3 percent.

These movements in expenditure per pupil seem to be directly related to the passage of the "baby bust" generation through the schools. For about one decade, beginning in the late 1960s, births in the United States were approximately 10 percent lower than they had been previously, and about 5 percent lower than in more recent years. Enrollment in grades kindergarten through eight hit a trough between about 1980 and 1986, although the decline began in 1970. Enrollment in grades 9 through 12 reached bottom in 1990. Expenditure declines did not match enrollment declines; thus, expenditure per pupil and the numbers of teachers per pupil rose.

The dropout problem.   One crucial measure of the success of a school system is its ability to produce high school graduates. Many central-city schools report dropout rates in excess of 25 percent, and some cities report dropout rates approaching 50 percent. This finding strongly suggests that the minimal standard (production of high school graduates) is frequently not met. There is particular concern that ghetto schools are producing a generation of blacks who will be unable to cope with the modern labor market. On careful examination, the facts show a more hopeful picture. In particular, there is a striking discrepancy between the data on dropout rates and independent data on the educational status of adults. Table 14.9 gives data since 1940 on the fraction of young adults (ages 25 to 29) who have completed high school, for all persons, and for blacks. In 1940, only 11.6 percent of young black adults had completed high school (median number of years completed was seven). By 1985, 80.6 percent had completed high school (as compared with 86.1 percent for the population as a whole). Note that the percentage of young black adults who failed to complete high school in 1980 is comparable to the percentage who failed to complete the fifth grade as recently as 1950.

Two questions emerge from the data in this table: What has caused the dramatic rise in completion rates for blacks, and why are the completion rates so strikingly at odds with dropout rates? Regarding the first question, there seem to be two forces at work. As can be seen in the table, there has been a tendency for high-school completion to rise for the population at large, and blacks have been part of this trend. Also, the rise in black completion rates coincides closely (with about a ten-year lag) with the wave of black migration to the urban sector.

Table 14.9 *Educational Attainment of 25- to 29-Year-Old Adults*

	All Persons		Blacks	
Year	Less than Five Years of School	High School Graduates	Less than Five Years of School	High School Graduates
1940	5.9	38.1	27.7	11.6
1950	4.7	52.1	16.8	22.2
1960	2.8	60.7	7.0	37.7
1970	1.7	73.8	3.2	55.4
1980	1.1	84.5	1.1	75.2
1985	0.7	86.1	0.4	80.6
1987	0.9	86.0	0.4	83.3
1988	1.0	85.7	0.3	80.6
1989	1.0	85.5	0.5	82.2

Source: Data from *Statistical Abstract of the United States* (Washington, D.C.: Government Printing Office, 1991).

The discrepancy between completion and dropout rates also appears to come from two sources. The dropout statistics, for one, are not very accurate (students who transfer to another school are sometimes listed as dropouts). In addition, many students who drop out eventually return and complete high school.

In summary, it is clear that the quality of black inner-city schools is much worse than that of white suburban schools. It is important, however, to recognize that the opportunities available to inner-city blacks are strikingly better than those of their sharecropper parents or grandparents.

What produces quality education?   Beginning in the mid-1960s, there has been a large volume of research on the question of what produces quality education, or to put it differently, what determines differences across people in educational attainment. By far the largest body of research has explored the determinants of standardized test scores. More recent research has concentrated on the relationship between education and subsequent earnings. Both of these strands of research will be discussed; interestingly, the two different strands yield somewhat contradictory conclusions.

The research based on test scores has shown that the quality of education depends crucially on the characteristics of parents and peers, and that variation in expenditure has relatively little influence on educational outcomes. This section discusses the research techniques that have been employed in arriving at this conclusion.

Suppose there is a sample of school districts, and for each district there is some measure of educational outcome (e.g., test scores or the fraction of students completing high school); call this measure Q. In addition, there are data on purchased inputs (possibly expenditure or teachers per pupil); call this variable E. Finally, there are data on the average socioeconomic characteristics *(SEC)* of people who live in the district. It is now possible to run a regression of a form such as

$$Q = a_0 + a_1E + a_2SEC, \tag{14.1}$$

where, for example, a_1 gives the statistical relationship between E and Q. In the simplest (and least satisfactory) educational studies, a_1 is taken as the *effect* of E on Q. In such studies, expenditure is uniformly found to be unassociated with Q. On the other hand, these studies consistently find that socioeconomic characteristics of parents and peers have a large and significant effect on educational attainment.

The finding that educational attainment (year-to-year improvement in test scores) is not responsive to reductions in class size or better pay and working conditions for teachers strikes many as highly implausible. The finding, however, is amazingly robust; it shows up in virtually every study of this sort.

In all likelihood, the failure of equations such as (14.1) to show any effect of E on Q is due in part to a subtle but important statistical phenomenon known as the *identification problem*. The identification problem is perhaps one of the most frequent sources of misinterpretation of statistical relationships, so it is worth exploring even aside from its relevance to our current discussion.

To see how the identification problem arises in the current context, consider first a more complete description of the determination of educational quality. Suppose that education is "produced" according to a relationship that looks very much like (14.1):

$$Q = \alpha_0 + \alpha_1E + \alpha_2Y, \tag{14.2}$$

where for simplicity Y (income) is used as the only *SEC*. The interpretation of (14.2) is that increasing E by one **causes** Q to rise by α_1, and a one dollar rise in Y causes Q to rise by α_2.

Now, invoke ordinary demand theory and assume that the quantity of education that will be demanded (voted for) by the electorate depends on the cost (i.e., E) and on the voters' income Y:

$$Q = \beta_0 + \beta_1E + \beta_2Y. \tag{14.3}$$

Before proceeding, it is useful to compare both (14.2) and (14.3) with (14.1). Is the a_1 coefficient in (14.1) an estimate of α_1 or β_1? The answer, in general, is that it is not an estimate of either α_1 or β_1; that is the identification problem. Because there are two different causal relationships between E and Q (namely, the production and demand functions), any observed statistical association, in general, cannot be identified as either the production or the demand coefficient.

The identification problem arises because the observed Q,E pairs are at intersections of production and demand functions, and it is not known which is being traced out by the various pairs.

There are various statistical techniques that, at least to some degree, address this problem. Most of these techniques involve estimating an equation much like (14.1), but choosing the observations in such a way that there is reason to believe that the relationship observed is the production rather than the demand function. In almost all of these studies, there is at least some question as to how successfully the researcher has sorted out the effects, however.[23] This possible problem should be recognized when looking at the findings. Bearing this caveat in mind, most studies find the following pattern:

1. Purchased inputs—teachers' salaries, teachers per pupil, and the capital plant—appear to have little or no influence on educational attainment.
2. On the other hand, educational attainment is very strongly related to parental background (including education and income) and the parental background of classmates.
3. Despite the first finding cited, there is strong evidence that the characteristics of the classroom environment matter. Some individual teachers consistently outperform others, as do some principals and schools. In other words, purchased inputs do matter after all, but high-quality purchased inputs generally do not cost any more than low-quality inputs.

If good teachers can improve the quality of education (and this finding exists virtually whenever anybody has tested for it), it seems strange that expenditure differentials between districts produce no observable effects. Perhaps this result is a manifestation of the identification problem. Another possibility is that teachers demand premium pay to go to "bad" school districts. If this happens, "good" school districts can get quality teachers more cheaply than "bad" districts, and expenditure differences between districts do not measure differences in the quality of purchased inputs. A final possibility is that administrators are unable or unwilling to pay higher than normal salaries to more effective teachers.

The evidence cited indicates that observable characteristics of schools have little apparent impact on educational outcomes, as measured in general by test scores. Recently, researchers have looked to other measures of educational success, with quite different findings. Card and Krueger (1992) have been able to match 1980 earnings data for

---

23. Dynarski, Schwab, and Zampelli (1989) have made a particularly careful attempt to disentangle the roles of parents as productive inputs and demanders, relying on a sample of California school districts where expenditure was out of the control of the parents (because of Proposition 13). School districts were forbidden from raising taxes, and, therefore, from raising expenditures. Presumably in this case, variation in expenditure is independent of demand, and its role in the production process can be isolated. Even here the evidence is not conclusive. Perhaps it works as follows: Parents demand a given quality of education. Forbidden by Proposition 13 from raising taxes to improve schools, they devote extra parental time to their children to make up the difference. (Despite the existence of this possible alternative explanation for their findings, the evidence of these authors is the latest and most convincing in a long line of findings that strongly indicates that parental and peer characteristics are much more important than expenditure levels in determining education quality.)

adults with the state and year in which they attended school, and with the number of years of education they attained. The sample is men born between 1929 and 1940; over this period there was substantial variation across states in teacher pay, classroom size, and the length of the school year.

Card and Krueger begin by defining the return to education as the percentage of wage increase associated with a change in education (e.g., an extra year of education).[24] Their findings are as follows:

1. The return to an extra year of schooling is higher the lower the pupil to teacher ratio. A 5 percent decrease in the pupil to teacher ratio is associated with a 0.4 percent increase in the return to schooling.
2. A 10 percent increase in teachers' pay[25] (relative to the average pay level at the time) is associated with a 0.1 percent increase in the return to schooling.
3. Though not quantified, it appears that pupils attending schools in which the return to education is higher tend to accumulate more years of schooling.

Taken together, these findings suggest that school quality, measured in a fairly traditional way, has a significant effect on the future economic well-being of students.

Thus, when earnings rather than test scores are taken as the measure of educational outcomes, there is now substantial evidence that the purchased inputs (mostly teachers) used by schools have a significant impact on the quality of education, and that central-city schools are substantially less effective than suburban schools, even after correcting for expenditure differences.

Education and the Tiebout mechanism.   If education is produced by a combination of purchased inputs, parents, and peers, then the Tiebout model of education takes on some strange new twists (the twists are particularly important if peers play a crucial role in the educational process). If peer group effects are significant, some important things happen. Various exclusionary practices such as zoning must be viewed as much more important policy tools available to jurisdictions. Exclusion of poor children from a wealthy district becomes valuable (to the residents of the wealthy jurisdiction) not only because the wealthy are saved from having to subsidize the poor, but also

---

24.   This "rate of return to education" is not the same as the normal rate of return to an investment, in which one asks how many dollars of return are earned on a dollar of investment. Here, one is asking how much the wage rises when a student graduates from high school or when the pupil to teacher ratio declines, and so on.

25.   Teachers' pay might influence the quality of education in two ways. First of course, higher quality might simply attract better people into the teaching profession. Second teachers who are paid more tend to stay in the teaching profession longer. Thus, higher pay seems to improve the average experience level of teachers.

because the wealthy are saved from having low-achievement pupils reduce the quality of their schools.

The same forces that make exclusion so attractive for the wealthy make it particularly sinister from the perspective of the poor. The one thing that would most effectively raise the quality of education for low-income children appears to be inclusion with higher-achieving students (recall that increasing expenditure appears to have only limited effectiveness). It must be noted that this achievement gain, which could be obtained by more mixing, carries a cost—reduced attainment of higher-achieving children.

Finally, it should be noted that the efficiency claim of the Tiebout hypothesis no longer holds if parents are inputs in the educational process. The efficiency claim of the Tiebout hypothesis is quite simple. If all people vote with their feet, and if a sufficient range of choice emerges, all people will be on their demand curves and all public services will be produced at minimum cost. In the presence of peer-group effects, however, Tiebout sorting does more than match up offerings with demand. If the cost of providing a given quality of education varies with where people live, then the location outcome that emerges from foot-voting may well not minimize the cost of education.

Proposals for reform.   This discussion of the Tiebout mechanism represents a good attempt to explain how education is "sold." Also considered has been the available evidence on how education is produced, and in particular, on the relationship between inputs and the educational outcome. It is now time to examine various proposals for improvement of the educational system.

Centralization.   Tiebout's model and observed reality are in full agreement: Children who live in rich suburban school districts receive much better education than do children who live in poor central-city school districts. There is some disagreement as to whether this finding is due to income differences across schools or expenditure differences. Whatever the immediate cause, it is clear that educational opportunities vary substantially across school districts.

The finding that parental and peer socioeconomic characteristics are important in determining educational outcomes has important and disturbing consequences. It means that educational opportunity cannot be equalized by giving compensatory aid to low-income school districts, and it further means that the centralization of educational finance (complete takeover by the state, for example) will not eliminate the incentive of wealthy people to keep poor people out of their school districts (Oates [1971]). As long as private schools are a viable option, the centralization of the public school system probably would cause an increase in upper-income attendance at private schools. In other words, preventing wealthy parents from fleeing to Tiebout suburbs is likely to induce a flight to private schools instead.

Wealthy parents who do not want to leave the central city already are faced with this choice. Not surprisingly, private-school patronage is much higher in central cities (particularly in the Northeast) than elsewhere. As shown in Table 14.10, in northeastern central cities, 20.3 percent of students were enrolled in private schools in 1979; the analogous figure for northeastern suburbs was 10.3 percent. In nonmetropolitan areas the analogous figure was 7.1 percent (*Current Population Reports* [1982]). Although this hypothesis has not been tested statistically, it appears that school districts with heterogeneous populations tend to drive a substantial fraction of their students into private schools.[26]

In turn, this increased reliance on private education results in reduced expenditure in public schools. One study (Brown and Saks 1975) reports that a 10 percent increase in the fraction of children in private schools results in a 4 percent decline in public school expenditure.

For these reasons, the centralization of finance and administration is at best a highly imperfect way to address the adverse distributional consequences of the Tiebout model. Even if everyone stayed within the public school system, the equalization of expenditure would go only a modest way toward equalizing quality.[27] Furthermore, with the viability of private schools, an attempt to provide the same quality of public education to wealthy and poor could result in an exodus of the wealthy from the public system, as well as decreased financial support for public schools.

Vouchers. Some economists, most notably Milton Friedman, have argued for a system of educational vouchers. The parents of each child would receive vouchers that could be redeemed at any accredited school, with no distinction between public and private. Schools would have to compete for students, and this competition would provide a healthy discipline. All students would be able to afford education up to the value of the voucher, so there would be a floor under expenditure, if not quality. Whether this system would lead to more racial and socioeconomic integration or equality, however, is not clear. The effect on educational quality also is unclear, given the demonstrated importance of peers and parents in the educational process.

---

26. For a more complete discussion see Hamilton and Macauley (1988).

27. Refer again to Table 14.4. Although it shows a consistent pattern of more spending per capita in suburbs than in central cities, note that expenditure per pupil is about the same in central cities and suburbs. The difference, of course, is that there are far fewer pupils per capita in the central cities.

Table 14.10 *Public and Private Elementary/Secondary School Enroll-ment by Region and Metropolitan Status, October 1979*

Region Metropolitan Status	Total Enrolled (in Thousands)	Enrolled in Public Schools (Percentage)
All regions:		
Total, all students	42,981	90.2%
Metropolitan	28,435	87.7
Central city	11,106	84.0
Outside central city	17,329	90.0
Nonmetropolitan	14,546	95.0
Northeast:		
Total, all students	9,734	87.5
Metropolitan	7,476	85.8
Central city	2,894	79.7
Outside central city	4,582	89.7
Nonmetropolitan	2,259	92.9
Midwest:		
Total, all students	11,198	88.5
Metropolitan	7,352	85.7
Central city	2,768	82.7
Outside central city	4,584	87.5
Nonmetropolitan	3,846	93.9
South:		
Total, all students	14,482	92.2
Metropolitan	7,887	89.3
Central city	3,450	87.6
Outside central city	4,437	90.6
Nonmetropolitan	6,595	95.8
West:		
Total, all students	7,567	92.1
Metropolitan	5,721	90.5
Central city	1,994	86.0
Outside central city	3,726	92.9
Nonmetropolitan	1,846	97.2

Region Metropolitan Status	Enrolled in Private Schools (Percentage)			
	Total	Religiously Affiliated	Unaffiliated	Affiliation not Reported
All regions:				
Total, all students	9.8%	8.2%	1.4%	0.2%
Metropolitan	12.3	10.4	1.6	0.3
Central city	16.0	13.5	2.1	0.4
Outside central city	10.0	8.4	1.3	0.2
Nonmetropolitan	5.0	4.0	0.9	0.1
Northeast:				
Total, all students	12.5	11.1	1.2	0.3
Metropolitan	14.2	12.6	1.2	0.4
Central city	20.3	18.6	1.2	0.6
Outside central city	10.3	8.9	1.2	0.2
Nonmetropolitan	7.1	5.9	1.1	0.1
Midwest:				
Total, all students	11.5	10.4	0.9	0.3
Metropolitan	14.3	12.7	1.3	0.3
Central city	17.3	15.2	1.5	0.5
Outside central city	12.5	11.2	1.2	0.2
Nonmetropolitan	6.1	5.9	0.0	0.2
South:				
Total, all students	7.8	5.7	1.9	0.1
Metropolitan	10.7	8.3	2.3	0.2
Central city	12.4	9.2	3.1	0.1
Outside central city	9.4	7.5	1.7	0.2
Nonmetropolitan	4.2	2.6	1.5	0.1
West:				
Total, all students	7.9	6.2	1.4	0.3
Metropolitan	9.5	7.4	1.8	0.3
Central city	14.0	10.9	2.7	0.4
Outside central city	7.1	5.5	1.3	0.3
Nonmetropolitan	2.8	2.4	0.3	0.1

Note: Details may not add to totals because of rounding.
Sources: Adapted with permission from National Center for Educational Statistics, Table 2.3, p. 62; after U.S. Department of Commerce, Bureau of the Census. *Current Population Survey,* unpublished tabulations.

Privatization of public schools.   Traditional private schools are different from public schools in two important respects. First of course, private schools charge tuition. Second private schools are free to admit and expel students selectively. Public schools, on the other hand, are required by law to accept all students who live within the attendance zone. There is substantial evidence that private schools produce more highly educated students than do public schools. The reasons for this gap are not clear. Perhaps private schools, having to compete for students, are more efficient than public schools. Perhaps they use admission and expulsion criteria to accept only those students who would do well in any environment. Perhaps tuition screens out parents who do not place a very high value on education.

Proposals (and actual steps) to privatize a few public schools are not proposals to create private schools. Rather, the proposal is that local governments hire private vendors to run their schools. The vendors will be paid by the governments and will not charge tuition. The vendors also will not be able to admit students selectively; they will be operating under the same guidelines in these respects as all public schools. Thus, the rationale for privatization is the conjecture that the public sector is simply mismanaging its educational resources and that the private sector can do better. There will be a wait through several years of experimentation before one can make a determination about the efficacy of privatization.[28]

The return to education and the distribution of income.   The gap between black and white earnings, and the gap between the earnings of the wealthy and the poor, shrank during the 1960s and 1970s. The 1980s, however, witnessed a significant widening of the gap between wealthy and poor, and between black and white. An important reason for these widening gaps is that the return to education rose dramatically during the 1980s. Since blacks and the poor are on average less well educated than whites and the wealthy, this rise in the return to education lead to a widening of the economic gap between black and white, and between wealthy and poor.

The return to education rose during the 1980s despite a steady increase in educational attainment levels. Most researchers believe that the rise in the return to education is due to increasing freedom of international trade. With elimination of many trade restrictions, Americans can more readily export their education—intensive high-tech products. At the same time, foreigners can more readily export their low-tech labor-intensive goods to the United States. These changes have placed a considerable premium on educational attainment.

---

28.   Many scholars believe that experimentation is one of the chief virtues of the federal system. If education, for example, is carried out by thousands of independent school districts, the innovative practices of some will prove successful, and other districts will be able to learn from their successes.

Regardless of the causes of the rise in the return to education, the relative effect on blacks, at least in the short run, has been harmful. If quality education is available, however, the higher return to education should stimulate higher levels of educational attainment in the future.

`Education: Summary.`   Despite the impression one gets from the popular press, many indicators of education show a fairly hopeful picture. Educational expenditure has risen dramatically in recent years. Teachers' salaries are up and class sizes, on the average, are down. High school completion rates are up, and the racial gap in educational attainment has been significantly reduced since 1970.

Central-city schools appear to be significantly poorer in quality than their suburban counterparts. More generally, the quality of education received by children appears to be closely tied to the income level of children's parents. The very rationale for placing education in the public sector seems to have been subverted by the workings of the Tiebout model.

☐ POLICE PROTECTION AND CRIME

Police protection is another local public service for which the output depends not only on purchased resources (e.g., patrol officers) but also on the characteristics of the clientele. Crime rates are significantly lower in wealthy low-density areas than in poor high-density areas.

The rate of violent crimes fell by almost 15 percent from 1980 through 1985, but then began to rise. By 1990, it was approximately 10 percent higher than it had been in 1980. Crimes against property shows a similar pattern, except that the rise from the middle of the decade was much less significant. Interestingly, despite the approximate constancy of the crime rate over the decade, the prison population has approximately doubled.

There is a widespread perception that drug-related crime has increased dramatically, and that the crime associated with drugs has had a significant effect on the population at large. Interestingly, the National Household Survey on Drug Abuse reports a 50 percent decline in drug use between 1985 and 1990. If the drug problem is more severe now than in the mid-1980s, it is apparently not because of increased drug use. According to a very careful study by Curie (1993), the nature of the drug-retailing mechanism changed dramatically during the 1980s, and this change has increased the exposure of neighborhoods to drug-related violence.[29] Until about 1980, the vast majority of retail drug sales took place in private, and between a buyer and seller who knew one another, at least casually. The 1980s witnessed the advent of the open-air

29.   The following material draws heavily on the report by Curie (1993).

drug market. An open-air market works without the private referrals typical of the previous market arrangement. Vendors stand on street corners and sell prepackaged drugs to passersby. Transactions happen very quickly. Dealers use pay phones to conduct some of their business, and convenience stores and abandoned or public housing as places of concealment in the event of a raid. In order to thrive, a seller must be able to work regularly on a given corner. This action requires dodging the police and sometimes fighting turf wars with potential competitors. According to Curie (1993), there are four necessary characteristics of a neighborhood that will attract an open-air drug market. (1) Dealers do not like clean, well-lighted neighborhoods; cleanliness is apparently a tip-off that neighbors will not tolerate the dealers. (2) Dealers need a legitimate cover for presence on the street, such as a bar, a convenience store, or a housing project. (3) Dealers are attracted to neighborhoods with many poorly supervised children. Such children are easy to recruit as salesmen and lookouts. (4) Markets require a steady stream of customers and a ready means of escape.

Several cities (the author cites Tampa in particular) have been quite successful in closing down open-air markets. Successful efforts to close down the open-air markets have had the following hallmarks: Enforcement of loitering laws, attention to street lighting, encouragement of neighborhood associations, and either boarding up or demolishing abandoned structures. In addition, some housing projects have required residents to show photographic identification for entry to the premises.

The open-air drug market is a much more serious threat to the stability of a neighborhood than is the private drug exchange that was the major means of distribution prior to the 1980s. Thus, understanding the mechanism whereby these markets work is crucial to controlling drug-related violence. It is much too early, however, to tell how successful local governments will be in attempting to eradicate open-air drug vendors.

☐ REGULATION

In addition to levying taxes and providing public services, local governments regulate private activities. The regulations are of two basic kinds: (1) Some natural spatial monopolies generally are regulated rather than are publicly owned, and (2) the use of land for any purpose is regulated through zoning ordinances and building codes.

Regulated Enterprises

There is little difference in economics between the provision of water and that of electric power, yet the former is generally a public enterprise and the latter is a regulated private enterprise. For no obvious reason, local governments have tended to deal with some natural monopolies through public ownership and to deal with others through regulation. Among the more recent industries to be regulated is cable television.

As compared with completely free enterprise, the regulation of monopoly has the obvious advantage of preventing monopoly pricing. The disadvantage, however, is that the regulator must monitor both the production and the pricing policies of the firm. Furthermore, the firm under regulation generally has an incentive to behave in an inefficient manner (see Averch and Johnson [1962]).

Perhaps a more important cost of regulation is that its scope has extended to industries for which there is no economic justification. In many cases, regulation is a blatant anticompetitive device enacted at the behest of the regulated industry. Local governments, for example, often regulate the number of taxicabs, with the result that the supply becomes restricted and the price is raised.[30]

Land-Use Regulation

Almost all local governments regulate the use of land with building codes and zoning ordinances. This section will explore the economic rationale for each of these types of regulations and then discuss some of the actual economic consequences of these regulations. Land-use controls have already been discussed as a fiscal tool—essentially, as a means for protecting the tax base. These controls, however, have other purposes and consequences.

Building codes. Building codes generally specify materials to be used in wiring and plumbing, as well such things as the configuration of windows and some aspects of interior wall location. They sometimes also specify standards for framing, foundation, and external building materials. The economic rationale for building codes is to protect the public from invisible defects in homes and other buildings (although the code generally covers visible aspects of the buildings as well). The notion is that a buyer cannot readily examine wiring, plumbing, and some aspects of structural integrity, and the code is required to keep the builder honest.

Many people object to codes as they are now generally constituted, because they require the use of specific materials rather than performance standards. If performance standards were imposed instead, builders would have an incentive to look for the cheapest way of satisfying the standard. For example, most codes specify a certain thickness of fiberglass insulation. Frequently, however, proper caulking and weather stripping would be a more productive way of achieving the same thermal resistance.

---

30. See the "Licensing Taxicabs" problem in Milton Friedman's *Price Theory* (1973, p. 282).

Zoning. A zoning map specifies which types of structures and activities can take place on each parcel of land. Sometimes, zoning is hierarchical: Land uses are ranked from most to least noxious. All activities are permitted on land zoned for the most noxious use. As we move up the hierarchy, the more noxious uses are excluded. Thus, for example, single-family homes can be built on land zoned for row houses, but not vice versa. More frequently, however, zoning is *exclusive use,* meaning that the land can be used only for the activity permitted on the zoning map. Broadly speaking, the economic justification for zoning rests on the notion that there are inherent inefficiencies in an unregulated land market. For a thorough discussion of both the institutions and economics of zoning, see Fischel (1985).

Inefficiencies in private land markets. The most obvious potential inefficiency in an unregulated land market is the existence of externalities from neighboring uses. For example, many industrial plants generate air, water, and noise pollution, as well as visual disamenities. Restricting the number of households exposed to the disamenities can mitigate their deleterious effects. This process is a major justification for segregation of residential from various types of nonresidential activities. Although private market forces probably generate a fair amount of segregation of uses in any event, the externalities may be sufficiently important that governmental intervention is appropriate.

Chapter 11 showed that the statistical evidence for neighborhood effects is very weak and that any externalities that do exist appear to be quite limited geographically. This finding raises doubts about the value of zoning to internalize neighborhood effects. The measurement of these neighborhood effects, however, as well as people's attitudes toward them, is far from perfect. Thus, one should be cautious in concluding that these externalities do not generate important land-market imperfections. By the same token, however, one might ask on what zoning officials will base their decisions about how to segregate land uses if there is no hard evidence on the magnitude (or even the direction, in some cases) of these externalities.

Some experts claim that externalities exist among various types of residential land uses. Apartments, rowhouses, and other high-density dwellings are said to create traffic, noise, and visual disamenities, justifying their separation from lower-density housing.

If high-density and low-quality housing impose costs on neighbors, however, zoning does not eliminate the problem; it just concentrates it in one place. The problem still exists, but the rich do not have to see it. An appropriate response to this type of neighborhood-effect problem would be to subsidize the consumption of low-income housing.

Also, some people believe that there is value to maintaining farmland and open spaces, largely for the visual amenities they produce.[31] This concept is tricky; within the boundaries of an urbanized area, the preservation of farmland also can be labeled *sprawl*.

Ecological reasons for land-use controls also exist, the most prominent being watershed management. As more land in the upstream part of a drainage area is covered with buildings and concrete, the ability of the land to absorb rainwater is diminished, which leads to increased flooding downstream. Private developers tend to ignore these external costs, and some sort of regulation is called for.

The final justification for zoning involves planning. Once local governments became the main providers of streets, sewers, and water, they faced the problem of predicting land-use density to determine street, water, and sewer-main capacity requirements. Making the correct prediction is extremely valuable; once buildings are in place, the cost of widening streets and laying bigger water mains can be very high. One solution to the prediction problem is to mandate—by zoning ordinance —that the prediction come true. Historically, this was one of the motivations behind zoning.

Most economists agree that there would be important inefficiencies in an unregulated private land market. The lack of evidence in support of neighborhood externalities may be due to difficulties in measuring the variables. Even if these externalities are unimportant, however, the problems of planning for roads, water, and sewers; watershed management; and, possibly, the preservation of farmland and areas of scenic beauty raise doubts about the efficiency of a private market.

There are important reasons, however, to doubt that the cure is an improvement over the problem. First it is unlikely that zoning officials can know the best locations for all economic agents. A distinction may be necessary between matters such as watershed and floodplain management on the one hand and neighborhood externalities on the other. The costs of increasing flooding downstream are demonstrable and reasonably easy to document, but the segregation of economic activities within an urban area might be another matter. It is hard to know which rules to apply in establishing zoning guidelines.

Second and more important, the actual objectives of zoning officials may go far beyond correcting market failures, and the pursuit of these other objectives may have some undesirable consequences from both the efficiency and equity perspectives. Zoning officials are either elected or appointed by elected officials. In either case, the constituency is the people who are eligible to vote in the jurisdiction. Therefore, the officials have an incentive to maximize the welfare of the current

31.   Some people also argue that a policy of preserving farmland is needed, specifically because of the value of the agricultural output. There seems, however, to be little substance to this argument. In a competitive land market, land would remain in agricultural production as long as the value of its marginal product were higher there than in urban uses. In the United States, the market value of agricultural land probably exceeds its social agricultural value, because the massive agricultural price-support system raises farmland values.

residents of the jurisdiction. They have no reason to be concerned with the welfare of nonresidents, yet zoning actions frequently have important consequences for nonresidents. Before exploring this further, we must examine the legal environment in which zoning takes place.

Under the constitutional system in the United States, government has two sources of power to regulate private activity, aside from the power to tax. The first is called *eminent domain,* which is the power to seize private property for public purposes, such as road building. The Constitution forbids the seizure of private property without just compensation. The sale of property, however, can be forced at a court-determined price, even if the landlord does not wish to sell. Thus, for example, it is impossible for one landowner to prevent a road from being built.

The other source of power over the private use of property is the *police power of the state.* Actions under police power do not require compensation. For example, if motorists are stopped at a roadblock checking for drunk drivers, the state is not required to compensate them for their time.

Under current Supreme Court rulings, almost all local land-use regulations are acts of police power rather than of eminent domain, so the government is not required to compensate the property owner for costs imposed by regulation. This feature has important economic consequences.

Assume that zoning authorities act selfishly, or rather that they act on behalf of the selfish interests of residents. In standard microeconomic theory, selfish behavior is guided by the invisible hand to yield an efficient outcome. When one of the selfish agents has the power to seize property without compensation, however, the invisible hand does not work. For example, suppose a plot of vacant land in a jurisdiction would be worth $100,000 in the absence of zoning. The land commands this price because of its valuable access to the CBD. The present value of the saving on commuting is roughly $100,000 if development occurs on this parcel rather than at the urban fringe, where land value is zero (remember Chapter 6; our hypothetical parcel is worth $100,000 because that is the present value of the commuting cost consumers can avoid by living on this parcel rather than at the periphery of the city). In other words, the market price of the land is a good estimate of the social value of using the land for urban development. Costs associated with using the land, however, also exist in the form of lost visual amenities and increased traffic congestion. If the costs exceed the benefits, efficiency dictates that the development not take place.

The problem with zoning is that our current institutions do not induce officials to weigh the costs as well as the benefits involved in the development of a parcel of land. Instead, the zoning board is likely to ask a much simpler question: Will any costs be imposed on current residents if the parcel is developed? If so, they are likely to deny permission to develop. Even if the benefits of development are $100,000 and externality costs are only $1,000, the zoning board has an incentive to deny the right to develop.

What has all of this to do with police power and eminent domain? Basically, in the previous example, the problem arose because the benefits of development were ignored in the zoning board's decision-making process; this result was due to the zoning board's indifference to the effects of its actions on the value of the parcel of land. The parcel was worth $100,000 in the absence of zoning restrictions; with restrictive zoning, the value might fall to $20,000. The $80,000 in lost property value is a measure of the (gross) social cost of the restriction. The authorities, however, have no reason to care whether the restriction reduces the value by $1, $100, or $100,000. From an economist's perspective, the zoning restriction in this example is equivalent to the seizure of $80,000 worth of property rights. On efficiency grounds, this seizure should take place only if the benefits of the restriction are worth at least $80,000. If the authorities respond to the wishes of the electorate, however, the property rights will be seized as long as the benefits are positive at all.

This example is not farfetched. As already shown, land values can vary manyfold according to how the land is zoned. The power of the local zoning board to take and give valuable property rights to citizens (all without compensation) is very great indeed. The possibilities for abuse, including unwarranted seizure and bribery, are obvious.

If zoning were an exercise of eminent domain, this problem would not arise. The $80,000 of property rights in the example still could be seized for the public benefit, but only with just compensation; that is, only by paying the owner the $80,000. Then the authorities would have to decide whether they wanted the property rights badly enough to pay for them; in other words, there would be a market test governing the use of land.

☐ Summary

Total governmental expenditure grew dramatically over the past half-century, rising from 9.9 percent of GNP in 1929 to 35.4 percent in 1985. Local governmental expenditure rose from 5.9 percent of GNP in 1929 to a high of 9.2 percent in 1975, falling to under 8 percent in 1983. In the first part of this chapter, these trends and their causes and consequences were examined. It was noted that the 1970s and early 1980s created particular financing problems for many central-city governments. Several of the reasons for these difficulties were discussed.

The second part of this chapter was concerned with the nature of the goods provided by local governments and the efficiency and distributional consequences of the current means of providing these goods. Of particular interest, we found that the amount of income redistribution that goes on at the local governmental level is much less than is commonly believed.

Questions and Problems

1. What would be the effect on central-city government finances of a negative income tax? Of a housing allowance?

2. The federal government can redistribute income by taxing high-income people and providing transfers either to low-income people or to local governments with large low-income populations. Which do you prefer and why?

3. What would be the effect of metropolitan area-wide local government on local taxes paid and governmental services received by poor central-city residents?

4. The tax revolt of the late 1970s was a revolt of middle-class suburban residents against local governments. Transfers to the poor appeared to be the object of their hostility, yet suburban governments transfer little money to the poor. How do you explain this?

References and Further Reading

Averch, Harvey, and Leland Johnson. "The Behavior of the Firm Under Regulatory Constraint." *American Economic Review* 52 (1962): 1058–1059.

Baumol, William. "The Macroeconomics of Unbalanced Growth: The Anatomy of Urban Crisis." *American Economic Review* 5 (1967): 414–426. A study of the long-run implications of low productivity growth in the government sector.

Babcock, Richard F. *The Zoning Game* (Madison: University of Wisconsin Press, 1966). A highly readable book of the legal and political environment in which zoning takes place.

Brown, B., and D. Saks. "The Production and Distribution of Cognitive Skills Within Schools." *Journal of Political Economy* 83 (1975): 571–594.

Card, David, and Alan B. Krueger. "Does School Quality Matter? Returns to Education and the Characteristics of Public Schools in the United States." *Journal of Political Economy* 100 (1992): 1–41.

Coleman, James, and Sara Kelly. "Education." In *The Urban Predicament*, edited by W. Gorham and N. Glazer (Washington, D.C.: Urban Institute, 1976). A review of the state of our knowledge regarding education.

Curie, Elliot. *Reckoning: Drugs, the Cities, and the American Future* (San Francisco, Hill and Wang, 1993).

Dynarski, Mark, Robert Schwab, and E. Zampelli. "Community Characteristics and Educational Production Functions." *Journal of Urban Economics* 26 No. 2 (1989): 250–263.

Ely, Richard. *Problems of Today* (New York: Crowell, 1888).

Fischel, William. *The Economics of Zoning Laws: A Property Rights Approach to American Land Use Controls* (Baltimore: Johns Hopkins University Press, 1985). Fischel presents a detailed discussion of the fact that zoning is an act of taking property rights without compensation.

Frieden, Bernard J. *The Environmental Protection Hustle* (Cambridge, Mass.: MIT Press, 1979). A provocative book on the forces underlying the environmental movement; it is rather one-sided, as the title suggests.

Friedman, Milton. *Price Theory* (Chicago, Aldine, 1973).

Getz, Malcolm. *The Economics of the Urban Fire Department* (Baltimore: Johns Hopkins University Press, 1979).

Hamilton, B. W. "Capitalization of Interjurisdictional Differences in Local Tax Prices." *American Economic Review* 66 (1976): 43–753.

Hamilton, B. W. "Local Government, the Property Tax and the Quality of Life: Some Findings on Progressivity." In *Public Economics and the Quality of Life,* edited by L. Wingo and A. Evans (Washington, D.C.: Resources for the Future, 1977). A discussion of capitalization with empirical evidence.

Hamilton, B. W., E. S. Mills, and D. Puryear. "The Tiebout Hypothesis and Residential Income Segregation." In *Fiscal Zoning and Land Use Controls,* edited by E. Mills and W. Oates. (Lexington, Mass.: D. C. Heath, 1975). An empirical examination of the link between local government structure and residential income segregation.

Hamilton, B. W., and Molly Macauley. "The Determinants and Consequences of the Public/Private School Decision." Working paper (Baltimore: Johns Hopkins University Press, 1988).

Hamilton, B. W., and Robert M. Schwab. "Expected Appreciation in Urban Housing Markets." *Journal of Urban Economics* 18 (July, 1985): 103–118. An examination of the determinants of actual and predicted capital gains for residential property.

Hulten, Charles. "A Method for Estimating Public-Sector Productivity Change." Working paper (Washington, D.C.: Urban Institute, 1982). A clever but difficult paper that estimates the rate of technological progress in the state and local public sectors.

Humphrey, Nancy, George Peterson, and Peter Wilson. *The Future of Cleveland's Capital Plant* (Washington, D.C.: Urban Institute, 1979). Chapter 1 gives a very nice summary of Cleveland's financial plight.

Inman, Robert P. "Fiscal Performance of Local Governments: An Interpretive Review." In *Current Issues in Urban Economics,* edited by Peter Mieszkowski and Mahlon Straszheim (Baltimore: Johns Hopkins University Press, 1979): 270–321.

Mieszkowski, Peter, and Mahlon Straszheim, eds. *Current Issues in Urban Economics* (Baltimore: Johns Hopkins University Press, 1979). A series of detailed up-to-date literature reviews. This book is the first source to turn to for more advanced discussions of both local public finance and other branches of urban economics. Especially useful are chapters by Inman, Oakland, Clotfelter, Mills, and Rubinfeld.

Mills, Edwin S. "An Economic Analysis of Urban Land Use Controls." In *Current Issues in Urban Economics,* edited by Peter Miezkowski and Mahlon Straszheim (Baltimore: Johns Hopkins University Press, 1979): 511–514.

Oakland, William. "Proposition 13: Genesis and Consequences." *National Tax Journal* 32 (June, 1979): 387–409. The discussion of Proposition 13 on which the section in this chapter is based.

Oates, W. E. "The Effects of Property Taxes and Local Public Spending on Property Values: An Empirical Study of Tax Capitalization and the Tiebout Hypothesis." *Journal of Political Economy* 77 (1969): 957–970. The original study of the effects of property taxes and expenditure on property values.

Oates, W. E. "On the Use of Local Zoning Ordinances to Regulate Population Flows and the Quality of Local Services." In *Essays in Labor Market Analysis,* edited by O. Ashenfelter and W. Oates (New York: Wiley, 1971): 201–219. A very good discussion of some interesting, but subtle, aspects of the Tiebout hypothesis.

Oates, W. E. "Fiscal Limitations: An Assessment of the U.S. Experience." Sloane working paper No. 5–81 (College Park: University of Maryland, July, 1981).

Peterson, George E. "Finance." In *The Urban Predicament,* edited by W.Gorham and N. Glazer (Washington, D.C.: Urban Institute, 1976). An excellent review of local government finance; it is more detailed than the first section of this chapter.

Reischauer, Robert, Peter Clark, and Peggy Cuciti. *New York City's Fiscal Problem* (Washington, D.C.: Congressional Budget Office, 1975). Has much more detail than this chapter's discussion of New York City's financial crisis.

Rubinfeld, Daniel L. "Judicial Approaches to Local Public-Sector Equity: An Economic Analysis." In *Current Issues in Urban Economics,* edited by Peter Mieszkowski and Mahlon Straszheim (Baltimore: Johns Hopkins University Press, 1979): 542–576.

Summers, A. S., and B. L. Wolfe. "Do Schools Make a Difference?" *American Economic Review* 67 (1977): 639–652. A careful examination of the determinants of educational attainment.

Tiebout, Charles. "A Pure Theory of Local Public Expenditure." *Journal of Political Economy* 64 (1956): 416–424. The original statement of the Tiebout hypothesis.

Vickrey, William. "Pricing in Urban and Suburban Transport." *American Economic Review* 53 (1963): 452–465.

U.S. Department of Commerce, Bureau of the Census. *Current Population Reports: Private School Enrollment, Tuition and Enrollment, Trends: October, 1979.* Series 23, No. 121 (Washington, D.C.: Government Printing Office, 1982). Detailed data on private schools and enrollment trends.

U.S. Department of Education. *The Condition of Education 1992* (Washington, D.C.: Government Printing Office, 1992).

15

Pollution and Environmental Quality

☐ Public and private concerns about pollution have increased enormously since World War II. Before the war, concern with pollution mostly came from small groups of conservationists who urged society to adopt the seemingly irrational policy of not using depletable natural resources.

All of that now has changed. Opinion polls show environmental problems to be high on the list of public concerns. Articles on the despoilation of the environment fill newspapers and magazines. Officials "pollute" the media with statements on pollution. Dozens of laws have been passed by federal, state, and local governments with the purpose of abating pollution. The intensity of concern with environmental problems slackened during the 1980s but has revived in the early 1990s.

The reasons for increased concern are not hard to find, although no one can work long with environmental problems and not realize the inadequacies of the data base. First there can be no doubt that the volume of wastes discharged into the environment has increased in recent decades. At a given state of technology and with a given mix of inputs and outputs, waste generation is about proportionate to the production of goods or to the level of real income. In 1991, real income and output were 4.5 times their 1961 levels. Improvements in technology and public policy undoubtedly imply that waste generation increased by less than output during this interval, but it cannot be doubted that the increase was large. Furthermore, modern technology produces some particularly persistent and harmful wastes that were unknown a few decades ago, such as atomic radiation and pesticides.

The second reason for increased concern is that pollution is more bothersome than it used to be. Popular writers refer to the revolution of rising expectations regarding the environment. It is a short step from that view to the position that a worsening of pollution is partly a matter of perception. Widespread prosperity has provided people with the income and leisure necessary to enjoy the environment through boating, camping, swimming, hiking, and skiing. Income elasticities of demand are high for such activities. Somewhat more subtle, but closely related, is the fact that people become much more concerned with the effects of pollution on health and mortality when urgent problems of massive unemployment and poverty have abated. Such concerns, however, are neither irrational nor frivolous.

Third the rapid urbanization of the country makes pollution worse than it used to be. Despite some views to the contrary, harmful waste discharges per capita are not greater in urban than in rural areas. The opposite actually is true, because some large waste-producing activities, such as agriculture and mining, occur predominantly in rural areas, and more resources are devoted to careful waste disposal in urban than in rural areas. The environment has the capacity to assimilate wastes. If that capacity is not exceeded, environmental quality remains intact. Large concentrations of people and economic activity, however, place great stress on the environment. Thus, the most serious deterioration in air and water quality has occurred in large metropolitan areas such as New York City, Chicago, and Los Angeles.

It has been shown that poverty, poor housing, and inadequate financing of local public services are by no means exclusively urban problems. Pollution is no exception. Some of the worst open dumps and littering of landscapes are in rural areas. Rural lakes and streams are frequently polluted. Even though urban areas have more than their share of air and water pollution, rural pollution is of concern to urban residents.

The most important difference between pollution concerns in recent years from those in earlier years is the growing concern about global pollution. In earlier years, most pollution was local, restricted to particular metropolitan areas, rivers, or estuaries. It is now clear that people have the capacity to affect the global environment. The best known and most studied global issues pertain to atmospheric pollution: global warming and ozone depletion.

☐ FACTS, INSTITUTIONS, AND BASIC ECONOMICS

What Is Pollution?

Although illustrations have been given, no limits have yet been placed on the concept of pollution. As pollution abatement has become an accepted goal, people have tended to include a variety of odious activities under the rubric of pollution. Air and water pollution are familiar concepts. Most people are used to describing pollution as the littering of the landscape with solid wastes. Some people would include excessive noise under the heading of pollution. Others would include a range of issues that relate to the beauty of urban and rural areas, social tensions, and other problems.

The term will be used narrowly in this chapter. Economic activity requires the withdrawal of materials from the environment. Most materials are eventually returned to the environment in ways more or less harmful to the use of the environment. The term *pollution* will be used to describe the impairment of the environment by the return or discharge of materials to it. The definition includes the usual categories of air, water, and solid-waste pollution, but it excludes a broad range of social and aesthetic issues sometimes classified as environmental. The reason for limiting the subject is not that the included problems are necessarily more important than the excluded ones, but that waste-disposal problems have important elements in common that are not shared by the excluded issues and that can be analyzed in certain ways. Air, water, and solid-waste pollution result from waste disposal, and they mostly involve materials that have potential economic value. These characteristics are not shared by an inadequate architectural environment, for example.

Materials Balance

The first step in thinking systematically about environmental problems is to place them in the context of the balance of materials. This concept leads to some of the fundamental insights regarding environmental problems.

All commodity production consists of the application of other inputs—labor, capital, and so on—to materials extracted from the environment in order to transform materials from their natural states into useful products. As materials are extracted and processed, large amounts of unwanted materials are separated and returned to the environment. Once the completed commodities lose their economic value, they too must be returned to the environment or be reused in the production process. The **materials balance** is an identity that equates exhaustive lists of sources and dispositions of materials. In its simplest form, it can be stated as follows: Materials extracted from the environment during the year must equal those in the system at the end of the year plus those returned to the environment during the year. Additions to the stock of materials in the economic system are *capital accumulation.* Thus, the materials balance also can be stated as follows: In any year, extraction of materials from the environment equals discharge to the environment plus capital accumulation.

The materials balance bears the same relationship to the national materials accounts that the identity between sources and dispositions of income bears to the national income accounts. Unfortunately, only fragmentary data are available concerning the components of the materials accounts. Capital accumulation is 10 to 15 percent of total production and is probably about the same proportion of materials output in the United States. Thus, returns to the environment in the

Table 15.1 *Weight of Basic Materials Production in the United States Plus Net Imports, 1965 (in Millions of Tons)*

Material	Weight
Agricultural	
Crops	364
Livestock	23.5
Fisheries	2
Subtotal	389.5
Forestry products	
Sawlogs	120
Pulpwood	54
Other	42
Subtotal	216
Mineral fuels	1,448
Other minerals	
Iron ore	245
Other metal ore	191
Other nonmetals	149
Subtotal	585
Total	2,638.5

Source: Adapted with permission from Kneese, Allen, Robert Ayres, and Ralph D'Arge. *Economics and the Environment* (Baltimore: Johns Hopkins University Press, 1970): 10.

United States equal about 85 to 90 percent of withdrawals from the environment.

Table 15.1 shows some private estimates of materials extraction plus net imports in the United States for 1965. The volume of extraction is enormous. The total in Table 15.1 comes to about 70 pounds of materials extracted from the environment per person per day, which excludes masses of construction material that are merely moved from one place to another without being processed. Of the total in the table, more than half is fuels. The remainder is divided about equally between nonfuel minerals and agricultural, forestry, and fishery products. Unfortunately, the numbers in the table are dated. For the early 1990s, 125 pounds per person per day is probably a good estimate of total withdrawals. The relationships among the numbers are probably as accurate today as they were in 1965.

Forms of discharges.   The materials balance indicates that about 85 percent of the roughly 125 pounds per person per day of materials withdrawn is returned to the environment. What happens to this enormous volume of discharges? Of the large volume of withdrawals in agriculture and minerals extraction industries, much is returned to the environment on the site from which it was extracted. Some such returns do no harm to the environment, but most extractive industries do great environmental damage unless materials are returned with care. Strip mining of coal is a controversial example in this category.

Smaller, but still large, parts of withdrawals are processed and incorporated in products. All such materials eventually are returned to the environment as discharges into air, water, or land. To which of these media wastes are discharged depends on the technical characteristics of products and production processes and on economic variables. Fuels, for example, are burned, discharging some materials into the air and leaving some as solid waste. The energy released is converted to heat, which eventually is discharged into the air. Solid waste from fuel results in part from noncombustible impurities, but also in part from incomplete combustion. The amount of such waste to be disposed of depends in part on the relative prices of fuels and high-quality combustion systems.

Most liquid waste, both in industry and households, is really solid waste that is either dissolved or conveniently floated away in water. For example, kitchen garbage appears as solid waste if it is put in the garbage can and as liquid waste if it is ground in the disposal and washed down the drain.

Thus, many wastes can be discharged as liquid, airborne, or solid, depending on the products produced, the production processes, and the treatment processes employed to convert wastes from one form to another. The effects of waste discharges on people and on the environment depend to a crucial extent on the form and place in which they are discharged. The materials balance tells us that most materials withdrawn must be returned to the environment, but it does not tell us the form in which they are returned or the medium to which they are returned. These forms depend on technical, economic, and governmental policy variables.

Amount of discharges. The materials balance tells us that, except for capital accumulation, the discharge of materials equals the withdrawal of materials. If the production of commodities and services were proportionate to material inputs, the only way to reduce the withdrawal and discharge of materials would be to reduce production and, therefore, living standards. Some environmentalists indeed have urged governments to reduce living standards systematically in order to preserve environmental quality. If that were the only way to achieve a livable environment, it would be justifiable. In the last part of the twentieth century, however, it is a counsel of despair. The previous subsection showed that environmental damage depends on not only the amount, but also the forms, of returns.

In addition, it is possible to reduce the withdrawals and discharges necessary to achieve a given living standard. Indeed, that is a normal characteristic of technological progress. For 150 years or so, the total material extraction per unit of goods produced has fallen gradually in the United States because an important characteristic of technological progress is learning how to make more efficient use of materials. In the early years of the century, for example, much of the content of crude oil was returned to the environment after fuel had been refined out. Now a wide range of products—plastics, chemicals, and medicines, for example—is made from previously discarded materials.[1]

Another way to reduce the withdrawal and discharge of materials necessary to produce a given living standard is to reuse materials. For example, trees are felled and processed into newspapers, and petroleum is pumped from the ground and processed into fuel for thermoelectric generators. Newspapers usually are returned to the environment by placing them in landfills. (A day or so after publication, a newspaper's consumption value is gone, although its physical condition has been unchanged by consumption.) Petroleum is mostly returned to the environment in the form of heat and gases released by combustion. The production and consumption of newspapers and electricity can be maintained, while reducing the withdrawal and discharge of petroleum, by burning used newspapers as fuel in thermoelectric plants. The return of newspapers to the environment is thereby unchanged, but the form of the return is altered. Less petroleum, however, needs to be withdrawn for thermoelectric generation.

Thus, the reuse of materials depends on both technical and economic variables. Many materials can be reused, but some only at great cost. The cost depends on the nature of the material and on the nature of the product in which it is incorporated. Many products can be designed to facilitate the reuse of the materials in them. Other materials are easy to reuse and are typically reused in large quantities. Steel is a good example. The greater the reuse of materials, the smaller is the volume of materials withdrawn and discharged to maintain given living standards.

Absorptive capacity of the environment. Finally, every aspect of the environment has a considerable capacity to absorb waste and regenerate itself. A stream can dilute any waste, and it can degrade and render organic wastes innocuous. If a stream is overloaded with organic wastes, however, it loses its capacity to degrade organic material. Extreme overloading occurs when so much organic material is discharged into the stream that it becomes *anaerobic* (that is, it loses all its dissolved oxygen). Its regenerative capacity is then virtually destroyed and may take a long time to return. An anaerobic stream cannot support fish life, and it stinks from the hydrogen sulfide gas it produces.

Chemical and other processes in the atmosphere also permit a stream to absorb limited amounts of waste without damage. For example, much of the sulfur discharged into the atmosphere eventually is converted to sulfuric acid and other compounds and is returned to the earth by precipitation. Particles discharged into the air eventually settle back onto the earth's surface. Much less is known about the chemical and other processes by which air restores its quality, however, than

---

1. Chapter 2 discusses another example—steel.

about those by which water restores its quality. Although hydrocarbons from automobile exhausts certainly seem to be a major factor, it is still not known, after many years of intensive study, just how smog is produced in Los Angeles and other cities. This finding is unfortunate, since, as Allen Kneese—the leading economist specializing in environmental problems—put it, "We are in somewhat the same position in regard to polluted air as the fish are to polluted water. We live in it" (Kneese, cited in Wolozin [1974]:33).

The environment also can degrade limited amounts of solid waste. Organic materials eventually rot, and ferrous metals rust. Problems arise, however, when the environment is overloaded, and modern technology produces materials such as glass, pesticides, and plastics that do not degrade except during periods that are long relative to human life.

Pollution of all forms is most serious in urban areas, because the overloading and subsequent impairment of the environment are most serious there. The concentration of people and affluence produce much more waste than the environment can absorb.

Unfortunately, it is not known how large parts of the materials withdrawn from the environment are returned. Most are returned as solid wastes, but most environmental damage is done by the relatively small amounts returned to the air and water environments.

Amounts and Effects of Pollutants

Air pollution. All pollutants discharged to the atmosphere are harmful to plants, animals, and humans in sufficient concentrations. Some are harmless in typical ambient concentrations; others have indirect effects that may be harmful. Some have effects that are local or regional, and some have global effects.

Best studied and documented are those that have local or regional effects. Table 15.2 gives data for the six pollutants that have the best known discharge magnitudes and effects. Effects of these six pollutants usually occur within a few miles or a few hundred miles of the points of discharge.

Table 15.2 *Air Pollution Emissions 1940 to 1990 (in Millions of Metric Tons per Year)*

Pollutant	1940	1950	1960	1970	1980	1990
Sulfur oxides	17.6	19.8	19.7	28.3	23.4	21.2
Nitrogen oxides	6.3	9.3	12.8	18.1	20.9	19.6
Reactive volatile organic compounds	18.6	21	23.8	27.5	22.7	18.7
Suspended particulates	23.1	24.9	21.6	18.5	8.5	7.5
Carbon monoxide	81.6	86.3	88.4	101.4	79.6	60.1
Lead[a]	n.a.	n.a.	n.a.	203.8	70.6	7.1

Source: Council on Environmental Quality, *Environmental Quality.* (Washington, D.C.: Government Printing Office 1991).
[a]Data not available

Most sulfur oxide discharges come from the combustion of fossil fuels in power plants, factories, and homes. Evidence is strong that it has harmful effects on human health at concentrations that were common in large metropolitan areas in the decades following 1950. Nitrogen oxides are discharged mainly from combustion in motor vehicles and stationary combustion systems. It has no known adverse health effects at recent concentrations, but it interacts with volatile organic compounds, especially hydrocarbons, in the presence of sunlight to produce ozone. Ozone dims sunlight and causes tearing and discomfort for many people, but appears not to have long-term health effects. Ozone generated in this way is local and is not to be confused with the global ozone problem, discussed below. Reactive volatile organic compounds come from many industrial processes, but mostly from automobile engines. Suspended particulates are small particles of solid matter, such as dust and ash, and come mostly from industrial sources. Particulates have documented adverse effects on human health. Most settle out of the atmosphere in the vicinity of the discharge. Carbon monoxide is a deadly poison, but evidence of adverse health effects from recent concentrations is difficult to find. Most carbon monoxide is discharged in automobile exhaust. Lead was formerly added to motor vehicle fuel and undoubtedly had adverse health effects, especially on people in the vicinity of filling stations.

Table 15.2 shows substantial progress in reducing atmospheric discharges of all the pollutants shown except nitrogen oxides. Similar trends have been experienced for large metropolitan areas.

Water pollution.   Humans have no feasible alternative to breathing air, so all of it should be fit to breathe. They drink, however, only a small part of the available water, so not all of it needs to be fit to drink. When most people think of water shortages and water pollution, they think of water for drinking and other domestic purposes. Domestic use, however, is only a small part of the water story.

The most important distinction regarding water use is between instream and withdrawal uses. *In-stream uses* are those for which water remains in its natural channel. The most important examples are commercial and sport fishing, pleasure boating, navigation, swimming, hydroelectric generation, and aesthetic use. The last example refers to many recreational activities—especially hiking, picnicking, and camping—that are enhanced by proximity to bodies of water.

Withdrawal uses are those that require water to be withdrawn from its natural channel. The major purposes of withdrawal are municipal use, industrial processing, cooling, and irrigation. Water withdrawn by municipalities for public water supply is for domestic, commercial, and public (for example, fire protection) uses. *Industrial processing* refers to a variety of industrial uses, many of which involve the washing away of wastes. *Cooling* means the use of water to dissipate heat, by far the most important example being the generation of thermoelectricity. *Irrigation* refers to the withdrawal of water for farm animals and crops.

Water quality is a complex notion with many dimensions, and quality requirements vary enormously among the many uses of water. For pleasure boating and aesthetic uses, the major quality requirements are the absence of odors, discoloration, and floating solids. Quality requirements vary among industrial processing uses, but for most, the major requirement is the absence of salts that corrode pipes. Noncorrosive properties are also important for cooling uses, as is temperature. Different kinds of fish can live in water of different qualities, and much is known about the effects of water quality on game fish.

The highest quality requirements are for municipal water, since it must be fit to drink. Public health authorities in the United States set stringent quality standards, although there are many unanswered questions about the effects of relaxing one or more standards. The United States, however, has largely avoided waterborne diseases endemic in countries that apply less strict standards for drinking water.

Swimming water is something of an enigma. Authorities set the same requirements for swimming water as for drinking water. Swimmers need not drink the water they swim in, however, and many people swim in water they should not drink. Various afflictions can result from swimming in poor-quality water, but little is known about the likely incidence at different levels of quality. Chlorine used to purify water in swimming pools may cause ear and other problems. With swimming, as with other water-quality requirements, there is an important subjective element in that people simply find it distasteful to swim in dirty water.

The subjective element in water-quality standards causes much confusion. It often is claimed that people do not like to drink reused water, regardless of its quality. To the extent that the reason is a misunderstanding about its quality, presumably people's feelings can be changed by education. To the extent that subjective feelings represent genuine tastes, however, they should not be ignored. We do not ignore the fact that some people pay $100 more for a color television than for a black-and-white one, although the preference is certainly subjective. With water use, however, people often want someone else to pay the cost. For example, New York City has long urged the federal government to build it a plant to desalt sea water so that New Yorkers can avoid reusing Hudson River water. No New York mayor has yet seen fit to ask the city's residents whether they are willing to pay for high-cost desalted water. If they are, outsiders should not object.

Not only do the various uses of water have different quality requirements, but they also have various effects on water quality. In the course of using water, humans discharge an enormous variety of wastes into streams and estuaries. The most important and best-documented category of waste discharge is organic material. Although there are many kinds of organic materials, most share the important characteristic of using dissolved oxygen in the water as they are degraded. The dissolved oxygen content determines the kind of fish and other life that can survive in the water and affects virtually every use of water. An anaerobic stream is useless for almost all the purposes that have been discussed. Thus, the most significant measure of water pollution is the rate at which organic discharges use oxygen, referred to as *biochemical oxygen demand* (BOD). The quality of the water in a stream is determined by the BOD of wastes discharged into it and by the rate at which the stream can replenish its oxygen from the atmosphere, called its *reaeration rate.*

Many kinds of wastes, however, are disposed of in waterways. Table 15.3 presents some recent data. It shows the numbers of measuring stations that recorded upward, downward, and no trend for concentrations of various pollutants from 1978 to 1987. Note that an upward trend represents deterioration in stream quality. For most pollutants, there are more upward than downward trends. In fact, the only large improvement recorded in the table is for the measures related to organic discharges, dissolved oxygen deficit, and bacteria. The reason for the improvement is that the federal government has had major programs to build sewage treatment plants and to regulate private organic discharges since the early 1960s. Other pollutants have been targeted only more recently and with less vigor.

Table 15.3 *Trends in Stream Water Quality, 1978 to 1987*

Water-Quality Indicators	NASQAN* Stations Analyzed	Flow-Adjusted Concentrations (Number of Stations)		
		Upward Trend	Downward Trend	No Trend
Common ions	393	91	42	260
Calcium	393	50	31	312
Magnesium	392	76	25	291
Sodium	393	55	29	309
Potassium	393	42	54	297
Sulfate	393	34	36	293
Chloride	392	65	32	295
Dissolved solids	388	84	22	282
Nutrients and suspended solids	389	67	61	261
Nitrogen	390	82	24	284
Phosphorus	389	12	69	308
Suspended solids	153	13	19	121
Dissolved oxygen deficit and bacteria	380	25	52	302
Oxygen deficit	316	12	39	265
Fecal coliform	390	24	51	315
Fecal streptococcus	366	20	36	310
Acidity and alkalinity	385	115	12	258
Acidity	387	91	12	284
Total alkalinity	385	82	9	298

Source: Data from Environmental Protection Agency. *Environmental Quality.* Table 32 (Washington, D.C.: Government Printing Office, 1992): 261.
*Analyses were made on data from the U.S. Geological Survey's National Stream Quality Accounting Network (NASQAN) stations.

Most of the pollutants listed in Table 15.3 come from a variety of sources. The nutrients come largely from runoff of fertilizers from farms. Acidity comes from industrial processes and from acid rain, the fallout from airborne sulfur discharges.

The data in Table 15.3 refer to streams. Lakes are more vulnerable because the water turns over slowly and does not reaerate as rapidly as does water in streams. The five Great Lakes, surrounded on all sides by urban, industrial, and agricultural activities, have a long history of serious pollution problems and have been well studied. Virtually all measurements of pollutants in the lakes show steady improvement in water quality from the mid-1970s to the late 1980s.

Solid wastes.   As has been seen, the economy in the United States generates enormous volumes of solid wastes. By far the most attention has been paid to municipal wastes, the paper, plastics, yard wastes, glass, and metal that are collected by local governments or their contractors. These wastes are the solid wastes generated in urban areas. The volumes increase annually. Roughly, the weight of municipal waste generated per month is about the weight of the population that generates it. Table 15.4 shows the volume of solid waste generated in the United States, by source.

By far the predominant form of disposal is the *sanitary landfill,* an open place where wastes are dumped and covered more or less carefully with dirt each day. A carefully managed landfill is a disamenity to nearby residents, and residents in many metropolitan areas successfully prevent the opening or expansion of landfills by lobbying, protests, and court cases. The news media often claim that we are running out of potential sites, but the problem is political, not physical. All the materials were extracted from the ground and all can be returned, although desirable sites become increasingly distant from metropolitan waste-generating areas as time passes. The important change in the last decade or two has been the increasing ability of local people to prevent the opening or

Table 15.4   *Solid Waste Discharges in the United States, 1977 (in Millions of Tons)*

Source	Waste
Municipal[a]	
Residential/commercial/industrial	145
Sewage sludge	5
Junked automobiles, construction/demolition	45
Industrial	
Nonhazardous	323–342
Hazardous	38–57
Radioactive	0.04
Total	556–594

[a]Does not include "uncollected," which was about one-quarter of the total in 1969.

Source: Data from Council on Environmental Quality. *Environmental Quality* (Washington, D.C.: Government Printing Office, 1981): 92.

expansion of needed facilities. The political process has proven incapable of compensating losers for facilities that are in the interests of metropolitan residents.

Political controversy over landfills has motivated increased efforts to reuse municipal solid wastes. By 1988, about 13 percent of municipal solid wastes was reused or composted. Metals are often recycled for uses similar to those that generated the waste. Glass can be reground for similar uses. Plastic, such as bags and cups, are among the most difficult materials. They do not degrade and are often difficult or impossible to reuse. They may generate toxic fumes if burned.

Atomic wastes.   Radioactive materials are used both by the military, for atomic weapons, and by the civilian economy, primarily for atomic electric plants. The hazards of atomic electric plants have received enormous attention since the near-disaster at Three Mile Island and the disaster at Chernobyl. About 20 percent of the electricity generated in the United States comes from atomic plants.

The mining, processing and generating of electricity from uranium, however, are no more hazardous than similar activities related to coal-fired plants. It is not difficult to build and manage an atomic electric plant that is practically free of health hazards. The qualification to this view is that the sloppy operation of an atomic plant can be a much greater disaster than the sloppy operation of a conventional thermal electric plant. Both Three Mile Island and Chernobyl occurred because of inexcusable carelessness. Occasional carelessness is, of course, a basic human characteristic, but back-up systems should prevent ordinary carelessness from resulting in disaster.

By far the most serious problem with radioactivity is waste disposal. Spent atomic fuel can be reprocessed and reused, but those procedures are not done in the United States because of local opposition to the facilities. Even if they were done, the fuel eventually becomes waste. Likewise, weapons-grade fuel eventually deteriorates and must be disposed of. There is no known or prospective way to "treat" atomic wastes in the ways that organic wastes can be treated and made innocuous. Estimates are that civilian and military atomic wastes will continue to be deadly for up to 10,000 years. Nothing else that humans do produces effects that can kill people for so many generations.

Shooting atomic wastes into space with rockets would be an acceptable but expensive solution if rockets were sufficiently reliable. One rocket explosion a few miles above the earth, however, would impose about the same health hazards as a small atomic war.

Practically the only thing to do with atomic waste is to store it. In this country, most is now stored above ground in containers that last no more than a century. Above-ground storage facilitates monitoring, and containers can be repaired or replaced safely as they age. The serious problems with above-ground storage are terrorists and war, which could generate disasters.

The difficulty with other kinds of storage is lack of access. Some Asian countries have dumped containers in the ocean, but they will last less than a century in salt water and are inaccessible. Most countries bury wastes underground. In a dry facility, the containers last a long time. The present intention of the United States is to bury containers under Yucca Mountain, about 100 miles from Las Vegas, Nevada. The plan is to keep the facility open about 50 years after it is filled, so it can be monitored, and then to seal it. It could be kept open indefinitely so that the radioactivity could be monitored, but that presumably would increase the risk of terrorist or military attack.

Local opposition to the Yucca Mountain facility is furious, despite the fact that it is on the site that has long been the major facility where the atomic bomb is tested. Yucca would receive both military and civilian wastes. Present proposals to reduce atomic weapons would add enormously to the weapons-grade materials that must be stored.

However this story makes one feel about the appropriate future of atomic energy, the fact is that large amounts of radioactive material are now lying around the country and they must be stored for thousands of years.

International issues.   Two distinct and important concerns have arisen with regard to the global atmospheric environment in recent years. First is the atmospheric concentration of greenhouse gases, especially carbon dioxide. Greenhouse gases reduce the repeat emission of solar energy from the earth's surface to outer space, thus warming the earth's atmosphere. Life could not exist on the planet without greenhouse gases. It is known that human activity has increased the global concentration of greenhouse gases since the industrial revolution, probably by about 25 percent. That increase poses no direct threat to human health, although a sufficiently high concentration would interfere with respiration. The near-term threat from increasing greenhouse gas concentration, however, is from global atmospheric warming. The global mean temperature has increased about 0.5 degree centigrade during the last century.

Discharges of greenhouse gas result from many phenomena, but primarily from fossil fuel combustion and from forest clearing and other changes in land use. There is a fixed amount of carbon in the planet. Much of it is in the oceans and in rocks. Photosynthesis fixes carbon in green matter and deforestation or burning of fossil fuels releases it.

Nobody knows how much of the increase in global temperature during the last century has resulted from human activity. It seems likely that industrialization and deforestation have been primary culprits. The atmospheric temperature fluctuates for natural reasons, however, and ice ages have alternated with warmer periods. Many elaborate computer models of the atmosphere have predicted that human activity should have increased atmospheric warming more than has actually occurred over the past century.

Why does global warming matter? Most eminent would be a partial melting of the Antarctic ice cap. (The Arctic ice cap floats on the ocean, so melting would have little effect on sea level.) Ocean levels have risen about 10 centimeters during the last century. Much urban development is very close to sea level, and predicted rises during the next half-century could badly disrupt many urban areas. Global warming might not be uniform. Higher tropical temperatures would harm most developing countries, though warming would make Canada and Siberia more habitable. (Most models predict that global warming would be concentrated in the higher latitudes.)

What should be done? The jury is still out on the seriousness of the problem, but it is not too soon to make plans and do research. International cooperation will be needed to solve the problems, and that proceeds slowly. A halt to deforestation is frequently advocated. People in developing countries in tropical climates, where most remaining forests are located, however, correctly argue that northern countries in the temperate zone cut down most of their trees during recent centuries and have no right to tell tropical countries that they cannot follow suit. Reduced fossil fuel combustion is equally problematic. Reduced industrial production is uninviting, and a switch to atomic fuel substitutes one set of environmental problems for another.

The problem of stratospheric ozone depletion is easier to understand, evaluate, and solve. The stratosphere extends from about 25 to 50 kilometers above the earth's surface. Ozone in the stratosphere retards the penetration of ultraviolet radiation to the earth's surface. A reduction in stratospheric ozone concentration would increase, and probably has already increased, skin cancer, eye damage, and other ills. Ozone depletion results from the discharge of chlorine, mainly contained in chlorofluorocarbons (CFCs), which gradually rise to the stratosphere, where chemical processes result in ozone depletion. These CFCs are widely used as coolants in air-conditioning and refrigeration systems, and as propellants in cans of shaving cream and such products. The CFCs rise slowly to the stratosphere and have resident times in the stratosphere of a decade or so. Thus, effects of discharge abatement would not be substantial for approximately a decade.

During the last couple of decades, important scientific efforts have been undertaken to measure ozone concentration. The efforts are complicated by the fact that depletion varies greatly by altitude and by location over the earth's surface, the worst depletion being over the South Pole. On a global average, the stratospheric ozone appears to have been depleted about 40 percent, and adverse health effects have almost certainly occurred in the southern part of South America.

The solution is straightforward: Reduce CFC discharges. Other coolants and propellants can be substituted, probably at higher cost. The United States and other industrialized countries now have programs to abate CFC discharges, including the substitution of other devices such as the pump spray, and to control leakage and the disposal of coolants from cooling systems. Although most CFC discharges come from the world's industrialized countries, air-conditioning and refrigeration are spreading rapidly in some tropical countries. Determined international cooperation will be needed to solve the problem.

Alternative Environmental Policies of the Government

It is easy to understand the fundamental reason for the pollution problem. Pollutants discharged into the environment are an *external diseconomy,* as the term was defined in Chapter 8. As has been shown, many kinds of production can use combinations of inputs that generate a range of kinds, amounts, and locations of waste.

In many cases, productive techniques that generate large amounts of harmful wastes are cheaper than other techniques. Furthermore, wastes can be discharged into the environment in many forms, depending on the ways they are treated. All forms of treatment, however, require valuable resources. Finally, the extent to which used products are reused or discharged into the environment depends on the relative costs of new and used materials. As also has been seen, people value a high-quality environment for health, aesthetic, and recreational reasons.

Producers can keep costs low by large and relatively harmful discharges into the environment. The cost of the resulting deterioration in environmental quality is borne by those whose use of the environment is impaired, but those who make the decisions regarding harmful discharges fail to take into account the costs that discharges impose. Although a high-quality environment is valuable, its value does not get counted in market transactions. Thus, too few resources are devoted to the reduction of waste discharges by recycling and to the treatment of wastes.

Why do producers and users of the environment not make private agreements to optimize discharges? Sometimes they do. Many agreements are made regarding waste disposal on private land. Air and flowing water, however, are *fugitive resources:* Their movements are hard to predict, and it is extremely difficult to compute the damage done to them by each discharger into the environment. The transaction costs of private agreements are so great for many environmental problems that private agreements are rare. The history of governmental policy toward the environment has been a history of a search for policies that regulate discharges into the environment without large transaction costs to the government and private sectors.

It has never been legal to discharge wastes freely into the air and water. The common law has long restricted activities that create nuisances. State laws about water-rights always have provided some protection for the rights of downstream users, and public-health laws have long imposed stringent restrictions on discharges into water used for the domestic water supply. These laws have been important, especially in protecting public health. From the point of view of optimum resource allocation, however, these laws are a patchwork created at different times and for many purposes, and they are extremely resistant to change. In the postwar period, the need for special laws that are aimed squarely at pollution has become clear.

Governmental collection and disposal.

The most straightforward governmental antipollution policy is construction and operation of facilities to collect, treat, and dispose of wastes. Public facilities are the predominant method of handling household and commercial sewage and solid wastes. Scale economies make it desirable for a single organization to perform these services for an entire metropolitan area. Such an organization should be either publicly owned or privately owned and publicly regulated. Both methods are employed in the United States, but the former predominates. Likewise, as has been seen, the federal government has assumed responsibility for the storage of radioactive wastes.

Regulation and enforcement.

Aside from the construction and operation of disposal facilities, the most common governmental antipollution program in the United States is discharge regulation. After more than a decade of experimentation with alternative approaches, the present program was laid down in laws passed in the early 1970s. All such laws have since been amended and extended many times. These laws established the Environmental Protection Agency (EPA) and empowered it to control air, water, and solid-waste discharges.

For air and water discharges, the procedure is similar. The EPA is instructed to calculate total discharge volumes into a stream or into the air over a metropolitan area that keep environmental quality at levels that protect public health and welfare. This task is enormous, especially for the large numbers of wastes discharged into water. Any firm or municipality that wants to discharge wastes into air or water must apply to the EPA for a permit to do so. The EPA attempts to restrict the total allowed by the permits issued to discharge volumes that meet its ambient goals of environmental quality.

For motor-vehicle emissions into the air, the procedure is somewhat different. Unlike other environmental provisions, the automobile pollution law enacted in 1970 specifies permitted automotive discharges; permitted discharges were to decrease gradually until, in 1976, discharges per car would be no more than 5 percent of discharges produced by the last uncontrolled cars, made in 1967. The goals have since been postponed several times because of energy crises and other events, but standards in effect in 1992 entail roughly 85 percent abatement from 1967 discharge levels.

Control of solid-waste discharges is still mainly the responsibility of states, which delegate most responsibility to local governments. The federal program is restricted to research and development, data collection, and encouragement to state and local governments to upgrade disposal facilities.

There can be no doubt that the governmental program has improved environmental quality since the early 1970s. The environmental trends shown in Tables 15.2 and 15.3 certainly show improvement because of governmental interventions. Nevertheless, almost all economists who have studied the programs are highly critical of governmental environmental programs. The programs are very expensive, and economists conclude that the benefits could have been obtained more cheaply.

The permit systems have become extremely complex. The EPA is now our largest regulatory agency, with more than 15,000 employees. The law requires the EPA to issue permits fairly, but literally every industrial, commercial, and governmental discharge facility is unique. The result is that there are rooms full of regulations about what facility can discharge what wastes. Inevitably, permit levels are negotiated between industrial and governmental officials. This process means that governmental officials become partners in major business decisions about new plant construction, expansion, or redesign of existing plants; design of new products; and important changes in industrial technology. As a result, business decision-making is slower, more bureaucratized, less innovative, and less responsive to market signals. To take an extreme example, about half of the government's billions of dollars of annual "superfund" expenditures to clean up toxic waste sites goes to litigation.

Inevitably, the EPA ends up issuing permits if specific antipollution measures have been taken, for example, secondary treatment plants, catalytic converters on cars, and so forth. The procedure emphasizes known and conventional devices, not those designed to optimize a particular situation. Most important, it emphasizes installation instead of operation of abatement devices. Two examples will illustrate.

For the most part, the EPA issues organic waste-discharge permits to municipalities if they construct secondary treatment plants, which can remove about 90 percent of organic wastes before discharge. Municipalities are happy to construct such facilities: Most of the money is provided in grants by federal and state governments, and local governments win the favor of construction contractors and unions by the resulting business. Municipalities, however, have no incentive to operate the treatment plants efficiently once they have been built, so many are operated at about half of their potential effectiveness.

New cars must meet stringent discharge limits stipulated in the law. Once cars are on the road, however, emissions are not checked except in a few states that have annual safety inspections. Emission-control devices do not continue to function properly longer than two or three years unless they are serviced and maintained. Furthermore, the car owner has a disincentive to maintain the devices, since the car's fuel mileage improves if the devices fail. The result is that new cars have technically sophisticated and expensive emission-control devices, but most cars on the road do not meet the legal standards. Much of the money spent to make a car meet extremely high standards when it is new is subsequently wasted.

Economists believe that the federal discharge-abatement program should encourage flexibility and innovation by which discharge goals are met and at which times they are met: Most important, they believe that the program should permit decentralized and market-oriented decision-making, in which businesses can make decisions about discharges on the basis of economic criteria and without negotiating every major decision with governmental officials.

Subsidies.   A federal grant program to subsidize the construction of municipal sewage treatment plants is a major part of the pollution-abatement program in the United States. Annual appropriations were in excess of $4 billion in the late 1970s, but fell during the 1980s. The program has resulted in treatment plant construction all around the country and certainly has reduced the volume of organic discharges to streams and estuaries by municipalities. It already has been pointed out that the discharge-abatement program places too much emphasis on facility construction and not enough on operation. The purpose of the subsidy program is political. In principle, the federal government should issue discharge permits, and the required abatement should be at the expense of those who generate the wastes. In the case of municipal sewage, the expense would be borne by local taxpayers. In fact, the federal government has almost no way to force local governments to comply with permits it issues. Local officials cannot be fined and jailed. About the only possibility is for the federal government to withhold grant funds for other purposes, such as housing subsidization, in the event of noncompliance. Such funds are given for urgent purposes— mostly to benefit the poor—and to withhold them would be unpopular. In the absence of large federal construction subsidies, many hard-pressed local governments probably just would not comply with federal permits.

Public officials frequently propose broad-based discharge-abatement subsidies. The proposal most studied is simple: A payment to all dischargers proportionate to the amount by which they abate discharges. Economists oppose such proposals on both efficiency and equity grounds. On efficiency grounds, subsidies do not achieve desired abatement economically. Subsidization would reduce discharges per unit of output, but the firm's improved revenue position would motivate it to increase output. The net effect could be an increase in polluting discharges. On equity grounds, subsidies are, in effect, payments to those who pollute by the remainder of society. This process hardly seems like a desirable way to redistribute income.

Such a subsidy scheme also would be an administrative nightmare. It would require the estimation of discharge volumes in the absence of subsidy payments. Dischargers would be motivated to exaggerate the volume of discharges they would have had. Especially with new or expanded production facilities, or new or modified products, estimation would be extremely difficult.

Effluent fees.   Almost all economists who have studied the subject favor a partial or total dismantling of the permit program and its replacement by an *effluent fee*. Effluent fees are extremely simple: Dischargers are permitted to discharge whatever quantity of wastes they wish, but they must pay the government a fee per unit of waste discharged. The fee for each major waste would be set by the government at the level it estimates would result in discharge volumes that equate marginal social benefits and marginal costs of abatement.

Setting effluent fees requires the same data and calculations that issuing permits requires—no more and no less.[2] The government must estimate the benefits and costs of abatement for either program, and it must meter actual discharges, at least on a sample basis. The great advantage of effluent fees over the permit program is that the government would be removed from business decision-making, and environmental decisions would be placed within the market context that firms are motivated to use and are experienced in using. Firms could design whatever abatement devices appeared to them to be the most economical means of achieving each abatement level. They would not need to obtain governmental permission for devices or discharge volumes.

Dischargers would be motivated to seek economical means of abatement as long as they discharged any wastes. Under a permit system, dischargers have no incentive to discharge less than the level provided by their permit.

Effluent fees have been better studied than almost any actual or potential governmental program. Their advantages in comparison with alternatives are overwhelming. They have been advocated by economists, business groups, and environmental groups. Other countries, especially West Germany and France, have tried them successfully. Why have they not been tried in the United States? The existing environmental program was put in place during the zenith of the environmental movement in the early 1970s. The mood of the country was similar to that of a crusade—not a time when politicians want to listen to economists talk about the dangers of governmental intrusion into

---

2.   Some critics of effluent-fee proposals claim that metering discharges would place an intolerable burden on dischargers or on the EPA. In fact, *no* pollution control program is possible without metering discharges, at least on a sample basis. The best way to handle metering would be a requirement that dischargers design a metering procedure that would be acceptable to the EPA. The EPA would then need to audit compliance on a sample basis. In fact, dischargers could be given the option of metering their discharges or of having the EPA do it for them and then charge the dischargers for the cost that the EPA incurred. In fact, no single policy would solve all environmental problems. Discharges of wastes that are highly toxic in small amounts could probably not be regulated by effluent fees. Evasion of the law over small amounts could be dangerous. Some other program is needed to monitor toxic discharges.

business. Since then, an enormous amount of human and physical capital has been invested in the permit program—designing it, implementing it, and learning to live with it. Furthermore, people's attention has shifted to fuel and other material shortages.

In fact, interest in introducing economic incentives into the environmental program is growing. Governmental officials are more interested in economic arguments now than they were a decade ago; the problems with the permit program have become more obvious, and more is known about the practical aspects of effluent fee programs. The EPA is moving to introduce better economic incentives into the program.

Marketable pollution rights. The notion of marketable pollution rights, worked out in some detail by Coolinge and Oates (1982), is an interesting variant of effluent fees. First a state or local government decides that the total amount of pollution (usually just point-source pollution) to be permitted in an area shall be X percent of the current level of pollution. Each existing fixed-site polluter then is granted a license to dump X percent of its current level of pollution. The final step allows holders of these pollution permits to buy or sell them at whatever price the market will bear. Once the "market" for pollution has cleared, the outcome will have the following features: (1) Pollution will be X percent of its original level, just as the government had wanted, and (2) every firm will face the same price of pollution, namely, the market price of pollution coupons.

This proposal has two advantages over the standard effluent-fee system. First the government knows in advance how much pollution will be reduced; with effluent fees, it can do little more than guess. Second the redistribution of wealth and the resistance to the plan would be much more modest under the marketable pollution-rights scheme. Under the effluent-fee system, many firms would be driven out of business because they would be unable to pay the fees (for several steel mills, this is a real possibility). The hardship under the marketable pollution-rights system would be much less severe. Suppose efficiency calls for a pollution reduction of 50 percent. Under an efficient effluent-fee scheme, a firm would be induced to reduce pollution by 50 percent, but it still would have to pay a fee on the other 50 percent. Under the marketable pollution-rights scheme, the same (efficient) 50 percent pollution reduction would be achieved without forcing the firm to pay a fee on the remaining 50 percent.

As this discussion makes clear, the difference between programs is basically a difference in who owns the property right to environmental quality. As such, many people argue that the marketable pollution-rights scheme passes out property rights to the wrong group of people—those who have polluted the environment in the past. The dispute is over a fair redistribution of property rights.

Materials reuse.   Although air and water pollution control is a cooperative federal-state program, its basic characteristics have been federal initiatives since the 1950s. However, solid-waste disposal, and hence reuse, is still mainly state and local responsibilities. Furthermore, most of the used products from which reusable materials come are in urban areas. Thus, solid-waste disposal and the recovery of materials are of great interest to urban governments.

Materials reuse responds strongly to prices of new materials. During times such as the early 1970s, when newly extracted materials—from food to metals to fuel—are scarce and expensive, recovery and reuse flourish. When new materials become relatively cheaper, as they did in the mid-1970s and especially in the 1980s, recovery and reuse languish.

Some materials are much easier to recover and reuse than others. Virgin copper is expensive, and much of it is used in such products as copper wire, from which the copper can be recovered cheaply. An automobile, by contrast, is a complex product containing many materials, and materials recovery and reuse require sophisticated technology.

Many government actions—mostly having to do with the tax system—favor the use of virgin instead of used materials. There is justification for governmental programs to promote reuse. Unfortunately, no one knows how much bias toward virgin materials is introduced by governments. In addition, solid-waste disposal is a chronic problem for local governments in metropolitan areas. Especially in central cities, land that can be used for landfills is almost nonexistent. Furthermore, local governments appear to be politically unable to contract with each other so that, for example, central-city governments can dispose of solid wastes in distant suburbs.

During the 1970s, several cooperative—federal, state, and local— solid-waste recovery and disposal experiments were carried out. Typically, a central facility was established to which municipal and industrial wastes could be brought. At the facility, materials would be separated and processed for reuse. Those for which there was no demand would be disposed of in landfills or incinerators. A typical activity of such facilities was the preparation of organic wastes to be used as fuel in thermoelectric plants. Such experiments have met with mixed success, but experience and high fuel prices, presumably, will guarantee eventual success. Experiments with "trash-to-steam" had continued in the 1980s, but success has been remarkably elusive.

A special local governmental solid-waste problem arises with sludge from municipal treatment plants. Traditionally, sludge has been burned, disposed of in landfills, or hauled to sea and dumped. Dumping at sea has been banned, however, creating a crisis in coastal cities. Promising experiments have processed sludge into fertilizer that can be used on farms and lawns. Easy processing results in an inexpensive and high-quality fertilizer. The biggest problem, however, is caused by heavy metals that are discharged into the sewage system by industry and that remain intact through treatment. Heavy metals in sludge that is process-ed into fertilizer may be taken up by plants and ingested by people or animals. People in the United States, fortunately, have been free of heavy metal poisoning, but experience elsewhere—especially in Japan—shows that heavy metal poisoning can lead to incurable illnesses and death.

Many questions are raised about cooperative solid-waste recovery and disposal facilities. Are they successful? To what extent is success the result of the large subsidies that facilities receive, and to what extent is it the result of their innovative activities? Should they be run by the government? It is too early to answer such questions.

☐ ENVIRONMENTAL AMENITIES AND URBAN ECONOMICS

This discussion of the environment and pollution has had little to do with urban economics per se—that is, with the workings of urban areas and their economies. Environmental economics, however, is a legiti-mate branch of urban economics in two important respects.

High Density

The first "urban" observation is that many environmental problems are not problems at all when population densities are small. High density creates a problem by increasing the number of victims of any environmental degradation. If air quality reduction imposes a cost of $100 per year per exposed resident, it is of much more quantitative importance in a city of 2,000,000 than in a town of 5,000 people.

In addition to increasing the number of pollution victims, and therefore, the social costs of pollution, a concentration of people and economic activity generally increases the density of pollutants as well. This finding is important, because damage generally rises more than proportionately with the volume of discharges—particularly when the pollutants are degradable. For example, up to a point, a stream is capable of degrading organic wastes with little adverse effect on water quality. Once the oxygen is gone, however, the stream cannot support fish life, and further decomposition of organic materials is anaerobic. This anerobic decomposition causes the foul smell of some sewage-laden streams. Thus, it is large volumes of pollutants that frequently give rise to environmental damage. The same applies to air pollution; many efflu-ents are innocuous at low densities.

These two uniquely urban components of the pollution problem—large numbers of victims and damage that rises more than proportionate-ly with discharges—mean that the per capita cost of pollution is likely to rise with city size. This finding, of course, means that the marginal cost of pollution is higher than the average cost. In other words, the increase in total pollution damage that results from the arrival of a new resident in a city is greater than the per capita pollution damage before the resident's arrival. The new resident increases total pollution cost because (1) he or she represents an additional victim of the existing level of pollution, and (2) the resident's presence adds to the existing level of pollution, imposing additional costs on others.

The economic analysis of this situation is much like that of road congestion. The marginal resident, in deciding where to live, takes account of the current pollution level in the city but ignores the effect his or her presence will have on the pollution endured by current residents. Some have argued that this process makes big cities too big in a market economy, because households do not face the proper migration incentives. The next chapter will return to this question in considering pollution and congestion problems at the same time.

Amenities, Rents, Wages, and Location

To implement an efficient system of effluent fees (or direct regulations), how much people are willing to pay for environmental improvement must be determined. This aspect is the crucial missing information when it comes to deciding how vigorously to pursue pollution abatement. How can one find out what air quality improvement is worth?

Urban economics provides one of the few reasonably reliable ways of answering this question. Through their behavior in urban land and labor markets, people provide a substantial amount of evidence regarding their demand for environmental quality.

Intraurban amenity variations. Although there are important qualifications, the basic principle to be explored is that intraurban differences in the value of environmental amenities (including, for example, air quality) are reflected in differences in property values. This principle already has been applied several times in this book—the land market, through spatial variation in rent, soaks up any geographic differences in attainable utility, regardless of whether these differences result from variation in access to the CBD, school quality, taxes, neighborhood amenities, or air quality.

In discussing neighborhood effects, however, conditions were described under which property value differences could be used quite stringently as pure measures of amenity differences. Most important, one must assume that all households have the same demand for the amenity. If demands vary among households—as a result of either income or differences in taste—property value differences generally yield an underestimate of the value of environmental quality. For example, suppose there is a city with two households (A and B) and two houses (a and b). Household A has a stronger demand for clean air than does Household B, and the air over House a is cleaner than that over House b. Household A will outbid Household B for House a, with clean air. In equilibrium, however, House a will command a rent premium equal only to the extent of Household B's preference for House a over House b, because this amount is all that Household A need offer to outbid Household B for the house with clean air. Notice that Household A would have been willing to pay a greater premium, but the market did not require it. In other words, the land market reveals Household B's willingness to pay for clean air, but it reveals nothing about Household A's (greater) willingness to pay.[3] So it always is with auctions: The winning bid is the maximum price the second-highest bidder is willing to pay. Obviously, this amount is less than what the highest bidder is willing to pay.

Despite these caveats, variations in property values contain much information about people's willingness to pay for environmental amenities. Polinsky and Rubinfeld (1977) use the property-value method to estimate the value to consumers of a 50 percent reduction in suspended particulates and sulfur dioxide for the St. Louis MSA. They calculate the mid-1970s value of the benefit to be about $900 per capita, which gives an annual benefit of roughly $90.[4]

Interurban amenity variations.   Researchers have looked at the effects of amenity variations among urban areas for a variety of reasons. One reason is that there is more variation among than within urban areas, so estimation possibilities are richer. Another reason, as will be shown, is that the data needs are more modest.

At several points it has been noted that studies of the determinants of rent (or value) variation are hampered by the difficulty of disentangling price from quantity. To examine the effects of amenities on rents, one first must gather data on rents of dwelling units. This task is a difficult one of data gathering and processing.

Most of these problems do not arise in studies of interurban amenity variations, because the value of these variations reveals itself not in land markets but rather in labor markets. (This discussion is based on an analysis in Chapter 6.) It works basically as follows: Suppose two urban areas are identical in size, air quality, and all other relevant characteristics. The land-rent gradient and the wage rates also are the same in both cities. Now air quality over one urban area is improved, making it a more desirable place to live. In the short run, this feature raises property values (that is, it shifts the land-rent gradient up) in the

---

3.   It may seen that this example works because of the small number of participants, but that is not so. The market clean-air premium generally will be smaller than the willingness to pay by the high-demand people as long as demands vary. See Polinsky and Rubinfeld (1977) for a thorough, but difficult, discussion of this problem.

4.   This amount is roughly the per capita cost of automobile emission standards at this time. Because automobiles contribute substantially less than half of all forms of air pollution except carbon monoxide (see Table 15.2), this estimate raises some doubt as to whether the benefits of the more stringent automobile-emission standards are worth the costs, at least in St. Louis.

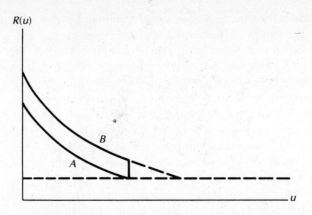

Figure 15.1   *Behavior of Land-Rent Function When Air Quality Improves*

clean city sufficiently to leave people indifferent between the two cities. The clean urban area's land-rent gradient now appears as curve *B* in Figure 15.1. It is not, however, an equilibrium gradient; land rent at the edge of the urban area does not fall to zero (or to the exogenous rent of agricultural land). Thus, developers have an incentive to increase the size of the urban area by converting land from agriculture to suburbia. In the process, land-market equilibrium is restored; the "tail" is added to the land-rent gradient in Figure 15.1. The land-rent gradient is still higher in the clean (curve *B*) than the polluted (curve *A*) urban area.

Thus, it might appear that a regression of property values on air quality and other determinants still would find an association between air quality and property values. This concept, however, is not true if population is included in the regression, as it should be. Chapter 6 showed that big urban areas should have higher land-rent gradients than small urban areas, and Chapter 7 provided evidence to support this prediction. In fact, in equilibrium, the height of the land-rent gradient is determined *only* by population and the amount of available land. There may be irregularities in the shape of the land-rent gradient due to within-urban area variations in amenities of various sorts. Aside from these "blips," however, the height must be governed only by population. The reason for this aspect is that rent must fall to zero (or to the exogenous agricultural rent) at the edge of the urban area to preserve equilibrium between rural and urban land users. The only observable statistical association is between population and land value, not between air quality and land value. Two urban areas of equal size, but different levels of air quality, have identical land-rent gradients. Two urban areas with different populations and the same air quality have different land-rent gradients.

Returning to the two-urban area example, the clean urban area is now larger and has a higher land-rent gradient than the smaller one, and the land market is in equilibrium. What about the labor market? Chapter 6 showed that workers insist on wage premiums to live in a large urban area (to compensate them for the greater commuting or land rent that life in the large urban area entails). Would such a wage premium exist in the large urban area with clean air? If it did, workers would prefer to live there rather than in the small, polluted urban area. It is true that the urban area is bigger and more costly to live in, but the wage premium compensates for this. In addition, the air is cleaner, so the net effect is that everyone prefers living in the big, urban area city rather than in the small, polluted one. This situation cannot persist in equilibrium.

The final equilibrium condition needed is this: After correcting for other determinants, interurban area wage differences must compensate workers for interurban area differences in amenities.

If wages vary among urban areas to compensate for variations in amenities, regression analysis should be able to estimate the size of the compensation workers require to endure various environmental disamenities.[5] Rosen (1979, pp. 100, 101) carried out such a study, which determined the following wage premiums: $15 per rainy day, $136 per 10 percent increase in suspended particulates, $50 per 10 percent increase in the crime rate, $290 per one-point increase in the unemployment rate, $120 per 10 percent *decrease* in population density, and $48 per 10 percent increase in population.[6]

Chapter 7 noted that the wage premiums for large-population and low-population densities closely agree with the values predicted by theory. The other numbers are plausible and interesting, and they tend to confirm that the labor market works basically in the previously indicated way. Rainy days, particulates, crime and unemployment are all associated with wage premiums, indicating that workers must be compensated for enduring them. The effect of particulates is somewhat larger than that estimated by Polinsky and Rubinfeld (1977). If a 10 percent reduction in particulates results in a wage reduction of $136, a 50 percent reduction in particulates would yield a $680 compensating wage reduction. With about 40 percent of the population in the labor force, this translates to $272 per capita, as compared with the $90 per capita estimated by Polinsky and Rubinfeld.[7] At this stage, these techniques for evaluating environmental amenities are not as refined as

5. As is always the case with regression analysis, it is necessary to include other determinants of wages (such as education and experience) to isolate the effects of amenities. These prices represent the mid-1970s. Late 1992 prices are about 2.6 times as high.

6. It might seem that high unemployment—indicating a depressed labor market —would be associated with low wages. Apparently, however, the compensation effect predominates; if an urban area has a reputation for high unemployment, workers insist on a wage premium to live there. In developing countries, this effect (originally observed by Harris and Todaro [1970]) is associated with an urban to rural wage ratio of two or more to one.

7. One problem might lie in the assumption that a 50 percent reduction in particulates is five times as valuable as a 10 percent reduction. As has been noted, the benefits of additional pollution abatement probably diminish rapidly as air quality improves.

might be hoped, although it is encouraging to see that the studies yield plausible results.

Firm location.   Chapter 2 discussed several determinants of firm location. It noted the historical importance of regional variations in input and output prices, as well as in the costs of transporting both inputs and outputs. It also showed, however, that both transport orientation and production-cost orientation have declined over the past two centuries as a result of declines in transport costs and reductions in regional input-cost variations. Increasingly, firms are footloose—not strongly tied to any location, at least for the traditional reasons. This finding, it has been argued, has led to an increase in amenity orientation —the tendency for firms to seek locations where working and living are enjoyable. It can now be seen that, at least in part, amenity orientation is labor-cost orientation. Firms may not be attracted to high-amenity regions at all (it is hard to imagine why they would be, if they want to maximize profit); rather, they may be attracted to low-wage regions. In the past, low-wage regions were regions with a temporary surplus of labor, such as the South. These disequilibriums, however, have largely disappeared as a result of massive migration of both firms and workers.[8] Most of the rather modest wage variations that remain appear to be compensation for amenity differences.[9]

☐ Summary

Pollution is defined as environmental deterioration resulting from the return of materials to the environment. The materials balance is an exhaustive list of sources and dispositions of materials used in economic activity. The practical ways to abate polluting discharges are to recycle more materials and alter the form of discharges by process changes and by treatment of wastes.

Pollutants are discharged into the environment as gases, liquids, or solid wastes. There is considerable evidence that air pollution affects mortality and morbidity, as well as property. Water pollution affects a large variety of water uses. Inadequate methods of solid-waste disposal mar the landscape and impair many uses of land.

8.   In Rosen's (1979) sample of 19 cities, the spread between the cities with the highest and lowest wages was about 30 percent.

9.   In another study of intercity wage variation, Hoch and Drake (1974) found that variation in environment, city size, and the like accounted for about 75 percent of the intercity variation in wages for several predominantly male occupations (janitor and mechanic, for example). The same variables, however, explained only about 40 percent of the wage variation for predominantly female jobs (accounting clerk, stenographer, and typist, for example). This finding suggests that men are better able to move in response to intercity wage differences than are women.

Economic theory shows that excessive pollution results unless discharges are controlled by governmental policy, because pollution costs are not borne by those who discharge wastes. Governmental policies to abate pollution may entail the public collection and disposal of wastes, regulation of discharges, subsidies for waste treatment, or fees for the discharge of wastes. In the United States, governmental pollution-abatement programs consist mainly of governmental collection, treatment, and disposal of wastes, as well as an elaborate permit program to regulate discharges. Only recently have governments shown interest in introducing economic incentives into pollution-control programs.

Solid-waste recovery and disposal are mainly local governmental responsibilities. Implementing effective recovery programs is a challenge to both government and private sectors.

Questions and Problems

1. What would be the effects on income distribution between wealthy and poor of more stringent controls on air and water pollution?

2. How would the following be affected by a fee levied on the discharge of sulfur into the atmosphere?
   a. Regulated electric utilities
   b. Manufacturers of atomic reactors
   c. Sulfur-mining companies

3. Evaluate the contention that polluters should be jailed as common criminals instead of merely being penalized by paying effluent fees.

4. *Depletion allowances* are percentages of gross revenues that mining firms are permitted to subtract before computing federal taxes for corporate profits. Suppose that, instead, they were required to depreciate their holdings like any other capital asset. What would be the effect on the reuse of materials?

5. How would you modify the materials balance to account for material and commodity imports and exports?

6. Suggest a method to measure the value of weather information to consumers when its predictability is observed to vary in a cross section of urban areas.

References and Further Reading

Baumol, William, and Wallace E. Oates. *The Theory of Environmental Policy.* (Englewood Cliffs, N.J.: Prentice-Hall, 1975). A technical, theoretical analysis of environmental economics.

Baumol, William, and Wallace E. Oates. *Economics: Environmental Policy and the Quality of Life* (Englewood Cliffs, N.J.: Prentice-Hall, 1979). A nontechnical and practical analysis of environmental programs.

Coolinge, Robert, and Wallace E. Oates. "Efficiency in Pollution Control in the Short and Long Runs: A System of Rental Emission Permits." *Canadian Journal of Economics* 15 (1982): 346–354.

Council on Environmental Quality. *Environmental Quality* (Washington, D.C.: Government Printing Office, 1991). The annual report of the federal executive office agency that advises the president on environmental issues.

Harris, J.R., and M. Todaro. "Migration, Unemployment and Development: A Two-Sector Analysis. *American Economic Review* 60 (1970): 126–142. An early model in which the market compensates for high urban unemployment with high wages.

Hoch, Irving, and Judith Drake. "Wages, Climate and the Quality of Life." *Journal of Environmental Economics and Management* 1 (1974) 268–295.

Kneese, Allen, Robert Ayres, and Ralph D'Arge. *Economics and the Environment* (Baltimore: Johns Hopkins University Press, 1970). A basic data source for the materials balance.

Kneese, Allen, and Charles Schultze. *Pollution, Prices and Public Policy* (Washington, D.C.: Brookings Institution, 1975). A careful analysis of the use of economic inventives in governmental policy making.

Lave, Lester, and Eugene Seskin. *Air Pollution and Human Health* (Baltimore: Johns Hopkins University Press, 1977). A careful statistical analysis of the health effects of air pollution.

Mills, Edwin. *The Economics of Environmental Quality* (New York: W. H. Norton, 1978). A textbook on environmental economics.

Polinsky, A. M., and D. Rubinfeld. "Property Values and the Benefits of Environmental Improvements: Theory and Measurement." In *Public Economics and the Quality of Life,* edited by Lowdon Wingo and Alan Evans (Baltimore: Johns Hopkins University Press, 1977): 154–180. An early use of property-value data to evaluate the demand for environmental quality.

Rosen, Sherwin. "Wage-based Indexes of Urban Quality of Life." In *Current Issues in Urban Economics,* edited by Peter Mieszkowski and Mahlon Straszheim (Baltimore: Johns Hopkins University Press, 1979). An estimate of the determinants of interurban wage differences.

Wolozin, Harold, ed. *The Economics of Air Pollution* (Morristown, N.J.: General Learning Press, 1974).

16

Sizes and Structures of Urban Areas

☐ Part One presented historical data on urban areas in the United States, with particular emphasis on the size distribution of cities and urban areas, the relationships among regions, and the degree of suburbanization of both residences and jobs. Now, having had the benefit of the material in intervening chapters, these topics are discussed further and the following questions are considered: Is population excessively concentrated in our largest urban areas—that is, are large urban areas too big relative to smaller ones? What have been the recent patterns of population movement between cities and suburbs, as well as among urban areas? What have been the causes of these movements, and is there evidence of market failures (leading, for example, to excessive suburbanization)?

It is invariably contended that the largest urban areas are too large and the smallest are too small. This belief may be more widely held than any other regarding social problems. It is believed by city planners, government officials, journalists, and scholars. It is held in wealthy and poor countries and in capitalist and socialist countries; it is held in African countries, where the largest urban area has only a few hundred thousand people, as well as in Japan, which has the world's largest urban area (some 25 million people). Many countries in Europe and Asia have official, although mostly ineffectual, governmental policies to discourage growth of the largest urban areas (Sundquist [1975]).

Also widely held is the view that metropolitan areas in the United States are excessively spread out or suburbanized. Chapter 4 showed that suburbanization proceeded rapidly and far after World War II. Most metropolitan suburbs are dominated by single-family houses on large lots. Journalists and planners complain that such low-density suburbs make wasteful use of land and fuel for heating, cooling, and transportation, and that they lead to undesirable life-styles. The phrase "slums and suburban sprawl" conveys the feeling of antipathy held by many toward suburbs. Most literature on the subject, however, leaves unclear whether the alleged deficiencies of suburbs are matters of efficiency or equity or whether they result from market failure, from locational preferences of people disapproved by authors, or from misguided governmental policies.

Although the beliefs analyzed in this chapter are widely held, they are less coherent than the problems analyzed in earlier chapters. An important task of this chapter will be to ask exactly what the alleged problem is, why it is a problem, and what—if anything—should be done about it.

☐ SIZE DISTRIBUTION OF URBAN AREAS

Theory

Chapter 4 presented data and analysis on the size distribution of urban areas. What reasons are there to believe that the size distribution resulting from the location decisions of residents and firms might not represent an efficient use of productive resources? Work by Tolley (1974) has been used to develop a coherent analysis of this subject, and much of the following is based on this analysis. It relies on the notion that market failure is due to external diseconomies. The basic theoretical analysis of market failure was presented in Chapter 8. Chapter 15 applied the analysis to problems of pollution. To build further on that analysis, this chapter will introduce the problem of urban size distribution in the context of environmental problems. It then will show how the analysis can be applied to other causes of market failure.

As Chapter 2 pointed out, input productivity varies among urban areas because of differences in comparative advantage and other considerations. If size of urban areas matter, it means that input productivity depends on that as well. Some inputs, notably labor, are mobile among urban areas. Massive urban migrations observed in the United States and elsewhere, as discussed in Chapter 2, represent input movements to the most advantageous locations.

The simplest situation to analyze is one in which there are two urban areas—one large and one small. The same product is produced in each urban area. A given labor supply, consisting of N identical workers, is to be allocated between the two urban areas. In Figure 16.1, A is the large and B is the small urban area in equilibrium. The number of workers in A is measured on the horizontal axis with the origin at the left vertical axis. Since N is fixed, N_B, the number of workers in B, is $N_B = N - N_A$. The length of the horizontal axis is N, so N_B is the distance from the right vertical axis to $N_A \cdot MP_{NA} \cdot P_A$ measures the value of the marginal product of workers in A, and $MP_{NB} \cdot P_B$ measures the value of their marginal product in B. Each MP is labor's marginal product, and each P is the local product price. $MP_{NB} \cdot P_B$ is measured from the right vertical axis, so it falls to the left. Assume that the labor market is competitive within and

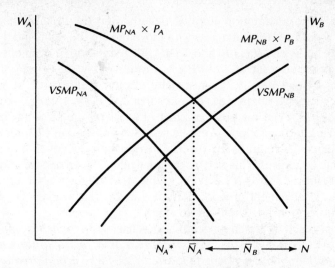

Figure 16.1   *Assignment of Population to Big and Small Cities*

between urban areas. As Chapter 5 showed, the wage rate equals the value of the marginal product in competitive equilibrium. Assume for the moment that workers care only about the local wage rates, W_A and W_B, respectively, in choosing between A and B. Then the labor force is in *locational equilibrium* when the wage rate is the same in both urban areas.[1] That occurs when $\bar{N}_A$ workers work in A and $\bar{N}_B = N - \bar{N}_A$ workers work in B.

Now suppose that not only commodity production, but also pollution discharges (e.g., into the air), increase as employment increases in each urban area. Assume for the moment that each firm's discharge damages the plants of other firms in the same urban area. (For example, discharges may peel paint from walls.) Then, as Chapter 15 showed, the social value of extra production from each firm is worth less than its market value; *from the market value of the marginal product must be subtracted the market value of the resulting additional pollution.* $VSMP_A$ and $VSMP_B$ show the social value of the marginal product of labor in A and B as functions of N_A and N_B. $VSMP_{NA}$ is below $MP_{NA} \cdot P_A$ at each value of N_A, and $VSMB_{NB}$ is below $MP_{NB} \cdot P_B$ at each value of N_B, showing that additional polluting discharge does harm.

Now make the crucial assumption that incremental damage from additional discharges is an increasing function of total discharges and, hence, of total output and labor input. For example, the incremental damage of the third ton per day of sulfur oxide discharge might be slight, but the incremental damage of the tenth ton per day might be much

---

1. This discussion abstracts from any wage premium that may exist in one city or the other to compensate for differences in costs or amenities. It is the real wage, not the money wage, that is equalized across urban areas.

greater.[2] The assumption implies that the vertical distance between $MP_{NA} \cdot P_A$ and $VSMP_{NA}$ increases with movement to the right, and that the distance between $MP_{NB} \cdot P_B$ and $VSMP_{NB}$ increases with movement to the left. Furthermore, at $\bar{N}_A$, $VSMP_{NA}$ is further below $MP_{NA} \cdot P_A$ than is $VSMP_{NB}$ below $MP_{NB} \cdot P_B$. A socially efficient labor force allocation between the two urban areas requires that $VSMP_{NA} = VSMP_{NB}$—that the value of the social marginal product of labor be the same in the two areas. This finding follows from the result, established in Chapter 8, that social efficiency requires the (social) marginal product of an input to be the same in all uses. This feature occurs when N_A^* workers live and work in A in Figure 16.1. If $N_A^* \neq \bar{N}_A$, it follows that efficient labor allocation requires a movement of workers from A to B—that workers be shifted from the large to the small urban area.

This result is based on common sense: *If incremental pollution damage increases with the size of the urban area, then market equilibrium causes too many workers to locate in the large urban area and too few to locate in the small urban area.* Before discussing the implications of the analysis for governmental attempts to improve resource allocation, it is important to explore the limits of the formal model in a less formal fashion.

First the theoretical model applies not only to pollution. Suppose, for example, that road congestion is an increasing function of an urban area's population. The analysis in Chapter 13 makes that a plausible assumption. Then assumptions analogous to those previously made imply that *unpriced congestion also causes large urban areas to be too large and small urban areas to be too small.* Certain other types of market failure may have similar implications for the relative sizes of urban areas. The possibility will be explored later.

Second the formal model assumes that the polluting discharges did not directly affect the welfare of residents. It might be thought that since polluting discharges reduce residents' welfare, the fact that the large urban area is more polluted than the small one would prevent excessive population in the large urban area. The congestion example shows, however, that this conclusion is false. As Chapter 13 showed, congestion is not adequately deterred by the fact that underpriced travel causes travelers direct welfare loss. Even though congestion hurts only those who travel in congested conditions, underpricing nevertheless causes excess crowding on roads. Likewise, in the pollution example, the fact that the large urban area is more polluted than the small urban area deters some, but not enough, people from living in the large urban area. To induce workers to live in the large urban area, equilibrium wages are made higher in the large than in the small urban area, inducing more production to locate in the small urban area than if pollution did not

---

2.   As was pointed out in Chapter 15, not only does a large urban area have more pollution victims than a small one, but also the large urban area's environmental capacity to absorb pollutants is more overloaded than the small urban area's capacity.

affect wages. However, this situation does not cause an optimum distribution of population between the two urban areas any more than the disutility of congested travel prevents congestion.

Third the analysis does not depend on there being only two urban areas. Imagine an entire distribution of urban sizes, as discussed in Chapter 4. Then, if the marginal damage from increased population in an urban area increases with the population of the urban area, it follows that a set of the largest urban areas is too large, and the remaining smaller urban areas are too small. In practice, damages from pollution are by no means uniquely correlated with the size of the urban area. They also depend on natural conditions (such as weather), on the industrial structure of the urban area, and on other variables. There is a tendency, however, for large metropolitan areas to be more polluted than small metropolitan areas.

The analysis so far, even in the light of the qualifying comments, suggests that externalities related to urban size render large urban areas too big and small ones too small. One more observation, however, casts critical doubt on the basic conclusion. One of the reasons for concentrating production in urban areas is the existence of agglomeration economies: Other things being equal, a firm's production costs are lower in a large urban area than elsewhere, essentially because a large urban area offers easy (that is, inexpensive) access to a rich variety of specialized inputs and markets. This finding is an external economy of large urban size. A firm that locates in an urban area increases the size of the urban area and, in the process, reduces production costs for other firms in the urban area. This cost reduction accrues to the incumbents—and not to the entrants—with the result that potential entrants have insufficient incentive to migrate to the urban area. The conclusion that emerges from looking only at this externality is that large urban areas are too small.

Unfortunately, no one knows the net effect of these external diseconomies and economies on the relative sizes of urban areas. As has been seen, there are forces working in both directions. The problem is that the magnitude of these externalities (particularly agglomeration economies) is difficult to measure. As the next section will show, however, even if it were known that the net effect of these externalities were to make large urban areas too big, the appropriate policy would not be to discourage people from living in large urban areas.

Policy Questions

What can governments do to remove the resource misallocation that results in an inappropriate urban size distribution? The immediate reaction of many people is to urge governments to undertake a variety of ad hoc programs to deter growth of large metropolitan areas. Many such programs would do great harm. In fact, the policy analysis is complex and must be undertaken with care.

If an external diseconomy were *technologically* linked to population, the policy solution would be simple. Suppose, for example, that pollution discharges were proportionate to population in an urban area. Then, the correct government policy would be a tax on each resident in each urban area equal to the difference between $MP_N \cdot P$ and $VSMP_N$, evaluated at the optimum population (N^*). The tax would be higher in larger urban areas, given the assumptions made in Figure 16.1.

Even in this simple situation, inappropriate policies frequently are urged on governments. The most common error is to urge taxes or other controls only on newcomers, say, on those who come to reside in the urban area after its population passes N^*. *Newcomers, however, are no more polluting than older residents; pollution is proportionate to total population.* The tax should exclude those to whom residence in the urban area is least valuable, and it should be levied on all residents. Taxes for the privilege of residing in large urban areas are understandably unpopular. Thus, government officials commonly think of indirect ways of discouraging growth of large urban areas. For example, steering federal defense and other contracts away from large urban areas frequently is proposed. All such proposals interfere with the optimum distribution of particular industries among urban areas and are therefore undesirable.

A crucial point, which is misunderstood in almost all discussions of governmental policies to change the urban size distribution, is that *external diseconomies are by no means technologically linked to urban population.* Chapter 15 showed that polluting discharges depend on how resources are allocated, not just on total population. Wastes can be treated before discharge, production processes and products can be modified so as to produce less waste, wastes can be transported to discharge points where they do less harm, and so forth. The appropriate governmental policy toward polluting discharges is controls or, better yet, effluent fees, on discharges.

It is likely that effluent fees should be higher, or controls more stringent, in large urban areas than elsewhere. The result indeed may be to shift population and employment somewhat from large to small urban areas. The main result, however, would be to reduce the polluting discharges resulting from a given total population and production in an urban area. Any effect on total population in an urban area would be incidental and probably small. Table 16.1 shows that air pollution tends to be worse in large urban areas than in small ones. The table, however, also reveals a substantial variation in pollution that is unrelated to population. It would take an enormous cut in the population of the Los Angeles MSA to improve its air quality much. Population redistribution is about as costly a pollution-control program as could be imagined.

If the analysis is taken a step further, it even becomes unclear that an optimum pollution-control program would shift people and jobs from large to small urban areas. Figure 16.1 assumed that polluting discharges affected production costs in the urban area but did not directly affect

Table 16.1 *Air Quality Trends in Major Urban Areas, 1980 to 1990*

MSA	1980	1985	1990
Atlanta	7	9	16
Boston	8	2	1
Chicago	na	4	3
Dallas	10	12	5
Denver	35	37	7
Detroit	na	2	3
Houston	10	30	35
Kansas City	13	4	2
Los Angeles	220	196	163
New York	119	21	10
Philadelphia	52	25	11
Pittsburgh	20	6	12
San Francisco	2	5	1
Seattle	33	26	2
Washington	38	15	5

Source: U.S. Environmental Protection Agency, Office of Air Quality Planning and Standards. *National Air Quality and Emissions Trends Report, 1990*. EPA-450/4-91-023 (Research Triangle Park, N.C.: Environmental Protection Agency, November, 1991).

residents' welfare. In fact, pollution affects both people and property, but the most important effects are on health. Consider a large, badly polluted urban area, and suppose an optimum effluent fee is levied on discharges in the urban area. The effluent fee has two effects. First it makes living and working in the urban area more expensive, inducing people to live and work elsewhere and thus shifting population to smaller urban areas. Second it makes the urban area more attractive as a place to live. In fact, an optimum set of effluent fees probably would improve the environmental quality in large urban areas relative to that in small urban areas. This second effect tends to increase population and employment in the large urban area. Thus, the two effects are offsetting, and it appears to be impossible to predict their net effect on the urban area's population without detailed data for the particular urban area.

The same analysis applies to every alleged external diseconomy. Chapter 13 showed that road congestion depends not only on the total population of an urban area, but also on resource allocation in the urban area. Congestion depends on the mix of automobile and public transit investments, on charges that discourage urban travel, and on locations of residences and workplaces. As with environmental problems, a governmental policy to reduce congestion by reducing the total population of an urban area would be about the most inefficient policy imaginable to reduce congestion. Appropriate programs to control congestion are directed at transportation-resource allocation, not at the urban area's total population. As with environmental programs, appropriate transportation programs to control congestion may affect the total population of an urban area, but the effects would be incidental and probably small.

The implication of this section can be summarized briefly: *If an activity distorts urban sizes, the activity should be controlled directly.*

Distortions in urban size are no more than symptoms of resource misallocation. To attack the urban size distribution directly is to attack the wrong variable. Tolley, Graves, and Gardner (1979) analyze a variety of causes of distortions in urban size and propose remedies for some.

It is useful at this point to recall the discussion of central place theory in Chapter 1. In particular, recall that there is an important economic rationale for the emergence of a few large urban areas. Some goods have scale economies associated with their production sufficient to make them inefficient to produce except at a small number of locations. According to central place theory, the disparity among goods in the degree of scale economies leads to a disparity of urban area sizes and, in particular, to a large number of small urban areas and a small number of large urban areas. At least roughly, this skewed size distribution of urban areas minimizes the sum of production and transportation costs for the goods we consume. Although there are clearly market failures of various sorts in any complex economy, the theoretical and empirical cases that large urban areas are too big are doubtful.

☐ SUBURBANIZATION

In Chapters 2 through 4, changes in the percentage of metropolitan residents living or working in central cities or suburbs were used as measures of suburbanization. It was pointed out that the measure is a poor one, because central-city boundaries are moved occasionally and because different central cities compose different fractions of their MSA populations and land areas.

The analysis in Chapter 7 suggests a measure of suburbanization that does not depend on locations of local governmental jurisdictional boundaries. It shows that urban population density can be approximated by an exponential function,

$$D(u) = D_0 e^{-\gamma u}, \tag{16.1}$$

where $D(u)$ is population per square mile u miles from the urban center, e is the base of the natural logarithm, and D_0 and γ are constants to be estimated from the data for each urban area. Equation (16.1) is an exact density function in special circumstances and an approximation otherwise. If u is placed at zero, then D_0 shows the density at the urban center. This notion is artificial, as few people live within a short distance of most urban centers, where most land is used for employment. For most urban areas, however, Equation (16.1) is a good approximation for distances more than one-half mile or so from the center, as was noted in Chapter 7. The term γ is positive if density decreases with distance from the urban center. Equation (16.1) has the general shape shown in Figure 7.1. The density function is flatter at each u the smaller is γ. It can be shown by differentiating Equation (16.1) with respect to u that 100γ is the percentage by which population falls per mile of distance from the urban center. For example, a γ of 0.3 implies that density falls 30 percent per mile of movement from the center.

A final property of Equation (16.1) shows the relationship between the exponential density function and suburbanization. If an urban areas's population grows by increasing D_0, leaving γ unchanged, the whole gradient shifts up, and the percentage of the urban population living within a fixed distance of the center remains unchanged. The percentage living within the central city, for example, remains unchanged. It is, therefore, natural to say that, of two exponential density functions, the smaller γ represents the more *suburbanized* urban area. The basic advantage of using γ as estimated from Equation (16.1) as a measure of suburbanization is that the measure does not depend on the location or movement of central-city boundaries.

As Chapter 7 discussed, Equation (16.1) has been estimated for many dozens of metropolitan areas in several dozen countries, some for as long ago as the early nineteenth century.

As noted in Table 7.2, the evidence indicates that residential-density gradients have been getting flatter, at least since 1880. Surprisingly, there is no evidence of an acceleration of suburbanization in recent decades. Indeed, in the era from 1880 to 1920, the density gradients for the four metropolitan areas with available data were falling about 50 percent faster than for the period from 1920 to 1963. Fragmentary evidence indicates that European metropolitan areas have been decentralizing since the early nineteenth century. Much more evidence indicates that the trend toward decentralization has been pervasive in non-Communist developed and developing countries during the post–World War II period. Decentralization has gone less far in other countries, but the speed of decentralization is greater in many countries—including Japan—than in the United States. Racial and school-related tensions and the widespread use of automobiles may play an important role in present-day suburbanization. If so, this finding is a case of new causes bringing about the continuation of a very old trend.

It is logical to ask what the determinants of suburbanization are by examining the determinants of residential-density gradients. This aspect suggests that a regression analysis should be run like the following:

$$\gamma = B_1 X_1 + B_2 X_2 + \ldots + B_n X_n, \qquad (16.2)$$

where γ is an urban area's density gradient (see Chapter 7), Xs are variables thought to influence the gradient, and Bs are the estimated coefficients that reveal how the Xs influence γ.

A study of this sort is useful for examining the causes of interurban differences in the degree of suburbanization, but it sheds little light on possible causes (such as the automobile) common to all urban areas. The broad historical pattern of suburbanization, revealed in Table 7.2, is not really amenable to detailed statistical analysis. Thus, attention is turned now to determinants of interurban variations in suburbanization (as measured by interurban differences in density gradients), as well as to what is known about the historical determinants of the decentralization.

Interurban Variation

The most important variable governing the steepness of a city's density gradient is the city's age. Old urban areas have much higher density central cities and steeper density gradients than do newer ones. Using a regression Equation like (16.2), Muth (1969) found that each decade of additional age increased the steepness of a city's density gradient by 0.08 (about 20 percent of the average value of the density gradients he estimated).[3] In other words, a 50-year-old MSA would have a density gradient about twice as steep as would an urban area of age zero.[4]

The next finding that emerges from studies such as those done by Muth (1969), Macauley (1985), and Mills (1992) is that big urban areas have flatter gradients than do small ones. This finding is contrary to the predictions of the model analyzed in chapters 6 and 7. In that model, the steepness of the gradient is independent of population. The discrepancy between model and fact may be due to the importance of subcenters in larger urban areas.

The other variable that is consistently associated with the steepness of the density gradient is the racial mix of the central city. If a large fraction of the central city's population is black, the density gradient tends to be flatter (that is, more suburbanized).

In addition to this information on the determinants of the steepness of density gradients, something is known about the manner in which the density gradients of urban areas' change through time. Bradbury, Downs, and Small (1982) found that city population growth (from 1970 to 1975) relative to suburban growth was influenced in the following ways: Cities grew slowly relative to the MSA if (1) old housing was more concentrated in the city than the suburbs, (2) the city had a high percentage of black population relative to the suburbs, (3) the suburban ring had a large number of municipalities, and (4) city taxes were high relative to the suburbs.[5]

The first finding suggests that MSAs with old central cities are suburbanizing more quickly than those with newer central cities. It has been noted already that old MSAs have steeper gradients than new ones and that cities of the past had steeper gradients than do today's cities. It appears that old cities carry a legacy of the past in the form of steep

---

3. Muth's (1969) variable was the number of decades since the MSA attained a population of 50,000.

4. Despite its large size, this coefficient was not statistically very significant in Muth's analysis.

5. Causation may go from high taxes to population loss or from population loss to high taxes. See Mills (1992).

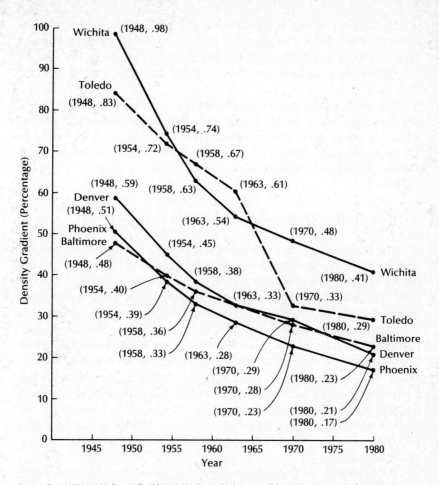

Source: From 1954–1963 data, Mills, Edwin S. *Studies in the Structure of the Urban Economy* (Baltimore: Johns Hopkins University Press, 1972): 40; 1970–1980 data, Macauley, Molly. *"Recent Behavior of Urban Population and Employment Density Gradients.* Working paper No. 124 (Baltimore, Johns Hopkins University, 1983).

Figure 16.2 *Density Gradients for a Sample of Urban Areas, 1948 to 1980*

density gradients. Not surprisingly, this legacy is being diminished with the passage of time, and its gradual disappearance can be seen in the more rapid suburbanization of old cities.

The same pattern was observed by Macauley (1985), who noted that density gradients that were steeper in 1948 tended to flatten more quickly over the next 30 years than did gradients that were relatively flat in 1948. Thus, there was much less variation among density gradients in urban areas in 1980 than in 1948. This convergence can readily be seen in Figure 16.2. It is apparent that old urban areas are gradually converting from high-density housing to lower-density, automobile-age housing.[6]

6. This finding does not imply that the housing stock is of lower density. One cause of reduced population density is reduction in the number of persons per room.

The second finding is straightforward: Racial antipathies cause more than one white person to leave the central city for every black entrant. This may be a purely race-related phenomenon or it may be due to variables such as income and income instability, which are correlated with race.

The third finding provides some support for the Tiebout hypothesis discussed in Chapter 14. Large numbers of suburban jurisdictions imply a rich variety of local governmental service offerings, which seem to attract people from the central city. The fourth finding also supports the Tiebout hypothesis (subject to caveat: see Mills [1992]).

Historical Trends and International Comparisons

The historical pattern of a gradual flattening of density gradients is not amenable to regression analysis. As will be seen, the most plausible causes of flattening gradients are rising incomes and falling transport costs. Because the trends in income, transport cost, and density have occurred together (for example, there are no important episodes of rising income, but there is constant transport cost), statistical analysis cannot be used to infer anything about the causes of decentralization. Note, however, that decentralization is what would be predicted as a result of rising income and falling transport cost. Chapter 6 showed that the price gradient becomes flatter with a fall in transport cost and possibly with a rise in income. As it is the rising price of housing (as the CBD is approached) that brings about higher density, it follows that a flattening of the price gradient leads to a flattening of the density gradient.

Population-density gradients in other developed countries are steeper than those in the United States. Chapter 7 noted that Japanese urban areas have gradients more than twice as steep as those in the United States. To a lesser degree, the same is true in western Europe. Gradients aside, urban density is higher in western Europe and Japan because land is much more scarce than in the United States. Table 16.2 gives average population densities for several countries in 1980. The stark fact emerges that land (relative to people) is very plentiful in the United States. To a good approximation, the only nations with lower population densities than the United States are those with large tracts of virtually uninhabitable land. Western European countries have average densities five to ten times that of the United States.[7]

One of the consequences of the scarcity of land in western Europe and Japan is that land is much more costly there than in the United States. It has been estimated that the market value of land in Japan is more than three times the GNP, as compared with about two-thirds the

---

7.   Alaska contributes to this gap. The population density for the contiguous 48 states is about 75 persons per square mile.

Table 16.2 *Average Population Densities, 1980 (in Persons per Square Mile)*

Country	Population Density	Country	Population Density
Mongolia	2.76	Austria	231.97
Libya	4.39	France	252.19
Australia	4.93	People's Republic of China	278.24
Iceland	5.79	Czechoslovakia	310.30
Canada	6.10	East Germany	413.32
Congo	11.66	Italy	490.44
Bolivia	13.20	India	519.13
Argentina	25.46	United Kingdom and Northern Ireland	592.48
U.S.S.R.	30.83	West Germany	642.49
Finland	36.74	Japan	810.97
Brazil	37.44	Belgium	842.18
United States	62.43	Taiwan	1,181.00
Spain	192.06	Singapore	10,575.22

Source: Data from *1983 World Almanac and Book of Facts* (New York: Newspaper Enterprise Association, 1982).

GNP in the United States (Mills and Ohta [1976]). In relation to incomes, land values are five times as high in Japan as in the United States. Inevitably, the result is that the Japanese economize on urban land. Homes, factories, and offices are built on tiny lots, so metropolitan areas are much higher in density and less decentralized than in the United States. Typical conditions in northern Europe are between those in Japan and the United States. The only industrialized countries in which densities and land values are as low as in the United States are Canada and Australia.

Density gradients are steeper in other countries partly because transport cost tends to be higher (high land values result in intense use of land for transport, among other things). Also, in many of these countries, income is lower than in the United States.

Racial mix, school quality, taxes, and demographics (see the "Return-to-the-City Movement" section later in this chapter), all have been linked statistically to suburbanization. Despite the importance of these phenomena, it is important to remember that the trend toward suburbanization is worldwide and at least a century old. The causes that have been noted in this paragraph are quantitatively insignificant in light of the broad historical experience.

Market Failure?

There is a widespread feeling in the United States that suburbanization is excessive. In part, this view rests on the accurate observation that suburbanization occurs at the expense of both the central city and rural land. Given a fixed population and land area, suburbanization reduces the stock of rural land and it provides an alternative to central-city living that reduces the demand for central-city housing. Suburbanization however, has benefits as well. Many households—particularly those with children—prefer low-density suburban living. Also, despite the pain of adjustment to lower density, current density levels of central cities may be higher than optimum, given the low cost of land and transportation. For an economist, the major question is whether there are inefficient market (and nonmarket) signals that have led to more suburbanization than would have occurred in a regime in which everyone faced efficient prices. A discussion of possible causes of excessive suburbanization follows.

Pollution.   Pollution is the easiest kind of market failure to analyze as a cause of excess decentralization. Suppose that air-polluting discharges are concentrated near the centers of urban areas, which is certainly true of discharges from motor vehicles and from combustion produced by space heating. Pollutants diffuse throughout the metropolitan area according to wind patterns. They become less concentrated, however, farther from discharge points, so air quality tends to improve somewhat with distance from the CBDs in most urban areas.

If air quality improves with distance and if people prefer clean to polluted air, the land-rent gradient that equalizes utilities between central and suburban locations is flatter than it would be otherwise. To understand this, recall that the role of the land-rent gradient is to soak up the utility gain associated with living close to the CBD. People gain utility by living close to the CBD as a result of reduced commuting needs. If air quality improves sufficiently with distance from the CBD, however, the utility differences between city and suburb are relatively small before accounting for land-rent differences. Therefore, in the presence of pollution that declines with distance from the CBD, a relatively flat land-rent gradient will be sufficient to equalize utilities between locations. For reasons discussed in chapters 6 and 7, the flatter the land-rent gradient, the flatter will be the density gradient. This mechanism is the one through which pollution might lead to a flattening of density gradients. This flattening is inefficient only to the extent that the pollution is inefficient. Even in an optimum world, pollution is probably higher in CBDs than suburban locations because of the higher concentration of economic activity. Only if the tendency for pollution to be worse in central locations is excessive will the resulting suburbanization be excessive.

The decentralizing effect of air pollution probably is not very important. The United States now has stringent controls on air-polluting discharges. Discharges are nevertheless somewhat greater near urban centers than in suburbs. It seems unlikely, however, that the difference in air quality is great enough to have much effect.

Transportation underpricing.   Chapter 13 suggested that urban transportation—especially during rush hours, when optimum congestion tolls are highest—is consistently underpriced in the United States. This finding means that the housing-price gradient, Equation 7.1, is flatter than it would be under efficient pricing. From this observation, it follows that the density gradient is flatter than it should be.

It is easy to calculate roughly how important this underpricing is. Chapter 7 argued that under reasonable assumptions, the density gradient would be about five times as steep as the housing-price gradient (with about the same steepness as the land-rent gradient). Suppose the price gradient is 0.04, giving a density gradient of 0.20. Also suppose that transportation is underpriced by 25 percent (the optimum congestion toll of Table 13.4 is 26.3 percent of full automobile transport cost, although it is approximately 35 percent of the full cost exclusive of parking). Under both optimum and inefficient transport pricing, the density gradient is about five times greater than the housing-price gradient. Thus, if the density gradient under inefficient pricing of transport were 0.20, the imposition of efficient congestion tolls would raise the gradient by 25 percent to 0.25. The effect of such a change would be fairly modest; the difference between a gradient of 0.20 and one of 0.25 represents roughly the amount of flattening that takes place every five years. To state it differently, consider an urban area with a central-city radius of eight miles. With a 0.20 density gradient, 47.5 percent of the population lives inside the central city; with a gradient of 0.25, the percentage living in the city rises to 59 percent.

It was noted that the optimum congestion toll appears to be more than 25 percent of marginal commuting cost, suggesting that these calculations have understated the centralizing effect of efficient pricing. There is, however, an important offsetting effect—under efficient pricing, congestion, and hence time cost, would decline. Thus, 25 percent may be approximately right after all.

Of course, all changes in density gradients are long run in nature, requiring the construction and alteration of dwellings. Presumably, the effect of an increase in urban travel cost to correct underpricing would be to slow down the decreases in gradients that occur for market reasons. No one should think, however, that even drastic increases in urban travel costs would dramatically reverse the long-term trend toward decentralization.

Land-use controls.   Chapter 14 discussed land-use controls for fiscal or exclusionary purposes. Although a wide range of such controls exists, zoning is perhaps the most important. An important zoning provision is the exclusion of all dwellings except single-family detached houses on lots no smaller than a stipulated minimum. Frequent minimums in many suburbs are one or two acres, but some are much larger. One purpose of such controls is to exclude dwellings with real estate taxes that would not pay the cost of local governmental services provided to its residents. The mechanism is to require all residents' housing to be of as high a quality and as low a density as is appropriate for a group of residents who are able to control zoning provisions. The typical procedure is for the initial residents to have relatively high incomes and to establish zoning provisions appropriate to their housing demand. As the metropolitan area grows and decentralizes, however, lower income residents who would move to the suburban community if the zoning provisions were absent are precluded from doing so. The result is inevitably to cause suburbs to be of lower density than they would be in the absence of zoning.

How large is the excessive decentralization resulting from low-density zoning? No one knows. Beyond a doubt, suburban-zoning provisions are consistent with the housing demands of most of the people who would live there, even in the absence of zoning restrictions. A sudden removal of all controls on the types and densities of suburban housing probably would slow the speed of metropolitan decentralization, but it would not reverse the direction.

The most important evidence that distortions from land-use controls are of modest proportions is that urban-density functions show little evidence of discontinuity as central-city boundaries are crossed. As was seen in Chapter 14, zoning controls on dwellings are much less important in central cities than in suburbs. If low-density zoning caused large resource misallocation, discontinuities in density functions would be expected at central-city boundaries. Such discontinuities, however, appear to be either nonexistent or small.

Favorable tax treatment of owner-occupied housing.   Chapter 11 showed that the federal income tax contains favorable provisions for owner-occupied housing and that these provisions make the user cost of capital for owner-occupied housing about 15 percent less than the rent per unit of comparable rental housing.

Do the favorable tax provisions cause excessive suburbanization? They do not directly, because they apply as much to central city as to suburban owner-occupied housing. However, high-income people prefer owner occupancy, as was seen in Chapter 11, and high-income people prefer single-family detached housing, and suburban communities tend to zone out multifamily housing. Thus, the favorable tax treatment of owner-occupied housing interacts with zoning to produce excessive suburbanization.

Energy costs.   The latter part of the 1970s was a period of rapidly rising fuel costs. The 1980s and early 1990s were periods of much lower energy costs, but the issues are still relevant. Many people are deeply concerned that low-density suburbs may be an inappropriate form of urban-resource allocation in a period of high-energy costs. The issue is not one of market failure, but rather one of adjustment from a form

appropriate for low-energy costs to one appropriate for high-energy costs. The issues fall into three categories.

The first category is heating and cooling costs. It requires only about one-third as much energy to heat and cool a high-rise apartment as it does to heat and cool a single-family detached house with the same number of square feet. Of course, energy requirements are less the better constructed and insulated any dwelling is, but the two-thirds savings is about the same for all construction materials, insulation types, regions of the country, and fuel types, provided similar dwellings are compared. For example, the two-thirds saving is about the same in the cold North as in the warm South. Heating and cooling are lost through outside walls, windows, doors, and roofs. The saving in high-rise buildings comes from shared walls, ceilings, and floors. Other housing types, such as garden apartments, are between the extremes for high-rise apartments and single-family detached houses.

The large fuel saving is no argument for requiring or subsidizing attached dwellings or for taxing or preventing detached dwellings. Provided fuel prices are at equilibrium levels, markets provide adequate incentive for fuel-efficient dwellings. *High fuel prices, however, are a powerful reason for local governments to abolish land-use controls that prohibit multifamily housing.* As Chapter 14 showed, the main purpose of land-use controls is exclusionary and of doubtful social benefit. In an era of high fuel prices, restrictions on multifamily housing are unforgivable.

The second issue in discussing energy costs is gasoline consumption from automobile use. Low-density suburbs probably entail somewhat longer trips for work and shopping. The fact of low density, however, does not necessarily mean that jobs and shops are far away. It has been shown that jobs are almost as suburbanized as residences. If households were to choose their homes and jobs *from the existing stock of homes and jobs* with more attention to the required commute, it would be possible to reduce total commuting greatly without recentralizing cities. If gasoline prices rise sufficiently to cause a major change in consumer behavior, it is not clear that the change will take the form of high-density living.

Two other observations should temper any conjecture that rising gasoline prices will halt the suburbanization of the last 100 years. First in real terms, the price of gasoline has not risen nearly as much as most people think; in fact, it has fallen since 1950, with the peak having occurred in 1975 (see Table 16.3). Second there is substantial evidence that the most important *long-run* response to a rise in the price of gasoline is the use of more fuel-efficient cars, not a reduction in the number of miles driven.

Even if the increase in gasoline price had been large (or if subsequent increases are large), the effect on location decisions is likely to be small for two reasons. First gasoline is a small part of commuting

Table 16.3 *Retail Price of Gasoline, Including Tax in Constant 1987 Dollars and Average Motor Vehicle Gas Mileage*

Year	Price (Dollars)	Automobile Gas Mileage	Gas Cost per Mile (Cents)
1950	$1.249	14.95	8.35
1955	1.221	14.53	8.40
1960	1.182	14.28	8.28
1965	1.109	14.15	7.84
1970	1.032	13.58	7.60
1975	1.194	13.52	8.83
1980	1.133	15.46	7.33
1985	1.196	18.20	6.57
1986	0.931	18.27	5.10
1987	0.957	19.20	4.98
1988	0.963	19.87	4.85
1989	1.060	20.31	5.22
1990*	1.217	20.92	5.82

*Preliminary data
Source: Russell, Milton. "Energy." In *Setting National Priorities: The 1978 Budget* (Washington, D.C.: Government Printing Office, 1979); and U.S. Energy Information Administration. *Monthly Energy Review* 6 (July, 1992): 187–188.

cost, as shown in Table 13.4. Second (related to the first reason), the total amount of money involved is modest.

Consider a household that drives 10,000 miles per year (about the average). Total gasoline cost is less than $600; however, probably no more than about 25 to 30 percent of this amount is consumed for CBD-bound trips, so the gasoline cost of trips toward the CBD is about $150. Even a doubling of this figure would have no important effect on a household earning $30,000 with a definite preference for the suburbs.

The third and most complex issue in energy costs is public transit. Beyond doubt, buses and subways require less energy per passenger mile than do cars. A passenger mile of car transportation requires at least 10 times as much fuel as a passenger mile in a nearly full bus. Thus, the higher motor-vehicle fuel prices are, the lower is the relative price of public transit compared with automobiles and the greater is the shift of demand to public transit travel.

Once again the magnitudes are important. Return to the example of Table 13.4. At a price of $1.00 per gallon, the gasoline required for the 8-mile trip considered there costs only about $0.40, or $0.05 per mile (assuming 20 miles per gallon). Suppose fuel prices rose by 50 percent. That increase would raise the cost of the trip by automobile by $0.20 to $6.27. It might raise the bus fare by $0.09, increasing the cost of the bus trip to $7.09. (Energy consumption per bus passenger mile is about 45 percent of energy consumption per auto passenger mile.) It is clear that even a drastic increase in fuel costs would have only a modest effect on modal choice; only those travelers who are nearly indifferent would switch modes.

There can be no doubt that low-density suburbs make it difficult to operate economical public transit systems. Chapter 13 showed that public transit systems require large numbers of travelers between particular origin-destination pairs. The relaxation of land-use controls on multifamily housing and small lots would help. A modal shift, however, toward public transit commuting will be a gradual process in metropolitan areas in the United States in any case, barring catastrophic fuel shortages.

☐ CITY-SUBURBAN INCOME DIFFERENCES

It has already been noted at several points that income tends to increase with distance from the CBD, giving rise to the familiar pattern of suburbs having higher incomes than their central cities. This observation, along with other relevant information, is summarized in Table 16.4. First note that, on the average, central city per capita incomes are only modestly smaller than suburban incomes, although per capita central-city income has fallen relative to suburban income during the 20-year period. Second income disparities are much larger in regions in the Northeast and the Midwest than in those in the South and West. Third it is clear that the per capita income comparisons over state the economic well-being of central-city residents. Per-household incomes are substantially lower in central cities, particularly in region in the Northeast and Midwest, reflecting the fact that city family sizes tend to be smaller than in suburbs. Also, the incidence of poverty (as of 1990) was more than two times higher in cities than suburbs (again, more so in the Northeast and the Midwest).

Table 16.4 *Comparison of City-Suburb Income by Region*

	1990			1980	1970
Region	Central City	Suburb	City/Suburb Ratio	City/Suburb Ratio	City/Suburb Ratio
Average household income					
United States	$26,052	$36,038	0.723	0.721	0.768
Northeast	25,108	39,699	0.632	0.614	0.733
Midwest	23,475	37,879	0.620	0.683	0.756
South	25,461	32,665	0.779	0.753	0.824
West	30,494	35,489	0.859	0.864	0.844
Average per Capita Income					
United States	$13,564	$16,063	0.844	0.864	0.947
Northeast	13,277	17,304	0.767	0.675	0.781
Midwest	12,664	16,829	0.753	0.844	0.954
South	13,237	14,721	0.899	0.910	0.926
West	15,057	15,845	0.950	0.984	1.019

Source: Data from U.S. Department of Commerce, Bureau of the Census. *Current Population Survey*. Various issues (Washington, D.C.: Government Printing Office).
Note: The average incomes are for median households. The population figures implied in the table are as of March in the following year.

The causes of this pattern continue to be subject to some dispute, with leading theories being the following:

1. The rent-offer curve for high-income people is flatter than that for low-income people; hence, the low-income people outbid the high-income people for central locations (see Chapter 6). Chapter 7 noted that the empirical evidence for this is weak.
2. Urban areas have been gradually built from the center outward, so the old (lower quality) housing is concentrated in the central city. That type of housing is what low-income people can afford, so that is where they live (see Chapter 7).
3. Various exclusionary activities have prevented low-income people from moving to the suburbs.

The correct explanation is surely a combination of the second and third of these possibilities, and possibly the first as well. There is little knowledge about the relative importance of these forces. The dramatic difference, however, between old "frostbelt" cities and new Sun Belt cities, as revealed in Table 16.4, lends considerable support to the second of these explanations.

☐ RETURN-TO-THE-CITY MOVEMENT

Beginning in the mid-1970s, a widely proclaimed return-to-the-city movement received substantial attention. The most exuberant reports suggested a massive influx of middle- and upper-income households to old city neighborhoods, resulting in a widespread revitalization of housing and improvements in central-city tax bases. In addition, the unhappy side effect of displacement received a substantial amount of attention.

Knowledge of the causes and future course of this movement is modest, at best. The patterns to date, however, give some evidence on both the causes and the future of the movement. The most important characteristic of the back-to-the-city movement is that it is very small. By one estimate, the average major city witnessed about 1,600 substantial renovations of dwelling units over the decade from 1968 to 1978 (with the bulk of the redevelopment coming in the last half of this period). For a typical major city, this amount constitutes about 1 percent of the housing stock, or a rate of redevelopment of about 0.1 percent per year. By way of contrast, in 1982, Baltimore had an estimated 7,000 abandoned dwellings; Philadelphia had 30,000; Detroit had 12,000; and New York City had 100,000.[8]

Comprehensive data on the characteristics of urban renovators are unavailable, but a common pattern emerges from surveys of renovated

8. These numbers were provided by Richard Davis of the Baltimore Department of Housing and Community Development.

Table 16.5 *Characteristics of Mount Pleasant and Capitol Hill Renovators Compared with All District of Columbia Residents*

| Characteristic | Renovators | | D.C. Residents | All First-Time Home Buyers |
	Mount Pleasant	Capitol Hill		
Have children under 19 years old	37%	21%	. . .	29%
White	77	94	25%	. . .
Earn income over $15,000	87	90	25	. . .
Have college degree	86	97	17	. . .
Age 30 to 34	44	48	11	34[a]

[a]The National Homebuying Survey does not use the "age 30 to 34" category; it reports 68 percent between the ages of 25 and 34. Probably more than half of these people are 30 to 34 years old.

Sources: Data from Gale, Dennis. "Neighborhood Resettlement: Washington, D.C." *Back to the City: Issues in Neighborhood Renovation,* edited by Shirley Laska and Daphne Spain (New York: Pergamon, 1980): 98–99; and National Association of Realtors. *National Homebuying Survey.* (Washington, D.C.: National Association of Realtors, 1981): 6.

neighborhoods. The renovators typically are young (20 to 35 years old), white, well educated, high-income, and typically either single or childless couples.[9] Table 16.5 summarizes the characteristics for the Mount Pleasant and Capitol Hill sections of Washington, D.C. To the extent that the data permit comparisons, the renovators are similar to all first-time home buyers, except renovators are more likely to be white and well educated.

The attraction of the central city for young whites is not a new phenomenon, as Figure 16.3 illustrates. In the 1960s, the migration flow of whites between the ages of about 20 and 30 was to central cities (in the cases of New York City, Boston, and Washington, D.C.) and of older whites and their children, out of central cities.

The big change in the 1970s was probably not in the inherent attractiveness of central cities but rather in demographics. As can be seen in Figure 1 (inside front cover), in this decade the first postwar babies became first-time homeowners. In addition, the young adults in the 1970s had fewer children than did their predecessors, further increasing the pool of people looking for the kind of housing central cities have to offer.

Figure 16.4, showing the probability of a person living in the central city—by age group, for 1970 and 1980—strengthens the view that there has not been a dramatic shift in preferences toward central-city living. For every age group, including young adults, the fraction living in central cities declined over the decade. Combining Figure 16.4 with Figure 1, we see that the maturing of the baby boom generation in the 1970s led to a temporary bulge in the population most likely to live in central cities (young adults).

9. This pattern has been observed in Washington, D.C., New Orleans, and Philadelphia among other cities. Case studies for all of these cities are discussed in Laska and Spain (1980).

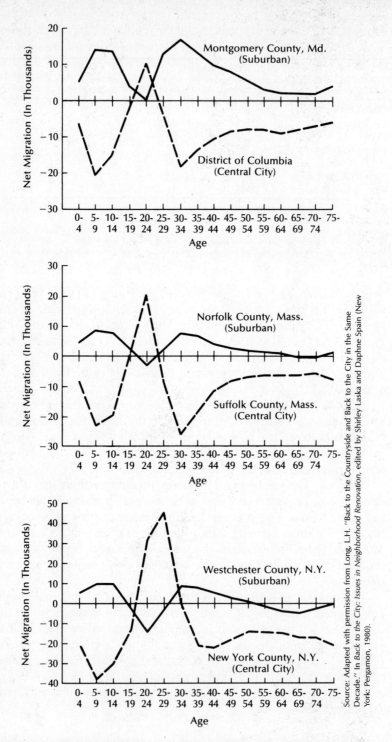

Source: Adapted with permission from Long, L.H. "Back to the Countryside and Back to the City in the Same Decade." In *Back to the City: Issues in Neighborhood Renovation,* edited by Shirley Laska and Daphne Spain (New York: Pergamon, 1980).

Figure 16.3 *Net Migration of White Population, 1960 to 1970, for Washington, D.C., Boston, Manhattan, and Selected High-Income Suburban Counties, by Age*

The cash flow problems facing first-time home buyers in the latter half of the 1970s (discussed in Chapter 10 and depicted in Figure 10.5) also may have contributed to the attractiveness of renovation. One way to reduce both the down payment and the monthly mortgage payments is to purchase a home in need of renovation and invest what has come to be called "sweat equity."

The meager evidence supports the notion that the upsurge in central-city renovation that began in the mid-1970s is largely or entirely a demographic phenomenon, possibly augmented by the cash-flow problems that first-time homebuyers faced in that period. As can be seen in Figure 1, Census Bureau projections indicate a rapid increase in the proportion of young adults up through the early 1990s, after which the low fertility of the 1970s (one of the apparent contributors to the present day return-to-the-city movement) will bring about a dramatic decline in the proportion of young adults. By that time, the young adult urban homesteaders of the 1970s and 1980s will be middle-aged. Whether they still will be childless and city dwellers are matters for speculation. So far, the behavior of this cohort is not strikingly different from that of previous cohorts at the same stage in life (except for the postponement of childbearing). If this cohort continues to adhere to the migration patterns depicted in Figure 16.3, the 1990s promises to be a big decade for the suburbs.

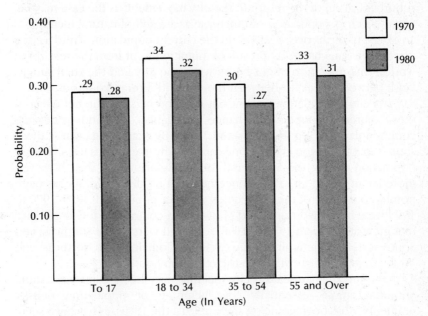

Sources: Data from U.S. Department of Commerce Bureau of the Census. *State and Metropolitan Area Data Book;* and *Statistical Abstract of the United States* (Washington, D.C.: Government Printing Office, 1973, 1983).

Figure 16.4 *Probability of Living in U.S. Central Cities, Given a Person's Age, 1970 and 1980*

☐ CENTRAL-CITY POPULATION LOSS

Despite the publicity surrounding urban homesteading, it was quantitatively insignificant compared with the massive migration out of many central cities. This section looks now at the magnitude and causes of central-city population loss.

Until the 1960s, it was extremely rare for a central city to lose population. During the 1960s, however, population declines in central cities became commonplace; by the 1970s, entire MSAs were losing populations. From 1980 to 1990, a total of 24 of the 75 largest cities lost population. The average loss of the population losers was over 6 percent for the decade. For the 10 cities that suffered the most rapid decline, the average decline was more than 10 percent. Thus, there is a relatively new phenomenon of a substantial number of cities losing a substantial portion of their populations.[10]

The MSA population losses are more recent and much smaller than those of the central city. Forty-eight of the nation's 320 MSAs in 1990 had lost populations since 1970. What is the cause of central-city population loss, and what do the trends foretell? The first step in addressing this question is to catalog the possible sources of central-city population change.

First a city's population can change even if the MSA population does not as a result of redistribution of people between city and suburbs— suburbanization or the return-to-the-city movement, as the case may be. Second a city's population can increase as a result of natural increase— an excess of births over deaths—in the current population. Third a city's population can change as a result of migration to or from the rest of the world. This migration might be between the city and the rural hinterland, between cities, or between the city and foreign countries.

If a city's population declines, it must be because the net effect of these sources of population change is negative. This finding became commonplace during the 1960s and 1970s. By examining each of these sources of population change, one can see why many cities began to lose population during the 1960s and 1970s. Before doing that, however, more about which cities are concerned will be discussed. As has been pointed out, most of the large cities that lost populations from 1970 to 1990 were in the Northeast and Midwest. In contrast, of the large cities that grew fastest from 1970 to 1990, nearly all were in the Southeast and Southwest. Decline is almost the exclusive domain of the Northeast and Midwest, and city growth is restricted to the South and West.

One of the causes of city decline has been suburbanization. Suburbanization—essentially the flattening of population density gradients—has been going on since at least the 1880s, as has been seen. On the average, the pace of suburbanization did not increase in the

---

10. The material in this paragraph and much of the subsequent material comes from Bradbury, Downs, and Small (1982).

1970s or 1980s, as compared with previous decades. It is true that in the absence of suburbanization there would have been only trivial city population loss (this finding is known, as MSA population loss was trivial), but it is not true that an upsurge of suburbanization is responsible for central-city losses.

For the nation as a whole, population growth through natural increase and immigration from abroad fell from 19 percent during the 1950s to 11 percent during the 1970s, and further to 9.8 percent during the 1980s. Thus, increase in total population as a potential source of city growth was much smaller in the 1970s than in the 1950s, and a bit smaller still in the 1980s.[11] Migration from farms essentially came to a halt after the great wave of black migration from the rural South in the 1950s and 1960s, as Chapter 2 noted. Quite simply, the reason is that there is hardly anyone left on farms. Thus, the traditional sources of urban population increase essentially disappeared beginning about 1970. Thereafter, any major changes in central-city populations have resulted from flows between cities and suburbs or between cities.

Chapter 2 discussed population flows between regions, noting that population has flowed from the Northeast and the Midwest to the West for many decades. These flows continued into the 1980s and, in fact, became much more visible because of the slowdowns of natural increase, international immigration, and rural-urban migration.

In large measure, cities of the Northeast and the Midwest began losing population in the 1960s and 1970s for two reasons. First the long-standing flows of population from these regions to the South and West were no longer offset to any important degree by the traditional sources of replacement—natural increase, rural-urban migration, and international migration. Second cities in the Northeast and Midwest, on the average, are much older than those in the South and West, and, as has been seen, older cities have been "suburbanizing" more quickly than newer ones.

Paradoxically, the same demographic forces that led to the modest return-to-the-city movement also contributed to decline in central-city population. With the population age distribution bulging with young adults and with the postponement of childbearing, the average household size fell by 16 percent between 1970 and 1990. This finding means that, on the average, an urban area's population could decline over this period by 16 percent with no reduction in the number of dwelling units occupied. In fact, the average household size was reduced by the large weight given to young childless adults (or young adults with few children), not by a reduction in household size in other adult-age groups. As has been seen, this young-adult group is the age group most attracted to central cities, so the reduction in household size should be most pronounced in central cities. For many cities, this fall in household size is the sole cause of population decline. Figure 2 (inside front

11.   In fact, it was smaller than in any decade in our history except the 1930s.

cover) shows the age distribution of central-city population for 1970 and 1980.

There is some reason to believe that this emptying out of old cities has about run its course. It already has been shown that the interregional wage differences of the past two centuries largely have been eliminated. This finding should diminish the rate of interregional migration. Also, the above-average suburbanization of older cities probably will slacken off, as population declines of the 1970s and 1980s have brought the population-density levels of these cities closely into line with those of new cities. Thus, the pattern of faster-than-average suburbanization in older cities probably will not continue very much longer. Finally, the wave of black migration to old northern cities—which has been linked to central-city population loss—has halted and, in fact, reversed in recent years. Evidence indicates that the pace of the population shift between regions has slowed in the 1980s and early 1990s. Bradbury, Downs, and Small (p. 35) reported reductions in growth and shrinkage rates of cities as early as the period from 1975 to 1980. That trend has continued into the 1990s.

☐ THE ECONOMIC DECLINE OF CENTRAL CITIES

The long-standing trend of suburbanization of both residences and jobs, and the concentration of poverty in central cities have already been discussed. In this section, much of the preceding material in this book will be built on to explore some of the causes and consequences of these central-city problems.

The economic problem can be seen most clearly by looking closely at the economic condition of central-city residents. In 1982, the central-city unemployment rate for black men was 23.4 percent; for whites, it was 9.5 percent. (Both of these figures are raised somewhat from their typical levels by the effects of the 1980 to 1981 recession.) Black male unemployment rates were very high in central cities for all educational levels and in all regions (though less severely so in the West). What is less well appreciated is that the unemployment picture has gotten much worse in central cities for both blacks and whites over the past 15 years (and, on some measures, the gap between black and white has increased). As Table 9.2 showed, the ratio of central-city to suburban poverty rates increased from about two to one in 1979 to about three to one in 1990. For both blacks and whites, the proportion of central-city men not even in the labor force (and, therefore, not counted as unemployed) has risen approximately 60 percent from 1969 to 1990.

Thus, the underlying facts are (1) things have gotten worse very quickly in the central-city labor market, and (2) although blacks have fared much worse than whites, the deterioration has been severe for both groups. Any explanation of this phenomenon must account for both of these facts.

One explanation can be ruled out very quickly. The deterioration is not due directly to black migration from the South when there were not enough jobs in northern cities. First the employment malaise has hit whites as well as blacks. Second as we have noted, the wave of black migration stopped in the early 1970s—shortly after the onset of the upturn in central-city unemployment but well before it reached today's proportions.

The spatial-mismatch hypothesis.   The most plausible explanation begins with an idea put forth by Kain (1968). Kain argued that much unemployment in the black population was caused by the fact that blacks were restricted to confined ghettos and that job opportunities were dispersed. He pointed out that postwar suburbanization had seriously aggravated this problem. (Since the publication of Kain's paper, the disappearance of entry-level jobs from central cities has accelerated, as has been seen.) He demonstrated empirically that the fraction of employees who are black (particularly in customer-contact jobs) declined dramatically with distance from the nearest black ghetto.

As an explanation for the trends noted, Kain's hypothesis has some problems. First the fact that black employment declines with distance from a ghetto may reflect nothing more sinister than the notion that blacks, like whites, prefer to work near their homes. Second Kain's theory does not explain the deterioration in black employment over the past 15 years (this finding is not surprising; his report was published in 1968). Third his paper does not explain why white men have suffered unemployment increases recently.

Kain's central idea is that, for some groups of people, jobs and homes are sufficiently remote from one another that the costs of searching for a job and commuting present serious obstacles to employment. So it is appropriate to ask whether this geographic mismatch has become more severe over the past 15 years and whether it is likely to have affected both blacks and whites. If it has, then the mismatch hypothesis takes on considerable additional plausibility.

The first piece of this puzzle is to note that central cities have disproportionately been the home of blacks and other minorities and the poor. We have already noted that there is a combination of benign and discriminatory explanations for this phenomenon. To reiterate briefly, the benign part of the explanation is that cities were built from the center out. Particularly in older cities, this finding means that the center was built at a time when we as a society were poorer. A consequence is that central-city housing tends to be small and lacking in amenities for which the modern middle class is willing to pay. The central city is thus the location at which old, relatively inexpensive, housing is available (through the filtering process) for today's poor and disadvantaged.

This benign, or natural-forces, explanation is augmented by a host of discriminatory practices that artificially depress the supply of moderate-income housing in the suburbs, and particularly discriminate against blacks.

Although the geographic spread between rich and poor has increased over the past 15 years, the patterns of home location by quality have existed since the first wave of upper-class suburbanization following the development of the streetcar. There is, however, one crucial reason for a pattern of increasing income segregation of American urban areas—the slowdown in the growth of urban population.

If filtering is the primary means of providing housing to low-income people, then the poor are geographically restricted to the places where old housing is abundant, and new housing will be built for the rich where vacant land is abundant. These sites are respectively the central cities and the suburbs. Up through the 1920s, and again right after World War II, American urban areas were growing with sufficient speed that new housing was constructed for people fairly far down the income distribution (there was not enough old housing for filtering to satisfy the demand). In such a world, residential location is not so tightly tied to the location of the existing housing stock, and we would expect more randomness in income-location patterns. (To take the extreme case, when Chicago grew in the nineteenth century from nothing to one million in 50 years, virtually everybody lived in new housing.) Thus, the slowdown in urban population growth over the past couple of decades naturally leads to intensified patterns of segregation.

There are several ways students might want to test this theory. With readily available census data, one can see whether residential segregation by income and race is more intense in urban areas that (1) are older and (2) have been growing more slowly in recent years.

With regard to the location of jobs, it will be seen that employment location patterns have undergone a change at least as dramatic in the past couple of decades as have residential patterns. The overall pattern is as follows:

1. Manufacturing has declined in relative importance throughout the United States economy.
2. Manufacturing has shown a modest movement out of larger MSAs in general.
3. There has been a massive exodus of manufacturing from old central cities.

As was noted at the end of Chapter 4, the major growth industry in old central cities has been professional services. (Following the lead of Kasarda, this sector is called "information processing.") Chapter 4 documents the reasons for this employment shift; now it is time to discuss the consequences.

The most significant consequence is also the most obvious: Entry-level jobs, for which high school education is sufficient, have been leaving central cities at a massive rate over the past two decades; there has been a dramatic replacement of these jobs with professional ones that require more educational background.

The specialty product of the modern city core is massive personal contact. This activity is precisely the type that "ought" to take place in an urban core. The activity is not particularly space intensive, and vertical transportation is probably at least as efficient as horizontal transportation. Thus, expensive land can be used to its fullest with high-rise office buildings. Once it became economically possible for manufacturing to leave the urban core—with the development of electric power, the automobile, and the truck—the urban core became available for office buildings.

By chance, the concentration of higher-education jobs downtown and the suburbanization of entry-level jobs occurred just as the preexisting location pattern of the housing stock was increasingly concentrating poor people in central cities. This set of events appears to be the primary reason for the massive increase in central-city unemployment (particularly, but far from exclusively, among blacks) over the past two decades.

This proffered explanation of the rapid increase in central-city unemployment must be regarded as both incomplete and tentative. It is tentative because it has not been thoroughly examined by scholars.[12]

The mismatch hypothesis is incomplete because it leaves unexplored another crucial question. Have jobs requiring low educational attainment been merely suburbanized or have they been disappearing from the national economy altogether? In the case of total manufacturing jobs, we know that employment in the United States has been rising slowly, suggesting suburbanization rather than total disappearance. The same appears to be true of entry-level service, retail, and wholesale jobs. Essentially what has happened with these jobs is that they have become suburbanized along with the population. These jobs have followed middle-class whites to the suburbs, and for central-city blacks without cars, they are virtually inaccessible.[13]

It appears that the most viable solution to the mismatch problem is increasing suburbanization of blacks and other victims of the mismatch (precisely as Kain advocated as early as 1968). Not only would it increase access of low-skilled people to jobs, but it is probably also the most promising way of increasing educational attainment. The return of entry-level jobs to the center city does not seem to be the answer. The CBD's comparative advantage for the forseeable future will be in

12.   One recent careful study finds little support for the spatial-mismatch hypothesis. Ellwood (1983) has examined the location patterns of black residences and jobs, and his empirical findings tend to refute the mismatch hypothesis. In particular, he finds that blacks who live near large concentrations of jobs do not fare much better than blacks who live far away from such concentrations.

13.   Kasarda has calculated the fraction of black and Hispanic city households with no automobile or truck in 1980 for Philadelphia, Boston, and New York. For Boston and Philadelphia, approximately half of these households lacked cars. For both groups, approximately 70 percent of New York City dwellers lacked private transportation.

information processing, requiring the employment of well-educated people. Employment opportunities for people with modest education will be in manufacturing and services associated with shopping, home maintenance, and the like. Each of these activities seems to have moved irrevocably to the suburbs or beyond.

Even after recognizing that it is the residences and not the jobs that must move, no solution has been found. Movement of poor and minority households to the suburbs involves the breakdown of discriminatory barriers. In addition, it may involve construction of new housing for low-income families. The latter will surely be a more costly way of providing low-income housing than the filtering mechanism that now provides most low-income housing. Perhaps a solution will be found through a combination of training, housing location, and transport policies.

Black suburbanization.   If it is true that the crisis of black central-city unemployment is due in part to spatial mismatch, then it seems clear that suburbanization of blacks must be at least an important part of the solution.

The Civil Rights Act of 1968 prohibits virtually all discriminatory acts with respect to both owner-occupied and rental housing. Until only a couple of decades before that date, government was frequently an active participant in residential discrimination. Racial covenants were legally enforceable until 1948 (zoning until 1917).

Since 1968, there have been substantial increases in black representation in American suburbs. According to calculations by Kain (1984), 18.1 percent of blacks in MSAs with more than one million in population lived in suburbs in 1970; by 1980, the figure had risen to 25 percent. He shows that the vast bulk of this suburbanization merely represents an expansion of the ghetto across the city-suburban boundary rather than true dispersal and mixing at the neighborhood level. He notes, however, that the number of all-white suburban jurisdictions declined markedly during the 1970s. Typical is the suburban ring around Chicago. In 1970, 69 of 117 suburban communities had fewer than 5 black households; by 1980, the figure had fallen to 15. The general pattern appears to be emerging in most suburban rings; formerly all-white suburbs almost everywhere have been acquiring small numbers of black households. By 1990, there were very few suburban communities that did not have a sprinkling of black residents.

Kain makes two crucial observations about these new black suburbanites. First the number of blacks living in largely white suburban communities is very small (well under 5 percent of the black population of the MSA). Second it is no longer true, as it was two decades ago, that the arrival of a few black households portends the switching of an entire neighborhood or jurisdiction to black occupancy. The reason is very simple. There are not enough blacks to "tip" even a small fraction of the suburban communities that now have a small number of black households. Thus, these influxes must remain fairly small. This finding is much different from the entry of a few blacks into a neighborhood in 1960 or even 1970, because (1) urban black populations are not growing as they were two decades ago, and (2) there recently have been so many small inroads made that they cannot all be followed up by massive flows. It is impossible to know yet whether this optimistic interpretation is correct. Recent changes in black residential location may be the first step in dramatic changes in both location patterns and attitudes.

We have emphasized that the deterioration of economic opportunity for central-city residents extends beyond the black (and growing Hispanic) population. Even a cursory examination, however, reveals that minorities bear the brunt of the social burden. The trend toward high black unemployment in the central city has been accompanied by many indications of severe stress in black urban social and family life, including dramatic increases in the numbers of female-headed households and teenage pregnancies.

There is some reason to believe that these problems have been exacerbated by the fact that blacks migrated to cities so quickly and in such large numbers. There has been remarkably little time for the development of stable community relationships, and urban black communities have been virtually lacking in the presence of an older generation capable of providing stability and leadership. With the end of black migration (largely a young-adult activity) and the passage of time, the age distribution of blacks will become more like that of other residents. Many researchers believe that a part of the problem facing urban black America is related to the turmoil brought about by the continuous wave of migration that ended in the early 1970s.

☐ Summary

There is widespread concern among government officials, scholars, and the public that the largest metropolitan areas are too big and that most urban areas are excessively decentralized. In both cases, much of the concern is misplaced. It is unlikely that any appropriate governmental intervention would have much effect on urban sizes or structures.

Large metropolitan areas are thought to be too large because externalities, such as environmental congestion-related ones, increase in importance with urban size. It does not follow, however, that appropriate intervention in solving the underlying problem would reduce the sizes of the large urban areas or not, changes in urban sizes would be incidental to the solution of the problem. The effect of governmental actions would be to alter resource allocation in metropolitan areas of a given size.

Suburbs in the United States are thought to be excessively decentralized for several reasons: centrally concentrated pollution discharges, underpricing of urban transportation, land-use controls, subsidization of owner-occupied houses, and high-energy costs. Thinking is confused on several issues, and a resolution of the problems probably would not have large effects on urban densities. Urban areas have decentralized in the United States and elsewhere for decades because of powerful market forces. To reverse the process would be unjustified and probably impossible.

Questions and Problems

1. In most countries, the share of the urban population living in the largest urban area falls as real income rises. Why do you think that is?

2. During the 1970s and early 1980s, the share of the urban population in the East and the Midwest decreased, and the share in the South, the West, and the Rocky Mountain region increased. What effect has the regional shift had on the size distribution of urban areas? What effect has it had on the use of energy?

3. Suppose all residential land-use controls were abolished. How many more people would live in multifamily housing by the end of the century? How much energy would be saved?

4. Suppose governmental programs returned typical density functions in the United States to their 1960 forms by the end of the century. What would be the percentage saving in energy use?

5. Do you think density gradients will continue to decline until metropolitan densities are uniform at all distances from the city center?

References and Further Reading

American Public Transit Association. *Transit Fact Book* (Washington: American Public Transit Association, 1981).

Beckmann, Martin, and John McPherson, "City Size Distributions in a Central Place Hierarchy: An Alternative Approach." *Journal of Regional Science* 10 (1970): 25–77. A theoretical model of urban size distribution.

Bradbury, Katharine, Anthony Downs, and Kenneth Small. *Urban Decline and the Future of American Cities* (Washington, D.C.: Brookings Institution, 1982). A careful and thoughtful study on the causes and consequences of central-city population loss.

Ellwood, David T. "The Spatial Mismatch Hypothesis: Are There Teenage Jobs Missing in the Ghetto?" (Cambridge, Mass.: National Bureau of Economic Research 1983). Working paper No. 1188.

Gale, Dennis E. "Neighborhood Resettlement: Washington, D.C." In Shirley Laska and Daphne Spain, eds. *Back to the City: Issues in Neighborhood Renovation* (New York: Pergamon, 1980). An analysis of neighborhood revitalization in Washington, containing a large amount of information on the characteristics of renovators and the types of houses involved.

Henderson, J. Vernon. *Economic Theory and the Cities* (New York: Academic Press, 1977). An advanced theoretical treaties on urban economics, including an analysis of distortions within and among urban areas.

Kain, John F. "Housing Segregation, Negro Employment, and Metropolitan Decentralization," *Quarterly Journal of Economics* 82 (May, 1968): 175–197. This very readable classic paper was the first to analyze carefully the relationship between residential location and unemployment.

Kain, John F. "Black Suburbanization in the Eighties: A New Beginning or a False Hope?" 1984. Paper presented at conference. The Agenda for Metropolitan America, sponsored by the Center for Real Estate and Urban Economics, University of California at Berkeley.

Laska, Shirley, and Daphne Spain, eds. *Back to the City: Issues in Neighborhood Renovation* (New York: Pergamon, 1980). A series of very good essays on several aspects of the return-to-the-city movement.

Long, Larry H. "Back to the Countryside and Back to the City in the Same Decade." In *Back to the City: Issues in Neighborhood Renovation,* edited by Shirley Laska and Daphne Spain. (New York: Pergamon, 1980). A good discussion of the demographic aspects of the back-to-the-city movement.

Macauley, Molly. "Estimation and Recent Behavior of Urban Population and Employment Density Gradients." *Journal of Urban Economics* 18 (1985) 251–260. An updating of density gradients from Edwin S. Mills's *Studies in the Structure of the Urban Economy,* along with new analysis and correction of some statistical flaws.

Mills, Edwin S. "The Measurement and Determinants of Suburbanization." *Journal of Urban Economics* 32 (November, 1992): 377–387. A recent statistical study of suburbanization.

Mills, Edwin S., and Katsutoshi Ohta. "Urbanization and Urban Problems." In *Asia's New Giant,* edited by Henry Rosovsky and Hugh Patrick (Washington, D.C.: Brookings Institution, 1976). A study of urban problems in Japan.

Muth, Richard. *Cities and Housing.* (Chicago: University of Chicago Press, 1969). Contains a careful analysis of density functions.

National Association of Realtors. *National Homebuying Survey,* annual (Washington, D.C.: National Association of Realtors). A good annual source of data on the housing market, including detailed characteristics of homebuyers and homes bought.

Peterson, Paul E., ed. *The New Urban Reality* (Washington, D.C.: Brookings Institution, 1985). A collection of scholarly interpretive essays on several aspects of the current urban scene. Of particular relevance to this chapter are the following: "Urban Change and Minority Opportunities," by John Kasarda, which was used in our discussion of the economic decline of central cities; "Islands of Renewal in Seas of Decay," by Brian Berry; and "The Urban Underclass in an Advanced Industrial Society," by William Wilson.

Real Estate Research Corporation. *The Costs of Sprawl.* (Washington, D.C.: Real Estate Research Corporation, 1974). A study of costs—government and private—of suburban developments at various densities.

Sundquist, James. *Dispersing Population* (Washington, D.C.: Brookings Institution, 1975). An analysis of European population-dispersal programs.

Tolley, George, Philip Graves, and John Gardner. *Urban Growth Policy in a Market Economy* (New York: Academic Press, 1979). Technical analyses of distortions in urban sizes.

Tolley, George. "The Welfare Economics of City Bigness." *Journal of Urban Economics* (1974): 324–345.

Yinger, John. "Measuring Racial Discrimination with Fair Housing Audits." *American Economic Review* 76 (December, 1986): 881–893. This paper reports finding extensive housing discrimination, as discovered through the employment of an audit, in which black and white auditors pose as prospective buyers or renters.

Wilson, William J. *The Truly Disadvantaged* (Chicago: University of Chicago Press, 1987). A provocative examination of the reasons for the deterioration of the socioeconomic condition of blacks.

17

Urbanization in Developing Countries

☐ Until 200 or 300 years ago, only a tiny fraction of people—rulers, courtiers, large landowners, and a few merchants—sustained over extended periods living standards that were substantially above the minimum required to subsist and reproduce. Then, England, much of northern Europe, and later, North America experienced important economic changes that culminated in continued rises in real incomes for a widening circle of ordinary people. By the early twentieth century, such economic growth had spread to a few places—notably, Japan— outside northern Europe and its former colonies in North America and Australia. Since the middle of the twentieth century, this growth has spread to many other countries—mostly former colonies in which almost everyone had lived at near subsistence living standards throughout history.

The high-income countries of northern Europe and North America have had high growth rates of per capita income for 100 or 200 years, averaging 1.5 to 3 percent annual real per capita growth during much of the period and interrupted by occasional devastating wars. Japan's rapid growth started late in the last century, but its people were reduced to near-subsistence living standards by World War II.

Since World War II, moderate numbers of countries—most starting at near-subsistence levels—have achieved growth rates that were previously unknown as sustained experiences. During the remarkably peaceful period from 1965 to 1990, among the world's growth leaders were Japan (4.7 percent), Singapore (7.0 percent), South Korea (7.0 percent), Switzerland (4.6 percent), Hong Kong (6.8 percent), and Thailand (4.2 percent). An even larger group of countries' achieved growth rates between 2 and 4 percent.

At the other extreme, some countries have achieved little or no growth. Living standards for Bangladesh's 110 million people were no higher in 1990 than they were in 1965. Many sub-Saharan African countries experienced decreasing living standards during the quarter century.

The questions of why and how economic growth occurs and actions that private groups, governments, and international organizations can take to foster growth have attracted the attention of some of the world's best economists, and several Nobel prizes have been awarded for this work. Introducing economics students to the complexities of economic development requires a book of its own. This chapter has the more limited purposes of analyzing the link between economic development and urbanization and a few of the problems that accompany urbanization in developing countries.

☐ CHARACTERISTICS OF DEVELOPING COUNTRIES

A few common features of developing countries play crucial roles in urbanization. Table 17.1 quantifies those characteristics for a sample of nations.

Income

As Table 17.1 reveals, real per capita GNP is between 50 and 100 times as high in rich countries as in poor ones, and relatively few countries have what might be called middle levels of GNP.[1] A 1990 per capita GNP of $1,000 is roughly equivalent to that of the United States in the early nineteenth century.[2] Almost all of the world's poorest countries are in sub-Saharan Africa and South Asia.

Income Growth

Some developing countries have fairly rapid rates of growth of GNP.[3] Much of this, however, is eaten up in population growth, so GNP per

---

1. Almost 70 percent of the nations listed in the original World Bank table have per capita incomes below $1,000 or above $7,000.

2. Comparisons of GNPs probably overstate international differences in standards of living because low income countries conduct more of their economic activities outside the realm of organized markets and, thus, much economic activity escapes inclusion in the GNP. Also, the GNP overstates income in all countries, because it includes expenditures required to replace depreciated capital. Despite these imperfections, GNP per capita is the most reliable and readily available measure of living standards. The United Nations and the World Bank compute purchasing power versions of GNP for a few countries. For example, using the purchasing power version, Bangladesh has per capita income of 4.7 percent of the level of per capita in the United States, whereas the data in Table 17.1 imply that it is only 0.5 percent.

3. Developing countries, like the rest of the world, generally suffered a slowdown in GNP growth in the 1970s.

person is growing only very slowly (generally, not fast enough to make substantial gain on developed countries). This pattern appears quite starkly in Column 7 of Table 17.1.

Differences in observed growth rates of per capita GNP produce enormous variations in living standards during short periods. A 7 percent growth rate doubles income in ten years. In less than one-half a century, a 7 percent growth rate raises living standards from among the lowest to among the highest (see Table 17.1). A 3 percent growth rate multiplies income almost 20 times in one century. It does not take long, at even modest growth rates, to raise living standards dramatically.

Population Growth

Columns 4 and 5 of Table 17.1 give annual rates of population growth between 1965 and 1980 and between 1980 and 1989, respectively. There is a strong tendency for growth rates to be higher in low-income than high-income countries. Population growth rates, however, slowed in most countries during the 1980s. The important exceptions were in African countries. Death rates have tended to fall in most countries, so the population growth rate accelerates unless birthrates also fall. In fact, the decline in mortality has contributed to a rise in birthrates in some places. The biggest improvement in mortality has occurred in infant and child mortality, and this improvement soon yields a large cohort of adults of childbearing age. Even with declines in average family size, the age distribution of the population in many developing countries is such that birthrates surely will remain high for many years. The average completed family size (after the birth of all children) has declined in some developing countries, however, as will be discussed. This finding may be due in part to improved educational attainment of the female population.

Level of Urbanization

The final important characteristic of developing countries is that they are inevitably less urbanized than developed countries, as Column 6 of Table 17.1 and Figure 3 (inside back cover) reveal. The reason for this figure is that urbanization is a concomitant of development. A less-developed country is almost necessarily one with a predominantly agricultural economy.

It is no great mystery why the urban share of the population correlates so strongly with the level of economic development. The basic pattern was seen in Chapter 3 on the urbanization of the economy in the United States, and it is being repeated in developing countries at present.

Table 17.1   Characteristics of Nations at Various Stages of Development

	GNP per Capita Rank 1977 (1)	GNP per Capita Rank 1989 (2)	(3)	Average Percentage Rate of Population Growth 1965–80 (4)	1980–89 (5)	Percent Urban (6)	GNP Growth per Capita 1965–89 (7)	Actual Growth Rate of Urban Population 1980–89 (8)	Calculated Growth Rate of Urban Population* (9)	Primacy (10)	Adult Literacy Rate (11)
Finland	20	3	$22,120	0.3%	0.4%	60.0%	3.2%	0.4%	0.7%	34%	100%
United States	7	5	20,910	1.0	1.0	75.0	1.6	1.2	1.3	2	99
Canada	10	8	19,030	1.3	0.9	77.0	4.0	1.1	1.2	4	98
United Arab Emirates	1	9	18,430	16.6	4.6	78.0	0.0	4.1	5.9	. . .	21
Singapore	30	19	10,450	1.6	1.2	100.0	7.0	1.2	1.2	100	86
Portugal	40	31	4,250	0.4	0.6	33.0	3.0	2.0	1.8	46	84
Panama	50	54	1,760	2.6	2.2	53.0	1.6	2.9	4.2	37	88
Peru	70	66	1,010	2.8	2.3	70.0	-0.2	3.1	3.3	41	85
Syria	60	68	980	3.4	3.6	50.0	3.1	4.4	7.2	32	60
Bolivia	80	81	620	2.5	2.7	51.0	-0.8	4.3	5.3	33	74
Ghana	90	97	390	2.2	3.4	33.0	-1.5	4.2	10.3	22	60
Central African Republic	100	98	390	1.9	2.7	46.0	-0.5	4.9	5.9	51	40
India	. . .	104	340	2.3	2.1	27.0	1.8	3.8	7.8	4	95
Sierra Leone	110	113	220	2.0	2.4	32.0	0.2	5.4	7.5	52	29
Chad	120	115	190	2.0	2.4	29.0	-1.2	6.5	8.3	43	25
Bangladesh	. . .	119	180	2.7	2.6	16.0	0.4	6.6	16.3	36	94

*Assumes no growth in rural population (column 5/column 6)
Source: Data from World Bank. *World Development Report* (New York: Oxford University Press, 1991).

Food is the prime requirement for life, and in the poorest countries, most production effort is devoted to agriculture. As economies develop, inputs and outputs shift from agriculture (the primary, or extractive, sector, sometimes including fisheries and forestry) to manufacturing (the secondary, or processing, sector, sometimes including construction) and services (the tertiary sector). In 1980, low-income countries had a weighted average of 72 percent of their labor forces in agriculture; in middle-income countries, the percentage was 43; and in industrial market economies, the percentage was 7 (*World Development Report,* 1987). Percentages of labor force in industry (manufacturing, mining, construction, electricity, water, and gas) and services, respectively, were as follows: low-income economies, 13 and 15 percent; middle-income economies, 23 and 34 percent; and industrial market economies, 35 and 58 percent. Over the entire range of development, the percentage of the labor force in agriculture varies from 75 to 93 in the lowest-income countries (Nepal, Ethiopia, and many African countries) to 3 to 6 percent in the highest-income countries (United States, Belgium, and West Germany).

Why does the massive shift from agriculture and into industry and services occur during economic development? One important reason is that demand shifts. At low-income levels, most income is spent on food; however, the income elasticity of demand for food is low and falls as income rises. The income elasticities of demand for manufactured products and services are large, and income shares spent on them rise with income. Thus, the 10- or 20-fold increase in income that occurs during development causes a massive shift of demand from food to manufactured products and services. Employers in the growing sectors offer relatively high wages and other input prices, and labor and other inputs move in directions of relatively high returns.

In addition, product prices of manufactured goods and services may fall relative to those of agricultural products. Technical progress may be faster in industry and services than in agriculture, and the accumulation of both physical and human capital may favor industry and services relative to agriculture. The relative price effects depend on whether the commodities are traded internationally and on the extent to which the economy is open. The easier a commodity is to trade and the more open the country, the more cost decreases result in production increases— with resulting labor and other input shifts—and the less the cost decreases result in price decreases.

Since the beginning of this book, powerful reasons have been shown for industry and services to be located in urban areas: Large markets permit scale and agglomeration economies to be exploited; production can locate where comparative advantage dictates and near water, road, and rail transportation facilities so that inputs and outputs can be shipped cheaply; and proximity to inputs produced in the same urban area permits savings on transportation costs.

☐ IMPLICATIONS OF URBANIZATION

Growth of Urban Population

Equation (17.1) expresses the accounting link among the total population growth rate (g_t), the rural and urban population growth rates $(g_r$ and g_w, respectively), and the fraction of population that is presently urban (U/P):[4]

$$g_t = [g_u \cdot U/P] + [g_r \cdot (1 - U/P)]. \qquad (17.1)$$

Equation (17.1) states that the growth rate of the entire population is equal to the urban growth rate times the fraction of the population that is urban plus the rural growth rate times the fraction of the population that is rural. Rearranging these, the growth rate of the urban population can be expressed as a function of the other variables:

$$g_u = \frac{g_t}{U/P} - g_r \frac{1 - U/P}{U/P}. \qquad (17.2)$$

Reference to the g_t (Column 5) and U/P (Column 6) numbers in Table 17.1 shows that it is almost inevitable for developing countries to have extremely rapid growth rates of urban population. If the rural population growth rate is zero, the urban population growth rate is the national growth rate divided by the fraction of the population that is urban.

The calculated annual growth rates of the urban populations, using Equation (17.2) and assuming that the rural population growth rate is zero, are shown in Column 9 of Table 17.1. The actual urban growth rates for the period from 1980 to 1986 are shown in Column 8. In all countries except Portugal, the calculated urban growth rate is at least as great as the actual growth rate, implying that the rural population is constant or increasing. The larger the positive difference between the calculated and actual growth rates, the faster the rural population is growing. Thus, the Portuguese rural population is decreasing, whereas those in India and Bangladesh are growing rapidly. The point of this calculation is that many developing countries have high agricultural population densities and relatively small percentages of urban populations. Furthermore, as economic growth proceeds, the application of new technology to agriculture and the price and income inelasticities of food demand results in rapid rural-urban migration until U/P is well above 50 percent. There is an enormous potential for urban growth, even if total population growth is at a modest pace, in many developing countries.

---

4. The reader can readily verify that this expression is correct. Clearly, Δpopulation = Δurban + Δrural. If this expression is divided through by total population, the left side becomes g_r. If Δurban/population is multiplied by urban/urban and terms are rearranged, we get $g_u \cdot U/p$. In a similar way (multiplying by rural/rural), we convert the last term to $g_r \cdot (1 - U/p)$. If we multiply Δurban/population by urban/urban and rearrange terms, we get $g_u \cdot U/P$. In a similar way, the last term is converted to $g_r \cdot (1 - U)/P$.

There are several additional valuable observations regarding the current urban population explosion in developing countries. First the same thing happened in currently developed countries in the nineteenth century, although on a more modest scale.[5] Second many observers believe that this rapid urbanization carries the seeds of its own end. As the fraction of population that is urban expands, the rate of urban population increase declines, as shown in Equation (17.2). In addition, completed family size tends to be smaller in urban areas than in rural areas, so the shift to an urban population reduces the growth rate of the total population (once the effects of the skewed age distribution have been eliminated).

Size of the Urban Sector

The high calculated rates of potential urban population growth have not been realized in any nation, although a few urban areas have achieved growth rates approaching 10 percent during brief periods. For the developing countries listed in Table 17.1, the actual average rate of urban population increase was 4.3 percent during the period from 1980 to 1989—considerably below the 7.5 percent calculated by assuming zero rural population increase. This finding means that urbanization is proceeding more moderately than the calculation suggests (although the urban population still doubles every 16 years). This action of course means that agricultural population density is being pushed still higher and that the period of rapid urbanization will continue for a longer period after the total population increase slows down.

The extremely rapid rate of urban population growth discussed previously has led many observers to conclude that urbanization is proceeding too quickly. A frequent component of these arguments is that urban growth is excessively concentrated in large metropolitan areas (that there is excessive *primacy,* which will be discussed later), that it is too concentrated in prosperous regions, and that it requires excessive expenditures on local governmental services. Related beliefs are that concentrations of low-income people in urban slums are undesirable and that cities are, in some ways, parasites living off the efforts and production of rural workers.

The belief that urbanization is proceeding too quickly seems to come from three sources. First, as Chapter 15 showed, externalities (pollution and congestion, basically) may imply that the equilibrium level of urbanization is excessive. Second many argue that urbanization should proceed more slowly on the grounds that rapid growth toward a given target is more costly and disruptive than slow growth. Third rapid

---

5.   The urban population of the United States grew at about 5 percent per year for the century between 1790 and 1890, but during this period the physical extent of the nation also was increasing rapidly. No single region realized a 5 percent annual growth of urban population for more than a few decades.

urbanization always has been accompanied by nostalgia for the bucolic life left behind.[6]

Migration to the urban sector is obviously migration from the rural sector. The first task in understanding the phenomenon, therefore, is to discuss the relationship between these two sectors.

Links between rural and urban sectors. In most developing countries, the product of marginal labor in agriculture is not far above zero. Because farming is frequently a cooperative family activity rather than an enterprise with wage labor, the marginal product requires careful definition. The relevant concept is the marginal product of a *laborer,* that is, the change in total output of the family farm if the number of working household members changes. Typically, the loss of a working member of a farm household results in little output loss because the same work load is shared by fewer workers.[7] When the farm household makes a family decision about whether to send one of its members to the urban labor market, it will compare the worker's *expected real wage* in the urban sector with the VMP in the rural sector. In the case of nearly zero agricultural marginal product, total household income rises if a migrant to the city can expect to make even a modest real wage.

The expected real wage is the wage paid in the urban sector less any urban wage premiums reflecting costs of urban life (urban housing cost and commuting, for example) and the risk of unemployment. Suppose, for example, that annual urban time and money commuting cost is $50. Just as in the open-city model of Chapter 6, the urban labor market must offer a wage premium of $50 to attract workers. In equilibrium, this premium covers all costs and disamenities associated with urban life. Thus, the equilibrium urban wage is equal to the rural VMP (that is, the VMP of a farm worker, which is sometimes not far above zero in developing countries) plus this wage premium that compensates for associated costs and disamenities. If the actual wage exceeds this compensation, workers migrate from the rural sector. In the typical case, where the rural marginal product is close to zero, the migration of a family member to the urban sector raises total family income, even if the expected real urban wage is small. In many developing countries, real urban wages are two to four times those in rural areas. Such urban premiums are far above equilibrium and are typically accompanied by rapid rural-urban migration.

Under what circumstances does the movement of a worker from the rural to the urban sector raise total welfare (in the sense discussed in Chapter 8)? Ordinarily, welfare is increased whenever the worker shifts

---

6.   For a particularly poignant statement of this nostalgia, see Oliver Goldsmith's "The Deserted Village," a classic English poem on rural life after the Enclosures, which permitted landowners to enclose their land so that others could not use it.

7.   For a fuller discussion, see Sen (1968).

from a low-VMP job to a high-VMP job. In the case of rural-urban migration, however, account also must be taken of the fact that there are costs associated with urban life (and employment) that are largely absent in rural life. The prime example is commuting, although, in fact, there are many such costs. Since commuting uses resources, welfare maximization requires that the gain in output resulting from migration be weighed against the increased demand on resources. In other words, optimality dictates that the flow of workers to the urban sector stop when the VMP of the urban worker exceeds the VMP of the rural worker and that this gap between the urban and rural VMPs is equal to the resource cost required by the last migrant. To return to numbers analogous to those in the previous paragraph, suppose that total commuting costs (including those of the migrant) rise by $50 per year by the entry of one more worker to the urban sector. Optimality dictates that the urban VMP exceed the rural VMP by $50; otherwise, the gain in output would be offset by the increased commuting requirement. Assuming wages are equal to the VMP in both rural and urban sectors, efficiency requires that there be an urban wage premium (of $50, in this example).

Markets give correct migration signals when the actual wage premium equals the optimum wage premium. This balance occurs whenever migrants are forced to pay all the costs (including congestion costs, in this example) associated with their move to the city. In other words, real wage differences serve as efficient signals about labor movement as long as there are no externalities associated with urban population growth.

This argument is the same made in the discussion of environmental quality in Chapter 15. It was argued there that whatever externality problems exist can be more efficiently handled with pricing methods than with controls on urban populations. In any case, it is not clear that the externalities are quantitatively important in developed countries. In developing countries, the story is less straightforward. First in societies with a high level of illiteracy and an urban population made up largely of recent immigrants from farms or peasant villages, it may be difficult to impose efficient externality fees. Second the extremely high density of many urban areas in developing countries suggests that externalities may be more severe in developing countries. The money value of the externalities however, is likely to be low. The demand for environmental amenities is highly income elastic (not surprisingly, at low incomes people prefer income to a nice environment). Similarly, the congestion externality is the imposition of time cost on others, as Chapter 13 indicated. When the opportunity cost of time is low, however, so is the money cost of congestion. To summarize, no evidence suggests that urban externalities are sufficiently important to justify restrictions on labor mobility, even if direct pricing policies are unavailable. Although facts on the magnitude of urban externalities in poor countries are scarce, there is no reason to believe that the equilibrium level of urbanization is nonoptimum.

Knowledge about a related topic is even sketchier. Suppose we accept the notion that unrestricted migration ultimately leads to an efficient level of urbanization. At the same time, it might be true that efficiency would be enhanced if the society approached that level of urbanization more slowly. The argument is that a given amount of growth can be accommodated at less cost if the growth takes place slowly instead of quickly. This finding might be true for a number of reasons. First urban life is quite different from village or farm life in the complexity of its rules and interactions. It is plausible that urban areas function more smoothly and with fewer bottlenecks if the proportion of people new to urban life is relatively small.[8] Second the construction of housing and other capital probably occurs under a special kind of increasing costs such that the total cost of building housing (or transport, water, or sewer) stock can be reduced if the construction is spread over several years.[9]

Although no quantitative information has been gathered, there may be some truth to these arguments. It does not follow, however, that governments should limit migration to cities. A decline in the rate of urban population growth implies an increase in the rate of rural population growth. For the sample of developing countries in Table 17.1, rural population growth has recently been about 1.5 percent (doubling farm population in about 47 years). For each 1 percent decline in urban population growth, the rural growth rate rises by about 0.5 percent. Because there is already surplus labor in the rural sector, any slowdown in the pace of urbanization would be harmful to the rural sector.[10]

The net effect of these considerations is that there is no basis for a presumption that slowing the rate of urbanization would be beneficial, once the effects of this policy on the rural sector have been accounted for. There also are equity issues here. All governmental programs to slow rural-urban migration inevitably slow migration of predominantly poor people. High-income urban residents designing these programs benefit at the expense of poor people who are precluded from migration.

---

8.   Recall that, at current population growth rates, about half of the population of a given urban area will have lived there for less than 16 years.

9.   In the investment literature, this factor is the distinction between the marginal efficiency of investment and the marginal efficiency of capital. At a rapid pace of investment, the marginal efficiency of investment falls below the marginal efficiency of capital because rapid investment is more expensive (for a given amount of total capital produced) than slower investment.

10.   Some researchers argue that rural development does not receive the attention it deserves in many national development strategies. The argument here, however, is that the return to capital investment in the rural sector would be high. It is plausible that such capital investment would be a substitute for labor, thus increasing the surplus of farm labor and increasing the pressure to migrate to the urban sector. It appears that some types of rural development—especially irrigation and the introduction of more productive plant strains—increase the demand for rural labor; however, the mechanization of planting, cultivating, and harvesting clearly displaces rural labor (see Ishizawa 1978).

Finally, educational opportunities for the poor are better in urban than in rural areas in most developing countries.

   Primacy. The term *primacy* refers to the size, or allegedly excessive size, of the largest metropolitan area in a country. More generally, the term sometimes refers to the claim that several of the largest metropolitan areas are too large.

   The percentage of the urban population living in the largest metropolitan area or areas varies enormously among countries. There is, however, a definitional issue. A country must have at least one urban area—its capital. If the country consists of sufficiently little additional territory, the share of its urban population living in the largest urban area is inevitably large. Singapore and Hong Kong are the extremes, being little more than city states. Some small African countries approximate the same situation. Guinea and Costa Rica, which contain 5 and 2.7 million people respectively, have 89 and 77 percent of their respective urban populations living in their national capitals.

   The definitional problem is more severe than the existence of national capitals. From an economic point of view, national boundaries are frequently arbitrary. A given distribution of population between farms, villages, and cities can yield vastly different primacy rates, depending on where the national boundary is drawn. Taking an example from the United States, the New York Consolidated Metropolitan Statistical Area's population is 7.2 percent of the national total. Were California and Texas to secede from the Union, however, this new nation would have a primacy ratio of 8.9 percent.

   Among countries with large populations, Thailand—with 55 million people—is the most primate, with 57 percent of its urban population in its largest metropolitan area, Bangkok. Mexico and the Philippines, each with 32 percent of their urban populations living in their capitals, are among the more primate of large developing countries. At the other extreme, India and China have only 4 and 2 percent of their respective urban populations living in their largest metropolitan areas.

   As a rule, large countries tend to be less primate than small countries (partly for the reason illustrated in the New York example), and high-income countries tend to be less primate than low-income countries. Beyond that, there are few regularities, as Column 10 of Table 17.1 indicates.

   Most developing and many developed countries have governmental policies to curtail the growth of their largest metropolitan area or areas. Mechanisms vary from requirements that people have permits or licenses to live or produce in the largest metropolitan area to subsidies to firms that produce elsewhere to policies to locate government-owned firms outside large metropolitan areas. Several countries—notably, Brazil and the United States—have moved their national capital to remove it from a large city or metropolitan area. Countries vary greatly as to the firmness with which such policies are applied.

The excessive primacy argument has the same basic components as the excessive urbanization argument just discussed: It maintains that some externality causes the private benefits of moving to the largest cities to exceed the social benefits. As in the case of excessive urbanization, the argument cannot be completely dismissed, although it should be recalled that there are external economies of large metropolitan size as well. The gap between marginal and average congestion costs may well be somewhat wider for large urban areas than small ones, and the same may be true of pollution costs. There is no evidence, however, concerning the quantitative importance of these considerations and no strong reason to believe that they are large. It is known on the one hand that policies to reduce the sizes of large urban areas have a cost (productivity is higher in large than small cities);[11] on the other hand, given our current knowledge, any benefit of shifting population and employment from large to small urban areas is conjectural.

There is, however, one key empirical finding on this subject. Henderson (1988) and others have found that, other things being equal, countries with centralized or unitary governments have more primate size distributions of urban areas than countries with federal systems of government. The United States, Brazil, India, and Malaysia have federal systems and dispersed size distributions of urban areas, whereas South Korea, Thailand, and the Philippines have centralized governments and highly primate city-size distributions.

The explanation is easy. In federal systems, states or provinces have some constitutional autonomy and can raise their own taxes to provide local governmental services (transportation, basic education, water supply, waste disposal, and so on) needed to make urban areas grow. In centralized governments, state or provincial and local governments receive their spending instructions, as well as much of their revenues, from the central government. National governments in such countries invariably pour money into the national capital to the neglect of other urban centers. The national capital is likely to have the best universities, public transit system, museums, convention centers, hospitals, and other services—provided, at least in part, with central governmental money.

Thus, governments in many developing countries try to undo with one hand what they have done with the other. Economic growth and social welfare inevitably suffer from such contradictory policies. The solution is also clear: Permit local governments to raise taxes locally and spend the money for the benefit of their constituents. Local autonomy would relate local governmental spending more closely to the needs and

---

11. According to one estimate for the United States (Sveikauskas 1975), a doubling of city size is associated with a 5.98 percent increase in labor productivity. It is an open question whether the same result would hold for developing countries, although there is surely some increase in labor productivity as city size increases. Big-city employers are willing to pay the wage premiums that have been discussed rather than move their operations to small cities or villages, presumably because labor is more productive in big cities.

wishes of the local populace, introduce competition among local governments, and disperse political power. These features are essentially the Tiebout model benefits discussed in Chapter 14.

Not all local governmental spending should be financed by locally raised taxes. Some regional and national considerations are involved. Local governments, however, should have much more autonomy than they have in most developing countries. In most countries, the third benefit of local autonomy is precisely the reason central governments do not permit it. Most central governments in developing countries are autocratic and are unwilling to share power with local governments or voters.

Much of the opposition to urbanization in general, and the growth of large cities in particular, is surely an expression of the wish that total population growth would slow. Urbanization probably could proceed more smoothly if urban populations were growing more slowly. It is inappropriate to cite this fact in isolation; however, the effect on the rural sector of slowing the pace of urbanization would be detrimental, as has been explained. The case for slowing the pace of urbanization is further weakened once it is recalled that urbanization is among the effective means of curbing population growth.

Poverty and Income Distribution

Low-income countries contain mostly low-income people. In 1989, GNP per capita was $180 in Bangladesh, $120 in Ethiopia, and $350 in China. No income distribution can permit lives of dignity for the majority of people if average incomes are at these levels. Economic growth is a prerequisite to decent living standards for most people in all low-income countries. Nevertheless, the income distribution differs greatly among countries, and most governments in low-income countries make more or less strong efforts to change the distribution. As was shown for the United States, poverty and income distribution are not inherently urban issues; as in the United States, however, they mostly arise in the context of urbanization. In most rapidly urbanizing countries, urban income per capita substantially exceeds rural income per capita.

The distribution of income varies considerably among countries whose income averages fall within a narrow range. Change in income distribution, however, follows a characteristic pattern as countries develop. The pattern was first perceived by Kuznets and has been studied by many economists during the 1970s and 1980s (Chenery [1979], Chap. 11).

Before discussing this pattern, some explanation of measures of inequality is needed. The best graphic representation of income distribution is the Lorenz curve, shown in Figure 17.1. To understand it, imagine a list of incomes in a country, going from the lowest income to the highest income. The poorest person has a certain share of total

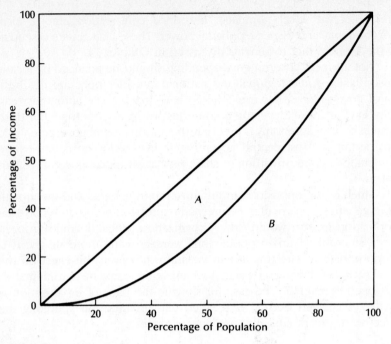

Figure 17.1   *Lorenz Curve*

income; the next poorest, a larger share; and so on. The Lorenz curve is a graph of population shares against these income shares, ordered from poorest to richest.

Since 0 percent of the people have 0 percent of the income and 100 percent of the people have 100 percent of the income, the Lorenz curve touches the lower left and upper right corners of the square. If everyone had the same income, x percent of the people would have x percent of the total income for any x between 0 and 100. Thus, the Lorenz curve would be the straight line shown in Figure 17.1. If there is any inequality, the poorest x percent of people must have less than x percent of the income for $0 < x < 100$. The smaller the income share of the poorest x percent of the people, the farther is the Lorenz curve below the straight line. Thus, the area between the straight line and the Lorenz curve, A in Figure 16.1, is a measure of inequality. Typically, A is divided by the total area under the straight line, $A + B$. Thus, the measure of inequality is

$$G = \frac{A}{A + B},$$

where G is called the *Gini coefficient.*

The larger is G, the greater is inequality. If G is 0, everyone has the same income. If G is 1, the highest-income person has all the income. For most countries, G is in the interval $0.3 \leq G \leq 0.6$.

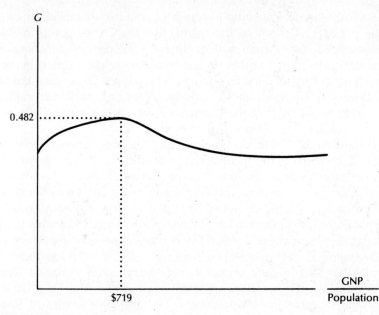

Figure 17.2   Kuznets Curve

The pattern perceived by Kuznets is that G is small in very low-income countries; it increases as average income rises from low levels; and it decreases after average income passes some modest level. Figure 17.2 shows an estimated Kuznets curve. Its characteristics are typical of recent estimates of Kuznets curves.[12] The income levels in Figure 17.2 are in purchasing power-adjusted 1991 U.S. dollars. The $2,525 income level at which the Gini coefficient peaks is about the income of Morocco. The Kuznets curve in Figure 17.2 implies that more than one-half the people in the world live in countries in which further growth means increased income inequality. It is not difficult to understand why people become agitated about this.

The variety of income distributions in the world's nations can be illustrated with recent World Bank data. The bank published only income shares by 20 percent population intervals (quintiles), but not Gini coefficients. Note that the share of the poorest 20 percent of the population cannot exceed 20 percent. If the poorest 20 percent have 10 percent of the total income, their incomes are half the country's average. Of the 20 high-income countries that the World Bank provides data for, Australia and the United States have the smallest shares going to the poorest 20 percent, 4.4 and 4.7 percent, respectively. The largest shares for the poorest 20 percent are Japan and Sweden, 8.7 and 8.6 percent, respectively.

12.   This estimate is taken from Becker (1987).

Such data are less plentiful in very poor countries. Bangladesh, one of the poorest countries in the world, has 10 percent going to the poorest 20 percent. Pakistan, with nearly twice the per capita income of Bangladesh, has moved farther up the rising part of the Kuznets curve, with 7.8 percent of total income going to the poorest 20 percent. Brazil and Botswana are both middle-income countries, with per capita incomes near the peak of the Kuznets curve, and 2.5 percent of total incomes going to the poorest 20 percent.[13]

If the Kuznets curve were steep enough at low-income levels, as average income rose, the income shares of low-income people would fall so rapidly that their per capita incomes would decrease. This subject is of intense concern in developing countries, and some scholars believe that low-income people do not benefit from economic growth. In fact, no careful estimate of the Kuznets curve implies that per capita incomes fall in any segment of the distribution as average incomes rise. There is no documented case in which the average income of a low-income segment has fallen as the overall average income has increased. The average income of a particular low-income group, however, may fall as the overall average income increases. The average incomes of low-income, small farmers, for example, might fall if mechanization—which favors large farms and drives down crop prices—occurred during development.

The Kuznets curve still is not understood in detail, but the basic explanation appears to be as follows. At very low-income levels, economic growth means that opportunities open up in particular places (mostly in urban areas and in certain industries—such as the modern manufacturing sector). Small groups of people are best placed to take advantage of these opportunities. A few entrepreneurial people may have money to invest, and small groups of workers have the education, skills, experience, and health to take part in the growing sectors. The incomes of such people rise well above the average, increasing inequality. Indeed, these reasons explain why incomes are not only higher but are also more unequal in urban than in rural areas in low-income countries. At later stages of development, a much larger segment of the labor force acquires the skills, health, and education needed to benefit from economic growth, so inequality decreases. Likewise, physical capital becomes plentiful relative to labor, and capital's share in GNP falls. Property income is always more concentrated in high-income groups than is labor income, so the decrease in the share of property income reduces inequality. In addition, inequality of property ownership probably falls as more people reach income levels at which they can save.

To summarize briefly, at very low income levels, human capital and probably physical capital become more unequally distributed as the economy develops; at higher developmental levels, however, both

---

13.   See World Bank (1991).

become less unequally distributed, and the share of relatively equally distributed human capital increases.

The possibilities for governmental intervention to redistribute income to low-income people are quite different in character in developing, as opposed to developed, countries. Traditional cash redistribution is difficult, in large part because record keeping and control are not well developed. In any case, such programs would have to be financed, probably through progressive taxation. Nations that desperately need investment funds are concerned about the effect of progressive taxation on the rate of saving.

In contrast, several types of in-kind transfers may offer important benefits.[14] Many of these in-kind transfers are aimed directly at increasing the productivity (and thereby the incomes) of low-income people. Health and educational services are the best examples. In countries with the lowest income, at least one-half of the adults typically are illiterate, and many more are only barely literate. Many studies show that the return to basic education is very high in these countries; however, children often obtain little or no education because there is no school in the town or village, schools are inconveniently located relative to the residences of the low-income people in cities, families cannot afford books or uniforms, or parents are unable or unwilling to send children to school.

Henderson (1988) found (for Brazil) that educational programs can improve the incomes of uneducated, as well as educated, workers. According to his estimates of urban production technology, educated labor is complementary to uneducated labor. In other words, the limited supply of educated people is a bottleneck that limits (for example) the level of manufacturing activity, which in turn limits employment opportunities for the uneducated. So an expansion in the supply of educated labor raises the productivity (and hence the wage) of uneducated labor (as well as that of people who receive the education).

Health is a serious problem in all low-income countries. Neighborhood or village clinics, "barefoot" (partially trained) doctors, and other health-related programs can improve the health, and thus the income-earning ability, of low-income people.

These productivity-enhancing programs of redistributive are attractive in that they offer the possibility of raising total income at the same time they equalize the distribution.[15] In developed countries, productivity-enhancing opportunities are less effective, since the cheapest (most cost-effective) of such activities already have been carried out. Illiteracy, chronic preventable diseases, and malnutrition are rare, so the most

14. Of course, in-kind transfers must be financed too, so the adverse effect on savings remains.

15. Remember, however, that the programs must be financed through taxation. This taxation distorts incentives, which in turn tends to depress total income. Nevertheless, the return to education, for example, is probably sufficiently high to offset this tendency.

obvious opportunities for simultaneously redistributing income and improving productivity are unavailable.[16]

The most widely publicized form of income redistribution in developing countries is land reform. Some researchers feel that this represents another case of productivity-enhancing redistribution, but the argument is inconclusive. Proposed reforms entail the seizure of large landholdings, their division into small plots, and the granting of ownership to peasants. If the original landlord is not fully compensated, or if the peasants receive title at below market price, land reform involves redistribution. Nevertheless, as an income redistribution vehicle, it tends to be haphazard. The beneficiaries are the peasants who are awarded title; in realistic programs, this reward involves only a minority of peasants. In an important sense, the beneficiaries are chosen at random.

Even so, in a low-income country, a major land-reform program can have a large effect on the distribution of income, because the share of property income is high in very low-income countries. The main reason is that in these countries most income originates in agriculture, and the share of property income is higher in agriculture than in manufacturing and services. Several South and Central American and African countries have some of the world's most unequal income distributions, and they have been subject to bloody civil wars in the 1970s and 1980s. The main reason for their extreme inequality of income is the concentration of land ownership in the hands of a few high-income people. Technically, government land-redistribution programs are not difficult, and several governments have carried them out successfully. In some countries, however, land redistribution is nearly impossible without bloodshed. Land redistribution can dramatically redistribute income to low-income peasants in low-income countries, but it also can be politically and economically disruptive if attempted by a weak government.

Is land reform a pure exercise in income transfer or does it also enhance agricultural productivity? There is no theoretical basis for predicting whether farm productivity will increase or decrease. The conversion of peasants from sharecroppers or wage laborers to entrepreneurs enhances their incentive to work efficiently; however, the subdivision of a large landholding may result in the loss of scale economies. In keeping with this ambiguous theoretical prediction, the evidence is mixed. The answer almost surely varies from country to country.

Land-reform policies may affect the rate of urbanization. Sen (1968) has found that labor use per acre is higher on small plots than on large ones, suggesting that the diversification of land ownership may retard

16. This comment is not to say that no such opportunities exist in developed countries. Such remaining opportunities are likely to be fairly expensive, however, and hence less cost-effective than those of developing countries.

urban migration.[17] In the long run, however, any effect of land reform (the creation of small owner-farmed landholdings) on fertility also must be considered.

Housing

The discussion in Chapter 11 about housing problems in the United States emphasized the durability of housing. In an urban area with a roughly constant population and a steady income growth, the durability and nonmalleability of housing lead to a chronic surplus of low-income housing and a chronic shortage of high-income housing. This imbalance creates benefits for the low-income people (housing is available at a low price), as well as a cost (housing is available only at certain locations and, frequently, in declining neighborhoods). Indeed, problems of decline and abandonment were seen to be due in part to the high cost of demolishing or renovating surplus low-income housing.

Urban areas in developing countries, by contrast, are characterized by rapid population increase and in some cases, low or zero growth of per capita income. Figure 17.3 captures the underlying facts for developing countries. With the passage of time, the size distribution of income (and therefore of housing demand) shifts from the solid to the dashed curve. For most developing countries, this shift is basically straight up (a rise in numbers) rather than to the right (a rise in per capita income, but little change in numbers). In the case of developing countries, the dynamics of income and population change do not create surpluses of low-income housing; instead, there is chronic shortage throughout the quality range.

Important observations emerge from the contrast between developing and developed countries. The most obvious is that filtering is almost nonexistent in developing countries. Low-income people generally do not live in hand-me-down housing and are not able to acquire their housing at a price below construction cost. Low-income people in developing countries generally live in new housing (with the population doubling every 14 years, almost everyone lives in new housing), frequently in illegal squatter settlements (to be discussed). In developed countries, low-income people can be found where there is old housing, frequently in the most central parts of the city.[18] In developing

17. Sen also found that small holdings had higher crop yields per acre, although this finding is subject to some dispute, as has been noted. For a recent discussion, see Rudra and Sen (1980).

18. Many developed countries do not exhibit the pattern discussed in Chapter 11. In Japan, for example, income does not show much variation with distance from the CBD. There are apparently three reasons for this: (1) a substantial amount of Japanese housing was destroyed during the war; (2) there was extremely rapid migration into Japanese cities after the war; and (3) Japanese housing traditionally has not been as durable as housing in the United States.

Number

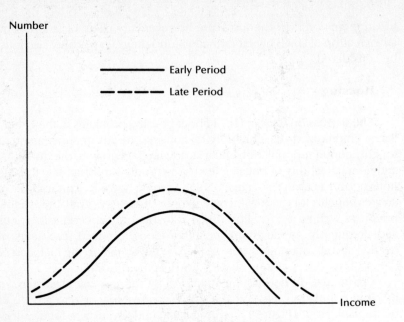

——————— Early Period

— — — — — Late Period

Income

Figure 17.3   *Size Distribution of Income and Housing Demand*

countries, by contrast, low-income people can be found where there is vacant land available for either legal or illegal development, which is frequently at the periphery.

Slums and Squatters

In all countries, housing quantity and quality vary greatly among residents. Slums exist in almost all countries. Most low-income countries, however, have a special problem almost unknown in high-income countries. There are millions of squatters in low-income countries. Bombay and Calcutta alone have at least one million each, and they are present in almost every city in South Asia, South America, and Africa.

A *squatter* is an illegal settler, almost always in an urban area. In fact, the term covers several distinct activities. Settlers may be illegal because they have no legal right to use the land (they neither own it nor have permission from the owner to use it); because it is not legal to build on the land (for example, because of land-use controls), although they have the legal right to use it; or because the structures in which they live are illegal (for example, they do not meet housing or building codes).

Typical squatters have low incomes and are relatively recent migrants to the urban area who cannot afford legal housing. They squat on government or privately owned land and build on the land whatever shelter they can, mostly with used or scrap materials and frequently with the help of friends.

Often, people squat on riverbanks, railroad rights-of-way, wide sidewalks, parks, land too hilly for normal development, land private owners have not developed, or simply open spaces surrounding apartment houses. In South America, squatters often settle on hills that are undeveloped because they are too steep to build on safely or too high for water and sewage services. In India, these sites may be on riverbanks or on sidewalks.

Not all squatters are low-income newcomers. Some are there because ownership rights are confused, because they are well organized and perhaps armed, because the government lacks the capability or political will to remove them, or just because squatting provides cheap housing. In some cases, squatters have constructed substantial dwellings and have improved them over the years.

There are good reasons why squatting is peculiar to developing countries. First, as Table 17.1 shows, urban population is growing rapidly and, as Figure 17.3 reveals, this feature leads to chronic shortage of existing low-income housing, so slums must be built new on vacant land. This pattern continues until per capita income growth accelerates and population growth slackens. It does not, however, follow from Figure 17.3 that newly built slums are illegal and lack the benefits of basic public infrastructure, such as a layout of lots and streets, or some sort of water supply and sewage disposal. The development frequently occurs illegally because governments lack the power to enforce property rights.

Squatters are a controversial subject everywhere. They may live in unsanitary and often dangerous places and many are unemployed and frequently politically troublesome. In addition, some settlements harbor criminals. Like other migrants, however, many squatters came to urban areas from the countryside in search of better living standards, education, and employment for themselves and their families. Surveys in several countries show that many urban squatters lived in much worse conditions in the rural villages they left.

What should governments do about squatters? Governmental policies fall in four categories, often followed approximately in sequence and with little consciousness of the evolution taking place.

First governments ignore squatters. They do not appear on master plans or housing registers. They may not be permitted to remain long in their illegal residences, so they do not get counted in censuses and other data. They are not provided educational, health, water, sewage, street, or transportation services.

Second governments try to remove squatters, often under pressure from owners of land on which squatters have taken up residence, from nearby legal residents, or from governmental agencies charged with health care, maintaining building codes, and administering public land on which squatters have located. In the 1960s, newspaper pictures appeared in the United States of South American governments destroying squatter settlements with bulldozers marked "Gift of the Alliance for

Progress" (the U.S. government foreign aid program for Latin America). Of course, squatters removed from one location frequently turn up in another, usually in the same city.

Third governments try relocation. Land is set aside (usually on the outskirts of the city where vacant land is available), and public housing is built (usually relatively high-quality, high-rise, concrete slab apartments). The squatters then are evicted from their illegal residences and offered the new apartments at subsidized rents or purchase prices. In general, relocation has not worked. The housing may be more costly than residents can afford, even with subsidized rents or purchase plans. Relocated squatters often resell or sublet their new quarters at market prices and end up back in slums, a little richer. More often, the new quarters are in the wrong places—far from places where residents find work—because public housing usually ignores the intimate relationship between work and residence of low-income people. Many low-income people—particularly recent migrants—work in the "informal sector," providing small services such as repairs, transportation of goods, and street vending of new and used goods. Typically, some family members process or repair goods in the residence while an adult buys, sells, seeks customers, and so on. Indeed, this informal sector self employment is traditionally the first type of job for the rural migrant. It provides subsistence income to new residents while they are looking for wage employment. For this purpose, the home must be where the business is carried on, and it must be close to customers. Public housing in some distant suburb satisfies neither of these requirements.

The fourth governmental policy is legalization. If the squatters are not too dangerously located—say, on a hillside subject to landslides or a riverbank subject to floods—the government gives the land or, more likely, sells it on concessionary terms to the residents, usually on the condition that the residents construct dwellings that meet minimum standards. Sometimes the government helps provide materials; usually, it provides "sites and services," meaning that the government lays out orderly plots and constructs paved paths, public latrines and water pumps, and some street lighting. The procedure often entails a modest subsidy to the residents, but it dramatically improves their incentives. They know they will own and can inhabit, rent, or sell whatever they build. The policy must be restricted to low-income residents to prevent large numbers of people from squatting somewhere and demanding that the land be given or sold cheaply to them, and the program usually requires that the recipient live on the plot for several years. Legalization generally takes place only some years after squatters have lived in squalor, and the plots offered are often so small that only genuinely poor people would want them.

From an economist's perspective, squatting and the evolution from illegal to legal status have two important aspects: wealth redistribution and resource allocation. The legalization or toleration of the permanent occupancy of squatter settlements involves a wealth redistribution from the former owners to the new de facto owners. Almost invariably this is pro-poor redistribution with compassion on its side.[19] The resource allocation effects are more troublesome. With squatting, the allocation of land to low-income housing passes no market or analogous efficiency test. Thus, there is no presumption that land goes to its best use. Second if existing squatter settlements are periodically legalized, with title given either free or at subsidized prices, the incentive to squat is enhanced. In addition, squatters frequently spend many years on their plots before it is clear what title will be recognized by the authorities. During this time, the original legal owners cannot sell the property, since they cannot assure the buyer that occupancy will be physically possible. The squatters have limited incentive to build substantial durable structures because of the possibility that they will be evicted and their structures either will be repossessed or, more likely, destroyed.

The most pathetic aspect of squatters is that governments often force them to be criminals. In many urban areas of developing countries, there is no place where it is legal to occupy the only housing that low-income migrants from rural areas can afford. Whatever other components there may be to governmental policy regarding squatters, it should certainly include legalization of dwellings in reasonable places that low-income residents can afford.

Urbanization and Capital Investment Needs

Urban life requires more physical capital than does rural life. Water provision and sewage disposal can be managed with only primitive capital in a rural setting, but the same service quality requires more elaborate and expensive investment in an urban area. Similarly, urban housing tends to be more costly than rural because of high land values. Formal education is more important in an urban than a rural setting in developing countries, and it requires the expenditure of resources. Finally, commuting and goods shipment require investments in road and rolling stock capacity that are largely unnecessary in rural life. Of course, there are economic benefits to urbanization, such as the realization of scale economies, but the investments must be incurred before the benefits accrue. A nation undergoing rapid urbanization is committed to a high level of investment in urban infrastructure. In other words, rapid growth in urban population places a heavy burden on investment funds and, of necessity, reduces the funds available for plant and equipment, as well as for agricultural modernization.

Lewis (1977) argues that it is the pace of urbanization, rather than poverty, that gives rise to the standard pattern of developing nations borrowing heavily from developed nations. He points out that the same

---

19. Many observers, however, feel that a more equal distribution of income—particularly in poor countries—reduces the total volume of saving. This process reduces investment, which retards development.

pattern existed in the middle of the nineteenth century, when the United States, Canada, Australia, and Argentina (the rapid urbanizers of that era) were heavy borrowers from France, England, and Germany, nations with cities that were already in place and that had excess loanable funds. These nineteenth-century debtor nations were, in fact, richer than were the lending nations, and they had real income levels comparable with those of many developing countries today.

Nevertheless, perspective is needed on the subject. The most important reason that governmental services and housing are more expensive in urban than in rural areas is that land is much more expensive in urban areas. It must be remembered that valuable urban land capitalizes the high productivity of urban areas. Thus, urban areas can generate tax revenues that can finance the extra costs of needed infrastructure, provided some of the high land rent is taxed for the purpose.

☐ Summary

Although sharing many features with the urbanization process in currently developed countries, developing countries have enough unique characteristics to ensure that urbanization is quite different from nineteenth-century America, for example.

Developing countries are, of course, much poorer than industrialized nations, but not substantially poorer than were the United States and Western Europe before industrialization. The most striking feature of urbanization in developing countries is the speed with which it is taking place, and the near-certainty that very rapid urbanization will proceed for several decades. This rapid growth of population, coupled with widespread poverty and illiteracy, causes urbanization in developing countries to have a different character from that in developed countries. There is essentially no filtering and abandonment of housing, since such a small fraction of the housing stock is old and of low quality (relative to demand). The poor are not concentrated in central cities, but more typically form squatter colonies on vacant land. A very large fraction of the cost of providing public services must continually go to the development of infrastructure (streets, lighting, water, and sewers). These durable investments place a serious drain on scarce funds, a problem that is much less significant in a society that is not undergoing rapid change.

It is relatively easy to see, in broad outline, how urbanization in developing countries differs from that in developed countries. It is much more difficult to see, however, what would constitute appropriate urbanization policies for developing countries. These policy problems offer one of the most important challenges facing urban economists.

Questions and Problems

1. Speculate as to the shape of the equation that relates percent of urban population to GNP per capita. What other explanatory variables would you include to increase the equation's explanatory power?

2. Of all the countries in the world, the United States has the largest fraction of its rural population employed outside of agriculture— more than 75 percent. In most countries, the percentage is below 25. Why?

3. Do you think that real urban wages in the United States exceed those in rural areas, as this chapter has indicated is common in developing countries? Why?

4. Do you think that the Kuznets curve applies to both urban and rural areas as economies grow? Why?

5. What governmental policy would you advocate toward urban squatters in developing countries if you were a World Bank official contemplating a loan program to alleviate the problem of inadequate housing?

References and Further Reading

Becker, Charles. "Urban Sector Income Distribution and Economic Development." *Journal of Urban Economics* 21, March (1987): 127–145. An analysis of urban and national income distribution as countries develop.

Beier, George, Anthony Churchill, Michael Cohen, and Bertrand Renaud. "The Task Ahead for Cities of Developing Countries," *World Development* 4, May (1976): 363–409. A discussion of the problems facing cities in developing countries.

Chenery, H. *Structural Change and Development Policy* (New York: Oxford University Press, 1979). A careful study of all aspects of developing policy.

Findlay, Ronald E. *International Trade and Development Theory* (New York: Columbia University Press, 1973). A textbook on economic development.

Henderson, J. Vernon. *Urban Development* (New York: Oxford University Press, 1988).

Ishizawa, S. "Labour Absorption in Asian Agriculture" (Washington, D.C.: International Labor Organization, 1978). A discussion of the relationship between agricultural employment and several other aspects of the production process.

Kravis, Irving, Alan Heston, and Robert Summers. *World Production and Income.* (Baltimore: Johns Hopkins University Press, 1982).

Lewis, W. Arthur. *The Evolution of International Economic Order* (Princeton: Princeton University Press, 1977). A monograph of twentieth-century economic development.

Lynn, Johannes. *Cities in the Developing World* (New York: Oxford University Press, 1983).

Rudra, Ashok, and A. K. Sen. "Farm Size and Labour Use." *Economic and*

Political Weekly 15, February (1980): 391–394. A brief discussion of farm size and labor productivity.

Sen, A. K. *Choice of Technique* (Oxford: Blackwell, 1968). An examination of the determinants of the input combinations used in the agricultural sector of developing countries.

Shukla, Vibhoti. *Urban Development and Regional Policy in India* (Delhi: Himalaya Publishing House, 1988).

Sveikauskas, Leo. "The Productivity of Cities." *Quarterly Journal of Economics* 89, August (1975): 393–413. An estimate of the relationship between productivity and city size.

World Bank, *World Development Report* (New York: Oxford University Press, 1991). Published annually.

Appendix

Regression Analysis

☐ Economists frequently refer to the notion that a change in one variable will bring about a change in another variable. A rise in income causes an increase in housing expenditure; an increase in distance from a CBD causes a decline in residential density. It is often important to make quantitative statements about these associations based on real-world observations, both to test theories and to make predictions. The standard statistical tool for making these quantitative statements is *regression analysis.*

Suppose the hypothesis that Y depends on X (e.g., housing expenditure depends on income) has been formed. The first step in any statistical study, obviously, is to gather the data. A sample of X and Y is depicted in the Figure A.1. Each point in the scatter diagram is called an *observation;* it is a matched set of values of each of the variables. For example, an observation would be the income and the housing consumption of a household.

The next step in a regression study is to choose a *functional form* for the regression equation; for example, the hypothesis that the relationship between X and Y is linear might be formed. A *linear regression* is the straight-line equation that most nearly passes through all the points on the scatter diagram; the equation of this best possible approximation is

$$Y = a_0 + a_1 X, \qquad \text{(A.1)}$$

and it is drawn in Figure A.1.[1] Many computer programs have been designed to find the straight line that gives the best fit to the observations. Finding the best fit entails finding the optimum values for the parameters a_0 and a_1; the computer gives us these parameters.

---

1. Formally, the *best possible approximation* generally means the line that minimizes the sum of the squares of the (vertical) distances of the observations from the regression line. These distances are known as *errors;* one such error is labeled ϵ in Figure A.1.

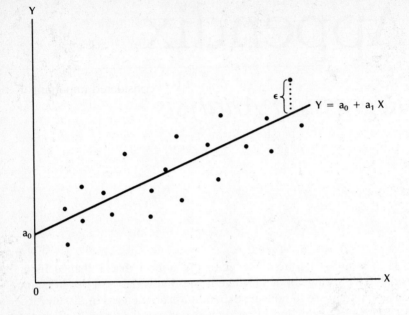

Figure A.1   *Scatter Diagram and Regression Line*

Notice that a_1 is equal to $\Delta Y/\Delta X$. Thus, for example, if X and Y are income and housing expenditure, respectively, it is possible to look at the results from a regression equation and know immediately how much (on the average) housing expenditure goes up with income.

How much Y goes up with X on the average is only part of the answer, however. It is also important to know how much confidence to place in this "on average" statement. Suppose, for example, that on average, housing expenditure goes up \$0.20 for every \$1.00 of extra income; $a_1 = \$0.20$. Is the expenditure change always between \$0.19 and \$0.21, or does it range anywhere between $-\$0.80$ and $+\$1.20$? How close do the points in a graph like Figure A.1 lie to the regression line? The first piece of information on this "goodness of fit" question is R^2, the fraction of the variation in Y explained by the variation in X. Because it is a fraction, it must lie between 0 and 1. If R^2 is 1, all the observations lie on the regresssion line; there are no errors. If R^2 is 0, knowledge of X is useless in predicting Y.

Sometimes there is reason to believe that Y depends on more than one variable; for example, urban land value might depend both on MSA population and air pollution. Just as before, observations are gathered (matched data on land value, city size, and air pollution) and a functional form, for example, linear, chosen:

$$Y = a_0 + a_1X_1 + a_2X_2, \tag{A.2}$$

where $Y =$ urban land value; $X_1 =$ MSA population; and $X_2 =$ level of air pollution.

Once again the computer finds the best-fit values of the parameters a_0, a_1, and a_2. The term a_2 tells how much land value changes as air pollution rises, *holding city size constant.* To determine the effect of air pollution on land value, it is important to include city size in the regression equation, even if this effect is not considered important. To see why, consider what would happen if it were left out and a regression analysis of land value on level of air pollution were run. Furthermore, suppose the following to be the true state of the world: Land value rises with city size but is unaffected by air pollution, but air pollution tends to be worse in big cities than in small cities. In such a world, air pollution is correlated with land value, simply because both are correlated with city size. Thus, a regression like Equation (A.1), where Y is land value and X is air pollution, will lead to the erroneous belief that high air pollution causes high land value. With a regression equation like (A.2), however, with city sizes being the other right-side variable, the effect of city size on land value is accounted for, and the regression analysis correctly finds that air pollution and land value are not correlated. The inclusion of other variables in the regression holds constant their effect, providing isolation of the effect of the variable of interest.

If two or more variables appear on the right side, the equation is called a *multiple regression.* With a multiple regression, R^2 continues to measure the fraction of the variation in Y explained by variation in the Xs. It gives no information, however, on the contribution of the individual variables to the explanation of the variation in Y. Returning to the previous example, suppose land value is regressed on city size and air pollution. As Chapter 15 discussed, air pollution is not expected to be associated with land value, after holding constant city size. Regression analysis can be used to see whether this is true. Basically, this means doing the following. Regress land value on just city size, and write down the R^2. Now regress land value on city size and air pollution. R^2 is not expected to rise significantly by including air pollution, because the theory says air pollution adds nothing to the explanation of rent differences between cities, after city size is corrected for.

The usual measure of whether R^2 rises significantly with the addition of another variable is the t-statistic. There is a t-statistic associated with each variable in the regression; its interpretation is as follows. If the t-statistic is greater than about 1.9 (in absolute value), the variable is of statistical significance. In the above example, the prediction is that the coefficient on the air-pollution variable will have a t-statistic smaller than about 1.9.

Acknowledgments

p. 141: From *Industrial Real Estate Market Survey* (Washington, D.C.: Society of Industrial Realtors, Spring 1988). Reprinted by permission of the National Association of Realtors; p. 190: From *Setting National Priorities: The Next Ten Years,* edited by Henry Owen and Charles Schultze (Washington, D.C.: The Brookings Institution, 1976). Reprinted by permission; p. 192: From *Public Expenditures, Taxes, and the Distribution of Income* by Morgan Reynolds and Eugene Smolensky. Copyright © 1977 Academic Press, Inc. Reprinted by permission of Academic Press, Inc., and Morgan Reynolds; pp. 240, 244: From "Low and Moderate Income Housing: Progress, Problems and Prospects" (Washington, D.C.: National Association of Home Builders, 1986). Reprinted by permission; p. 242; From *Annual Housing Survey.* Part C (Washington, D.C.: National Association of Home Builders, 1974, 1983). Reprinted by permission; pp. 274, 275: From *Real Estate Status Report* (Washington, D.C.: National Association of Realtors, March, 1982). Reprinted by permission; p. 274: From *National Homebuyers Survey* (Washington, D.C.: National Association of Realtors, 1981). Reprinted by permission; p. 300: From *The Full Costs of Urban Transport* by Theodore Keeler et al. Reprinted by permission of the author; p. 332: Data from "Finance" by George E. Peterson in *The Urban Predicament,* edited by W. Gorham and N. Glazer (Washington, D.C.: Urban Institute, 1976, Table 6). p. 341: From "Local Government, the Property Tax and the Quality of Life: Some Findings of Progressivity" by B. W. Hamilton in *Public Economics and the Quality of Life,* edited by L. Wingo and A. Evans. Copyright © 1977 by Resources for the Future, Inc. Reprinted by permission; p. 373: From *Economics and the Environment* by Allen Kneese, Robert Ayres and Ralph D'Arge. Copyright © 1970 by Resources for the Future, Inc. Reprinted by permission; p. 409: From *Studies in the Structure of the Urban Economy* by Edwin S. Mills. Copyright © 1972 by Johns Hopkins University Press. Reprinted by permission; and from "Recent Behavior of Urban Population and Employment Density Gradients," Johns Hopkins Working Paper No. 124, 1983, by Molly Macauley. Reprinted by permission; p. 416: From "Energy" by Milton Russell in *Setting National Priorities: The 1978 Budget,* edited by J. Pechman (Washington, D.C.: The Brookings Institution, 1977). Reprinted by permission; p. 419: From *National Homebuyers Survey* (Washington, D.C.: National Association of Realtors, 1981). Reprinted by permission; p. 420: From "Back to the Countryside and Back to the City in the Same Decade" by Larry Long in *Back to the City: Issues in Neighborhood Renovation,* edited by Shirley Laska and Daphne Spain. Copyright © 1980 by Pergamon Press, Inc. Reprinted by permission; p. 436: From *1980 World Tables:* Copyright © 1980 by Johns Hopkins University Press. Reprinted by permission.

Photo Credits

cover photo: Chicago, © Andy Caulfield/The Image Bank; p. 1: Boston, © Southwick, Stock, Boston; p. 88: El Paso, © Monkmeyer Press Photo; and p. 175: slum, © Maher, Stock, Boston.

462

Index

Abandonment of housing, 146,
246–251. *See also* Demolition
of housing; Slums
Absorptive capacity of environment,
375–376
Adjustable rate mortgages,
223
Agglomeration economies of urban
areas, 20, 118, 122, 403
Agricultural population densities,
437–439
Agricultural revolution, 59
Agriculture. *See also entries
beginning with* Rural
in developing countries, 435–437
and industries, labor distribution
between, 58–60
land for, 147, 363
technological progress in, 58–60
Aid to Families with Dependent
Children, 188, 189, 321n
Air pollution, 376–377, 385, 393n,
404, 412
Alonso, William, 13n
Amenities, environmental, 391–396,
441
Amenity orientation of firms, 39
Annexation of land by cities, 75
Apgar, William, 128n
Asabere, Paul K., 138
Atomic wastes, 381–382
Automatic vehicle identification
(AVI), 295
Automobile pollution, 377, 385, 386,
393n
Automobile travel:
in city growth, 30
congestion caused by, 287–297
costs of, 288–305, 415–417
versus public transit systems,
279–284, 415–417
Average cost in automobile travel,
288–290
Average population densities, 4,
410–411
Averch, Harvey, 362

Bailey, Martin J., 261
Balloon (frame) construction

technique, 27
Basic (export base) employment, 16,
46
Basic welfare theorem, 159
Beach, Alfred Ely, 27n, 28n
Becker, Charles, 447n
Beer industry, 36
Bessemer process, 26
Best possible approximation in
regression analysis, 459–461
Biochemical oxygen demand (BOD),
379
Birch, David, 128n
Black Americans:
in central cities, 283, 307–308,
408–410, 428–429
discrimination against, 106,
256–257, 259–262, 307–308,
346, 425
reduction of discrimination,
193–194, 428
migrations of, 45, 50–51, 258
poverty of, 181–185, 193–194
prejudice against, 410
segregation of, housing, 256–259,
307–308
suburban job access of, 307–308
suburbanization of, 428–429
urbanization of, 182–185
Bobrick, Benson, 27n, 29n
Bradbury, Katharine, 408, 442n
Break-even point for pretax and
aftertax income, 187–188
Brown, A. Theodore, 56n
Brown, B., 22n, 29n, 41n, 42n, 356
Budget constraints, household, 107,
109, 171, 328–329
Building codes, 362
Burchell, Robert, 249n
Burt, Martha, 263
Bus systems, 298–303
Business cycles, central-city
sensitivity to, 333–334

Capital:
cost of, 202–203, 206,
207
human, 448
Capital accumulation, 372